macroeconomics

THEORIES AND POLICIES

THEORIES AND POLICIES

macro

Richard T. Froyen

University of North Carolina,
Chapel Hill

economics

Macmillan Publishing Co., Inc.
NEW YORK

Collier Macmillan Publishers
LONDON

About the cover: The figure on the cover is an abstract representation that approximates the percentage rates of inflation and unemployment from 1953 through August, 1982. The blue line is the unemployment rate and the red is the inflation rate.

Copyright © 1983, Macmillan Publishing Co., Inc.

Printed in the United States of America

Macmillan Publishing Co., Inc.
866 Third Avenue, New York, New York 10022

Collier Macmillan Canada, Inc.

Library of Congress Cataloging in Publication Data

Froyen, Richard T.
  Macroeconomics, theories and policies.

  Includes index.
  1. Macroeconomics. I. Title.
HB172.5.F76   339   82-15217
ISBN 0-02-339780-2   AACR2

Printing: 2 3 4 5 6 7 8   Year: 3 4 5 6 7 8 9 0

ISBN 0-02-339780-2

To Linda
Katherine, Sara, and Andrea

preface

The period since 1970 has been a challenging one for macro-economists. The key variables in macroeconomics—the levels of output, inflation, and unemployment; rates of interest; and foreign exchange rates—while behaving in interesting ways have proved difficult to explain and predict. The period since 1970 has also been an active one in macroeconomic theory. It has been a period of controversy, but also of progress in at least clarifying the issues on which macroeconomists are divided. The decade of 1970's saw a broadening of the issues in the *monetarist–Keynesian* controversy. Additionally, a new challenge to the neo-Keynesian position, the *new classical* economics, emerged. At the end of the decade, neo-Keynesian policy prescriptions were also under attack from a group that has come to be called the *supply-side* economists. Finally, the post-1970 period has been an active one in terms of macroeconomic policy. The decade of the 1970s began with President Nixon's *New Economic Policy,* and the decade of the 1980s with President Reagan's *Economic Recovery Program,* with many major policy shifts in between.

In this book I have tried to explain macroeconomics, inclusive of the above-mentioned recent developments, in a coherent way, but without glossing over the fundamental disagreements among macroeconomists on issues of both theory and policy. The major modern macroeconomic theories are presented and compared. Within this framework, the important topics and issues in macroeconomics are developed in full. Important areas of agreement as well as differences are discussed. An attempt is made to demonstrate that the controversies among macroeconomists center on well-defined issues that have their basis in theoretical differences in the underlying models.

An effort is made to interrelate macroeconomic theory and policy, recent policy actions as well as not so recent ones. The behavior of economic variables is considered in relation to developments in economic theory; for example, the simultaneously high inflation and unemployment rates of the 1970s are considered in relationship to the development of the monetarist theory of the *natural rate of unemployment* and the new classical *rational expectations* view. The development of the original *classical economics* and the Keynesian revolution against the classical view are also explained with reference to their historical settings.

Specific distinguishing features of the approach taken here are:

—a detailed analysis of the monetarist and new classical challenges to the neo-Keynesian position

—an up-to-date summary of the modern neo-Keynesian position, including the neo-Keynesian response to the monetarist and new classical critics

—an extensive treatment of monetary policy which considers the optimal strategy for monetary policy including the merits of intermediate targeting on monetary aggregates. Also, the question of reserves versus an interest rate as a short-run operating target for money stock control is examined within the context of the recent shift in Federal Reserve operating procedure.

—an analysis of the recent slowdown in output growth, capital formation and growth in labor productivity in the United States. It is within this context of intermediate-run growth that the views of the *supply-side* economists are considered, along with the neo-Keynesian perspective on such intermediate-run growth. Also, within this context the economic policy initiatives of the Reagan administration that have come to be known as "Reaganomics" are analyzed.

—a thorough coverage of money demand which discusses recent difficulties in predicting money demand, the effects of ongoing innovations in the financial sector, and the recent redefinition of the monetary aggregates.

—an analysis of the question of rules versus discretion in macroeconomic policymaking. Rules for monetary policy as well as a constitutional amendment for balancing the Federal budget are considered. These issues are examined in the context of the interventionist versus noninterventionist policy positions of the different schools of macroeconomic theory. The *public choice* view of macroeconomic policymaking is also examined.

The organization of the book is as follows. Part I (Chapters 1–2) discusses the subject matter of macroeconomics, the recent behavior of the U.S. economy and questions of measurement. Part II presents the major macroeconomic models or systems, beginning with the classical system (Chapters 3–4). Consideration of the classical system at the start is useful because the Keynesian model can then be viewed as an attack on the classical orthodoxy. The recent challenges to the neo-Keynesian position can then be rooted in the parts of the classical model that provide starting points for their analysis: the quantity theory of money for the monetarists and the classical labor market clearing assumptions and choice-theoretic based behavioral functions for the new classical economists. The classical analysis is also useful for a later examination of the policy prescriptions of the supply-side economists.

The Keynesian model is analyzed in detail in Chapters 5–8. Beginning from a very simple model, more complex models are built up to incorporate: monetary influences, wage and price flexibility, changing price expectations and shocks to aggregate supply. Chapters 9 and 10 present the monetarist model. Chapter 9 focuses on the monetarists' view of the importance of money and Chapter 10 develops the monetarists' theory of the natural rate of unemployment. Chapter 11 examines the new classical view, often termed the *rational expectations* theory, as well as the neo-Keynesian critique of this view. Chapter 12 summarizes and compares the different models.

Part III presents extensions and considers parts of the models in greater detail. The chapters here and in Part IV are designed to be self-contained so that the instructor can choose topics as time and interest allow. Chapter 13 is a more detailed examination of the components of private sector demand: consumption and investment spending. Chapter 14 considers money demand and Chapter 15 the money supply process. Chapter 16 returns to the supply side of macroeconomic models to discuss long-run equilibrium growth and the determinants of growth over intermediate-run periods, periods too long to fit the short-run framework of the models in Part II, but not necessarily situations of long-run equilibrium. As noted above, it is in this context that supply-side economics is examined. Chapter 17 considers *open-economy* macroeconomics. An appendix to the chapter develops an open-economy macroeconomic model.

Part IV deals with macroeconomic policy, fiscal and incomes policies in Chapter 18 and monetary policy in Chapter 19. An appendix to Chapter 19 considers the supply-side economists' proposal for monetary policy, a return to a gold standard. A historical appendix to Part IV describes major macroeconomic policy actions over the period since the Great Depression of the 1930s.

In the section on macroeconomic models, the conceptual approach taken here is to develop each model within the aggregate demand-aggregate supply framework in order to facilitate comparisons among the models. Throughout the book the aim is to provide a clear and rigorous, primarily graphical and verbal analysis. Other pedagogical features are the explanatory captions provided for the graphs in the text, end-of-chapter questions, and a list of selected readings following each chapter.

An instructor's Manual to accompany the text contains summaries of chapter objectives, answers to all end-of-chapter questions, and test materials that include problems, essay questions, and multiple-choice questions. A Study Guide, co-authored by Lawrence Davidson and myself, contains a review outline, problems, multiple-choice questions, and exercises on concepts and techniques for each chapter.

Acknowledgments

Many people have been helpful in the preparation of this book. The readers recruited by Macmillan to review the manuscript at various stages have provided comments which led to many substantial improvements. These readers were: Lawrence Davidson, Indiana University; Ed Day, University of Louisville; Gary Gigliotti, Rutgers University; John Lapp, North Carolina State University; Thomas McCaleb, Florida State University; Richard Selden, University of Virginia; John Trapani, University of Texas-Arlington; Doug Waldo, University of Florida; and Warren Weber, Virginia Polytechnic Institute. I am particularly grateful to Lawrence Davidson who in addition to his comprehensive reviews provided many additional comments in discussions with me concerning the book. He is also my co-author for the study guide which accompanies the text. My editors at Macmillan, Anthony English, Charles Place and Chip Price, have provided encouragement and numerous useful suggestions. I am especially grateful to Chip Price for suggested alterations in the final stages of preparing the manuscript and for comments on some of the last parts of the book to be written. I am indebted to Arthur Benavie, Michael Salemi, and Roger Waud, colleagues here at the University of North Carolina, for their comments and suggestions and for the great deal I have learned from them on the subject matter of this book. I am likewise indebted to the many graduate and undergraduate students whom I have taught here for what I have learned from them about the teaching of macroeconomics and the subject itself.

Other important debts are to Linda Froyen who prepared the index and proofread the manuscript and to Becky Engebretsen who cheerfully and expertly typed many drafts of the material in this book. I am grateful to John Travis, at Macmillan, for his competent supervision of the production process.

Weaknesses or errors that remain, despite such aid, are my responsibility.

R.T.F.

contents

part two

macroeconomic models

9 MONETARISM (I): THE IMPORTANCE OF MONEY   238

10 MONETARISM (II): THE NATURAL RATE OF UNEMPLOYMENT   270

14 MONEY DEMAND: THEORY AND EVIDENCE   374

15 THE MONEY SUPPLY PROCESS   412

APPENDIX AN OPEN ECONOMY MACROECONOMIC MODEL 507

part four economic policy

18 FISCAL AND INCOMES POLICIES 522

introduction and measurement

chapter

1.1 WHAT IS MACROECONOMICS?

This book examines theories and policy questions in the branch of economics called *macroeconomics*. The British economist Alfred Marshall defined economics as the "study of mankind in the ordinary business of life; it examines that part of individual and social action which is most closely connected with the attainment and with the use of the material requisites of wellbeing."[1] In macroeconomics we study this "ordinary business of life" in the aggregate; that is, we look at the behavior of the economy as a whole. The key variables we study include the level of total output in the economy, the aggregate price level, the levels of employment and unemployment, levels of interest rates, wage rates, and rates of foreign exchange. The subject matter of macroeconomics includes factors that determine both the levels of these variables and the way in which the variables change over time: the rate of growth of output, the inflation rate, changing unemployment in periods of boom and recession, appreciation or depreciation in foreign exchange rates.

Macroeconomics is a policy-oriented part of economics. Much of our analysis will focus on the way in which macroeconomic varia-

[1]Alfred Marshall, *Principles of Economics*, 8th ed. (New York: Macmillan, 1920), p. 1.

2

INTRODUCTION

bles are affected by government policies. To what degree can government policies affect the level of output and employment in the economy? To what degree is inflation the result of unfortunate government policies? What government policies are optimal in the sense of achieving the most desirable behavior of aggregate variables such as the level of unemployment or the inflation rate?

On these policy questions we will find considerable disagreement among economists. In large part the controversy over policy questions stems from differing views of the factors that determine the aggregate variables listed above. Questions of theory and policy are interrelated. In our analysis we will examine different macroeconomic theories and the policy conclusions that follow from these theories. It would be more satisfying to present *the* macroeconomic theory and policy prescription. Satisfying, but such a presentation would be misleading because there *are* fundamental differences among what can be termed schools of macroeconomists. In comparing different theories, however, we will see that there are substantial areas of agreement as well as disagreement. Controversy does not mean chaos. The aim of the approach taken here will be to isolate the key issues that divide macroeconomists, and to explain the theoretical basis for each position.

Over the past decade public interest in macroeconomic issues has grown. The reason is simple. The 1970s were a decade of unstable economic growth, high inflation, and high unemployment. In stable times we take for granted the behavior of the economy as a whole and concentrate on our individual economic decisions. When the macroeconomy misbehaves, when individuals cannot find jobs although they have the required skills, when the value of the earnings of the employed are eroded by high inflation rates, then we become more interested in the behavior of aggregates. With the increased interest in macroeconomics has also come a dissatisfaction with the explanation of economic events and the policy prescriptions provided by the established macroeconomic theory. Recent years have been, as economist James Tobin calls them, "troubled times" for macroeconomics. We will analyze the macroeconomic orthodoxy as it existed when the 1970s began, what is termed "neo-Keynesian economics." The roots of neo-Keynesian theory as an attack on an earlier orthodoxy, the *classical economics*, will be explained. We will then examine the challenges to the neo-Keynesian position, theories that have come to be called *monetarism* and the *new classical economics*. How each theory explains the events of the 1970s and the policies each group of economists propose to provide for better future performance of the economy will be a central concern of our analysis.

To start, it is useful to examine the performance of some important macroeconomic variables in the United States over recent years.

1.2 POST–WORLD WAR II U.S. ECONOMIC PERFORMANCE

Our goal here and in the next section is to sketch the broad outline of U.S. macroeconomic performance over the post–World War II period and suggest some of the central questions to be addressed in our later analysis. We will put off detailed definitions of the aggregates discussed here until Chapter 2, which deals with the measurement of macroeconomic variables. Tables 1.1 to 1.3 provide data for selected postwar years for several important macroeconomic variables. Table 1.1 shows the level output for the United States for the years 1953–1981. The table also shows the growth rate in output for each year. The output measure in the table is *real* gross national product (GNP). Gross national product measures current production of goods and services and by real is meant that the measures in Table 1.1 have been corrected for price change. The figures measure growth in the actual quantity of goods and services produced.

As the table shows, output has increased substantially over the 1953–81 period, rising from $623.6 billion in 1953 to $1509.6 billion in 1981. Looking at the data in more detail, it can be seen that

Table 1.1 Real Output in the United States, 1953–1981

Year	GNP (billions)	Percentage Change in GNP	Year	GNP (billions)	Percentage Change in GNP
1953	$ 623.6	3.8	1970	$1085.6	−0.2
1954	616.1	−1.2	1971	1122.4	3.4
1955	657.5	6.7	1972	1185.9	5.7
1956	671.6	2.1	1973	1255.0	5.8
1957	683.8	1.8	1974	1248.0	−0.6
1958	680.9	−0.4	1975	1233.9	−1.1
1959	721.7	6.0	1976	1300.4	5.4
1960	737.2	2.2	1977	1371.7	5.5
			1978	1436.9	4.8
1961	756.6	2.6	1979	1483.0	3.2
1962	800.3	5.8	1980	1480.7	−0.2
1963	832.5	4.0	1981	1509.6	1.9
1964	876.4	5.3
1965	929.3	6.0
1966	984.8	6.0
1967	1011.4	2.7
1968	1058.1	4.6
1969	1087.6	2.8

Source: *Economic Report of the President,* 1982.

Figure 1.1 Rate of Growth in GNP in the United States, 1953–1981 (percent)

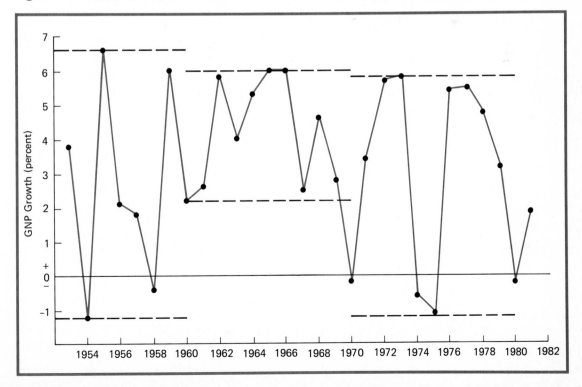

GNP growth in the period since 1970 has been more irregular than was the case for the 1961–69 period. In fact, real GNP has declined in four of the last twelve years. The 1961–69 period was one of steady expansion. In this respect the 1970s were more like the decade of the 1950s, when, as can be seen from the table, there were two years when GNP fell. The instability of GNP growth in the period since 1970 can also be seen from Figure 1.1, which plots the GNP growth rate for the period 1953–1981. Fluctuations since 1970 have been substantially greater than for the 1960s and more similar to the pattern of the 1950s. In other respects, however, the 1970s were quite dissimilar to the 1950s, as will be seen below.

Table 1.2 shows the unemployment rate, the percentage of the labor force that was not employed, for each year since 1953. The instability in output growth in the 1970s is mirrored in the fluctuations in the unemployment rate over this period. Similarly, the strong steady expansion of the 1960s is reflected in a steady decline in unemployment rate. Also notice that relative to the 1960s or the 1950s, the average unemployment rate for the 1970–81 period has been high, 6.4 percent, compared with 4.9 percent for the 1953–60 period and 4.7 percent for the 1961–69 period.

Table 1.3 gives data for the rate of inflation for 1953–1981. The

Table 1.2   U.S. Unemployment Rate, 1953–1981

Year	Unemployment Rate (percent)	Year	Unemployment Rate (percent)
1953	2.9	1970	4.9
1954	5.5	1971	5.9
1955	4.4	1972	5.6
1956	4.1	1973	4.9
1957	4.3	1974	5.6
1958	6.8	1975	8.5
1959	5.5	1976	7.7
1960	5.5	1977	7.0
Average (1953–60)	4.9	1978	6.0
		1979	5.8
1961	6.7	1980	7.1
1962	5.5	1981	7.6
1963	5.7	Average (1970–81)	6.4
1964	5.2		
1965	4.5		
1966	3.8		
1967	3.8		
1968	3.6		
1969	3.5		
Average (1961–69)	4.7		

Source: *Economic Report of the President*, 1982.

Table 1.3 U.S. Inflation Rate, 1953–1981

Year	Inflation Rate (percent)	Year	Inflation Rate (percent)
1953	0.6	1970	5.5
1954	−0.5	1971	3.4
1955	0.4	1972	3.4
1956	2.9	1973	8.8
1957	3.0	1974	12.2
1958	1.8	1975	7.0
1959	1.5	1976	4.8
1960	1.5	1977	6.8
Average (1953–60)	1.4	1978	9.0
		1979	13.3
1961	0.7	1980	12.4
1962	1.2	1981	8.9
1963	1.6	Average (1970–81)	8.0
1964	1.2		
1965	1.9		
1966	3.4		
1967	3.0		
1968	4.7		
1969	6.1		
Average (1961–69)	2.6		

Source: *Economic Report of the President,* 1982.

Figure 1.2 U.S. Inflation and Unemployment Rates, 1953–1981 (percent)

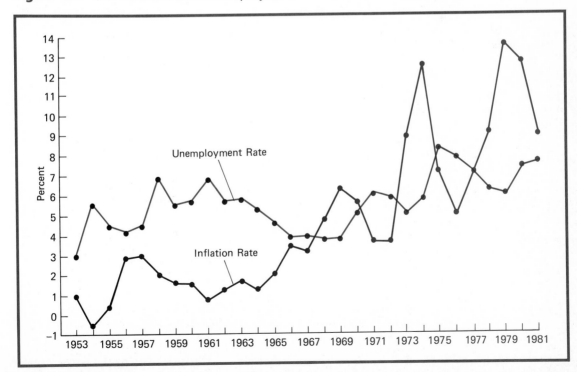

measure of inflation in the table is the percentage increase in the consumer price index, one of several measures of the aggregate price level to be discussed in Chapter 2. As can be seen from the table, the inflation rate in the 1950s was low and relatively stable. In the late 1960s an upward trend in the inflation rate is apparent. This upward trend continued and was intensified in the 1970s. It can also be seen that there is much greater variability in the annual inflation rate figures over the period since 1970. This variability, as well as the upward trend, is apparent in the plot of the inflation rate series in Figure 1.2.

Figure 1.2 also shows a plot of the annual unemployment rate for 1953–81. It is interesting to note that in the early portion of this period, through the late 1960s, a negative relationship between the

Figure 1.3A
Relationship Between
Inflation and
Unemployment,
1953–1969

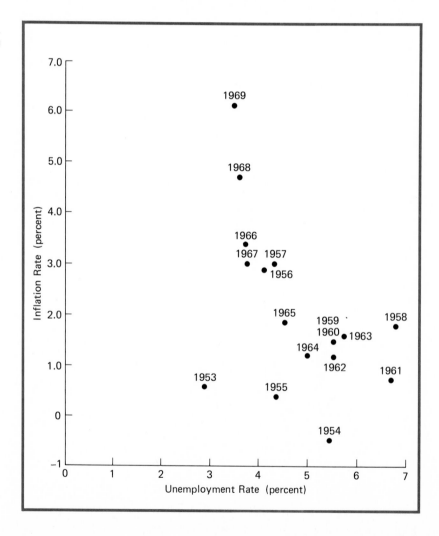

inflation rate and the unemployment rate is obvious; years of relatively high rates of inflation are years of relatively low unemployment. In the period since 1970, no such negative relationship is evident. In fact, during the 1973–75 period the unemployment and inflation rates both rose sharply.

This change in the relationship between the inflation rate and unemployment rate can be seen in Figure 1.3. In the figure the inflation rate is measured on the vertical axis and the unemployment rate is measured on the horizontal axis. Observations until 1970 shown in part *A* of the figure seem to trace out a negative

Figure 1.3B
Relationship Between
Inflation and
Unemployment,
1970–1981

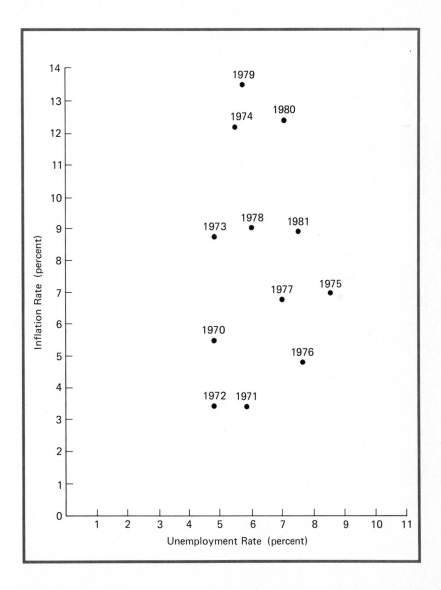

relationship between the two series. The post-1970 observations plotted in part *B*, however, show no clear relationship between the inflation and unemployment rates.

1.3 CENTRAL QUESTIONS IN MACROECONOMICS

The data for output growth, unemployment, and inflation in the foregoing tables and figures suggest some important macroeconomic questions.

First, why has the behavior of output, employment, and inflation become so unstable in the period since 1970? In contrast, what factors explain the steady expansion of output in the 1960s or the price stability of the 1950s? To answer these questions requires a general explanation of the determinants of output, employment, and the price level over periods of several years—that which is termed the *cyclical* behavior of the economy. The macroeconomic theories we consider below attempt to do just this.

Second, why have both the unemployment rate *and* the inflation rate been so high during substantial portions of the post-1970 period? What became of the negative relationship that seemed to exist between unemployment and inflation during earlier years (Figure 1.3*A*)?

The presence of both high inflation rates and high unemployment rates during the 1970s was especially puzzling to macroeconomists. The experience of the 1950s and 1960s had led economists to explain substantial inflation as a symptom of too high a level of total demand for output. Substantial unemployment was considered the result of inadequate demand. Such an explanation is consistent with the negative relationship between inflation and unemployment during the 1953–69 period as exhibited in Figure 1.3*A*. When demand was high, the inflation rate was high and unemployment was low; when demand was low, the inflation rate was low but unemployment was high. But this line of reasoning cannot explain simultaneously high unemployment and high inflation. Total demand for output cannot be both too high and too low.

The events of the 1970s have caused economists to reconsider and modify earlier theories of inflation and unemployment, as we will see in our analysis below. An important part of this reconsideration of existing theory will concern the role of total demand for output, what is termed *aggregate demand*, in determining output, employment and inflation.

1.4 A PREVIEW OF THE TEXT

We begin in Chapter 2 with a consideration of the measurement of macroeconomic variables. In that chapter we tie the variables considered in later chapters to their counterparts in the U.S. economy. Chapters 3 to 12 (Part II) present and compare four major schools of macroeconomic theory: the classical theory (Chapters 3 and 4), Keynesian economics (Chapters 5 to 8), monetarism (Chapters 9 and 10), and the new classical economics (Chapter 11). These chapters will examine the models that each of these groups of economists have constructed to analyze the cyclical or short-run behavior of macroeconomic variables. We also examine the policy conclusions that follow from each of these models. In Chapter 12 we summarize the major issues on which macroeconomists are divided. Chapters 13 to 17 (Part III) consider elements of the models in Part II in more detail and extend the models in various ways. Finally, in Chapters 18 and 19 (Part IV) we consider macroeconomic policy.

Review Questions

1   What are some of the important variables that comprise the subject matter of macroeconomics? How does macroeconomics differ from microeconomics, the other major branch of economic theory?

2   Compare the behavior of inflation, output growth, and the unemployment rate of the U.S. economy in the 1970s with the behavior of the same variables for the 1960s; for the 1950s. In which decade was the performance of the macroeconomy, as measured by these variables, the most "desirable"? the least desirable?

3   There appears to have been a shift in the output–inflation relationship between the 1953–69 and 1970–81 periods. Explain the nature of this shift.

4   Using the *Economic Report of the President* or other sources for the most recent years, update the data in Tables 1.1 to 1.3.

chapter 2

In subsequent chapters we examine a number of *macroeconomic models*. Such models are simplified representations of the economy which attempt to capture important factors determining aggregate variables such as output, employment, and the price level. The elements of such models are hypothesized theoretical relationships among aggregative economic variables, including macroeconomic policy variables. To understand such theoretical relationships it is best to begin by carefully defining the real-world counterparts of the variables that appear in our models. It will also prove useful to consider some of the accounting relationships that exist among these variables, since we make use of such relationships in the construction of our theoretical models. We begin by describing the key variables measured in the *national income accounts*.

2.1 THE NATIONAL INCOME ACCOUNTS

One reads with dismay of Presidents Hoover and then Roosevelt designing policies to combat the Great Depression of the 1930s on the basis of such sketchy data as stock price indices, freight car loadings, and incomplete indices of industrial production. The fact was that comprehensive measures of national income and output did not exist at the time. The Depression and with it the growing role of government in the economy emphasized the need for such

MEASUREMENT OF MACROECONOMIC VARIABLES

measures and led to the development of a comprehensive set of national income accounts.[1]

The central measures in the national income accounts are gross national product (GNP) and the closely related concept of national income (NI). We explain each in turn.

2.2 GROSS NATIONAL PRODUCT

Gross national product is a measure of all currently produced final goods and services evaluated at market prices. A number of aspects of this definition require clarification.

Currently produced: GNP includes only currently produced goods and services. It is a flow measure of output per time period, for example per quarter or per year, and includes only goods and services produced during this time interval. Such market transactions as exchanges of previously produced houses, cars, or factories

[1]Simon Kuznets, winner of the 1971 Nobel prize in economics played a pioneering role in the development of national income accounting. See Simon Kuznets, *National Income and Its Composition, 1919–38* (New York: National Bureau of Economic Research, 1941). During World War II the Commerce Department took over the maintenance of the national income accounts. National income accounts data are published in the *Survey of Current Business.* Historical data series can be found in *Business Statistics,* biennial supplement to the *Survey,* as well as in the Commerce Department's publication, *National Income and Product Accounts of the United States, 1929–76.*

would not enter into GNP. Exchanges of assets, such as stocks and bonds, are examples of other market transactions that do not directly involve current production of goods and services and are therefore not in GNP.

Final goods and services: only the production of *final* goods and services enters gross national product. Goods that are used in the production of other goods rather than being sold to final purchasers, what are termed intermediate goods, are not counted separately in GNP. Such goods show up in GNP because they contribute to the value of the final goods in whose production they are used. To count them separately would be double counting. To give an example, we would not want to count the value of flour used in making bread separately, then again when the bread is sold.

There are, however, two types of goods used in the production process which are counted in GNP. The first of these are currently produced *capital goods*—business plant and equipment purchases. Such capital goods are ultimately used up in the production process but within the current period only a portion of value of the capital good is used up in production. This portion, termed *depreciation*, is the part which can be thought to be embodied in the value of the final goods that are sold. If capital goods were not separately included in GNP, it would be equivalent to assuming that they depreciated fully in the current time period. In gross national product, the whole value of the capital good is included as a separate item. In a sense this is double counting since, as just noted, the value of depreciation is embodied in the value of final goods. *Net national product*, defined as gross national product minus depreciation, is an aggregate output measure that avoids such double counting and is therefore conceptually preferable to GNP. There is, however, no error-free way of measuring depreciation, so in practice GNP is often considered the more useful measure.

The other category, containing essentially intermediate goods, which is part of GNP is *inventory investment*—the net change in inventories of final goods awaiting sale or of materials used in the production process. Additions to inventory stocks of final goods belong in GNP because they are currently produced output. To get the timing of national product correct, they should be counted in the current period as they are added to stocks; they should not be counted later when they are sold to final purchasers. Inventory investment in materials similarly belongs in GNP because it also represents currently produced output whose value is not embodied in *current* sales of final output. Notice that inventory investment can be negative as well as positive. If final sales exceed production, for example, due to a rundown of inventories (negative inventory investment), GNP will fall short of final sales.

Evaluated at market prices: GNP is the *value* of goods and services using the common measuring rod of market prices. This is the trick to being able to measure apples plus oranges plus railroad cars plus. . . . But this does exclude from GNP goods that are not sold in markets, such as the services of homemakers or output of home gardens, as well as nonreported output from illegal activities such as the sale of narcotics, gambling, and prostitution.[2] Also, since it is a measure of the value of output in terms of market prices, GNP, which is essentially a *quantity* measure, will be sensitive to changes in the average price level. The same physical output will correspond to a different GNP level as the average level of market prices varies. To correct for this, in addition to computing gross national product in terms of current market prices, a concept termed *nominal* GNP, the national income accountants also calculate *real* GNP, which is the value of national product in terms of constant prices from a base year. The way in which the latter calculation is made is discussed below.

GNP can be broken down into the components shown in Table 2.1. The values of each component for selected years are also given in the table. The data in the table suggest a number of trends and patterns which will be of interest to us later.

The consumption component of GNP consists of the household sector's purchases of currently produced goods and services. Consumption can be further broken down into consumer durable

[2]For some services that are not actually sold on the market, the Commerce Department does try to *impute* the market value of the service and include it in GNP. An example is the services of owner-occupied houses, which the Commerce Department estimates based on rental value.

Table 2.1 Nominal GNP and Its Components, Selected Years[a] (billions of dollars)

Year	GNP	Consumption	Investment	Government Purchases of Goods and Services	Net Exports
1929	103.4	77.3	16.2	8.8	1.1
1933	55.8	45.8	1.4	8.2	0.4
1939	90.9	67.0	9.3	13.5	1.2
1945	212.4	119.5	10.6	82.8	−0.5
1950	286.5	192.0	53.8	38.5	2.2
1960	506.5	324.9	75.9	100.3	5.5
1970	992.7	621.7	144.2	220.1	6.7
1980	2626.1	1672.8	395.3	534.7	23.3

[a]Components may not sum to total due to rounding error.
Sources: *Economic Report of the President*, January 1981; *Federal Reserve Bulletin*, June 1981.

goods (e.g., automobiles, televisions), nondurable consumption goods (e.g., foods, beverages, clothing), and consumer services (e.g., medical services, haircuts). Consumption is the largest component of GNP, between 60 and 65 percent of GNP in recent years.

The investment component of GNP in Table 2.1 consists of three subcomponents. The largest of these is business fixed investment, which amounted to $296.0 billion, 75 percent of the total investment in 1980. Business fixed investment consists of purchases of newly produced plant and equipment—the capital goods discussed above. The second subcomponent of investment is residential construction investment, the building of single- and multifamily housing units, which in 1980 totaled $105.3 billion. The final subcomponent of investment is inventory investment, which is the change in business inventories. As noted above, inventory investment may be positive or negative. In 1980, inventory investment was minus $5.9 billion, meaning that there was a decline of $5.9 billion in inventories during that year.

Over the years covered by the table, investment was a volatile component of GNP, ranging from 2.5 percent of GNP in 1933 to 18.8 percent of GNP in 1950. Such volatility is a feature of investment behavior which has implications for the construction of the macroeconomic models considered below.

Since the figures in Table 2.1 are for *gross* rather than net national product, no adjustment for depreciation has been made. The investment total in the table is gross investment, not net investment (net investment would equal gross investment minus depreciation). In 1980, for example, depreciation, which is also called the capital consumption allowance, was $287.3 billion. Therefore, net investment was $108 billion (395.3 − 287.3) and net national product was $2338.9 billion (2626.1 − 287.3, where the discrepancy in the decimal is due to rounding).[3]

The next component of gross national product in the table is government purchases of goods and services. This is the share of the current output of goods and services bought by the government sector, which includes the federal government as well as state and local governments. It is important to note that not all categories of government spending are part of gross national product because not all government spending represents a demand for currently produced goods and services. Government transfer payments to

---

[3]In 1933, depreciation was $7.4 billion. Since gross investment was only $1.4 billion, *net* investment was negative. This means that the capital stock declined in that year since gross investment was insufficient to replace the portion of the capital stock that wore out.

individuals (e.g., social security payments) and government interest payments are examples of categories of spending that are not included in GNP. From the table it can be seen that government's share in gross national product has increased in the post–World War II period relative to the prewar period. In 1929, government purchases of goods and services were 8.5 percent of GNP. Not surprisingly, in 1945, during World War II, the government component of GNP, swollen by the military budget, had risen to 39 percent. But in the postwar period the government sector did not return to its prewar size. Government purchases of goods and services were approximately 20 percent or one-fifth of GNP in both 1960 and 1980. Trends in the size of the government budget—both purchases of goods and services and other components not included in the national income accounts—will be given some detailed analysis in a later chapter when we consider *fiscal* or government budget policy.

The final component of GNP given in Table 2.1 is net exports. Net exports equals total (gross) exports minus imports. These items represent the direct contribution of the foreign sector to GNP. Gross exports are currently produced goods and services sold to foreign buyers. They are a part of gross national product. Imports are purchases by domestic buyers of goods and services produced abroad and should not be counted in gross national product. Imported goods and services are, however, included in the consumption, investment, and government spending totals in GNP.[4] Therefore, we need to subtract the value of imports to arrive at the total of domestically produced goods and services. Net exports remain as the (net) direct effect of foreign-sector transactions on GNP.

Before turning from the product to the income side of the national income accounts, it should be noted that the breakdown of GNP into consumption, investment, government purchases, and net exports (exports minus imports) results from the attempt to group purchases by type of buyer—rather than, for example, by type of product. This is done with an eye toward explaining the levels of such components by isolating the factors that motivate each group of purchasers. Consumers in general would be expected to be influenced by household incomes, businesses by profit opportunities, the government by macroeconomic policy considerations, and so on. Not all the macroeconomic theories discussed below use a sectoral approach to modeling GNP determination, but one, the Keynesian theory, does.

---

[4]Also, the value of imported intermediate products is reflected in these totals.

2.3 NATIONAL INCOME

National income is the sum of all factor earnings from current production of goods and services. Factor earnings are incomes of factors of production: land, labor, and capital. Each dollar of GNP is one dollar of final sales, and if there were no charges against GNP other than factor incomes, GNP and national income would be equal. There are, in fact, some other charges against GNP which cause national income and GNP to diverge, but the two concepts are still closely related. The adjustments required to go from GNP to national income, with figures for the year 1980, are shown in Table 2.2.

The first charge against GNP that is not included in national income is depreciation. The portion of the capital stock used up must be subtracted from final sales prior to computing national income; depreciation represents a cost of production, not factor income. Making this subtraction gives us net national product. From this total, both indirect taxes—sales and excise taxes—and the net amount of some additional items labeled "other" in the table are subtracted to yield national income. An indirect tax such as a sales tax represents a discrepancy between the market price of a product, which includes the tax (the amount entered in GNP), and the proceeds of the seller, from which factor incomes are paid. The "other" entry in Table 2.2 includes relatively minor adjustments for some additional discrepancies between factor earnings and the market prices of items included in GNP.[5]

Table 2.3 shows the components of national income and the level of each component in 1980. Compensation of employees, which includes wage and salary payments as well as supplementary benefits, is the largest element in national income, 75.3 per-

---

[5]An example of the type of item included in the "other" category is bad debts to the business sector, which would be termed a business transfer payment. Since such debts are uncollected, they are not factor earnings, yet they represent sales included in GNP.

Table 2.2
Relationship of Gross National Product and National Income, 1980[a]
(billions of dollars)

Gross national product	2626.1
Minus: Depreciation	287.3
Net national product	2338.9
Minus: Indirect taxes	212.3
Other	5.2
National income	2121.4

[a]Subtotals may not sum to total due to rounding.
Source: *Survey of Current Business*, April 1981.

Table 2.3 **Components of National Income, 1980 (billions of dollars)**	Compensation of employees	1596.5
	Corporate profits	182.7
	Proprietors' Income	130.6
	Rental income of persons	31.8
	Net interest	179.8
		2121.4

Source: *Survey of Current Business,* April 1981.

cent in 1980. Corporate profits were 8.6 percent of national income in that year. The next item in the table, proprietors' income, is the income of unincorporated business. In 1980 this amounted to 6.2 percent of national income. The final two items are rental income of persons and net interest income, which totaled 1.5 and 8.5 percent of national income, respectively.

Below we return to the discussion of national income and derive some useful relationships between national income and national product. First we consider two other income concepts.

2.4 PERSONAL AND PERSONAL DISPOSABLE INCOME

National income is a measure of income earned from current production of goods and services. For some purposes, however, it is useful to have a measure of income received by *persons* and regardless of source. For example, we noted above that consumption expenditures by households would be influenced by income. The relevant income concept would be one of all income received by persons. Also, we would want a measure of income after deducting personal tax payments, since income needed to make tax payments could not be used to finance consumption. *Personal income* is the national income accounts measure of the income received by persons from all sources. When we subtract personal tax payments from personal income we get a measure of *disposable (after-tax) personal income.*

In order to go from national income to personal income we have to subtract elements of national income that are not received by persons and add income of persons from sources other than current production of goods and services. The necessary adjustments are shown in Table 2.4. The first items subtracted from national income are the portions of the corporate profits item in the national income accounts which are not paid out as dividends to persons. The portion of corporate profits not paid out in dividends

Table 2.4
Relationship of National Income, Personal Income, and Disposable Income, 1980

National income	2121.4
less	
corporate profits tax payments, undistributed profits and valuation adjustment	128.3
contributions to social security	203.7
plus	
government transfer payments to persons	283.8
net government interest payments	30.1
business transfer payments	10.5
Personal income	2113.8
less	
personal tax and nontax payments	338.5
Personal disposable income	1775.3

Source: *Survey of Current Business,* April 1981.

includes corporate profits tax payments, undistributed profits (retained earnings), and a valuation adjustment made by the Commerce Department to correct for a distortion of reported profits figures due to inflation. The first two of these should require no explanation. The details of the valuation adjustment need not concern us here except to recognize that since this adjustment was made to the corporate profits entry in national income, but did not actually affect profits that can be paid out to persons, it must be subtracted in computing personal income.[6] Also subtracted from national income in computing personal income are contributions to social security by the employer and employee. Such payroll taxes are included in the employee compensation term in national income but go to the government, not directly to persons.

The items added in going from national income to personal income are payments to persons that are not for current production of goods and services. Government transfer payments to persons (social security benefits, welfare payments, etc.) are one such category. Net government interest payments (interest on outstanding government bonds) are also payments that are not in return for a productive service and are not included in national income.[7] They do comprise personal income, however. Business transfer payments are items such as cancellation of bad debts from persons and gifts from business to the household sector (which includes nonprofit foundations).

With these adjustments we can calculate personal income, which equaled $2113.8 billion in 1980. We then subtract personal

[6]We return to the discussion of the reasons why inflation distorts reported corporate profit figures in Chapter 16.

[7]Interest payments from the business sector to persons are considered payments for a productive service and are included in national income. This is the net interest entry in Table 2.3.

Table 2.5
Disposition of Personal Income, 1980

Personal income	2113.8
less	
personal tax and nontax payments	338.5
Personal disposable income	1775.3
less	
personal consumption expenditures	1672.8
personal transfer payments to foreigners (net)	1.2
Personal saving	101.3

Source: *Survey of Current Business,* April 1981.

tax and nontax payments, where nontax payments are such items as fines and license fees, to get personal disposable income, which was equal to $1775.3 billion in 1980.[8]

The next question to which we turn is the allocation or disposition of personal income into personal outlays and personal saving. The disposition of personal income is shown in Table 2.5, together with 1980 figures. As above we see that a portion of personal income ($338.5 billion in 1980) goes for personal taxes. The remainder is personal disposable income. Personal disposable income is divided between personal outlays and personal saving. Personal outlays are predominantly personal consumption expenditures ($1672.8 billion in 1980), the household sector's demand for currently produced goods and services. The other, very small, component of personal outlays are net personal transfers to foreigners ($1.2 billion in 1980), items such as gifts to foreigners by individuals or nonprofit organizations. Personal saving ($101.3 billion, or 5.7 percent of personal disposable income in 1980) is the portion of personal disposable income which is not paid out in taxes or as personal outlays. It should be noted that personal savings is not measured independently in the national income accounts but is defined residually to make the dispositions sum to total personal income.

2.5 SOME NATIONAL INCOME ACCOUNTING IDENTITIES

The interrelationships among gross national product, national income, and personal income form the basis for some accounting

---

[8]The personal income and disposable personal income figures on Table 2.4 differ from the figures in the actual national income accounts tables in one respect. Consumer interest payments have been excluded. In the actual accounts, such payments, which totaled $46.4 billion in 1980, are included in personal income and then subtracted below as a personal outlay. Such consumer interest payments are not included in any of the models below and we have simply ignored them.

definitions or *identities* which are used in the construction of the macroeconomic models considered below. In deriving these identities in this section we will simplify the national income accounting structure by ignoring a number of items discussed above. This simplified accounting structure will be carried over into the models in the next section.

The simplifications we impose are as follows:

1. The foreign sector will be omitted. This means that we drop the net exports term from GNP (Table 2.1) and the net foreign transfers item from personal outlays in breaking down the disposition of personal income (Table 2.5). The foreign sector is reintroduced into our models in Chapter 17, where questions of international macroeconomics are considered.

2. Indirect taxes and the other discrepancies between GNP and national income will be ignored (Table 2.2). We assume that national income and national product or output are the same. *The terms national "income" and "output" are used interchangeably throughout this book.*

3. Depreciation will also be ignored (except where explicitly noted). Therefore, gross and net national product will be identical.

4. Several simplifications will be made in the relationship between national income and personal disposable income (Table 2.4). We assume that all corporate profits are paid out as dividends; there are no retained earnings or corporate tax payments and there is no valuation adjustment (see Table 2.4). We assume that all taxes, including social security contributions, are assessed directly on households. Also, business transfer payments will be ignored. Consequently, we can specify personal disposable income as national income (or output) minus tax payments (Tx) plus government transfers (Tr), which include government interest payments. Letting *net* taxes (T) equal tax payments minus transfers (Tx − Tr), we have (personal) disposable income (DI) equal to national income (Y) minus net taxes (DI $\equiv Y - T$). With these simplifications we have the following accounting identities.

Gross national product (Y) is defined as

$$Y \equiv C + I_r + G \tag{2.1}$$

that is, as consumption (C) plus *realized* investment (I_r) plus government purchases of goods and services (G).[9] The subscript (r) on the investment term is included since below we shall want to distinguish between this *realized* investment total which appears in

---

[9]It is important to distinguish identities such as (2.1), which are indicated by the three-bar symbol ($\equiv$), and equations, which will be indicated with the usual equal sign ($=$). Identities are relationships that follow from accounting or other definitions and therefore hold for any and all values of the variables.

the national income accounts and the *desired* level of investment spending.

From the income side of the national income accounts, again making use of simplifications 1 to 4 above, we have the identity

$$Y - T \equiv C + S \tag{2.2}$$

which states that all disposable income, which equals national income (Y) minus *net* tax payments (T = tax payments minus transfers), goes for consumption expenditures or personal saving. We can write (2.2) as

$$Y \equiv C + S + T$$

and since Y is both national income and output, we can combine (2.1) and (2.2) to write

$$C + I_r + G \equiv Y \equiv C + S + T \tag{2.3}$$

This identity states that expenditures on GNP ($C + I_r + G$) must by definition be equal to the dispositions of national income ($C + S + T$) and will be useful below in the construction of the Keynesian macroeconomic model. By canceling the consumption term (C) on both the left and right in (2.3), we can rewrite this fundamental identity as

$$I_r + G \equiv S + T \tag{2.4}$$

This form of the expenditures–income identity will also be employed below.

2.6 MEASURING PRICE CHANGES: REAL VERSUS NOMINAL GNP

So far the figures we have been discussing are for *nominal* GNP, which is the output of currently produced goods and services evaluated at current market prices or in current dollar terms. Since gross national product is the value of currently produced goods and services measured in market prices, it will change when there is a change in the overall price level as well as when the actual volume of production changes. For many purposes we want a measure of output that varies only with the quantity of goods produced. Such a measure would, for example, be most closely related to the level of employment; more workers are not needed to produce a given volume of output simply because it is sold at a higher price. To construct a measure of output which changes only when quantities and not prices change, what is termed *real* GNP, we measure output in terms of constant prices or constant-valued dollars from a base year. Using 1972 as a base year, for example, we can compute the value of GNP in 1929, 1975, or 1980 in terms of the price level or value of the dollar in 1972. Changes in GNP in 1972-valued dollars would then measure quantity changes between these years.

Column 1 of Table 2.6 shows the nominal GNP for the same years as those given in Table 2.1 as well as for some additional recent years. Column 2 shows the values of real GNP as measured in 1972 prices for each of these years. In 1972, real and nominal income are the same, of course, since base-year prices are current prices. In prior years, since current prices were lower than 1972 prices, real GNP is higher than nominal GNP. Conversely, in years after 1972, when prices were higher, nominal GNP exceeds real GNP.

As can be seen from the table, the real GNP figures tell a somewhat different story from the nominal figures. The decline in real GNP between 1929 and 1933 was much less than the decline in nominal GNP, although it was still a sharp decline (30 percent). This was because part of the fall in nominal GNP came from a decline in the aggregate price level between these two years. In more recent years, it can be seen that while nominal GNP rose by over $200 billion from 1973 to 1975, real GNP actually declined during that period. Again in 1980 there was a rapid increase in nominal GNP and a fall in real GNP. In both cases prices were increasing rapidly but the level of real economic activity was de-

Table 2.6 Nominal and Real GNP, Selected Years (billions of dollars)	(1)	(2)	(3)
Year	Nominal GNP	Real GNP	Implicit GNP Deflator (Column 1 ÷ Column 2 × 100)
1929	103.4	315.7	32.8
1933	55.8	222.1	25.1
1939	90.9	319.8	28.4
1945	212.4	560.4	37.9
1950	286.5	534.8	53.6
1960	506.5	737.2	68.7
1970	992.7	1085.6	91.4
1972	1185.9	1185.9	100.0
1973	1326.4	1255.0	105.7
1974	1434.2	1248.0	114.9
1975	1549.2	1233.9	125.6
1976	1718.0	1300.4	132.1
1977	1918.0	1371.7	139.8
1978	2156.1	1436.9	150.1
1979	2413.9	1483.0	162.8
1980	2626.1	1480.7	177.4

Source: *Economic Report of the President,* 1981.

INTRODUCTION AND MEASUREMENT

clining. Such inflationary recessions will receive considerable attention in our later analysis. Finally, it can be seen from the table that real GNP has approximately doubled in the past two decades. Nominal GNP has risen by a factor of about 5 during the same period, both as a result of this real growth and, additionally, due to the increase in the aggregate price level.

The ratio of nominal GNP to real GNP is a measure of the value of current production in current prices relative to the value of the same goods and services in the base-year prices. This ratio is then a measure of the aggregate price level relative to the base year— what is called a price index. We can measure changes in the aggregate price level by comparing the ratios of nominal to real GNP in different years. These ratios (nominal GNP ÷ real GNP) are shown in column 3 of Table 2.6, where they are multiplied by 100 (following the procedure in the national income accounts) to construct an index that will be equal to 100 in the base year. This index is called the *implicit GNP deflator*.

First, consider a comparison of this ratio between the base year and some other year, for example 1980. In the base year real and nominal GNP are the same and the value of the implicit price deflator is 100. In 1980 the value of the implicit price deflator was 177.4 (the ratio of nominal to real GNP was 1.774). GNP at current prices in 1980 (nominal GNP) was 77.4 percent greater than 1980 GNP in 1972 prices (real GNP). This means that the aggregate price level had risen by 77.4 percent from 1972 to 1980. We can also use the implicit GNP deflator to measure price changes between two years neither of which is the base year. For example, in 1979 the value of the deflator was 162.8, compared to a value of 177.4 in 1980. As measured by this index, therefore, the rise in the aggregate price level or the rate of inflation between 1979 and 1980 was 9.0 percent:

$$[(177.4 - 162.8) \div 162.8] \times 100 = 9.0$$

Similarly, between 1929 and 1933 the value of the implicit GNP deflator fell from 32.8 to 25.1, indicating a decline in the aggregate price level or a deflation (over four years) of 23.5 percent:

$$[(25.1 - 32.8) \div 32.8] \times 100 = -23.5$$

The ratio of nominal to real GNP is termed a deflator because we can divide nominal GNP by this ratio to correct for the effect of inflation on GNP—to deflate GNP. This is obvious since

$$\text{GNP deflator} = \frac{\text{nominal GNP}}{\text{real GNP}}$$

$$\text{real GNP} = \frac{\text{nominal GNP}}{\text{GNP deflator}}$$

Less obvious is why the adjective *implicit* is attached to the name of this price index. The GNP deflator is an implicit price index in that we first construct a quantity measure, real GNP, and then compare the movement in GNP in current and constant dollars to gauge the changes in prices. We do not try, directly or explicitly, to measure the average movement in prices. Two examples of explicit price indices are considered in the next section.

2.7 THE CONSUMER PRICE INDEX AND THE PRODUCER PRICE INDEX

Since the GNP deflator measures changes in the prices of all currently produced goods and services, it is the most comprehensive and in that sense the preferable measure of the rate of price change. Two other price indices are, however, widely reported and have their particular uses and advantages.

The *consumer price index* (CPI) measures the retail prices of a fixed "market basket" of approximately 400 goods and services purchased by consumers. The CPI is an explicit price index in the sense that it directly measures movements in the weighted average of the prices of the goods and services in the market basket through time. The CPI may be considered the price index most relevant to consumers since it measures only the prices of goods and services directly purchased by them. Many government pensions, including the level of social security benefits and many wage rates are indexed to the CPI, meaning they have provisions for automatic increases geared to increases in the CPI.

Another widely reported explicit price index is the *producer price index* (PPI), which measures the wholesale prices of approximately 2800 items. Since these items sold at the wholesale level include many raw materials and semifinished goods, movements in the producer price index signal future movements in retail prices, such as those measured in the CPI. Both the consumer price index and the producer price index have the advantage that they are available monthly, whereas the implicit GNP deflator is available only quarterly.

All three price indices generally move in similar ways, as can be seen from Table 2.7, which gives the annual inflation rates for the years 1971–80 and the average annual inflation rate for the decade as a whole as measured by the three price indices we have discussed. The differences in the movements in the indices reflect their different composition. The producer price index, for example, gives a larger weight to raw materials than either of the others and therefore rose substantially more than the CPI or GNP deflator in

		Table 2.7		
Year	**GNP Deflator**	**Consumer Price Index**	**Producer Price Index**
1971	5.0	4.3	3.1
1972	4.2	3.3	3.1
1973	5.7	6.2	9.1
1974	8.7	11.0	15.3
1975	9.3	9.1	10.8
1976	5.2	5.8	4.2
1977	5.8	6.5	6.0
1978	7.3	7.7	7.8
1979	8.5	11.3	11.0
1980	9.0	13.5	14.2
1970–80	6.9	7.9	8.5

**Table 2.7
Annual Rates of
Inflation as
Measured by
Various Price
Indices, 1971–80[a]**

[a]For comparability with the GNP deflator, the CPI and PPI figures are year to year inflation rates. Note that the CPI figures in Table 1.3 are December to December changes and therefore differ somewhat from the figures here.
Sources: *Economic Report of the President*, 1981; *Survey of Current Business*, April 1981.

the 1973–75 period of rapidly rising prices for crude oil (and other basic commodities).

2.8 MEASURES OF CYCLICAL VARIATION IN OUTPUT

Most of the analysis in this book focuses on short-run or cyclical movements in output and employment—fluctuations over periods of perhaps one to four years. Only in Chapter 16 do we consider the factors determining the growth of output over longer-run periods. In the short run, fluctuations in output and employment come primarily from variations in actual output around *potential output,* where potential output is defined as the level of real output that the economy could produce at high rates of resource utilization. Such short-run movements in output consist of changes in the utilization rates of labor and capital. It is in the longer run that growth of potential output, which implies growth in the available quantity of factors of production (capital and labor), becomes an important determinant of the growth of output. We have already discussed the measurement of actual real output (real GNP); what remains for this section is to explain the measurement of potential real output and thus of deviations of actual GNP from potential GNP.

The official U.S. estimates of potential GNP are compiled by the President's Council of Economic Advisors. The first step in making such estimates is to choose benchmark measures of high resource utilization. Potential income is then estimated as the level of *real*

GNP that would be forthcoming at those benchmark high utilization rates. In the 1960s the Council simply estimated potential GNP as the output level that corresponded to a 4 percent unemployment rate; that is, a 4 percent unemployment rate was taken as the benchmark level of high unemployment. This reflected an assumption that at an unemployment rate of 4 percent of the labor force, existing unemployment was of a frictional or seasonal nature—workers between jobs, just entering or reentering the labor force, or workers whose employment has a seasonal pattern. These early estimates made no allowance for the utilization rate of capital.

In recent years the procedure for estimating potential GNP has been modified in two ways.[10] First, the new estimates also take explicit account of the utilization rate of capital. The benchmark utilization rate for capital is assumed to be 86 percent; that is, "high employment" of the capital stock is assumed to mean that 86 percent of existing plant capacity is in use.

The second difference from the earlier estimates is that the unemployment rate which is assumed to correspond to a high or full-employment level is no longer assumed to have been a constant 4 percent. In the revised estimates, the benchmark unemployment rate used to compute potential output is still assumed to be 4 percent until 1965 but is assumed to rise thereafter to 4.9 percent by 1973 and to 5.1 percent beginning in 1975. This increase in the benchmark for a high utilization rate for labor was made because of changes in the age–sex composition of the labor force, which seem likely to have raised the levels of frictional and seasonal unemployment that would exist even in a high-employment situation. Specifically, young workers and female workers have increased relative to older male workers as a proportion of the labor force. Since the former groups include a greater number of new entrants or reentrants to the labor force, and tend to change jobs more frequently as well as to combine spells of employment with periods of alternative activity (school or work in the home), they would be expected to have more frequent episodes of frictional or seasonal unemployment. Therefore, the Council of Economic Advisors estimates that the level of unemployment corresponding to a high- or "full"-employment rate has been rising in recent years.

The revised estimates of potential GNP for the 1956–80 period, together with the corresponding actual GNP figures, are shown in

[10]For the methods used in early estimates of potential output, see the *Economic Report to the President*, 1962, or Arthur Okun, "Potential GNP: Its Measurement and Significance," an appendix to his book *The Political Economy of Prosperity* (Washington, D.C.: Brookings Institution, 1970). The revisions of the potential output series are described in the *Economic Report of the President*, 1977, 1979.

Table 2.8		(1)	(2)	(3)
Potential GNP, Actual GNP, and the GNP Gap, 1956–1980 (billions of dollars)	Year	Potential GNP	Actual GNP	GNP Gap (Potential minus actual GNP)
	1956	675.9	671.6	4.3
	1957	699.3	683.8	15.5
	1958	723.5	680.9	42.6
	1959	748.5	721.7	26.8
	1960	774.4	737.2	37.2
	1961	801.2	756.6	44.6
	1962	829.0	800.3	28.7
	1963	859.7	832.5	27.2
	1964	892.9	876.4	16.5
	1965	927.6	929.3	−1.7
	1966	963.5	984.8	−21.3
	1967	999.2	1011.4	−12.2
	1968	1035.0	1058.1	−23.1
	1969	1072.0	1087.6	−15.6
	1970	1110.4	1085.6	24.8
	1971	1150.3	1122.4	27.9
	1972	1191.7	1185.9	5.8
	1973	1234.9	1255.0	−20.1
	1974	1277.5	1248.0	29.5
	1975	1320.6	1233.9	86.7
	1976	1365.1	1300.4	64.7
	1977	1411.4	1371.1	40.3
	1978	1459.3	1436.9	22.4
	1979	1492.1	1483.0	9.1
	1980	1548.5	1480.7	67.8

Sources: *Economic Report of the President,* 1981; Federal Reserve Bank of St. Louis.

columns 1 and 2 of Table 2.8. Column 3 of the table gives potential GNP minus actual GNP, termed the *GNP gap*. The GNP gap measures the amount by which actual GNP fell short of potential GNP. Figure 2.1 plots the movements in potential and actual GNP for the same years.

Looking at either the figures in the table or the graph in Figure 2.1, one can trace the cyclical course of output in recent years. The recession that began in 1957 and a second recession beginning in 1960, before there had been a full recovery from the first, show up as sizable shortfalls of GNP relative to potential GNP. There is a slow recovery back toward potential income in the 1961–65 period. In the 1966–69 period the economy was overheated, with actual GNP exceeding potential GNP. This was the period of high Vietnam war expenditures imposed on an economy already operating at high resource utilization rates. The result was to push employment above a sustainable rate for the long run (as meas-

Figure 2.1 Potential and Actual GNP, 1956–1980

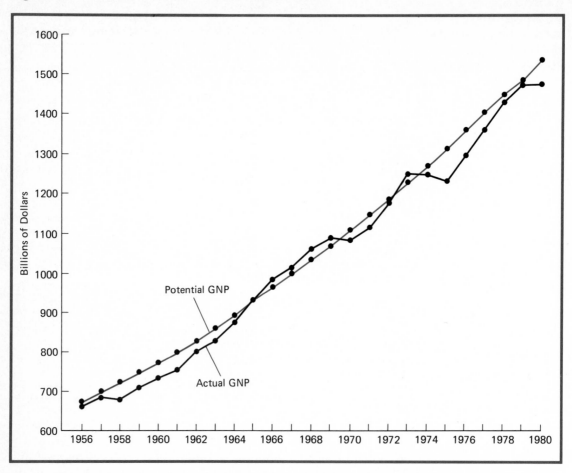

ured by the benchmark high employment rate). Another result, as we will see later in our discussion, was an accelerating inflation rate as demand came to exceed capacity.

In the wake of restrictive economic policies, the boom conditions of the late 1960s gave way to a relatively mild recession in 1970–71, followed by a strong expansion which pushed actual above potential income by 1973. There followed the most severe of the post–World War II recessions, with output falling to nearly $90 billion below potential output in 1975. Despite a recovery beginning in the second quarter of 1975, actual GNP still fell short of potential GNP by $9.1 billion in 1979, and then slipped down sharply during the recession in 1980.

The fluctuations in actual output around the level of potential

INTRODUCTION AND MEASUREMENT

output, as illustrated in Table 2.8 and Figure 2.1, together with the associated variations in other important macroeconomic aggregates, such as employment, prices, and interest rates, form the subject matter for much of the analysis to come.

2.9 CONCLUSION

We have now discussed the real-world counterparts to the central variables that will appear in the models of the next section—with one exception. The exception is money. The quantity of money is a key variable in all the models that we consider later. Control of the quantity of money through *monetary policy* is one important type of stabilization policy. The question of the definition of money turns out to be somewhat more complicated than it would seem at first glance and is best put off until later when questions of money supply and demand are examined in detail. For now it will be adequate to take the term "money" in our models to refer to the stock of currency plus demand deposits (deposits on which checks may be written).[11]

We shall return to questions of measurement at several later points. In addition to further discussion of the empirical definition of money (Chapter 14), we also need to consider measures of our international transactions (Chapter 17) and go into more detail concerning the federal government budget (Chapter 18). Some other variables (e.g., the wage rate and the interest rate) will be defined as they are encountered in our analysis. At this point it seems time to turn to the task of explaining rather than just measuring the behavior of macroeconomic variables.

Review Questions

1 Define the term *gross national product* (GNP). Explain carefully which transactions in the economy are included in GNP.

2 What is the difference between net national product and gross national product? Why is this difference important?

3 Define the term *national income* (NI). Why is national income not equal to gross national product?

4 Define the terms *personal income* and personal *disposable in-*

[11]In 1980, the definitions of the *money aggregates* in the official U.S. statistics were revised. The differences between the old and new definitions are discussed in Chapter 14.

come. Conceptually, how do these income measures differ from national income? Of what usefulness are these measures?

5   Three price indices were considered in this chapter: the GNP deflator, the consumer price index, and the producer price index. Explain the differences between these different measures of *the* price level.

6   Using the data in Table 2.6, compute the change in the price level between 1972 and 1976; between 1950 and 1970; between 1950 and 1980.

7   Explain the concept of *potential income*. How would you interpret a situation such as that in the late 1960s when the economy was above *potential* income?

Selected Readings

ABRAHAM, W. I., *National Income and Economic Accounting*. Englewood Cliffs, N.J.: Prentice-Hall, 1969.

NORDHAUS, WILLIAM, and TOBIN, JAMES, "Is Growth Obsolete?" in *Economic Growth*, 50th Anniversary Colloquium, Vol. 5. New York: National Bureau of Economic Research–Columbia University Press, 1972.

OKUN, ARTHUR, "Potential GNP, Its Measurement and Significance," *1962 Proceedings of the Business and Economic Statistics Sections of the American Statistical Association*, pp. 98–104. Also reprinted as an appendix to Arthur Okun, *The Political Economy of Prosperity*. Washington, D.C.: Brookings Institution, 1970.

RUGGLES, NANCY, and RUGGLES, RICHARD, *The Design of National Income Accounts*. New York: National Bureau of Economic Research–Columbia University Press, 1970.

U.S. DEPARTMENT OF COMMERCE, "The National Income and Product Accounts of the United States: An Introduction to the Revised Estimates for 1929–80," *Survey of Current Business*, 60 (December 1980), Part 1, pp. 1–45.

PART two

macroeconomic models

3

The chapters of this part trace the development of several competing macroeconomic theories. This approach, rather than the discussion of a unified macroeconomic theory, is made necessary by the existence of differing explanations of the economic phenomena described in Chapter 1 and correspondingly different positions on central macroeconomic policy questions. We begin with an analysis of the *classical* macroeconomic model (Chapters 3 and 4). Succeeding chapters discuss the *Keynesian* model (Chapters 5 to 8), the *monetarist* model (Chapters 9 and 10), and the *new classical* model (Chapter 11). The final chapter in the part summarizes the positions of these different "schools" of macroeconomic theory.

3.1 THE STARTING POINT

The term "macroeconomics" originated in the 1930s. That decade witnessed substantial progress in the study of aggregative economic questions. The forces that determine income, employment, and prices had been receiving greater attention since about the turn of the century, after a long period in which microeconomic questions dominated the field of economics. The world depression that began in 1929 added urgency to the study of such macroeconomic questions. The products of such research were a number of theories of the "business cycle" and accompanying sets of policy

CLASSICAL MACROECONOMICS (I): EQUILIBRIUM OUTPUT AND EMPLOYMENT

prescriptions for stabilizing economic activity. One such theory and one set of policy conclusions swept the field and was to become a new orthodoxy in macroeconomic thought. The book containing this theory was *The General Theory of Employment, Interest and Money* by John Maynard Keynes, and the process of change in economic thinking that resulted from this work has been called the Keynesian Revolution. But revolution against what? What was the old orthodoxy? Keynes termed it "classical economics" and it is this body of macroeconomic thought that we study in this chapter and the next.

The ideas that formed the Keynesian revolution, as well as the evolution of these ideas in the post-Keynesian period, are the central focus of our analysis. A prerequisite for this analysis is a knowledge of the classical system that Keynes attacked. Classical theory also plays a more positive role in the later development of macroeconomics. Although many early Keynesian writers viewed the classical theory as ready for the scrap heap of outmoded ideas, with time such overreaction subsided, and modern *neo-Keynesian* economics contains many ideas that originated with the classical economists. The classical model also provides the starting point for the two main challenges that have been mounted against the neo-Keynesian theory, those of the *monetarists* and of the *new classical economists*.

Keynes used the term "classical" to refer to virtually all economists who had written on macroeconomic questions prior to 1936.

More conventional modern terminology distinguishes between two periods in the development of economic theory prior to 1930. The first, termed *classical*, is the period dominated by the work of Adam Smith (*Wealth of Nations*, 1776), David Ricardo (*Principles of Political Economy*, 1st ed., 1817), and John Stuart Mill (*Principles of Political Economy*, 1st ed., 1848). The second, termed the *neoclassical* period, had as its most prominent English representatives Alfred Marshall (*Principles of Economics*, 8th ed., 1920) and A. C. Pigou (*The Theory of Unemployment*, 1933). The theoretical advances distinguishing the classical and neoclassical periods related primarily to microeconomic theory. Keynes felt that the macroeconomic theory of the two periods was homogeneous enough to be dealt with as a whole. Our treatment here follows Keynes in that respect. A distinction should, however, be made between what the classical economists referred to as "normal" equilibrium analysis and their disequilibrium analysis, which they referred to as the abnormal or "pathological" case, where equilibrium had been disturbed.

To the classical economists the normal or equilibrium level of income at any time was a point of full employment, or in terms of the variables described in Chapter 2, a point where actual output was equal to potential output. Equilibrium for a variable refers to a state where all the forces acting on that variable are in balance and where there is no tendency for the given variable to move from that point. It was an important tenet of classical economists that only such full-employment points could be positions of even short-run equilibrium. Away from full employment the classical economists assumed that there were forces not in balance acting to bring output to the full-employment level. The classical equilibrium economics examined the factors that determined the level of full-employment output along with the associated levels of other important aggregates, such as employment, prices, wages, and interest rates.

The classical economists observed that the economy did not always satisfy the conditions for such full-employment equilibrium. The classical *disequilibrium* analysis attempted to explain the forces that cause prices, output, interest rates, and other aggregative variables to deviate from normal levels and, more ambitiously, to explain the movement of the variables through time while they were out of equilibrium. We deal for the most part with the classical equilibrium theory. This was the theory attacked by Keynes and it is also, for the most part, elements of the equilibrium theory which provide a basis for the monetarist and new classical theories. An example of the classical disequilibrium approach is discussed in an appendix to Chapter 4.

3.2 THE CLASSICAL REVOLUTION

The classical economists attacked a body of economic doctrines known as *mercantilism*. Mercantilist thought was associated with the rise of the nation-state in Europe during the sixteenth and seventeenth centuries. Two general tenets of mercantilism that the classical writers attacked were bullionism, a belief that the wealth and power of a nation were determined by its stock of precious metals, and the belief in the need for state action to direct the development of the capitalist system.

An adherence to bullionism led countries to attempt to secure an excess of exports over imports and, hence, earn gold and silver through foreign trade. Methods used to secure this favorable balance of trade included export subsidies, import duties, and development of colonies to provide export markets. State action was assumed to be necessary to cause the developing capitalist system to act in line with the interests of the state. Foreign trade was carefully regulated and export of bullion prohibited in many places to serve the ends of bullionism. The use of state action was also advocated on a much broader front to develop home industry, reduce home consumption, and develop both human and natural resources.

In contrast to the mercantilists, classical economists emphasized the importance of *real* factors in determining the *Wealth of Nations* and stressed the optimizing tendencies of the free market in the absence of state control. Classical analysis was primarily *real* analysis; the growth of an economy was the result of increased stocks of the factors of production and advances in techniques of production. Money played a role only in facilitating transactions as a means of exchange. Most *real* questions in economics could be answered without an analysis of the role of money. The classical economists were mistrustful of government and stressed the harmony of individual and national interest when the market was left unfettered with government regulation, except for those necessary to see that the market remained competitive. Both of these aspects of classical economics, the stress on real factors and the belief in the efficacy of the free market mechanism, developed in the course of controversies over long-run questions, concerns about the determinants of long-run economic development. These classical positions on long-run issues were, however, important in shaping classical economists' views on short-run questions.

The attack on bullionism led classical economists to stress that money had no intrinsic value. Money was held only for the sake of the goods that could be purchased with it. It was on the role of money as a means of exchange that the classical economist focused. Another role that money had played in the mercantilist view was as a spur to economic activity. In the short run many of the mercantilists argued that an increase in the quantity of money would lead to an increase in demand for commodities and would stimulate production and employment. For the classical economists to ascribe this role to money in determining real variables, even in the short run, was dangerous in light of their deemphasis of the importance of money.

The classical attack on the mercantilist view of the need for state action to regulate the capitalist system also had implications for short-run macroeconomic analysis. One role for state action in the mercantilist view was to assure that markets existed for all goods produced. Consumption, both domestic and foreign, must be encouraged to the extent that production advanced. The classical response is stated by John Stuart Mill:

> In opposition to these palpable absurdities it was triumphantly established by political economists that consumption never needs encouragement.[1]

As in other areas, the classical economists felt that the free market mechanism would work to provide markets for any goods that were produced: "The legislator, therefore, need not give himself any concern about consumption."[2] The classical doctrine was that in the aggregate, production of a given quantity of output will generate sufficient demand for that output; there could never be a "want of buyers for all commodities."[3] Consequently, classical economists gave little explicit attention to factors that determine the aggregate demand for commodities or to policies to regulate aggregate demand.

There were, then, two general features of the classical analysis which arose as part of their attack on mercantilism.

1. The classical economics stressed the role of real as opposed to monetary factors in determining real variables such as output and employment. Money had a role in the economy only as a means of exchange.
2. The classical economics stressed the self-adjusting tendencies of the economy if left free of government intervention. Government policies to ensure an adequate demand for output were among those state actions considered by the classical economics to be unnecessary and generally harmful.

[1]Mill J. S., "On the Influence of Consumption on Production," in *Essays on Economics and Society*, Vol. IV of Collected Works. (Toronto: University of Toronto Press, 1967), p. 263.
[2]Ibid., p. 263.
[3]Ibid., p. 276.

We turn now to the model constructed by the classical economists to support these positions.

3.3 PRODUCTION

A central relationship in the classical model is the *aggregate production function*. This production function, which is based on the technology of the individual firms, provides a relationship between the level of output and the level of factor inputs. For each level of inputs the production function shows the resulting level of output and can be written in the form

$$y = F(\bar{K}, N) \tag{3.1}$$

where y is real output, K the stock of capital (plant and equipment), and N the quantity of the homogeneous labor input.[4] For the short run the stock of capital is assumed to be fixed, as indicated by the bar over the symbol for capital. The state of technology and the population are also assumed to be constant over the period considered. For this short-run period output varies solely with variations in the labor input (N) drawn from the fixed population. In Figure 3.1a we plot the output that will be produced by the efficient utilization of each level of labor input. As drawn, the production function has several characteristics of interest. At low levels of labor input (below N'), the function is assumed to be a straight line. Since the slope of the line gives the increment in output that is forthcoming for a given increment in labor input, this straight-line (constant-slope) portion of the curve exhibits constant returns to increases in labor input. For very low levels of labor utilization it might be presumed that additional workers could be applied to a given amount of plant and equipment without a fall in the productivity of the last worker added. For the most part, however, we will be considering situations to the right of N', between N' and N'', where adding additional labor input will result in an increment to output, but where the size of the increments to output declines as more labor is employed. Past N'', increments to labor produce no increment to output.

In Figure 3.1b we plot the increment to output per increment to the labor input, termed the *marginal product of labor* (MPN). The marginal product of labor curve is the slope of the production function ($\Delta y/\Delta N$) in Figure 3.1a. As N increases below N', the line is

---

[4]Functional notation such as that used in (3.1) will be utilized at numerous points in our analysis. In each case such equations have the interpretation that the function involved (in this case F) is a relationship that determines a unique value of the left-hand variable (in this case y) for each combination of the levels of the *arguments* of the function (in this case K and N).

Figure 3.1
Production Function
and Marginal Product
of Labor Curves

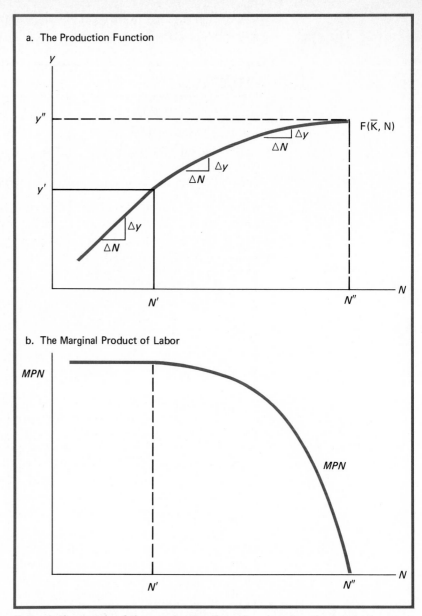

a. The Production Function

b. The Marginal Product of Labor

Part *a* is the graph of the production function showing the level of output (*y*) for each level of employment (*N*). As employment rises, output rises but at a diminishing rate. The slope of the production function ($\Delta y/\Delta N$) is positive, but diminishes as we move along the curve. The marginal product of labor (*MPN*), plotted in Part *b*, is the increment to output as a result of the addition of one further unit of labor input. The marginal product of labor is measured by the slope of the production function ($\Delta y/\Delta N$) and is a downward sloping curve when plotted against the level of employment.

flat, representing the constant marginal product of labor. Past N', the marginal product of labor is positive but declining and the curve crosses the horizontal axis at N''.

The short-run production function plotted in Figure 3.1a is a technological relationship which determines the level of output given the level of labor input (employment). The classical economists assumed that the quantity of labor employed would be determined by the forces of demand and supply in the labor market.

3.4 EMPLOYMENT

The purchasers of labor services are the firms that produce commodities. To see how the aggregate demand for labor is determined, we begin by considering the demand for labor on the part of an individual firm, denoted the ith firm. In the classical model the firms are considered to be perfect competitors who choose their output level so as to maximize profits. In the short run, output is varied solely by changing the labor input, so that choice of the level output and quantity of the labor input are essentially one decision. The perfectly competitive firm will increase output until the marginal cost of producing a unit of output is equal to the marginal revenue received from its sale. For the perfectly competitive firm marginal revenue is equal to product price.[5] Since labor is the only variable factor of production, the marginal cost of each additional unit of output is the marginal labor cost. Marginal labor cost will equal the money wage rate divided by the number of units of output produced by the additional unit of the labor input. Above, we defined the units of output produced by the incremental unit of labor employed as the marginal product of labor (MPN). Thus marginal cost for the ith firm (MC_i) is equal to the money wage rate (W) divided by the marginal product of labor for that firm (MPN_i):[6]

$$MC_i = \frac{W}{MPN_i} \qquad (3.2)$$

[5]Recall that the perfectly competitive firm faces a horizontal product demand curve. By assumption the firm is so small a portion of the market that its own increase in output can be sold without depressing product price. The analysis could be reformulated for the firm facing a downward-sloping demand curve without substantively changing the conclusions that we shall reach in this section.

[6]The i superscript does not appear on the price or wage variables since these are uniform across firms. The marginal product of labor for each firm (MPN_i) is derived from the production function for each firm, assumed to be identical over all firms; that is,

$$Y_i = F(K_i, N_i)$$

for each firm.

If, for example, the wage rate is $6 per hour and the additional unit of labor input will produce 3 units of output, the marginal cost of a unit of output would be $2.

The condition for short-run profit maximization will be

$$P = \text{MC}_i = \frac{W}{\text{MPN}_i} \tag{3.3}$$

Alternatively, (3.3) can be written as

$$\frac{W}{P} = \text{MPN}_i \tag{3.4}$$

In this form the condition for profit maximization is that the real wage paid by the firm must equal the marginal product (which is measured in units of the commodity, i.e., in real terms).

From this condition for profit maximization we can see that plotted against the real wage, the demand for labor schedule for the firm will be the marginal product of labor schedule, as illustrated in Figure 3.2. At a real wage such as 3.0 (e.g., a money wage of $6 and a product price of $2), the firm will hire 500 units of labor. At a quantity of labor below 500, say 400, the marginal product of labor (4.0 at 400) exceeds the real wage (3.0). The payment to the worker in real terms is less than the real product he produces. Profits would be increased by hiring additional units of labor. Alternatively, at quantities of labor input above 500, if the real wage is 3.0, the real wage will be above the marginal product of labor. The payment to labor will exceed the real product of the marginal worker, and marginal cost will exceed product price. The firm will reduce labor input to increase profit.

Thus the profit-maximizing quantity of labor demanded by a firm at each level of the real wage is given by the quantity of labor input that equates the real wage and marginal product of labor. The marginal product curve is the firm's demand curve for labor. This implies that labor demand depends inversely on the level of the real wage. The higher the real wage, for example, the lower the level of labor input that will equate the real wage to the marginal product of labor. In Figure 3.2, if the wage were 4.0 instead of 3.0, labor demand would be 400 instead of 500. The aggregate demand curve for labor is the horizontal summation of the individual firms' demand curves. For each real wage this curve will give the sum of the quantities of labor input demanded by the firms in the economy. We write this aggregate labor demand function as

$$N^d = f\left(\frac{W}{P}\right) \tag{3.5}$$

where in the aggregate, as with individual firms, an increase in the real wage lowers labor demand.

Figure 3.2
Labor Demand Curve
for a Firm

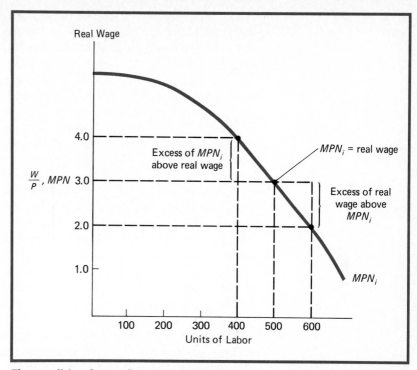

The condition for profit maximization by the firm is met at the point where the real wage (W/P) is equated with the marginal product of labor (MPN). If the real wage is 3.0 then the firm will maximize profits by hiring 500 units of the labor input. At a lower labor input, 400 units, the marginal product of labor (4.0) exceeds the real wage of 3.0 and the firm can increase profits by hiring additional labor. At a higher labor input, 600 units, the marginal product of labor (2.0) falls short of the real wage of 3.0 and the firm will increase profits by reducing the number of labor units employed.

The last relationship necessary for determining employment, and hence output, in the classical system is the labor supply curve. Labor services are supplied by the individual workers in the economy. As was the case with the labor demand relationship, the labor supply curve can best be explained by first considering an individual's labor supply decision. The classical economists assumed that the individual attempts to maximize utility or satisfaction. The level of utility depended positively on both real income, which gave the individual a command over goods and services, and on leisure. There is, however, a trade-off between the two goals since income is increased by work that reduces available leisure time.

Consider, for example, how individual j allocates one 24-hour period between leisure hours and hours worked: N_j^s, his supply of labor. Figure 3.3a illustrates the nature of the choice facing the individual. On the horizontal axis we measure hours of work per day. The zero point is at the right-hand corner and work hours are measured from right to left to a maximum of 24. Leisure is equal to 24 minus hours worked. Real income is measured on the vertical axis and is equal to the real wage W/P multiplied by the number of hours the individual works (N_j^s). The curved lines in the graph (labeled U_1, U_2, U_3) are *indifference curves*. Points along one of these lines are combinations of income and leisure which give equal satisfaction to the individual; hence he is indifferent as to which point along a given curve he achieves. The slope of the indifference curve gives the rate at which the individual is willing to trade off leisure for income, that is, the increase in income he would have to receive to be just as well off after giving up a unit of leisure, increasing N_j^s by a unit. Notice that as drawn, the curves become steeper as we go from right to left. For the eighteenth hour of work one would require greater compensation to maintain a given utility level than for the fifth hour of work. The hour of leisure the individual gives up (sleep, no doubt) in the former case would have more subjective value than the hour given up in the latter case. Curves higher and to the right represent progressively greater levels of utility. All points along U_2, for example, yield greater satisfaction than any point on U_1. The individual attempts to achieve the highest possible indifference curve.

The straight-line rays originating at the right-hand origin give the budget lines facing the individual. Starting from the origin (no work, all leisure) the individual can trade off leisure for income at a rate equal to the hourly real wage W/P; the slope of the budget line is the real wage. The higher the real wage, the steeper the budget line, reflecting the fact that at a higher real wage if we increase hours of work by 1 unit (move 1 unit to the left along the horizontal axis) we will receive a larger increment to income (move farther up the vertical axis along the budget line) than would have been the case at the lower real wage. Three such budget lines, corresponding to real wage rates of 2.0, 3.0, and 4.0, are shown in Figure 3.3a.

To maximize utility for any given real wage rate, the individual will choose the point where the budget line corresponding to that wage rate is tangent to one of his indifference curves. This point will have the property that the rate at which he is able to trade off leisure for income (the slope of the budget line) is just equal to the rate at which he is willing to make that trade-off (the slope of his indifference curve). In Figure 3.3a, at a real wage of 2.0 the worker will choose point A, where he supplies 6 hours of labor services, has 18 hours of leisure, and has a real income of 12. At real wage rates of 3.0 and 4.0, respectively, points B and C are chosen. As the

Figure 3.3
Individual Labor
Supply Decision

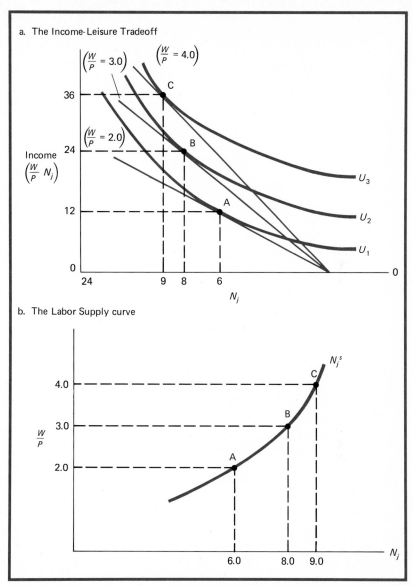

a. The Income-Leisure Tradeoff

$\left(\dfrac{W}{P} = 3.0\right)$ $\left(\dfrac{W}{P} = 4.0\right)$

$\left(\dfrac{W}{P} = 2.0\right)$

Income $\left(\dfrac{W}{P} N_j\right)$

36

24

12

0

24   9   8   6

N_j

C

B

A

U_3

U_2

U_1

b. The Labor Supply curve

$\dfrac{W}{P}$

4.0

3.0

2.0

6.0   8.0   9.0

N_j

N_j^s

A

B

C

Part *a* depicts the individual's labor–leisure choice. The individual will supply labor (N_j) up to the point where the rate at which labor may be traded
for income in the marketplace, which is given by the real wage (W/P), is
equated with the rate at which the individual is willing to trade labor (give
up leisure) in return for income which is measured by the slope of the
individual's indifference curves (U_1, U_2, U_3). At a real wage of 2.0, 6 hours
of labor will be supplied (point A); at a real wage of 3.0, 8 hours of labor
will be supplied (point B); at a real wage of 4.0, 9 hours of labor will be
supplied (point C). In Part *b* these amounts of labor supplied for given
values of the real wage are plotted to give the individual's labor supply
curve (N_j^s).

figure is constructed, more labor services are supplied at the higher real wage rates.

In Figure 3.3*b*, we construct the labor supply curve for the *j*th individual. This supply curve consists of points such as *A, B,* and *C* from Figure 3.3*a*, giving the amount of labor the individual will supply at each real wage rate. The aggregate labor supply curve would be obtained by horizontally summing all the individual labor supply curves and would give the total labor supplied at each level of the real wage. This aggregate labor supply curve can be written as

$$N^s = g\left(\frac{W}{P}\right) \tag{3.6}$$

Two features of the classical labor supply theory require further comment. First, note that the wage variable is the *real wage*. The worker receives utility ultimately from consumption, and in making the labor–leisure decision his concern is with the command over goods and services he receives for a unit of his labor. If, for example, his money wage rose from $2 per hour to $4 per hour while all product prices doubled, he would supply the same amount of labor after the change as before.

Second, by the construction of Figure 3.3, the labor supply curve is positively sloped; more labor is assumed to be supplied at higher real wage rates. This reflects the fact that a higher real wage rate means a higher price for leisure in terms of forgone income. At this higher price we assume that the worker will choose less leisure. This effect is analogous to the "substitution effect" in the theory of consumer demand. There is another effect, the equivalent of the "income effect" in consumer demand theory. As the real wage increases, the worker is able to achieve a higher level of real income. At higher levels of real income, leisure may become more desirable relative to further increments to income. With successive increases in the real wage a point may be reached where the worker chooses to supply less labor as the real wage increases and consumes more leisure. At this point the income effect outweighs the substitution effect; the labor supply curve assumes a negative slope and bends back toward the vertical axis. Almost certainly, at extremely high wage rates we would reach a backward-bending portion of the labor supply curve and perhaps wage rates need not be so "extremely" high. Although the empirical evidence on this question is inconclusive, we will assume that for wage rates which have been observed in industrialized nations, the aggregate labor supply curve does have a positive slope; the substitution effect outweighs the income effect.

To this point the following relationships have been derived:

$$y = F(\bar{K}, N) \qquad \text{(aggregate production function)} \quad (3.1)$$

$$N^d = f\left(\frac{W}{P}\right) \qquad \text{(labor demand schedule)} \qquad (3.5)$$

$$N^s = g\left(\frac{W}{P}\right) \qquad \text{(labor supply schedule)} \qquad (3.6)$$

These relationships, together with the equilibrium condition for the labor market,

$$N^s = N^d \qquad (3.7)$$

determine output and employment in the classical system, as illustrated in Figure 3.4. Part *a* of the graph shows the determination of the equilibrium levels of employment (N_0) and the real wage ($W/P)_0$ at the point of intersection between the aggregate labor demand and labor supply curves. This equilibrium level of labor input (N_0) results in an equilibrium level of output (y_0) given by the production function as shown in Figure 3.4*b*.

3.5 THE DETERMINANTS OF OUTPUT AND EMPLOYMENT IN THE CLASSICAL MODEL

We are now in a position to consider which factors in the economy are the ultimate determinants of output and employment in the classical theory, those factors that determine the positions of the labor supply and demand curves and the determinants of the position of the aggregate production function. Of equal interest is consideration of factors that do *not* affect equilibrium employment and income according to classical theory.

One property common to the determinants of the positions of the schedules in Figure 3.4 is that they are, for the most part, constant in the short run. The production function will be shifted by technical change which alters the amount of output forthcoming for given input levels. As graphed in Figure 3.4*b*, the production function will also shift as the capital stock changes over time. The state of the technology and the level of the capital stock are, however, factors that change only in the long run. The labor demand curve is the marginal product of labor curve, the slope of production function curve. Consequently, if the production function does not shift, the position of labor demand curve will be fixed. From our derivation of the labor supply curve, it can be seen that this relationship would be changed as the labor force varies (the number of individual labor supply curves to be summed to get aggre-

Figure 3.4
Classical Output and
Employment Theory

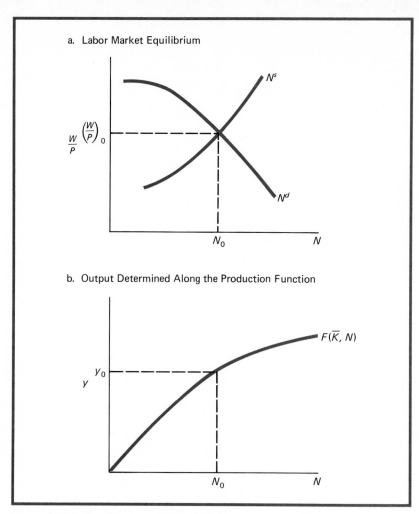

a. Labor Market Equilibrium

b. Output Determined Along the Production Function

Part *a* depicts the determination of labor market equilibrium at the level of the real wage $\left(\frac{W}{P}\right)_0$, which just equates labor supply and demand. The resulting equilibrium level of employment is N_0. Once the equilibrium level of employment is determined we find the equilibrium level of output, y_0, along the production function curve in Part *b*.

gate labor supply is changed) or as the individual preference function expressing his labor–leisure trade-off (U_1, U_2, U_3 in Figure 3.3a) shifts. Again, changes in these variables would be expected in the long run but not in the short run.

A second common feature of the factors determining output in the classical model is that they are all variables that affect the supply side of the market for current output—the amount that firms choose to produce. *In the classical model, the levels of output and employment are determined solely by such supply factors.*

Since the supply-determined nature of output and employment is a crucial feature of the classical system, it is worthwhile demonstrating this property of the model more formally. To do so it is necessary to give further consideration to the properties of the labor supply and demand functions just discussed. Figure 3.5*a* reproduces the aggregate supply and demand curves for labor. In

Figure 3.5
Labor Market Equilibrium and the Money Wage

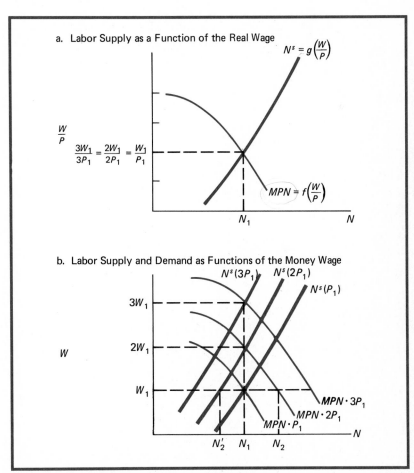

Part *a* shows the determination of equilibrium employment (at N_1) where labor supply equals labor demand. In Part *b* labor supply and demand are plotted as functions of the money wage. Increases in the price level (from P_1 to $2P_1$ then to $3P_1$) shift the labor supply and demand schedules upward proportionately. The money wage rises proportionately with the price level (from W_1 to $2W_1$ then to $3W_1$). The real wage and level of employment are unchanged.

Figure 3.5*b* we plot labor supply and labor demand as functions of the money wage (W). First consider the form of each of the latter relationships. For labor supply, we can draw a positively sloped curve such as $N^s(P_1)$, which gives the amount of labor supplied for each value of the money wage. Since workers are interested in the real wage there will be a different curve for each price level. For a given money wage each price level will mean a different real wage and, hence, a different amount of labor supplied. At a price level of $2P_1$, just double P_1, the labor supply curve in Figure 3.5*b* shifts to $N^s(2P_1)$. Notice that less labor is supplied for any money wage because at the higher price level a given money wage corresponds to a lower real wage. A rise in the price level shifts the labor supply curve (plotted against the money wage) upward to the left. The fact that the individual worker is interested *only* in the real wage can be seen from the fact that the same level of labor (N_1) is supplied at a money wage of W_1 and a price level of P_1 (real wage W_1/P_1) as at money wage and price combinations of $2W_1, 2P_1$ and $3W_1, 3P_1$ (real wage = W_1/P_1 at both points). Equiproportional increases (or decreases) in both money wages and the price level leave the quantity of labor supplied unchanged.

Now consider the labor demand curve plotted against the money wage, where in Figure 3.5 we use the fact that the labor demand $\left[f\left(\dfrac{W}{P}\right) \right]$ and marginal product of labor (MPN) schedules are equivalent. Recall that the condition met at all points along the demand curve is

$$\frac{W}{P} = \text{MPN} \tag{3.8}$$

If we want to know the quantity of labor that will be demanded at any money wage, as was the case for the quantity supplied, the answer depends on the price level. Given the money wage the firm will choose the level of employment where

$$W = \text{MPN} \cdot P \tag{3.9}$$

At successively higher price levels ($P_1, 2P_1, 3P_1$) the labor demand curve plotted against the money wage shifts to the right. For a given money wage more labor is demanded at higher price levels (N_1 at P_1, N_2 at $2P_1$, N_3 at $3P_1$) since that money wage corresponds to a lower real wage rate.[7] Again notice that the demand for labor

[7]Condition (3.9) has a simple economic interpretation. For profit maximization the money wage paid to the incremental worker (W) must just equal his contribution to the firm's revenue. His contribution to money revenues equals his marginal product multiplied by product price (MPN · P), which is termed his marginal revenue product.

depends only on the real wage. Equiproportional increases in the money wage and the price level from (W_1, P_1) to $(2W_1, 2P_1)$, and $(3W_1, 3P_1)$ leave labor demand unchanged at level N_1. They leave the real wage unchanged at W_1/P_1, which corresponds to the demand N_1 in Figure 3.5a.

The information in Figure 3.5 is useful in constructing the classical aggregate supply function—a relationship that makes clear the supply-determined nature of output in the classical model. The aggregate supply curve is the macroeconomic analogue to the microeconomic concept of the firm's supply curve. For the firm, the supply curve gives the output forthcoming at each level of the product price. For the perfectly competitive firm profits are maximized, as we have seen, where marginal cost (W/MPN_i for the ith firm) equals product price (P), or equivalently where

$$\text{MPN}_i = \frac{W}{P} \tag{3.10}$$

the marginal product of labor equals the real wage. Since the money wage is taken as given by the firm in deciding on optimal output, the supply curve for the firm will be positively sloped as a function of price. Higher prices will mean lower real wages, and consequently the firm will demand more labor and produce more output. In constructing the aggregate supply curve for the economy we will not be able to assume that the money wage remains fixed as output and labor input are varied. The money wage must vary to maintain equilibrium in the labor market. With this difference, the aggregate supply curve will address the same question as its microeconomic analogue: How will the level of output supplied vary when we change the product price?

In Figure 3.6 we construct the classical aggregate supply function. Consider output supplied at the three successively higher price levels, P_1, $2P_1$, and $3P_1$, which were plotted in Figure 3.5. At price level P_1 and money wage W_1, employment was N_1 and we will assume that the resulting output is y_1, as shown in Figure 3.6.[8] How will output supplied vary as we go to a price level of $2P_1$? At a price level of $2P_1$, *if* the money wage remained at W_1, we can see from Figure 3.5b that labor demand would increase to N_2. The higher price would mean a lower real wage and firms would try to expand both employment and output. The money wage will not, however, remain at W_1. At a price level of $2P_1$ the labor supply curve in Figure 3.5b will have shifted to $N^s(2P_1)$, and at a money wage of W_1, labor supply will be only N_2' units. There will be an

[8] This output level would be read from the production function curve given in Figure 3.4.

Figure 3.6
Classical Aggregate
Supply Curve

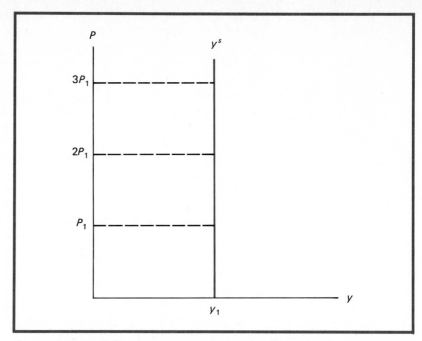

The vertical classical aggregate supply curve reflects the fact that higher values of the price level require proportionately higher levels of the money wage for labor market equilibrium. The real wage, employment, and, therefore level of output are the same at P_1, $2P_1$ and $3P_1$. The vertical aggregate supply curve implies that output is completely supply-determined in the classical system.

excess demand for labor equal to $(N_2 - N_2')$ units and the money wage will rise.

The process at work here will be one of some firms responding to higher prices by attempting to expand employment and production. To expand employment they raise money wages in an effort to bid workers away from other firms. Firms that lag in the process of raising money wages suffer higher quit rates and lose workers. This process of rising money wages will stop only when the money wage has increased sufficiently to reequilibrate supply and demand in the labor market. As can be seen in Figure 3.5b, this happens at a money wage of $2W_1$, where the money wage has increased proportionately with the price level. At this point the initial real wage is restored and employment is back at its original level. Consequently, output supplied at price level $2P_1$ is equal to y_1, the output level for price level P_1. At a still higher price level of $3P_1$, the money wage would rise to $3W_1$, but again output would be unchanged at y_1. *The aggregate supply curve is vertical.* Higher prices provide a spur to output only if they are not matched by proportionately higher money wages—only if they lower the real wage. Given the assumptions we have made, however, equilibrium in the labor market requires that money wages rise proportionately with prices to maintain the unique equilibrium real wage in that market.

The vertical aggregate supply curve in the classical model illustrates the supply-determined nature of output. An aggregate demand curve could be constructed and added to Figure 3.6, but whatever the shape and position of such a curve, it would clearly not affect equilibrium output. For output to be in equilibrium we must be on the supply curve; output must be at y_1.

The question raised above of which factors do not play a role in the classical theory of output and employment can now be answered. All factors, such as the quantity of money, levels of government spending and taxation, and level of autonomous investment by the business sector—to the degree that they affect only aggregate demand—will not affect equilibrium output. This rather striking property of the classical theory follows from the vertical classical aggregate supply curve. The classical aggregate supply curve is vertical, as we have just seen, due to the assumptions that we have made about the labor market. It is worthwhile to recognize explicitly the nature of these assumptions. Generally, the foregoing portrayal of the labor and product markets can be characterized by the term "auction market." Labor and output are assumed to be traded in markets which are continually in equilibrium and where all participants make bid and offer decisions on the basis of announced real wage rates and product prices. A contemporary market that has characteristics similar to these would be a stock exchange. Two assumptions implicit in this classical representation of the labor market are:

1. Perfectly flexible prices and wages.
2. Perfect information on the part of all market participants about market prices.

For whatever time period we assume that the equilibrium model determines employment and output, it must be the case that equilibrium is achieved. If such a model is to explain employment and output in the short run, prices and wages must be perfectly flexible in that time period.

The auction market characterization of the labor market above also requires that market participants have perfect information about market prices. Both suppliers and purchasers of labor must know the relevant trading prices. This requires that when selling and buying labor at a given money wage rate W, both workers and employers know the command over commodities that will result from such a wage (W/P).

These two assumptions, essential for the nature of the classical equilibrium theory of employment and output, are elements of the classical theory that Keynes attacked. Prior to considering the nature of that attack, we discuss the other major elements of the classical equilibrium theory and the classical economists' own analysis of the results of weakening these assumptions.

Review Questions

1 In what respects was the classical attack on mercantilism important in shaping the classical economists' views on macroeconomic questions?

2 Explain the concept of an aggregate production function. How would you expect the production function in Figure 3.1 to be affected by an increase in the average and marginal productivity of labor for a given output level, due for example to increased education of the labor force? How would such a shift in the production function affect the levels of output, employment and price in the classical model?

3 Explain the classical theories of labor supply and demand. Why is the labor demand schedule downward sloping when plotted against the real wage while the labor supply schedule is upward sloping on the same graph?

4 Suppose that there were a tax on the income labor suppliers received for working. For example, assume that the tax rate is t_0^y and, therefore, the after-tax real wage received for one hour of labor supplied is only $(1 - t_0^y) \dfrac{W}{P}$. Show how the presence of such a tax would affect the derivation of the individual and aggregate labor supply schedules, as illustrated in Figure 3.3. Would a change in this tax rate on income from t_0^y to some higher rate t_1^y have any effect on output and employment in the classical system?

5 We termed the classical view of the labor market an *auction market* characterization. What assumptions underlie this characterization?

6 In microeconomics we would expect to find the supply curve for the firm to slope upward to the right when drawn against price. The classical aggregate supply curve is based on this microeconomic theory of the firm but is vertical. Why?

7 What factors are the major determinants of output and employment in the classical system? What role does aggregate demand have in determining output and employment?

Selected Readings

ACKLEY, GARDNER, *Macroeconomic Theory*. New York: Macmillan, 1961, Chaps. 5–8.
MAKINEN, GAIL, *Money, the Price Level, and Interest Rates*. Englewood Cliffs, N.J.: Prentice-Hall, 1977, Chaps. 1–4.

4

Our task in this chapter is to complete the discussion of the classical model. This requires an analysis of the classical theory of the determination of the price level and the interest rate. Next we consider the policy conclusions that emerge from the classical equilibrium model. We then analyze the role of rigid money wages in the classical system. It will be seen that money wage rigidity can explain the existence of unemployment in the classical system. The appendix to the chapter considers a disequilibrium classical model. The disequilibrium model attempts to explain the transition of the economy from one equilibrium position to another.

4.1 THE QUANTITY THEORY OF MONEY

To understand the determination of the price level in the classical system, it is necessary to analyze the role of money in the classical model. The starting point for the classical theory of money was the equation of exchange, which was in fact an identity relating the volume of transactions at current prices to the stock of money times the turnover rate of each dollar. In the form used by the most prominent American quantity theorist Irving Fisher, this identity was expressed as

$$MV_T \equiv P_T T \qquad (4.1)$$

THE CLASSICAL SYSTEM (II): MONEY, PRICES, AND INTEREST

where M is the quantity of money, V_T the transaction velocity of money, P_T the price index for the items traded, and T the volume of such transactions. This relationship is an identity because of the *ex post* definition of velocity. If, for example, over a given period the value of transactions in current dollars ($P_T T$) was \$3600 billion and the money stock (M) were \$300 billion, we could *define* the transactions velocity (or turnover rate) of money as the average number of times the average dollar was used in transactions:

$$V_T \equiv \frac{P_T T}{M} = \frac{3600}{300} = 12 \qquad (4.2)$$

The transaction variable (T) would include not only sales and purchases of newly produced goods but also exchanges of previously produced goods and financial assets. Another expression of the equation of exchange focuses only on income transactions:

$$MV \equiv Py \qquad (4.3)$$

M is again the quantity of money and V is now the income velocity of money, the number of times the average dollar is used in a transaction involving current output (income). The price index for currently produced output is given by P and the level of current output by y. Again this relationship would be an identity as long as income velocity were defined residually, as the level necessary to make the equality hold:

$$V \equiv \frac{Py}{M} \qquad\qquad (4.4)$$

In the form (4.3), the variables in the equation of exchange are easier ones to measure and are more central to our concerns in analyzing the classical theory, so it is on this form of the equation of exchange that our interest will be focused.

The equation of exchange is a "truism" and by itself does not explain the variables it contains. Fisher and other quantity theorists, however, postulated that all the *equilibrium* values of the elements in the equation of exchange with the exception of the price level were determined by other forces. Thus the equation of exchange served to determine the price level. As Fisher put it:

> We find that, under the conditions assumed, the price level varies (1) directly as the quantity of money in circulation (M), (2) directly as the velocity of its circulation (V), (3) inversely as the volume of trade done by it (T). The first of these three relations is worth emphasis. It constitutes the "quantity theory of money."[1]

The level of real output (or transactions) was a measure of real economic activity. As we have seen in Chapter 3, the classical economists regarded this variable as supply determined. Most simply, money was assumed to be a metallic money such as gold, but considering paper money and bank deposits does not seriously complicate the analysis as long as we confine ourselves to equilibrium situations. The important assumption was that the quantity of money was exogenously controlled by the monetary policy authority.

In equilibrium, Fisher argued that the velocity of money was determined by the payments habits and payments technology of the society. To give some examples, factors such as the average length of the pay period, practice of using charge accounts or bank charge cards, and prevalence of trade credit among businesses will all affect the velocity of circulation. Shorter pay periods will lead to smaller average money holdings over the pay period for any given income level, hence an increase in velocity. Frequent use of charge accounts by consumers or trade credit by businesses will also increase velocity, the number of transactions per unit of money. According to Fisher and other quantity theorists, the equilibrium level of velocity was determined by such institutional factors and could be regarded as fixed for the short run.

If velocity is a predetermined constant and not simply defined residually to equate MV and Py, the equation of exchange is no longer merely a definition. With the volume of output fixed from

---

[1]Irving Fisher, *The Purchasing Power of Money* (New York: Macmillan, 1922).

the supply side, the equation of exchange now expresses a relationship of proportionality between the exogenously given money stock and the price level:

$$M\bar{V} = P\bar{y} \tag{4.5}$$

or

$$P = \frac{\bar{V}}{\bar{y}} M \tag{4.6}$$

The bar over the V and y indicates that these terms can be taken as given. Equation (4.6) indicates the dependence of the price level on the stock of money. A doubling of M will just double P, or an x percent increase in M will lead to an x percent increase in P. This is the basic result of the quantity theory of money; *the quantity of money determines the price level.*

While the mathematics of the quantity theory may be clear from (4.5) and (4.6), what about the economics? How do changes in the money stock affect the price level? This question will be answered more easily after considering another variant of the quantity theory, the Cambridge or cash balances approach.

The *Cambridge approach*, named after Cambridge University, the academic home of its originators Alfred Marshall and A. C. Pigou,[2] again demonstrated a proportional relationship between the exogenous quantity of money and the aggregate price level. The foundation of this relationship was, however, less mechanistic than the transactions or Fisherian (after Irving Fisher) version of the quantity theory considered above. Marshall began by focusing on the individual's decision on the optimal amount of money to hold. Some money will be held due to the convenience that money provides in transactions as compared to other stores of value. Money also provides security by lessening the possibility of inconvenience or bankruptcy from failing to be able to meet unexpected obligations. But as Pigou notes, "currency held in the hand yields no income," so money will be held only in so far as its yield in terms of convenience and security outweighs the income lost from not investing in productive activity or satisfaction lost by not simply using the money to puchase goods for consumption. On these criteria, how much money will it be optimal to hold?

Marshall and the other Cambridge economists assumed that the demand for money would be a proportion of income and wealth. In most formulations the distinction between income and wealth was neglected and the Cambridge equation was written as

[2]John Maynard Keynes, who was also at Cambridge University, participated in the development of this approach to the quantity theory in the earlier "pre-Keynesian" phase of his career.

$$M^d = kPy \qquad (4.7)$$

Money demand (M^d) was assumed to be a proportion (k) of nominal income, the price level (P) times the level of real income (y). Since the primary desirable property of money was its usefulness for transactions, it followed logically that the demand for money would depend on the level of transactions, which may be supposed to vary closely with the level of income. The proportion of income that would be optimal to hold in the form of money (k) was assumed to be relatively stable in the short run, depending as in the Fisherian formulation on the payments habits of the society.

In equilibrium the exogenous stock of money must equal the quantity of money demanded:

$$M = M^d = kP\bar{y} \qquad (4.8)$$

With k treated as fixed in the short run and real output ($\bar{y}$) determined, as before, by supply conditions, the Cambridge equation also reduces to a proportional relationship between the price level and money stock. As in the Fisherian approach, the quantity of money determines the price level.

The formal equivalence of the Cambridge equation and Fisher's version of the equation of exchange can be seen by rewriting (4.8) as

$$M \frac{1}{k} = P\bar{y} \qquad (4.9)$$

It can then be seen from a comparison with Fisher's equation (4.5) that the two formulations are equivalent with V equal to $1/k$. If, for example, all individuals wish to hold an amount equal to one-fifth of the nominal income in the form of money, the number of times the average dollar is used in income transactions will be five.

While the two formulations of the quantity theory are formally equivalent, the Cambridge version represents a step toward more modern monetary theories. The Cambridge focus was on the quantity theory as a theory of the demand for money. The proportional relationship between the quantity of money and the price level resulted from the fact that the proportion of nominal income people wished to hold in the form of money (k) was constant and the level of real output was fixed by supply conditions. Following up on Pigou's analysis of the alternatives to holding wealth in the form of money, Keynes was to attack the quantity theory by providing a new theory of money demand. The monetarists, as we will see, also take the Cambridge form of the quantity theory as the starting point for their theory of money demand.

Additionally, the Cambridge focus on the quantity theory as a theory of money demand leads naturally to an answer to the question raised above about the mechanism by which money affects the general price level. Let us suppose that we begin at equilibrium and then consider the effects of doubling the quantity of money. Initially, there will be an excess of money supply over the amount demanded. Individuals try to reduce money holdings to the optimal proportion of income by putting this excess into alternative uses of consumption and investment in production activities. They increase their demand for goods for both consumption and investment. This increased demand for commodities puts upward pressure on prices. If output is unchanged, as it would be in the classical model, and k is constant, a new equilibrium will be reached only after the general price level is doubled. At that point nominal income and, hence, money demand will have doubled. This was the direct link in the classical system between money and prices; an excess supply of money led to increased demand for commodities and upward pressure on the general price level.

Thus the quantity theory was the *implicit* theory of aggregate demand within the classical system. We can use the quantity theory to construct an aggregate demand curve which together with the vertical aggregate supply curve will illustrate the determination of price and output in the classical system.

The construction of the aggregate demand curve is illustrated in Figure 4.1. For concreteness we assign some numerical values to the variables with which we are concerned. Let the value of k be one-fourth and, hence, velocity be 4. Initially, let the stock of money be 300 units. For either (4.8) or (4.5) to hold, $P \times y$ (nominal income) must be equal to 1200 (4 $\times$ 300). In Figure 4.1 with price on the vertical axis and real output on the horizontal axis, the line labeled $y^d(M = 300)$ connects all the points where $P \times y$ equals 1200 units.[3] Points lying on the schedule for example are real income levels of 300 and 600 with accompanying price levels of 4.0 and 2.0, respectively.

Now consider a higher value of the money stock, for example, 400 units. To satisfy either (4.8) or (4.5) with k still equal to one-fourth ($V = 4$), $P \times y$ must now equal 1600. The schedule $y^d(M = 400)$ corresponding to M of 400 lies above and to the right of the $y^d(M = 300)$ schedule and shows all $P \times y$ combinations of 1600. An increase in the money stock shifts the aggregate demand curve to the right.

For a given stock of money, we trace out a downward-sloping

---

[3]The schedule $y^d(M = 300)$ and the other such aggregate demand curves are constructed to have the property that the area under the curve ($P \times y$) is equal at all points along the schedule. Such a curve is a rectangular hyperbola.

Figure 4.1
Classical Aggregate
Demand Curve

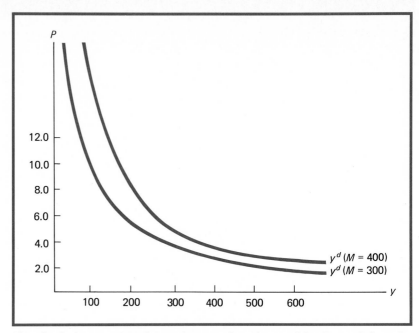

The classical aggregate demand curve plots the combinations of the price level (P) and real income (y) consistent with the quantity theory equation $Py = M\bar{V}$, for a given money stock (M) and fixed velocity ($\bar{V}$). With $M = 300$ and velocity assumed to be 4, points such as $P = 12.0$ and $y = 100$ or $P = 6.0$ and $y = 200$ ($Py = 1200 = M\bar{V}$ in each case) lie along the aggregate demand schedule. An increase in the money stock to $M = 400$ shifts the aggregate demand schedule to the right.

aggregate demand curve which can be put together with the vertical aggregate supply curve constructed in Figure 3.6 to illustrate the determination of price and output in the classical model. This is done in Figure 4.2.

Figure 4.2 reproduces the vertical aggregate supply curve (y_1^s) from Figure 3.6 and also contains several aggregate demand schedules [$y^d(M_1)$, $y^d(M_2)$, $y^d(M_3)$] drawn for successively higher values of the money stock (M_1, M_2, M_3). As just explained, increasing the money stock shifts the aggregate demand curve upward to the right. Because the supply curve is vertical, increases in demand do not affect output. Only the price level increases. Also note that for a given value of k (or V), *a change in the quantity of money is the only factor that shifts the aggregate demand curve.* Since the equilibrium value of k (V) was considered to be stable in the short run, aggregate demand varied only with the stock of money.

This classical theory of aggregate demand has been termed an

Figure 4.2

Aggregate Supply and
Demand in the
Classical System

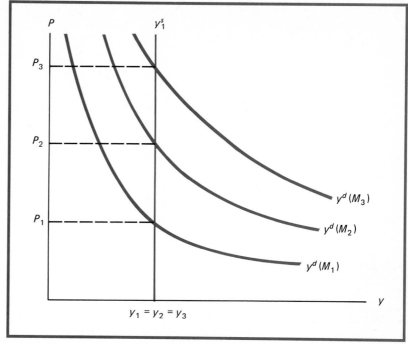

Successive increases in the money stock, from M_1 to M_2 and then to M_3, shift the aggregate demand curve to the right, from $y^d(M_1)$ to $y^d(M_2)$ to $y^d(M_3)$. The price level rises from P_1 to P_2 then to P_3. Output, which is completely supply determined, is unchanged ($y_1 = y_2 = y_3$).

implicit theory and it is worthwhile to consider its nature more carefully. The theory is not explicit in the sense of a theory that focuses on the components of aggregate demand and explains the factors that determine their level. Instead, in the classical theory a given value of MV [or $M(1/k)$] implies a level of $P \times y$ that must pertain for equilibrium in the money market—for money demand to equal the existing supply. If money demand exceeds (falls short of) money supply, there will be a spillover to the commodity market as individuals try to reduce (increase) their expenditures on commodities. Points along the y^d schedule are points where firms and households are in equilibrium with regard to their money holdings and, hence, are also at equilibrium rates of expenditures on commodities. It is in this sense that the classical theory of aggregate demand is an implicit one. Equilibrium levels of commodity demand are those price–output combinations that provide equilibrium in the money market and implicitly equilibrium levels of commodity demand.

4.2 THE CLASSICAL THEORY OF THE INTEREST RATE

In the classical system the components of aggregate commodity demand—consumption, investment, and government spending—play their explicit role in the determination of the equilibrium interest rate. It is, in fact, the interest rate which guarantees that exogenous changes in the particular components of demand do not affect the aggregate level of commodity demand.

The equilibrium interest rate in the classical theory was the rate at which the amount of funds that individuals desired to lend were just equal to the amount others desired to borrow. For simplicity we assume that borrowing consists of selling a standard bond, a promise to pay certain amounts in the future. Lending consists of buying such bonds. Later we will have to consider the properties of bonds in more detail, but for now the simplest assumption will be that the standard bond is a "perpetuity," a bond that pays a perpetual stream of interest payments with no return of principal.[4] The rate of interest measures the return to holding such bonds and equivalently the cost of borrowing. The interest rate will depend on the factors that determine the levels of bond supply (borrowing) and bond demand (lending).

In the classical system the suppliers of bonds were the firms, which financed all investment expenditures by the sale of bonds, and the government, which might sell bonds to finance spending in excess of tax revenues.[5]

The level of the government deficit (excess of spending over revenues) as well as the portion of the deficit the government might choose to finance by selling bonds to the public are exogenous policy variables. In the classical model the level of business investment was a function of the expected profitability of investment projects and the rate of interest. The expected profitability of investment projects was assumed to vary with expectations of product demand over the life of these projects, and the state of these expectations was subject to exogenous shifts.

For a given expected profitability, investment expenditures var-

---

[4]Also, for simplicity no resale market for such bonds is allowed. This and the other simplifying assumptions may be dropped without substantive change in the analysis.

[5]The word "might" is used concerning the government's sale of bonds to finance a deficit because the alternative of financing the deficit by printing money is available to the government. Also note that "investment" refers to expenditure by firms on plant, durable equipment, and inventories—investment in the national income accounts sense. The term "investment" does *not* refer to the purchase of financial assets such as bonds.

ied inversely with the interest rate. The classical economists explained this relationship as follows. A firm would have a number of possible investment projects offering various expected returns. It could rank these projects in order of the level of expected profits. The rate of interest represents the cost of borrowing funds to finance these investment projects. At a high interest rate fewer of these projects will be profitable net of interest costs. At successively lower rates of interest (lower borrowing costs) more and more projects will become profitable, net of interest costs, and investment will increase. Later we will look at investment in more detail but obtain the same general result. Investment depends inversely on the rate of interest. Thus, on the supply (borrowing) side of the bond market, government bond supply is exogenous and the business supply of bonds equals the level of investment expenditure. Investment varies inversely with the interest rate and is also influenced by exogenous shifts in the expected profitability of investment projects.

On the demand (lending) side of the bond market are the individual savers who purchase the bonds.[6] In the classical model saving was taken to be a positive function of the rate of interest. The act of saving is the act of foregoing current consumption in order to have a command over consumption goods in a future period, a trade-off of current consumption for future consumption. As the interest rate increases the terms of the trade-off become more favorable. A dollar saved today will be earning a higher interest return for the saver, a greater command over consumption goods in future periods. The classical economists assumed that individuals would take advantage of this more favorable trade-off of consumption in the future for consumption today; they would save more at higher rates of interest.

But saving need not go into bonds; money is also a potential store of wealth. Since money paid no interest, the classical economists assumed that bonds would always be preferred as a store of wealth. As discussed above, some money would be held for the convenience and security it offered. Wealth accumulated through new saving, however, would be held in the form of bonds. Classical economists did believe that people might shift their wealth into the form of money in times of severe general economic distress. At such times, with bank panics and bankruptcies being prevalent, people might worry about bond default and "hoard" money, but for normal times the classical assumption was that saving was a demand for bonds.

Determination of the interest rate in the classical system is illus-

---

[6]Households may lend to each other but this is not formally considered in the simple classical system, saving can be considered net saving of households.

trated in Figure 4.3. Saving (s) is plotted as an upward-sloping function of the rate of interest. Saving provides the demand for bonds, or as the classical economists called it, the supply of loanable funds. Investment (i) is a negatively sloped schedule plotted against the interest rate. Investment plus the exogenously determined government deficit ($g - t$), all of which we assume to be financed by selling bonds, equals bond supply. In the classical terminology this is the demand for loanable funds. In the diagram, r_0 is the equilibrium interest rate, the rate of interest that equates the demand and supply for bonds or loanable funds.

The interest rate plays a stabilizing role in the classical system, as can be seen by examining the effects of a change in the expected profitability of investment. Recall that in the short run, investment depends on the interest rate and the expected future profitability of investment projects. Let us suppose that due to some exogenous event (e.g., fear of a future war) business managers in general revise downward their expectation about such future profits from investment. This would have the effect of reducing investment and, hence, reducing the demand for loanable funds *at each interest rate*.

Figure 4.4 illustrates the effect of this autonomous decline in

Figure 4.3
Interest Rate Determination in the Classical System

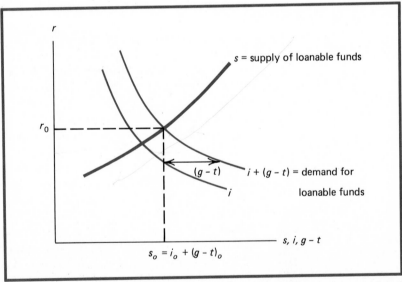

The equilibrium interest rate r_0 is the rate which equates the supply of loanable funds, which consists of new saving (s), with the demand for loanable funds, which consists of investment (i) plus the bond-financed government deficit ($g - t$).

MACROECONOMIC MODELS

Figure 4.4

Autonomous Decline
in Investment Demand

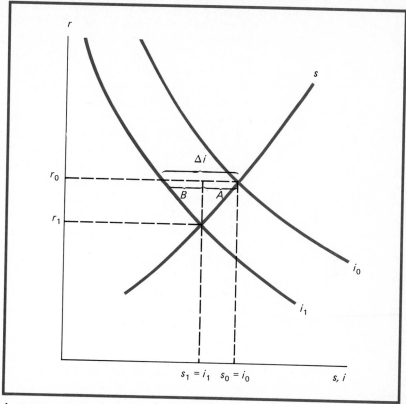

An autonomous decline in investment shifts the investment schedule to the left from i_0 to i_1—the distance Δi. The equilibrium interest rate declines from r_0 to r_1. As the interest rate falls there is an interest rate induced increase in investment—distance B. There is also an interest rate induced decline in saving, which is an equal increase in consumption—distance A. The interest rate induced increases in consumption and investment just balance the autonomous decline in investment ($A + B = \Delta i$).

investment demand. For simplicity we assume that the government budget is balanced ($g = t$), so there is no government borrowing. Investment is the only source of the demand for loanable funds. The fall in expected profitability of investment projects is shown as a shift in the investment schedule downward from i_0 to i_1. At a given rate of interest, the amount of the decline in investment is measured by Δi in Figure 4.4

At the initial equilibrium interest rate of r_0, the supply of loanable funds exceeds demand, putting downward pressure on the rate of interest. As the interest rate falls, saving declines, which means that current consumption increases. The amount of this decline in saving and the equal increase in current consumption demand is given by the distance marked A in Figure 4.4.[7] Also, investment is somewhat revived by the decline in the interest rate. This interest rate induced increase in investment is measured by the distance B in Figure 4.4. Equilibrium is restored at interest rate r_1 with saving (the supply of loanable funds) again equal to investment (the demand for loanable funds). At the new equilibrium the increase in consumption (fall in saving) plus the increase in investment caused by the drop in the interest rate, the distance $A + B$ in Figure 4.4, is just equal to the original autonomous decline in investment demand, the distance Δi in Figure 4.4. Owing to the adjustment of the interest rate, the sum of private sector demands $(c + i)$ is unaffected by the autonomous decline in investment demand.

This stabilizing role of the interest rate is quite important to the classical system. The interest rate adjustment is the first line of defense for full employment. Shocks that affect consumption demand, investment demand, or as we will see shortly, government demand will *not* affect the demand for output as a whole. Even if they did, of course, there would be no effect on output or employment. This is because of the self-adjusting properties of the classical labor market as reflected in the vertical aggregate supply curve—the second line of defense for full employment.

4.3 POLICY IMPLICATIONS OF THE CLASSICAL EQUILIBRIUM MODEL

In this section we analyze the effects of monetary and fiscal policy actions within the classical model. We consider the effects that various policy shifts will have on output, employment, the price level, and the interest rate.

Fiscal Policy

First we consider the effects of an increase in government spending. To avoid also bringing in a monetary policy change, we will assume that the money stock is fixed. We also assume that tax collections (t) are fixed; the increased government expenditures are financed by selling bonds to the public. It should be clear from our analysis to this point that increased government spending will *not* affect the equilibrium values of output or the price level. This must be the case since we constructed both the aggregate demand and aggregate supply curves, which together determine output and the price level, without reference to the level of government

---

[7]It is important here to note that as saving declines there is a dollar-for-dollar increase in current consumption. Real income is fixed, as are taxes, so all changes in saving are mirrored in changes in current consumption.

spending. Since output is not affected by changes in government spending, employment must also be unaffected. To understand these results it is necessary to examine the effects on the interest rate of a change in government spending.

The effect in the loanable funds market of a change in government spending financed by a sale of bonds to the public is shown in Figure 4.5. We assume that prior to the increase in government spending the government budget was in balance ($g - t = 0$). The government deficit is then equal to the increase in spending ($\Delta g = g - t$). Initially, with no government deficit the demand for loanable funds comes only to finance investment and is given by schedule i in Figure 4.5. The increase in government spending

Figure 4.5

Effect of Increase in Government Spending in the Classical Model

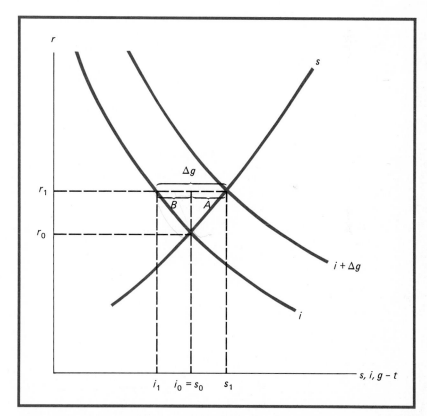

An increase in government spending shifts the demand for loanable funds schedule to the right from i to $i + \Delta g$, a distance Δg. The equilibrium interest rate rises from r_0 to r_1. The rise in the interest rate causes a decline in investment from i_0 to i_1, a distance B, and an increase in saving, which is an equal decline in consumption, from s_0 to s_1, a distance A. The decline in investment and consumption just balances the increase in government spending ($A + B = \Delta g$).

shifts the demand for loanable funds to the $i + \Delta g$ schedule in Figure 4.5. Note that the distance of the horizontal shift in the curve, the increase in the demand for loanable funds at a given interest rate, measures the amount of the increase in government spending. This amount is measured by the distance Δg in Figure 4.5.

The increase in government spending creates an increased demand for loanable funds as the government sells bonds to the public to finance the new spending. This creates an excess of borrowers over lenders at the initial interest rate r_0 and the interest rate is pushed up to r_1. The increase in the interest rate has two effects. Saving increases from s_0 to s_1; this is the distance A in Figure 4.5. As was explained in the preceding section, an increase in saving is mirrored by an equal decline in consumption demand. Second, investment declines with the higher interest rate. At r_1 we can read the new level of investment as i_1. The investment decline is the distance B in Figure 4.5.

It can be seen from the figure that the amount of the decline in consumption demand, which equals the amount of increased saving (distance A), plus the decline in investment (distance B) just equals the amount of the increase in government spending (Δg). The increase in government spending financed by selling bonds to the public pushes the interest rate up by enough to "crowd out" an equal amount of private expenditure (consumption plus investment). Private expenditures are discouraged because the higher interest rate causes households to substitute future consumption for current consumption—to save more. Investment declines because fewer projects appear profitable with higher borrowing costs. It is this crowding out that keeps aggregate demand from increasing when the government component of demand rises. Since aggregate demand is not changed, increases in government expenditures financed by bonds do not affect the price level.

An analysis similar to that above would produce an analogous result for a change in tax policy.[8] A tax cut, for example, would raise the equilibrium interest rate but would not affect aggregate demand and, hence, would not affect the price level, assuming that the tax cut was bond financed.

What about the effects of an increase in government spending or a tax cut where the government prints money to either finance the new spending or to replace revenues lost by the tax cut? Here since the quantity of money is changed, the price level will be changed proportionately. We have previously analyzed the way in which an

---

[8]Note that the analysis here deals with the relationship between fiscal policy variables and aggregate demand. Additional fiscal policy effects on the supply side of the economy are considered in Chapter 16. There we will find that changes in government spending and changes in tax policy might have quite different supply-side effects.

increase in the money stock would shift the aggregate demand curve up along the vertical aggregate supply curve, raising the price level (Figure 4.2). In the classical system the source of the increase in the money stock does not matter. A given change in the money stock has the same effect whether it enters the economy to finance an increase in government spending or in another manner. Put differently, and this is the crucial point, *neither the increase in government spending nor the tax cut have independent effects on aggregate demand.*

Monetary Policy

The role of money in the classical system has been dealt with already and here we simply need to summarize our findings. The quantity of money determines the price level and, for a given real income, the level of *nominal* income in the classical system. In this sense monetary policy was quite important to classical economists. Stable money was a requirement for stable prices.

In another sense money was not important. The quantity of money did not affect the equilibrium values of the real variables in the system: output, employment, *and the interest rate.* The supply-determined nature of output and employment was the subject of Chapter 3. The theory of the equilibrium interest rate we have constructed here is a real theory that did not mention the quantity of money. Factors determining the interest rate were real investment demand, real saving, and the real value of the government deficit—what the classical economists called the forces of "productivity and thrift."

To the classical economists, money was a "veil" determining the nominal values in which we measure such variables as the level of economic activity, but having no effect on real quantities.

4.4 THE CLASSICAL SYSTEM WITH RIGID MONEY WAGES—ONE EXPLANATION OF UNEMPLOYMENT

So far we have been assuming that the money wage is perfectly flexible. It is the instantaneous adjustment of the money wage which guarantees that the labor market will be in equilibrium. Thus, in the classical system perfect money wage flexibility is a requirement for full employment.

The classical economists recognized that wages might be somewhat rigid, especially in the downward direction. There were several reasons for such downward rigidity in wages. Consider the response of the money wage to a change that produced a fall in the demand for labor. Clearly, workers might try to avoid the fall in the money wage required to reequate supply and demand. Individual workers in the type of "auction" market setting by which the classical economists characterized the labor market would have little power to keep their wage from falling in response to market conditions. The classical economists, however, witnessed the growth of organized labor unions and congresses of unions. They recognized that labor organizations might effectively resist wage cuts required to maintain equilibrium in the labor market during periods when the demand for labor was declining. Disruptions, work slowdowns, strikes, and even a general strike were weapons that could be used by organized labor for this purpose.

Second, government policies might make the money wage inflexible in a downward direction. The most obvious example of government policies that keep wages from falling would be minimum wage laws. In addition, during periods when the level of economic activity was falling, government often tried to keep wages and prices from falling, believing that this would minimize economic distress. An example was Franklin Roosevelt's attempt in 1933–34 to get employers to agree to codes limiting wage cuts.

The effect of such downward rigidity in the money wage in the classical system can be analyzed within the graphical framework of Chapter 3 (see Figure 3.5). In Figure 4.6 we plot both labor supply and demand as functions of the *money* wage. As explained in Chapter 3, each schedule must be drawn for a given price level; the curves will shift as shown in Figure 3.5 when the price level changes.

In Figure 4.6 we assume that labor supply and demand are given initially by $N^s(P_1)$ and $N^d(P_1)$, respectively, where P_1 is the initial price level. Equilibrium in the labor market would be at N_1 with money wage W_1 and the real wage W_1/P_1. Assume instead, however, that the money wage is fixed at $\bar{W}$, a level too high for equilibrium, and does not fall despite the fact that at $\bar{W}$ labor supply $\bar{N}_1^s$ exceeds labor demand $\bar{N}_1^d$. The wage is assumed to be rigid at this level, owing, for example, to organized labor's resistance to a wage cut following a decline in labor demand. In this situation firms will hire labor only up to the point where the marginal product of labor equals the real wage. This results in employment of $\bar{N}_1^d$, the point on the labor demand curve corresponding to $\bar{W}$. Labor supply is $\bar{N}_1^s$ at $\bar{W}$, so there is unemployment equal to $\bar{N}_1^s - \bar{N}_1^d$. Thus a possible explanation for unemployment which is consistent with the classical system is that wages are rigid in the downward direction.

If wages are rigid downward, it will no longer be the case that the levels of employment and output are completely supply determined; the aggregate supply curve will no longer be vertical. To see this, consider the effect on employment of an increase in the price level from P_1 to a higher value P_2, as illustrated in Figure 4.7.

Figure 4.6

Effects of a Rigid
Money Wage in the
Classical System

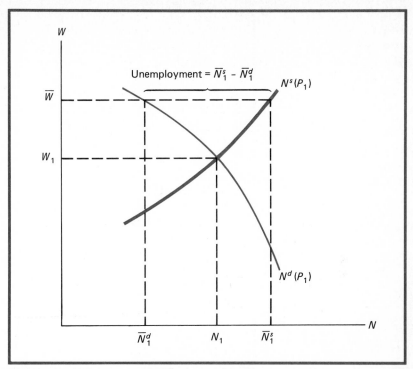

The equilibrium point for the labor market with price level P_1 is at a money wage W_1 and level of employment N_1. If the money wage is fixed at $\bar{W}$ above W_1, employment will be determined by labor demand, $\bar{N}_1^d$, and there will be unemployment equal to $(\bar{N}_1^s - \bar{N}_1^d)$.

The increase in the price level with the money wage held at $\bar{W}$ will reduce the real wage and shift the demand for labor curve to the right to $N^d(P_2)$. The fall in the real wage does cause labor supply to decline. The labor supply schedule shifts to the left to $N^s(P_2)$. As long as there is unemployment, however, and supply exceeds demand, this fall in supply has no effect. In other words, as long as the real wage is too high for equilibrium, demand—not supply—is the factor constraining employment. A fall in the real wage increases employment. In Figure 4.7 the increase in the price level to P_2 is just sufficient to achieve equilibrium employment N_1. The rise in the price level is sufficient to generate a real wage $\bar{W}/P_2$ equal to W_1/P_1.

The implications of a rigid money wage for the slope of the aggregate supply curve and for the output effects of changes in aggregate demand can be seen from Figure 4.8. At price level P_1 and the fixed money wage $(\bar{W})$, output would be at $\bar{y}_1$, the level produced with employment $\bar{N}_1^d$ in Figure 4.6. In the figure this price level (P_1)

Figure 4.7
Effect of a Price
Increase When the
Money Wage is Rigid

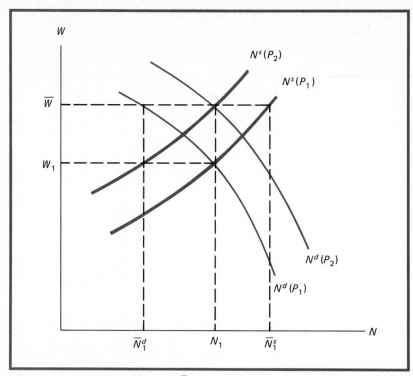

With the money wage fixed at $\overline{W}$, an increase in the price level from P_1 to P_2 will shift the labor demand schedule from $N^d(P_1)$ to $N^d(P_2)$. Employment will rise from $\overline{N}_1^d$ to N_1. The increase in price will also shift the labor supply schedule leftward from $N^s(P_1)$ to $N^s(P_2)$, but given the initial excess supply of labor this will not prevent the expansion in employment.

is shown to be consistent with the money stock being at M_1, giving the aggregate demand curve $y^d(M_1)$. At a price level of P_2, as we have seen in Figure 4.7, employment would increase to N_1. Output would then increase to output y_1. The price level could be pushed up to P_2 if the money stock were increased to M_2, shifting the aggregate demand curve to $y^d(M_2)$.

The aggregate supply curve would be upward sloping at price levels below P_2 since over that range $\overline{W}/P$ would be above the equilibrium value in Figure 4.6. Movements of the price level above P_2 would not increase output supplied. At P_2 with wage $\overline{W}$, labor supply equals labor demand. Further increases in the price level would simply lead to proportionate increases in the money wage. The money wage is not assumed to be rigid in the upward direction, so at price levels above P_2 the derivation of the aggregate supply curve remains as discussed in Chapter 3.

To summarize, downward money wage rigidity was one expla-

Figure 4.8
Classical Aggregate
Supply Curve With a
Rigid Money Wage

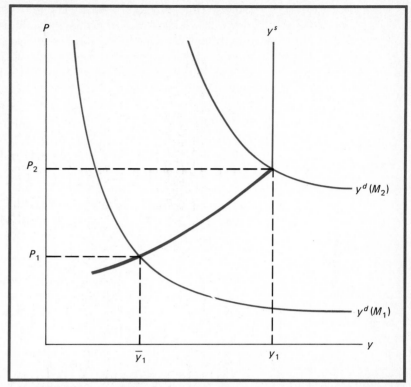

At price level P_1 output is at $\bar{y}_1$. An increase in the money stock from M_1 to M_2 will shift the aggregate demand schedule from $y^d(M_1)$ to $y^d(M_2)$; the price level will rise to P_2 and in the case of a rigid money wage output will rise to y_1. At price level P_2 the labor market is assumed to be in equilibrium at the fixed money wage $\bar{W}$ (see Figure 4.7); further increases in aggregate demand will not increase output.

nation of unemployment in the classical system. If unemployment was caused by such downward rigidity—if the real wage was too high for full employment—then an increase in the money stock would increase employment. A higher money stock would also increase aggregate demand. The price level would rise and the real wage fall toward its equilibrium value. Notice that fiscal policy should still have no independent effect. Fiscal policies that left the money stock unchanged would not shift the aggregate demand curve, as we saw in the preceding section. This is unrelated to whether the money wage is rigid or flexible. Since fiscal policy changes would not shift the aggregate demand curve, in the case of a rigid money wage such actions would affect neither the price level nor employment.

Monetary policy could affect the level of output with a rigid money wage, but that does not mean that such policy actions were viewed as desirable by the classical economists. If there was unemployment because the money wage was being maintained at too high a level, then a fall in the money wage was the preferable way to lower the real wage and restore full employment. To use monetary policy to raise the price level would encourage organized labor to attempt to push wages above equilibrium levels and depend on the government to validate this wage inflation with an expansionary monetary policy. Changes that would increase wage flexibility by restricting the power of organized labor to fix money wages were also recommended by classical economists.

4.5 THE CLASSICAL EQUILIBRIUM SYSTEM: CONCLUSION

Our analysis of the classical equilibrium system has been quite detailed since the properties of the system are crucial to the theories we consider later. The Keynesian theory is an attack on the classical system. The monetarist and new classical economic frameworks are reformulations of the equilibrium classical system.

The classical economists stressed the *self-adjusting tendencies of the economy*. Free from destabilizing government actions, the private sector would be stable and full employment would be achieved. The first of these self-stabilizing mechanisms is the interest rate, which adjusts to keep shocks to sectoral demands from affecting aggregate demand. The second set of stabilizers in the classical system are freely flexible prices and money wages, which keep changes in aggregate demand from affecting output. As we saw when we considered the effects of a rigid money wage, such price and wage flexibility is crucial to the full-employment properties of the classical system. The inherent stability of the private sector led the classical economists to what can be termed *noninterventionist* policy conclusions. To be sure, many of the interventionist mercantilist policies that the classical economists opposed (tariffs, trading monopolies, etc.) were a far cry from the macroeconomic stabilization policies of today, but the model itself argues for nonintervention in a very general sense.

A second central feature of the classical system is the *dichotomy between the factors determining real and nominal variables*. In the classical theory real factors determined real variables. Output and employment depended primarily on population, technology, and capital formation. The interest rate depended on productivity and thrift. Money was a veil determining the nominal values in which quantities were measured, but monetary factors did not play a role in determining these real quantities (assuming wage flexibility).

In the next theoretical system we consider—the Keynesian theory—we will see that the policy conclusions which emerge are much more interventionist. We will also see that monetary and real variables are much more interrelated in the Keynesian system.

Review Questions

1 Explain the role that money plays in the classical system. Specifically, in the classical model, what role does money have in determining real output, employment, the price level, and the interest rate? Explain how money affects these variables; or, if money has no effect on some of them, explain why this is the case.

2 What are the differences between the Fisherian and Cambridge versions of the quantity theory of money?

3 Define the term *velocity of money*. What factors determine the velocity of money in the classical system? What is the relationship between the velocity of money and the Cambridge k?

4 Explain how aggregate demand is determined within the classical model. What would be the effects on output and the price level as a result of an increase in aggregate demand?

5 The classical economists assumed that velocity was stable in the short run. But suppose that due to a change in the payments mechanism, for example greater use of credit cards, there was an exogenous rise in the velocity of money. What effect would such a change have on output, employment, and the price level within the classical model?

6 Explain how the interest rate is determined in the classical theory.

7 Explain the way in which the interest rate works in the classical system to stabilize aggregate demand in the face of autonomous changes in components of aggregate demand such as investment or government spending.

8 Using graphs such as those in Figures 4.3 and 4.5, analyze the effects of a tax cut in the classical model. How will the tax cut affect the equilibrium values of real income, the price level, and the rate of interest?

9   What are the major policy conclusions of classical economics? Explain how these policy conclusions follow from the key assumptions of the classical theoretical system.

10   How are the classical policy conclusions modified if we assume that the money wage is rigid rather than perfectly flexible?

11   Suppose that we are in the situation depicted in Figure 4.6 where the money wage is fixed (at $\bar{W}$) above the equilibrium level. Using a graphical analysis combining Figures 4.6 and 4.8, show the effects on output and employment of a policy action, such as some type of anti-union legislation, which resulted in an exogenous fall in the money wage to a level $\bar{W}'$, below $\bar{W}$ but still above the equilibrium money wage (W_1).

Selected Readings

ACKLEY, GARDNER, *Macroeconomic Theory*. New York: Macmillan, 1961, Chaps. 5–8.

FISHER, IRVING, *The Purchasing Power of Money*. New York: Macmillan, 1922, especially Chap. 4.

MAKININ, GAIL, *Money, the Price Level and Interest Rates*. Englewood Cliffs, N.J.: Prentice-Hall, 1977, Chaps. 1–4.

PATINKIN, DON, "On the Short-Run Non-neutrality of Money in the Quantity Theory," *Banca Nazionali del Lavora Quarterly Review*, 25 (March 1972), pp. 3–22.

PIGOU, A. C., "The Value of Money," *Quarterly Journal of Economics*, 32 (1917–18), pp. 38–65. Reprinted in Friedrich Lutz and Lloyd Mints, eds., *Readings in Monetary Theory*. Homewood, Ill.: Irwin, 1951.

The Classical System: Disequilibrium Analysis

Next, we consider an example of the classical analysis of disequilibrium positions, the short-run behavior of the economy when it is displaced from the classical full-employment equilibrium. Of what importance was such disequilibrium analysis within the classical system?

In later chapters, we will see that *for the long run,* all the other schools of macroeconomic theory that we consider will reach conclusions quite similar to those of the classical equilibrium model. The distinguishing feature among different models we consider will be their short- to medium-run properties, what they imply for periods of perhaps one to five years. Would the classical economists have applied their equilibrium model to explain the behavior of the economy over this time frame? Whether the equilibrium model would be useful for describing the behavior of the economy in the short run depends on the speed with which the economy returns to equilibrium when disturbed by some exogenous shock. If the adjustment is quite fast, we would normally expect to be close to equilibrium. The equilibrium model would be a useful guide to the behavior of the economy even in the short run. If the speed of adjustment to equilibrium were slow, we could not generally expect the economy to be in the neighborhood of its equilibrium position and the equilibrium model would be of little value for analyzing short-run economic behavior. It seems clear that at least some of the classical economists felt that the speed of adjustment of the economy was fast enough so that the model could be useful in the short run. In this case there was little need for disequilibrium analysis. Such classical economists, and policymakers accepting their analyses, applied the classical equilibrium model without much qualification about the need for a lengthy period of adjustment before the model's conclusions would hold.

Other classical economists recognized the need for disequilibrium analysis: the need to examine a "transition period" from one equilibrium to another. The classical view of how long such transition periods might be was not always made explicit. For some at least, the period was taken as possibly quite long. Irving Fisher believed that the transition period might last for 10 years. We will examine Irving Fisher's model as an example of the classical disequilibrium analysis.[1]

A.1 GENERAL FEATURES OF CLASSICAL DISEQUILIBRIUM MODELS

Fisher's model, dating from the 1920s, is a good example of the later classical disequilibrium analysis. A general feature of such models is that the elements of the classical model that were amended were the theories of price and interest-rate determination. No formal disequilibrium analysis was applied to the labor market. As Fisher points out: "The amount of trade is dependent, almost entirely, on other things than the quantity of currency, so that an increase of currency cannot, even very temporarily, very greatly increase trade." In or out of equilibrium, output and employment were for the most part determined by real factors, such as population, the state of technology, and the level of capital accumulation.

Another general feature of classical disequilibrium analysis is that during transition periods there is an interaction between the money market and the loanable funds market which is absent in the equilibrium model. Out of equilibrium, the rate of interest is not determined by real factors alone. Changes in the supply of money and changes in money demand will affect the interest rate.

A third general feature of the classical disequilibrium model is the presence of some misperception on the part of the economic agents in the system. At least some of the economic agents fail to understand fully the effects that a shock, such as a change in the money stock, will have on the economy. The disequilibrium persists until these agents' behavior comes to be based on correct expectations. Up to that point they are changing their behavior in

[1]Fisher's model is presented in Chapter 4 of *The Purchasing Power of Money* (New York: Macmillan, 1922).

response to new information which shows their previous expectations to have been wrong. Any rigidities in the system, such as contracts that fix variables such as the price level and the interest rate for various periods, will lengthen the period of adjustment to a new equilibrium. Such arrangements will lock agents into decisions based on misinformation. This classical view of misperceptions interacting with rigidities in the economy as the source of disequilibrium will reappear in different forms in all the short-run models we consider in future chapters.

A.2 FISHER'S MODEL OF THE TRANSITION PERIOD

As an example of Fisher's analysis of the transition from one equilibrium point to another, we consider, as he did, the effect of a change in the amount of government issued money or currency in the system. Later classical models such as Fisher's make a distinction between such government-issued money and bank deposits. Money would then be defined as the sum of currency plus bank deposits, where we will use the following symbols:

$$M = \text{quantity of money} = C + D$$

$$C = \text{currency}$$

$$D = \text{bank deposits}$$

The Fisherian version of the quantity theory would be, as stated previously,

$$MV = Py \tag{A.1}$$

with M as just defined. As explained above, we will be able to assume that changes in y caused by a change in M are minor and can be ignored. Out of equilibrium, however, we will *not* be able to assume that V is relatively stable. Systematic changes in V play an important part in the adjustment to a change in the quantity of money.

Another feature of the classical system that requires modification when we consider the classical disequilibrium model is the supply of loanable funds. We assumed that in equilibrium the supply of loanable funds was the new saving that took place. Out of equilibrium we will have to consider the effect of a change in bank deposits on the supply of loanable funds. This change reflects not only the switch to disequilibrium analysis but the fact that we are now including a banking system in the model. We could have included a banking system in our equilibrium analysis with little effect on our result; it is out of equilibrium that this change in the model is important.

Bank deposits are created by increases in the banking system's purchase of earning assets.[2] In the classical disequilibrium models the bank's only earning asset was "loans." An increase in deposits came from an expansion of bank lending. Any increase in bank lending, thus any increase in bank deposits, must be included in the supply of loanable funds. Alternatively, any decrease in bank loans and deposits will decrease the supply of loanable funds. The total supply of loanable funds is then the sum of new saving plus (minus) the increase (decrease) in bank deposits.

What determines the change in bank deposits or loans? In Fisher's model the volume of bank lending was assumed to be positively related to the rate of interest. As we will see below, bank lending was also assumed to be affected by the reserve position of the bank. Banks were assumed to hold currency as a reserve asset either because of some regulation or simply to protect against deposit outflows. The ratio of reserves to deposits will affect the bank's willingness to increase loans. For now, however, we neglect this effect.

Figure A.1 shows graphically the determination of the interest rate with this modification in the supply of loanable funds. In the graph and throughout this section we will assume that the government budget deficit is zero and, consequently, there is no borrowing by the government. The demand for loanable funds is by firms that borrow to finance investment. The interest rate will move to equate the level of investment (demand for loanable funds) with the sum of the supply of new savings *plus* the increase in bank deposits, the latter factor being the banking sector's supply of loanable funds. In the figure this equilibrium occurs at r_0.

As shown in Figure A.1, r_0 is also the rate at which there is no increase or decline in bank deposits (or loans). Above r_0 banks are assumed to desire to increase their volume of existing loans. Below that rate they want to cut back the volume of loans. Clearly, for other positions of the investment schedule the equilibrium in the loanable funds market would occur at other points along the $(s + \Delta D)$ schedule with a nonzero value for ΔD. Such points would be positions of equilibrium for the loanable funds market and we consider such positions below. It is important to note that they would not be positions of overall equilibrium for the economy. Bank deposits are a component of the money stock and if the volume of deposits is either increasing or decreasing, the money stock is changing. From the quantity theory equation (A.1), we know that price or velocity must then change. The system is in full equi-

---

[2]This process of deposit creation is considered in Chapter 15.

Figure A.1
Loanable Funds
Market With a
Banking Sector

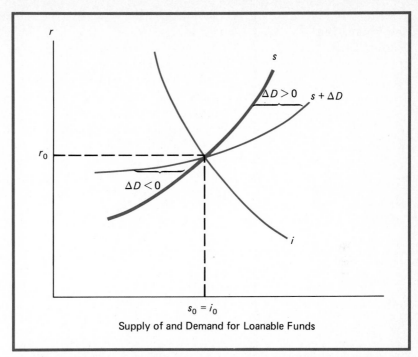

Supply of and Demand for Loanable Funds

With the addition of a banking system, the supply of loanable funds will
include the increase or decrease in bank deposits (= loans), ΔD, as well as
new saving (s). The equilibrium at interest rate r_0 is one where ΔD equals
zero and therefore the level of bank deposits is constant.

librium only at a position such as that shown in Figure A.1, when
the volume of bank deposits is not changing.

Using Fisher's version of the quantity equation with this modification in the market for loanable funds we are now able to analyze
how the system moves from one equilibrium position to another in
response to a shock. In our example the shock is an increase in
currency.

An increase in the quantity of money (currency plus demand
deposits) coming as a result of the increase in currency will shift
the aggregate demand curve to the right, increasing the price level
as shown in Figure A.2. The aggregate demand curve shifts from
$y^d(M_0V_0)$ to $y^d(M_1V_0)$, as the quantity of money is assumed to increase from M_0 to M_1. Note that in Figure A.2 we label each position of the aggregate demand curve as corresponding to a given
value of the money stock and a given value of velocity. An increase
in either the money stock or the level of velocity will shift the y^d
schedule out to the right (will increase Py). Since we were previously assuming velocity to be constant, changes in M were the only

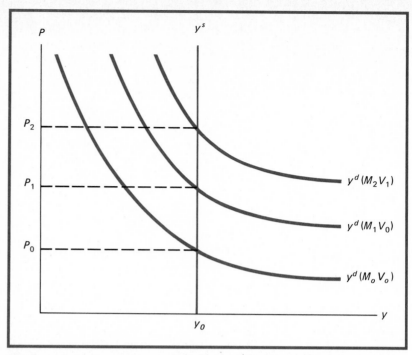

The aggregate demand curve shifts from $y^d(M_0V_0)$ to $y^d(M_1V_0)$ due to the initial increase in the currency component (C) of the money stock (M). The second shift in the aggregate demand curve, from $y^d(M_1V_0)$ to $y^d(M_2V_1)$ comes as a result of the increase in the bank deposit (D) component of the money stock and the rise in velocity during the boom.

factor that shifted the aggregate demand curve, but as we will see, velocity will vary over the transition period between points of equilibrium.

Now we come to the central feature of Fisher's disequilibrium analysis. As prices rise, from P_0 toward P_1 in Figure A.2, business profits are assumed to increase. This is because costs are not assumed to rise immediately in proportion to the increase in price. The failure of costs to rise proportionately with price could be due to a lag in the adjustment of the money wage, since workers may fail to recognize that prices are rising. Alternatively, workers may be locked into previous contracts that fix the money wage. This type of misperception on the part of workers was recognized as a possibility by classical economists and it will be important in later short-run models we consider, but it was not the crucial misperception in Fisher's model.

The crucial cost that did not rise proportionately with price in

Fisher's model was interest cost, the cost of borrowing money. Presumably, the lender of money would be interested in the real purchasing power he received when the loan was repaid. Thus to get 5 percent return in real terms would require a 7 percent nominal interest rate if the inflation rate were 2 percent, but a 9 percent nominal interest rate if the inflation rate were 4 percent. While Fisher believed that in equilibrium situations lenders would require increases in the nominal interest rate to compensate for any increases in the inflation rate, he believed that this adjustment was "slow and imperfect." Thus at first lenders continued to think of "a dollar as a dollar." Their behavior is not initially affected by the inflation caused by an increase in the money stock. In terms of Figure A.1, this means that the inflation does *not* shift the supply of loanable funds schedule (the $s + \Delta D$ curve).

Firms then find that the interest component of their costs has not risen proportionately with price. Profits have increased and firms wish to take advantage of this increasing profitability by expanding their enterprises. Investment increases. The formulation above is Fisher's. A more modern version might state that as inflation occurs the firms are not fooled and do not believe that "a dollar is a dollar." They expect inflation to continue. Their perceived *real* borrowing cost is the nominal rate of interest minus their expected inflation rate, which we denote $\dot{P}^e$. It is this real rate of interest $(r - \dot{P}^e)$ that determines the level of investment.

If investment depends on the real rate of interest, then in a graph such as Figure A.1 there will be a different investment schedule corresponding to each expected inflation rate. An increase in the expected inflation rate will shift the schedule out to the right. This is because with a higher expected inflation rate any nominal interest rate will correspond to a lower real interest rate and, hence, to a higher level of investment.

With either Fisher's original formulation or this more modern version, the result is the same. The increase in prices caused by the increase in currency will increase investment demand. We show this effect in Figure A.3.

Initially, the economy is in equilibrium at r_0, with s_0 equal to i_0. The increase in currency, which increased aggregate demand, causes prices to begin to rise. Firms perceive that inflation is going on and this shifts the investment curve to i_1 in Figure A.3. Initially, lenders are unaffected. At r_0 there is now an excess demand for loanable funds and the interest rate starts to rise. As the nominal interest rate rises, individuals save more. If increases in saving were the only way in which the supply of loanable funds could be increased, a new equilibrium position would be reached at r_1', with saving again equal to investment. Notice that this position would

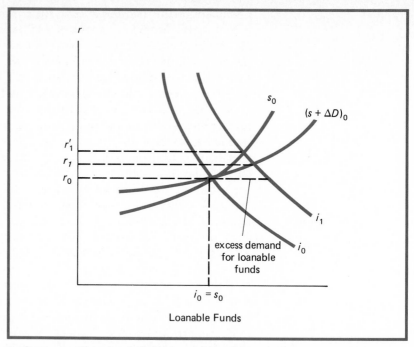

As firms perceive the inflation resulting from an increase in the money stock, the investment schedule shifts from i_0 to i_1. The interest rate rises from r_0 to r_1. There is an increase in bank lending and, therefore, deposits. Due to increased bank lending, the interest rate does not rise sufficiently (to r_1') to re-equilibrate saving and investment.

be potentially consistent with equilibrium for the economy as a whole at price level P_1, since there would, by assumption, be no factor leading to a further increase in the money stock.

New savings are, however, not the only source of loanable funds. When the investment schedule shifts to i_1, we move up the $s + \Delta D$ schedule and there is an increase in bank lending and, hence, deposits as well as an increase in savings. The new equilibrium is at interest rate r_1. At r_1 there has been an expansion of bank deposits and consequently an additional increase in the money stock. This additional increase in the money stock produces another shift to the right in the aggregate demand curve.

In this way Fisher believed that an increase in the money stock would set off what becomes for a time a self-generating inflationary boom. Fundamentally, it is the failure of the interest rate to rise sufficiently to reequilibrate savings and investment which causes the boom. The expansion of loans and deposits by the banking system is responsible for this maladjustment of the interest rate.

As the inflationary boom develops there is an additional self-generating aspect to the process. As inflation goes on, people holding money realize that the value of their money is declining and they try to hold less money. As Fisher put it; "We all hasten to get rid of any commodity which, like ripe fruit, is spoiling on our hands." In terms of the Cambridge version of the quantity theory ($M = kPy$), k falls as individuals choose to hold a smaller proportion of their income in the form of money. In terms of Fisher's version of the quantity theory given in (A.1), velocity ($V = 1/k$) increases. This increase in velocity is an additional factor shifting out the aggregate demand curve in Figure A.2.

At the end of one stage of this boom process the aggregate demand curve would be at a position such as $y^d(M_2V_1)$ in Figure A.2. The money stock has been pushed up from M_1 to M_2 by the increase in bank deposits (Figure A.3). Velocity has risen from V_0 to V_1 for the reason just explained. Just as the initial increase in aggregate demand caused by the rise in the currency component of the money stock triggered the first phase of the boom, this new increase in the money stock and *in the velocity of money* sets off a second phase as prices now rise from P_1 to P_2 in Figure A.2.

This inflationary part of the transition period can be summarized as follows:

1. Prices rise.
2. The rate of interest rises but not sufficiently to reequate saving and investment.
3. Profits increase, loans expand.
4. The volume of bank deposits and, hence, the money stock increase.
5. Velocity rises.
6. The price level continues to rise due to the changes noted in steps 4 and 5. We then go back to step 1 and repeat the process.

Where does the boom end? The bankers are the economic agents who are acting under a misperception—they fail to perceive the decline in their real interest earnings as a result of inflation. The boom ends when they recognize this and raise the nominal interest rate sufficiently to choke off the boom. Such recognition may be forced on them because the expansion of loans, as interest rates are kept too low, will cause problems for the bank. If there are legal reserve requirements mandating that a specific percentage of the value of deposits be held as currency, banks will eventually find reserves difficult to obtain and they will have to cut back on the growth of loans. Even without such laws, banks will find it unsound to expand loans too far with limited reserves. Thus Fisher felt that bankers would ultimately push the interest rate to a high enough level to end the boom.

Fisher did not, however, think that equilibrium would be restored at this point. He believed that the interest rate would overshoot the equilibrium level. The interest rate would move to too high a level for stable prices. Firms trying to renew loans would no longer find favorable rates. Many firms that had counted on such rates to make their investment projects profitable would go bankrupt. Banks that were overextended would fail. The resulting loss of confidence would create "runs" on banks as people try to convert deposits into currency. This would lead to further bank failures and cause even sound banks to be hesitant to make loans.

The volume of bank lending and, therefore, bank deposits now declines and we move into a downward and deflationary phase of the cycle. This downward process mirrors the upswing with the

Figure A.4
Interest Rate
Adjustment in the
Downswing

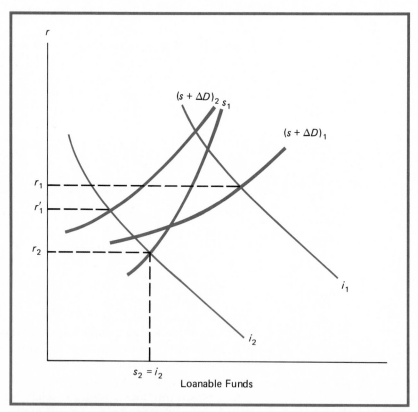

The equilibrium at the peak of the boom is at interest rate r_1. The level of bank lending and consequently the money stock fall as the deflationary part of the cycle begins. The investment schedule shifts downward from i_1 to i_2. The supply of loanable funds schedule shifts to the left from $(s + \Delta D)_1$ to $(s + \Delta D)_2$. The interest rate falls from r_1 to r_1', but not sufficiently (to r_2) to re-equilibrate saving and investment.

MACROECONOMIC MODELS

same self-generating features, but now they lead to a cumulative fall in prices. Again the key element causing the process is the maladjustment of the interest rate. The interest rate does begin to fall once this downward phase gets under way, but not quickly enough to equilibrate savings and investment. This aspect of the downswing is illustrated in Figure A.4. All the schedules labeled with the subscript 1 refer to the situation at the peak of the boom. Those with a subscript 2 refer to the situation after the downswing is in progress.

Banks begin to retrench after bankruptcies and bank failures begin. This shifts the supply of loanable funds back to a position such as $(s + \Delta D)_2$. Bank loans and deposits decline. This drop in the money stock (deposits plus currency) causes the price level to fall. As in the upswing, firms perceive the change in prices. In this case firms see that falling prices are raising the real interest rate and cutting profits. This shifts the investment schedule to i_2. For a new equilibrium at a stable price level the interest rate must fall to r_2, where investment and saving are equal, with no increase or decrease in bank deposits.

With the banking system in such disarray, this is not possible. Instead, we move to interest rate r_1', where the total supply of loanable funds—saving plus the change in bank lending (in this case a negative amount)—is equal to investment. The interest rate falls relative to its value at the peak of the boom, but not by enough. Recovery must await improvement of the financial condition of the banking system and restoration of confidence in bank deposits.

A.3 CLASSICAL DISEQUILIBRIUM ANALYSIS: CONCLUSION

Fisher believed that, together, the upward and downward phases of the process described above would last for about 10 years. He also believed that although the system did tend toward an eventual equilibrium position, new shocks to the system would prevent that equilibrium from being achieved. It would seem to follow that the economy would generally be in the midst of such transitions and the further development of the classical *disequilibrium* model would have been his main interest. Instead, Fisher devoted the rest of the book from which we have taken this model to the description of the equilibrium version of the quantity theory. Later in the book he describes the transition period as a minor phenomenon and in describing the equilibrium properties of the classical system, he notes: "Some of the foregoing propositions are subject to slight modifications during transition periods."

Neither Fisher nor the other classical economists developed a complete theory of the behavior of the economy away from the full-employment norm. Fisher's own model, which we have examined as an example of the classical disequilibrium analysis, is an interesting model of a credit cycle—of money "misbehaving." Several aspects of the model, such as the relationship between the interest rate and expected inflation and the role of misperceptions in generating disequilibrium, reappear in more modern models of the economy in the short run. However, Fisher's model, as well as other classical disequilibrium models, failed to provide a systematic theory of the determination of output and employment when these variables were not at their full-employment levels and to link that analysis with the behavior of credit markets in disequilibrium. To do this required the development of a theory of the aggregate demand for output and a theory of the role of money as an asset and not just a medium of exchange. These were to be the two accomplishments of Keynesian economics.

chapter 5

5.1 THE PROBLEM OF UNEMPLOYMENT

Keynesian economics developed against the background of the world depression of the 1930s. The length and severity of the decline in economic activity that occurred at that time were unprecedented. The effect of the depression on the U.S. economy can be seen in Figure 5.1, which shows the annual unemployment rates for the years 1929–41. The unemployment rate rose from 3.2 percent of the labor force in 1929 to 25.2 percent of the labor force in 1933, the low point for economic activity during the Depression. Unemployment remained over 10 percent throughout the decade. Real GNP fell by 30 percent between 1929 and 1933 and did not reach the 1929 level again until 1939.

The British economist John Maynard Keynes, whose book *The General Theory of Employment, Interest and Money* is the foundation of the Keynesian system, was more heavily influenced by events in his own country than those in the United States. In Great Britain high unemployment began in the early 1920s and persisted into and throughout the 1930s.[1] The high unemployment in Great

---

[1]The unemployment rate in Great Britain was above 10 percent as early as 1923 and remained above 10 percent, except for one brief fall to 9.8 percent, until 1936, the year in which *The General Theory* was published.

THE KEYNESIAN SYSTEM (I): THE ROLE OF AGGREGATE DEMAND

Britain led to a debate among economists and policymakers over the causes of unemployment and the proper policy response to increased unemployment. Keynes was a prominent participant in this debate, during the course of which he was to develop his revolutionary theory of macroeconomics.

According to Keynes's theory, the high unemployment in Great Britain and the United States (as well as in other industrialized countries) was the result of a deficiency in *aggregate demand*. Aggregate demand was too low because of inadequate investment demand. Keynes's theory provided the basis for economic policies to combat unemployment. Policies should be aimed at stimulating aggregate demand. At the time of the depression Keynes favored fiscal policy measures, primarily government spending on public works projects, to stimulate demand. More generally, the Keynesian theory argues for the use of monetary and fiscal policies to regulate the level of aggregate demand. To understand the revolutionary nature of this theory it is useful to consider the state of macroeconomic thinking about unemployment as an economic policy question at the time Keynes's thought was developing.

The word "unemployment" did not come into common usage until about the turn of the century and it continued to be used in quotation marks for some time. Classical economists clearly recognized the human cost of unemployment, as stated feelingly, for example, by Alfred Marshall.

Figure 5.1
U.S. Unemployment
Rate, 1929–1941
(percent)

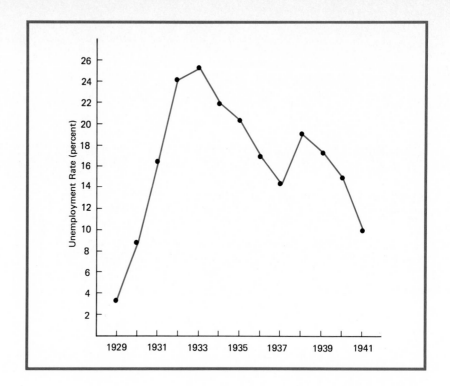

Forced interruption to labour is a grievous evil. Those, whose livelihood is secure, gain physical and mental health from happy and well-spent holidays. But want of work, with long continued anxiety, consumes a man's best strength without any return. His wife becomes thin; and his children get, as it were, a nasty notch in their lives, which is perhaps never outgrown.[2]

But Marshall had little to say about the causes of unemployment. He noted that unemployment existed in early times and argued that knowledge was the cure, in that knowledge would increase the skills of labor and also keep laborers and firms from making poor economic decisions which result in business failures and unemployment. When Marshall offered suggestions for ways in which to diminish fluctuations in unemployment, the following was the first given.

Those causes of discontinuity which lie within our scope, and are remediable, are chiefly connected in some way or other with the want of knowledge; but there is one which is willful: it is fashion. Until a little while ago only the rich could change their clothing at the capricious order of their dressmakers: but now all classes do it.

[2]Alfred Marshall, *Money, Credit and Commerce* (London: Macmillan, 1922), p. 260.

MACROECONOMIC MODELS

The histories of the alpaca trade, the lace trade, the straw hat trade, the ribbon trade, and a multitude of others, tell of bursts of feverish activity alternating with deadening idleness.[3]

To the modern reader this analysis must appear quaint; it was hardly a sound basis for meaningful solutions to the unemployment problem of Britain in the 1920s. Marshall and the other economists relying on the classical equilibrium theory had little else to offer. In the classical system unemployment could result from downward rigidity of the money wage. Money wage cuts could be, and were, suggested as a possible remedy for unemployment. The money wage, however, fell in the United States by one-third between 1929 and 1933 without stopping the rise in unemployment. Just as wage cuts did not appear to provide an adequate remedy to the depression, rigid money wages did not provide a satisfactory explanation of the massive unemployment. The failure of the money wage to fall in response to a decline in the demand for labor would result in unemployment, but why was the demand for labor falling so disastrously? Was not the decline in labor demand the ultimate source of the unemployment? Recently, economists have tried to explain the depression in ways not inconsistent with the classical model, but economists at the time were dissatisfied and were casting about for alternatives to the orthodox classical analysis.

Much of the debate over economic policy in Great Britain at that time focused on the question of the desirability of government spending on public works as a cure for unemployment, what we would now term as expansionary fiscal policy action. The argument advanced by Keynes and others was that such actions would increase output and employment. Such expenditures would stimulate output and employment both directly and indirectly because they would increase the income and hence consumer expenditure of those employed by the public works projects, thus generating secondary employment.

Those arguing against this view drew primarily on the classical equilibrium analysis that we have presented. Fiscal policy actions, unless financed by money creation and thus changes in monetary policy, would not affect either employment or the price level. If public works projects were financed by money creation, the price level but not the levels of output or employment would be affected. This classical theory was the basis for the official position of the Conservative Party in Great Britain, which was in power for the bulk of the 1920s and early 1930s. As Winston Churchill explained this position: "It is the orthodox Treasury dogma, steadfastly held,

[3]Ibid.

that whatever might be the political or social advantages, very little employment can, in fact, as a general rule, be created by state borrowing and state expenditure."

In the United States, policy prescriptions consistent with the classical position were also influential. Far from trying to raise demand and stimulate output and employment, during the height of the Depression, in 1932, the administration of Herbert Hoover engineered a large income tax increase. Hoover's reason for increasing tax rates was to balance the federal budget. Higher tax rates were needed to balance the budget in the wake of falling tax revenues as income declined. Since in the classical system fiscal policy had no effect on income, prudent budget management had come to mean simply balancing spending with tax revenues. When Franklin Roosevelt ran against Hoover for the presidency in 1932, he attacked Hoover for failing to succeed in balancing the budget and argued for cuts in government spending. Would not the income tax increase or cut in government spending lower aggregate demand, output, and employment? Not in the classical system, since output and employment were supply determined. In any case, in the classical model fiscal policy did not affect aggregate demand. As we will see, such a tax increase or spending cut is just the opposite of the "correct" policy action as indicated by the Keynesian model.

To sum up, the situation in the early 1930s was one of massive unemployment which was regarded as not well explained by the classical system and for which classical economics provided no remedy. Many economists and political figures argued in favor of various policy actions, including public works projects, to try to increase aggregate demand. The classical economists pointed out that such policies would not work in the classical system, where output and employment were not demand determined. As Keynes pointed out: "The strength of the self-adjusting school depends on its having behind it almost the whole body of organized economic thinking and doctrine of the last hundred years."[4] Keynes ranged himself among the "heretics" to the classical view of the self-adjusting properties of the economy. Of the heretics, he wrote: "They are deeply dissatisfied. They believe that common observation is enough to show that facts do not conform to the orthodox reasoning. They propose remedies prompted by instinct, by flair, by practical good sense, by experience of the world—half right, most of them, half wrong."[5] Keynes felt that the heretics would never prevail until the flaw in the orthodox classical theory had been found. He believed that flaw to be the lack of an explicit the-

[4]John M. Keynes, *Collected Works*, Vol. 13 (London: Macmillan, 1973), p. 489.
[5]Ibid., pp. 488–89.

ory of the aggregate demand for output and, hence, of the role of aggregate demand in determining output and employment. We discuss next the theory provided by Keynes and his followers to fill this gap in the classical system.

Our analysis of the Keynesian system will proceed as follows. In the remainder of this chapter we analyze a very simple version of the Keynesian model. This model will be useful in developing the basic elements of Keynes's theory of aggregate demand. Our simple model will neglect complications that come from allowing for the effects of money and interest rates in the model. It will also neglect the effect of changes in the price level and the level of the money wage. Money and interest rates are introduced into the model in Chapter 6. Chapter 7 analyzes policy effects in the resulting version of the Keynesian model. Chapter 8 takes account of the effects of price and wage changes in the Keynesian system. There, we explain the Keynesian theory of aggregate supply.

5.2 THE SIMPLE KEYNESIAN MODEL: CONDITIONS FOR EQUILIBRIUM OUTPUT

A central notion in the simple Keynesian model is that for a level of output to be an equilibrium level requires that output be equal to aggregate demand. In our simple model this condition for equilibrium can be expressed as

$$Y = E \tag{5.1}$$

where Y is equal to total output (GNP) and E equals aggregate demand or desired expenditures on output. Aggregate demand (E) consists of three components: household consumption (C), desired business investment demand (I), and the government sector's demand for goods and services (G). Thus in equilibrium we have

$$Y = E = C + I + G \tag{5.2}$$

The simple form of (5.2) and of the identities discussed below result from neglecting a number of complexities in the definitions of gross national product and national income. These simplifications, which were discussed in Chapter 2, are noted here briefly again. Exports and imports do not appear in (5.2). Here we will be dealing with a "closed" economy, neglecting foreign trade. Depreciation is also neglected, so we will not need to distinguish between gross national product and net national product. We also assume that gross national product and national income are equivalent. This means that we do not include in the model the items that cause a discrepancy between the two totals (primarily indirect business taxes). A final assumption has to do with the units in which each of the variables is measured. For this section we assume that *the aggregate price level is fixed*. All variables are *real* variables and all changes are changes in real terms.

With national product Y also measuring national income, we can write

$$Y \equiv C + S + T \tag{5.3}$$

Equation (5.3) is an accounting definition or identity stating that national income, all of which is assumed to be paid to households in return for factor services, is either consumed (C), paid out in taxes (T), or if it goes to neither purpose, it is saved (S).[6] Additionally, from the fact that Y is national product we can write

$$Y \equiv C + I_r + G \tag{5.4}$$

Equation (5.4) *defines* national product as equal to consumption, plus realized investment (I_r), plus government spending.

Using the definitions given in (5.3) and (5.4), we can rewrite the condition for an equilibrium level of income given in (5.2) in two alternative ways which will help us to understand the nature of equilibrium in the model. Since, by (5.2), in equilibrium Y must equal $(C + I + G)$, and from (5.3), Y is defined as $(C + S + T)$ *in equilibrium*,

$$C + S + T \equiv Y = C + I + G$$

or, equivalently,

$$S + T = I + G \tag{5.5}$$

In similar fashion, from (5.2) and (5.4) we can see that in equilibrium

$$C + I_r + G \equiv Y = C + I + G$$

or, by canceling terms,

$$I_r = I \tag{5.6}$$

There are then three equivalent ways in which to state the condition for equilibrium in the model:

$$Y = C + I + G \tag{5.2}$$

$$S + T = I + G \tag{5.5}$$

$$I_r = I \tag{5.6}$$

---

[6]The model does not allow for retained earnings. All profits are assumed to be paid out as dividends. Also, firms are assumed to make no tax payments; all taxes are paid by households.

To help us interpret the meaning of these conditions, we turn to the flowchart given in Figure 5.2. Each of the magnitudes in the chart (each of the variables in our model) is a flow variable. They are measured in dollars per period. In the national income accounts they are measured as billions of dollars per quarter or year. The flow marked with the uppermost arrow in the diagram is the flow of national income from the business sector to the household sector. This flow consists of payments for factor services (wages, interest, rents, dividends). Such payments are assumed to sum to national income, which is equal to national product. There is a corresponding flow from the household sector to the business sector, consisting of the factor services supplied by the household sector. This flow and similar flows are not shown in the diagram because they are not money flows.

National income is distributed by households into three flows. There is a flow of consumption expenditures which goes back to the business sector as a demand for the output produced. Thus the inner loop of our diagram depicts a process whereby firms produce output (Y), which generates an equal amount of income to the household sector, which in turn generates a demand for the output produced (C).

All of national income does not return directly to the firms as a demand for the output produced. There are two flows out of the household sector in addition to consumption expenditure. These are the saving flow and the flow of tax payments. If we regard the inner loop of our diagram, linking the households (as suppliers of

Figure 5.2 Circular Flow of Income and Output

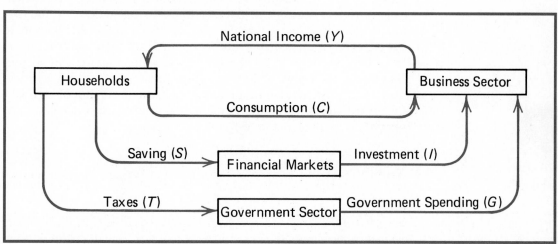

factor services and demanders of output) and the business sector (as suppliers of output and demanders of factor services), as the central income and output generating mechanism, the saving and tax flows are *leakages* from this central loop.

The saving leakage flows into the financial markets. By this we mean that the part of income that is saved is held in the form of some financial asset (currency, bank deposits, bonds, equities, etc.). The tax flow is paid to the government sector. The tax flow in the diagram is *net* taxes, that is, gross tax payments minus transfer payments from the government to the household sector (social security benefits, welfare payments, unemployment compensation, etc.). Consequently, when we talk below about a tax increase or tax cut, this can be interpreted equivalently as a change in the opposite direction in the level of such transfer payments.

Although each dollar of output and, hence, national income does not directly generate one dollar of demand for output on the part of the household sector, this does not mean that total demand must fall short of output. There are additional demands for output on the part of the business sector itself for investment, and from the government sector. In terms of our circular flow diagram, these are *injections* into the central loop of our diagram. The investment injection is shown as a flow from financial markets to the business sector. The purchasers of the investment goods are actually the firms in the business sector themselves. These purchases must, however, be financed by borrowing in financial markets. Thus the dollar amount of investment represents an equivalent flow of funds lent to the business sector. Government spending is a demand for the output of the business sector and is shown as a money flow from the government to the business sector.

We are now in a position to examine the three equivalent expressions for equilibrium given by (5.2), (5.5), and (5.6). Production of a level of output Y generates an equivalent amount of income to households. A portion of this income, equal to consumption demand (C), returns directly to the firms as a demand for that output. The level of output will be an equilibrium level if this directly generated demand (C), when added to desired investment expenditures of firms (I) and government spending (G), produces a total demand equal to Y, that is, if

$$Y = C + I + G \tag{5.2}$$

From the second version of the condition for equilibrium income

$$S + T = I + G \tag{5.5}$$

we see that a flow rate of output will be an equilibrium rate if the leakages ($S + T$) from the central loop of our flow diagram are just balanced by injections ($I + G$) into this central income and output circular flow. This assures that the amount of income households do not spend on output $(S + T)$, and therefore the amount of output that is produced but not sold to households $(Y - C \equiv S + T)$, is just equal to the amount the other two sectors wish to buy $(I + G)$. This is equivalent to saying that total output equals aggregate demand and is thus equivalent to the first way of stating the condition for equilibrium.

The third way of expressing the condition for equilibrium, equation (5.6) $(I = I_r)$, states that in equilibrium desired investment must equal actual or realized investment. What does it mean for desired investment to differ from realized investment? The GNP accountant computes investment as the total volume of business spending on plant and equipment, plus inventory investment, the increment (or decline) in inventories. For the first two of these categories of spending we can assume that desired spending equals actual spending as recorded by the GNP accountant. It is in the last category, inventory investment, that desired and realized totals may differ. The GNP accountant will record all goods that are produced by a firm and not sold as inventory investment—*whether such investment was intended or not.*

To see how realized and intended inventory investment can differ, consider what happens when a level of output $(Y \equiv C + I_r + G)$ is produced that exceeds aggregate demand $(E = C + I + G)$. In this case

$$Y > E$$
$$C + I_r + G > C + I + G \tag{5.7}$$
$$I_r > I$$

where $I_r - I$ is the unintended inventory accumulation. The amount by which output exeeds aggregate demand $(I_r - I)$ will be unsold output over and above the amount of inventory investment that the firm desired. This excess will be *unintended inventory accumulation.*

In the reverse situation, where aggregate demand exceeds output, we have

$$E > Y$$
$$C + I + G > C + I_r + G \tag{5.8}$$
$$I > I_r$$

where $I - I_r$ is the unintended inventory shortfall. Demand is greater than output and the firms sell more than was planned. Inventories end up at less than the desired level. The equilibrium point $(I = I_r)$ is a level of production which after all sales are made leaves inventory investment at just the level desired by the firms.

As can be seen from (5.7) or (5.8), this is the level where output equals aggregate demand and hence is equivalent to the other two ways of expressing the condition for equilibrium in the model.

Looked at from this third way of expressing the condition for equilibrium in the model, it is easy to see the reason why there can not be an equilibrium at any other point. If at a given level of output firms are accumulating undesired inventories or are seeing their inventories depleted, there will be a tendency for the level of output to change. If production exceeds demand $(Y > E)$, firms are accumulating unwanted inventories $(I_r > I)$ and there will be a tendency for output to fall as firms cut production to reduce the level of inventories. If, alternatively, demand is outstripping production $(E > Y)$; there will be an inventory shortfall $(I_r < I)$ and a tendency for output to rise as firms try to prevent further falls in inventories. Only when aggregate demand equals output will firms be satisfied with their current level of output. There will be neither an unintended inventory buildup or shortfall and, therefore, no tendency for output to change. This is what is meant by equilibrium.

5.3 THE COMPONENTS OF AGGREGATE DEMAND

We have expressed the condition for equilibrium in the simple Keynesian model in terms of the components of aggregate demand. To see the factors that determine the level of income, we need to consider the factors that affect the components of aggregate demand: the determinants of consumption, investment, and government spending. We look at each of these in turn. The determinants of saving and the role of taxes also enter into our discussion.

Consumption

Consumer expenditure is the largest component of aggregate demand, amounting to between 60 and 65 percent of GNP in recent years. Consumption plays a central role in the Keynesian theory of income determination.

Keynes believed that the level of consumer expenditure was a stable function of disposable income, where disposable income (Y_D) in our simple model is national income minus tax payments $(Y_D = Y - T)$. Keynes did not deny that variables other than income could have some effect on consumption, but he felt that income was the dominant factor determining consumption. As a first approximation other influences could be neglected.

MACROECONOMIC MODELS

The specific form of the consumption–income relationship proposed by Keynes was as follows:

$$C = a + bY_D \qquad a > 0, \quad 0 < b < 1 \qquad (5.9)$$

Figure 5.3 graphs this relationship. The intercept term a, which is assumed to be positive, is the value of consumption where disposable income equals zero. As such, a can be thought of as a measure of the effect on consumption of variables other than income, variables not explicitly included in this simple model. The parameter b, the slope of the function, gives the increment to consumer expenditure per unit increase in disposable income. In notation we will use frequently

$$b = \frac{\Delta C}{\Delta Y_D} \qquad (5.10)$$

where the differencing symbol Δ indicates the change in the variable it precedes. The value of the increment to consumer expenditure per unit increment to income (b) is termed the *marginal propensity to consume* (MPC). The Keynesian assumption is that consumption will increase with an increase in disposable income

Figure 5.3
Keynesian
Consumption Function

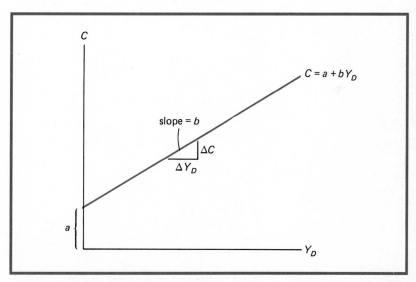

The consumption function shows the level of consumption (C) corresponding to each level of disposable income (Y_D). The slope of the consumption function ($\Delta C/\Delta Y_D$) is equal to the marginal propensity to consume (b), the increase in consumption per unit increase in disposable income. The intercept for the consumption function (a) is the (positive) level of consumption at a zero level of disposable income.

($b > 0$), but that the increase in consumption will be less than the increase in disposable income ($b < 1$).

From the definition of national income previously discussed,

$$Y \equiv C + S + T \tag{5.3}$$

we can write

$$Y_D \equiv Y - T \equiv C + S \tag{5.11}$$

which shows that disposable income is by definition consumption plus saving. Thus a theory of the consumption–income relationship will also implicitly determine the saving–income relationship. In the case of the Keynesian theory, we have

$$S = -a + (1 - b)Y_D \tag{5.12}$$

If consumption is a units with Y_D equal to zero, then *at that point*

$$S \equiv Y_D - C$$
$$= 0 - a$$
$$= -a$$

If a 1-unit increase in disposable income leads to an increase of b units in consumption, the remainder of the 1-unit increase $(1 - b)$ is the increase in saving:

$$\frac{\Delta S}{\Delta Y_D} = 1 - b \tag{5.13}$$

This increment to saving per unit increase in disposable income $(1 - b)$ is called the *marginal propensity to save* (MPS). The graph of the saving function is shown in Figure 5.4.

Figure 5.4
Keynesian Saving
Function

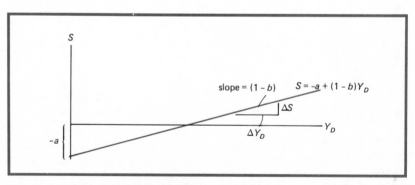

The saving function shows the level of saving (S) corresponding to each level of disposable income (Y_D). The slope of the saving function is equal to the marginal propensity to save $(1 - b)$, the increase in saving per unit increase in disposable income. The intercept for the saving function $(-a)$ is the (negative) level of saving at a zero level of disposable income.

Investment

The level of investment was also a key variable in the Keynesian system. Changes in desired business investment expenditure were one of the major factors which Keynes thought were responsible for changes in income.

As noted above, Keynes believed that consumption was a stable function of disposable income. This did not imply that the level of consumption expenditures would not vary over time. It did imply that in the absence of other factors which caused income to change, consumption expenditures would not be an independent source variability in income. Consumption was primarily *induced* expenditure, by which we mean expenditure that depends directly on the level of income.

To explain the underlying causes of movements in aggregate demand and, hence, income, Keynes looked to the *autonomous* components of aggregate demand. These were the components that were determined, for the large part, independently of current income. When these expenditure components varied, they caused income to vary. Keynes believed that investment was the most highly variable of the autonomous components of aggregate demand. He believed that it was the variability of such investment spending that was primarily responsible for the instability in income.

Table 5.1 contains figures for investment and consumption as percentages of gross national product in selected years. The years shown in the table contrast investment and consumption spending in prosperous years (1929, 1955, 1973) with corresponding spending in subsequent depression or recession years (1933, 1958, 1975). Investment spending does appear to be more volatile and is a logical choice as a factor explaining income variability. The question remains: What determines investment?

Keynes suggested two variables as the primary determinants of investment expenditures in the short run. These variables were the interest rate and the state of business expectations.

Table 5.1 **Consumption and Investment as a Percentage of Gross National Product, Selected Years**	Year	Investment	Consumption
	1929	15.7	74.8
	1933	2.5	82.1
	1955	17.1	63.5
	1958	13.8	64.5
	1973	16.1	62.6
	1975	12.5	64.0

In explaining the relationship between investment and the rate of interest, Keynes's analysis did not differ from the classical view. Again the level of investment is assumed to be inversely related to the level of the interest rate. At higher interest rates there are fewer investment projects that have a prospective return high enough to justify borrowing to finance them. This link will be important in Chapter 6. For now, since we have not explained how the interest rate is determined in the Keynesian model, we neglect this effect of the interest rate on investment. We focus instead on the second factor determining investment, the expected yield on investment projects. It was shifts in such expectations about the future profitability of investment projects that Keynes believed to be the major cause of the instability in investment.

Business managers' expectations about the future profitability of investment projects are a central element in Keynes's analysis of the sources of economic instability. Keynes emphasizes the "uncertain knowledge" upon which expectations of the future must be based. In planning a project that will produce output over 20 or 30 years, in order to know how profitable the project will be, a manager would need a great deal of knowledge about the future. He would need to know the future demand for the product, which would require knowledge about future consumer tastes and the state of aggregate demand. He would need knowledge about future costs, including money wages, interest rates, and tax rates; a well-grounded forecast of such variables cannot be made that looks 20 or 30 years into the future.

Nevertheless, investment decisions are made. Keynes felt that rational managers faced with the need to make decisions under such extreme uncertainty formed expectations using the following techniques:

1. They tended to extrapolate past trends into the future, ignoring possible future changes, unless there was specific information about a prospective change.
2. "Knowing that our own individual judgment is worthless, we endeavor to fall back on the judgment of the rest of the world which is perhaps better informed. That is, we endeavor to conform with the behavior of the majority or the average. The psychology of a society of individuals each of whom is endeavoring to copy the others leads to what we may strictly term a *conventional* judgment."[7]

Keynes believed that an expectation formed in this manner would have the following property.

[7]John M. Keynes, "The General Theory of Employment," *Quarterly Journal of Economics*, February 1937, p. 214.

In particular, being based on so flimsey a foundation, it is subject to sudden and violent changes. The practice of calmness and immobility, of certainty and security, suddenly breaks down. New fears and hopes will, without warning, take charge of human conduct. The forces of disillusion may suddenly impose a new conventional basis of valuation. All these pretty, polite techniques, made for a well-panelled board room, are liable to collapse. At all times the vague panic fears and equally vague and unreasoned hopes are not really lulled, and lie but a little way below the surface.[8]

To summarize, expectations of the future profitability of investment projects rested on a very precarious base of knowledge and Keynes felt that such expectations could shift frequently, at times drastically, in response to new information and events. Consequently, investment demand was unstable. Investment expenditure is the component of autonomous expenditures which Keynes believed to be responsible for instability in the behavior of income.

Government Spending and Taxes

The level of government spending (G) is a second element of autonomous expenditures. Government spending is assumed to be controlled by the policymaker and, therefore, does not depend directly on the level of income.

We will assume that the level of tax receipts (T) is also controlled by the policymaker and is an exogenous policy variable. A more realistic assumption would be that the policymaker sets the tax rate and that tax receipts vary with income. This would complicate our calculations somewhat but would not change the essential conclusions (more complex tax structures are discussed in Chapter 18, where we consider fiscal policy in more detail).

5.4 DETERMINING EQUILIBRIUM INCOME

We now have all the elements needed to determine the level of equilibrium income. The first form of the condition for an equilibrium level of income was

$$Y = C + I + G \tag{5.2}$$

The autonomous expenditure terms I and G are given; these are the exogenous variables. Consumption was seen in the preceding subsection to be given by

$$C = a + bY_D = a + bY - bT \tag{5.9}$$

[8]Ibid., pp. 214–15.

where the second equality uses the definition of disposable income $(Y_D \equiv Y - T)$.

Substituting the definition for consumption given by (5.9) into the equilibrium condition (5.2), we can solve for $\bar{Y}$, the equilibrium level of income, as follows:

$$Y = C + I + G$$

$$Y = a + bY - bT + I + G$$

$$Y - bY = a - bT + I + G$$

$$Y(1 - b) = a - bT + I + G$$

$$\bar{Y} = \frac{1}{1 - b}(a - bT + I + G) \qquad (5.14)$$

In Figure 5.5 the determination of equilibrium income is depicted graphically. The level of income is measured along the horizontal axis and the components of aggregate demand are measured along the vertical axis. The 45° line is drawn to split the

Figure 5.5

Determination of Equilibrium Income

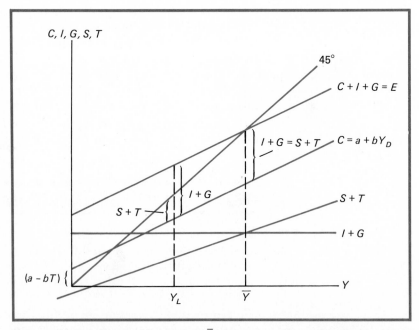

The equilibrium level of income is $\bar{Y}$, the point where the $C + I + G = E$ schedule intersects the 45° line. At that point aggregate demand equals output $(C + I + G = Y)$. Also at $\bar{Y}$, the $S + T$ and $I + G$ schedules intersect so $S + T = I + G$. At a level of income below $\bar{Y}$, Y_L, aggregate demand exceeds output $(C + I + G > Y)$. At points above $\bar{Y}$, output exceeds aggregate demand.

MACROECONOMIC MODELS

positive quadrant of the graph. All points along the line marked 45° have the property that the value of the variable measured on the vertical axis is equal to that of the variable measured on the horizontal axis. The consumption function ($C = a + bY_D$) is shown on the graph and we have also plotted the ($C + I + G$) or aggregate demand (E) schedule, which is obtained by adding the autonomous expenditure components investment and government spending to consumption spending at each level of income. Since the autonomous expenditure components (I, G) do not depend directly on income, the ($C + I + G$) schedule lies above the consumption function by a constant amount. Similarly, the line plotting these autonomous expenditure components alone, the $I + G$ line, is horizontal, reflecting the fact that their level does not depend on Y. The final line, marked $S + T$ in the graph, plots the value of saving plus taxes. This schedule slopes upward because saving varies positively with income.

The equilibrium level of income is shown in the graph at the point where the ($C + I + G$) schedule crosses the 45° line and aggregate demand is therefore equal to income (Y). At this point it must also be true that the ($S + T$) schedule crosses the ($I + G$) schedule. This reflects the equivalence of our various expressions of the equilibrium condition as discussed in Section 5.2. That this must be the case in the graph can be seen as follows. The distance between the consumption schedule and the 45° line is always ($S + T$), by definition ($Y \equiv C + S + T$). The distance between the consumption schedule and the ($C + I + G$) line is clearly always equal to ($I + G$). Where the ($C + I + G$) schedule hits the 45° line, these two distances ($S + T$) and ($I + G$) are equated. Also note that at $\overline{Y}$, actual investment is just equal to desired investment ($C + I + G = Y \equiv C + I_r + G$; therefore, $I = I_r$).

The understanding of the properties of an equilibrium level of income is aided by considering why other points on the graph are not points of equilibrium. Consider a level of income below $\overline{Y}$, for example the point marked Y_L in Figure 5.5. A level of income equal to Y_L will generate consumption as shown along the consumption function. When this level of consumption is added to the autonomous expenditures ($I + G$), the total aggregate demand exceeds income; the ($C + I + G$) schedule is above the 45° line. Equivalently, at this point $I + G$ is greater than $S + T$, as can be seen from the graph. It also follows that with demand outstripping production, desired investment will exceed actual investment at points such as Y_L ($C + I + G > Y \equiv C + I_r + G$; therefore, $I > I_r$). There will be an unintended inventory shortfall at such points below $\overline{Y}$ and therefore a tendency for output to rise.

Analogously, at levels of income above $\overline{Y}$ in Figure 5.5, output will exceed demand (the 45° line is above the $C + I + G$ schedule), unintended inventory investment will be taking place ($Y \equiv C + I_r + G > C + I + G$; therefore, $I_r > I$), and there will be a tendency for output to fall. It is only at $\bar{Y}$ that output is equal to aggregate demand; there is no unintended inventory shortfall or accumulation and, consequently, no tendency for output to change.

Returning to our mathematical expression for equilibrium income, equation (5.14), we can rewrite this equation in a form that gives the essence of Keynes's view of the income determination process. Our expression for equilibrium consists of two parts:

$$\bar{Y} = \frac{1}{1 - b}(a - bT + I + G)$$

$$\bar{Y} = \left(\begin{matrix}\text{autonomous expenditure}\\ \text{multiplier}\end{matrix}\right) \times \left(\begin{matrix}\text{autonomous}\\ \text{expenditures}\end{matrix}\right)$$

(5.15)

The first term, $\left(\dfrac{1}{1 - b}\right)$, is what we will refer to as the *autonomous expenditure multiplier*. Note that b is the fraction of any increment to disposable income that will go to consumption, what we termed the marginal propensity to consume (MPC). The term $1/(1 - b)$ or $1/(1 - MPC)$ is then 1 divided by a fraction and, hence, some number greater than 1. Some examples are:

$$b = 0.5: \quad \frac{1}{1 - b} = \frac{1}{1 - 0.5} = \frac{1}{0.5} = 2$$

$$b = 0.8: \quad \frac{1}{1 - b} = \frac{1}{1 - 0.8} = \frac{1}{0.2} = 5$$

$$b = 0.9: \quad \frac{1}{1 - b} = \frac{1}{1 - 0.9} = \frac{1}{0.1} = 10$$

We call this term the autonomous expenditure multiplier because every dollar of autonomous expenditure is multiplied by this factor to get its contribution to the level of equilibrium income.

The second term in the expression is the level of autonomous expenditures. We have already discussed two elements of autonomous expenditures, investment (I) and government spending (G). The first two terms (a and $-bT$) require a few words of explanation. These terms measure the autonomous component of consumption expenditures (a) and the autonomous effect of tax collections on aggregate demand ($-bT$), which also works through consumption. Consumption is for the most part induced expenditures, as explained above. The two terms (a and $-bT$), however, affect the amount of consumption *for a given level of income* (Y). In terms of Figure 5.5, they determine the height of the consumption function. Like G and I, they affect the amount of aggregate demand

MACROECONOMIC MODELS

for a given level of income rather than being themselves directly determined by income. They are thus appropriately included as autonomous factors affecting aggregate demand.

Keynes's theory in its simplest form can be stated as follows. Since consumption is a stable function of income, the marginal propensity to consume will be stable. Changes in income will come primarily from changes in the autonomous components of aggregate demand, especially from changes in the unstable investment component of aggregate demand. A given change in an autonomous component of aggregate demand will cause a larger change in equilibrium income due to the multiplier, for reasons we explain below. Equation (5.15) makes clear that in the absence of government policies to stabilize the economy, income will be unstable due to the instability of investment. From (5.15) it may also be seen that by appropriate changes in government spending (G) and taxes (T), the government could counteract the effects of shift in investment. Appropriate changes in G and T could keep the sum of the terms in parentheses (autonomous expenditures) constant even in the face of undesirable changes in the I term. This is the basis for the interventionist policy conclusions that Keynes reached.

Before giving examples of such stabilization policies, we need to consider the workings of the autonomous expenditure multiplier in more detail.

5.5 CHANGES IN EQUILIBRIUM INCOME

Consider the effect on equilibrium income of a change in autonomous investment demand. We assume that the other components of autonomous expenditures, the other items in parentheses in (5.15), are fixed. We solve for the change in equilibrium income from (5.15) as follows:

$$\Delta \bar{Y} = \frac{1}{1 - b} \Delta I \tag{5.16}$$

or

$$\frac{\Delta \bar{Y}}{\Delta I} = \frac{1}{1 - b} \tag{5.17}$$

A 1-unit change in investment causes a change in income of $\left(\frac{1}{1-b}\right)$ units. If b is 0.8, for example, Y changes by 5 units for each 1-unit change in investment. Why does income change by a multiple of the change in investment, and why by the precise amount $\left(\frac{1}{1-b}\right)$?

One way of explaining the process which is behind the multiplier is to consider an analogy with the "ripple effect" of a stone dropped in a pond. There is the initial effect as the stone disturbs the water. Added to this is the effect on the rest of the water surface as the water displaced by the stone disturbs the adjoining water in a process that spreads out and with intensity that diminishes as the distance from the initial point of impact increases. The investment change is the initial disturbance; let us assume this equals 100 units. As some firms experience increased demand due to this increased investment, their output increases. In consequence, their payments to factors of production (wages, rents, interest, dividends) increase. To the households this is an increase in income and, since taxes are fixed, an equal increase in disposable income. Consumption will then increase, although by less than the increase in income. This is the beginning of the indirect effects of the shock. With ΔI equal to 100 as assumed, if the MPC were 0.8, for example, there would now be an additional 80 units of consumer demand.

The process will not stop here, since this 80 units of new consumer expenditure, with the resulting increase in production, generates a second-round increase in income for some households of 80 units. There will be a further increase in consumer demand (64 units if the MPC is 0.8). The reason then for income rising by more than the autonomous rise in investment is that the rise in investment leads to induced increases in consumer demand as income increases.

Why is the increase in income per dollar increase in investment just equal to $\left(\dfrac{1}{1-b}\right)$? With the other elements of autonomous expenditures fixed, we can write the change in equilibrium income as investment varies as

$$\Delta Y = \Delta I + \Delta C \tag{5.18}$$

To restore the equality of income and aggregate demand, equilibrium income must rise by an amount equal to the increase in investment (ΔI) plus the income induced increase in consumer demand. Rearranging terms in (5.18), we have

$$\Delta Y - \Delta C = \Delta I$$

or[9]

$$\Delta S = \Delta I \tag{5.19}$$

Condition (5.19) can also be seen to follow from our second way of expressing the condition for equilibrium income:

$$S + T = I + G \tag{5.5}$$

[9]Note that tax collections are fixed, so $\Delta Y = \Delta Y_D$. Thus $\Delta Y = \Delta Y_D \equiv \Delta C + \Delta S$ and, therefore, $\Delta Y - \Delta C = \Delta S$.

With T and G fixed, for equilibrium S must rise by the amount of the increase in I, as required by (5.19). To restore equilibrium income must rise by enough to generate new saving equal to the new investment. Put differently, the amount of the increase in income must be such that after the induced consumption demand is satisfied, sufficient new output will be left to satisfy the increased investment demand.

Since ΔS is equal to $(1 - b)\,\Delta Y$, we have, from (5.19),

$$(1 - b)\,\Delta Y = \Delta I$$

$$\frac{\Delta Y}{\Delta I} = \frac{1}{1 - b} = \frac{1}{1 - \text{MPC}} = \frac{1}{\text{MPS}} \qquad (5.20)$$

If, for example, b equals 0.8, the marginal propensity to save ($\text{MPS} = 1 - b$) is equal to 0.2. Each dollar increase in income will generate 20 cents worth of new saving and a five-dollar increase in income will be required to generate the one dollar of new saving to balance a one-dollar increase in investment. The value of the multiplier in this case will be 5.

The effects of an increase in autonomous investment expenditure are illustrated graphically in Figure 5.6. Initially, with invest-

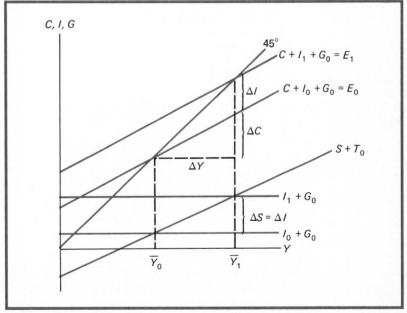

Figure 5.6
Effect on Equilibrium Income of an Increase in Autonomous Investment from I_0 to I_1

An increase in autonomous investment from I_0 to I_1 shifts the aggregate demand schedule upward from $C_0 + I_0 + G_0 = E_0$ to $C_0 + I_1 + G_0 = E_1$. The $I + G$ schedule shifts up from $I_0 + G_0$ to $I_1 + G_0$. Equilibrium income rises from $\bar{Y}_0$ to $\bar{Y}_1$.

ment at I_0 and government spending and taxes at G_0 and T_0, equilibrium income is at $\bar{Y}_0$. Now let investment increase to the higher level I_1. The aggregate demand (E) schedule shifts up by the amount $(\Delta I = I_1 - I_0)$, from E_0 $(= C + I_0 + G_0)$ to E_1 $(= C + I_1 + G_0)$. The $(I + G)$ schedule shifts up by the same amount. Equilibrium is restored at $\bar{Y}_1$, where income is now equal to the higher value of aggregate demand. Note that the increase in income is equal to the initial increase in investment plus an induced increase in consumption as shown in the graph. Note also that at the new equilibrium, saving has increased by the same amount as the increase in investment.

The multiplier concept was central to Keynes's theory because it explained how shifts in investment due to changes in business expectations set off a process that caused not only investment but consumption to vary. The multiplier showed how shocks to one sector were transmitted throughout the economy. Keynes's theory also implied that other components of autonomous expenditure affect the overall level of equilibrium income. The effect on equilibrium income of a change in each of the two policy-controlled elements of autonomous expenditures, government spending and taxes, can be calculated from (5.15).

We proceed just as we did in considering the effects of a change in investment, and let one component of autonomous expenditures change while each of the others is held constant. For a change in government spending (G), we have

$$\Delta \bar{Y} = \frac{1}{1 - b} \Delta G$$

$$\frac{\Delta \bar{Y}}{\Delta G} = \frac{1}{1 - b} \qquad (5.21)$$

For a change in taxes, we have

$$\Delta \bar{Y} = \frac{1}{1 - b} (-b) \Delta T$$

$$\frac{\Delta \bar{Y}}{\Delta T} = \frac{-b}{1 - b} \qquad (5.22)$$

For government spending we see that a one-dollar increase has just the same effect as we found for a one-dollar increase in investment. Both are one-dollar increases in autonomous expenditures. The multiplier process whereby the initial increase in income generates induced increases in consumption is just the same for an increase in government spending as for investment. In terms of Figure 5.6, an increase in government spending of ΔG units would

114

shift up the $(C + I + G)$ schedule by just the same amount as an equal increase in investment.

From the expression given in (5.22), we see that the effect of an increase in taxes is in the opposite direction from those of either an increase in government spending or investment. A tax increase will lower the level of disposable income $(Y - T)$ for any level of national income (Y). This will shift the aggregate demand schedule down since it reduces consumption spending *for any level of national income*. The effect on equilibrium income from a tax increase is illustrated in Figure 5.7. We assume that taxes rise by ΔT from T_0 to T_1. The aggregate demand schedule shifts from $(C + I + G)_0$ down to $(C + I + G)_1$. This is the consequence of the downward shift in the consumption function shown to result from the rise in taxes from T_0 to T_1. Equilibrium income falls from $\overline{Y}_0$ to $\overline{Y}_1$.

Notice that the aggregate demand schedule shifts down by $(-b\,\Delta T)$, that is, by only a fraction (b) of the increase in taxes. This is because at a given level of income, a one-dollar increase in taxes

Figure 5.7
Effect on Equilibrium Income of an Increase in Taxes from T_0 to T_1

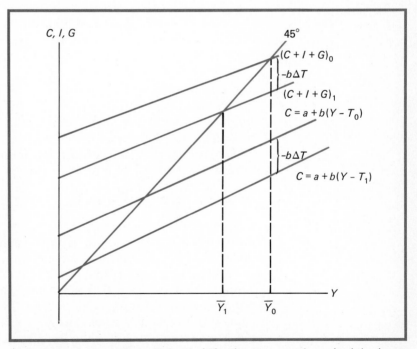

An increase in taxes from T_0 to T_1 shifts the consumption schedule downward from $C = a + b(Y - T_0)$ to $C = a + b(Y - T_1)$. The aggregate demand schedule also shifts downward, from $(C + I + G)_0$ to $(C + I + G)_1$. Equilibrium income falls from $\overline{Y}_0$ to $\overline{Y}_1$.

reduces disposable income by one dollar but lowers the consumption component of aggregate demand by only b dollars. The rest of the one-dollar decline in disposable income is absorbed by a fall of $(1 - b)$ dollars in saving. Unlike changes in government expenditures and investment, which have a dollar-for-dollar effect on autonomous aggregate demand, a one-dollar change in taxes shifts the aggregate demand schedule by only a fraction $(-b)$ of one dollar. It is this fraction $(-b)$ times the autonomous expenditure multiplier $\left(\dfrac{1}{1-b}\right)$ that gives the effect on equilibrium income of a one-dollar change in taxes $\left(\dfrac{-b}{1-b}\right)$.

There is a relationship between the absolute values of tax and government expenditure multipliers, which can be seen from the following examples:

$$b = 0.5: \qquad \frac{1}{1-b} = \frac{1}{1-0.5} = 2; \qquad \frac{-b}{1-b} = \frac{-0.5}{1-0.5} = -1$$

$$b = 0.8: \qquad \frac{1}{1-b} = \frac{1}{1-0.8} = 5; \qquad \frac{-b}{1-b} = \frac{-0.8}{1-0.8} = -4$$

$$b = 0.9: \qquad \frac{1}{1-b} = \frac{1}{1-0.9} = 10; \qquad \frac{-b}{1-b} = \frac{-0.9}{1-0.9} = -9$$

The tax multiplier is always one less in absolute value than the government expenditure multiplier. This fact has an interesting implication for the effects of an increase in government spending accompanied by an equal increase in taxes, a balanced budget increase. To find the effects of such a combination of policy changes, we add the two policy multipliers to get

$$\frac{\Delta \bar{Y}}{\Delta G} + \frac{\Delta \bar{Y}}{\Delta T} = \frac{1}{1-b} + \frac{-b}{1-b} = \frac{1-b}{1-b} = 1$$

A one-dollar increase in government spending financed by a one-dollar increase in taxes will increase equilibrium income by just one dollar. This result, often termed the *balanced budget multiplier*, simply reflects the fact that tax changes have a smaller per dollar impact on equilibrium income than do spending changes. The value of 1 for the multiplier results because the tax multiplier is just one less in absolute value than the spending multiplier. The latter result does not carry through in many more complex models, but the result that tax changes affect aggregate demand by less per dollar than changes in government spending is a quite general one.

5.6 FISCAL STABILIZATION POLICY

Since the level of equilibrium income is affected by changes in government spending and taxes, these fiscal policy instruments can be varied to offset the effects of undesirable shifts in private investment demand. In other words, the government can use these fiscal policy instruments to stabilize the total of autonomous expenditures and, therefore, equilibrium income, even if the investment component of autonomous expenditures is unstable.

An example of such a fiscal stabilization policy is illustrated in Figure 5.8. The economy is assumed to be in equilibrium at a full-employment level $\bar{Y}_F$, with aggregate demand at E_F equal to $(C + I_0 + G_0)$. We assume that from this point there is a decline in autonomous investment from I_0 to I_1, as a result of an unfavorable change in business expectations. In the absence of a policy action,

Figure 5.8
An Example of Fiscal Stabilization Policy

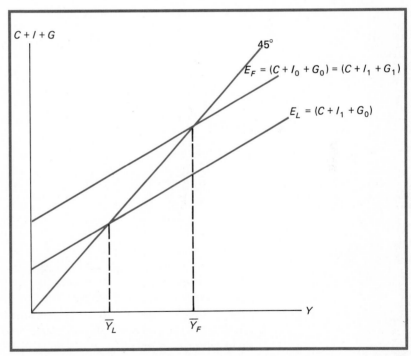

A decline in autonomous investment expenditure from I_0 to I_1 would shift the aggregate demand schedule downward from $E_F = (C + I_0 + G_0)$ to $E_L = (C + I_1 + G_0)$. A compensating increase in government spending from G_0 to G_1 will shift the aggregate demand schedule back to $C + I_1 + G_1 = E_F = C + I_0 + G_0$. Equilibrium income will again be at $\bar{Y}_F$.

aggregate demand declines to E_L, equal to $(C + I_1 + G_0)$. The new level of equilibrium income is below full employment at $\bar{Y}_L$.

Within the model an appropriate fiscal policy response would be to increase government spending by an amount sufficient to restore equilibrium at $\bar{Y}_F$. In the graph, a rise in government spending from G_0 to G_1 shifts the aggregate demand curve back up to where aggregate demand is again E_F, now equal to $(C + I_1 + G_1)$. Alternatively, a tax cut could have been used to restore the initial level of aggregate demand. Since the tax multiplier is smaller, the appropriate tax cut would be somewhat larger than the required spending increase, but in theory this poses no particular problem.

5.7 SUMMARY

The model in this chapter is seriously incomplete. We need to consider money and interest rates and to explain the behavior of prices and wages before we complete our analysis of the Keynesian system. Several features of the Keynesian system are highlighted by considering this simple model, however, and these will carry over to more complex models.

The simple model clearly illustrates the role of aggregate demand in determining income in the Keynesian system. As we will see later, it overstates the role of aggregate demand. Still a key feature of all the Keynesian models we consider is that demand plays a crucial role in income determination. In the Keynesian view, changes in the autonomous elements of aggregate demand, especially investment demand, were key factors causing changes in the equilibrium level of income. Via the multiplier process such changes in autonomous expenditures also caused induced changes in consumption spending. Inadequate investment, and as a consequence a low level of aggregate demand, was the Keynesian explanation for massive unemployment in the depression of the 1930s.

The model also illustrates the role of fiscal stabilization policy in managing aggregate demand to cushion equilibrium output from shifts in the unstable investment demand. While the simple expressions we derive for the government expenditure and tax multipliers will require modification below, the principles behind them remain intact.

Review Questions

1   Explain how the origins of the Keynesian Revolution can be found in the problem of unemployment.

2 Interpret each of the three ways of writing the condition for equilibrium income in the simple Keynesian model [equations (5.2), (5.5), (5.6)]. Explain why the three ways of writing the equilibrium condition are equivalent.

3 Carefully explain the difference between realized and desired investment. In which component of investment does the discrepancy between the two totals occur?

4 Explain Keynes's theory of how expectations affect investment demand. How is this theory related to Keynes's view that aggregate demand would be unstable in the absence of government stabilization policies?

5 In the simple Keynesian model an increase of one dollar in autonomous expenditure will cause equilibrium income to increase by a multiple of this one-dollar increase. Explain the process by which this happens.

6 Explain carefully why the tax multiplier ($\Delta Y/\Delta T = -b/1 - b$) is negative and why it is smaller in absolute value than the government expenditure multiplier ($\Delta Y/\Delta G = 1/1-b$).

7 Suppose that for a particular economy, for some time period, investment was equal to 100, government expenditure was equal to 75, net taxes were fixed at 100, and consumption (C) given by the consumption function

$$C = 25 + 0.8Y_D$$

where Y_D is disposable income and Y is GNP.
a. What is the level of equilibrium income (Y)?
b. What is the value of the government expenditure multiplier ($\Delta Y/\Delta G$)? the tax multiplier ($\Delta Y/\Delta T$)?
c. Suppose that investment declined by 40 units to a level of 60. What will be the new level of equilibrium income?

8 Suppose that initially equilibrium income was 200 units and that this was also the full-employment level of income. Assume that the consumption function is

$$C = 25 + 0.8Y_D$$

and assume that from this initial equilibrium level, we now have a decline in investment of 8 units. What will be the new equilibrium level of income? What would be the increase in government spending required to restore income to the initial level of 200? Alternatively, what reduction in tax collections would be sufficient to restore an income level of 200?

9 Suppose that government spending was increased by 10 units and that this increase was financed by a 10-unit increase in taxes. Would equilibrium income change or remain the same due to these two policy actions? If equilibrium income would change, in which direction would it move, and by how much?

10 Suppose that instead of a fixed level of taxes we had an income tax so that

$$T = t_1 Y$$

where t_1 was the income tax rate. Following the procedure of Section 5.4, derive an expression for equilibrium income ($\bar{Y}$) analogous to (5.14) for this case where the level of tax collections depends on income. What is the expression equivalent to the autonomous expenditure multiplier $\left(\dfrac{1}{1-b} \right)$ for this case of an income tax?

11 In question 7, assume that beginning from the initial equilibrium position (investment equal to 100, government expenditure equal 75, and net taxes fixed at 100), there was an autonomous fall in consumption and increase in saving such at the consumption function shifted from

$$C = 25 + 0.8Y_D$$

to

$$C = 5 + 0.8Y_D$$

a. Find the change in equilibrium income resulting from this autonomous increase in saving.
b. Calculate the actual level of saving before and after the shift in the consumption and, therefore, saving function. How do you explain this result?

Selected Readings

ACKLEY, GARDNER, *Macroeconomics: Theory and Policy*. New York: Macmillan, 1978, Chaps. 6 and 7.

BRANSON, WILLIAM, *Macroeconomic Theory and Policy*, 2nd ed. New York: Harper & Row, 1979, Chap. 3.

HUTCHISON, T. W., *A Review of Economic Doctrines*. London: Oxford University Press, 1953, Chap. 24.

KEYNES, JOHN M., "The General Theory of Employment," *Quarterly Journal of Economics*, February 1937, pp. 209–23.

KLEIN, LAWRENCE, *The Keynesian Revolution*, 2nd ed. New York: Macmillan, 1966.

SURREY, M. V. C., *Macroeconomic Themes*. London: Oxford University Press, 1976, Chap. 1: readings pertaining to the material in the present chapter and the following three chapters on the Keynesian system.

chapter 6

In Chapter 5 we were able to ignore the interest rate and monetary policy only because we neglected the effect of the interest rate on investment or other components of aggregate demand. Here we explain the role of the interest rate and money in the Keynesian system and construct a model which shows how both the equilibrium interest rate and equilibrium level of income are jointly determined. In Chapter 7 we use this model to provide a more realistic view of how income depends on aggregate demand and will make clear how monetary policy can affect income via an effect on aggregate demand. We will also see how the results in Chapter 5 concerning fiscal policy are modified by the inclusion of a money market in the model.

6.1 THE ROLE OF MONEY IN THE KEYNESIAN SYSTEM

Fundamental to Keynes's theory of money was his view that money affected income via an effect on the interest rate. An increase in the money stock, for example, would lower the interest rate, which, in turn, would increase the level of aggregate demand and income. There are then two links we need to examine in the chain of events connecting changes in the money stock and changes in income. The first is the relationship between money

THE KEYNESIAN SYSTEM (II): MONEY, INTEREST, AND INCOME

and the interest rate. The second is the effect of the interest rate on aggregate demand. In the next two subsections we look at these relationships, beginning with the latter one.

Interest Rates and Aggregate Demand

We have already considered the reasons why business investment demand would depend on the interest rate. Briefly, an investment project will be pursued only if its expected profitability exceeds the cost of borrowing to finance the project by an amount sufficient to justify the risks of the project. At a high interest rate (borrowing cost), fewer projects will satisfy this criterion.

When considering the possible influences of the interest rate, we also need to consider components of aggregate demand other than business investment. The first of these is residential construction investment. Residential construction is a component of investment in the national income accounts, but the reason such investment will be affected by the level of the interest rate requires further explanation. The value of newly constructed houses enters the GNP accounts as the houses are built. One element of building cost will be the cost of short-term borrowing to finance construction of the house. Higher interest rates will mean higher costs to the builder and, other things equal, this will discourage housing starts.

Additionally, an important factor determining the rate of new housing construction is the overall state of demand for houses, existing and newly constructed. Most purchases of houses are financed by long-term borrowing in the mortgage market, and high interest rates include high rates of mortgage interest. High mortgage rates increase the cost of buying a house and reduce the demand for new and existing homes. This reduced demand in the housing market will lower the volume of new residential construction. We will see later that in addition to the direct effect of high interest rates discouraging housing demand, periods of high interest rates often make funds to finance mortgage lending quite scarce. Thus it is not only the high cost but also the reduced availability of mortgage funds which limits housing demand in periods of high interest rates. For these reasons, residential construction is the component of aggregate demand that is most sensitive to interest rate changes.

There are additional components of aggregate demand which are not counted as investment by the GNP accounts, but which would be included in a broader definition of investment and which may be affected by interest rate changes. The first of these is consumer expenditures on durable goods. Such expenditures are counted as current-quarter consumption in the national income accounts, but to the consumer the purchase of a car or an appliance such as a refrigerator or television set is clearly a form of investment. Such purchases are often financed by borrowing, especially in the case of new-car purchases. Higher interest rates will raise the cost of such purchases when one includes the financing cost, and should lower this component of aggregate demand. Several early studies did not reveal much evidence of an effect of interest rates on consumer durable purchases, but later studies do seem to find evidence of this effect.

A final component of aggregate demand that may be affected by interest rates is a subcomponent of government spending. Government spending in the national income accounts includes state and local government spending for services, consumption goods, and investment goods. In the models constructed here we take government spending to be exogenously fixed by the policymaker. The actual policymaker would be the federal government, and the appropriate policy variable is federal government expenditures. State and local government spending can more properly be considered to be included with private consumption and investment spending. Much of state and local government investment spending is financed by borrowing through bond issues. High interest rates should, in theory, increase such borrowing costs and discourage this part of state and local government expenditures. There are, however, many determinants of the level and timing of such state and local government spending projects, and how important the effect of interest rates is in practice remains uncertain.

Within the simple model of Chapter 5 the effects on aggregate demand and equilibrium income of a change in the level of the interest rate are illustrated in Figure 6.1. Initially, we assume that the economy is in equilibrium at $\bar{Y}_0$ with aggregate demand at E_0 equal to $(C + I + G)_0$, corresponding to an interest rate of r_0. A decline in the interest rate to r_1 shifts the aggregate demand curve up to E_1, equal to $(C + I + G)_1$. This shift represents the combined effects of the interest rate on business investment, residential construction investment, consumer expenditures on durable goods, and state and local government investment spending. Equilibrium income rises to $\bar{Y}_1$.

Clearly, one important factor determining the extent of the change in equilibrium income $(\bar{Y}_1 - \bar{Y}_0)$ that will occur for a given change in the interest rate is the size of the shift in aggregate demand caused by the change in the interest rate. The more sensitive the various components of aggregate demand discussed above are to interest rate changes, the larger will be the shift in the aggregate demand function in Figure 6.1 and the greater will be the effect on equilibrium income. The interest sensitivity of aggregate demand will therefore be important in determining how effective

Figure 6.1

Effects on Aggregate Demand and Equilibrium Income of a Decline in the Rate of Interest

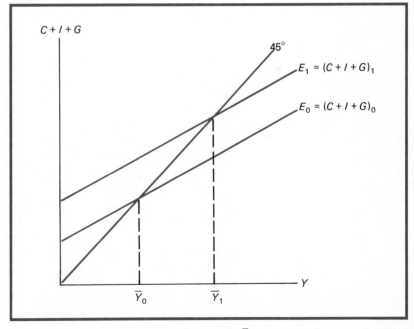

The initial level of equilibrium income is $\bar{Y}_0$ corresponding to a level of aggregate demand $E_0 = (C + I + G)_0$ at the initial interest rate r_0. A decline in the interest rate to r_1 increases aggregate demand to $E_1 = (C + I + G)_1$; equilibrium income rises to $\bar{Y}_1$.

monetary policy, which works through interest rates in the Keynesian system, will be in affecting equilibrium income. In the models we consider we represent the effect of interest rates on aggregate demand as simply an effect on I, the investment component of aggregate demand. The discussion of this section should, however, be kept in mind to understand the process we are trying to represent. To account fully for the effects of interest rates on aggregate demand, we must consider investment as broadly defined to include the effects of interest rates on the other components of aggregate demand discussed here.

The Keynesian Theory of the Interest Rate

The next relationship we consider is that between the quantity of money and the rate of interest. Once we have done this, we can complete our analysis of the way in which money influences equilibrium income. Keynes believed that the quantity of money played a key role in determining the rate of interest and structured his theory of interest-rate determination in such a way as to highlight that role.

Keynes begins with some simplifying assumptions. First, he assumes that all financial assets can be divided into two groups (1) money and (2) all nonmoney assets, which we will term "bonds." Money can be thought of as the narrowly defined money stock, which includes only currency and demand deposits. The bond category includes actual bonds plus other long-term financial assets, primarily corporate equities. The long-term versus short-term distinction between the bond and money assets was the distinction Keynes emphasized. Additionally, as long as we stick to a narrow definition of money (currency plus demand deposits), bonds are the interest-bearing assets and money pays no interest.[1] For the purposes of our discussion we will initially consider the bonds to be homogeneous in all respects. As we did in our discussion of the classical system, we assume that bonds are perpetuities, promises to pay fixed amounts at fixed intervals throughout the future (e.g., one dollar per year), with no repayment of principal.

Within this simplified framework Keynes considers the way that individuals will decide how to allocate their wealth between the two assets, money and bonds. At a point in time, wealth (Wh) is fixed at some level, and since bonds and money are the only stores of wealth, we have

---

[1]NOW (negotiated order of withdraw) accounts, which are virtually identical to commercial bank demand deposits, do pay interest. However, the interest rate on such accounts is subject to a legally fixed ceiling rate well below the level of market interest rates. Allowing for such an exogenous interest rate on deposits in the Keynesian model would not have a substantive effect on our analysis. NOW accounts and other new substitutes for commercial bank demand deposits are discussed in Section 14.1.

$$\text{Wh} \equiv B + M \qquad (6.1)$$

The equilibrium interest rate on bonds will be that rate at which the demand for bonds is just equal to the existing stock of bonds. It might seem most natural to develop a theory of the equilibrium interest rate by studying the factors that directly determine the supply of and demand for bonds. Keynes did not proceed in this manner. Note that given (6.1), there is only one independent portfolio decision, the split between money and bonds. If for an individual wealth is equal to $1000, the decision to hold $300 in the form of money implicitly determines that bond holdings will be the remainder, $700. In terms of equilibrium positions this means that if a person is satisfied with the level of his money holdings relative to total wealth, he is by definition [equation (6.1)] satisfied with his bond holdings; he is at the optimal split of his fixed wealth between the two stores of value. To say, for example, that the demand for money exceeds the supply is to say in the aggregate that the public is trying to increase the proportion of wealth held in the form of money. This is definitionally the same as to say that

Figure 6.2
Determination of the Equilibrium Interest Rate in the Keynesian Model

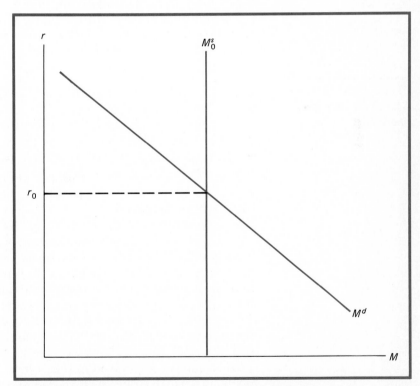

In the Keynesian system, the equilibrium interest rate (r_0) is the interest rate which equates money supply and money demand.

the supply of bonds exceeds the demand; the public is trying to reduce the proportion of wealth held as bonds.

Consequently, there are two equally correct ways to describe the equilibrium interest rate. The equilibrium interest rate is that rate which equates the supply of and demand for bonds. Alternatively, the equilibrium interest rate can be viewed as that rate which equates the supply of money with the demand for money. Equilibrium in one market implies equilibrium in the other, so the interest rate that equilibrates one market *must* equilibrate the other. Keynes chose the latter of these perspectives because he wished to emphasize the relationship between monetary factors and the interest rate.

This Keynesian view of interest rate determination is illustrated in Figure 6.2. The money supply is assumed to be fixed exogenously by the central bank at M_0^s. The equilibrium interest rate is r_0, the rate at which money demand, given by the money demand schedule M^d in the graph, is just equal to the fixed money supply.

In a more fundamental sense the equilibrium rate of interest is determined by factors affecting the supply of money and money demand. In the case of supply the major factor will be the policies of the central bank. We turn now to the factors Keynes believed determined money demand, the factors determining the position and slope of the M^d schedule in Figure 6.2.

The Keynesian Theory of Money Demand

Keynes considered three motives for holding money. The analysis proceeds as if there were separate money demands for each of the motives. It is not presumed that any individual can say which dollars of his money holdings are kept for each of the three motives, but Keynes believed it was useful to look at the separate motives behind the overall level of money holdings.

Transactions Demand

The first motive for holding money that Keynes considered was the *transactions motive*. Money is a medium of exchange, and individuals hold money for use in transactions. Money bridges the gap between the receipt of income and eventual expenditures. The amount of money held for the transactions purpose would vary positively with the volume of transactions in which the individual engaged. Income was assumed to be a good measure of this volume of transactions, and thus the transactions demand for money was assumed to depend positively on the level of income.

When money is received in one transaction it could be used to buy bonds, which would then be sold to get money again when the time came for an expenditure. The gain from doing so would be that interest would be earned for the time the bonds were held.

Brokerage fees involved in buying bonds and the inconvenience of a great number of such transactions would clearly make purchases of bonds for small amounts to be held for short periods unprofitable. Some money will be held for transactions. Still, there is room to economize on transaction balances by such bond purchases. Since the return to be gained is interest earnings on bonds, we would expect that the incentive to economize on transaction balances would be greater the higher the interest rate. Consequently, in addition to depending positively on income, the transactions demand for money would be expected to be negatively related to the rate of interest.

Keynes did not place much emphasis on the interest rate when discussing the transactions motive for holding money, but it has proven to be of importance, especially for the business sector's transaction demand. Firms with high volumes of transactions can by cash management practices reduce considerably their average holdings of money. The incentive to make the expenditures required for such careful cash management depends on the level of rate of interest.

Precautionary Demand

Beyond the money held for planned transactions, Keynes believed that additional money balances were held in case unexpected expenditures became necessary. Money would be held for use in possible emergencies, to pay unexpected bills such as medical bills or repair bills of various types. Money held for this motive Keynes termed the *precautionary demand* for money. He believed that the amount held for this purpose would depend positively on income. Again, the interest rate might be a factor if people tended to economize on the amount of money held for the precautionary motive as interest rates rose. Since the motives for holding precautionary balances are similar to those for transactions demand, we will simplify our discussion here by subsuming the precautionary demand under the transaction demand category, transactions being expected or unexpected ones. The precautionary demand for money will receive separate treatment when we return to the subject of money demand in Chapter 14.

Speculative Demand

The final motive for holding money that Keynes considered was the *speculative motive*. This was the most novel part of Keynes's analysis of money demand and we consider the speculative motive in some detail. Keynes began with the question of why an individual would hold any money above that needed for the transactions and precautionary motives when bonds pay interest and money does not. Such an additional demand for money did exist, Keynes believed, only because of uncertainty about future interest rates and the relationship between changes in the interest rate and the market price of bonds. If interest rates were expected to move in such a way as to cause capital losses on bonds, it was possible that these expected losses would outweigh the interest earnings on the bonds and cause an investor to hold money instead. Such money would be held by those "speculating" on future changes in the interest rate. To see the way in which such speculation works, we need to begin by analyzing the relationship between the interest rate and the level of bond prices. After that the details of Keynes's theory are considered.

Consider the case of a perpetuity, which is what we have been assuming the bonds in our model to be. Suppose that at some point in the past you paid the then prevailing market price $1000 to buy a government bond that entitles you to payment of $50 per year, termed the *coupon payment*. You bought a perpetual bond at a price of $1000, at a market interest rate of 5 percent (50/1000 = 0.05 or 5 percent). How much would this bond be worth if you tried to sell it today? The value of a financial asset that entitles the owner to a coupon payment of $50 per year will depend on the *current* market rate of interest. First, suppose that the current market rate of interest is 5 percent, the same as the interest rate that prevailed when you bought the bond. In this case the bond would still sell for $1000; at that price it would yield the current interest rate of 5 percent.

Next consider the case where the market interest rate has risen to 10 percent over the time since you purchased the bond. The going price today for a bond with a coupon payment of $50 per year is $500 (50/500 = 0.10 or 10 percent). Your bond has no particular feature that will enable you to sell it for more. Even though you paid $1000, given the rise in interest rates, you will be able to sell it only at a *capital loss* for $500, the price that makes it competitive at *current* market rates. *A rise in the market interest rate results in a capital loss on previously existing bonds.*

If, instead, from the time you purchased the bond the market interest rate had fallen, then the value of your bond would have increased. If the interest rate had declined from 5 to 2 percent, the bond price would have increased from the $1000 you paid to $2500. At that price your bond, which has a coupon of $50 per year, will pay 2 percent (50/2500 = 0.02 or 2 percent). Thus *a decline in interest rates results in a capital gain on previously existing bonds.* With this relationship between bond prices and interest rate changes in mind, we return to the question of the relative desirability of money and bonds.

The expected returns on the two assets can be expressed as follows:

return on money = 0

return on bonds = interest earnings $(= r)$ $\quad$ (+) expected capital gain
$$\text{or}$$
(−) expected capital loss

The return on money is zero, since it earns no interest and because its value is not subject to capital gains or losses as interest rates change.[2] Money clearly has a fixed price. The bond will pay an interest rate of r. The expected return on bonds will equal this interest return plus or minus any expected capital gain or loss. For reasons just discussed, an investor would expect a capital gain if he expected interest rates to fall and a capital loss if he expected interest rates to rise. It is this uncertainty about the future course of interest rates that is crucial to Keynes's analysis.

Suppose that an investor believes that interest rates will fall. Bonds then clearly have the higher expected return. They pay interest and are expected to yield a capital gain. If interest rates are expected to rise, however, it is possible that the expected capital loss on bonds will outweigh the interest earnings. The expected return on bonds would be negative in such a case and money would be the preferred asset. Money held in anticipation of a fall in bond prices (a rise in interest rates) is Keynes's speculative demand for money.

To this point we have a relationship between the level of money demanded and expected future *changes* in interest rates. Keynes converts this to a relationship between money demanded and the *level* of the interest rate by an assumption about the way in which people form expectations about future interest rate changes. He assumes that investors have a relatively fixed conception of the "normal" level of the interest rate. When the actual interest rate is above the normal level, investors expect the interest rate to fall. When the interest rate is below the normal rate, a rise in the interest rate is expected.

Given this assumption about the way expectations about future movements in interest rates are formed, we can develop a relationship between the level of the speculative demand for money and the interest rate. We do so first for an individual investor and then consider the corresponding aggregate relationship.

For the individual investor the demand curve for speculative balances is shown in Figure 6.3a. Here we let M_i^2 represent the speculative demand for money by the ith individual and let M_i^1 equal his transactions demand. We have then

---

[2]Notice that so far we are not allowing for the effect of commodity price changes. The *real* value of money declines proportionately with increases in the aggregate price level. So, however, does the real value of bonds; therefore, the relative returns would not be directly affected by allowing for changes in the price of output.

Figure 6.3
Individual Investor's
and Aggregate
Speculative Demand
Curves for Money

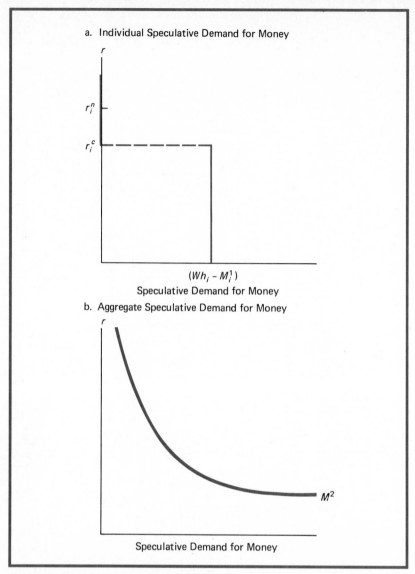

a. Individual Speculative Demand for Money

$(Wh_i - M_i^1)$
Speculative Demand for Money

b. Aggregate Speculative Demand for Money

M^2

Speculative Demand for Money

The individual's speculative demand for money is shown in Part *a*. At any interest rate above the critical rate (r_i^c) the speculative demand for money is zero. Below the critical interest rate, the individual shifts into money. Part *b* shows the aggregate speculative demand for money schedule (M^2). As the interest rate becomes lower it falls below the critical rate for more individuals and the speculative demand for money rises.

132   MACROECONOMIC MODELS

$$M_i^1 + M_i^2 \equiv M_i$$

and (6.2)

$$M_i + B_i \equiv \text{Wh}_i$$

where M_i, B_i, and Wh_i are the individual's total money holdings, bond holdings, and wealth, respectively.

Following Keynes's theory the individual is assumed to have a preconceived view of the normal level of the interest rate. This is shown as r_i^n in Figure 6.3. Since at all rates of interest above r_i^n, interest rates are expected to fall, bonds will be preferred to money as an asset. The speculative demand for money will be zero and bond holdings will equal $(\text{Wh}_i - M_i^1)$. The speculative demand for money will also be zero for interest rates over a certain range below r_i^n. If the interest rate is not too far below r_i^n, the interest earnings on the bond will be greater than the small expected capital loss. The expected capital loss will be small because only a small rise in r will be expected as r returns to r_i^n.

There is a level of the interest rate below r_i^n, however, at which the expected capital loss on bonds, which increases as the interest rate declines below r_i^n, will come to just equal the interest earnings on the bond. We term this value of the interest rate the individual's *critical* interest rate (r_i^c). Below this rate, money will be preferred. The individual will sell bonds and hold speculative balances of $(\text{Wh}_i - M_i^1)$, which means that he will be holding all his wealth in the form of money.

Different individuals were assumed by Keynes to have different views as to what was a "normal" interest rate. Thus there is no specific critical rate of interest that if approached would trigger a massive shift of funds between money and bonds. Instead, as the interest rate fell, beginning for example at a very high rate where there was very little speculative demand, declines in the interest rate would move the rate successively below the critical rates of different investors. The lower the interest rate, the more investors would find that given their view of the normal rate, money was the preferred asset. At very low values of the interest rate, almost all investors would come to expect that the interest rate would rise substantially in the future ($r < r_i^c$) and money would be almost universally preferred as an asset. Proceeding in this manner we can construct the aggregate demand for speculative balances shown in Figure 6.3b.

The curve is smooth, reflecting the gradual increase in the speculative demand for money at successively lower interest rates. The curve flattens out at a very low rate of interest, reflecting the fact that at this low rate, there is a general expectation of capital losses on bonds which outweigh interest earnings. At this rate increments to wealth would be held in the form of money, with no further drop in the interest rate. Keynes termed this situation the "liquidity trap" and it will play a role in our later analysis. For the most part, however, we will assume that we are on the downward-sloping portion of the speculative demand for money curve.

The Total Demand for Money

We have looked at the three motives for holding money in the Keynesian system and can now put these together to construct the total money demand function. The transactions demand and the precautionary demand were seen to vary positively with income and negatively with respect to the interest rate. The speculative demand for money was negatively related to the interest rate. Taken together, then, we can write total money demand as

$$M^d = L(Y, r) \qquad (6.3)$$

where Y is income and r is the interest rate. A rise in income increases money demand; a rise in the interest rate leads to a fall in money demand. Below, we make the simplifying assumption that the money demand function is of a linear form:

$$M^d = c_0 + c_1 Y + c_2 r \qquad c_1 > 0, \quad c_2 < 0 \qquad (6.4)$$

Equation (6.4) expresses the same information as (6.3) but assumes that we can plot the money demand function as a straight line on our graphs. The parameter c_1 is the increase in money demand per unit increase in income and c_2 gives the amount by which money demand declines per unit increase in the interest rate.

The Effects of an Increase in the Money Stock

In Figure 6.4 we plot this linear Keynesian money demand schedule [equation (6.4)] as a function of the interest rate and illustrate the effect that an increase in the money supply will have in the money market.

The money demand function M^d is downward sloping; a decline in the interest rate, for example, will increase the demand for money. To fix the position of the money demand function, we must fix the level of income. The curve in Figure 6.4 is drawn for a level of income Y_0. An increase in the level of income would shift the curve to the right, reflecting the fact that, for a given interest rate, money demand will increase with income. The money supply is assumed to be an exogenously controlled policy variable set initially at M_0^s.

Now consider the effects of an increase in the money stock to the level shown by the M_1^s schedule in Figure 6.4. At the initial equilibrium level of the interest rate r_0, after the money stock increases there will be an excess supply of money. At r_0 people will not be content to hold the new money ($\Delta M = M_1^s - M_0^s$). They will attempt to decrease their money holdings by buying bonds. The in-

Figure 6.4
Equilibrium in the Money Market

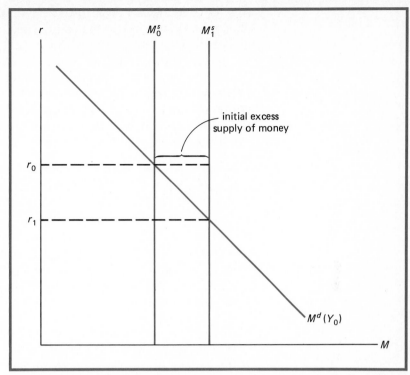

An increase in the money stock from M_0^s to M_1^s causes an initial excess supply of money. The equilibrium interest rate falls from r_0 to r_1 to restore equilibrium in the money market.

crease in the demand for bonds will decrease the rate of interest suppliers of bonds (borrowers) have to pay to sell their bonds. The fall in the interest rate will cause the demand for money to rise and a new equilibrium is reached at interest rate r_1.

It may seem that we are now ready to analyze the effects of monetary policy in the Keynesian system. In this subsection we have seen how changes in the money supply affect the interest rate. In the preceding subsection we saw how a change in interest rates affected aggregate demand. Can we not simply combine Figure 6.4 with Figure 6.1 to examine sequentially the effect on income of a change in the money supply? Unfortunately, we cannot.

In Figure 6.4 we analyzed the effects of a change in the money supply in the money market not allowing any effects in other markets. Specifically, we held income constant (at Y_0) to fix the position of the money demand function. Now as the interest rate drops from r_0 to r_1, we can see from Figure 6.1 (assuming that subscripts have the same meaning in both diagrams) that income increases from Y_0 to Y_1. This rise in income will shift the money demand schedule in Figure 6.4 to the right. There will be a further change in the interest rate back toward r_0 and consequently a further change in income. What we need to find is the effect of changes in the money stock on the equilibrium values of the interest rate and income level, equilibrium values for both the money and commodity markets. We do have all the relationships required for this, but we will need a new framework in which to fit them together. This new framework is the IS–LM model, to which we now turn.

6.2 THE IS–LM CURVE MODEL

Our task in this section is to find the values of the interest rate and level of income which simultaneously equilibrate both the commodity market and the money market. Note that since equilibrium in the money market implies equilibrium in the bond market, such a combination will equilibrate all three of these markets (commodities, money, and bonds). First, we identify combinations of income and the interest rate that will equilibrate the money market, neglecting the commodity market. Next, we identify combinations of income and the interest rate that are equilibrium values for the commodity market. These two sets of equilibrium combinations of interest rate and income levels are then shown to contain one combination that equilibrates both markets. To find a unique point of equilibrium we will have to assume that policy variables, including the money stock, government spending, and taxes, are held fixed at some levels. Other autonomous influences on income and interest rates (e.g., the state of business expectations that affects investment) must also be assumed to be fixed. We will see that these policy variables and other exogenous influences determine the positions of the equilibrium schedules for the money and product markets, termed below the LM and IS schedules. In Chapter 7 we will see how these policy variables and other exogenous influences affect the equilibrium values of income and the interest rate.

Money Market Equilibrium: The LM Curve

Construction of the LM Curve

We explained above that money demand in the Keynesian model was assumed to depend positively on the level of income because of the transactions demand. Money demand also varied inversely with the rate of interest, owing to the speculative demand for money and because the amount of transactions balances held at any income level would decline as the interest rate (the opportunity cost of holding such balances) increased. We expressed this relationship as

$$M^d = L(Y, r) \qquad\qquad (6.3)$$

or in a linear form

$$M^d = c_0 + c_1 Y + c_2 r \qquad c_1 > 0, \quad c_2 < 0 \qquad (6.4)$$

Now we wish to find all the combinations of r and Y that will equilibrate money demand with a fixed money stock, denoted M_0^s. The schedule of such points is termed the *LM schedule* since along this schedule money demand, for which we use the symbol L [equation (6.3)], is equal to the money stock (M). For simplicity we discuss the case where money demand is given by the linear form (6.4). For this case the condition that must be satisfied for money market equilibrium, the LM curve equation, can be written as

$$M_0^s = M^d = c_0 + c_1 Y + c_2 r \qquad\qquad (6.5)$$

We have already considered the nature of equilibrium in the money market. In Figure 6.5, for example, three separate demand for money schedules are drawn corresponding to three successively higher levels of income, Y_0, Y_1, and Y_2. As income increases from Y_0 to Y_1, then from Y_1 to Y_2, the money demand curve shifts to the right when plotted against the interest rate. The points where

Figure 6.5
Equilibrium Positions
in the Money Market

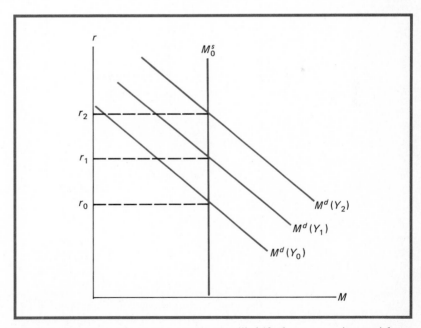

Increases in income from Y_0 to Y_1 to Y_2 will shift the money demand function from $M^d(Y_0)$ to $M^d(Y_1)$ then to $M^d(Y_2)$. Equilibrium in the money market will require successively higher interest rates r_0, r_1, r_2 at higher levels of income Y_0, Y_1, Y_2.

these money demand schedules intersect the vertical line, giving the value of the fixed money stock, are points of equilibrium for the money market. The income–interest rate combinations at which equilibrium occurs, (Y_0, r_0), (Y_1, r_1), and (Y_2, r_2), are points along the LM or money market equilibrium curve. These points are plotted in Figure 6.6. Proceeding in this manner we can find the equilibrium value of the interest rate for each level of income and construct the complete LM schedule shown in Figure 6.6.

Notice that the LM curve slopes upward to the right. At higher levels of income, equilibrium in the money market occurs at higher interest rates. The reason for the positive slope for the LM curve is the following. An increase in income (e.g., from Y_0 to Y_1 in Figures 6.5 and 6.6) will increase money demand at a given interest rate, since transactions demand varies positively with income. To restore demand to a level equal to the fixed money stock, the interest rate must be higher (r_1 instead of r_0 in Figures 6.5 and 6.6). The higher interest rate will result in a lower speculative demand for money and lower the transactions component *corresponding to*

Figure 6.6
The LM Curve

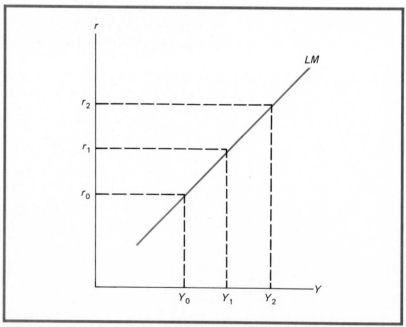

The *LM* schedule shows the combinations of income (Y) and the interest rate (r) which equilibrate the money market. Equilibrium combinations such as (r_0, Y_0), (r_1, Y_1) and (r_2, Y_2) from Figure 6.5 are points along the LM schedule. As we saw in Figure 6.5, at higher levels of income higher interest rates are required for money market equilibrium; the *LM* schedule slopes upward to the right.

MACROECONOMIC MODELS

any level of income. The interest rate must rise until this decline in money demand is just equal to the initial income-induced increase in transactions demand.

To complete our discussion of the LM curve, two questions need to be considered. First, we want to know what determines the value of the slope of the LM curve. We know that the curve is upward sloping, but is it steep or is it relatively flat? The slope of the LM curve will be important for our discussion of policy effects below. The second question concerns the position of the LM curve in our graph—what factors shift the schedule?

Factors Determining the Slope of the LM Schedule

To see which factors determine the slope of the LM schedule, we begin by considering the effect on money market equilibrium of an increase in income, ΔY, for example from Y_0 to Y_1 in Figures 6.5 and 6.6. The income-induced increase in money demand as a result of this change will equal $c_1 \Delta Y$, where c_1 is the parameter giving the increase in money demand (for transaction purposes) per unit increase in income from (6.4). The interest rate will have to rise by enough to offset this income-induced increase in money demand. The higher the value of c_1, the larger the increase in money demand per unit increase in income and, hence, the larger upward adjustment in the interest rate required to restore total money demand to the level of the fixed money stock. The higher the value of c_1, the steeper will be the LM curve. The value of c_1 is, however, not a subject of much debate. Controversy on this subject centers around the second factor that determines the slope of the LM curve.

For a given income-induced increase in money demand (a given c_1), the amount by which the interest rate has to rise to restore total money demand to the value of the fixed money stock depends on how elastic (sensitive) money demand is with respect to changes in the rate of interest.[3] In (6.4) the interest elasticity of money demand will depend on the value of c_2, which determines the amount of the change in money demand for a given change in the interest rate ($c_2 = \Delta M^d/\Delta r$). This relationship between the interest elasticity of money demand and the slope of the LM curve is illustrated in Figure 6.7.

Part *a* of the figure illustrates the case of a low interest elasticity

[3]The concept of elasticity refers to the percentage change in a variable x which results from a 1 percent change in another variable. In the case of the interest elasticity of money demand, the elasticity is negative. A 1 percent increase in the interest rate will cause money demand to decline. In the text, the term "high elasticity" refers to the absolute value of the elasticity. If money demand is very responsive to changes in the interest rate, we say that money demand is highly elastic. If money demand is not very responsive to interest rate changes, we term this a low interest elasticity or low interest sensitivity of money demand.

Figure 6.7 Interest Elasticity of Money Demand and the Slope of the LM Curve

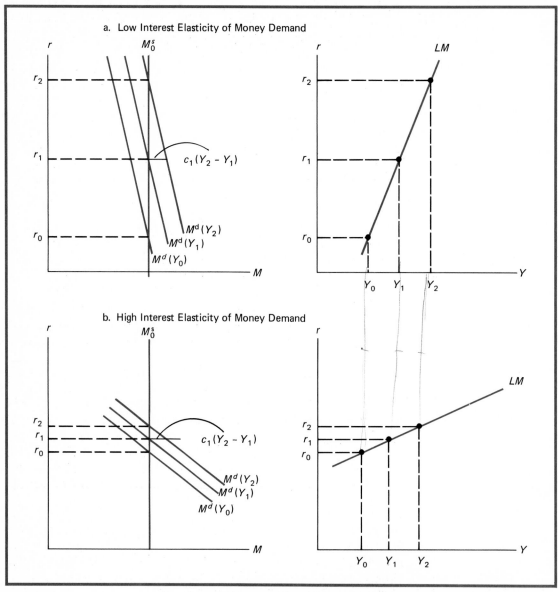

a. Low Interest Elasticity of Money Demand

b. High Interest Elasticity of Money Demand

The relatively steep money demand schedule in Part *a* reflects the assumption that the interest elasticity of money demand is low (in absolute value). With a low interest elasticity of money demand, the *LM* schedule is relatively steep. In Part *b* money demand is assumed to highly interest elastic and as a result the money demand schedule is relatively flat. The *LM* schedule in this case is also relatively flat.

MACROECONOMIC MODELS

of money demand. The money demand curve is steep, reflecting the fact that large changes in the interest rate will not change the level of money demand by very much. To see how the slope of the LM schedule is related to the interest elasticity of money demand, consider how money market equilibrium changes as we consider progressively higher income levels. Increases in income from Y_0 to Y_1 and then to Y_2 will shift the money demand schedule to the right in Figure 6.7a, from $M^d(Y_0)$ to $M^d(Y_1)$, then to $M^d(Y_2)$. These increases in income cause increases in the transactions demand for money equal to $c_1(Y_1 - Y_0)$ and $c_1(Y_2 - Y_1)$, respectively. Since a given increase in the interest rate will not reduce money demand by much (c_2 is small in absolute value), the interest rate will have to rise by a large amount to reduce money demand back to the fixed M_0^s level. This fact is reflected in the LM curve in Figure 6.7a, which is quite steep.

The case where money demand is highly interest elastic is shown in Figure 6.7b. Here the money demand curve is quite flat. A small drop in the interest rate, for example, will increase money demand significantly. Here again the money demand curve shifts to the right as income increases from Y_0 to Y_1, then to Y_2. The graph is constructed such that the increase in income and the value of c_1 from (6.4) are the same as in Figure 6.7a. Thus the income-induced increases in money demand are the same in Figure 6.7a and b. Notice that in Figure 6.7b the interest rate must rise by a relatively small amount to restore equilibrium in the money market. As a consequence, the LM curve in Figure 6.7b is relatively flat. If money demand is highly responsive to changes in the interest rate (c_2 is large), a relatively small rise in the interest rate will offset the income-induced increases in transaction balances as income rises from Y_0 to Y_1, then to Y_2.

Two special cases for the slope of the LM curve result from the interest elasticity of money demand taking on the value of zero or, alternatively, becoming extremely high.

First consider the case where money demand is completely interest insensitive [c_2 equals zero in (6.4)]. Beginning at some initial equilibrium, consider the rise in the interest rate required to re-equilibrate the money market if income were to be increased. To have income at a higher level would mean increased transactions demand for money. With money demand completely unresponsive to changes in the interest rate there is no possible rise in the interest rate that would reduce money demand back to the level of the fixed money supply. In this special case a rise in the interest rate is assumed not to cause people either to reduce the speculative demand for money or to economize on transactions balances. Consequently, only one level of income can be an equilibrium level. To see this clearly, notice that with c_2 equal to zero, (6.4) becomes

$$M^d = c_0 + c_1 Y$$

and the LM curve equation (6.5) is given by

$$M_0^s = c_0 + c_1 Y$$

Consequently, with M fixed at M_0^s, for equilibrium we must have

$$Y = \frac{M_0^s - c_0}{c_1} \qquad \text{(6.6)}$$

Only this one level of income can be an equilibrium level for the money market.

The LM curve for this case is shown in Figure 6.8, and we will refer to this case as the classical case. This is a classical case because the Keynesian money demand function *when c_2 equals zero* does not differ substantively from the classical money demand function. As in the classical theory (Section 4.1), money demand depends only on income. The distinguishing feature of the Keynesian theory of money demand was the negative relationship between money demand and the interest rate.

The alternative extreme case is where the interest elasticity of money demand becomes extremely large, approaching infinity. What would cause this to happen? We saw from our discussion of Keynes's theory of the speculative demand for money that as the

Figure 6.8
LM Curve: The
Classical Case

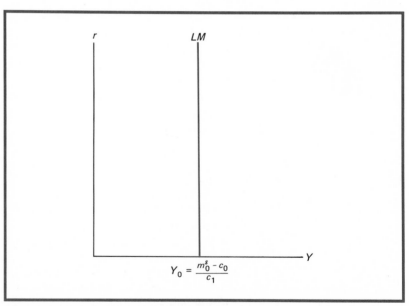

The *LM* schedule will be vertical if money demand is completely interest insensitive.

MACROECONOMIC MODELS

interest rate becomes very low relative to what is considered a normal value, a consensus would develop viewing future interest rates increases as likely. In this situation, with expected future capital losses outweighing the small interest earnings on bonds, the public would hold any increase in money balances with only a negligible fall in the interest rate. It is in this range of the money demand schedule that the interest elasticity of money demand has become extremely high. This case, which Keynes termed the *liquidity trap*, is illustrated in Figure 6.9. Notice that here we have to abandon the linear form of the Keynesian money demand function which we have been discussing. In the liquidity-trap case we are considering a change in the slope of the money demand function. The function becomes very flat at low interest rates.

In Figure 6.9a, consider first the money demand schedules $M^d(Y_0)$ and $M^d(Y_1)$ corresponding to the income levels Y_0 and Y_1 shown in Figure 6.9b. Relative to income levels Y_2 and Y_3, these are low levels of income. Consequently, $M^d(Y_0)$ and $M^d(Y_1)$ are to the left of $M^d(Y_2)$ and $M^d(Y_3)$ in Figure 6.9.

At such low income levels, with the money stock at M_0^s, the equilibrium interest rate is so low that we are on the very flat portion of the money demand schedule. Within this range a rise in income, from Y_0 to Y_1 for example, requires only a very slight rise in the interest rate to restore equilibrium in the money market; money demand is highly responsive to changes in interest rate. In this range the LM curve in Figure 6.9 is nearly horizontal.

Notice that at higher levels of income, between Y_2 or Y_3, for example, an increase in income would require a larger increase in the interest rate to restore equilibrium in the money market. Here the equilibrium interest rates are such that we are not in the liquidity trap. The interest elasticity of money demand is lower over this portion of the money demand schedule.

We return to this liquidity trap case and to the classical case of the vertical LM curve when we consider policy effects in the model below.

Factors That Shift the LM Schedule

Two factors that will shift the LM curve are changes in the exogenously fixed money stock and shifts in the money demand function. These are the two factors that we have set at given levels in order to determine the position of the LM curve. The money stock is assumed to be a policy variable and when we consider an increase in the money stock, for example, we mean by this a exogenous policy action changing the setting of this policy instrument to a new fixed level.

We have already considered shifts in the money demand schedule drawn against the interest rate *as the level of income changes.*

Figure 6.9
Keynesian Liquidity
Trap

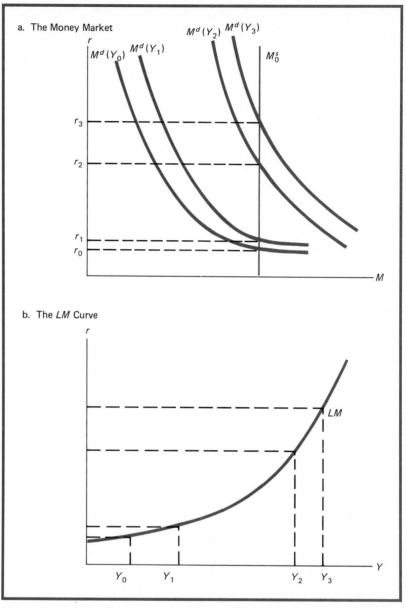

At very low levels of income, Y_0 and Y_1, equilibrium in the money market in Part *a* occurs at points along the flat portion of the money demand schedule where the elasticity of money demand is extremely high. Consequently, the *LM* schedule is nearly horizontal over this range of low income levels. At higher income levels such as Y_2 and Y_3, money market equilibrium is at steeper points along the money demand curves $M^d(Y_2)$, $M^d(Y_3)$ and the *LM* curve becomes steeper.

This is *not* what is meant here by a shift in the money demand *function*. A shift in the money demand function means a change in the amount of money demanded for given levels of the *interest rate and income*, what Keynes called a shift in *liquidity preference*. To give an example, if very unsettled economic conditions increase the probability of firms going bankrupt and, hence, the default risk on bonds, the demand for money might increase. This would be a shift in individuals' portfolios away from bonds and toward holding an increased amount of money for given levels of the interest rate and income.

Consider first the effect on the LM schedule of an exogenous change in the money stock. Figure 6.10 illustrates the effects of an increase in the money stock from M_0^s to M_1^s. With the initial money stock M_0^s, the LM curve is given by LM_0 in Figure 6.10*b*. Along this initial LM curve an income level of Y_0, for example, would be a point of money market equilibrium for an interest rate value of r_0, as shown at point *A* on the graph. Equilibrium in the money mar-

Figure 6.10 Shift in the LM Curve With an Increase in the Quantity of Money

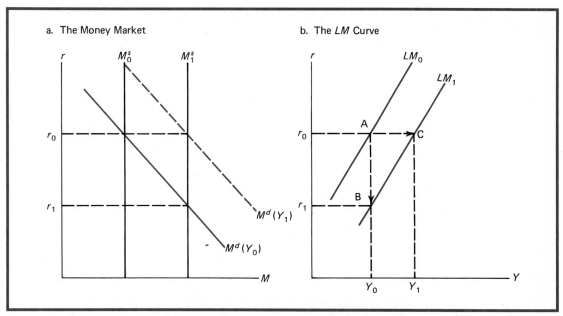

Initially with money stock M_0^s, the interest rate r_0 will be an equilibrium rate when income is at Y_0 in Part *a*. This r_0, Y_0 combination is one point (A) on the LM schedule, LM_0. If the money stock is increased to M_1^s, r_0 will be an equilibrium interest rate in the money market only with a higher income level Y_1. This r_0, Y_1 combination is one point (C) on the new LM schedule LM_1. The increase in the money stock shifts the LM schedule to the right.

ket for income level Y_0 is also shown in Figure 6.10a at the intersection of the M_0^s and $M^d(Y_0)$ curves.

An increase in the money stock from M_0^s to M_1^s can be seen in Figure 6.10a to reduce the level of the equilibrium interest rate to r_1 for a given level of income Y_0. With income fixed, for the new higher money stock to be equal to money demand the interest rate must be lower, to increase the speculative demand for money and transactions demand for a given income level. In terms of the LM curve in Figure 6.10b, the point on the new LM schedule (for money stock M_1^s) that gives the equilibrium interest rate for income level Y_0 will be at interest rate r_1. This income–interest rate combination (Y_0, r_1) is a point on the new LM curve, LM_1, as shown at point B on the graph.

In general, with a higher money stock for a given level of income, the interest rate that equilibrates the money market will be lower. The new LM curve, LM_1, will lie below the initial curve LM_0, as shown in Figure 6.10b.

Alternatively, consider the point on the new LM curve that gives the equilibrium level of income corresponding to interest rate r_0. At M_0^s the income level Y_0 was an equilibrium level for interest rate r_0 (point A). With the money stock M_1^s, for r_0 to be an equilibrium value in the money market, income would have to be higher at Y_1, higher by an amount that would shift the money demand schedule in Figure 6.10a out to the dashed schedule shown in the graph. With a higher money stock and a given interest rate, for there to be equilibrium in the money market, income must be at a higher level. The point on the new LM schedule LM_1, corresponding to r_0, must lie to the right of point A. This point is shown as point C in Figure 6.10b. Thus the new LM curve, LM_1, with the higher money stock M_1^s will lie to the right of the original LM schedule in Figure 6.10b.

In sum, *an increase in the money stock will shift the LM schedule downward and to the right.* Clearly, as can be verified by reversing the foregoing analysis, a decline in the money stock will shift the LM schedule upward and to the left.

Consider next the effect on the position of the LM curve of a shift in the money demand function. Assume that there is a increase in money demand for a given level of income and the interest rate. A possible reason for such a shift, as suggested above, would be a loss of confidence in bonds. The effects of such an increase in money demand are illustrated in Figure 6.11.

Figure 6.11a shows an initial equilibrium in the money market corresponding to income level Y_0. Initially, money demand is given by $M_0^d(Y_0)$. The equilibrium interest rate is r_0, as shown at point A on the initial LM curve LM_0 in Figure 6.11b. Now we assume that the money demand function shifts to $M_1^d(Y_0)$, an increase in money

Figure 6.11 Shift in the LM Curve With a Shift in the Money Demand Function

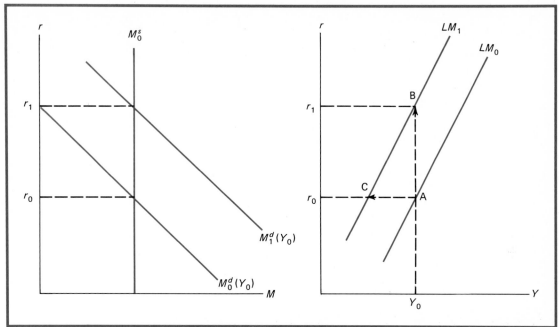

A shift in the money demand *function* which shifts the money demand schedule upward from $M_0^d(Y_0)$ to $M_1^d(Y_0)$ in Part *a* raises the equilibrium interest rate for a given income level. The *LM* schedule in Part *b* shifts upward to the left from LM_0 to LM_1.

demand for a given level of income. Note here that it is the *function* that shifts, from $M_0^d(Y_0)$ to $M_1^d(Y_0)$. At the unchanged level of income, Y_0, equilibrium in the money market requires an interest rate of r_1. The point on the new LM curve, LM_1 in Figure 6.11*b*, for a given level of income Y_0 will be above the old LM schedule. This point is shown as point *B* in Figure 6.11*b*.

Similarly, to maintain equilibrium in the money market at r_0 after the shift in the money demand curve would require a fall in income to a level below Y_0, which would shift the schedule in Figure 6.11*a* back down to the level of the original $M_0^d(Y_0)$ line. Thus the point on LM_1 at r_0 is to the left of LM_0. This point is shown as point *C* in Figure 6.11*b*.

A shift in the money demand function which increases the demand for money at a given level of both the interest rate and income shifts the LM schedule upward and to the left. A reverse shift in money demand lowering the amount of money demanded at given levels of income and the interest rate can be seen by analogous reasoning to shift the LM curve downward to the right.

MONEY, INTEREST, AND INCOME

147

The LM Schedule: Summary
We now know all we need to know about the LM curve. The LM curve:

1. Is the schedule giving all the combinations of values of income and the interest rate which produce equilibrium in the money market.
2. Slopes upward to the right.
3. Will be relatively flat (steep) if the interest elasticity of money demand is relatively high (low).
4. Will shift downward (upward) to the right (left) with an increase (decrease) in the quantity of money.
5. Will shift upward (downward) to the left (right) with a shift in the money demand function, which increases (decreases) the amount of money demanded at given levels of income and the interest rate.

Product Market Equilibrium: The IS Curve

Construction of the IS Schedule
The condition for equilibrium in the product market is

$$Y = C + I + G \tag{6.7}$$

An equivalent statement of this equilibrium condition was seen to be

$$I + G = S + T \tag{6.8}$$

The product market equilibrium schedule, which is termed the *IS curve,* is most often constructed from this second form of the equilibrium condition, although the same results could be derived using (6.7).

We will proceed, as we did with the money market, by finding the set of interest-rate and income-level combinations that produce equilibrium, in this case equilibrium for the product market. Next we examine the factors that determine the slope and position of this product market equilibrium schedule.

To begin we consider a simplified case where we neglect the government sector (i.e., G and T equal zero). The more general case is considered below. For this simple case we can rewrite (6.8) as[4]

$$I(r) = S(Y) \tag{6.9}$$

Here we indicate the dependence of investment on the interest rate and of saving on the level of income. Our task in constructing the IS schedule is to find combinations of the interest rate and level of income that equate investment with saving.

Figure 6.12 illustrates the construction of the IS curve for this

---

[4]The label IS comes from this simple version of the product market equilibrium curve, an equality between investment (I) and saving (S).

Figure 6.12 Construction of the IS Curve ($T = G = 0$)

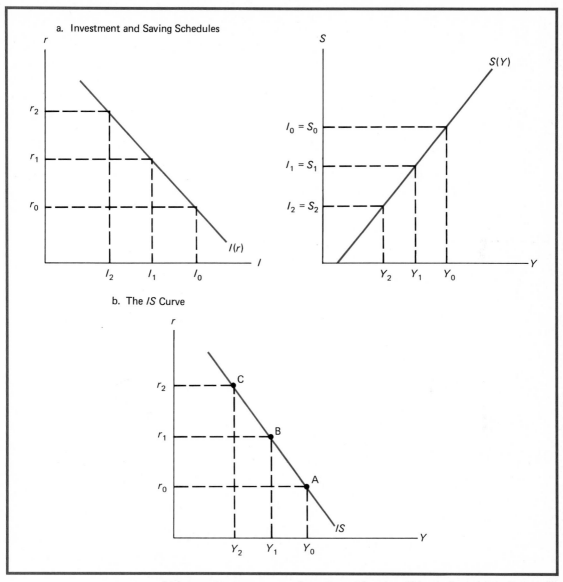

a. Investment and Saving Schedules

b. The IS Curve

At interest rates r_0, r_1, r_2, investment levels will be I_0, I_1 and I_2 in Part a. To generate levels of saving S_0, S_1, S_2, equal to these levels of investment income must be at Y_0, Y_1, and Y_2, respectively. Therefore, interest rate income combinations (r_0, Y_0), (r_1, Y_1) and (r_2, Y_2) are points (A, B, C) along the IS schedule in Part b.

simple case. In Figure 6.12*a* investment is plotted as a negatively sloped function of the interest rate; a decline in the interest rate will increase investment expenditures. Saving is depicted as a positively sloped function of income, the slope being the positive marginal propensity to save.

Consider an interest rate of r_0. For this level of the interest rate, investment spending will be the amount I_0 as shown along the investment schedule. An amount of saving just equal to I_0 is shown as S_0 along the saving function. This level of saving will result if income is at Y_0. Thus for the interest rate r_0, a point of product market equilibrium will be at Y_0. To reiterate, an interest rate of r_0 will correspond to investment demand equal to I_0. To have an equal amount of saving S_0, income must be at Y_0. This interest rate–income combination (r_0, Y_0) is one point on the IS curve, shown as point A in Figure 6.12*b*.

Now consider a higher value of the interest rate, such as r_1. At interest rate r_1 investment will be I_1, a smaller amount than at the lower interest rate r_0. For equilibrium, saving must be at S_1, lower than S_0. This saving level is generated by income level Y_1, which is lower than Y_0. Thus a second point on the IS curve will be at r_1 and Y_1, point B on Figure 6.12*b*. Notice that for the higher interest rate, the corresponding equilibrium income level is lower. *The IS curve will have a negative slope.* By choosing additional interest rate values such as r_2 in Figure 6.12*a* and finding the corresponding income level for equilibrium Y_2, where $I_2 = S_2$, we can find additional points on the IS curve in Figure 6.12*b*, such as point C. In this way we trace the complete set of combinations of income and interest rate levels that will equilibrate the product market.

Factors That Determine the Slope of the IS Schedule

The next topic we consider concerns the factors that determine the degree of the slope of the IS curve. We know that the curve will be negatively sloped, but will it be steep or flat? As was the case with the LM curve, this question is of interest because we will see below that the steepness of the IS curve will be a factor determining the relative effectiveness of monetary and fiscal stabilization policies.

In constructing the IS curve we have looked at how investment changes as we vary the interest rate and then at the required change in income to move saving to equal the new investment level. In considering the steepness of the IS curve, we are asking whether as we look at progressively lower interest rates, for example, equilibrium in the product market requires much higher income levels (the curve is relatively flat) or only slightly increased income levels (the curve is steep). This will depend on the slopes of the investment and saving functions. Figure 6.13 illustrates how the slope of the IS curve is related to the slope of the investment

Figure 6.13 Interest Elasticity of Investment and the Slope of the IS Curve

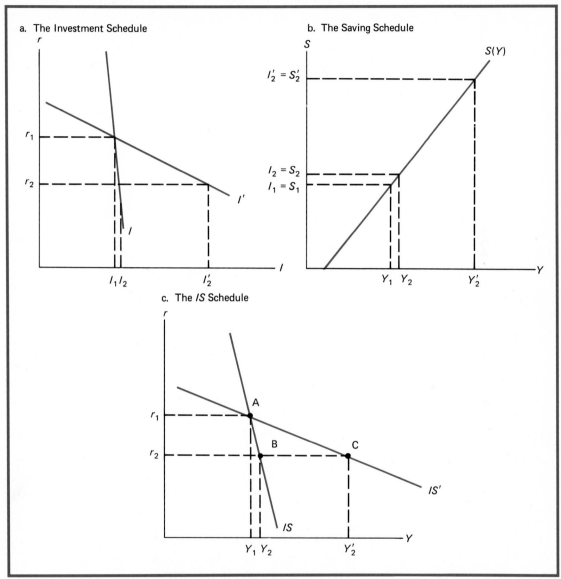

a. The Investment Schedule

b. The Saving Schedule

c. The IS Schedule

Where the investment schedule is steep (*I*) in Part *a*, a fall in the interest rate will increase investment by only a small amount. Only a small increase in saving and, hence, income will be required to restore product market equilibrium. Therefore the IS schedule in Part *c* (*IS*) in this case will be steep. Where the investment schedule is relatively flat (*I'*), investment will increase by more with a fall in the interest rate. Saving and therefore income must then increase by more; the *IS* schedule for this case (*IS'*) will be relatively flat.

function. Two investment schedules are depicted in Figure 6.13a. The schedule labeled I is drawn to be very steep, indicating that investment is not very sensitive to changes in the interest rate; the interest elasticity of investment demand is low.[5] The schedule I' is drawn for the case where investment is more sensitive to movements in the interest rate. For either investment schedule the graph is constructed so that an interest rate of r_1 corresponds to an investment level of I_1 (the curves have different intercepts on the interest-rate axis). Equilibrium in the product market for this interest rate will be at Y_1, as can be seen from Figure 6.13b (at that point, $I_1 = S_1$). This will be one point along the product market equilibrium schedules that we construct corresponding to each of these investment schedules. These product market equilibrium schedules, IS for investment schedule I, and IS' for investment schedule I', are shown in Figure 6.13c. They have a common point at (Y_1, r_1), point A.

Now consider the point along each of these equilibrium schedules corresponding to a lower interest rate r_2. If investment is given by schedule I in Figure 6.13a, at the lower interest rate r_2 investment will be increased to I_2. Equilibrium in the product market would require an equal increase in saving to S_2, which would require that income be at Y_2 in Figure 6.13b. Along the IS schedule we move to point B in Figure 6.13c. Notice that since investment was assumed to be relatively insensitive to changes in the interest rate, the increase in the level of investment when the interest rate falls to r_2 is small. Consequently, the required increase in saving and, therefore, income in Figure 6.13b was small. The IS curve is steep in this case; lower levels of the interest rate correspond to only slightly higher levels of income along the product market equilibrium curve.

Now consider the case where investment is given by the flatter schedule I' in 6.13a. At the lower interest rate r_2, investment will be at I'_2. The level of income corresponding to r_2 along the investment-equals-saving curve for this case, IS' in Figure 6.13c, would be Y'_2 at point C. Saving must increase to S'_2, and this requires income level Y'_2. In this case investment is more highly interest elastic and increases by a greater amount as the interest rate falls to r_2. Consequently, saving must be increased by a greater amount than in the case where investment was interest inelastic, and for this income must increase by more. The product market equilibrium schedule (IS') is flatter for the case where investment is more sensitive to the interest rate.

[5]The concept of elasticity is defined in footnote 3. Here, as in the case of money demand, the interest elasticity is negative; an increase in the interest rate lowers investment demand. By saying that elasticity is low, we again refer to the absolute value of the elasticity.

This, then, is the first of the factors determining the slope of the IS curve. The curve will be relatively steep if the interest elasticity of investment is low. The curve will be flatter for higher (absolute) values of investment interest elasticity.

One extreme case for the slope of the IS curve is where the interest elasticity of investment demand is zero; investment is completely insensitive to the interest rate. In this case the investment schedule in Figure 6.13a will be vertical and as the reader can verify with a graphical analysis analogous to that above, the IS curve will also be vertical. For this case a fall in the interest rate from r_1 to r_2 would not increase investment at all. Consequently, equilibrium in the product market would require the same level of saving and, hence, income at r_2 as at r_1. This means that the IS curve would be vertical. Below we consider the implications of a vertical IS curve for the effectiveness of monetary and fiscal policies.

The second factor affecting the slope of the IS curve is the slope of the saving function. Until we consider more elaborate theories of consumption, we do not encounter much controversy over the slope of the saving function in Figure 6.13b, which is equal to the marginal propensity to save. Consequently, in this section the value of the MPS will not play much of a role in our discussion of the factors determining the slope of the IS curve or, as we see below, the relative effectiveness of monetary and fiscal policy. It can be shown, however, that the IS curve will be relatively steeper, the higher the MPS.

To see this, first note that the higher the value of the MPS, the steeper will be the saving function in Figure 6.13b (saving increases by more per unit of income). Once we have determined the slope of the investment schedule we fix the increase in investment for a given change on the interest rate. A given decline in the interest rate, for example, then leads to a given increase in investment and for product market equilibrium along the IS curve, saving must be higher by the same amount. If the MPS is relatively high, then a smaller increase in income will generate this new saving than would be the case if the MPS were low. Thus for a given fall in the interest rate, the amount by which income would have to be increased for a new point of equilibrium in the product market would be smaller (larger) the higher (lower) the value of the MPS. This means that the IS curve is relatively steeper, other factors being as given, the higher the MPS.

Factors That Shift the IS Schedule

Next we consider the factors that determine the position of the IS curve and changes that will shift the schedule. Here we drop the assumption that government expenditures and taxes are zero; we bring the government sector back into the model. With the government sector in the model the condition for product market equilibrium is given by (6.8), which we rewrite as

$$I(r) + G = S(Y - T) + T \qquad (6.10)$$

Notice that saving must now be written as a function of *disposable income* $(Y_D = Y - T)$, which differs from income by the amount of tax collections.

Construction of the IS curve for this more general case is illustrated in Figure 6.14, which should be compared to Figure 6.12. In part *a* we plot both the investment function and the level of investment plus government spending. Note that the $I + G$ schedule is downward sloping only because investment depends on the rate of interest. The $I + G$ schedule lies to the right of the I schedule by the fixed amount of government spending. In Figure 6.14*b* the saving schedule is plotted against the level of income. Saving plus taxes $[S(Y - T) + T]$ is also plotted. Since we are assuming that tax collections are fixed exogenously, the saving plus taxes schedule lies above the saving schedule by a fixed distance (equal to T).

Consider an interest rate such as r_0 in Figure 6.14. At this interest rate the level of investment [which can be read from the $I(r)$ curve] plus the fixed level of government spending equals $I_0 + G$. For equilibrium this must be balanced by an equal total of saving plus tax collections, given by $S_0 + T$ in Figure 6.14*b*. The level of income that generates this level of saving plus tax collections is given by Y_0. Thus one point along the IS curve is point A in Figure 6.14*c*, corresponding to interest rate r_0 and income level Y_0. If we consider a higher interest rate, such as r_1, investment would be less; hence, with government spending unchanged, investment plus government spending would be at the lower level $I_1 + G$. For equilibrium a lower level of saving plus taxes would be required. This level is shown as $S_1 + T$ in Figure 6.14*b*, where it should be noted that the change is only in the saving component, since taxes are fixed. For this lower level of saving, income must be at Y_1, below Y_0 in Figure 6.14*b*. The corresponding point on the IS curve is point B in Figure 6.14*c*.

By similar reasoning the reader can establish that an interest rate of r_2 will require an income level of Y_2 for equilibrium in the product market (point C in Figure 6.14*c*). Proceeding in this manner, the complete IS schedule is constructed.

We can now look at factors that would cause a shift in the IS curve. From the equilibrium condition given by (6.10) it can be seen that a change in either the level of government spending (G) or the level of taxes (T) will disturb an initial product market equilibrium position—this will be a shift in the IS curve. Additionally,

Figure 6.14 IS Curve With the Addition of a Government Sector

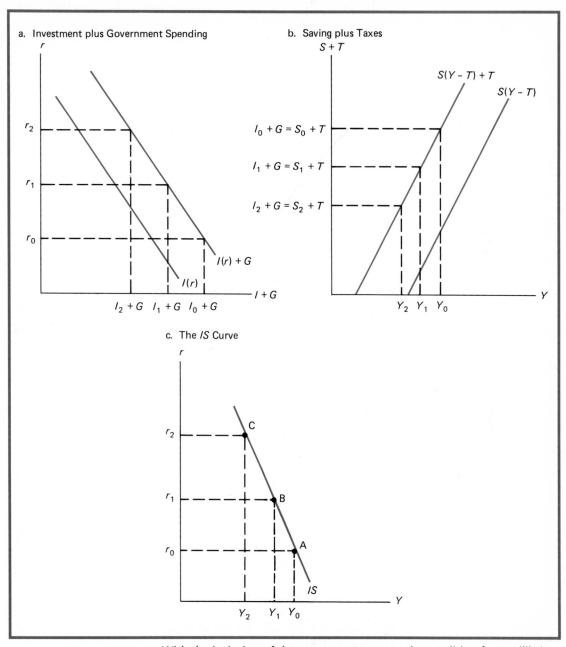

a. Investment plus Government Spending

b. Saving plus Taxes

c. The *IS* Curve

With the inclusion of the government sector, the condition for equilibrium in the goods market becomes $I + G = S + T$. At an interest rate of r_1 in Part *a*, investment plus government spending will be equal to $I_1 + G$. Therefore, equilibrium in the goods market requires that saving plus taxes, as shown in Part *b*, be equal to $S_1 + T (= I_1 + G)$, which will be the case at an income level Y_1. Thus the combination r_1, Y_1 is one point (B) along the *IS* schedule in Part *c*.

an autonomous investment change that shifts the investment function will shift the IS curve. The precise nature of this autonomous change in investment is explained below. Generally note that the factors that shift the IS curve are the factors that determine autonomous expenditures in the simple Keynesian model of the preceding chapter. The reason for this should become clear as we proceed.

Consider first the effects of a change in government spending. The shift in the IS curve when government spending increases from an initial level G_0 to a higher level G_1 is illustrated in Figure 6.15. For the initial level of government spending the IS schedule is given by IS_0 in Figure 6.15c. An interest rate of r_0, for example, will be an equilibrium level for the product market if income is at Y_0, as shown at point A on IS_0. At interest rate r_0, investment plus government spending will be $I_0 + G_0$, as shown in Figure 6.15a. As shown in Figure 6.15b, an income level of Y_0 generates saving plus taxes just equal to this amount of government spending plus investment ($S_0 + T_0 = I_0 + G_0$).

Now let government spending increase to G_1. In Figure 6.15a it can be seen that this shifts the investment plus government spending schedule out to the right. At a given interest rate, investment will be unchanged and the sum of investment plus government spending will be higher by the increase in government spending ($\Delta G = G_1 - G_0$). Equilibrium in the product market will require an equally higher level of saving plus taxes, shown as $S_1 + T_0$ in Figure 6.15b. This level of saving plus taxes will be forthcoming at income level Y_1 above Y_0. Thus a given interest rate r_0 will, for equilibrium in the product market, require a higher level of income when government spending is increased. The increase in government spending will shift the IS curve to the right to IS_1 in Figure 6.15c, where at r_0 the point of equilibrium is at point B, corresponding to the higher income level Y_1.

It will be useful to establish here the amount by which the IS curve shifts to the right, the horizontal distance from A to B in Figure 6.15c. For each 1-unit increase in government spending with taxes assumed unchanged to restore equilibrium *at a given interest rate* in the product market, saving must be higher by 1 unit. This can be readily seen by looking at (6.10). So the question of the distance of the horizontal shift in the IS curve (e.g., distance $A - B$) is that of the amount of the increase in income required to generate new saving equal to the increase in government spending. Since the increase in saving per unit increase in income is given by the MPS equal to $(1 - b)$, the required increase in income (the horizontal shift in the IS curve) will be $\Delta G\left(\dfrac{1}{1 - b}\right)$,

Figure 6.15 Shift in the IS Curve with an Increase in Government Expenditures from G_0 to G_1

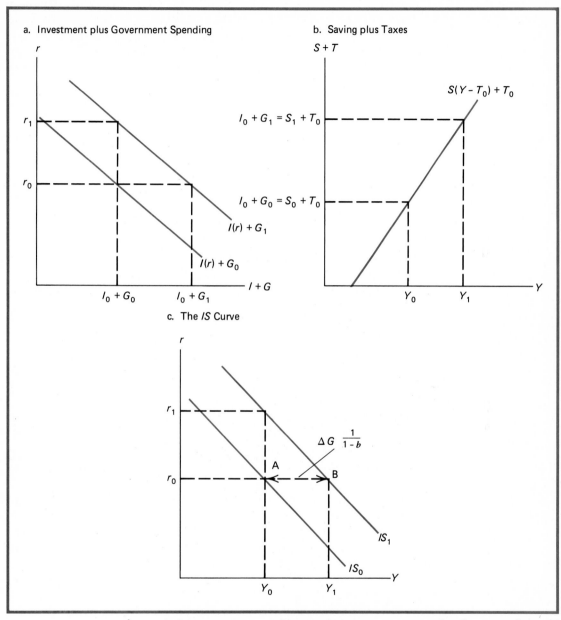

a. Investment plus Government Spending

b. Saving plus Taxes

c. The IS Curve

At interest rate r_0, an increase in government spending increases the total of investment plus government spending from $I_0 + G_0$ to $I_0 + G_1$. To maintain the condition $I + G = S + T$, with a fixed level of taxes, saving must rise from S_0 to S_1 which requires income to be Y_1 instead of Y_0. At interest rate r_0, the equilibrium point in the product market is point B instead of point A. An increase in government spending shifts the IS schedule to the right from IS_0 to IS_1.

$$\Delta G = \Delta S = (1 - b)\Delta Y|_{r_0}$$

$$\Delta G \frac{1}{1 - b} = \Delta Y|_{r_0} \tag{6.11}$$

where the subscript r_0 on the ΔY term indicates that we are computing the increase in the value of Y that will be required to maintain equilibrium in the product market *at interest rate r_0*. This is the amount of the horizontal shift in the IS schedule.

Notice that the amount of the horizontal shift in the IS curve per unit increase in G is $\dfrac{1}{1 - b}$, the autonomous expenditures multiplier from Chapter 5. This should not be surprising. In looking at the horizontal distance that the curve shifts, we are holding the interest rate constant, which fixes investment. Once investment is assumed given, our model is identical to that in Chapter 5. We are looking for the increase in income that will come with investment fixed, government spending rising, and with a consequent induced increase in consumption. This is the same question analyzed in Chapter 5, and reassuringly, we get the same answer.

Next consider the shift in the IS curve with a change in taxes. The effect on the position of the IS curve of a tax increase from T_0 to T_1 is depicted in Figure 6.16. For each one-dollar increase in taxes *at a given income level,* taxes are higher by one dollar and saving is less by $(1 - b)$ dollars. The latter effect follows since an increase of one dollar in taxes lowers disposable income by one dollar and reduces saving by the MPS $(1 - b)$. Since for a given income level the decline in saving is less than the increase in taxes, an increase in taxes will shift the $S + T$ schedule upward. In Figure 6.16*b* an increase in taxes from T_0 to T_1 will shift the schedule from $[S(Y - T_0) + T_0]$ to $[S(Y - T_1) + T_1]$.

At an interest rate such as r_0 in Figure 6.16*a*, we can find the level of government expenditures plus investment along the $I(r) + G$ schedule at $I_0 + G_0$. Equilibrium in the product market requires an equal amount of saving plus taxes. Initially, with taxes at T_0, the equilibrium level of saving plus taxes is $S_0 + T_0$, and this requires income to be at Y_0. This combination of (r_0, Y_0) is a point on the initial IS curve IS$_0$, point A in Figure 6.16*c*.

After the tax increase, for equilibrium in the product market at r_0 we must still have the same total of saving plus taxes. This is the case because there has been no change in investment plus government spending. With the higher level of taxes, for saving plus taxes to be unchanged, saving and therefore income, must be lower. The new level of income required for product market equilibrium is given by Y_1 in Figure 6.16*b*. The corresponding point on the new IS curve is point B in Figure 6.16*c*. The increase in taxes shifts the IS curve to the left.

Figure 6.16 Shift in the IS Curve with an Increase in Taxes from T_0 to T_1

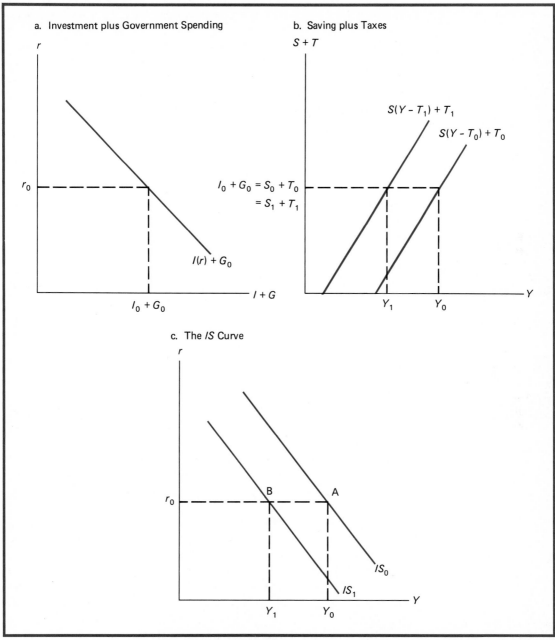

a. Investment plus Government Spending

b. Saving plus Taxes

c. The IS Curve

An increase in taxes shifts the $S + T$ schedule to the left in Part b. At interest rate r_0, which fixes $I_0 + G_0$, with higher taxes, saving and therefore income must be lower to maintain the condition $I + G = S + T$. After the tax increase an income level of Y_1 (point B) rather than Y_0 (point A) will clear the product market for interest rate r_0. The IS curve has shifted leftward from IS_0 to IS_1.

As with the change in government spending, we can calculate the magnitude of the horizontal shift in the IS curve as a result of an increase in taxes. *For a given rate of interest* a tax change does not affect the left-hand side of the equilibrium condition for the product market [equation (6.10)]; investment and government spending are unchanged. So for equilibrium at the same interest rate, the right-hand side must also be unchanged; saving plus taxes must be unchanged. This requires that the increase in taxes be just balanced by a decline in saving,

$$0 = \Delta S + \Delta T$$

We can express the change in saving as

$$\Delta S = (1 - b)\,\Delta(Y - T) = (1 - b)\,\Delta Y - (1 - b)\,\Delta T$$

So for (6.10) to hold requires that

$$\Delta S + \Delta T = 0$$

$$(1 - b)\,\Delta Y - (1 - b)\,\Delta T + \Delta T = 0$$

$$(1 - b)\,\Delta Y - \Delta T + b\,\Delta T + \Delta T = 0$$

$$(1 - b)\,\Delta Y + b\,\Delta T = 0$$

$$(1 - b)\,\Delta Y = -b\,\Delta T$$

$$\Delta Y|_{r_0} = \frac{-b}{1 - b}\,\Delta T \qquad\qquad (6.12)$$

where again in (6.12) the subscript r_0 is used on the ΔY term to indicate that this is the change in the income level that at interest rate r_0 will be an equilibrium value for the product market. From (6.12) it can be seen that, as demonstrated above, income must be lower for product market equilibrium at r_0 with a higher level of taxes. Also, it can be seen that the amount by which the IS curve shifts to the left for a 1-unit increase in taxes, $\left(\dfrac{-b}{1 - b}\right)$, is just equal to the tax multiplier from the simple Keynesian model of Chapter 5. When we consider the horizontal shift in the IS curve per unit change in taxes, we are fixing the interest rate which fixes investment. Thus we are calculating the change in equilibrium income per unit change in taxes for a given level of investment. This is what was given in Chapter 5 by the tax multiplier $\left(\dfrac{-b}{1 - b}\right)$.

The last factor we consider which shifts the IS curve is an autonomous change in investment. By this is meant a shift in the investment schedule as drawn against the interest rate. For example, an increase in expectations about the future profitability of investment projects will increase the level of investment demand corre-

sponding to each interest rate shifting the $I(r)$ schedule and hence the investment plus government spending schedule to the right in Figure 6.15a. This rightward shift in the $I(r)$ schedule, by the amount of the autonomous increase in investment, will have exactly the same effect on the IS curve as an equal increase in government spending, analyzed in Figure 6.15. Both changes shift the investment plus government spending schedule, and as was seen in the discussion above, this shifts the IS curve to the right by $\frac{1}{1-b}$ units per unit increase in government spending, or in this case, autonomous investment expenditures.

In this section we have considered the various factors that shift the IS schedule. We have also generalized the analysis to allow for a government sector and hence enable us to see how fiscal policy variables affect the position of the IS schedule. Since the new variables considered, government spending and taxes, were exogenous, the slopes of the investment plus government spending schedule and of the saving plus taxes schedule were the same as those for the investment and saving schedules considered in the preceding section. Since it is the slopes of these functions that were shown to determine the slope of the IS curve and since they are unchanged, the addition of the government sector to the model in this section requires no revision of the previous discussion of the slope of the IS curve.

The IS Schedule: Summary

In the last two subsections we derived the following results concerning the IS curve, the equilibrium schedule for the product market:

1. The IS curve slopes downward to the right.
2. The IS curve will be relatively flat (steep) if the interest elasticity of investment is relatively high (low).
3. The IS curve will shift to the right (left) when there is an increase (decrease) in the level of government expenditures.
4. The IS curve will shift to the left (right) when the level of taxes increases (declines).
5. An autonomous increase (decrease) in investment expenditures will shift the IS curve to the right (left).

The IS and LM Curves Combined

In Figure 6.17 we combine the LM and IS schedules. The upward-sloping LM schedule shows all the points of equilibrium for the money market. The downward-sloping IS schedule shows all the points of equilibrium for the product market. The point of intersection between the two curves, point E in the figure, is the (only) point of general equilibrium for both markets. As pointed out at

Figure 6.17
IS and LM Curves
Combined

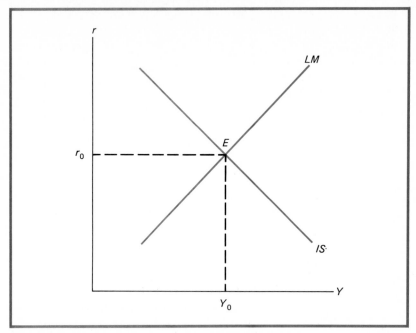

The point of intersection of the *IS* and *LM* curves gives the combination of the interest rate and income level (r_0, Y_0) which produces equilibrium for both the money and product markets.

the beginning of our discussion, if the money market is in equilibrium, the bond market must also be in equilibrium. Thus the interest rate and income level at the intersection of the IS and LM schedules in Figure 6.17, denoted r_0 and Y_0, are values that produce a simultaneous equilibrium for the money market, product market, and bond market.

As was the case with the simpler Keynesian model in Chapter 5, the nature of equilibrium in the IS–LM curve model can be better understood by considering why points other than the point of intersection of the two curves are not points of equilibrium. Figure 6.18 shows a number of points off the IS and LM curves (A, B, C, D).

First consider points above the LM schedule such as points A and B. At all points above the LM schedule there will be an excess supply of money (XS_M). At the level of income for either point A or B, the corresponding interest rate is too high for money market equilibrium. With an excess supply of money there is downward pressure on the interest rate, as indicated by the downward-directed arrow. There is a tendency to move toward the LM schedule. Similarly, at points below the LM schedule, such as points C and D, there will be an excess *demand* for money (XD_M) and consequently there will be upward pressure on the interest rate.

Figure 6.18
Adjustment to
Equilibrium in the *IS–
LM* Curve Model

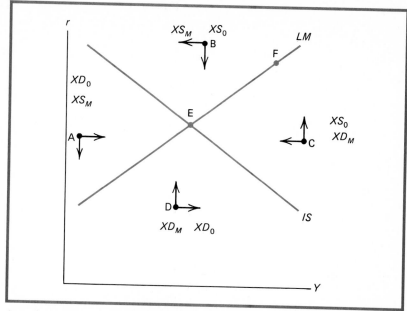

At points such as A, B, C, D, there are either excess supplies or demands in
the money and product markets, and therefore pressures for the interest
rate and output to change. At point F, the product market is out of equilibrium and there is pressure for output to change. Only at point E are both
the money and product markets in equilibrium with no pressure for change
in either the interest rate or level of output.

Now consider the same points in relation to the IS curve. At
points such as *B* and *C*, to the right of the IS schedule output will
exceed aggregate demand or, analogously, saving plus taxes will
exceed investment plus government spending. At the levels of the
interest rate for either point *B* or *C*, the corresponding output level
that will just equate investment plus government spending to saving plus taxes, an output level given by the point along the IS
curve, is below the actual output level. There is an excess supply of
output (XS_O), and therefore a downward pressure on output, as
indicated by the arrows pointing to the left. Correspondingly, at
points to the left of this IS schedule, such points *A* and *D*, actual
output is below the level that will just clear the product market.
There is an excess demand for output (XD_O) and there will be upward pressure on output, as indicated by the rightward-directed
arrows at these points.

Finally, note that points on one schedule but not on the other
will also be *disequilibrium* points relative to one of the two markets. A point such as *F*, for example, is a point of equilibrium for
the money market but is a point of excess supply for the product

market. Similarly, any point along the IS curve other than point E would result in disequilibrium in the money market. It is only at point E that both the money and product markets are in equilibrium. There is no excess demand or supply in either the money or product market, and therefore there are no pressures for the interest rate or output to change. This is the condition for equilibrium in the IS–LM curve model.

Having seen how the equilibrium levels of income and the interest rate are determined in the IS–LM curve model, our next task will be to see how these equilibrium values are affected by monetary and fiscal policy variables as well as by other shocks to the model.

Review Questions

1 Explain the Keynesian theory of interest rate determination. What differences do you see between this theory and the classical theory of the interest rate?

2 How would the level of aggregate demand be affected by a rise in the interest rate in the Keynesian theory? Which components would be affected most strongly?

3 What are the three motives for holding money according to Keynes's theory of money demand? Explain each motive.

4 What property is shared by all points along the LM schedule? along the IS schedule?

5 Explain why in the IS–LM curve model, the IS curve is negatively sloped and the LM curve is positively sloped.

6 What factors determine the magnitude of the slope of the IS schedule; that is, what factors determine whether the curve is steep or flat?

7 What variables will shift the position of the IS schedule? Explain the way a change in each variable will shift the schedule (to the left or to the right).

8 What factors determine the magnitude of the slope of the LM schedule; that is, what factors determine whether the curve is steep or flat?

9 Trace through the procedure for deriving the IS schedule, as was done in Figure 6.14, for the case where rather than a fixed level of taxes (T), we have taxes depending on income

$$T = t_1 Y$$

where t_1 is the marginal income tax rate. Will the IS curve for this case be steeper or flatter than for the case where the level of taxes is fixed?

10   What variables will shift the position of the LM schedule? Explain the way in which a change in each variable will shift the schedule (to the left or to the right).

11   What condition would be required for the LM schedule to be vertical? What condition would be required for the alternative extreme case where over a range the LM schedule became nearly horizontal?

12   Why are we assured that when the money and product markets are in equilibrium the bond market will also be in equilibrium?

13   Explain why at a point such as B in Figure 6.18, there is downward pressure on both the level of output and the interest rate.

Selected Readings

HICKS, JOHN, "Mr. Keynes and the Classics: A Suggested Interpretation," *Econometrica*, 5 (April 1937), pp. 147–59. Reprinted in John Hicks, *Critical Essays in Monetary Theory*. London: Oxford University Press, 1967. See also Chap. 8 in that volume, "The 'Classics' Again," and Chap. 9, "Monetary Theory and History—An Attempt at Perspective."

LAIDLER, DAVID, *The Demand for Money*. New York: Dun-Donnelley, 1977, Chap. 1.

MAKINEN, GAIL, *Money, the Price Level and Interest Rates*. Englewood Cliffs, N.J.: Prentice-Hall, 1977 Chaps. 5–8.

ROBERTSON, D. H., "Mr. Keynes and the Rate of Interest," in D. H. Robertson, *Essays in Monetary Theory*. London: Staples Press, 1940.

chapter 7

In this chapter we use the IS–LM curve model to analyze the effects of various policy actions on the equilibrium levels of income and the interest rate. Other factors that can affect the levels of income and the interest rate are also considered. The groundwork for this analysis was established in Chapter 6. Equilibrium levels of income and the interest rate are those given by the intersection of the IS and LM curves. The factors that change these equilibrium levels are the factors that shift either the IS or the LM curve, considered in Chapter 6. Here we need only to see how such shifts affect income and the interest rate when the two schedules are considered jointly. We do this in Section 7.1. In Section 7.2 we see how the magnitude of the effects of different policies depend on the slopes of the IS and LM curves. The slopes of the IS–LM curves were shown in Chapter 6 to depend on various features of the economic system, the most important being the interest sensitivity of investment and of money demand. In Section 7.2 we see how policy effectiveness depends on these factors.

7.1 FACTORS AFFECTING EQUILIBRIUM INCOME AND THE INTEREST RATE

Monetary Influences: Shifts in the LM Schedule

Consider the effects on income and the interest rate of changes in the quantity of money. Figure 7.1 illustrates the effect of an increase in the quantity of money from M_0 to M_1. Initially, assume that the IS and LM schedules are IS_0 and LM_0 in Figure 7.1. In-

THE KEYNESIAN SYSTEM (III): POLICY EFFECTS IN THE IS–LM MODEL

come and the interest rate are at Y_0 and r_0, respectively. As we saw in Chapter 6, an increase in the quantity of money shifts the LM schedule to the right to a position such as LM_1 in Figure 7.1. Consequently, the interest rate falls from r_0 to r_1 and income rises from Y_0 to Y_1.

The economic process producing these results is straightforward. The increase in the money stock creates an excess supply of money, which causes the interest rate to fall. As the interest rate falls, investment demand is increased and this causes income to rise, with a further income-induced increase in consumption demand. A new equilibrium is achieved where the fall in the interest rate and rise in income jointly increase money demand by an amount equal to the increase in the money supply. This occurs at the point where the new LM curve intersects the IS curve.

A decline in the money stock would have effects just opposite to those above. The LM curve would shift to the left. The equilibrium level of income would fall. The equilibrium interest rate would rise.

The other factor that was seen in Chapter 6 to shift the LM schedule is a shift in the money demand function. Consider, for example, an increase in money demand *for given levels of income and the interest rate*. Such a portfolio shift away from bonds into money will shift the LM schedule to the left. As people try to reduce their bond holdings in order to increase their money holdings, the interest rate will rise. The higher interest rate will cause income to decline. An increase in money demand, in the sense of a

Figure 7.1

Effects of an Increase in the Quantity of Money from M_0 to M_1

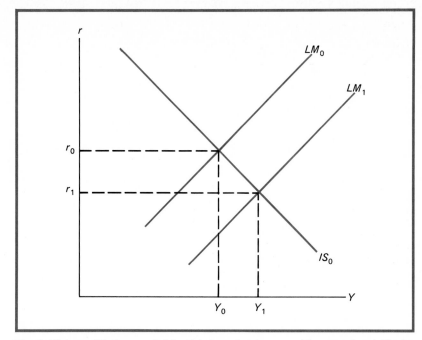

The initial equilibrium point is at interest rate r_0 and income level Y_0. An increase in the money stock from M_0 to M_1 shifts the LM schedule to the right from LM_0 to LM_1. The interest rate falls from r_0 to r_1 and income rises from Y_0 to Y_1.

shift in the function such that more money is demanded at a given level of income and interest rate, would have the same effect as a decline in the money stock. Equilibrium income would fall and the interest rate would rise. A reverse portfolio shift toward holding more bonds and less money would have the reverse effects.

Real Influences: Shifts in the IS Schedule

Fiscal policy variables are one set of factors that shift the IS schedule and hence affect equilibrium income and the interest rate in the model. In Figure 7.2 we illustrate the effects of one fiscal policy shift, an increase in government spending from G_0 to G_1. The initial positions of the IS and LM schedules are given by IS_0 and LM_0 in Figure 7.2. The initial equilibrium values of income and the interest rate are Y_0 and r_0, respectively. The increase in government spending to G_1 will, as shown in Chapter 6, shift the IS schedule out to the right to a position such as IS_1 in Figure 7.2. The equilibrium level of income will rise, as will the equilibrium level of the interest rate.

The force pushing up the level of income is the increase in aggre-

Figure 7.2
Effects of an Increase in Government Spending from G_0 to G_1

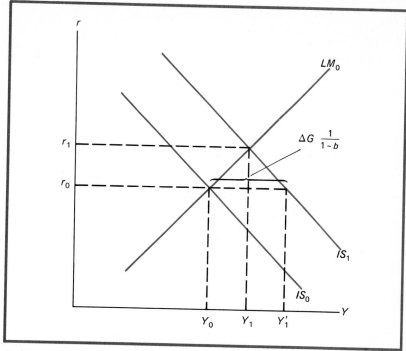

An increase in government spending shifts the *IS* schedule to the right from IS_0 to IS_1. Income rises from Y_0 to Y_1; the interest rate rises from r_0 to r_1.

gate demand both directly as government demand rises and then indirectly due to an income-induced increase in consumer expenditures. The forces pushing up the interest rate require some explanation. Notice that the LM schedule does not shift. At a given level of income, equilibrium in the money market, and therefore in the bond market, is undisturbed by the government spending change. It is the rise in income in response to the fiscal policy shift that necessitates the interest rate adjustment. As income increases, the transactions demand for money rises. The money stock is not changed, so the attempt to increase transactions balances requires a decline in the demand for bonds. It is this income-induced increase in money demand and decline in bond demand that causes the interest rate to rise.

In the aggregate, the public cannot increase money holdings; the money stock is fixed. The attempt to do so, however, will push up the interest rate, reducing the speculative demand for money and causing individuals to economize on the amount of transactions balances held for any level of income. At the new equilibrium the interest rate must rise sufficiently such that the net money demand is unchanged even though income is higher.

It was shown in Chapter 6 that the horizontal distance by which the IS curve shifts when government spending increases is equal to $\Delta G \left(\dfrac{1}{1-b} \right)$ where ΔG equals $(G_1 - G_0)$. The distance of the shift in the IS curve is the increase in government spending times the autonomous expenditure multiplier from the simple (no money market) Keynesian model. This horizontal distance equals the amount by which income would have increased in that simple model. In Figure 7.2 this increase in equilibrium income would have been to Y_1'. When we take into account the required adjustment in the money market, it can be seen that income rises by less than this amount, to Y_1 in Figure 7.2. Why?

The difference between the simple Keynesian model and the IS–LM curve model is that the latter includes a money market. When government spending increases, as we have just seen, the rate of interest must rise to maintain equilibrium in the money market. The increase in the interest rate will cause a decline in investment spending. The decline in investment spending will partially offset the increase in aggregate demand resulting from the increase in government spending. Consequently, the increase in income will be less than that in the simple Keynesian model, where investment was taken as completely autonomous.[1] By neglecting the necessary increase in the interest rate and consequent decline in investment that accompany an increase in government spending, the simple Keynesian model overstated the effect of an increase in government spending.

Next consider the effects in the model of an increase in the level of tax collections (T), as illustrated in Figure 7.3. An increase in tax collections from T_0 to T_1 will, as shown in Chapter 6, shift the IS curve to the left. In the figure this is shown as a shift in the IS curve from its initial position IS_0 to the position IS_1. As can be seen, the level of income declines from Y_0 to Y_1. The interest rate also declines, from r_0 to r_1.

Income falls as taxes rise because the tax increase lowers disposable income $(Y - T)$ and causes consumption to decline. The reason for the drop in the interest rate parallels that for the income-induced interest rate increase when government spending was increased. As income declines due to the tax increase, money demand declines and bond demand increases. This causes the interest rate to fall.

---

[1]Note that the increase in the interest rate and consequent decline in investment come only *because* income has increased. Thus the decline in investment cannot completely offset the increase in income caused by the increase in government spending.

Figure 7.3
Effects of an Increase
in Taxes from T_0 to T_1

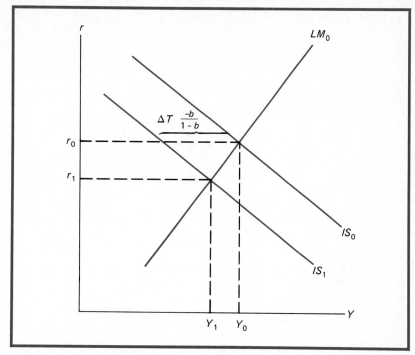

An increase in taxes shifts the *IS* schedule to the left from IS_0 to IS_1. Income falls from Y_0 to Y_1 and the interest rate falls from r_0 to r_1.

As was the case with a change in government spending, notice in Figure 7.3 that income falls by less than the horizontal distance of the shift in the IS curve. The horizontal distance by which the IS curve will shift with a change in taxes is, as explained in Chapter 6, equal to $\Delta T \left(\dfrac{-b}{1-b} \right)$, the tax multiplier from the simple Keynesian model times the change in taxes. Thus it is again true that in the IS–LM curve model, fiscal policy multipliers are reduced relative to our results for the simple Keynesian model. For the case of a tax increase, the reason for this is that the decline in the interest rate discussed above will cause investment to rise, partially offsetting the decline in consumption caused by the tax increase. The simple Keynesian model assumed investment to be fixed, neglected this offset, and hence overstated the effects of the tax increase.

A decrease in taxes would have just the opposite effects of the tax increase. The IS curve would shift to the right and both income and the interest rate would rise. Similarly, a decline in government spending would have effects just opposite to those for the increase in government spending discussed above.

Within the IS–LM curve model we can derive a result similar to the balanced budget multiplier in Chapter 5, that is, a multiplier giving the effect on income of a change in government spending financed by an equal change in tax collections $\left(\dfrac{\Delta Y}{\Delta G} + \dfrac{\Delta Y}{\Delta T}\right)$. Figure 7.4 illustrates the effects of an increase in government spending financed by an increase in taxes *of an equal amount*.

As above, the increase in government spending shifts the IS curve to the right, from IS_0 to IS_1' in Figure 7.4. The horizontal distance by which the curve shifts is $\Delta G\left(\dfrac{1}{1-b}\right)$ as shown in the graph. The increase in taxes will shift the IS curve back to the left by an amount equal to $\Delta T\left(\dfrac{-b}{1-b}\right)$, or equivalently since ΔT equals ΔG by $\Delta G\left(\dfrac{-b}{1-b}\right)$. In Figure 7.4 this is shown as a shift from IS_1' to IS_1. The crucial point to note here is that the initial

Figure 7.4
Effects of an Increase in Government Spending Financed by an Equal Increase in Tax Collections

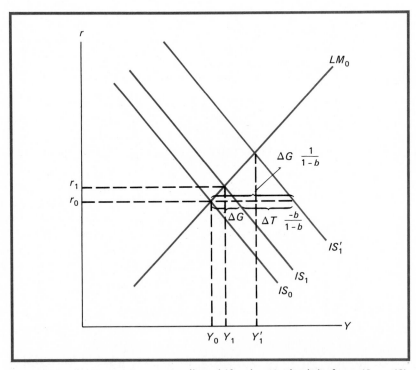

An increase in government spending shifts the *IS* schedule from IS_0 to IS_1'. An increase of an equal amount in taxes shifts the *IS* schedule to the left from IS_1' to IS_1. The *IS* curve does not, however, shift all the way back to IS_0. Income rises from Y_0 to Y_1 and the interest rate rises from r_0 to r_1.

MACROECONOMIC MODELS

shift to the right caused by the increase in government spending is only partially offset by the increase in taxes,

$$\Delta G \left(\frac{1}{1-b} \right) + \Delta G \left(\frac{-b}{1-b} \right) = \frac{\Delta G - b\,\Delta G}{1-b}$$

$$= \Delta G \left(\frac{1-b}{1-b} \right) = \Delta G \qquad (7.1)$$

There is a net shift to the right in the IS curve by the distance ΔG, the amount of the balanced increase in the size of the government budget. This is the result that parallels the balanced budget multiplier of Chapter 5.

As with the other fiscal policy actions considered above, however, the actual change in income will be less than the horizontal shift in the IS curve, and therefore, less than the multiplier from the simple model, which for this case was unity. As can be seen from Figure 7.4, the net shift in the IS curve from IS_0 to IS_1 increases income to Y_1, an increase of less than ΔG, and causes the interest rate to rise to r_1. As was the case with expansionary fiscal policy actions considered previously, the interest rate must rise to clear the money market as income increases. This causes investment demand to decline and explains why income rises by less than in the simple Keynesian model.

To summarize, as was the case in the simple Keynesian model, government spending changes have a greater per-dollar effect on income than do tax changes. As a consequence, a change in the size of the budget holding the deficit constant (an equal change in spending and taxes) will cause income to change in the same direction as the change in the size of the government budget.

Fiscal policy variables are not the only factors that can shift the IS schedule. Any autonomous change in the aggregate demand for output will have this effect. One such change is an autonomous change in investment demand, by which is meant a shift in the function giving the level of investment for each level of the interest rate. Such a change would occur, for example, if, as a result of some exogenous event, the expected profitability of investment projects changed.

Figure 7.5 illustrates the effects of an autonomous decline in investment demand. In Figure 7.5a the investment schedule is plotted. The initial schedule is $I_0\,(r)$. The autonomous decline in investment of ΔI shifts the schedule to the left to $I_1\,(r)$, reducing the level of investment at each rate of interest. In Figure 7.5b this autonomous decline in investment demand shifts the IS schedule to the left, from IS_0 to IS_1. Income falls from Y_0 to Y_1. The interest rate declines from r_0 to r_1. Income declines because investment demand at the initial interest rate has fallen (from I_0 to I_1' in Figure 7.5a).

Figure 7.5
Effects of an
Autonomous Decline
in Investment Demand

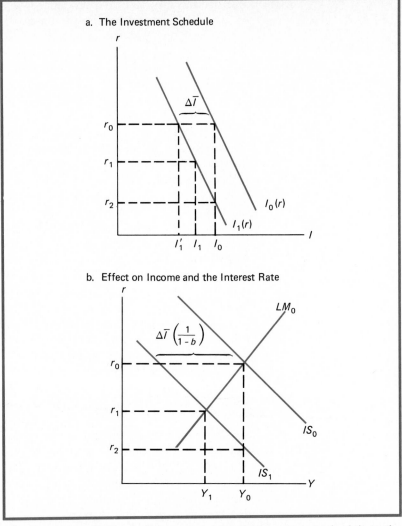

a. The Investment Schedule

b. Effect on Income and the Interest Rate

An autonomous decline in investment shifts the investment schedule to the left in Part *a*. At the initial interest rate r_0 this shift would cause investment to fall from I_0 to I_1'. The shift in the investment function causes the *IS* schedule in Part *b* to shift to the left from IS_0 to IS_1. Equilibrium income falls from Y_0 to Y_1 and the equilibrium interest rate falls from r_0 to r_1. As a result of the fall in the interest rate, investment is revived somewhat to I_1 in Part *a*.

As income falls there is also an income-induced decline in consumption spending. The interest rate decline is also income induced, as was the case when we considered the interest rate effects of fiscal policy changes. The decline in income causes money demand to fall and bond demand to rise; consequently, the interest rate falls.

Notice that the decline in the interest rate causes investment to return somewhat toward its initial level. At the new equilibrium investment, demand is at I_1 in Figure 7.5a, having increased from I'_1 to I_1 as a result of the decline in the interest rate.

It is of interest to compare the effects of an autonomous decline in investment in the IS–LM curve version of the Keynesian model, with the effect of the same shift within the classical model analyzed previously (Section 4.2). There the interest rate played a stabilizing role such that a change in investment demand did not affect aggregate demand. The interest rate fell sufficiently to restore aggregate demand to its initial level. In the IS–LM model the interest rate adjustment is stabilizing but incomplete. For income to be unchanged when there is an autonomous decline in investment, the interest rate would have to fall to the level r_2 in Figure 7.5b. At that level of the interest rate, income would be at the original level Y_0 along the new IS schedule IS_1. In Figure 7.5a it can be seen that at level r_2, the interest rate has fallen sufficiently to return investment to its initial level I_0. The interest rate falls only to r_1, however; the offset to the initial autonomous drop in investment demand is incomplete.

There is one case where the offset will be complete, that is, where the interest rate would fall to r_2. This is where the LM schedule is vertical. In that case, when the IS schedule shifted from IS_0 to IS_1 we simply move down the vertical LM schedule to a new equilibrium at the initial income level Y_0 and with the interest rate having declined to r_2. The vertical LM schedule was termed a classical case, so it should not be too surprising that classical conclusions result from that assumption. An explanation of these classical results for the vertical LM curve case is provided in the next section.

7.2 THE RELATIVE EFFECTIVENESS OF MONETARY AND FISCAL POLICY

In Section 7.1 we examined the qualitative effects of monetary and fiscal policy actions within the IS–LM curve model, as summarized in Table 7.1. As can be seen from the table, both monetary and fiscal policy instruments can be used to affect the level of income. In this section we examine the relative effectiveness of the two types of policy actions. By "effectiveness" will be meant the size of the effect on income of a given change in the policy variable.

Table 7.1

Effects of Monetary and Fiscal Policy Variables[a]

Effect of on	M	G	T
Y	+	+	−
r	−	+	−

[a]M, money stock; G, level of government spending; T, taxes. A + sign indicates that a change in the policy instrument causes the variable in that row (Y or r) to move in the same direction. A − sign indicates the reverse.

There are additional aspects to the question of macroeconomic policy effectiveness, such as the predictability and speed of policy effects, but these will be postponed until later. The effectiveness of each type of policy (monetary and fiscal) will be shown to depend on the slopes of the IS and LM curves, which in turn are determined by certain behavioral parameters of our model.

Policy Effectiveness and the Slope of the IS Schedule

First we examine how the slope of the IS curve influences the effectiveness of monetary and fiscal policy. As we saw earlier, the crucial parameter determining the slope of the IS schedule is the (absolute value of the) interest elasticity of investment. If investment demand is highly interest elastic, meaning that a given rise in the interest rate will reduce investment by a large amount, the IS curve will be relatively flat. The lower the value of the interest elasticity of investment demand, the steeper will be the IS curve.

Here and when we consider the influence on policy effectiveness of the slope of the LM curve below, we proceed as follows. First, we compare the effects of monetary and fiscal policy on income when the schedule, here the IS curve, is steep and when it is flat. The monetary policy action considered will be an increase in the money stock. The fiscal policy action considered will be an increase in government spending. Since both tax changes and spending changes work by shifting the IS schedule, tax changes and government spending changes are effective or ineffective in the same circumstances. No separate evaluation of tax policy effectiveness is required.

As a measure of whether fiscal policy actions are effective or not, we will compare the effect of the policy action on income with the effect predicted by the simple Keynesian model. In moving to the IS–LM curve model, we added a money market to the Keynesian system. By comparing the effect of fiscal policy in the IS–LM model with the effect in the simple Keynesian system, where fiscal policy variables are major determinants of income, we see how the addition of the money market modifies our previous results. The distance of the horizontal shift in the IS curve for a given fiscal policy action equals the effect on income in the simple Keynesian model (e.g., $\Delta Y = \Delta G \left(\dfrac{1}{1-b} \right)$, for a government spending change). Consequently, to evaluate the effectiveness of fiscal policy on the graphs below, we compare the change in income with the horizontal shift in the IS curve.

To evaluate the effectiveness of monetary policy we will compare the effect on income of the change in the money stock with the horizontal distance of the shift in the LM schedule. The horizontal shift in the LM schedule when the money stock changes is equal to $\Delta M \left(\dfrac{1}{c_1} \right)$, where c_1 is the coefficient on income in the money demand function [equation (6.4)]. The coefficient c_1 gives the amount of the increase in money demand per unit of income; therefore, $\Delta M \left(\dfrac{1}{c_1} \right)$ gives the increase in income that could occur for an increase in the money stock if *all* new money balances went to support increased transactions demand for money due to increased income. This would be the amount of the increase in income for a given level of the interest rate, and thus the amount of the horizontal shift in the LM schedule. This distance measures the maximum possible increase in income for a given increase in the money stock.

Monetary Policy Effectiveness and the Slope of the IS Schedule

Figures 7.6a and b show the effects of an increase in the quantity of money for two differently sloped IS schedules. In each case the increase in the money stock shifts the LM schedule from LM_0 to LM_1. In Figure 7.6a the IS schedule is steep, reflecting a low interest elasticity of investment demand. As can be seen from the graph, monetary policy is relatively ineffective in this case. Income rises very little as a result of the increase in the money stock.

In Figure 7.6b the slope of the LM schedule has been kept the same as in Figure 7.6a. The size of the horizontal shift in the LM schedule, $\Delta M \left(\dfrac{1}{c_1} \right)$, which fixes the size of the policy action, has also been kept the same. The only difference is in the slope of the IS schedule. In Figure 7.6b that schedule is drawn to be much flatter, reflecting a higher interest elasticity of investment demand. As can be seen, monetary policy becomes more effective when the IS schedule is flatter.

The difference in monetary policy effects in the two graphs should not be surprising. Within the IS–LM curve model, monetary policy affects income by lowering the interest rate and stimulating investment demand. If investment demand is little affected

Figure 7.6 Monetary Policy Effects and the Slope of the *IS* Schedule

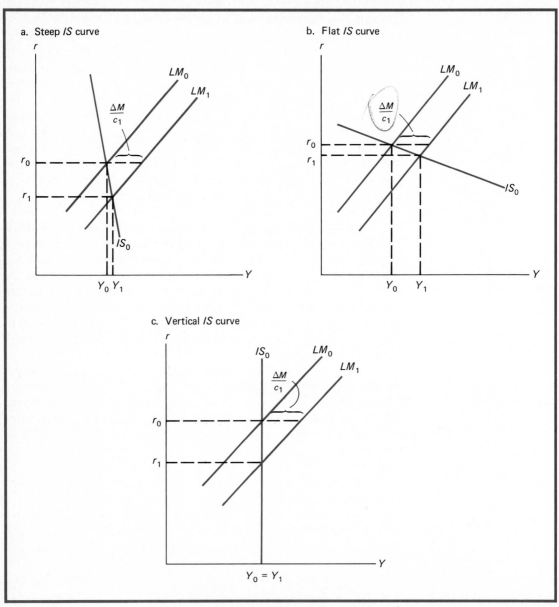

An increase in the money stock shifts the *LM* schedule to the right from LM_0 to LM_1. This expansionary monetary policy action has only a small effect on output in Part *a*, where the *IS* curve is steep, but a much larger effect in Part *b*, where the *IS* curve is relatively flat. In Part *c*, where the *IS* curve is vertical, the increase in the money stock has no effect on equilibrium income.

MACROECONOMIC MODELS

by interest rate changes, which is the assumption in Figure 7.6*a*, monetary policy will be ineffective. In Figure 7.6*b*, where the interest sensitivity of investment is assumed to be substantially greater, monetary policy has correspondingly greater effects. Our first result in this section is then that monetary policy will be ineffective when the IS schedule is steep, that is, when investment is interest inelastic. Monetary policy will be more effective the higher the interest elasticity of investment, and thus the flatter the IS schedule.

Here and below we consider several extreme cases for the slopes of the IS or LM schedule. We return to a discussion of these cases when making comparisons of the Keynesian and monetarist positions in later chapters. Consideration of such extreme cases should also be helpful in understanding our results in the "normal" cases.

The first such extreme case is that of the vertical IS schedule. As discussed earlier, the IS curve will be vertical if investment is completely insensitive to changes on the interest rate (interest elasticity equals zero). The effects of an increase in the money stock for this case are shown in Figure 7.6*c*. If the IS curve is vertical, as shown in the graph, increasing the money stock simply shifts the LM schedule down along the IS schedule. The interest rate falls until money demand increases by enough to restore equilibrium in the money market, but income is unchanged. To increase income the increase in the money stock and resulting fall in the interest rate must stimulate investment demand. When the IS curve is vertical, investment will not be affected by monetary policy because, by assumption, investment demand does not depend on the interest rate. It should be clear that the steeper the IS curve, the closer we come to this extreme case and the less effective is monetary policy.

Fiscal Policy Effectiveness and the Slope of the IS Schedule

Figures 7.7*a* and *b* show the effects of an increase in government spending in the case of a steep IS schedule (7.7*a*) and a relatively flat IS schedule (7.7*b*). In both cases the increase in government spending shifts the IS schedule from IS_0 to IS_1. The horizontal distance of the shift in the curve $\Delta G \left(\dfrac{1}{1-b} \right)$ is the same in both cases, meaning that the size of the policy action as well as the autonomous expenditure multiplier from the simple Keynesian model are equal in both cases. As can be seen from these graphs, fiscal policy is much more effective in the case where the IS schedule is steep (Figure 7.7*a*).

The steep IS curve case is where investment is relatively interest inelastic. What we have found is that the less sensitive investment

Figure 7.7 Fiscal Policy Effects and the Slope of the *IS* Schedule

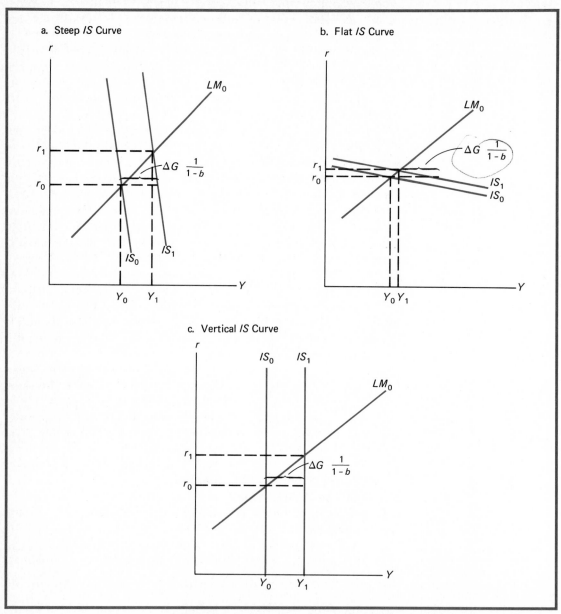

In each part of the figure an increase in government spending shifts the *IS* curve to the right from IS_0 to IS_1. In Part *a*, where the *IS* curve is steep, this expansionary fiscal policy action results in a relatively large increase in income. This fiscal policy action is much less effective (the increase in income is much smaller) in Part *b* where the *IS* curve is relatively flat. Fiscal policy is most effective in Part *c*, where the *IS* curve is vertical.

MACROECONOMIC MODELS

is to the interest rate, the greater will be the effect of a given fiscal policy action. To see why this is so, consider the role of the interest-rate change in the adjustment to a new equilibrium after an increase in government spending. As income increases following the rise in government spending, the interest rate must rise to keep the money market in equilibrium. This rise in the interest rate will cause investment to decline, partially offsetting the expansionary effect of the government spending increase. It is this interest rate–induced decline in investment that causes the income response in the IS–LM curve model to fall short of the response given by the multiplier from the simple Keynesian system; that is, income rises by less than the horizontal shift in the IS schedule.

How important is this effect on investment, which is often referred to as "crowding out"? One factor determining the importance of such crowding out of private investment is the slope of the IS curve. If investment is not very sensitive to changes in the interest rate, the assumption in Figure 7.7a, then the interest rate increase will cause only a slight drop in investment, and income will rise by almost the full amount of the horizontal shift in the IS curve. Alternatively, if investment is highly interest sensitive, the assumption in Figure 7.7b, then the rise in the interest rate will reduce investment substantially, and the increase in income will be reduced significantly relative to the prediction of the simple Keynesian model.

The case of the vertical IS curve shown in Figure 7.7c may again be instructive. Here investment is completely interest insensitive. The increase in government spending causes the interest rate to rise, but this does not result in a decline in investment. Income increases by the full amount of the distance of the horizontal shift in the IS curve. In this case the simple Keynesian model does not overstate the effects of fiscal policy because there is no crowding out of private investment expenditures.

A comparison of the results in this subsection with those in the preceding subsection shows that fiscal policy is most effective when the IS curve is steep (low interest elasticity of investment), while monetary policy is most effective when the IS curve is flat (high interest elasticity of investment). This is due to the different role that the interest rate plays in transmitting the effects of these policy actions. Monetary policy affects income via an effect on interest rates. Consequently, the greater the effect of interest rates on aggregate demand, *ceteris paribus*, the greater will be the effects of a given monetary policy action. In the case of fiscal policy, the interest rate change acts to offset the fiscal policy effects. A larger interest elasticity of investment will mean that more of the expansionary effect of an increase in government spending will be offset by an interest rate–induced decline in investment, and thus the greater will be the "crowding out" effect. Fiscal policy will be more effective, again *ceteris paribus*, the lower the interest elasticity of investment.

Policy Effectiveness and the Slope of the LM Schedule

The slope of the LM schedule has been shown to depend most crucially on the interest elasticity of money demand. A high interest elasticity of money demand will cause the LM schedule to be relatively flat. At progressively lower values of the interest elasticity of money demand, the LM curve will become steeper. If money demand is completely insensitive to the interest rate (interest elasticity is zero), the LM schedule will be vertical. In this section we see how monetary and fiscal policy effectiveness depend on the slope of the LM schedule and, hence, on the interest elasticity of money demand.

Fiscal Policy Effectiveness and the Slope of the LM Schedule

Figure 7.8 illustrates the effects of an increase in government spending for three separate assumptions concerning the slope of the LM schedule. In Figure 7.8*a* the LM schedule is rather flat, in 7.8*b* the schedule is steep, and in 7.8*c* the LM schedule is vertical. In each case the increase in government spending is assumed to shift the IS curve from IS_0 to IS_1. The slope of the IS curve is the same in each graph. The size of the increase in government expenditure is also the same. As can be seen from the graph, the effect on income of this expansionary fiscal policy action is largest when the LM schedule is relatively flat (Figure 7.8*a*) and less for the case where the curve is relatively steep (Figure 7.8*b*). In the extreme case where the LM schedule is vertical, the increase in government spending has no effect on equilibrium income.

Fiscal policy is seen to be most effective when the interest elasticity of money demand is high, making the LM schedule relatively flat. The reason for this result again concerns the effect of the interest rate adjustment on investment following the fiscal policy shift. The increase in government spending causes income to rise. As income rises, the demand for transactions balances increases, and to reequilibrate the money market with an unchanged stock of money requires a rise in the interest rate. The rise in the interest rate must lower the speculative demand for money and cause individuals and corporations to economize on the use of transactions balances. If money demand is highly sensitive to changes in the interest rate, only a small rise in the interest rate will be required to restore equilibrium in the money market. This is the case in Figure 7.8*a*, where the interest rate rises by only a small amount from r_0 to r_1.

Since in this case there is only a small increase in the interest

Figure 7.8 Fiscal Policy Effects and the Slope of the *LM* Schedule

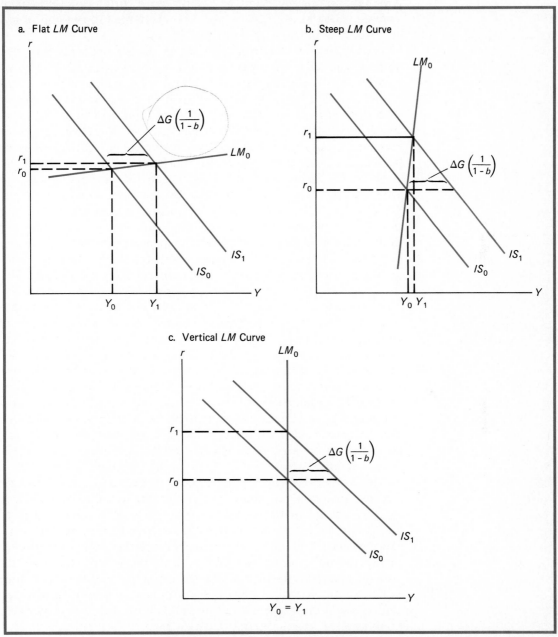

a. Flat *LM* Curve

$\Delta G \left(\dfrac{1}{1-b} \right)$

b. Steep *LM* Curve

$\Delta G \left(\dfrac{1}{1-b} \right)$

c. Vertical *LM* Curve

$\Delta G \left(\dfrac{1}{1-b} \right)$

In each part of the figure an increase in government spending shifts the *IS* schedule to the right from IS_0 to IS_1. Fiscal policy is most effective in Part *a* where the *LM* schedule is relatively flat, less effective in Part *b* where the *LM* curve is steeper, and completely ineffective in Part *c* where the *LM* curve is vertical.

POLICY EFFECTS IN THE IS–LM MODEL

rate, other things being equal, the decline in investment due to the interest rate increase will be small.[2] With little crowding out of private investment, income rises by nearly the full amount of the horizontal shift in the IS curve.

For the case where money demand is relatively interest inelastic (Figure 7.8b), a greater increase in the interest rate (from r_0 to r_1 in Figure 7.8b) is required to reequilibrate the money market as income rises. The larger increase in the interest rate leads to a larger decline in investment spending, offsetting more of the expansionary effect of the increase in government spending. Consequently, the increase in income for the case of the steeper LM curve (Figure 7.8b) is a smaller proportion of the horizontal shift in the IS curve.

If money demand is completely insensitive to changes in the interest rate (Figure 7.8c), only one level of income can be an equilibrium level—the level that generates transactions demand just equal to the fixed money stock. An increase in aggregate demand, caused by an increase in government spending, creates an upward pressure on income at a given interest rate. There is an excess demand for goods (G is higher, C and I are unchanged). However, the attempt to increase income (or a temporary rise in income) leads to an increased demand for transactions balances and causes the interest rate to rise. *Equilibrium* income cannot, in fact, be higher than Y_0, since there is no possible increase in the interest rate that will reequilibrate the money market at a higher level of income. A new equilibrium will be achieved when in the attempt to acquire transaction balances to support a higher income level, an attempt that must fail in the aggregate, individuals bid the interest rate up by enough to return aggregate demand to its initial level. In Figure 7.8c this occurs at interest rate r_1. At that point private investment has declined by an amount just equal to the increase in government spending. Crowding out is complete in this case.

The vertical LM case was referred to above as a "classical" case because the classical economists failed to take account systematically of the dependence of money demand on the interest rate. Implicitly, they assumed that money demand was completely interest inelastic. Notice that in this classical case our fiscal policy results are quite classical in nature, even though in other respects (the relationships underlying the IS curve) the model we are using is Keynesian in nature.[3] An increase in government expenditures affects the interest rate but not the level of income. Crowding out is complete.

At the end of Section 7.1 we saw that for this case of a vertical

---

[2]The primary "other thing" being held equal in this case is the amount by which a given increase in the interest rate will cause investment to decline—the interest elasticity of investment.

[3]The classical analysis of fiscal policy effects is discussed in Section 4.3.

LM curve, an autonomous change in investment demand would also leave income unchanged. The interest rate adjustment would have completely offset the initial drop in investment demand in the case considered there. Again here for changes in the government component of autonomous expenditures, the interest rate adjusts fully, so that total aggregate demand ($C + I + G$) is not affected by the shift.

A necessary element, then, in the Keynesian view that changes in autonomous expenditure resulting from such fiscal policy actions do affect income is the belief that money demand does depend on the rate of interest. This belief follows from considering the role that money plays as an asset, as an alternative store of wealth to bonds. The classical view of money focused simply on its role in transactions, and thus the classical economists were led to neglect the role of the interest rate in determining money demand. It can be seen from the analysis here that Keynes's theory of the relationship between money demand and the interest rate was a crucial part of his theory of how autonomous changes in aggregate demand affected income.

Monetary Policy Effectiveness and the Slope of the LM Schedule

Figure 7.9 shows the effects of an increase in the quantity of money for the same three assumptions about the LM schedule as those considered above. In part a, the LM schedule is relatively flat. In part b the LM curve is steeper, and in part c the schedule is vertical. In each case the increase in the money stock shifts the LM schedule by an equal amount from LM_0 to LM_1; that is, the horizontal shift in the LM schedule equal to $\Delta M/c_1$ is the same in each graph.

As can be seen from the figure, monetary policy is least effective in Figure 7.9a, where the LM schedule is relatively flat (the interest elasticity of money demand is high). The effect on income of the increase in the money stock is successively greater as we consider Figure 7.9b, where the interest elasticity of money demand is lower, and then Figure 7.9c, where the interest elasticity of money demand is zero and the LM curve is vertical.

The reason for this can be seen by comparing the fall in the interest rate that results from the money stock increase in each case. The increase in the money stock will at the initial level of income and the interest rate create an excess supply of money, causing the interest rate to fall. This fall in the interest rate will stimulate investment and, hence, income. The interest rate must decline to a point where the lower interest rate and higher income level have increased money demand by an amount equal to the increase in the money supply. In Figure 7.9a, where money de-

Figure 7.9 Monetary Policy Effects and the Slope of the *LM* Schedule

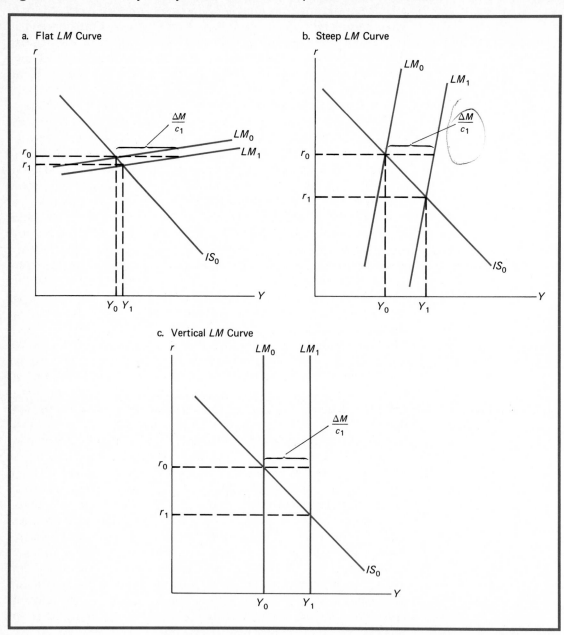

a. Flat *LM* Curve

b. Steep *LM* Curve

c. Vertical *LM* Curve

In each part of the figure an increase in the money stock shifts the *LM* schedule to the right from LM_0 to LM_1. Monetary policy is least effective in Part *a* where the *LM* curve is relatively flat, more effective in Part *b* where the *LM* curve is steeper, and most effective in Part *c* where the *LM* curve is vertical.

MACROECONOMIC MODELS

mand is very interest sensitive, a small drop in the interest rate is all that is required for this purpose. Consequently, the increase in investment and, hence, income will be small in this case. With a highly interest elastic demand for money, as the interest rate falls, individuals substantially increase their speculative balances and economize less on transactions balances. Most of the newly created money is used for these purposes and relatively little ends up as transactions balances required by a higher level of income.

In Figure 7.9*b* the interest elasticity of money demand is lower and a larger fall in the interest rate is required to reequilibrate the money market following the increase in the money stock. As a consequence, investment, and therefore income, increase by a greater amount. In Figure 7.9*c,* where money demand is completely interest inelastic, there is again a fall in the interest rate following an increase in the money supply. Here the fall in the interest rate itself does nothing to increase the demand for money and restore equilibrium in the money market, since in this case money demand does not depend on the interest rate. The fall in the interest rate will, however, cause investment and income to rise. The rise in income will continue until all the new money is absorbed into additional transaction balances. Clearly, this is the maximum possible increase in income for a given increase in the money stock, since all of the new money balances end up as transaction balances required by the higher income level. None of the new money is siphoned off as an increase in speculative demand as the interest rate falls. There is also no tendency for the amount of transactions balances held for a given income level to rise as the interest rate falls.

To summarize, the effect on the level of income of a given increase in the money stock will be greater the lower the interest elasticity of money demand.

As was the case in our discussion of the IS schedule, we find here that the condition which makes monetary policy most effective makes fiscal policy least effective. Monetary policy effectiveness increases as the interest elasticity of money demand is reduced. Fiscal policy is more effective the higher the interest elasticity of money demand. The reason for this difference is again the differing role of the interest rate adjustment in transmitting monetary and fiscal policy effects. For the case of monetary policy, which affects income via an effect on the interest rate, the *greater* the interest rate response, the more effective the policy action will be. As we have just seen, the interest rate response will be greatest when the interest elasticity of money demand is low (i.e., the LM schedule is steep).

For the case of fiscal policy where the interest rate response, with the resulting crowding out of investment, offsets part of the effect of the policy action, the income response will be greater the *smaller* the interest rate response. A high interest elasticity of money demand reduces the effect of a fiscal policy action on the interest rate (compare parts *a* and *b* of Figure 7.8). Therefore, fiscal policy is most effective when the interest elasticity of money demand is high (i.e., the LM schedule is flat).

7.3 SUMMARY

In Section 7.1 we examined the effects of monetary and fiscal policy actions on income and the interest rate assuming that the IS–LM curves had normal slopes, where by "normal slopes" is meant that the slopes of both the IS and LM schedules were in an intermediate range—neither so steep or so flat as to make either monetary or fiscal policy impotent. In Section 7.2 the relationships between the slopes of the IS and LM schedules and the relative effectiveness of monetary and fiscal policies were examined in some detail. The results of that analysis are summarized in Table 7.2.

A relevant question to consider at this point is that of which of the cases in the table actually characterizes the economy. What are the actual slopes of the relationships in our economy that correspond to the model's IS and LM curves? We will see in our later analysis that this question is still subject to dispute. Issues concerning the slopes of the IS and LM schedules form a part of the controversy between the Keynesians and the next group of macroeconomists whose theoretical system we will analyze, the monetarists. There is also some divergence between the positions of some of the earlier Keynesians and current-day Keynesians on the

Table 7.2
Relative Monetary and Fiscal Policy Effectiveness and the Slopes of the IS and LM Curves

	Monetary Policy	
	IS Curve	**LM Curve**
Steep	ineffective	effective
Flat	effective	ineffective

	Fiscal Policy	
	IS Curve	**LM Curve**
Steep	effective	ineffective
Flat	ineffective	effective

issue of the slopes of these schedules. These differences are analyzed below. Here we confine ourselves to the position of the modern-day Keynesians or, as we term them, the neo-Keynesians. The neo-Keynesian view is that both the IS and LM curve slopes are in the intermediate or normal range, where both monetary and fiscal policies are effective in controlling income. Our results in Section 7.1—summarized in Table 7.1—characterize the neo-Keynesian position.

There is one qualification to this view that both types of policy will be effective. This qualification concerns monetary policy, which the neo-Keynesians would *not* expect to be effective in a depression situation such as that experienced by the United States in the 1930s. The neo-Keynesian view of the ineffectiveness of monetary policy in such a situation is illustrated in Figure 7.10. The depression period was characterized by low levels of both interest rates and income—an intersection of the IS and LM schedule at a point such as that shown at Y_0 and r_0 in Figure 7.10.

At such a low level of interest rates the elasticity of money de-

Figure 7.10
Monetary Policy Ineffectiveness in a Depression Situation

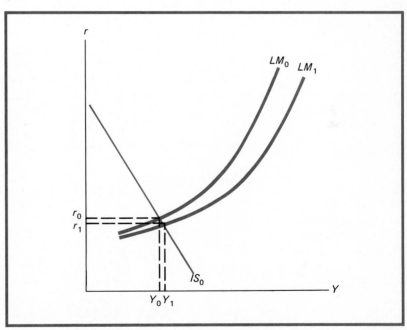

At the low levels of income and the interest rate that would prevail in depression conditions, the neo-Keynesians would expect that the economy would be on the nearly horizontal range of the LM curve and that the IS curve would be very steep. Consequently, monetary policy would be ineffective in this situation.

mand would be expected to be quite high, for reasons discussed in the previous chapter. Such a situation approaches the liquidity-trap case.[4] This high value of the interest elasticity of money demand contributes to the ineffectiveness of the monetary policy. Further, in such depression conditions the neo-Keynesians believe that the IS schedule would be relatively steep; investment would be relatively interest inelastic. A depression is characterized by a low rate of utilization of existing plant and equipment. With such excess capacity, the neo-Keynesians believe it unlikely that investment would respond much to changes in the interest rate.

Overall, because increases in the money stock would not lower the interest rate very much (the LM schedule would be flat) and because investment would be unresponsive to interest rate changes (the IS curve would be steep), the neo-Keynesians do not feel that monetary policy would be effective in depression conditions. This view parallels Keynes's original analysis. It is important to note, however, that this argument applies only to conditions such as those of a depression. It is *only* a qualification to the general neo-Keynesian view that both monetary and fiscal policy are effective in controlling income.

Review Questions

1 Within the IS–LM curve model, show how income and the interest rate are affected by each of the following changes.
a. An increase in government spending.
b. An autonomous decline in investment spending.
c. An increase in taxes.
d. An increase in the money stock.
e. An increase in government spending financed by an equal increase in taxes.
In each case explain briefly why the changes in income and the interest rate occur.

2 What would be the effect within the IS–LM curve model of an autonomous increase in saving which was matched by a drop in consumption, that is, a fall in a in the consumption function?

$$C = a + b(Y - T)$$

[4]At such a low level of the interest rate, the speculative demand curve for money would be quite flat. With a consensus that future interest rate increases were likely, an increase in the money supply would be absorbed with very little fall in the rate of interest.

Which curve would shift? How would income and the interest rate be affected?

3   Explain the relationship between the effectiveness of monetary policy and the interest elasticity of investment. Will monetary policy be more or less effective the higher the interest elasticity of investment demand? Explain. Now explain the relationship between the effectiveness of fiscal policy and the interest elasticity of investment demand. Why do the two relationships differ?

4   Explain the relationship between the effectiveness of monetary policy and the interest elasticity of money demand. Will monetary policy be more or less effective the higher the interest elasticity of money demand? Explain. Now explain the relationship between fiscal policy and the interest elasticity of money demand. Why do the two relationships differ?

5   Suppose we had a case where the interest elasticity of *both* money demand and investment were quite low. Would either monetary or fiscal policy be very effective? How would you interpret such a situation?

6   We saw that the interest rate played a stabilizing role in the classical system, adjusting so that a shock to one component of demand, a decline in autonomous investment for example, would not affect aggregate demand. Does the interest rate perform a similar stabilizing function in the Keynesian model?

7   How do the fiscal policy multipliers in the IS–LM model compare to those from the simple Keynesian model of Chapter 5? Are they larger or smaller? Why?

8   In what sense is the situation where the LM schedule is vertical a "classical case"?

9   Why would Keynesian economists be pessimistic about the ability of monetary policy to stimulate output in a situation such as the Great Depression of the 1930s? In such a depression situation what type of policy would be effective?

Selected Readings

BRANSON, WILLIAM, *Macroeconomic Theory and Policy*. New York: Harper & Row, 1979, Chaps. 4 and 5.

8

The preceding three chapters analyzed the determination of income in the Keynesian system assuming that the price level and the level of the money wage were fixed. With these assumptions in the Keynesian model, output is determined solely by aggregate demand. We have gone this far assuming wages and prices constant not because of the plausibility of that assumption but because the fixed price–fixed wage version of the Keynesian system highlights the role of aggregate demand. This theory of aggregate demand was Keynes's central contribution. The demand-determined nature of output in this fixed price–fixed wage Keynesian model stands in sharp contrast to the supply-determined nature of output in the classical system. In this chapter we examine the Keynesian system when prices and wages are not held constant and see that supply factors as well as demand factors play a role in determining output. In this sense the models considered in this chapter are a synthesis of the classical and Keynesian systems. We will see, however, that the key feature in the Keynesian system continues to be the fact that aggregate demand is a factor (here not the only factor) determining aggregate output.

We proceed as follows. In Section 8.1 we illustrate the demand-determined nature of output (income) in the Keynesian system. Here we construct a Keynesian aggregate demand curve. In Section 8.2 this Keynesian aggregate demand curve is put together

THE KEYNESIAN SYSTEM (IV): AGGREGATE SUPPLY

with the classical supply side to form a model of price and output determination. It will be seen that as long as we retain the classical assumptions of perfect information in the labor market and perfect price and wage flexibility,[1] the substitution of the Keynesian aggregate demand curve does not change the classical nature of the model. As long as the supply curve remains vertical, as it does if the foregoing labor market assumptions are made, aggregate output will be determined independently of the assumptions made about the demand side of the model. For aggregate demand to play a role in output determination, which means for the model to be a Keynesian model, the classical labor market assumptions of perfect information and perfect wage and price flexibility must be modified.

The alternative Keynesian assumptions about the supply side of the economy are analyzed in Sections 8.3 and 8.4. In these sections we develop the Keynesian aggregate supply function. In Section 8.5 we see how shifts in this aggregate supply function play a role in determining price and output in the Keynesian model. Section 8.6 considers the policy implications of such supply shocks. The final section of the chapter compares the classical and Keynesian systems.

[1]See Section 3.5.

8.1 THE KEYNESIAN AGGREGATE DEMAND CURVE

The simple model of Chapter 5 presented Keynes's theory of the aggregate demand for output. The essential notion embodied in the simple Keynesian model was that for a level of output to be an equilibrium level, aggregate demand must just equal output. In Chapters 6 and 7 the effect of the interest rate on investment, and hence on aggregate demand, was considered. There it was shown that for an output (Y) and interest rate (r) combination to be an equilibrium point, output must equal aggregate demand and it must also be true that money demand equals money supply.

What guarantees that this level of output will also be equal to aggregate supply—equal to the amount the business sector will choose to produce? No supply considerations were included in these versions of the Keynesian model. We were able to ignore the supply side due to the assumption that the price level and the level of the money wage were fixed. The assumption we were implicitly making about the aggregate supply curve of output is depicted graphically in Figure 8.1. We were assuming that any level of output demanded would be forthcoming at the given price level. Supply was assumed to be no constraint on the level of output.

Such an assumption could be a plausible approximation of conditions where the levels of output being considered are far below the capacity of the economy. In these conditions, for example during the depression of the 1930s, increases in output might not put upward pressure on the level of the money wage, given the high level of unemployment. Also, the marginal productivity of labor (MPN) might not fall as more labor is employed when we begin at a low level of employment (see Figure 3.1). As a consequence, the cost of producing additional units of output $\left(\dfrac{W}{\text{MPN}} \right)$ might be expected to remain constant even with increases in output. In more normal conditions, an increase in output would be expected to put upward pressure on both the wage and price levels. We would expect the supply curve to be upward sloping.

In this more general case of the upward-sloping aggregate supply curve, we cannot assume that price is given (supply is no constraint) and simply determine output by determining aggregate demand. Output and price will be jointly determined by supply and demand factors. The Keynesian aggregate supply curve will be discussed below (Sections 8.3 and 8.4). Here we construct the Keynesian aggregate demand curve, the relationship between ag-

Figure 8.1
Aggregate Supply
Curve in the Fixed-
Price Keynesian Model

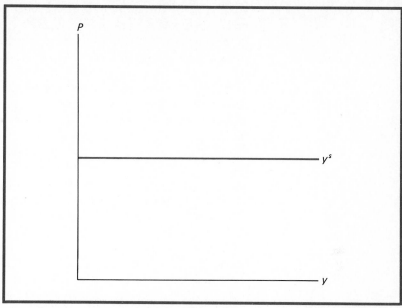

In previous chapters on the Keynesian model where we assumed the price level was fixed and output was determined by aggregate demand, we were implicitly assuming that the aggregate supply curve was horizontal. Supply was no constraint on the level of output.

gregate demand and the price level implied by the Keynesian model.

The factors that determine aggregate demand in the Keynesian system have been analyzed in detail. These are the factors that determine the positions of the IS and LM curves and, therefore, the income–interest rate combination that equilibrates the money market and causes output to equal aggregate demand. In constructing an aggregate demand schedule we want to find the level of output demanded for each price level. To do this we need to examine how the position of the IS and LM schedules and consequently the level of interest rate and output, *which must be considered output demanded*, are affected by price changes.

The condition of equilibrium along the IS schedule is

$$i(r) + g = s(y) + t \qquad (8.1)$$

where i = investment
$\quad g$ = government spending
$\quad s$ = saving
$\quad t$ = taxes
$\quad y$ = output

AGGREGATE SUPPLY

Here we return to the notation used in Chapters 3 and 4, where lowercase letters were used to denote real (constant dollars) magnitudes with capital letters used for the corresponding nominal (current dollar) magnitudes. To see how the price level influences the position of the IS schedule, consider how each of the variables in (8.1) is affected by price changes.

Two of the variables, government spending (g) and the level of taxes (t), are assumed to be fixed by the government in *real terms;* that is, we have been and will continue to assume that their real levels are unaffected by price changes. The level of investment is also assumed to be determined in real terms—a given interest rate determines a level of real investment. Changes in the price level do not directly affect investment. Changes in the price level may affect investment indirectly if they affect the interest rate, but for a given interest rate there will be no effect on real investment.

Similarly, *real* saving is assumed to depend on real income and is not directly affected by changes in the price level. Since none of the four terms in (8.1), the IS curve equilibrium condition, depends directly on the price level, a change in the price level does not shift the IS curve.

What about the LM schedule? The equilibrium condition for the money market, the LM schedule equation, is

$$m = \frac{M}{P} = L(y, r) \tag{8.2}$$

The condition equates the real stock of money $\left(m = \dfrac{M}{P}\right)$ with the demand for money in real terms (demand for real money balances). The real money stock is equal to the exogenously fixed *nominal* money stock divided by the price level.

The Keynesian theory of the demand for money considered in Chapter 6 related the demand for money in *real* terms to the level of *real* income and to the interest rate, although as long as prices were held constant there was no need to distinguish between changes in real and nominal values. People wish to hold a certain amount of real money balances for a given volume of transactions measured in real (constant dollar) terms, where the level of real income is a proxy for the real volume of transactions. Consequently, equilibrium in the money market occurs when the demand for real money balances is just equal to the real money stock. It is the nominal money stock, however, which can be exogenously fixed by the monetary authority—not the real money stock. Any change in the price level will affect the real money stock and consequently shift the LM schedule.

Figure 8.2*a* illustrates this effect of the price level on the position of the LM schedule. Three price levels are considered, where

Figure 8.2

Construction of the
Aggregate Demand
Schedule

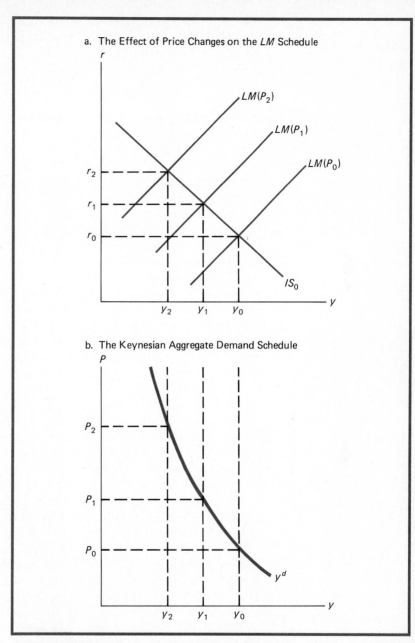

a. The Effect of Price Changes on the *LM* Schedule

b. The Keynesian Aggregate Demand Schedule

At successively higher price levels P_0, P_1, P_2 the *LM* schedule in Part *a* is shifted further to the left. This results in successively lower levels of aggregate demand y_0, y_1, y_2. These combinations of price and aggregate demand are plotted to give the negatively sloped aggregate demand schedule in part *b*.

$P_2 > P_1 > P_0$. Notice that as we consider the effect of a price increase from P_0 to P_1, then from P_1 to P_2, at the higher price level the LM schedule is shifted to the left. The effect of a higher price level is the same as that of a fall in the nominal stock of money; both reduce the real money stock $\left(\dfrac{M}{P} = m \right)$. The LM schedule shifts to the left, raising the interest rate and lowering investment and aggregate demand.

In Figure 8.2b we plot the level of the aggregate demand for output corresponding to each of the three price levels considered. This schedule labeled y^d is our aggregate demand schedule. It gives the level of output demanded at each price level. As can be seen from the construction of the aggregate demand curve, this level of output demanded is the equilibrium output level from the IS–LM curve model, the output level which for a given price level just equates output and aggregate demand while simultaneously clearing the money market.

The aggregate demand curve reflects monetary influences (factors that affect the LM schedule) as well as direct influences on aggregate demand (factors affecting the IS schedule). Factors that increase the level of equilibrium income in the IS–LM curve model (increase the level of output demanded at a given price level) will shift the aggregate demand curve to the right. Factors that cause equilibrium income to decline in the IS–LM curve framework will shift the aggregate demand schedule to the left.

Consider, for example, the effect of an increase in the money stock as shown in Figure 8.3. From an initial position LM_0 (P_0) the increase in the money stock will shift the LM schedule to LM_1 (P_0) as shown in Figure 8.3a. Equilibrium income for a given price level, P_0 in the figure, would increase from y_0 to y_1. The aggregate demand curve shown in Figure 8.3b would shift to the right, from y_0^d to y_1^d.[2] Notice that the distance of horizontal shift in the aggregate demand curve is $(y_1 - y_0)$, the amount of the increase in equilibrium income in the IS–LM curve model. This is the increase in income and aggregate demand that results *at a given price level.* Similarly, changes in government expenditures or taxes which shift the IS schedule will shift the aggregate demand schedule such that the distance of the horizontal shift in the curve will equal the amount of the change in equilibrium income from the IS–LM curve model—the amount of the change in aggregate demand for a given price level.

---

[2]For simplicity, the Keynesian aggregate demand curve here and in later graphs is drawn as a straight line rather than the actual nonlinear curve in Figure 8.2. The exact curvature of the aggregate demand curve is not important for our analysis.

Figure 8.3

Effect on Aggregate
Demand of an
Increase in the Money
Stock

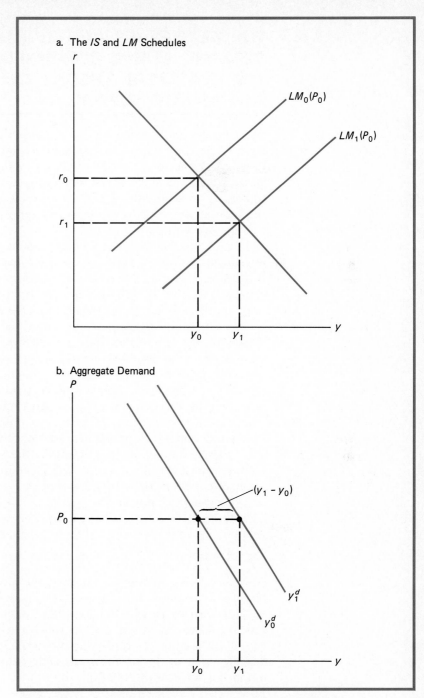

a. The *IS* and *LM* Schedules

b. Aggregate Demand

An increase in the money stock shifts the LM schedule in Part *a* to the right
from $LM_0(P_0)$ to $LM_1(P_0)$ and shifts the aggregate demand schedule to the
right from y_0^d to y_1^d in Part *b*.

8.2 THE KEYNESIAN AGGREGATE DEMAND CURVE COMBINED WITH THE CLASSICAL THEORY OF AGGREGATE SUPPLY

When prices and wages are not assumed constant, knowing the effects of policy actions on demand is not enough to determine their effects on income. The effect on income will depend on the assumptions we make about aggregate supply. This is illustrated in Figure 8.4, where the effect of an increase in government spending is compared for three different assumptions about the shape of the aggregate supply function.

In each case the increase in government expenditures shifts the aggregate demand schedule to the right, from y_0^d to y_1^d in Figure 8.4. If the supply curve is given by y_2^s, a horizontal schedule, then output increases by the full amount of the horizontal shift in the aggregate demand schedule. Recall from Section 8.1 that this is the increase in equilibrium income from the IS–LM curve model which implicitly assumed that the supply curve was horizontal. If the supply curve is upward sloping (y_1^s), prices will rise and the increase in income will be less, $y_1 - y_0$ compared with $y_2 - y_0$ in Figure 8.4. If the supply curve were vertical (y_0^s in Figure 8.4), there would be no increase in income even though aggregate demand increased. Clearly, then, the effects of policy changes on income will depend on the assumption made concerning aggregate supply. In this section we consider the implications of making the "classical" assumptions about supply while maintaining the Keynesian apparatus behind the aggregate demand schedule.

The classical analysis of aggregate supply was explained in Chapter 3. The central elements of this analysis are illustrated graphically in Figure 8.5. In the labor market both labor supply and demand depend solely on the real wage $\left(\dfrac{W}{P}\right)$, which is as-

sumed to be known to all. Further, the labor market is assumed always to be in equilibrium with the perfectly flexible money wage, adjusting to equate supply and demand. The labor market has the characteristics of an "auction" market. The equilibrium in the labor market is graphed in Figure 8.5a. As shown in Figure 8.5b, for a given level of employment output will be determined along the production function, the relationship giving the output produced by each amount of labor, given the fixed capital stock.

As explained in Chapter 3, since a change in the price level will not shift the labor supply curve, labor demand curve, or production function, the classical assumptions result in a vertical aggre-

MACROECONOMIC MODELS

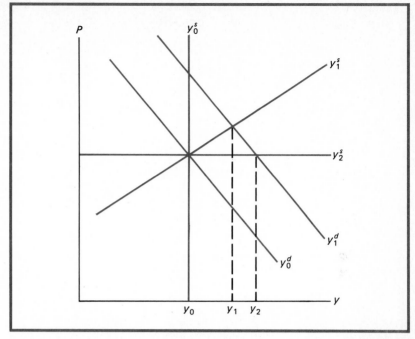

An increase in government spending shifts the aggregate demand curve
from y_0^d to y_1^d. If the aggregate supply curve is horizontal (y_2^s) output increases from y_0 to y_2. If the aggregate supply curve slopes upward to the
right (y_1^s) output increases only to y_1. If the supply curve is vertical (y_0^s)
output is unchanged at y_0.

gate supply curve (Section 3.5). With the classical assumptions
concerning the supply side, the aggregate supply curve would be
given by y_0^s in Figure 8.4; output would be completely supply determined. Factors such as changes in government spending, taxes,
and the money stock which shift the demand schedule would not
affect the equilibrium income. This is the case even though the
Keynesian theory of aggregate demand is used to construct the
aggregate demand curve, for with the classical supply assumptions the form of the aggregate demand curve is irrelevant for income determination.

The effect of a shift in the aggregate demand curve resulting
from a change in the level of government expenditures is illustrated in Figure 8.6 for this case where the classical labor market
assumptions are made. The increase in government spending
shifts the IS schedule from IS_0 to IS_1 in Figure 8.6a and shifts the
aggregate demand curve from y_0^d to y_1^d in Figure 8.6b. If prices were
fixed, output would increase to the level given by y_1' in both figures.
Prices will not, however, remain constant. As can be seen in Figure

Figure 8.5
Classical Supply
Assumptions

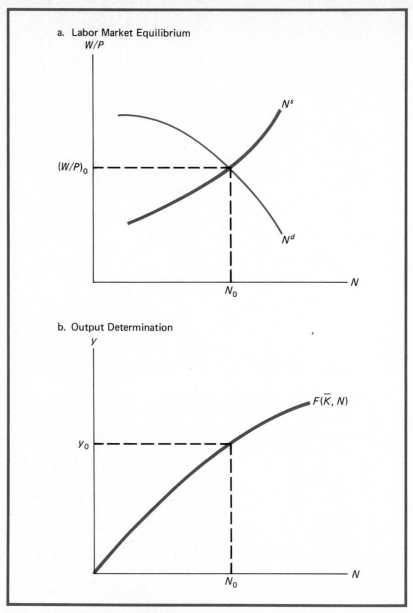

a. Labor Market Equilibrium

b. Output Determination

In the classical model, employment (N_0) is determined at the point where labor supply and demand, both as functions of the real wage, are equated (Part *a*). Equilibrium output (y_0) can then be determined using the production function relationship (Part *b*).

Figure 8.6
Effect of an Increase
in Government
Expenditures With
Classical Assumptions
About the Labor
Market

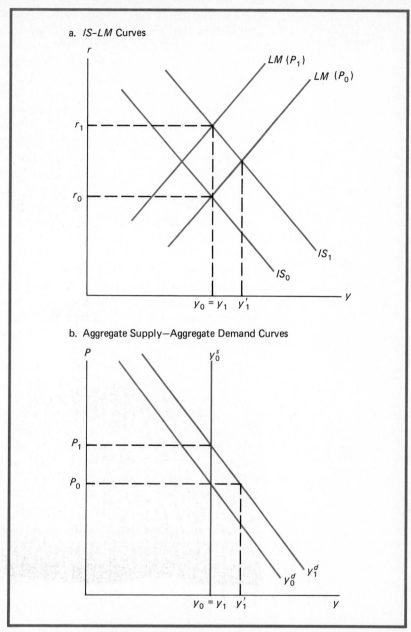

a. *IS-LM* Curves

b. Aggregate Supply—Aggregate Demand Curves

An increase in government expenditures shifts the *IS* schedule to the right from IS_0 to IS_1 (Part *a*) and shifts the aggregate demand schedule to the right from y_0^d to y_1^d (Part *b*). In the classical case the aggregate supply curve (y_0^s) is vertical. The increase in aggregate demand causes the price level to rise from P_0 to P_1 but the level of output is unchanged at y_0. The increase in the price level shifts the *LM* schedule in part a from $LM(P_0)$ to $LM(P_1)$.

8.6*b*, at the initial price level of P_0, aggregate demand exceeds supply. Prices will rise to the level P_1, where demand is reduced just back to the initial level y_0. The increase in prices will lower the real money stock (from M/P_0 to M/P_1). This will shift the LM schedule from LM (P_0) to LM (P_1) in Figure 8.6*a*.

It is worth stopping here to consider why prices must rise by an amount just sufficient to shift the LM schedule in Figure 8.6*a* to a point where it intersects the IS_1 schedule at the initial income level (y_0). The price level must increase until demand returns to the initial level y_0. As we saw in constructing the aggregate demand schedule, increases in the price level lower the real money stock $\left(\dfrac{M}{P}\right)$, which in turn pushes up the interest rate and lowers investment. With the classical vertical supply curve, prices must rise until interest rates have been pushed up and investment has declined by just enough to restore equilibrium at y_0. This occurs when the LM schedule has shifted to the left by just enough to intersect the new IS schedule IS_1 at the original income level.

From the analysis of this section it can be seen that *the classical theory of aggregate supply based on the classical "auction market" characterization of the labor market is fundamentally incompatible with the Keynesian system.* The central feature of Keynesian analysis is the theory of aggregate demand and the influence of aggregate demand on output and employment. With the classical assumptions about aggregate supply, leading to the vertical supply curve, there is *no* role for aggregate demand in the determination of output and employment. It was therefore necessary for Keynes and his followers, in addition to developing a theory of aggregate demand, to attack the classical supply assumptions and develop a Keynesian theory of the supply side. This Keynesian theory of aggregate supply is the subject of the next two sections.

8.3 THE KEYNESIAN MODEL WITH A FLEXIBLE PRICE LEVEL AND A FIXED MONEY WAGE

Keynes believed that the money wage would not adjust sufficiently in the short run to keep the economy at full employment. In the classical system both labor supply and demand were functions of the real wage and, as we saw (Figure 8.5), the intersection of the labor supply and demand curves determined an equilibrium real wage and level of employment. Wage bargains are, however, set in terms of money wages and one assumption crucial to the classical model is that the money wage was perfectly flexible. Adjustments in the money wage were required to equate labor supply and labor demand—to keep the economy at full employment.

The Keynesian view of why money wages would not continually adjust to keep the economy at full employment is dealt with in the next section. Here we will simply assume that while prices are perfectly flexible, the money wage is fixed. The purpose of this analysis is to show that within the Keynesian system rigidity of the money wage will result in the possibility of unemployment. Further, if the money wage is rigid, both monetary and fiscal policies will affect output and employment. If the money wage is rigid, aggregate demand will play a role in the determination of output. Analysis of the variable price–fixed wage version of the Keynesian system also serves as a prelude to consideration of the model in the next section, when both the money wage and the price level are allowed to vary.

Keynes's concern was with the downward rigidity of the money wage—the failure of the money wage to fall sufficiently to restore full employment when the demand for labor was less than supply. If the demand for labor were to exceed supply, he would have expected money wages to rise quickly. Thus the only situations to which we would want to apply the fixed-wage model are those where there is unemployment, an excess supply of labor.

With the money wage fixed and labor supply greater than labor demand, the actual level of employment will be determined by demand. Firms will be able to hire the amount of labor they demand at the going wage and are not forced to hire more. Keynes did not object to the classical theory of labor demand. According to this theory, as explained in Chapter 3, the profit-maximizing firm demands labor up to the point where the real wage $\left(\dfrac{W}{P}\right)$ is equal to the marginal productivity of labor (MPN) or equivalently to the point where

$$W = \mathrm{MPN} \cdot P \qquad (8.3)$$

the money wage paid to labor is just equal to the money value of the marginal product (the marginal revenue product) of labor. Since with an excess supply of labor and a fixed money wage, employment depends only on labor demand, the determination of employment is as depicted in Figure 8.7. At a fixed money wage $\bar{W}$, labor demand and, therefore, employment will be N_0.

Notice that the labor demand schedule, the schedule giving the money value of the marginal product of labor corresponding to each level of employment (the $\mathrm{MPN} \cdot P_0$ schedule in Figure 8.7), depends on the price level. The number of workers firms will hire, and as a consequence the amount of output they will supply, will

Figure 8.7
Employment With a
Fixed Money Wage

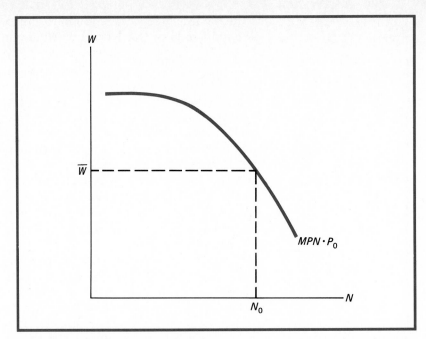

With the money wage fixed at $\overline{W}$, employment will be at N_0, the amount of labor demanded.

depend on the price level. This relationship between output supplied and the price level is developed in Figure 8.8.

Figure 8.8a shows the level of employment that will result at three successively higher price levels, P_0, P_1, and P_2, with the money wage fixed at $\overline{W}$. An increase in the price level (from P_0 to P_1, then from P_1 to P_2) will increase the money value of the marginal product of labor corresponding to any level of employment and therefore increase labor demand for a given money wage. The labor demand ($MPN \cdot P$) schedule shifts to the right and employment increases. As employment increases, output is shown to rise in Figure 8.8b, where we have plotted the aggregate production function giving the level of output for each level of employment.

Figure 8.8c combines the information from Figures 8.8a and 8.8b to show for each price level the resulting level of output supplied. Higher price levels result in higher levels of supply; the aggregate supply function is upward sloping. This is the same relationship as for the classical model with rigid wages (Section 4.4). Until the supply side of the labor market is considered, Keynes had no quarrel with the classical supply analysis. As in the classical model, one would expect that at some level of income (y_f in Figure 8.8c), full employment would have been reached and further in-

206

Figure 8.8 Derivation of the Keynesian Aggregate Supply Curve When the Money Wage Is Fixed

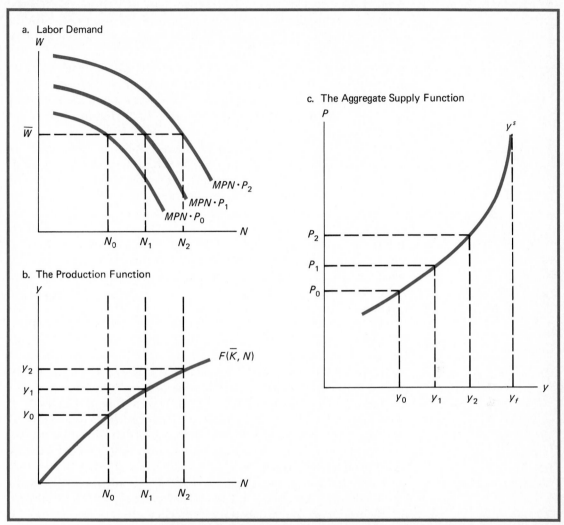

a. Labor Demand

b. The Production Function

c. The Aggregate Supply Function

Part *a* shows the levels of employment, N_0, N_1, N_2, for three successively higher price levels P_0, P_1, P_2. Part *b* shows the levels of output, y_0, y_1, y_2, which will be produced at these three levels of employment. In Part *c* we put together the information in Parts *a* and *b* to show the level of output supplied at each of the three price levels. Notice that at higher price levels, employment and, hence, output supplied increases—*the aggregate supply curve (y^s) is upward sloping.*

creases in price would lead to an excess demand for labor and upward pressure on money wages. Money wages are not assumed to be rigid upward, so once full employment is reached, money wages can be assumed to rise proportionately with prices, with no effect on output. The aggregate supply curve becomes vertical at this full-employment level.

Below full employment the supply curve will not be vertical; shifts in the aggregate demand curve will change the level of output. The effects of an increase in the money stock and the effects of an increase in government spending are illustrated in Figures 8.9 and 8.10, respectively.

In Figure 8.9a an increase in the money stock is shown to shift the LM schedule from LM_0 (P_0) to the schedule marked LM_1 (P_0). This is the shift in the LM curve as a direct result of the change in the money stock. This increase in the money stock shifts the aggregate demand schedule to the right in Figure 8.9b, from y_0^d to y_1^d. At the initial price level P_0, output would be increased to y_1', as shown in Figure 8.9. But for output supplied to increase, prices must rise and the new equilibrium is reached not at y_1' but at y_1, where the price level has risen to P_1. The rise in price shifts the LM schedule in Figure 8.9a to LM_1 (P_1).

Thus we find the same type of Keynesian results from an increase in money stock as we did for the fixed-price IS–LM curve model in Chapter 7. Output and employment will rise and the interest rate will fall, from r_0 to r_1 in Figure 8.9a. When the price level is allowed to vary, the increase in output will be less than when the price level is fixed. Output rises to y_1 instead of y_1'. This is because the increase in the price level reduces the real money stock (M/P), which *partially* offsets the effects of the increase in the nominal quantity of money. The interest rate falls only to r_1, not to r_1'. As a consequence, this expansionary monetary policy action has a smaller effect on investment and, hence, on output.

The situation is much the same with fiscal policy effects. Again the results are Keynesian in that fiscal policy does affect output, but again the effect of a given policy action will be smaller in magnitude when the price level is variable than for the case where we assumed that the price level was fixed. The effects of an increase in government spending are illustrated in Figure 8.10.

An increase in government spending shifts the IS curve from IS_0 to IS_1 in Figure 8.10a. The increase in government spending has no direct effect on the LM schedule, which is initially given by $LM_0(P_0)$. The increase in aggregate demand as the IS curve shifts right is reflected in Figure 8.9b in the shift of the aggregate demand curve from y_0^d to y_1^d. Output increases to y_1 and the price level rises to P_1. The increase in the price level decreases the real money stock (M/P), causing the LM schedule to shift from $LM_0(P_0)$ to

Figure 8.9
Effects of an Increase in the Money Stock When the Price Level Is Flexible

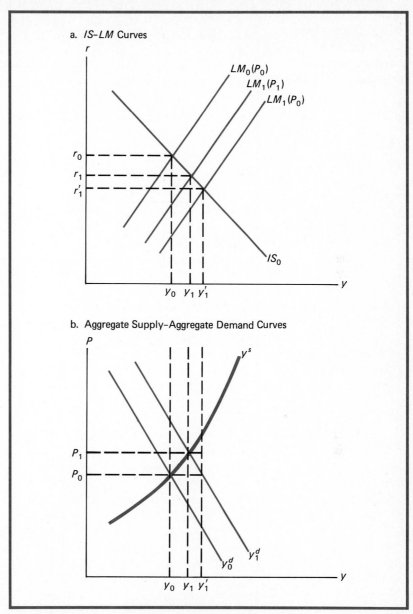

a. *IS–LM* Curves

b. Aggregate Supply–Aggregate Demand Curves

An increase in the money stock shifts the *LM* schedule to the right from $LM_0(P_0)$ to $LM_1(P_0)$ (Part *a*) and shifts the aggregate demand curve to the right from y_0^d to y_1^d (Part *b*). The increase in aggregate demand causes output to rise from y_0 to y_1 and the price level to rise from P_0 to P_1. The increase in the price level shifts the *LM* schedule from $LM_1(P_0)$ to $LM_1(P_1)$.

Figure 8.10
Effects of an Increase
in Government
Spending When the
Price Level Is Flexible

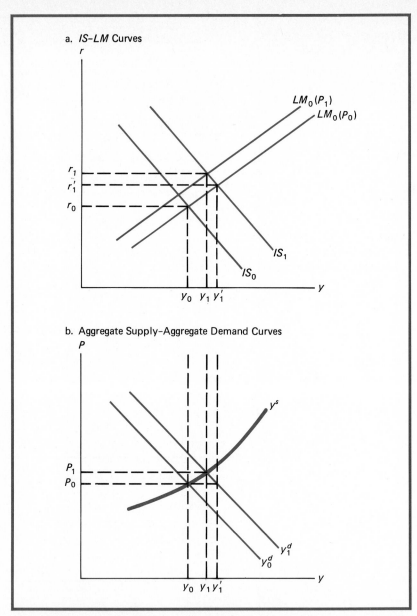

a. *IS–LM* Curves

b. Aggregate Supply–Aggregate Demand Curves

An increase in government spending shifts the *IS* curve from IS_0 to IS_1 (Part
a) and shifts the aggregate demand curve from y_0^d to y_1^d (Part *b*). The increase in aggregate demand causes output to rise from y_0 to y_1 and the
price level to rise from P_0 to P_1. The increase in the price level shifts the *LM*
schedule from $LM_0(P_0)$ to $LM_0(P_1)$.

MACROECONOMIC MODELS

$LM_0(P_1)$ in Figure 8.10a. Output rises only to y_1, not to y_1', the increase in output that would have occurred had the price level remained fixed.

8.4 LABOR SUPPLY AND VARIABILITY IN THE MONEY WAGE

In this section we bring the supply side of the labor market into the picture. We examine the differences in the Keynesian and classical views of labor supply and then examine a version of the Keynesian model where both the aggregate price level and the money wage are allowed to vary.

The Classical and Keynesian Theories of Labor Supply

The classical economists believed that the supply of labor depended positively on the real wage,

$$N^s = g\left(\frac{W}{P}\right) \tag{8.4}$$

The reasoning behind this formulation was that individuals maximized utility, which depended positively on real income and on leisure. A rise in the real wage increased the income that could be gained from an hour's labor or, looked at in reverse, increased the opportunity cost of taking one hour of leisure. Consequently, an increase in the real wage was assumed to increase labor supply.[3] Suppliers of labor were assumed to know the real wage, and a perfectly flexible money wage was assumed to adjust to bring the supply of labor and demand for labor into equality.

The Keynesian theory of labor supply begins with the observation that the wage bargain is struck in terms of the money wage, not the real wage. The Keynesian theory offers a number of reasons why the money wage will not quickly adjust (especially in the downward direction) to maintain equilibrium in the labor market. The following factors are among those which have been offered by Keynesian economists as explanations for the "rigidity" of money wages.

1. The first explanation is one due to Keynes. He argued that workers are interested in their relative as well as their absolute wage. There exists in any labor market a set of wage differentials between workers with different trades and skills. Much of the work of wage bargaining is to arrive at a relative wage structure accept-

[3]As explained in Section 3.4, the increase in the real wage will increase labor supply only if the "substitution effect" (leisure is now more expensive in terms of income forgone) outweighs the "income effect" (with a higher income level leisure may be more desirable and workers may choose to supply less labor). We continue here to assume that the substitution effect dominates.

able to labor and management. Wage differentials can be measured by relative money wages, since price-level changes affect all wages symmetrically.

Keynes believed that one reason workers would resist money wage cuts even as the demand for labor fell was that they would see the wage cuts as eliminating existing wage differentials, as "unfair" changes in the structure of relative wages. Workers in one firm or industry would see changes in money wages as changes in relative wages because they would have no assurance that if they accepted a cut in money wages, workers in other sectors of the labor market would do the same. Notice that a decline in the real wage due to a rise in prices would not be seen by labor as affecting the structure of relative wages. Because of this Keynes believed that declines in real wages due to price-level increases would meet much less resistance from labor than an equivalent fall in the real wage from a money wage cut.

2. The next factor leading to stickiness in the money wage level is a more purely institutional one. In the unionized sector of the labor market wages are set by long-term labor contracts, most often of two or three years' duration. Such contracts typically fix the money wage levels for the life of the contract. The money wage will not respond to events, such as a decline in labor demand, over the life of the contract. Indexation of the money wage set in the contract (i.e., provisions that tie changes in the money wage to changes in the price level) provides some flexibility in the money wage over the length of the contract. In the United States, however, where there is any indexation of labor contracts it is generally incomplete. Thus fixed-money-wage contracts impart stickiness to the money wage.

Once such a labor contract is signed, the decision of how much labor to hire is left to the employer. A labor supply curve such as the classical labor supply function in Figure 8.5 no longer plays any role in determining employment. The firm hires the profit-maximizing amount of labor at the fixed real wage. This is the characterization of the labor market in the preceding section.

3. Even in segments of the labor market where there is no explicit contract fixing the money wage, there is often an implicit agreement between employer and employee that fixes the money wage over some time period. In particular, such implicit contracts keep employers from cutting money wages in the face of a fall in the demand for their products and consequent decline in labor demand. The incentive for employers to refrain from attempting to achieve such wage cuts, or alternatively from hiring workers from among the pool of the unemployed who might be willing to work for a lower wage, is their desire to maintain a reputation as a "good employer." Firms might achieve a temporary gain by a re-

duction in labor costs by forcing a money wage cut, but this could be more than counterbalanced by the effect of poor labor relations with existing employees and difficulties in recruiting new employees. Keynesians believe that the "conventions" of the U.S. labor markets are such that firms find it in their interest to cut the length of the workweek or have temporary layoffs of workers in response to falls in demand rather than to seek money wage cuts.

These Keynesian observations about the supply side of the labor market provide explanations for downward rigidity in the money wage. These observations are justifications for the type of model used in the preceding section, which assumed the money wage to be fixed. A fixed money wage is an extreme version of a sticky wage and Keynesian economists certainly do not believe that the money wage is completely rigid even in the short run. Still, if the response of the money wage to unemployment is small and slow to materialize, results based on the assumption of a fixed money wage will be approximately correct for the short run. They will certainly be closer to reality than results based on the classical assumption that the money wage moves instantaneously to clear the labor market.

In addition to the foregoing explanations of why the money wage will not move instantaneously to keep the labor market in equilibrium, the Keynesians have another objection to the classical view of the supply side of the labor market. The classical theory assumes that the supplier of labor knows the real wage. The Keynesians argue that since the labor bargain is in terms of the money wage, we can assume that the worker knows the money wage but not the price level. As explained above, through implicit or explicit contracts, the worker agrees to provide labor services over some period, let us say for a year. He has no way of knowing the value that the aggregate price level will take on over the coming year. It is this aggregate price level that will determine the purchasing power of any money wage he agrees to in a current wage bargain. As a consequence, the Keynesians believe that decisions about labor supply depend on the current money wage and the *expectation* of the aggregate price level. Further, the Keynesian view has been that workers' expectations about the price level depend for the most part on the past behavior of prices.

To see the implications of the Keynesian view of the worker bargaining for a known money wage with only imperfect information about the behavior of prices, we will construct a Keynesian labor supply curve, which we can then compare with the classical labor supply curve [equation (8.4)]. We will then consider a model where the money wage is perfectly flexible, but labor supply is given by the Keynesian version of the labor supply function. In this analysis we will be neglecting the factors enumerated above, which the

Keynesians believe cause the money wage to be sticky. The purpose of this analysis is to show that *even if the money wage were perfectly flexible*, with the Keynesian version of the labor supply curve, the aggregate supply curve would not be vertical. Output and employment would not be completely supply determined; aggregate demand would also play a role. In reality the Keynesians believe that the money wage *is* sticky in the downward direction and much of the unemployment we observe is the result of the failure of the money wage to clear the labor market. Imperfect information about prices is, however, an important additional factor which the Keynesians believe explains fluctuations in output and employment.

The Keynesian labor supply function can be written as follows:

$$N^s = t\left(\frac{W}{P^e}\right) \tag{8.5}$$

where W is the money wage, an increase in which would be expected to result in an increase in the quantity of labor supplied. An increase in the money wage for a given value of the expected price level (P^e) would increase labor supply, since it would be viewed by workers as an increase in the real wage. An increase in the expected price level will cause labor supply to decline. Fundamentally, the worker is assumed to be interested in the real wage, not the money wage, and he reduces his supply of labor when he perceives that real wage has declined. The difference between the Keynesian and classical labor supply functions is that in the Keynesian version the worker must form an expectation of the price level. Labor supply therefore depends on the *expected* real wage. In the classical system workers know the real wage. Labor supply depends on the *actual* real wage.

The Keynesian theory of labor supply is incomplete without an assumption about the way in which workers form an expectation of the price level (P^e). The Keynesian assumption is that such price expectations are based primarily on the past behavior of the price level, adjusting only slowly over time. Thus

$$P^e = a_1 P_{-1} + a_2 P_{-2} + a_3 P_{-3} + \cdots + a_n P_{-n} \tag{8.6}$$

where P_{-i} ($i = 1, 2, 3, \ldots$) is the price level from i periods back and the $a_1, a_2, \ldots, a_n$ are the weights given to a number of past observations on the price level in forming the expectation of the current period value of the price level. Clearly, there is additional information that might prove useful in accurately predicting the behavior of prices. The Keynesian assumption is that the cost of gathering and processing such additional information is high enough so that the price expectations of labor suppliers are reasonably accurately represented by a simple formulation such as (8.6). As we will see in later chapters, this assumption has not gone unchallenged.

If expectations about the price level for the current period are assumed simply to adjust slowly to the past behavior of prices, then we are assuming that they do not change as a result of current economic conditions. In analyzing the effects of various policy changes, for example, we can take P^e as constant. In the longer run (after many short periods have passed) we will need to take account of how stabilization policies affect P^e, because such policies will have affected actual price levels from past periods.

The Keynesian Aggregate Supply Curve with a Variable Money Wage

Figure 8.11 illustrates the construction of the aggregate supply curve, where labor supply is given by (8.5) and the money wage is assumed to adjust to equate labor supply and labor demand. In Figure 8.11a labor supply (N^s) and labor demand are plotted as functions of the money wage. As in previous analysis, labor demand is assumed to depend on the real wage and firms are assumed to know the price level at which they will be able to sell their individual products. The labor demand curve will shift to the right with an increase in the price level. In Figure 8.11a we show labor demand curves for three successively higher price levels, P_0, P_1, and P_2, respectively.

The labor supply curve is drawn for a given value of the *expected* aggregate price level. As explained above, this expected price level is assumed to be fixed in the short run. With the fixed labor supply curve, increases in the price level shift the labor demand curve along the supply curve, with the result that for a higher price level the equilibrium levels of employment and the money wage are increased. The process at work here is as follows. The increase in price (from P_0 to P_1, for example) causes an excess demand for labor at the old money wage (W_0). The money wage is bid up and for a given value of P^e an increase in the money wage causes more workers to accept jobs (or increase hours worked in existing jobs); employment rises.

At the higher levels of employment N_1 and N_2, corresponding to the higher price levels P_1 and P_2, output will be correspondingly higher at the levels shown by y_1 and y_2 in Figure 8.11b. Thus a higher price level corresponds to a higher level of output supplied. This information is reflected in the upward-sloping aggregate supply curve, plotting output supplied for each price level (points such as P_0, y_0; P_1, y_1; and P_2, y_2). This is the Keynesian aggregate supply function, with the assumption that the money wage is variable.

Policy Effects in the Variable-Wage Keynesian Model

Since the variable-wage Keynesian aggregate supply curve is still upward sloping (nonvertical), changes in aggregate demand that shift the aggregate demand curve will affect the level of output.

Figure 8.11 Derivation of the Keynesian Aggregate Supply Curve When the Money Wage Is Variable

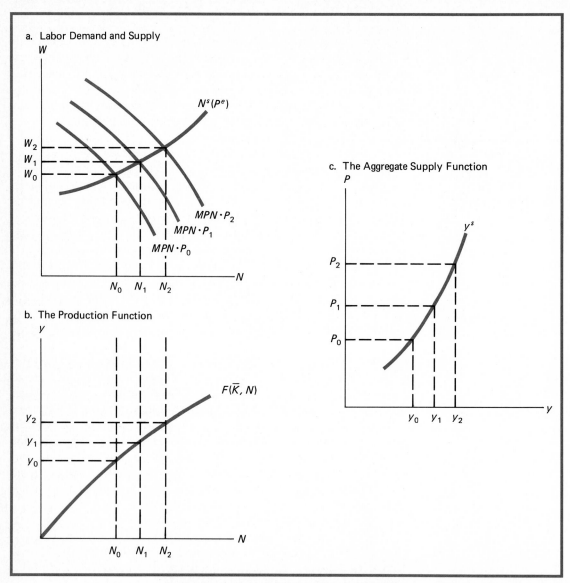

Part *a* shows the equilibrium levels of employment N_0, N_1, N_2, corresponding to successively higher values of the price level P_0, P_1, P_2. Part *b* gives the level of output y_0, y_1, y_2 which will be produced at each of these employment levels. Part *c* combines the information in Parts *a* and *b* to show the relationship between the price level and output supplied. At higher values of the price level, output supplied increases; as in the fixed wage case, *the aggregate supply curve* (y^s) *is upward sloping.*

MACROECONOMIC MODELS

Increases in the money stock or level of government expenditures will shift the aggregate demand curve to the right, increasing both the level of output and the aggregate price level. Graphical illustrations of such policy shifts would be *qualitatively* the same as Figures 8.9 and 8.10.

Suppose that we compare the effects on price and output from a given change in aggregate demand when the money wage is variable with the effects for the case where we assumed the money wage is fixed. Is there a predictable *quantitative* difference? The answer is yes. When the money wage is variable, a given increase in aggregate demand will cause output to increase by less than for the case in which the money wage is fixed. When the money wage is variable, an increase in aggregate demand will cause the price level to rise by more than when the money wage is fixed. The reason for these results is that the aggregate supply curve when the money wage varies will be steeper than for the case where the money wage is fixed. As the aggregate demand curve is shifted to the right along the steeper aggregate supply curve, the increased demand results less in increased output and more in increased price.

The reason why the aggregate supply curve is steeper in the variable-money-wage case is illustrated in Figure 8.12. In Figure 8.12a the labor market response to an increase in the price level is illustrated for the fixed- and variable-money-wage cases. If the money wage is fixed at $\bar{W} = W_0$, an increase in the price level from P_0 to P_1 shifts the labor demand curve from $MPN \cdot P_0$ to $MPN \cdot P_1$ and employment rises from N_0 to N_1. Output supplied can be seen from Figure 8.12b to rise from y_0 to y_1. The aggregate supply curve will be given by $y^s(W = \bar{W})$ in Figure 8.12c.

With a variable money wage when the labor demand curve shifts from $MPN \cdot P_0$ to $MPN \cdot P_1$, as a result of the increase in price, employment rises only to N_1'. The money wage must rise from W_0 to W_1 to get workers to increase labor supply. This increase in the money wage dampens the effect of the original increase in labor demand. Since employment increases by less than in the fixed-wage case, output supplied also increases by less, rising only to y_1', as shown in Figure 8.12b. The increase in the price-level leads to a smaller rise in output supplied, and this is reflected in the steeper aggregate supply curve for the variable-money-wage case, as shown in Figure 8.12c, the $y^s(W \text{ variable})$ curve.

As shown in Figure 8.13, with the steeper aggregate supply curve an increase in aggregate demand will have a smaller output effect. A shift in the aggregate demand curve from y_0^d to y_1^d will increase output from y_0 to y_1 in the fixed-money-wage case but only to y_1' in the variable-money-wage case. Price will rise by more in the variable-money-wage case, to P_1' as opposed to P_1 for the case where the money wage is fixed. Policy multipliers giving out-

Figure 8.12 Keynesian Aggregate Supply Curves for the Fixed- and Flexible-Money-Wage Cases

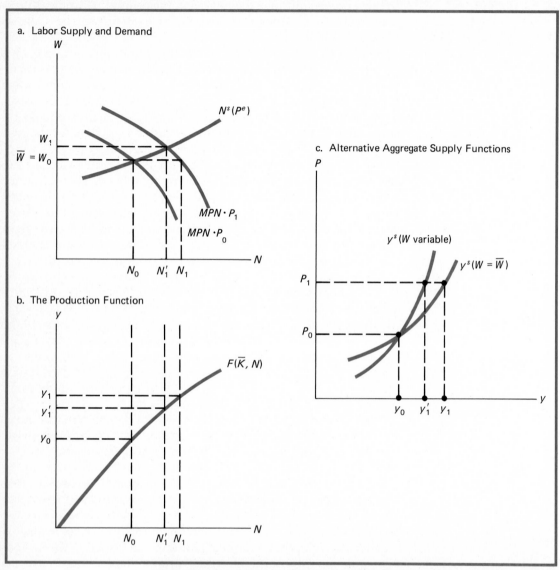

a. Labor Supply and Demand

b. The Production Function

c. Alternative Aggregate Supply Functions

The aggregate supply schedule in Part *c* for the case where the money wage is variable [y^s(*W* variable)] is steeper than for the case where the money wage if fixed [y^s($W = \overline{W}$)]. This is because the increase in employment (Part *a*) with a rise in price and therefore the increase in output (Part *b*) are smaller in the case where the money wage is variable than for the case where it is fixed. In essence, this follows because the rise in the money wage in the variable wage case dampens the effect on employment and output from an increase in the price level.

MACROECONOMIC MODELS

Figure 8.13
Effect of an Increase in Aggregate Demand in the Fixed- and Variable-Money-Wage Cases

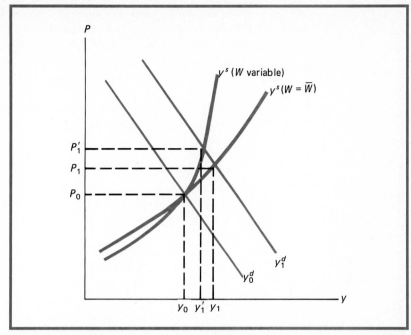

Since the aggregate supply curve in the variable money wage case [$y^s(W$ variable)] is steeper than for the fixed wage case [$y^s(W = \overline{W})$], a shift to the right in the aggregate demand curve will increase output by a smaller amount (from y_0 to y_1') in the variable wage case than in the fixed wage case (from y_0 to y_1).

put effects for changes in the money stock or for changes in government spending, factors that affect output via aggregate demand, will be smaller for the variable-money-wage case than for the fixed-money-wage case.

At this point it is useful to draw together some conclusions from the preceding two sections concerning the way in which allowing price and wage flexibility affects the policy implications of the Keynesian system.

In Section 8.3 we saw that when the price level was assumed to vary (the money wage still fixed), policy multipliers were reduced relative to their values in the simple IS–LM curve model of Chapter 7, where both the price level and the money wage had been fixed. In that simple IS–LM curve model the implicit assumption was that the aggregate supply curve was horizontal. Supply was no barrier to an increase in output. In the model in Section 8.3 we were taking account of the fact that in normal circumstances, as output increases the marginal product of labor declines. Since the unit cost of producing additional units of output is the money wage divided by the marginal product of labor, firms will supply a greater output only at a higher price—even if the money wage is fixed. The aggregate supply curve was seen to be upward sloping, and increases in aggregate demand consequently had smaller output effects than for the case of the horizontal aggregate supply curve.

When the money wage is also assumed to be variable, the implied aggregate supply curve becomes steeper. Now as output is increased, not only does the marginal product of labor decline, causing an increase in unit costs (W/MPN), but the rise in the money wage required to induce workers to supply more labor will also push up unit cost. As a result, any increase in output supplied will require a larger increase in price; the aggregate supply curve is steeper. Aggregate demand changes have still smaller output effects.

In the classical system the aggregate supply curve was vertical; output was completely supply determined. The price and wage were assumed to be perfectly flexible. In the simple IS–LM curve model, output was completely demand determined. Prices and wages were completely rigid. The models in the preceding two sections, by introducing price and wage flexibility in the Keynesian system, have brought the Keynesian results closer to those of the classical model. Still the models in these sections remain "Keynesian" in the important sense that aggregate demand still plays a role in determining the level of output. The aggregate supply curve is not vertical in the short run.

8.5 THE EFFECTS OF SHIFTS IN THE AGGREGATE SUPPLY FUNCTION

So far in our development of the Keynesian theory of aggregate supply we have focused on how taking account of supply factors changes the role of aggregate demand in determining output. The output and employment effects of changes in aggregate demand— shifts in the aggregate demand function—will depend on the slope of the aggregate supply function. In addition, supply factors have an independent role in determining output and employment. There can be shifts in the aggregate supply curve and such shifts will affect output, employment, and the price level.

In recent years such shifts in the supply curve have played an important part in the Keynesian explanation of price, output, and employment movements. In fact, without taking account of shifts in the aggregate supply schedule, the recent behavior of price, output, and employment is unexplainable within a Keynesian framework. In this section we consider the effects of shifts in the aggregate supply function and also see the role that such "supply shocks" play in the Keynesian explanation of recent economic developments.

The Recent Behavior of Price and Output

Figure 8.14 plots the levels of real income and the aggregate price level (GNP deflator) for the years 1973–81. Notice that while the price level increased substantially in each year, there were several declines in the level of real output. The relationship between changes in real output and changes in the aggregate price level can be seen in Table 8.1, giving the annual rates of change for real GNP and the GNP deflator for the years 1973–81. From Table 8.1 it is also clear that during this period the years with the greatest growth in real output were not those with the largest rates of price increase. In fact, the three years when output declined (1974, 1975, and 1980) were three of the four most inflationary years of the period.

This pattern of price and output changes is inconsistent with the Keynesian model unless shifts in the aggregate supply curve are taken into account. To see this, consider Figure 8.15. In Figure 8.15a, movements in output and price are caused by shifts in the aggregate demand curve (from y_0^d to y_1^d, then to y_2^d). In this case increases in price (from P_0 to P_1, then to P_2) would *always* be accompanied by increases in output (from y_0 to y_1, then to y_2). The demand schedule shifts to the right along the fixed upward-sloping supply curve, increasing both price and output. Shifts to the left in the aggregate demand curve would cause *both* output and price to fall. Therefore, shifts in the aggregate demand schedule do not provide an explanation for the behavior of price and output in years such as 1974, 1975, and 1980, where output fell but price rose, and in fact the rate of price increase accelerated.

In Figure 8.15b, it can be seen that shifts to the left in the aggregate supply curve (from y_0^s to y_1^s and to y_2^s) would result in price increases (from P_0 to P_1, then to P_2) associated with declines in output (from y_0 to y_1, then to y_2). Such "supply shocks" could explain the U.S. economy's recent experience with inflationary recessions—periods where output declines and prices increase.

Factors That Shift the Aggregate Supply Schedule

The question remains of the causes of shifts in the aggregate supply schedule—the nature of the supply shocks referred to above. Recall that points on the aggregate supply schedule give the desired output of the firms in the economy for each value of the aggregate price level. Each firm, and therefore firms in the aggregate, will choose the level of output that maximizes profits. This

Figure 8.14
Real GNP and the
Aggregate Price Level,
1973–1981

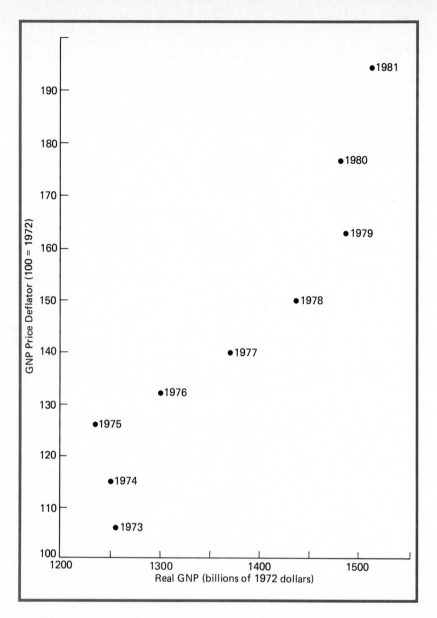

implies, as discussed in Chapter 3, that firms produce up to the point where price P is equal to marginal cost:

$$P = \mathrm{MC} \tag{8.7}$$

Marginal cost is the addition to total cost due to increasing the use of variable factors of production to increase output. In our analysis above we assumed that labor was the only variable factor

Year	Growth in Real GNP	Increase in GNP deflator
1973	5.8	5.7
1974	−0.6	8.7
1975	−1.1	9.3
1976	5.4	5.2
1977	5.5	5.8
1978	4.8	7.3
1979	3.2	8.5
1980	−0.2	9.0
1981	1.9	9.1

of production. In this case the marginal cost of producing an additional unit of output was the money wage (W), the amount paid for an additional unit of labor, divided by the marginal product of labor (MPN). Marginal cost (W/MPN) increased as output increased because as more labor was hired, the marginal product of labor (MPN) declined. Additionally, in the variable-wage model of the preceding section, in order to get workers to supply additional labor, the money wage had to be increased, a further factor causing marginal cost to rise as output increased. These two factors, the declining marginal product of labor and increasing upward pressure on money wages as output and employment increase, explain why the aggregate supply schedule is upward sloping.

A shift in the aggregate supply schedule, for example a shift upward to the left as in Figure 8.15*b*, means that after the shift, firms will produce less for a given price or, put differently, firms will find it optimal to continue to produce the same output, only at a higher price. From (8.7) it can be seen that any factor that causes marginal cost to increase *for a given output level* will cause such a shift upward and to the left in the aggregate supply schedule. If marginal cost increases for a given output, then to continue to meet condition (8.7) *at a given price* the firm must decrease output. As output declines, marginal cost will decline (MPN will rise and W will fall) and equality (8.7) can be restored. Alternatively, price would have to rise by the amount of the increase in marginal cost for the firm to find it optimal to continue to produce the same level of output.

This is half the story; the next question is to determine the factors that will change marginal cost for a given output level. Such factors are often termed *cost push* factors because they affect price independently of the level of demand, acting by shifting the supply curve. One set of such cost push factors are factors that affect the money wage demands on the part of labor at a given level of employment; these are factors that shift the labor supply curve as

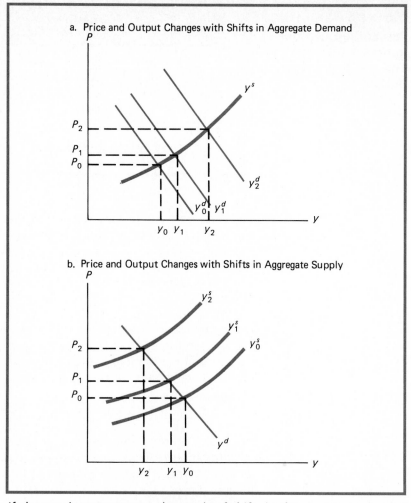

a. Price and Output Changes with Shifts in Aggregate Demand

b. Price and Output Changes with Shifts in Aggregate Supply

If changes in output were the result of shifts in the aggregate demand schedule along a fixed supply schedule as in Part *a*, we would expect a positive relationship between price and output changes. If, on the other hand, output changes resulted from shifts in the aggregate supply schedule along a fixed demand schedule as in Part *b*, we would expect a negative association between price and output changes. Shifts to the left in the aggregate supply curve can provide an explanation for the behavior of the U.S. economy in years such as 1974, 1975, and 1980 (see Table 8.1).

that schedule is drawn, for example, in Figure 8.11. So far we have considered one factor that will shift the labor supply schedule, a change in the worker's expectation about the aggregate level of price (P^e).

In the preceding section we assumed that the laborers' expected price level depended on the past behavior of prices and, hence, was given in the short run. Over time, however, as new information is received, the workers will adjust their price expectation. Figure 8.16 shows the effect on labor supply and on the aggregate supply curve as a result of an increase in the workers' expectation concerning the current aggregate price level.

Suppose that as a result of observed past increases in the aggregate price level, workers' expectation of the current price level rises from P_0^e to P_1^e. As a result, the labor supply schedule shifts to the left in Figure 8.16a, from $N^s(P_0^e)$ to $N^s(P_1^e)$. Less labor will be supplied at each level of the money wage because with the higher expectation about the aggregate price level, a given money wage corresponds to a lower real wage. Looked at from the firm's point of view, a higher money wage would have to be paid to obtain a given quantity of labor. At the initial price level P_0, the shift in the labor supply schedule will reduce employment (from N_0 to N_1). Consequently, output at price level P_0 falls (from y_0 to y_1), as can be seen in Figure 8.16b. The aggregate supply schedule shifts to the left in Figure 8.16c [from $y^s(P_0^e)$ to $y^s(P_1^e)$].

We see then that any factor that shifts the labor supply curve upward to the left, lowering labor supply for a given money wage or, what amounts to the same thing, increasing the money wage at which a given amount of labor will be supplied, will shift the aggregate supply schedule to the left. Such shifts in the labor supply function will play an important part in our analysis of the longer-run adjustment of output and employment to policy changes.

If we broaden our analysis to allow for variable factors of production other than labor, it follows that an autonomous increase in the price of any variable factor of production will increase marginal cost for a given output level and will shift the aggregate supply schedule to the left.

In particular, autonomous increases in the price of raw materials will have this type of cost push effect. The Keynesians believe that recent increases in the world price of raw material inputs to the production process, primarily energy inputs, have caused large increases in production cost for a given level of output and have resulted in significant shifts to the left in the aggregate supply schedule, increasing the domestic aggregate price level and reducing real GNP.

In addition to the direct effects that increases in raw material prices have on the aggregate supply schedule, such supply shocks have indirect effects which come through an effect on labor supply. Increases in raw material prices, for example the price of imported oil and other energy products, push up the domestic price level. As domestic prices rise and enough time passes for these price increases to be perceived by the suppliers of labor, the workers' ex-

Figure 8.16 Shift in the Aggregate Supply Function With an Increase in the Expected Price Level

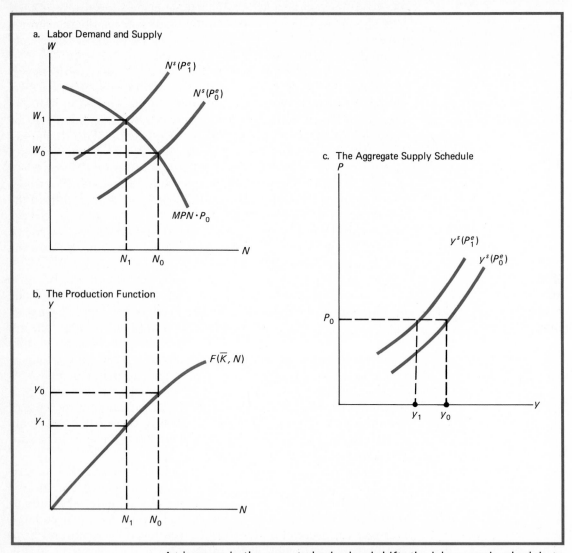

a. Labor Demand and Supply

b. The Production Function

c. The Aggregate Supply Schedule

An increase in the expected price level shifts the labor supply schedule to the left from $N^s(P_0^e)$ to $N^s(P_1^e)$ in Part a. At a given price level, P_0, employment declines from N_0 to N_1 and output falls from y_0 to y_1 (Part b). This decline in output for a given price level is reflected in a shift to the left in the aggregate supply function from $y^s(P_0^e)$ to $y^s(P_1^e)$ in Part c.

pectation about the aggregate price level (P^e) will increase. As was just explained, such as increase in the expected price level will cause a shift to the left in the aggregate supply curve, further increasing the price level and causing an additional decline in real output.

The Keynesian explanation of the large price increases and output declines in the 1974–75 period and more recently in 1979–80 relies on such direct and indirect effects of supply shocks. The key supply shock in the 1974–75 period was the fourfold increase in the price of crude oil on the world market following the formation of the OPEC cartel. The 1979 disruption of the world oil market following the Iranian revolution again precipitated a huge increase in crude oil prices. The Keynesian view of the effects of such supply shocks can be represented graphically, as in Figure 8.17. The initial increase in oil prices and resulting increase in the price of other energy sources (coal, natural gas, etc.), which would come

Figure 8.17
Effects of an An Autonomous Increase in the World Price of Energy Inputs

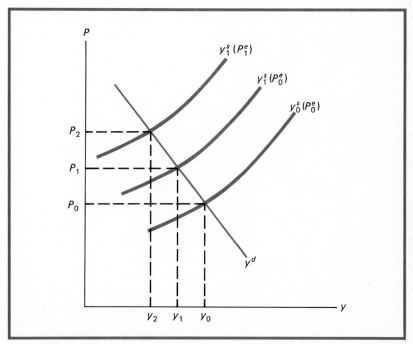

An autonomous increase in the price of energy inputs shifts the aggregate supply schedule to the left from $y_0^s(P_0^e)$ to $y_1^s(P_0^e)$; output falls from y_0 to y_1 and the price level rises from P_0 to P_1. As labor suppliers perceive the rise in the price level, the expected price level rises from P_0^e to P_1^e. The aggregate supply schedule shifts farther to the left to $y_1^s(P_1^e)$. Output falls to y_2 and the price level rises to P_2.

as a result of the attempt of energy users to substitute other fuels for the higher-priced oil, would cause a shift in the aggregate supply schedule from $y_0^s(P_0^e)$ to $y_1^s(P_0^e)$. Output would decline from y_0 to y_1 and price would rise from P_0 to P_1. This would be the direct effect of the supply shock. As prices of energy-related products and of all products that use such energy inputs in the production process—a virtually all-inclusive category—rose, labor suppliers would in time perceive the increase in price; the expected price level would rise (from P_0^e to P_1^e). There would be a further shift to the left in the aggregate supply schedule, from $y_1^s(P_0^e)$ to $y_1^s(P_1^e)$. Price would further increase to P_2 and output would decline to y_2.[4]

8.6 SUPPLY SHOCKS AND AGGREGATE DEMAND POLICY

Supply shocks, such as the energy price shock just analyzed, create a dilemma for macroeconomic policymakers, a dilemma that concerns the proper response of monetary and fiscal policy to such supply shocks.

To see the nature of the policymaker's dilemma, first consider the case where there is no response of monetary or fiscal policy in the wake of an unfavorable energy price shock. In this case the situation would be as illustrated in Figure 8.17. The supply shock would cause output to fall and prices to rise. In Figure 8.18 this outcome is shown as a fall in output from y_0 to y_1 and a rise in the price level from P_0 to P_1 as a result of a shift to the left in the supply schedule from y_0^s to y_1^s.

Instead, to avoid increased unemployment, the policymaker could try to offset some or all of the unfavorable output effect of the supply shock by increasing the level of aggregate demand through expansionary monetary and/or fiscal policies. To offset all of the unfavorable output effect of the supply shock, the policymaker would expand demand by enough to shift the aggregate demand schedule from y_0^d to y_H^d in Figure 8.18, thereby restoring output to the initial level y_0. The policymaker accommodates the supply shock by increasing aggregate demand sufficiently to support the same level of output even with higher energy prices. No-

[4]This secondary shift in the supply schedule due to the adjustment in price expectations explains why supply shocks have inflationary effects which persist for a number of quarters rather than just causing a one-time rise in the price level. Such persistence may also be due to accommodating increases in aggregate demand, as discussed in the next section.

Figure 8.18

Aggregate Demand
Responses to a Supply
Shock

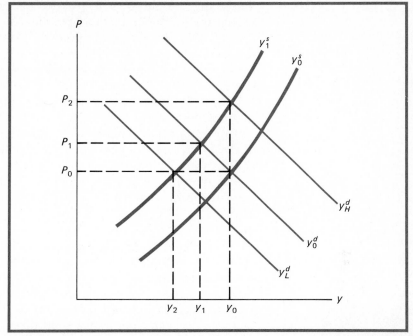

A supply shock shifts the aggregate supply schedule from y_0^s to y_1^s; output will fall from y_0 to y_1 and the price level will rise from P_0 to P_1. The policymaker could increase aggregate demand to y_H^d and offset the unfavorable output effect of the supply shock, but then price would rise further to P_2. Alternatively, he could lower demand to y_L^d to offset the price effect of the supply shock, but in this case output would fall by more, to y_2.

tice, though, that in doing so the policymaker exacerbates the inflationary effect of the supply shock. With an accommodating aggregate demand policy the price level rises to P_2, a higher level than P_1, when there was assumed to be no accommodation.

An alternative policy response would be to try to offset the price rise due to the supply shock by lowering aggregate demand through restrictive monetary and fiscal policies. Such policies could offset all the unfavorable price effects of the supply shock by shifting the aggregate demand schedule from y_0^d to y_L^d in Figure 8.18. Even given the new supply schedule y_1^s, with demand at this low level the initial price level P_0 is restored. Notice, however, that the effect of the restrictive aggregate demand policy is to worsen the output effect of the supply shock. Output falls to y_2 below y_1, the level of output with no demand response.

We see, therefore, that accommodation of the supply shock can offset the unfavorable output effect of the supply shock only by increasing the unfavorable price-level effect. On the other hand, restrictive aggregate demand policies as a response to the supply shock, although helpful in reducing the unfavorable price effect of the shock, do so only at the cost of worsening the output effect. This is the dilemma that faces policymakers in the face of a supply shock such as the oil price increase in 1974. In the Keynesian view, it is the fact that in the presence of supply shocks aggregate demand policy cannot by itself prevent both price increases and declining output that explains why even well-designed policy actions of the 1970s (and the neo-Keynesians do not claim that all policy actions were well designed) did not produce attractive outcomes.

The inability of aggregate demand policy to offset simultaneously the unfavorable price and output effects of supply shocks has also led neo-Keynesians to look for supply-side policies which might directly offset the unfavorable shift in the aggregate supply curve due to increases in energy prices. Such policies would be aimed at shifting the aggregate supply curve downward to the right by reducing the marginal cost of producing a given output. Among the policy actions considered in this light are reductions in sales or excise taxes and reductions in the employer's portion of the social security tax. Since such taxes are a part of the cost of producing (and selling) output, reductions in these tax rates would be cost-reducing disturbances that could offset the effect of unfavorable supply shocks.[5] We will discuss these cost-reducing tax policies further when we return to the economics of the supply side in Chapter 16.

8.7 KEYNES VERSUS THE CLASSICS

The last four chapters have analyzed the Keynesian view of macroeconomics. What are the major differences between this Keynesian view and the classical macroeconomic theory that Keynes attacked? In this chapter we have seen how the Keynesian system can be summarized by the aggregate supply and aggregate demand relationships. The classical model can be expressed in the same manner, as was done in Chapter 4. A convenient way to summarize the differences between the Keynesian and classical theories is to examine the differences between the respective aggregate demand and aggregate supply relationships in the two models.

---

[5]The price level (P) is inclusive of excise or sales taxes, so it is appropriate to view payment of these taxes as a cost of producing and selling the product. The employer's portion of the social security tax, which in 1980 was 6.65 percent of the first $29,700 of an employee's wage, represents an element in the cost of the labor input.

Keynesian Versus Classical Theories of Aggregate Demand

The classical model did not contain an explicit theory of aggregate demand. The *quantity theory of money* provided an implicit classical theory of aggregate demand. Using the quantity theory relationship

$$MV = Py \qquad (8.8)$$

with the assumption that V is constant, we can determine Py for a given value of M. This relationship gives the rectangular hyperbola $y^d(M_0)$ plotted in Figure 8.19a for M equal M_0. This was the classical aggregate demand curve. The nominal demand for goods (Py) depended on the quantity of money.

The economic logic behind this relationship was clearest for the Cambridge form of the quantity theory:

$$M = M^d = kPy \qquad (8.9)$$

Since k is equal to $1/V$, (8.8) and (8.9) are equivalent. From (8.8) it can be seen that an increase in M will for a given value of Py and an assumed constant k cause an excess supply of money. The classical theory assumed that this excess supply of money would be reflected in an excess demand for goods.

Increases in the demand for output by one sector of the economy, government demand or autonomous investment demand, for example, would not affect aggregate demand in the classical system. Such changes in sectoral demands would cause adjustments in the interest rate. The interest rate played a stabilizing role in the classical system and assured that such changes in sectoral demand could not change aggregate demand. For example, an increase in government spending financed by selling bonds to the public would in the classical model cause the interest rate to rise until private spending had declined by just the amount of the increase in government spending. Aggregate demand would be unchanged (Section 4.3). *Only monetary factors shift the classical aggregate demand curve.*

The Keynesian aggregate demand curve is shown in Figure 8.19b. Although both the classical and Keynesian aggregate demand curves are downward-sloping schedules when plotted against price, there is an important difference between them. Whereas the classical aggregate demand schedule shifts only when the stock of money changes, the position of the Keynesian aggregate demand curve depends on variables such as the level of government spending (g_0), the level of tax collections (t_0), and the level of autonomous investment expenditures ($\bar{\imath}_0$) in addition to the quantity of money (M_0). As we have seen, the Keynesian aggregate demand function will shift when any of these other factors are

Figure 8.19
Classical and Keynesian Aggregate Supply and Demand Curves

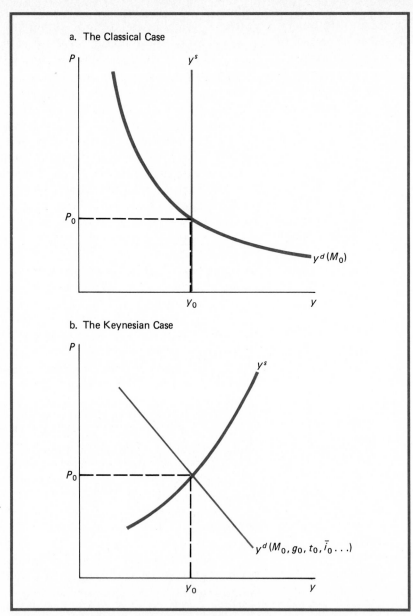

a. The Classical Case

b. The Keynesian Case

The classical aggregate supply schedule is vertical while the Keynesian aggregate supply schedule slopes upward to the right. The classical aggregate demand schedule depends only on the level of the money stock (M_0), while in the Keynesian system aggregate demand also depends on the levels of fiscal policy variables (g_0, t_0), the level of autonomous investment ($\bar{I}_0$), and other variables as well.

varied. The interest rate does not completely insulate aggregate demand from changes in sectoral demands in the Keynesian system. This difference in the determinants of aggregate demand in the Keynesian and classical models produces important differences in their respective explanations of the sources of instability in the economy and the usefulness of various stabilization policies.

Keynes believed that the instability of investment demand was the major cause of cyclical fluctuations in income. Autonomous changes in investment demand due to changes in expectations would cause shifts in the aggregate demand function and consequently instability in price and output. Fiscal policy could be used to cause offsetting changes in aggregate demand and potentially stabilize aggregate demand even though investment demand were unstable.

In the classical view there is neither a need for government policy to stabilize aggregate demand in the face of investment instability nor would fiscal policy be able to perform such a function. For a given stock of money, the aggregate demand curve will be unaffected by either autonomous changes in investment or by changes in fiscal policy variables. To the classical economists the only source of instability in aggregate demand is from changes in the quantity of money. The only remedy is stable money. The business cycle is a "dance of the dollar," to use Irving Fisher's phrase. This classical view followed naturally from the quantity theory of money.

This difference between the Keynesian and classical economists over the degree to which monetary factors determine aggregate demand explains the difference between these two schools in the debate over the usefulness of public works projects (changes in g) as a remedy for unemployment (see Section 5.1). As we will see later, there is a similar dispute between the Keynesians and the modern-day successors to the quantity theorists, the monetarists, over the usefulness of fiscal stabilization policy.

Keynesian Versus Classical Theories of Aggregate Supply

The key difference between the classical and Keynesian aggregate supply functions concerns the slope of the function. The classical aggregate supply function, shown in Figure 8.19a, is vertical. The vertical supply function results from the classical assumptions about the labor market. Labor supply and demand are assumed to depend only on the real wage, which is known to all. The money wage is assumed to be perfectly flexible, adjusting instantaneously to equate supply and demand. Since the aggregate supply curve is vertical, output and employment are completely supply determined. Aggregate demand plays no systematic role in the determination of output.

In the *short run* the Keynesian aggregate supply curve slopes upward to the right. We would expect the curve to be quite flat at levels of output well below full capacity and to become steeper as full capacity output is approached. The Keynesian view of aggregate supply (Sections 8.3 and 8.4) emphasizes the stickiness of the money wage and the failure of market participants to perceive the real wage correctly. As a consequence, the labor market will not be in continual equilibrium at full employment. Actual output and employment will not be completely determined by the supply factors that determine *full employment* output. Shifts in the aggregate demand function will move the economy along the upward sloping supply function, causing output to change. In the Keynesian system the level of aggregate demand is an important factor determining the level of output and employment.

As we saw in Chapter 3, the classical economists recognized that a rigid money wage would result in an aggregate supply curve that was not vertical. With a rigid money wage, output would not be completely supply determined. In such a situation, aggregate demand, which in the classical model is totally determined by monetary factors, would affect output.

The fact that with a rigid money wage, output is affected by aggregate demand even in the classical model has led some economists to conclude that the only important difference between the classical and Keynesian models is that Keynes assumed the money wage was fixed, whereas the classical economists assumed the money wage to be perfectly flexible. Such an interpretation underestimates the contribution of Keynesian economics. As we have seen, the Keynesian theory of aggregate demand differs considerably from that of the classical economists. Also, the Keynesian theory of aggregate supply does not rest *only* on the assumption of an institutionally rigid money wage, although, as we saw in Section 8.4, the Keynesians do believe that wages are sticky in the downward direction. A Keynesian aggregate supply curve can also result where the money wage is flexible, but labor suppliers have imperfect information about the level of the real wage. Differing views of the labor market certainly are, however, an important source of the differing conclusions reached in the classical and Keynesian models.

The Keynesian aggregate supply curve in Figure 8.19*b* was termed a short-run supply curve, to emphasize that it pertained to a short period of time not to a long-run equilibrium situation. Factors such as explicit long-term labor contracts, implicit contracts, and resistance to wage cuts seen as cuts in the relative wage would slow but not permanently prevent the necessary wage adjustment to return the economy to a full-employment level. Imperfect information about the real wage on the part of labor suppliers would also be a short-run phenomenon. Eventually, expectations would approach the actual value of the price level and, hence, of the real wage. The Keynesians would not deny that eventually the economy would approach full employment. But such long-run "classical" properties of the economy are to the Keynesians unimportant. They agree with Keynes that

> this *long run* is a misleading guide to current affairs. *In the long run* we are all dead. Economists set themselves too easy, too useless a task if in tempestuous seasons they can only tell us that when the storm is long past the ocean is flat again.[6]

Keynesian Versus Classical Policy Conclusions

Given the differences in their models, it is not surprising that the Keynesian and classical economists reach quite different policy conclusions. The classical economists stressed the self-adjusting tendencies of the economy. If left free from destabilizing government policies, the economy would achieve full employment. The classical economists were noninterventionist in that they did not favor active monetary and fiscal policies to stabilize the economy. Such policies to affect aggregate demand would have no effects on output or employment given the supply-determined nature of those variables in the classical system.

The Keynesians view the economy as unstable due to the instability of aggregate demand, primarily the private investment component of aggregate demand. Aggregate demand does affect output and employment in the Keynesian view. Consequently, swings in aggregate demand will cause undesirable fluctuations in output and employment in the short run. These fluctuations can be prevented by using monetary and fiscal policies to offset undesirable changes in aggregate demand. The Keynesians are interventionists, favoring active policies to manage aggregate demand.

Review Questions

1 Carefully explain why the Keynesian aggregate demand curve is downward sloping when plotted against the price level.

2 Derive the Keynesian aggregate demand curve for the case where investment is completely interest inelastic and therefore the IS schedule is vertical (follow the procedure in Figure 8.2). Explain the resulting slope of the aggregate demand curve for this case.

[6]John M. Keynes, *A Tract on Monetary Reform*, (London: Macmillan, 1923), p. 80.

3   In what sense is the classical theory of aggregate supply "fundamentally incompatible" with the Keynesian system?

4   Why are fiscal policy multipliers smaller in magnitude in the variable price–fixed wage version of the Keynesian model than in the fixed-price IS–LM model? Why are these multipliers still smaller when we allow the money wage as well as the price level to be variable?

5   Analyze the effects of an increase in the money stock within the Keynesian model, where both the price level and money wage are assumed to be variable. Include in your answer the effects on the level of real income, the price level, the interest rate, and the money wage.

6   In the Keynesian system increases in aggregate demand can lead to increases in output because the money wage rises less than proportionately with the price level in response to such increases in demand. This is necessary since firms will hire more workers only if the real wage (W/P) falls. Explain the possible reasons why the money wage does not adjust proportionately with the price level in the short-run Keynesian model.

7   Why are supply shocks of such importance to the neo-Keynesian explanation of the behavior of price and output during the course of the 1970s?

8   Assume that there is an exogenous decline in the price of imported oil. Using the graphical analysis in this chapter, explain how such a shock would affect output and the price level. Explain the role that inflationary expectations play in this adjustment.

9   Explain the dilemma that is created for policymakers by unfavorable supply shocks.

10   "Money is more important in the Keynesian system than in the classical system." Do you agree? Or would you maintain that the opposite is true?

11   What do you see as the essential differences between the classical and Keynesian theories of aggregate supply?

12   What do you see as the essential differences between the classical and Keynesian theories of aggregate demand?

13   Compare the effects of an expansionary fiscal policy action, an increase in government spending financed by government bond sales to the public for example, in the Keynesian and classical models. Include in your answer the effects of this policy shift on the level of real income, employment, the price level, and the rate of interest.

Selected Readings

BRANSON, WILLIAM, *Macroeconomic Theory and Policy*. New York: Harper & Row, 1979, Chaps. 6–9.

GRAMLICH, EDWARD, "Macro Policy Responses to Price Shocks," *Brookings Paper on Economic Activity*, No. 1, (1979), pp. 125–66.

MODIGLIANI, FRANCO, "Liquidity Preference and the Theory of Interest and Money," *Econometrica*, 12 (January 1944), pp. 45–88. Reprinted in Friedrich Lutz and Lloyd Mints, *Readings in Monetary Theory*. Homewood, Ill.: Irwin, 1951.

MODIGLIANI, FRANCO, "The Monetary Mechanism and Its Interaction with Real Phenomena," *Review of Economics and Statistics*, 45 (February 1963), supplement, pp. 79–107.

SMITH, WARREN, "A Graphical Exposition of the Complete Keynesian System," *Southern Economic Journal*, 23 (October 1956), pp. 115–25. Reprinted in Thomas Havrilesky and John Boorman, *Current Issues in Monetary Theory and Policy*. Arlington Heights, Ill.: AHM Publishing Corp., 1980.

chapter 9

9.1 INTRODUCTION

The Keynesian attack on the classical orthodoxy was successful. A debate continued between the classical economists and the Keynesians, but by 1950 Keynesian economics was well established as a new orthodoxy. Keynes died in 1946, but his successors took up the task of refining his theories and applying them to the policy questions facing Western nations as they converted to peacetime economies in the aftermath of World War II. This is the environment in which monetarism, the first of the major attacks on the Keynesian position, had its origins.

Rather than attempt to give a capsule definition of monetarism, we follow the example of many previous authors and instead list a number of propositions that characterize the monetarist position. This strategy is not without risks. As Milton Friedman, the central figure in the early development of monetarism, notes: "One man's 'characteristic monetarist proposition' is not another's."[1] The characteristic monetarist propositions advanced here are:

1. The supply of money is the dominant influence on nominal income.
2. In the long run, the influence of money is primarily on the price

[1] An alternative list of monetarist propositions is given in Thomas Mayer, *The Structure of Monetarism* (New York: Norton, 1978).

MONETARISM (I): THE IMPORTANCE OF MONEY

level and other *nominal* magnitudes. In the long run, *real* variables, such as real output and employment, are determined by real, not monetary, factors.

3. In the short run the supply of money does influence real variables. Money is the dominant factor causing cyclical movements in output and employment.

4. The private sector of the economy is inherently stable. Instability in the economy is primarily the result of government policies.

From these four propositions we will see that there follow two policy conclusions:

1. Stability in the growth of the money stock is crucial for stability in the economy. Such stability is best achieved by setting a constant growth rate for the money stock.

2. Fiscal policy, by itself, has little systematic effect on either real or nominal income. Fiscal policy is not an effective stabilization tool.

Our procedure in explaining monetarism will be first to clarify the meaning of each of the foregoing statements and then to consider its theoretic basis.

The first of the monetarist propositions is that the level of economic activity in current dollars is determined primarily by the stock of money. An important element in this proposition is that the direction of influence or causation is assumed to be from money to income. For the most part, changes in the money stock are assumed to *cause* changes in nominal income. The level and rate of growth of the money stock are assumed to be determined primarily by the actions of the government central bank.

The second monetarist proposition can perhaps be clarified by restating it in a negative manner. Restated this way, proposition 2 asserts that in the long run the level of economic activity measured in real (inflation corrected) dollars does not depend on the quantity of money. In the longer run the level of real output will be determined by real factors such as the stock of capital goods, the size and quality of the labor force, and the state of technology. If in the long run the level of real economic activity is not affected by the quantity of money while the level of economic activity in nominal terms is almost completely determined by the stock of money, it is clear that the long-run effect of money is on the price level.

Proposition 3 states that in the short run, real output and employment are strongly influenced by changes in the stock of money. Prices are influenced as well, but in the short run prices, including wage rates (the price of labor), are not perfectly flexible. Thus, when the quantity of money changes, in the short run, prices do not make the full long-run adjustment. Output and employment are also affected.

The fourth monetarist proposition asserts that the private sector (businesses and households) is not the source of instability in the economy. As one prominent monetarist, Karl Brunner, puts it, the private sector is "essentially a shock-absorbing, stabilizing and self-adjusting process. Instability is produced dominantly by the operation of the government sector." The government causes instability in the economy primarily by allowing instability in the growth of the money stock, the major determinant of the level of economic activity. In the monetarist view the government can also destabilize the economy by interfering with the normal adjustment mechanisms in the private economy. Mandatory controls on prices and wages are the most obvious example of government interference with such adjustment properties. Other examples are usury ceilings on interest rates, rent controls, and minimum wage laws.

The two policy corollaries follow from the four monetarist propositions. Given propositions 1 and 3, the importance of stable money growth for a stable economy is evident. The reason for favoring a constant growth rate will be elaborated below.

If monetary factors dominate the determination of nominal income and short-run real income, little role is left for other systematic influences. The term "dominate" does, however, allow for some ambiguity. Does it mean that movements in the money stock explain 55 percent of the systematic movement in income, or 95 percent? This question is important in assessing the role of fiscal policy (and other factors) in determining the level of economic activity. As stated, our second policy conclusion allows little independent role for fiscal policy. This seems consistent with the position of monetarists such as Milton Friedman. Other monetarists would not accept such a strong form of this policy proposition, but the general monetarist position has been that fiscal policy is not an effective stabilization tool.

In considering the basis for these monetarist propositions and policy conclusions, it is convenient to divide the analysis into two parts. First we examine the reasons why the monetarists ascribe such predominance to money (i.e., the basis of propositions 1 and 3). We postpone until Chapter 10 the question of what monetary policy cannot do, the basis for proposition 2. Although proposition 4 is not given separate consideration, it will be of importance at a number of points in our discussion of monetarism.

9.2 THE REFORMULATION OF THE QUANTITY THEORY OF MONEY

The first stage in the development of monetarism centered around redefining the quantity theory of money in the light of Keynes's attack on the quantity theory. The central monetarist figure in this period was Milton Friedman, a professor of economics at the University of Chicago from 1946 until his retirement in 1977 and since that time a senior research fellow at the Hoover Institution.

We have examined the quantity theory of money in our consideration of classical economics (Section 4.1). Friedman describes the quantity theory in the following way:

> In monetary theory, that analysis was taken to mean that in the quantity equation $MV = PT$ the term for velocity could be regarded as highly stable, that it could be taken as determined independently of the other terms in the equation, and that as a result changes in the quantity of money would be reflected either in prices or in output.[2]

Put simply, this is proposition 1 of monetarism as stated above. (Notice that the stability of velocity means not only that changes in M will cause changes in PT, but that *only* changes in M can cause changes in PT.)

As Friedman pointed out, the quantity theory of money had come into disrepute, together with the rest of classical economics, as a result of the Great Depression of the 1930s. Friedman felt that

[2]Milton Friedman, *The Counter-revolution in Monetary Theory* (London: Institute of Economic Affairs, 1970).

the events of the 1930s had been improperly assessed and did not in fact offer evidence against the quantity theory of money. He did, however, see the need to restate the quantity theory in terms that took account of Keynes's contribution. His purpose in doing this was to reassert the importance of money. To see why he felt that this was needed, it is best to start by considering the role (or lack of a role) which some early Keynesians attributed to money as a determinant of the level of economic activity.

Money and the Early Keynesians

Our analysis of the Keynesian system made clear that within that framework money was one of a number of important determinants of the level of economic activity. But velocity was not constant or independently determined; it was systematically determined within the system. Factors other than money could also affect the level of economic activity. Consider, for example, the response of the system to an increase in government spending as depicted in Figure 9.1.

The increase in government spending from G_0 to G_1 shifts the IS curve from $IS(G_0)$ to $IS(G_1)$. Income rises from y_0 to y_1 and the

Figure 9.1
Effects of an Increase in Government Spending: The Keynesian View

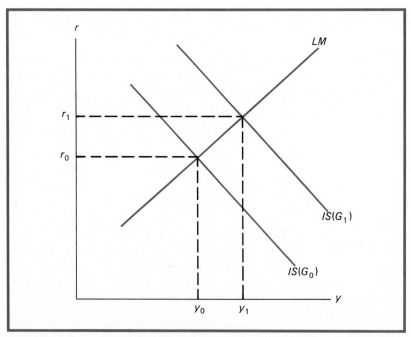

An increase in government spending shifts the *IS* schedule to the right. The equilibrium interest rate rises and the equilibrium level of income rises. Since the money stock is unchanged and income has risen, the velocity of money, the ratio of income to the money stock, has increased.

MACROECONOMIC MODELS

interest rate will increase from r_0 to r_1. The money stock is held constant here, with the increased government spending assumed to be financed by selling bonds to the public. The higher level of income causes a higher transactions demand for money. To bring money demand back into equality with the unchanged money supply, a rise in the interest rate is required. At the higher interest rate the speculative demand for money will have declined and the demand for transaction balances *at a given level of income* will also have fallen. Thus the same money stock can support a higher income level. This is what we found in our earlier analysis of the Keynesian system. Another way to express this finding is to say that velocity varies positively with the interest rate.

Since velocity is variable in the Keynesian system, there is no one level of income corresponding to a given level of the money stock. It would not be even an approximately accurate statement of the Keynesian view to state that in the short run nominal or real income was determined solely by the level of the money supply. This is not to say that the Keynesians believe that money is unimportant; they do not. The quantity of money is one of the key determinants of income in the Keynesian system. As we saw in Chapter 7, an increase in the quantity of money, for example, would shift the LM curve to the right in Figure 9.1. Income would rise and the interest rate would fall. There is no reason in the Keynesian system to view these changes as small.

Many of the *early* Keynesian economists (circa 1945–50) did, however, believe that money was of little importance and monetary policy of little use as a stabilization tool. Their view was based on empirical judgments about the slopes of the IS–LM curves, which, as we saw in our analysis of the Keynesian system, are important in determining the relative effectiveness of monetary and fiscal policy. Influenced by the experience of the Depression, they believed that the LM schedule was quite flat and the IS schedule quite steep—the configuration which we have argued above would be characteristic of depression conditions (see Section 7.3). Figure 9.2 shows this configuration of the IS–LM curves and illustrates the ineffectiveness of an increase in the quantity of money which shifts the LM curve from LM_0 to LM_1. In this case monetary policy is "doubly doomed." The LM curve is very flat around the point of equilibrium, reflecting a very high, almost infinite interest elasticity of money demand. This is a situation approaching the liquidity trap. A given change in the money stock does very little in terms of lowering the interest rate, the first link in the chain connecting the stock of money and level of income in the Keynesian model.

Further, the IS curve is very steep, nearly vertical, reflecting the assumption that aggregate demand is highly interest inelastic. A drop in the interest rate would not increase investment by a signif-

Figure 9.2
Early Keynesian View
of Monetary Policy
Ineffectiveness

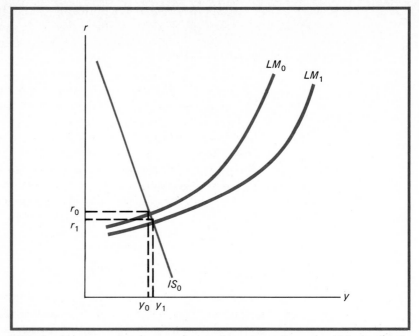

With the *IS* curve quite steep and over the range where the *LM* schedule is nearly horizontal, an increase in the quantity of money, which shifts the *LM* schedule from LM_0 to LM_1, has little effect on income.

icant amount. This combination of an assumed high interest elasticity of money demand and low interest elasticity of the demand for output led early Keynesian economists to the conclusion that the quantity of money was unimportant.

What role was there for monetary policy? During World War II much of the war expenditure had been financed by selling bonds to the public at relatively low interest rates. Keeping the interest rate on bonds low and stable would have the desirable effects of keeping the cost of interest payments on the debt low and protecting the capital value of the bonds for the investors (recall that bond prices and interest rates vary inversely). Low interest rates would also mean that monetary policy would make whatever limited contribution it could to strengthening aggregate demand. Since early Keynesian economists feared a return to the severe depression conditions of the 1930s, this was another desirable feature of low interest rates. Thus low and stable interest rates became the goal of monetary policy. To achieve this goal the monetary authority cooperated with the Treasury to "peg" or fix the levels of interest rates and in doing so, as we will see in a moment, they surrendered control over the quantity of money.

There was a further element in the view of the early Keynesians that made pegging the interest rate desirable. Following Keynes, they felt that the demand for money was highly unstable.[3] The LM curve was not only flat (in the relevant range) but shifted around in an unpredictable way. These shifts would lead to unpredictable interest-rate changes and consequent instability in financial markets. Such changes could be avoided by pegging the interest rate.

It will be useful for our later analysis to examine just what the monetary authority does when it pegs the interest rate and the implications of pegging interest rates for money stock control. Consider the situation where there is one type of bond, a perpetuity paying a fixed amount per period. In this case, as we saw in Section 6.1, the price of the bond is inversely related to the current market interest rate. The price of the bond (PB) can be expressed as

$$PB = \frac{C}{r}$$

or, equivalently,

$$r = \frac{C}{PB} \tag{9.1}$$

where C is the number of dollars of interest the bond pays per period (the coupon payment) and r is the interest rate expressed as a decimal. If C is \$100 and r is 0.05 (5 percent), the bond will sell for \$2000 ($100 \div 0.05 = 2000$).

If the monetary authority wished to peg the interest rate at 5 percent, it would maintain the price of the bond at \$2000 by standing ready to buy or sell bonds at that price. As long as the monetary authority will sell the bond at \$2000, no investor will pay a higher price to buy from another bond holder. The interest rate cannot fall below 5 percent [from (9.1) note that $r = C \div PB = 100 \div 2000 = 0.05$]. Similarly, since the monetary authority will buy bonds for \$2000, no bond holder will sell for less to a private buyer. The interest rate will not rise above 5 percent. As long as the monetary authority has a sufficiently large holding of bonds, which in practice it does, it can fix the price of bonds and peg the interest rate.

But now what happens to the quantity of money? The monetary authority buys or sells bonds by exchanging them for money. We

___

[3]What is meant here by instability in money demand is that the money demand *function* would shift in an unpredictable manner. As discussed in Chapter 6, such shifts in the money demand function are changes in the quantity of money demanded for given levels of income and the interest rate. The effects on the LM schedule from such shifts in the money demand function are discussed in Section 6.2.

consider the details of the process later but for now assume that the monetary authority simply prints new money to pay for bonds it purchases from private bond holders and retires from circulation the money earned from sales of bonds. Since in order to peg the interest rate the monetary authority must stand ready to exchange money for bonds on demand, the quantity of money will be determined not by the monetary authority but by the desire of the private sector to hold bonds. *The monetary authority can peg the interest rate, but in doing so it surrenders to the private sector control of the quantity of money.*

To understand better the demand-determined nature of the quantity of money in a system where the monetary authority is pegging the rate of interest, it is useful to consider our IS–LM graph in such a situation, as shown in Figure 9.3. The graph contains three possible IS curves, IS_0, IS_1, and IS_2, corresponding to successively higher levels of aggregate demand. We assume that the monetary authority pegs the interest rate at $\bar{r}$. This is represented in Figure 9.3 by the perfectly horizontal LM schedule, $\overline{LM}$, at interest rate $\bar{r}$. The LM curve in this case is flat even though the interest elasticity of money demand is not infinite. We are not

Figure 9.3
IS–LM with the
Interest Rate Pegged

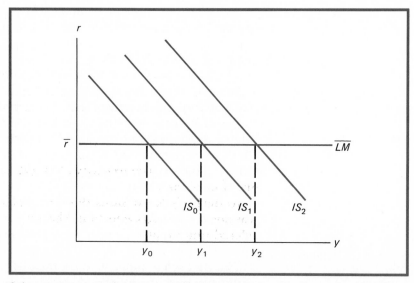

If the monetary authority pegs the interest rate at $\bar{r}$, the *LM* curve effectively becomes horizontal. Increases in aggregate demand which shift the *IS* schedule from IS_0 to IS_1, then to IS_2, will increase income from y_0 to y_1 then to y_2. The monetary authority supplies the additional money required for increased transactions balances as income rises. The quantity of money becomes demand determined.

MACROECONOMIC MODELS

assuming that there is a liquidity trap. With the interest rate pegged, it is the fact that the monetary authority will buy and sell bonds—increase or decrease the money stock—to prevent any movements in the interest rate, which makes the LM schedule flat. It is the money supply that is now perfectly elastic.

Now we can see how the quantity of money in the system will be determined. Recall that in the Keynesian model, money demand is given by

$$M^d = L(y, r) \tag{9.2}$$

With r fixed at $\bar{r}$, money demand varies solely with income. With the interest rate pegged, the money stock will be determined by this demand for money, and, therefore, by the level of income. Consider what happens as aggregate demand increases from IS_0 to IS_1 then to IS_2 in Figure 9.3. With the IS curve at IS_0, income will be at y_0 and money demand will be

$$M_0^d = L(y_0, \bar{r}) \tag{9.3}$$

With the increase in aggregate demand shifting the IS schedule to IS_1 and then IS_2, income rises from y_0 to y_1 and then y_2 in Figure 9.3. As a result of the increase in income, money demand increases to

$$M_1^d = L(y_1, \bar{r})$$

and then

$$M_2^d = L(y_2, \bar{r}) \tag{9.4}$$

To increase its money holdings, the private sector must sell bonds. Normally, this would result in a fall in bond prices, but the monetary authority prevents this by buying any bonds the public wants to sell at existing bond prices. As income rises the monetary authority supplies the additional money required for increased transaction balances. The quantity of money is determined by the demand for money.

To the early Keynesians this loss of control of the money stock was not considered important. The quantity of money was not considered important.

Friedman's Restatement of the Quantity Theory: The Weak Form

It is at this point that Milton Friedman enters the story. Contrary to the view of the early Keynesians, Friedman argued that the demand for money was stable. Contrary to the near-liquidity-trap characterization, Friedman maintained that the interest elasticity of money demand was certainly not infinite and was in fact "rather small." The quantity of money, far from being unimportant, was the dominant influence on the level of economic activity.

The analysis on which Friedman's conclusions rest began with a restatement of the classical quantity theory of money. Friedman's version of the quantity theory is closest to the Cambridge approach we considered. That approach focused on the demand for money. The central relationship was

$$M^d = \bar{k}Py \tag{9.5}$$

expressing a proportional relationship between money demand (M^d) and the level of nominal income [price (P) times real income (y)]. The factor of proportionality (k) was taken as constant in the short run.

Friedman emphasizes the fact that the quantity theory was, as can be seen from (9.5), a theory of money demand. It was because k was treated as a constant by the Cambridge economists and the *nominal* supply of money (M) was treated as being set exogenously by the monetary authority that the Cambridge equation could be transformed into a theory of nominal income,

$$M = M^d = \bar{k}Py$$

$$M\frac{1}{\bar{k}} = Py \tag{9.6}$$

or the alternative form (where V, the velocity of money, equals $1/k$).

$$M\bar{V} = Py \tag{9.7}$$

where the bar over k or V indicates that these magnitudes do not vary. Friedman examined the changes in the Cambridge theory of money demand that must be made in the light of Keynes's theory of money demand. Then he investigated the validity of transforming this revised version of the Cambridge theory into a theory of nominal income.

Keynes's theory of money demand stressed the role of money as an asset in addition to its role in transactions. In studying the factors that determined how much money people would hold, Keynes was then naturally led to consider factors that determined the desirability of money relative to other assets. He made the simplifying assumption that other assets were a homogeneous enough group that he could lump them together under the category "bonds." He then considered how an individual allocated his wealth between money and bonds. The key factors which he thought determined the split were the level of income and the level of the interest rate. Put in terms of the Cambridge equation, Keynes focused on the interest rate as the primary determinant of k, the amount of money balances one would hold for a given level of income. A rise in the interest rate led to a fall in k or, equivalently, a rise in velocity; this is what we saw in the preceding subsection. Since k was a variable, not a constant, the Cambridge equation could not by itself provide a theory of nominal income.

Friedman accepted Keynes's emphasis on the role of money as an asset. With this as a basis he sets out his own theory of the demand for money. Again income is one determinant of money demand and, as with Keynes, one can view Friedman's analysis as providing a theory of what determines the Cambridge k, money holdings as a proportion of nominal income. Friedman's money demand function can be written as follows:

$$M^d = L(P, y, r_B, r_E, r_D) \tag{9.8}$$

where P = price level
$\quad y$ = real income
$\quad r_B$ = nominal interest rate on bonds
$\quad r_E$ = nominal return on equities
$\quad r_D$ = nominal return on durable goods

Money demand is assumed to depend on nominal income, the product of the first two arguments in the demand function. An increase in nominal income would increase money demand.[4] For a given level of nominal income, Friedman assumes, as does Keynes, that the amount of money demanded will depend on the rate of return offered on alternative assets. The money demand function given by (9.8) is a simplification of Friedman's equation and includes the rates of return on the major alternatives to money as an asset. These are bonds, the asset Keynes focused on, equities (shares of stock in corporations), and durable goods, such as consumer durables, land, and houses. Durable goods do not pay an explicit interest rate or dividend rate. Their return would be the expected increase in the price of the good over the period for which it is held. Thus the expected rate of inflation is also a determinant of money demand. An increase in the rate of return on any of these alternative assets causes the demand for money to decline.

Friedman's theory differs from Keynes's in several respects. First, Friedman views the money demand function as stable. The variables in the equation determine the quantity of money that will be demanded; the function is not assumed to shift erratically. Keynes's view was that the demand for money function was unstable, shifting with changes in the public confidence in the economy.

Second, Friedman does not segment his money demand into components representing transaction balances, speculative demand, and a precautionary demand. Money, like other "goods," has a number of attributes that make it useful, but Friedman does

---

[4]There is a difference between the concept of income in Keynes's theory and Friedman's income variable, which he calls "permanent income." Friedman's permanent income concept is discussed in Chapter 13.

not find it helpful to specify separate demands based on each of the uses of money.

The third difference between Keynes's and Friedman's money demand theories is that Friedman includes separate yields for bonds, equities, and durable goods. Keynes focused on the choice of money versus bonds. It is not clear how much of a substantive difference this is, since what Keynes termed "bonds" can be considered more broadly as at least including equities. Often this has not been done, however, and Keynesian analysis has focused narrowly on the money versus bonds choice. Friedman makes explicit the possibility of other substitutions and also allows for a shift from money directly into commodities (durable goods) as rates of return change.

Friedman's money demand theory can be used to restate the Cambridge equation as follows:

$$M^d = k(r_B, r_E, r_D)Py \tag{9.5'}$$

where instead of a constant k we now have k expressed as a function of the rates of return on the assets which are alternatives to holding money. A rise in the rate of return on any one of these alternative assets would cause k to fall, reflecting the increased desirability of the alternative asset. In these terms Friedman can be seen to have restated the quantity theory, providing a systematic explanation of k, an explanation that takes account of the Keynesian analysis of money's role as an asset.

If this is the restated quantity theory, how would we characterize a modern quantity theorist? How would he differ from a Keynesian? In Friedman's view, a quantity theorist must believe that:

1. The money demand function is stable.
2. This demand function plays an important role in determining the level of economic activity.
3. The quantity of money is strongly affected by supply factors.

In Friedman's version of the Cambridge equation, the equilibrium condition in the money market is

$$M = M^d = k(r_B, r_E, r_D)Py \tag{9.9}$$

With a stable money demand function, an exogenous increase in the money stock must lead to a rise in Py or must cause declines in r_B, r_E, and r_D (which will cause k to rise), with indirect effects on Py.[5] A quantity theorist must believe that the money demand

---

[5]Notice that a fall in the rates of return on the alternative asset to money (r_B, r_E, r_D) will increase money demand for a given income level and therefore raise k.

function is in fact stable. He must believe that changes in the money stock do come mostly from the supply side as a result of central bank policies. Finally, he must believe that such changes in the quantity of money are important in determining nominal income; much of the effect of a change in M does come in the form of a change in Py.

In what way does a quantity theorist differ from a Keynesian? The answer to this question depends on whether the term "Keynesian" refers to the position of the early Keynesians described in the preceding subsection or more generally to the neo-Keynesian theory presented earlier. Friedman's theory as outlined so far is clearly antithetical to the early Keynesian position. The early Keynesians believed that the money demand function was unstable, that the interest elasticity of money demand was extremely high, and that as a consequence, changes in the quantity of money did not have important predictable effects on the level of economic activity. In Friedman's view the quantity theorist believes that the money demand function is stable and that the quantity of money is an important determinant of the level of economic activity. Further, Friedman believes, as we will see shortly, that the interest elasticity of money demand is low.

Vis-a-vis the early Keynesians, it is hard with hindsight not to conclude that Friedman's view was the more correct. Today few economists share the view of the early Keynesians that money is unimportant. In the United States the importance of money was demonstrated by the failure of the policy of pegging interest rates. The post–World War II period did not see a return to the depression conditions of the 1930s, as many of Keynes's followers expected. Instead, inflation became a problem. Consumers forced to save during the war due to rationing and shortages satisfied a pent-up demand for consumer durables and semidurables from automobiles to baby carriages. Strong demand encouraged investment spending to convert plant from production of war materials to consumer goods.

With aggregate demand growing and the interest rate pegged at a low level, the situation was similar to that depicted in Figure 9.3 as the IS curve moves from IS_0 to IS_1, then to IS_2. At each step the monetary authority must increase the money stock to keep the interest rate from rising as the demand for transactions balances grows. This growth in the money stock contributes to the inflationary spiral. In the United States such a process continued until the Federal Reserve stopped cooperating with the Treasury to peg interest rates at low levels and began to exert independent control over the money stock.

What about the differences between the quantity theory as outlined so far and the neo-Keynesian position? Here there is no clear distinction. The neo-Keynesians believe that money is important. During the postwar period there was accumulating evidence that the demand for money function was stable.[6] Estimates of the money demand function did show significant interest elasticity, larger than suggested by Friedman's own analysis, but certainly not indicating a liquidity trap. Overall, if a quantity theorist need only subscribe to the three beliefs listed by Friedman, a neo-Keynesian can in fact be a quantity theorist.

Friedman's Restatement of the Quantity Theory: The Strong Form

The quantity theory view embodied in the three propositions listed above is, however, what may be termed a *weak quantity theory* view—weak in at least two senses. First, it is not sufficient to establish the quantity theory postulate which we attributed to the classical quantity theory: that the price level would move proportionately with the money stock. Second, the weak quantity theory is not sufficient to establish the first and third of the monetarist propositions listed in the introduction: that the supply of money is the dominant influence on nominal income and in the short run on real income as well. The weak quantity theory position is that money matters for such variables but not that it is the only major systematic influence on them. There is a strong modern quantity theory position offered by Friedman and others which is consistent with these two monetarist positions. In the short run, it is not consistent with the classical view of the proportionality of money and prices, although this proportionality is assumed to hold in the long run. It is this strong quantity theory position which differs sharply from the neo-Keynesian position.

The strong quantity theory position extends the quantity theory from a theory of money demand to a theory of nominal income. We have seen how the Cambridge quantity theorists did this with the assumption of a constant k [see (9.6) or (9.7)]. Friedman points out that his version of the quantity theory can also be turned into a theory of nominal income if the variables in his money demand function [equation (9.8)] other than nominal income (r_B, r_E, r_D) have little effect on money demand. This being the case, these variables will have little effect on k. Money holdings as a proportion of income (k) will be nearly constant. Since Friedman does not believe that money demand is completely independent of these rates of return, the theory of nominal income which results from assuming that k is a constant will only be an approximation. But then

---

[6]Innovations in the financial sector during the 1970s have cast doubt on the stability of the demand function for M1 (demand deposits plus currency). This is, however, more a matter of the proper definition of money as new types of deposits have come into being than a question of the stability of the demand for money properly defined. The questions of the proper definition of money and recent instability of the M1 money demand function are discussed in Chapter 14.

any theory will hold only approximately. Friedman and others have done empirical work which convinces them that such a strong quantity theory position, which can be written as

$$Py = \frac{1}{k}M \qquad (9.10)$$

is a better approximation than that given by simple representations of the Keynesian view. It is this strong quantity theory that is required for statements by Friedman such as: "I regard the description of our position as 'money is all that matters for changes in *nominal* income and for *short-run* changes in real income' as an exaggeration but one that gives the right flavor to our conclusions"; or, "appreciable changes in the rate of growth of the stock of money are a necessary and sufficient condition for appreciable changes in the rate of growth of money income."[7] This strong quantity theory position is a central element of monetarism. It is this strong quantity position that produces policy conclusions sharply at odds with neo-Keynesian views, as we will see in the next section. Prior to that, it is useful to represent this strong quantity theory position in terms of the IS–LM diagram and the aggregate supply–aggregate demand framework used to explain the Keynesian position. This will facilitate comparisons between the monetarists and the neo-Keynesians, and in the course of representing the strong quantity theory position in these terms we will explain one further difference between the monetarists and the neo-Keynesians. In Figure 9.4 we have drawn the IS–LM curves as the strong quantity theorist would. The LM curve is nearly, but not quite, vertical, reflecting Friedman's view that the interest elasticity of money demand is quite low.

Another divergence from the Keynesian position concerns the slope of the IS curve. Here a flatter IS curve is consistent with the monetarist position that aggregate demand is quite sensitive to changes in the interest rate. The neo-Keynesians also believe that the interest rate affects aggregate demand and would not argue that the IS curve should be nearly vertical as we drew it for the model of the early Keynesians (Figure 9.2). The difference between the neo-Keynesians and monetarists on this point is one of degree. The monetarists argue that the Keynesians restrict channels by which the interest rate affects aggregate demand to an effect on investment via a change in the cost of borrowing funds. The mone-

[7]These two quotations are from Milton Friedman, "A Theoretical Framework for Monetary Analysis," in Robert Gordon, ed., *Milton Friedman's Monetary Frameworks* (Chicago: University of Chicago Press, 1974), p. 27; and Milton Friedman and Anna Schwartz, "Money and Business Cycles," *Review of Economics and Statistics*, 45 (February 1963), supplement, pp. 32–64, respectively.

Figure 9.4
IS–LM: A Monetarist
Version

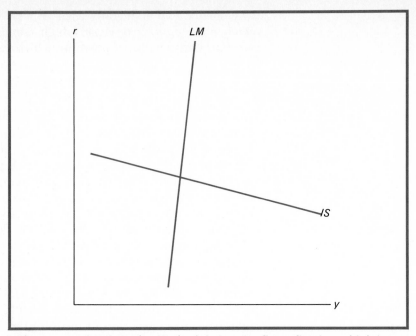

In the monetarist view, the *IS* schedule is quite flat reflecting a high interest elasticity of aggregate demand. The *LM* schedule is nearly vertical reflecting a very low interest elasticity of money demand.

tarists argue that this is too narrow an interpretation of the effects
of interest rates, resulting in part from the tendency of the Keynesians to think of "bonds" as just one class of financial assets, rather
than as all assets other than money.

In his theory of money demand, Friedman did not lump all nonmoney assets into one category. He separately considered bonds,
equities, and durable goods, avoiding Keynes's simplification of
aggregating to just "bonds" and money. The monetarists believe
that if it is recognized that a change in *the* interest rate is really a
change in all these yields, its effects go beyond the effects of a
change in borrowing cost to firms that buy investment goods. In
addition, a change in *the* interest rate means a change in the prices
of corporate stock, the prospective return on real estate and holding durable goods as well. The monetarists believe that the interest
rate plays a more important role in determining aggregate demand than was allowed in the neo-Keynesian model.

Figure 9.4 is adequate to bring out several of the features of the
monetarist view that differ from that of the neo-Keynesians, but it
is deficient in one respect. We have generally used the IS–LM
curves by themselves to show how real GNP and the interest rate

were determined, with the price level held constant. A constant price level, even as a short-run approximation, is *not* an assumption made by the monetarists. Figure 9.5 shows how the monetarist view would be represented in the aggregate supply–aggregate demand framework of previous chapters.

Three positions for the aggregate demand curve are shown in the graph, $y^d(M_0)$, $y^d(M_1)$, and $y^d(M_2)$, corresponding to three values of the money stock, M_0, M_1, and M_2. Recalling the monetarist (strong quantity theory) formula, giving nominal income

$$Py = \frac{1}{k} M \qquad (9.10)$$

the monetarist position can be represented as asserting that changes in M are *required* for significant shifts in the aggregate demand curve. Money is the only important systematic influence on aggregate demand.

Figure 9.5

Aggregate Supply and Demand: The Monetarist View

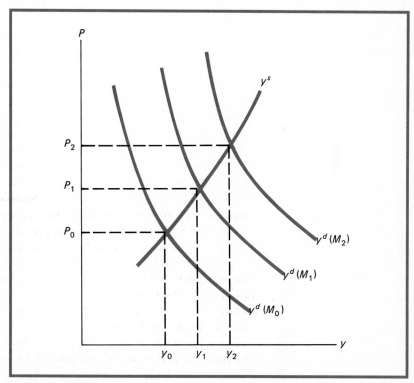

In the monetarist view, the position of the aggregate demand schedule is determined primarily by the level of the money stock. Increases in the money stock from M_0 to M_1 then to M_2 shift the aggregate demand schedule from $y^d(M_0)$ to $y^d(M_1)$ then to $y^d(M_2)$.

We have left unanswered the question of what determines aggregate supply. What determines the slope of the aggregate supply curve and, consequently, the proportion of a money-induced rise in nominal income which goes to increase output and the proportion that goes to increase price? This is the central question of the next chapter. Prior to that we analyze the differing views of the monetarists and neo-Keynesians on the relative effectiveness of fiscal and monetary policies. Here the issue is the effect of the policies on aggregate demand. Whether the change in aggregate demand primarily affects prices or output is not crucial to this analysis, and we will revert to using the IS–LM curve graph to illustrate these policy differences.

9.3 MONETARY AND FISCAL POLICY: MONETARISTS VERSUS NEO-KEYNESIANS

Fiscal Policy

The monetarist and neo-Keynesian frameworks produce quite different views about the effectiveness of fiscal policy changes. The monetarist view on the effectiveness of fiscal policy has been expressed by Milton Friedman in several places. Since there is a great deal of controversy on this question, it is best to quote him directly: "I come to the main point—in my opinion, the state of the budget by itself has no significant effect on the course of nominal income, on deflation, or on cyclical fluctuations."[8] In reference to the Keynesian proposition that fiscal policy was effective Friedman wrote: "The 'monetarists' rejected this proposition and maintained that fiscal policy by itself is largely ineffective that what matters is what happens to the quantity of money."[9] The most optimistic assessment he has given of fiscal policy effects is that they are "certain to be temporary and likely to be minor."

When Friedman discusses the independent effects of fiscal policy, the question at issue, he means the effects of changes in the government budget *holding constant the quantity of money in the system.* Consider an increase in government spending. If tax rates are not changed, which has been the usual assumption we have made when considering one policy change at a time, the new spending must be financed by printing money or by selling bonds. Similarly for a tax cut, if spending is to be unchanged, lost tax revenues must be replaced by sales of bonds to the public or by printing new money.

If a tax cut or spending increase is financed by printing new

[8]Milton Friedman and Walter Heller, *Monetary Versus Fiscal Policy* (New York: Norton, 1969), p. 51.
[9]Friedman, *Counter-revolution*, p. 18.

money, we have both a monetary policy action (M increases) and a fiscal policy action (G increases or T falls). In terms of the IS–LM framework, both the IS and LM curves shift. Monetarists *do not* argue that this type of policy change will be ineffective. They do argue that the policy effect will come only because the stock of money changes. The controversy is over what Friedman refers to above as the effect of a change in the federal budget *by itself,* meaning without an accompanying change in the quantity of money. This would mean in the case of a tax cut or spending increase that the deficit created by these actions would be financed completely by sales of bonds to the public. The monetarist position is that such policy actions will have little systematic effect on nominal income (prices or real output) over short-run periods of perhaps one to three years.

The reasons the monetarists reach this conclusion can be seen from Figure 9.6. There we consider the effects of an increase in government spending when we accept the monetarist assumptions about the slopes of the IS and LM curves. An increase in government spending from G_0 to G_1 shifts the IS curve to the right, from IS_0 to IS_1. Recall from our analysis of the Keynesian system that the size of the change in government expenditure affects the size of the horizontal shift in the IS curve. The IS_0 and IS_1 curves have been drawn to reflect an increase in government spending of approximately the same amount as that depicted in Figure 9.1, the last time we analyzed an increase in government spending in the neo-Keynesian model.[10] The effect of the increase in government spending in the monetarist case (Figure 9.6) is primarily to cause the interest rate to rise (from r_0 to r_1). The level of income is changed only slightly (from y_0 to y_1). Why?

In essence, the explanation for these results has already been supplied in the discussion about the dependence of the relative effectiveness of monetary and fiscal policy on the slopes of the IS and LM curves, in particular on the assumed magnitudes of the interest elasticities of money demand and of investment demand. The monetarists assume that the interest elasticity of money demand is small; the LM curve is steep. The increase in government spending increases aggregate demand initially. As income begins to rise, the demand for transactions balances increases. With the money stock fixed, this puts upward pressure on the interest rate, which rises until money supply and demand are again equal. If money demand is interest inelastic, a large increase in the interest rate is required to reequilibrate money demand with the fixed money supply.

---

[10]The horizontal shift in the IS curve will be equal to $\Delta G[1/(1 - b)]$, where b is the marginal propensity to consume (see Section 6.2).

Figure 9.6
Effects of an Increase
in Government
Spending: The
Monetarist Case

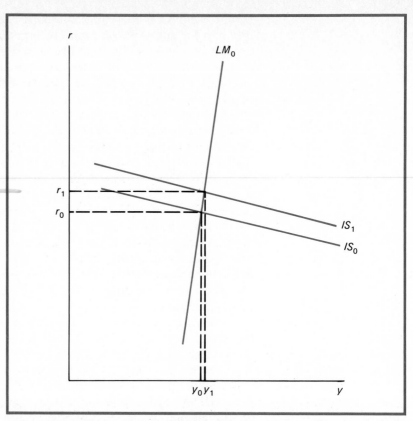

An increase in government spending shifts the *IS* schedule from IS_0 to IS_1. With the relatively flat *IS* schedule and nearly vertical *LM* schedule, this fiscal policy action has little effect on income (*y* rises only from y_0 to y_1).

The IS curve is relatively flat in the monetarist view. Investment demand is highly sensitive to changes in the interest rate. Therefore, the rise in the interest rate required to keep the money market in equilibrium will cause private-sector aggregate demand to decline substantially as government spending begins to stimulate income. This reduction in private sector aggregate demand is what we referred to earlier as "crowding out." In the monetarist model such crowding out occurs almost dollar for dollar with an increase in government spending. On net, aggregate demand and, hence, income is increased very little by an increase in government spending.

Although the analysis so far provides sufficient reason why a monetarist might expect little increase in income as a result of an expansionary fiscal policy, it leaves out one key element in the monetarist analysis of crowding out.

MACROECONOMIC MODELS

We saw in our analysis of the Keynesian system that the equilibrium interest rate was that rate at which the public's demand for money was equal to the exogenously given money supply. Since total wealth was fixed, and wealth consisted of bonds plus money, equilibrium in the money market guaranteed equilibrium in the bond market. Keynes ignored the effect on the interest rate of the ongoing increments to wealth that resulted from new saving or changes in bond supply that come as a result of financing business investment *or a government deficit*. The important implication of this assumption for our analysis here is that the Keynesian model neglected any *direct* upward pressure on interest rate that would come as a result of the government selling bonds to the public to finance a budget deficit. This is not to say that the Keynesians neglected all sources of upward pressure on interest rates from deficit spending. As income was increased, money demand increased, and with a fixed money stock the interest rate had to rise to restore equilibrium in the money market. By *direct* effect what is meant here is the upward pressure on interest rates that is created by the sale of the new bonds *at a given level of income*. The Keynesians implicitly assume that the supply of new government bonds to finance a government deficit is so small relative to the outstanding stock of bonds of all kinds that the direct effects of such bond sales on interest rates are negligible.[11]

The monetarists disagree. They argue that the government bond sales will directly create upward pressure on interest rates, an additional source of crowding out. The monetarists believe that if the money stock is held constant, the public will be willing to buy new bonds, thus shifting their portfolio of assets more toward bonds and away from money, only if the interest rate they earn on bonds is increased. This *portfolio effect* can be illustrated as follows.

We rewrite the Keynesian money demand function to include a wealth variable, where we assume that an increase in wealth (Wh) would cause an increase in the demand for money,

$$M^d = L(y, r, \text{Wh}) \qquad (9.11)$$

Where since wealth (Wh) equals bonds (B) plus money (M), we can equivalently write this demand function as

$$M^d = L(y, r, B + M) \qquad (9.12)$$

At a given level of income and of the interest rate, an increase in wealth coming from an increase in the stock of bonds creates an increased demand for money to restore the initial proportions of money and bonds.

[11]Recall here that the category "bonds" includes all nonmoney financial assets.

Now consider the effects that an increase in government spending financed by bonds would be having on income perhaps eight quarters (two years) after the policy change was initiated. We depict this graphically in Figure 9.7. To be concrete, suppose that government spending is increased by 10 units at an annual rate and then is maintained at this new level. In Figure 9.7 the effect of this increase in government spending is shown by the rightward shift in the IS curve from IS_0 to IS_1. This results in an increase in y from y_0 to y_1. At the end of two years, if tax collections and the money stock were held constant, 20 units (10 per year for two years) of new bonds would have been sold to the public to finance this new spending.[12] The increase in bond supply would increase wealth and, hence, increase the demand for money *at given levels of y and r*. This increase in the demand for money will shift the LM curve to the left from LM_0 to LM_1,[13] causing income to decline to y_2. The interest rate is pushed even farther, up to r_2. In the graph income is shown to have declined even relative to y_0, the equilibrium level of income in the absence of any fiscal policy action. This is not the necessary or even the most likely case. What is assured is that this direct crowding out will cause income to decline relative to y_1. Since the monetarists believe that the original increase from y_0 to y_1 is likely to be minor, they expect the net effect of a debt-financed fiscal policy action to be small, with even the direction of the effect uncertain.

As noted above, the neo-Keynesians disregard this direct crowding out. Any wealth effect of newly created bonds on money demand (the leftward shift in the LM curve in Figure 9.7) in the short run is assumed to be negligible. In the longer run the neo-Keynesians would agree that there are effects from growth of *all* asset supplies and demands. To focus only on the wealth effect on money demand from an increase in government bonds is too narrow a perspective for this long-run analysis. In any case the neo-Keynesians argue that the short run (two to four years) is the relevant policy horizon. In contrast to Friedman's assessment, the neo-Keynesians believe that the effects on income of bond-financed fiscal policy actions will be substantial and will persist for several years. This makes fiscal policy a useful stabilization tool.

Monetary Policy

Both the monetarists and the neo-Keynesians believe that monetary policy actions will have substantial and sustained effects on nominal income. The early Keynesians did, as we have seen, doubt

[12]Since in reality tax collections will move with the level of income even if tax rates are unchanged, some of the new spending will be financed by increased tax collections. This would mean fewer bonds would have to be sold and the magnitude of the direct crowding out discussed here would be lessened.

[13]The reasons an increase in the demand for money, for given levels of y and r, will shift the LM curve to the left are discussed in Section 6.2.

Figure 9.7
Direct Crowding Out
in the *IS–LM* model

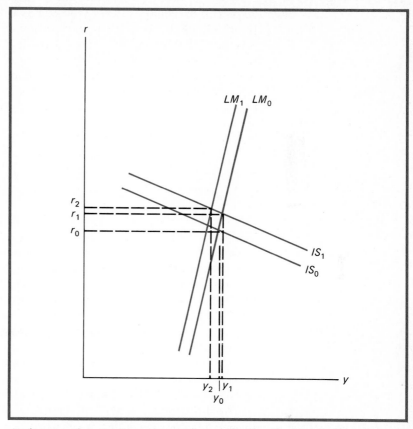

An increase in government spending shifts the *IS* schedule from IS_0 to IS_1 which in the monetarist view has a small expansionary effect on income which rises from y_0 to y_1. The sale of bonds to finance the increased government spending increases wealth and causes the *LM* schedule to shift to the left from LM_0 to LM_1, reducing income to y_2.

the effectiveness of monetary policy. At one stage in the debate over monetarism and the quantity theory of money (perhaps circa 1945–50) it might have been correct to refer to the Keynesians as "fiscalists" relying solely on fiscal policy, in contrast to the monetarist reliance on monetary policy. This is certainly not the case today. The difference between neo-Keynesians and monetarists over monetary policy concerns not *whether* monetary policy can affect income but *how* monetary policy should be used to stabilize income.

The Monetarist Position
The monetarists believe that changes in the quantity of money are the dominant influence on changes in nominal income and for the

short run on changes in real income as well. It follows that stability in the behavior of the money stock would go a long way toward producing stability in income growth. Friedman would in fact trace most past instability in the growth of income to unstable money growth. Because of the importance of money and because of what Friedman regards as past mistakes in money management, his position on monetary policy is as follows:

> My own prescription is still that the monetary authority go all the way in avoiding such swings by adopting publicly the policy of achieving a specified rate of growth in a specified monetary total. The precise rate of growth, like the precise monetary total, is less important than the adoption of some stated and known rate.[14]

To give an example, the monetary authority might announce and achieve a target rate of growth in M1 (currency plus checkable deposits) of 5 percent per year. The monetarists believe that nominal income growth would then be approximately 5 percent per year. If the trend growth in real income were 3 percent per year, the price level would rise by about 2 percent per year. The 5 percent level is not crucial, but whatever level is picked the monetarists want a *constant growth rate in the money stock.*

Such a policy would take away from the monetary authority the ability to regulate the quantity of money to try to offset other shocks that might affect the level of economic activity. Why is it that this is not regarded as a great loss by the monetarists?

The monetarist view of income determination with a constant money growth rate policy is illustrated in Figure 9.8. If a constant growth rate policy is followed, the level of the money stock at any one point in time (t) has been fixed exogenously. Since in the monetarist view the demand function for money is stable, this means that the position of the LM curve is fixed exogenously, at LM_{t0} in Figure 9.8. The IS curve may be shifted around due to other shocks to the economy. In Figure 9.8, depending on the values of these other shock variables (fiscal policy, export demand, etc.), we assume that the IS curve may be at IS_{t0}, IS_{t1}, or IS_{t2}. If the LM curve is steep, as it is drawn in Figure 9.8 and as the monetarists assume, these shifts in the IS curve will *for a given LM curve* have little destabilizing effect on income. In Figure 9.8 such shocks would cause income to vary only between y_{t0} and y_{t2}. Further, recall that the monetarists believe that left to itself the private sector is quite stable. This does not mean that there will be no shocks to the IS curve due to the private sector, but the fluctuations from this source should be relatively minor.

[14]Milton Friedman, "The Role of Monetary Policy," *American Economic Review*, 58 (March 1968), p. 16.

Figure 9.8

Income Determination with a Constant Growth Rate for Money: The Monetarist View

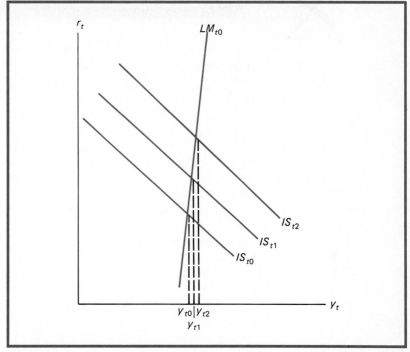

If a constant money growth rate policy is followed, at a point in time, t, the position of the LM schedule will be fixed at LM_{t0}. If the LM schedule is very steep, as the monetarists believe, then even if there are shifts in the IS schedule (from IS_{t0} to IS_{t1} to IS_{t2}), income will vary only over the narrow range y_{t0} to y_{t2}.

To summarize, the monetarists believe that money is the primary determinant of nominal income and of real income in the short run. Stabilizing money growth will remove the major source of instability in income determination. There are still other sources of instability, but these are not major because given the level of the money stock a given shock will not have a great impact (the LM curve is steep). Further, shocks of large magnitude are not likely because of the essential stability of the private sector.

If one accepts the reasoning that one will do pretty well with such a constant growth rate monetary rule, the question still remains: "Why not the best?" Why not use monetary policy, which is very potent, to offset even minor shocks that affect income? Why not "fine tune" the economy? Friedman's answer to this question is:

> We simply do not know enough to be able to recognize minor disturbances when they occur or to be able to predict either what their

effects will be with any precision or what monetary policy is required to offset their effects.[15]

Friedman and other monetarists believe that changes in the money
stock will have a strong effect on the level of income, but they
believe that money affects income with a lag. The bulk of the effect
of a monetary action today will, they believe, come only after 6 to
18 months. Thus, to offset a minor shock, one must be able to predict its size and when it will affect the economy several quarters in
advance. Friedman and other monetarists simply do not feel that
we know enough about the economy to do this. In the past they
believe that in trying to offset minor shocks, the monetary authority has destabilized income more often than not. To Friedman,
"the best is often enemy to the good."[16]

Contrast with the Keynesians

We have already examined the neo-Keynesian view of monetary
policy. In this view monetary policy is one of the main tools that
can be used by the policymaker to stabilize income. The neo-
Keynesians believe that both monetary and fiscal policy variables
should be actively adjusted to offset shocks to the economy which
would otherwise be destabilizing. Franco Modigliani, one of the
leading neo-Keynesians, expressed this view (which he characterized as nonmonetarist) as follows:

> Nonmonetarists accept what I regard to be the fundamental practi-
> cal message of *The General Theory:* that a private enterprise economy
> using an intangible money *needs* to be stabilized, *can* be stabilized,
> and, therefore, *should* be stabilized by appropriate monetary and
> fiscal policies.[17]

The neo-Keynesians favor active discretionary monetary as well as
fiscal policy actions. They oppose the constant money growth rate
policy espoused by Friedman and other monetarists. What are the
reasons for the differing views of the monetarists and Keynesians
on this issue?

The first explanation for these differing views about the proper
conduct of monetary policy is the disagreement between the monetarists and neo-Keynesians concerning the need for active stabilization policies. Whereas the monetarists view the private sector as
stable and "shock absorbing," the neo-Keynesians see the private
sector as shock producing and unstable. This is not to say that the

[15]Ibid., p. 14.
[16]Ibid., p. 14.
[17]*The General Theory* was Keynes's major work on macroeconomics. Franco
Modigliani, "The Monetarist Controversy, or Should We Forsake Stabilization Policies?" *American Economic Review*, 67 (March 1977), p. 1.

neo-Keynesians believe that without government stabilization policies we would constantly experience depressions and hyper-inflations, but rather that shocks we experience would result in substantial prolonged deviations from conditions of full employment and price stability. They believe that this would be the case even with a fixed rate of growth in the money stock.

This type of situation is depicted in Figure 9.9. Shocks to the economy from sources such as autonomous changes in investment demand will in the absence of offsetting monetary and fiscal policies cause the IS curve to move among positions such as IS_{t0}, IS_{t1}, IS_{t2}. This will cause income to vary substantially over the range of y_{t0}, to y_{t2}. Since neo-Keynesians believe private sector demand is unstable, they view such shifts in the IS curve as likely. The neo-Keynesians do not believe that money plays such a dominant role in income determination; thus in Figure 9.9 the LM curve is much less steep than in the monetarist case (Figure 9.8). Consequently these shifts in the IS curve do produce large changes in income.

Figure 9.9
Income Determination with a Constant Growth Rate for Money: A Neo-Keynesian View

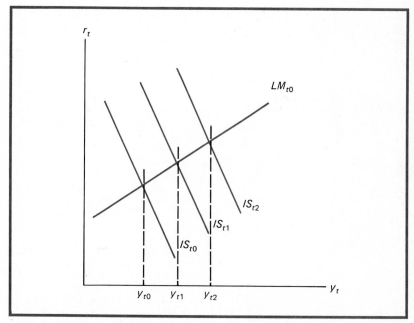

Even if a constant money growth rate policy is followed and the position of the LM schedule at time period t is fixed at LM_{t0}, the neo-Keynesians believe there can still be substantial variability of income (over the range y_{t0} to y_{t2}) in response to shocks to aggregate demand (shifts in the IS curve from IS_{t0} to IS_{t1} to IS_{t2}).

A second source of the differing views of the monetarist and neo-Keynesian is also evident from Modigliani's statement. He believes that we *can* stabilize the economy. We can predict shocks that will hit the economy and design policies to combat them. To be sure, there will be (have been) errors, but overall such policies will result in a more stable economic performance than we would have with fixed policy rules. Modigliani characterizes the fixed rule policy as equivalent to

> arguing to a man from St. Paul wishing to go to New Orleans on important business that he would be a fool to drive and should instead get himself a tub and drift down the Mississippi: that way he can be pretty sure that the current will eventually get him to his destination; whereas if he drives, he might take a wrong turn and, before he notices he will be going further and further away from his destination and pretty soon he may end up in Alaska, where he will surely catch pneumonia and he may never get to New Orleans.[18]

To Friedman and the monetarists adopting the constant growth rate rule puts the economy on a safe route and does not sacrifice much. To the neo-Keynesians, viewing money as only one of the major determinants of income and viewing the contribution of other factors such as investment decisions as unstable, the loss from such a constant growth rate rule is much greater and they oppose such policy rules.

Summary

In this section we presented the different views of the monetarists and neo-Keynesians on the relative effectiveness of monetary and fiscal policy.

The monetarist view is that fiscal policy actions have little independent effect on the level of economic activity. This view stems from the strong quantity theory position we analyzed. This policy view is essentially a corollary to the monetarist proposition that money is the dominant factor determining nominal income. The neo-Keynesians believe that fiscal policy actions exert significant and sustained influence on the level of economic activity. They reject the strong quantity theory position.

On monetary policy, the difference between the monetarists and the neo-Keynesians is not about the potential of monetary policy to significantly affect the level of economic activity—both believe that monetary policy has strong effects. They differ on what they view as the proper role for monetary policy. The monetarists are *noninterventionists*. They favor a constant growth rate in the

[18]Ibid., p. 13.

money stock that will then create an environment in which the stable private sector of the economy can function effectively. The neo-Keynesians are *interventionists* or policy *activists*. They see the need for active discretionary monetary and fiscal policies to keep an unstable private economy on track.

In Chapter 10, when we analyze the monetarist view of why money affects only nominal, and not real, variables in the longer run, we will see additional reasons for the noninterventionist views of the monetarists. Again the neo-Keynesians will disagree.

Review Questions

1   Compare the neo-Keynesian and monetarist views on how the velocity of money is determined. How do their differing views on velocity affect their respective policy conclusions?

2   Why were the early Keynesian economists so pessimistic about the effectiveness of monetary policy?

3   Compare Milton Friedman's formulation of the money demand function with the Keynesian specification in previous chapters.

4   How does the weak quantity theory position described in the text differ from what was termed the strong quantity theory or monetarist position?

5   Show how the IS and LM curves look in the monetarist view. Use these IS and LM curves to illustrate the monetarist conclusions about the relative effectiveness of monetary and fiscal policy.

6   Compare the monetarist and neo-Keynesian views on the proper conduct of fiscal policy. For both the monetarists and neo-Keynesians, explain not only the conclusion they reach concerning fiscal policy, but also how that conclusion is related to their respective theories.

7   Compare the monetarist and neo-Keynesian views on the proper conduct of monetary policy. For both the monetarists and neo-Keynesians, explain not only the conclusion they reach concerning monetary policy, but also how the conclusion is related to their respective theories.

8   Within the monetarist framework, money is the key variable in determining the level of economic activity. It would seem

to follow that the monetary authority should pursue an activist strategy of varying the money stock to offset other shocks to the economy. Therefore, it is surprising that monetarists favor a constant rate of growth for the money stock. Comment.

9　Analyze the effects of a decrease in taxes from T_0 to T_1 in the monetarist framework. In your answer be sure to take account of the financing of the deficit that results from the tax cut. How are the equilibrium levels of income and the interest rate affected by the tax cut?

Selected Readings

BRUNNER, KARL, "The Role of Money and Monetary Policy," Federal Reserve Bank of St. Louis *Review*, 50 (July 1968), pp. 9–24.

BRUNNER, KARL, "The Monetarist Revolution in Monetary Theory," *Weltwirtschaftliches Archiv*, 55 (March 1970), pp. 1–30.

CARLSON, KEITH, and SPENCER, ROGER, "Crowding Out and Its Critics," St. Louis Federal Reserve Bank *Review*, 57 (December 1975), pp. 2–17. Reprinted in Thomas Havrilesky and John Boorman, *Current Issues in Monetary Theory and Policy*. Arlington Heights, Ill.: AHM Publishing Corp., 1980.

FRIEDMAN, MILTON, "The Quantity Theory of Money—A Restatement," in Milton Friedman, ed., *Studies in the Quantity Theory of Money*. Chicago: University of Chicago, 1956. Reprinted in Milton Friedman, *The Optimum Quantity of Money and Other Essays*. Chicago: Aldine, 1969.

FRIEDMAN, MILTON, "A Monetary and Fiscal Framework for Economic Stability," *American Economic Review*, 38 (June 1948), pp. 245–64. Reprinted in Friederick Lutz and Lloyd Mints, eds., *Readings in Monetary Theory*. Homewood Ill.: Irwin, 1951.

FRIEDMAN, MILTON, and HELLER, WALTER, *Monetary Versus Fiscal Policy*. New York: Norton, 1969.

FRIEDMAN, MILTON, and SCHWARTZ, ANNA, "Money and Business Cycles," *Review of Economics and Statistics*, 45 (February 1963), supplement, pp. 32–64. Reprinted in Milton Friedman, ed., *The Optimum Quantity of Money and Other Essays*. Chicago: Aldine, 1969.

GORDON, ROBERT J., ed., *Milton Friedman's Monetary Framework*. Chicago: University of Chicago Press, 1974.

MAKINEN, GAIL, *Money, the Price Level, and Interest Rates*. Englewood Cliffs, N.J.: Prentice-Hall, 1977, Chaps. 9 and 12.

MAYER, THOMAS, *The Structure of Monetarism*. New York: Norton, 1978.

MODIGLIANI, FRANCO, "The Monetarist Controversy, or Should We Foresake Stabilization Policies?" *American Economic Review*, 67 (March 1977), pp. 1–19. Reprinted in Thomas Havrilesky and John Boorman, *Current Issues in Monetary Theory and Policy*. Arlington Heights, Ill.: AHM Publishing Corp., 1980.

POOLE, WILLIAM, *Money and the Economy: A Monetarist View.* Reading, Mass.: Addison-Wesley, 1978.

SMITH, WARREN, "A Neo-Keynesian View of Monetary Policy," in *Controlling Monetary Aggregates.* Boston: Federal Reserve Bank of Boston, 1969.

chapter 10

The preceding chapter focused on the monetarist analysis of the importance of money. We examined the basis for the monetarist belief that the supply of money is the dominant influence on nominal income. We also saw that for the *short run*, the monetarists believe that changes in the money stock are the primary determinant of fluctuations in real output and employment. In this chapter we consider a limitation that the monetarists place on the importance of money, a limitation expressed in the second of the monetarist propositions.

2. In the long run the influence of money is primarily on the price level and other *nominal* magnitudes. In the long-run, real variables, such as real output and employment, are determined by real, not monetary factors.

The theoretical basis for this proposition is the theory of the "natural" rate of unemployment developed by Milton Friedman.[1]

According to the natural rate theory, there exists for any economy an equilibrium level of output and an accompanying rate of unemployment determined by the supply of factors of production, technology, and institutions of the economy (i.e., determined by real factors). This is Friedman's natural rate. Changes in the level

---

[1]The theory of the natural rate of unemployment was also developed independently by Edmund Phelps of Columbia University. See, for example, the contributions by Phelps and others in Edmund Phelps, ed., *Employment and Inflation Theory* (New York: Norton, 1970).

MONETARISM (II): THE NATURAL RATE OF UNEMPLOYMENT

of aggregate demand, which Friedman believes are dominated by changes in the supply of money, can cause temporary movements of the economy away from the natural rate. Expansionary monetary policies, for example, can move output above the natural rate and move the unemployment rate below the natural rate for a time. The increased demand resulting from such an expansionary policy would also cause prices to rise. In the short run the price adjustment would not be complete, as it would be in the classical theory, where increases in demand cause prices to rise but do not affect output. *The monetarists do not agree with the classical position that output is completely supply determined even in the short run.*

Friedman does believe that there are equilibrating forces which cause the levels of output and employment to return to their natural rate over a longer period. It is not possible in Friedman's view for the government to use monetary policy to maintain the economy permanently at a level of output that holds the unemployment rate below the natural rate. It is at least not possible for the policymakers to do so unless they are willing to accept an ever-accelerating rate of inflation. To see why this is the case, we will look at Friedman's description of the effects of an expansionary monetary policy (Section 10.1). Next we compare Friedman's analysis with the Keynesian view of how expansionary policies affect employment and inflation (Section 10.2). This chapter concludes with a summary of the important differences between the monetarist and Keynesian views (Section 10.3).

10.1 THE ROLE OF MONETARY POLICY: A MONETARIST VIEW

The natural rate of unemployment is defined by Friedman as that rate of unemployment "which has the property that it is consistent with equilibrium in the structure of *real* wage rates."[2] Thus the natural rate of unemployment or the corresponding natural rate of employment will be a level such that labor demand equals labor supply at an equilibrium real wage. Such a situation is depicted in Figure 10.1a.

The labor demand schedule is the familiar marginal product of labor schedule (MPN). Labor supply is an increasing function of the real wage. Labor supply and demand are equated at N^*, the natural rate of employment. Only at this level of employment is there no tendency for the real wage to change. The natural rate of unemployment can be found simply by subtracting those employed from the total labor force to find the number unemployed and expressing this number as a percent of the total labor force. Using another familiar device, the production function in Figure 10.2b, we can find the level of output that will result from an employment level N^*. This is the natural level of output, y^*.

As can be seen from Figure 10.1, the natural rates of output and employment depend on the supply of factors of production and the technology of the economy—supply-side factors. The natural rates of output and employment do *not* depend on the level of aggregate demand. All this is much the same as in the classical system; the difference between the monetarists and the classical economists is that the monetarists do not assume that the economy is necessarily at these natural levels of employment and output in the short run.

Monetary Policy in the Short Run

Friedman considers the effects in the short run and the long run of an increase in the rate of growth in the money stock. Let us suppose that we begin with a situation where the economy is in equilibrium at the natural rate of unemployment and of output. Also suppose that the money stock (and hence nominal income) has been growing at a rate equal to the rate of growth of real output. Thus the price level is assumed to have been stable for some time. Suppose now that the rate of growth in the money stock is increased above the rate consistent with price stability. For concreteness, assume that the rate of growth in the money stock rises from 3 percent to 5 percent.

The increase in the rate of growth of the money stock will stimu-

[2]Milton Friedman, "The Role of Monetary Policy," *American Economic Review,* 58 (March 1968), p. 8.

Figure 10.1
Natural Rates of Employment and Output

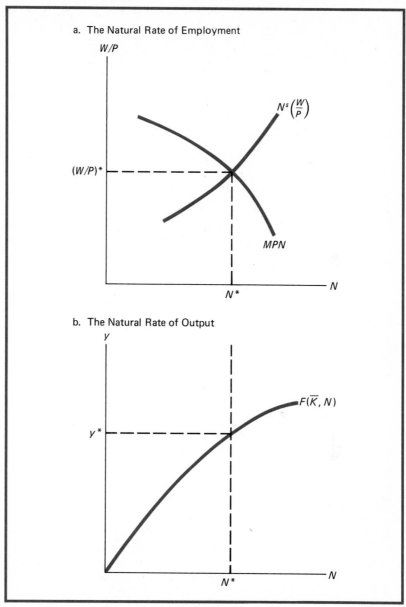

a. The Natural Rate of Employment

b. The Natural Rate of Output

The natural rate of employment (N^*) is determined at the point where labor supply and demand, both as functions of the real wage, are equated (Part a). The natural rate of output (y^*) is then determined along the graph of the production function (Part b).

late aggregate demand and, as a consequence, nominal income. The *short-run* consequences of this increase in aggregate demand are described by Friedman as follows:

> To begin with much or most of the rise in income will take the form of an increase in output and employment rather than in prices. People have been expecting prices to be stable, and prices and wages have been set for some time in the future on that basis. It takes time for people to adjust to a new state of demand. Producers will tend to react to the initial expansion in aggregate demand by increasing output, employees by working longer hours, and the unemployed by taking jobs now offered at former nominal wages. This much is pretty standard doctrine.[3]

The standard doctrine to which Friedman refers was the notion of a *Phillips curve*. The Phillips curve was a negative relationship between the unemployment rate (U) and the inflation rate ($\dot{P}$), such as that plotted in Figure 10.2. High rates of growth in aggregate demand would stimulate output and hence lower the unemployment rate. Such high rates of growth in demand would also cause an increase in the rate at which prices were rising (i.e., raise the inflation rate). Thus the Phillips curve postulated a trade-off between inflation and unemployment; lower rates of unemployment could be achieved but only at the cost of higher inflation rates.[4] In the description above of the immediate effects of an increase in the rate of growth in the money stock, Friedman is agreeing with this notion of a trade-off between inflation and unemployment *in the short run*. He is, in fact, arguing that the terms of the trade-off will be rather good in the short run since much of the increase in nominal income will be in the form of an increase in *real* output with prices rising to a lesser extent.

Monetary Policy in the Long Run

The distinctive element in Friedman's analysis comes in his view of the long-run effects of monetary policy. It is here that the notion of the natural rate of unemployment comes into play. We have just considered the short-run effects of an increase in the rate of growth of the money stock from 3 percent to 5 percent. In terms of Figure 10.2 the original equilibrium was with stable prices ($\dot{P} = 0$) and unemployment equal to the natural rate assumed to be 6 percent (point *A* in Figure 10.2). As a result of the increase in the rate of growth in the money stock, we assume that the economy moves to a new *short-run* equilibrium with unemployment reduced to 4 percent, and an inflation rate at 2 percent (point *B* in Figure 10.2). The

[3]Ibid., p. 10.
[4]The Phillips curve derives its name from the British economist A. W. H. Phillips, who studied the trade-off between unemployment and wage inflation (a key element in price inflation) in the British economy.

Figure 10.2
The Phillips Curve

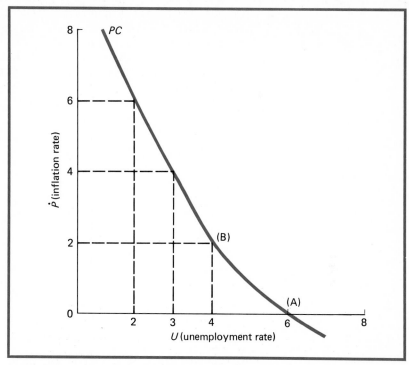

In the short run an increase in the rate of growth in the money stock moves the economy from point A to point B along the short-run Phillips curve. Unemployment declines and the inflation rate rises.

expansionary aggregate demand policy has succeeded in lowering the unemployment rate to a level below the natural rate.

Friedman accepts this outcome:

> But it describes only the initial effects. Because selling prices of products typically respond to an unanticipated rise in nominal demand faster than prices of factors of production, real wages received have gone down—though real wages anticipated by employees went up, since employees implicitly evaluated the wages offered at the earlier price level. Indeed, the simultaneous fall *ex post* in real wages to employers and rise *ex ante* to employees is what enabled employment to increase. But the decline *ex post* in real wages will soon come to affect anticipations. Employees will start to reckon on rising prices of the things they buy and to demand higher nominal wages for the future. "Market" unemployment is below the natural level. There is an excess demand for labor so real wages will tend to rise toward their initial level.[5]

Let us consider this explanation in some detail. Friedman points

[5]Friedman, "Role of Monetary Policy," p. 10.

THE NATURAL RATE OF UNEMPLOYMENT   **275**

out that in the short run, product prices increase faster than factor prices, the crucial factor price being the money wage. Thus the real wage (*W/P*) falls. This is a *necessary* condition for output to increase, for firms must be on their labor demand curve in Figure 10.1. Firms expand employment and output only with a decline in the real wage.

Friedman does not argue that workers are always on the labor supply curve shown in Figure 10.1. That curve expresses labor supply as a function of the actual real wage and Friedman does not assume that workers know the real wage. In the short run, after a period of stable prices, workers are assumed to evaluate nominal wage offers "at the earlier price level." While prices have risen, workers have not yet seen this, and will increase labor supply if offered a higher money wage *even if this increase in the money wage is less than the increase in the price level, even if the real wage is lower.* In the short run, labor supply increases because the *ex ante* or expected real wage is higher due to the higher nominal wage and unchanged view about the behavior of prices. Labor demand increases because of the fall in the *ex post* level of the actual real wage paid by the employer. Consequently, unemployment can be pushed below the natural rate.

This situation is only temporary, for workers eventually observe the higher price level and demand higher money wages. In terms of Figure 10.1, the real wage has been pushed below (*W/P*)*, the wage that clears the labor market once labor suppliers correctly perceive the price level and, hence, the real wage. At a lower real wage there is an excess demand for labor, which pushes the real wage back up to its equilibrium level, and this rise in the real wage will cause the level of employment to return to the natural rate shown in Figure 10.1.

The implications for the Phillips curve of this longer-run adjustment back to the natural rate are illustrated in Figure 10.3. The schedule labeled PC($\dot{P}^e = 0$) is the short-run Phillips curve from Figure 10.2. Here we have made explicit the fact that the curve is drawn for a given expected rate of inflation on the part of the suppliers of labor, in this case stable prices ($\dot{P}^e = 0$, where $\dot{P}^e$ is the expected rate of inflation). We have already analyzed the process whereby an increase in the rate of growth of the money stock from 3 percent to 5 percent moves the economy in the short run from point *A* to point *B*.

As suppliers of labor come to anticipate that prices are rising, the Phillips curve will shift upward to the right. Suppliers of labor will demand a higher rate of increase in money wages and, as a consequence, a higher rate of inflation will now correspond to any given unemployment rate. If money growth is continued at 5 percent, the economy will return to the natural rate of unemployment

Figure 10.3

Short-Run and Long-Run Phillips Curves

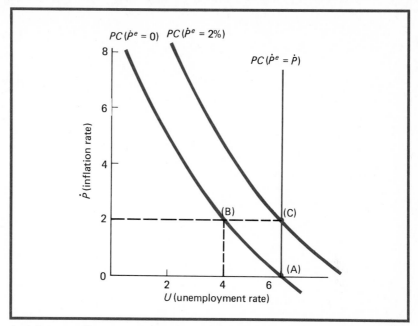

As labor suppliers come to anticipate the higher inflation rate, the short-run Phillips curve shifts from $PC(\dot{P}^e = 0)$ to $PC(\dot{P}^e = 2\%)$. The unemployment rate returns to the natural rate of 6 percent; the inflation rate remains higher at 2 percent (we move from point B to point C).

of 6 percent, but now with an inflation rate of 2 percent instead of the initial stable price level. In terms of Figure 10.3, this longer-run adjustment moves the economy from point B to point C.

The policymaker may not be content with this return to 6 percent unemployment (the natural rate) and may still pursue a target unemployment rate below the natural rate. In this case he will again increase the rate of growth in the money stock. Let us suppose that this time he increases money stock growth to from 5 percent to 7 percent. The effects of this further expansion of aggregate demand are illustrated in Figure 10.4 and can be analyzed as above. Until the suppliers of labor come to anticipate the further increase in the inflation rate, there will be an expansion of employment. The economy would move to a point such as D in Figure 10.4, with the unemployment rate below the natural rate of unemployment.

Suppliers of labor will after a time come to anticipate the higher inflation rate that corresponds to a 7 percent growth in the money stock. The short-run Phillips curve will shift to the schedule labeled $PC(\dot{P}^e = 4\%)$ and the economy will return to the natural rate of unemployment, with the inflation rate increased to 4 percent (7

Figure 10.4
Effect of an Attempt
to "Peg" the
Unemployment Rate
Below the Natural
Rate

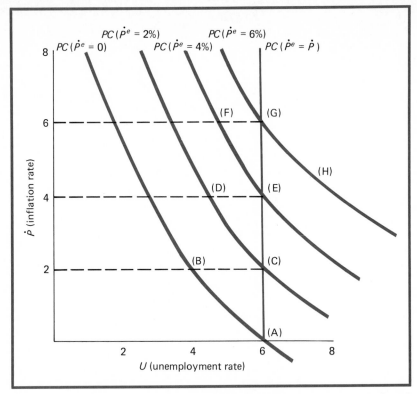

Additional increases in money growth, to 5 percent, then 7 percent, then 9 percent, result in each case in temporary reductions in unemployment (movements from C to D and E to F, for example). But in the longer run we simply move up the vertical Phillips curve (to points like E and G, for example).

percent money growth minus 3 percent growth in real income). In terms of Figure 10.4 we move from point D to point E. If the policymaker persists in his attempt to "peg" the unemployment rate, he will again increase money stock growth, for example to 9 percent. This will move the economy in the short run to point F, but in the longer run to point G, with a still higher rate of inflation.

Eventually, one expects that the policymaker will be led to conclude that inflation has become a more serious problem than unemployment (or he will be replaced by a different policymaker who has this view) and the acceleration of inflation will stop. Notice, however, that when inflation has persisted for a long time, inflationary expectations become built into the system. At a point such as point G in Figure 10.4, expansionary aggregate demand policies have increased the expected (and actual) inflation rate to 6 percent (9 percent money growth minus 3 percent growth in real income). An attempt to lower inflation by slowing the rate of growth in the money stock, let us suppose all the way back to the initial noninflationary 3 percent, will *not* immediately move the economy back to a point such as the initial point (*A*). In the short run we would move along the short-run Phillips curve which corresponds to an expected inflation rate of 6 percent, to a point such as point *H* in Figure 10.4, with high inflation and unemployment above the natural rate. Just as it took time for suppliers of labor to recognize that the rate of inflation had increased and, hence, to demand a faster rate of growth in money wages, it will take time for them to recognize that the inflation rate has slowed and for them to modify money wage demands to a level compatible with price stability. In the meantime, in the monetarist view, the economy must suffer from high inflation and high unemployment.

In the monetarist view, expansionary monetary policy can only temporarily move the unemployment rate below the natural rate. Put somewhat differently, there is a trade-off between unemployment and inflation only in the short run. In terms of Figures 10.3 and 10.4, the downward-sloping short-run Phillips curves *which are drawn for given expected inflation rates* illustrate the short-run trade-off between unemployment and inflation. The long-run Phillips curve showing the relationship between inflation and unemployment *when expected inflation has time to adjust to the actual inflation rate ($\dot{P} = \dot{P}^e$)—when inflation is fully anticipated*—is vertical, as shown in Figures 10.3 and 10.4

Friedman's theory of the natural rate of unemployment and output is the theoretical foundation for the monetarist belief that in the long run the influence of the money stock is primarily on the price level and other nominal variables. Real variables such as output and employment have time to adjust to their natural levels in the long run. Those natural rates of output and employment depend on real variables such as factor supplies (labor and capital) and technology.

Policy Implications of the Natural Rate Hypothesis: The Monetarist View

The theory of the natural rate of unemployment implies that the policymaker cannot "peg" the unemployment rate at some arbitrarily determined target rate. Attempts to lower the unemployment rate below the natural rate by increasing the rate of growth in aggregate demand will be successful only in the short run. The unemployment rate will gradually return to the natural rate and the lasting effect of the expansionary policy will be a higher inflation rate.

Monetarists believe that the natural rate theory strengthens the case for noninterventionists policies—most important, their suggestion of a constant money growth rate policy. The monetarists believe that the record of the past 20 years provides evidence that interventionist or activist policies to affect unemployment have resulted in only short-run gains and have been responsible for the increased inflation rates in the United States and other industrial countries.

Table 10.1 shows annual unemployment, inflation, and money growth rates for the United States for 1961–71. According to the monetarist interpretation, the expansionary policies of the mid-1960s succeeded in temporarily lowering the unemployment rate from an average rate of 5.8 percent for the 1961–64 period to an average rate of 3.8 percent for the 1965–69 period. In the monetarist view this decline in unemployment resulted from the increase in the rate of growth in the money stock beginning in 1964, which is evident in the table. The natural rate theory would suggest that at first the increased money growth would stimulate output and employment, the effect on prices coming with a longer lag. Consequently, the theory would have predicted the higher inflation rates observed in the table for the later 1960s. The natural rate theory would also have predicted the reversal of the downward movement in the unemployment rate. The average unemployment rate for 1970–71 being 5.4 percent, while the inflation rate remained high relative to the early 1960s.[6]

Although the monetarist explanation is not the only one for the figures shown in Table 10.1, the behavior of the U.S. economy, especially since the early 1970s, has directed increased attention to the natural rate theory. The natural rate theory provides one ex-

---

[6]The inflation rate did fall from 5.5 percent in 1970 to 3.4 percent in 1971, but this was in part due to mandatory price and wage controls instituted on August 15, 1971. The inflation rate prior to the imposition of controls was still in excess of 5 percent.

Table 10.1 Unemployment, Inflation, and Money Growth Rates for the United States, 1961–1971	Year	Unemployment Rate[a]	Inflation Rate[b]	Money Growth Rate[c]
	1961	6.7	0.7	2.1
	1962	5.5	1.2	2.2
	1963	5.7	1.6	2.9
	1964	5.2	1.2	4.0
	1965	4.5	1.9	4.2
	1966	3.8	3.4	4.7
	1967	3.8	3.0	3.9
	1968	3.6	4.7	7.2
	1969	3.5	6.1	6.1
	1970	4.9	5.5	3.8
	1971	5.9	3.4	6.7

[a]Civilian unemployment rate (percent).
[b]Annual percentage rate of change in the consumer price index.
[c]Annual percentage rate of growth in M1 (currency held by the public plus demand deposits).

planation of the simultaneously high rates of inflation and unemployment experienced during this period.

10.2 A KEYNESIAN VIEW OF THE OUTPUT–INFLATION TRADE-OFF

Friedman's theory of the natural rate of unemployment is a theory explaining both the short-run and long-run relationship between inflation and unemployment. The Phillips curve expressing this relationship between inflation and unemployment is, according to Friedman, downward sloping in the short run but vertical in the long run. What is the Keynesian view of the Phillips curve, and how does it differ from the natural rate theory? How can the Keynesians defend activist policies to affect output and employment if the natural rate theory is correct and such policies have only a temporary effect on output and employment? These are the questions considered in this section.

The Phillips Curve: A Keynesian Interpretation

The Keynesian view of the relationship between the rate of inflation and the levels of employment and output follows directly from the theory of how price and output are determined. That theory was considered in Chapter 8. Here we relate that theory to the concept of the Phillips curve.

The Short-run Phillips Curve

Figure 10.5 shows the effect on price, output, and employment of a sequence of expansionary policy actions increasing aggregate demand. The version of the Keynesian model here is the same as in Section 8.4. The money wage is flexible and labor supply is assumed to depend on the expected real wage (W/P^e), the known money wage divided by the expected price level.

In the Keynesian system an expansionary aggregate demand policy might be a monetary policy action such as the increase in the rate of growth in the money stock analyzed in the preceding section, or it might be a fiscal policy action such as a series of increases in government spending. In either case the effect of the policy will be to produce a series of shifts in the aggregate demand schedule as shown in Figure 10.5a. As can be seen from Figure 10.5, the effects of these increases in aggregate demand will be to increase ouput (from y_0, to y_1, to y_2, then to y_3) and employment (from N_0, to N_1, to N_2, then to N_3), as well as the price level (from P_0, to P_1, to P_2, then to P_3). As employment increases, the unemployment rate will decline. The level of the money wage will also increase.

Figure 10.5 Short-Run Effects of Increases in Aggregate Demand in the Keynesian Model

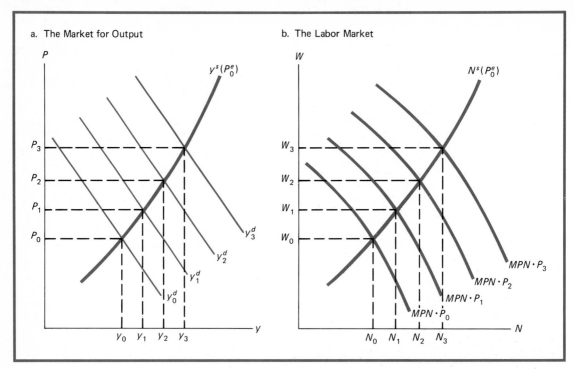

a. The Market for Output

b. The Labor Market

An expansionary aggregate demand policy such as an increase in the rate of growth in the money stock will cause a series of shifts to the right in the aggregate demand schedule (from y_0^d to y_1^d to y_2^d to y_3^d). In the short run, output, the price level, and the level of employment will all rise.

These results can be interpreted in terms of a Phillips curve relationship. The more quickly aggregate demand grows, the larger the rightward shifts in the aggregate demand schedule, and, *ceteris paribus*, the faster will be the rate of growth in output and employment. For a given growth in the labor force, this means that the unemployment rate will be lower the faster the rate of growth in aggregate demand. As can also be seen from the example in Figure 10.5, increases in aggregate demand cause the price level to rise, so, again *ceteris paribus*, the faster the growth of aggregate demand, the higher the rate of inflation.

The Keynesian model then would also imply a trade-off between inflation and unemployment. High rates of growth in demand would correspond to low levels of unemployment and high rates of inflation. Slower growth in aggregate demand would mean a lower inflation rate but a higher rate of unemployment. The

MACROECONOMIC MODELS

Phillips curve implied by the Keynesian model is downward sloping.

But is this a short-run or a long-run relationship? Notice that so far we are holding the expected price level constant. We are considering the effects of increases in demand in the short run. As explained in Chapter 8, the Keynesians view the expected price level as depending primarily on the past behavior of prices. Thus, as successive periods go by with increases in the actual price level, the expected price level will rise. In the longer run we must take account of the effects of such increases in the expected price level. Since we did not do so in Figure 10.5, our results there and the Phillips curve relationship derived from them pertain to the short run. To emphasize this, we have labeled the labor supply curve $N^s(P_0^e)$ and the aggregate supply curve $y^s(P_0^e)$, to indicate that these curves are drawn for the initial value of the expected price level. In Figure 10.6 we label the Phillips curve implied by the example in Figure 10.5 as the short-run Phillips curve, PC(short-run).

What we have found then is that in the short run the monetarists and the Keynesians would agree that the Phillips curve is downward sloping: there is a trade-off between inflation and unemployment.

Figure 10.6
The Phillips Curve:
The Keynesian
Perspective

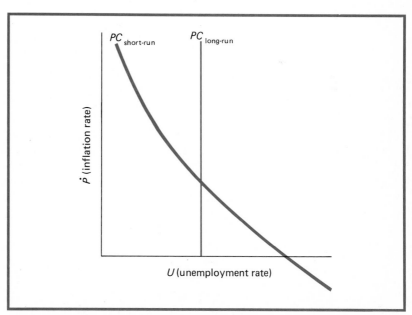

In the short run, the Phillips curve implied by the Keynesian model is downward sloping. In the long run in the Keynesian model, as in Friedman's analysis, the Phillips curve is vertical.

The Long-Run Phillips Curve

The long run differs from the short run in that in the long run the expected price adjusts to the actual price. The suppliers of labor perceive the inflation that has come as a result of the expansionary aggregate demand policy. Notice that, as was the case in Friedman's description of the short-run effects of an increase in aggregate demand, employment increases in the Keynesian model only because the increase in price lowers the real wage and increases the demand for labor. The increase in price is not perceived by the labor suppliers as a fall in the real wage. Their expectation of the price level (P^e) is assumed not to have changed. In fact, the quantity of labor supplied increases as the money wage (W) rises (see Figure 10.5b). This situation changes in the longer run when the expected price adjusts to the actual price.

The longer-run adjustment of output and employment to an increase in aggregate demand is illustrated in Figure 10.7. Recall that in the Keynesian system, labor supply depends on the expected real wage:

$$N^s = t\left(\frac{W}{P^e}\right) \tag{10.1}$$

where the effect of the money wage on labor supply is positive and the effect of an increase in expected price is negative. As the expected price rises, the labor supply curve in Figure 10.5b will shift to the left. Less labor will be supplied at any money wage (W) since a given money wage corresponds to a lower expected real wage (W/P^e) after an increase in the expected price level. This shift in the labor supply curve is shown in Figure 10.7b. As the expected price level rises to P_1^e, to P_2^e, and then to P_3^e, the labor supply curve shifts to $N^s(P_1^e)$, to $N^s(P_2^e)$, then to $N^s(P_3^e = P_3)$.

As the labor supply curve shifts to the left, the level of employment for any given price level declines. We move back up on a given labor demand curve (which is drawn for a given price level). The increase in expected price will lower employment for any price level and, therefore, lower output supplied at any price level. The aggregate supply curve will also shift upward to the left with each increase in expected price, reflecting this decline in output supplied at a given price level. These shifts in the supply curve are illustrated in Figure 10.7a.

The labor supply and aggregate supply curves will continue to shift to the left until expected price and actual price are equal. The *long-run* equilibrium position is shown in Figure 10.7, where the labor supply curve is $N^s(P_3^e = P_3)$ and the aggregate supply curve is $y^s(P_3^e = P_3)$. At this point notice that income and employment have

MACROECONOMIC MODELS

Figure 10.7 Long-Run Effects of Increases in Aggregate Demand in the Keynesian Model

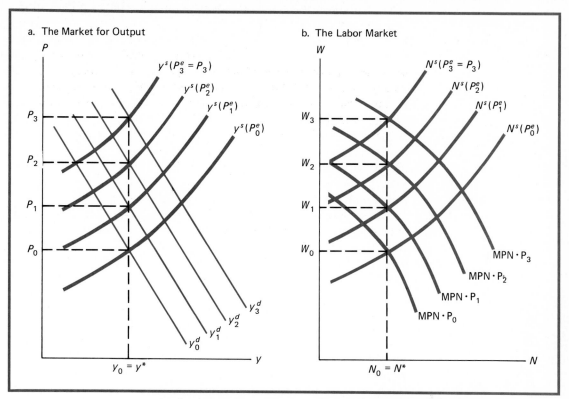

a. The Market for Output

b. The Labor Market

In the long run, leftward shifts in the labor supply schedule and consequently leftward shifts in the aggregate supply schedule reverse the increases in output and employment which come as a result of the expansionary aggregate demand policy (represented by the shifts to the right in the aggregate demand schedule). Output and employment return to their initial levels y_0 to N_0 which can be interpreted as their natural rates (y^*, N^*).

returned to their initial levels y_0 and N_0. This must be the case because output and employment can be maintained above y_0 and N_0 only as long as the expected price is below the actual price, that is, only as long as labor suppliers underestimate the inflation caused by the expansionary aggregate demand policy. Once the suppliers of labor correctly perceive the increases in the price level, they will demand increases in the money wage proportionate to the increase in the price level. At this point the real wage will have returned to its initial level ($W_3/P_3 = W_0/P_0$). Both labor supply and labor demand will have returned to their initial levels. Consequently, employment and output will be at their initial levels of N_0 to y_0.[7] We therefore arrive at a conclusion equivalent to Friedman's natural rate theory. An increase in the level of aggregate demand will increase the level of output and employment and as a consequence lower the unemployment rate only in the short run. As shown in Figure 10.6, the long-run Phillips curve is vertical in the Keynesian view as well as the monetarist. Why, then, do the Keynesians and monetarists reach different conclusions on the usefulness of activist policies to stabilize output and employment?

Stabilization Policies for Output and Employment: The Keynesian View

To see why Keynesian acceptance of the concept of the natural rate does not lead to acceptance of the monetarist noninterventionist policy position, we must begin by recognizing that the natural rate is a *long-run* concept. Acceptance of the natural rate concept has the clear policy implication that the levels of employment and output cannot be permanently pegged at some arbitrarily picked government target level. The theory of the natural rate by itself, however, in the Keynesian view, tells us relatively little about the desirability of policies aimed at *stabilizing* income and employment in the short run.

The aim of such stabilization policies is (or should be) to keep the economy at its equilibrium level in the face of shocks to aggregate demand or supply. In other words, the aim of *stabilization* policies is, as the name implies, to offset what would otherwise be destabilizing influences on output and employment. The focus of such policies is on the short run, with agreement among both Keynesians and monetarists that in the long run output and employment will tend toward their natural levels.

The monetarist noninterventionist policy conclusion is based, to a large extent, on the propositions discussed in Chapter 9. The private sector is basically stable if left to itself. Thus one would not expect large destabilizing shocks to private sector demand for output. Even if there were such shifts in private sector demand (undesired shifts in the IS schedule), they would have little effect on output if the money stock were held constant, due to the steepness of the LM schedule (see Figure 9.8). There may be small shocks that will cause output and employment to deviate somewhat from the

---

[7]In this discussion of the *long-run* effects of an increase in aggregate demand we are ignoring some elements of the Keynesian theory of labor supply which explain why the money wage is sticky in the *short run* (see Section 8.4). We are not, for example, allowing for the effects of implicit or explicit labor contracts, which prevent the money wage from adjusting to changes in demand conditions. Such factors are important in explaining the short-run behavior of the labor market. They are, however, factors that can slow but not ultimately prevent the adjustment to the long-run equilibrium position.

natural rate, but Friedman and other monetarists do not believe that our knowledge of the economy allows us to predict such shocks and design policies with sufficient precision to offset them.

One could still argue that left to itself the private sector produces equilibrium levels of output and employment that are "undesirable." Unemployment might be "too high." It could then be proposed that the role of monetary policy was to assure that unemployment and output were at "desirable" levels. The theory of the natural rate of unemployment shows that monetary policy cannot fulfill this role and indicates that attempts to achieve such arbitrary unemployment targets will have destabilizing effects on the price level in the long run. The natural rate theory therefore buttresses the monetarist noninterventionist policy proposition.

If one does not accept the other propositions of the monetarists, and as we have seen the Keynesians do not, there is still a possible short-run role for stabilization policies, whether monetary or fiscal. The Keynesians believe that private sector aggregate demand is unstable, owing primarily to the instability of investment demand. The Keynesians believe that *even for a given money stock*, such changes in private sector aggregate demand can cause large and prolonged fluctuations in income. Consequently, they believe that monetary and fiscal policies should be used to offset such undesirable changes in aggregate demand and stabilize income around its long-run equilibrium level.

An example of the type of destabilizing shock the Keynesians would expect is illustrated in Figure 10.8. Here we assume that due to an autonomous decline in investment demand, the aggregate demand schedule shifts from y_0^d to y_1^d. In the short run, output will decline below the natural rate y^* to y_1. In the long run, suppliers of labor will make a downward adjustment of their expected price level as they observe the lower actual prices. Just as the aggregate supply curve shifted upward to the left when the expected price rose, it will now shift to the right as the expected price level declines. Workers now see a given money wage as representing a higher expected real wage. Labor supply and hence output and employment for a given price level will increase. The aggregate supply curve will eventually shift to position $y^s(P^e = P)$ in Figure 10.8, where output has returned to the natural rate. This adjustment will be made slower by the existence of implicit and explicit labor contracts and other factors that make the money wage sticky downward, because with a lower price level the money wage must fall to restore employment to the natural rate level.

The Keynesians do not deny that this supply adjustment will take place. They do believe, however, that the required fall in the money wage will come only after a relatively long and economi-

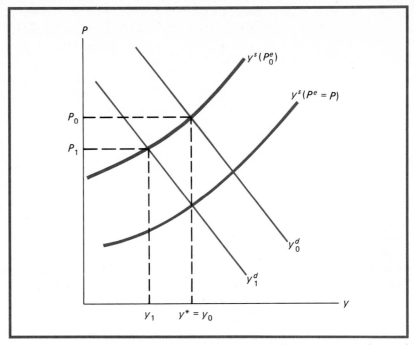

A decline in autonomous investment will cause the aggregate demand schedule to shift from y_0^d to y_1^d. In the short run output will fall below $y^* = y_0$ to y_1. In the long run the aggregate supply schedule would shift out to $y^s(P^e = P)$ as labor suppliers come to expect a lower price level corresponding to lower aggregate demand. Rather than wait for this adjustment, the Keynesians advocate aggregate demand management policies, in this case an expansionary policy to restore the level of aggregate demand to y_0^d.

cally costly adjustment period—the costs being the lost output due to being at y_1 instead of y^*. In such a case the Keynesians favor the use of monetary and fiscal policy to offset the decline in aggregate demand due to the fall in autonomous investment. An increase in government spending could, for example, shift the aggregate demand curve back to y_0^d and restore output and employment to their natural rates.

To summarize, the Keynesians believe that the supply adjustments required to keep output and employment at their natural rates in the face of shifts in aggregate demand will take place only after a long period of time. Rather than wait for such supply adjustments, they favor activist monetary and fiscal policies to manage aggregate demand.

10.3 THE MONETARISTS VERSUS THE KEYNESIANS: A SUMMARY

This chapter and the preceding one considered the basis for the several propositions of monetarism. We have also considered the Keynesian view on the issues raised by the monetarists. We conclude this discussion of monetarism by summarizing the major differences between the Keynesian and monetarist views. As with the Keynesian–classical dispute (Chapter 8), it is useful to consider separately issues pertaining to aggregate demand and aggregate supply.

Monetarist Versus Keynesian Theories of Aggregate Demand

Monetarist and Keynesian views of the aggregate supply and aggregate demand curves are displayed in Figure 10.9. For the case of aggregate demand, the striking feature of the monetarist view is that the level of aggregate demand is determined primarily by the level of the money stock. Changes in the money stock are believed by the monetarists to be the major factors causing movements in aggregate demand and movements in nominal income.

As drawn, the aggregate demand curve in Figure 10.9a depends only on the quantity of money. Such a characterization reflects what Friedman termed an "exaggeration but one that gives the right flavor" to the monetarist conclusions. This is the strong form of the monetarist position. The monetarists do not deny that there are some *nonsystematic* influences causing aggregate demand to deviate from the level predicted on the basis of the level of the money stock. The monetarists, however, argue that changes in money stock are the dominant factor causing appreciable systematic movements in aggregate demand and, therefore, nominal income.

Because they believe that changes in the money stock are the dominant factor causing changes in aggregate demand, they believe that stable growth in the money stock is a requirement for economic stability. They advocate a constant growth rate rule for the money stock. Since movements in aggregate demand are dominated by monetary factors, the monetarists deny the usefulness of fiscal stabilization policies.

The Keynesian aggregate demand schedule (y^d) is shown in Figure 10.9b. In the Keynesian view the level of aggregate demand does not depend on the level of the money stock (M_0) alone. In addition, the Keynesians believe that there are other variables which have *important* and *systematic* effects on aggregate demand. These other influences include fiscal policy variables [the level of

Figure 10.9

Monetarist and
Keynesian Aggregate
Supply and Demand
Curves

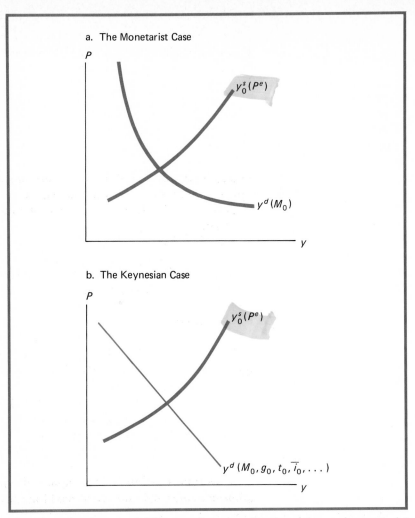

a. The Monetarist Case

P

$y_0^s(P^e)$

$y^d(M_0)$

y

b. The Keynesian Case

P

$y_0^s(P^e)$

$y^d(M_0, g_0, t_0, \overline{i}_0, \dots)$

y

There is no fundamental difference between the Keynesian and monetarist
views of aggregate supply. The position of the monetarist aggregate demand schedule (Part *a*) depends primarily on the level of the money stock
(M_0). The Keynesian aggregate demand function depends not only on the
money stock (M_0) but also on the levels of fiscal policy variables (g_0, t_0),
autonomous investment ($\overline{i}_0$), and other variables as well.

government spending (g_0) and taxes (t_0)], the level of autonomous
investment demand ($\overline{i}_0$), as well as other factors that would cause
autonomous changes in demand (exports, autonomous shifts in
consumer demand, etc.). The Keynesians believe that private sector aggregate demand is unstable, primarily but not solely as a
result of instability of investment demand. They favor activist fis-

cal and monetary policies to stabilize aggregate demand. Stable money growth alone will not produce economic stability because of the unstable behavior of the nonmonetary factors which are important in determining demand.

Monetarist Versus Keynesian Theories of Aggregate Supply

There is no apparent difference between the monetarist aggregate supply curve as drawn in Figure 10.9*a* and the Keynesian counterpart as drawn in Figure 10.9*b*. This similarity reflects the agreement between the Keynesians and monetarists that the aggregate supply curve is upward sloping in the short run. An increase in aggregate demand will increase both output and price in the short run in either model. Both groups, as we have seen, believe that there is a trade-off between unemployment and inflation in the short run.

In both the monetarist and Keynesian cases, as indicated by the labeling of the curves, the upward-sloping aggregate supply function is drawn for a given value of the expected price. In the longer run, when the expected price has had time to adjust, output will have to approach its natural rate. In effect, the long-run supply curve is vertical; only one level of output is a long-run equilibrium level. That level is independent of the level of aggregate demand.

To the monetarists the fact that output can be influenced by aggregate demand only in the short run is seen as buttressing their case for a constant growth rate. They emphasize the possible long-run destabilizing effects of government policies aimed at pegging the level of output at a rate below the natural rate. Since they believe that the private sector is inherently stable, they do not see a useful purpose for government policies aimed at stabilizing output and employment in the short run.

The Keynesians, since they believe that private sector aggregate demand is unstable, *do* see a need for short-run stabilization policies. Although they are not unmindful of the possibility that government policies can be a source of instability in the economy, the Keynesians are more optimistic than the monetarists about the ability of the monetary and fiscal authorities to design effective stabilization policies. In the Keynesian view the existence of *long-run* natural rates of employment and output has little bearing on the need for or effectiveness of short-run stabilization policies.

Review Questions

1   Explain the concept of the natural rate of unemployment. What are the implications of Milton Friedman's theory of the natural rate of unemployment for the effectiveness of economic stabilization policies?

2   Explain why the monetarists believe that monetary policy affects output and employment in the short run but not in the long run. What is the crucial difference between the short run and the long run?

3   Contrast the monetarist and Keynesian views of the relationship between real output (or employment) and the level of aggregate demand in both the short run and the long run. Contrast the conclusions that monetarists and Keynesians draw from this analysis of the aggregate demand–output relationship for the usefulness of activist policies to stabilize output and employment. To what degree do differences in the theoretical analysis explain the differences in policy conclusions?

4   Explain the concept of the Phillips curve. Is there any difference between the monetarist and neo-Keynesian views of the Phillips curve?

5   Within the monetarist framework, would an expansionary fiscal policy action have effects in the short run and long run which are similar to those of the expansionary monetary policy analyzed in Section 10.1?

6   Summarize what you believe to be the essential differences between the monetarist and neo-Keynesian positions.

7   A supply shock such as the exogenous increase in the price of oil analyzed in Section 8.5 would have no effect on real or nominal income within the monetarist model. This follows because such a supply shock would not affect the quantity of money which is the dominant factor determining nominal income and, in the short run, real income as well.

Do you agree or disagree with the above statement? Explain.

8   Contrast the monetarist and classical views on the short-run effects of an increase in the quantity of money.

Selected Readings

ACKLEY, GARDNER, *Macroeconomics: Theory and Policy*. New York: Macmillan, 1978, Chaps. 13–15.

FRIEDMAN, MILTON, "The Role of Monetary Policy," *American Economic Review*, 58 (March 1968), pp. 1–17. Reprinted in Milton Friedman, *The Optimal Quantity of Money and Other Essays*. Chicago: Aldine, 1969.

GORDON, ROBERT J., "Recent Developments in the Theory of Inflation and Unemployment," *Journal of Monetary Economics*, 2 (April 1976), pp. 185–219.

GORDON, ROBERT J., "The Theory of Domestic Inflation," *American Economic Review*, 67 (February 1977), pp. 128–34.

HUMPHREY, THOMAS, "Changing Views of the Phillips Curve," Federal Reserve Bank of Richmond Monthly *Review*, July 1973, pp. 2–13. Reprinted in Thomas Havrilesky and John Boorman, *Current Issues in Monetary Theory and Policy*. Arlington Heights, Ill.: AHM Publishing Corp., 1980.

RASCHE, ROBERT, "A Comparative Static Analysis of Some Monetarist Propositions," St. Louis Federal Reserve Bank *Review*, 55 (December 1973), pp. 15–23. Reprinted in Thomas Havrilesky and John Boorman, *Current Issues in Monetary Theory and Policy*. Arlington Heights, Ill.: AHM Publishing Corp., 1980.

SANTOMERO, ANTHONY, and SEATER, JOHN, "The Inflation–Unemployment Trade-off: A Critique of the Literature," *Journal of Economic Literature*, 16 (June 1978), pp. 499–544.

SURREY, M. J. C., *Macroeconomic Themes*. London: Oxford University Press, 1976, Chap. 7.

TOBIN, JAMES, "Inflation and Unemployment," *American Economic Review*, 62 (March 1972), pp. 1–18.

VANE, HOWARD, and THOMPSON, JOHN, *Monetarism: Theory Evidence and Policy*. New York: Wiley, 1979, Chap. 4.

chapter 11

As mentioned in Chapter 10, the simultaneously high inflation and unemployment of the 1970s created an increased interest in the monetarist theory of the natural unemployment rate. The natural rate theory provided a possible explanation of this recent phenomenon: namely, both high inflation and unemployment were the result of attempts to reverse excessive aggregate demand growth in a climate of high inflationary expectations (see the discussion of Figure 10.4). But not all those sympathetic to the natural rate theory subscribed to the other features of monetarism—the monetarism of Chapter 9. The last school of macroeconomic theory we discuss, the new classical economics, developed against this backdrop of high unemployment and inflation in the 1970s and shares with monetarism the idea of a natural rate of unemployment. We will see, in fact, that the new classical economists are even more skeptical than the monetarists about the usefulness of activist aggregate demand stabilization policies. The new classical economists do not, however, necessarily hold to a belief in the dominant influence of money on aggregate demand and on nominal economic activity.

Additionally, the new classical economics is a more fundamental attack on the Keynesian theoretical system than is monetarism. The monetarists accepted much of the theoretical contribution of Keynesian economics. To be sure, the monetarists and Keynesians reached very different policy conclusions and differed on a number

THE NEW CLASSICAL ECONOMICS

of empirical questions.[1] But in the preceding two chapters we presented no distinct monetarist theoretical models. The new classical economists, a group that includes Robert Lucas of the University of Chicago, Thomas Sargent and Neil Wallace of the University of Minnesota, Robert Barro of the University of Rochester, and Bennett McCallum of the University of Virginia, have attacked the neo-Keynesian theoretical structure as "fundamentally flawed." These economists argue, as we will see below, that we must go back to the methodology of the classical economics as a basis for constructing useful macroeconomic models.

This chapter will proceed by first presenting the new classical economists' critique of Keynesian macroeconomics, focusing especially on the differences in the policy conclusions of the two groups (Section 11.1). Next, we will take a broader look at the new classical economics, indicating the new classical economists' own suggestions of useful avenues for future research and examining the classical roots of their approach (Section 11.2). The Keynesian response to the criticisms of the new classical economists is then considered (Section 11.3). The last section (Section 11.4) of the chapter summarizes the current state of the continuing and intense controversy between the Keynesians and new classical economists.

[1] The stability of the private sector, the interest elasticity of money demand, and the importance of fiscal policy "crowding out," to name a few.

11.1 THE NEW CLASSICAL ATTACK

We have already had reason to quote Franco Modigliani's neo-Keynesian view that a private enterprise economy needs to be, can be, and should be stabilized by active government aggregate demand management. The monetarists' view to the contrary has also been examined. The central policy tenet of the new classical economics is that stabilization of *real* variables such as output and employment *cannot* be achieved by aggregate demand management. The values of such variables *in both the short run and the long run* are insensitive to *systematic* aggregate demand management policies. In other words, in the new classical view, systematic monetary and fiscal policy actions that change aggregate demand will not affect output and employment even in the short run.

While the monetarists questioned the necessity and desirability of activist policies to affect output and employment, and questioned the effectiveness of *fiscal* policy actions, they believed that systematic *monetary* policy actions had real effects in the short run. The new classical objection to the use of activist stabilization policies is thus even more far reaching than that of the monetarists.

A Review of the Keynesian Position

To see the basis for this new classical policy position we need to consider the new classical economists' critique of Keynesian macroeconomics. A good starting place is a review of the neo-Keynesian analysis of the relationships among real output, employment, and aggregate demand, as discussed in Section 10.2. Consider the effects in the neo-Keynesian model of an expansionary policy action, for example an increase in the money stock. In the short run such a policy action would increase aggregate demand. The aggregate demand curve would shift to the right along the upward-sloping aggregate supply schedule (as illustrated, for example, in Figure 10.5a). The price level and level of real output would rise. Parallel to the increase in real output is a rise in employment as labor demand increases, with the rise in prices shifting the labor demand schedule to the right along the upward-sloping (drawn against the money wage) labor supply schedule (as illustrated, for example, in Figure 10.5b).

Crucial to these results was the fact that the positions of both the aggregate supply schedule and labor supply schedule were fixed in the short run. The position of both these schedules depended on the value of the expected price level (P^e), which was assumed to depend primarily on past prices and not to change with current policy actions.

In the longer run, the level of the expected price level converged to the actual price level and we saw that both the aggregate supply schedule and the labor supply schedule shifted to the left. The initial levels of employment and real output were restored, with only the price level and the money wage left permanently higher due to the increase in the money stock (see Figure 10.7). Output and employment remained above their long-run equilibrium levels (natural rates) only for as long as it took labor suppliers to perceive correctly the change in the price level that resulted from the expansionary policy action. As long as our attention is confined to monetary policy actions, the monetarists would agree with the foregoing analysis of an increase in aggregate demand, although as we saw in Chapter 9, they draw different policy conclusions from this analysis than do the Keynesians.

The Rational Expectations Concept and its Implications

The new classical economists do not agree with the analysis above. In particular, they would not accept the difference between the short-run and long-run results in this Keynesian or monetarist analysis of the effects of aggregate demand on output and employment. The focal point of their criticism is the Keynesian (and monetarist) assumption concerning the formation of price expectations. This formulation assumes that labor suppliers form an expectation of current aggregate price level (or future inflation rate) on the basis of the past behavior of prices. In practice, the Keynesians and monetarists have assumed that such price expectations adjust slowly over time and can be assumed to be fixed for the analysis of policy effects over relatively short periods. Thus, above we *defined* the short run as that period of time over which such expectations were fixed.

The new classical economists have criticized such formulations of expectations formation as "naive in the extreme." Why, they ask, would rational economic agents forming an expectation of the price level, for example, rely only on past values of the price level? Why especially would they do so when in general such behavior results in their being *systematically* wrong when there are shifts in aggregate demand? We have in fact been assuming that following changes in aggregate demand, the increase in the money stock considered in the preceding subsection for example, labor suppliers fail to perceive the effect that the demand shift will have on price. The new classical economists argue that economic agents will not persist in making such systematic errors.

The new classical economists propose that economic agents will form "rational" expectations, rational in the sense that they will not make avoidable systematic errors. According to the hypothesis of rational expectations, expectations *are formed on the basis of all the available relevant information concerning the variable being predicted.* Furthermore, the rational expectations hypothesis maintains that individuals *use available information intelligently; that is, they understand the way in which the variables they observe will affect the variable they are trying to predict.* According to the rational expectations hypothesis, then, expectations are, as the originator of the concept, John Muth, suggested, "essentially the same as the predictions of the relevant economic theory,"[2] based on available information. What does the rational expectations assumption imply about the way labor suppliers form price expectations?

If expectations are rational, then in forming a prediction of the value of the aggregate price level for the current period, labor suppliers will use all relevant past information, not just information about the past behavior of prices. In addition, they will use any information they have about the current values of variables that play a role in determining the price level. Most important from the standpoint of the effects of aggregate demand management policy, labor suppliers will take account of any anticipated (expected) policy actions in forming their price forecasts. Further, they are assumed to understand the relationship between such aggregate demand policies and the price level.

If such rational forecasts of the price level are in fact made by labor suppliers, then the analysis of the preceding subsection must be modified in an important way. To see this we will analyze the effects of the same expansionary policy action considered above, a one-time increase in the money stock. To analyze the effects of such a change with the assumption that expectations are rational, we must begin by specifying whether the policy change was anticipated or not.[3] We will see that anticipated and unanticipated policy changes have very different effects when expectations are assumed to be rational. As a first case we assume that the policy change was anticipated. This might be because the policymaker announces the policy change. Alternatively, the public may anticipate the policy change because the policymaker is known to act in certain systematic ways. For example, if the policymaker systematically responds to an increase in unemployment in one period by increasing the money stock in the next period (to counteract unemployment), the public will come to anticipate an increase in the money stock for period t when they observe an increase in the unemployment rate of period $t - 1$.

To begin, consider the characterization of equilibrium output and employment in the new classical analysis as illustrated in Fig-

[2]John Muth, "Rational Expectations and the Theory of Price Movements," *Econometrica*, 29 (July 1961), p. 316.
[3]The terms "expected" and "anticipated" or "unexpected" and "unanticipated" are used interchangeably here. Generally, policy shifts will be referred to as either *anticipated* or *unanticipated*, whereas we will refer to *expected* levels of variables, including policy variables.

ure 11.1. The crucial difference between the new classical case and the neo-Keynesian case concerns the variables that determine the positions of the labor supply and the aggregate supply schedules. As in the neo-Keynesians theory, we are assuming here that labor supply depends on the expected real wage, the known money wage divided by the expected price level:

$$N^s = t\left(\frac{W}{P^e}\right) \tag{11.1}$$

Consequently, it will again be the case that the position of the labor supply schedule, and therefore the aggregate supply schedule, will depend on the expected price level. Increases in the expected price level will shift both schedules to the left.

In the new classical model, however, with the assumption of rational expectations the expected price level will depend on the expected levels of the variables in the model that actually determine the price level. These include the *expected* levels of the money

Figure 11.1 Output and Employment in the New Classical Model

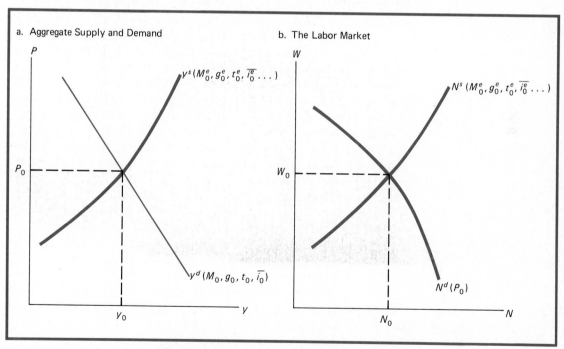

The distinctive feature of the new classical model is that both the aggregate supply and labor supply schedules depend on the rationally formed expectations of current variables including monetary and fiscal policy variables (M_0^e, g_0^e, t_0^e).

stock (M^e), the level of government spending (g^e) and tax collections (t^e), the expected level of autonomous investment ($\bar{\imath}^e$), and possibly other variables.[4] The dependence of the expected price level, and hence the positions of the labor supply and aggregate supply schedules on these variables, is indicated by the labeling of these curves in Figure 11.1. Especially important for the new classical policy conclusion is the fact that the positions of the labor supply and aggregate supply schedules depend on the expected levels of the policy variables (e.g., M^e, g^e, t^e).

Now consider the effect of a fully anticipated increase in the money stock from M_0 to M_1, as depicted in Figure 11.2. Initially, assume that the aggregate demand, aggregate supply, and labor market supply and demand schedules are at the same positions as in Figure 11.1, with actual and expected variables subscripted zero (0). The increase in the money stock will shift the aggregate demand schedule out to $y^d(M_1, g_0, t_0, \bar{\imath}_0)$. If the supply schedule did not shift, output would rise from y_0 to y_1' and the price level would increase from P_0 to P_1'. With the rise in the price level the labor demand curve shifts to the right (to the dashed schedule $N^d(P_1')$ in Figure 11.2). *If the labor supply curve did not also shift,* employment would rise (from N_0 to N_1'). In the neo-Keynesian or monetarist frameworks, with the expected price level unrelated to the level of policy variables, the positions of the aggregate supply curve and labor supply schedules would be fixed in the short run and our analysis would be complete.

But as can be seen in Figure 11.2, in the new classical case the positions of the labor supply and aggregate supply schedules are not fixed in the short run. The expansionary policy action was assumed to be fully anticipated. Therefore, the level of the *expected* money stock also increases. This will increase the *expected* price level since with rational expectations labor suppliers will understand the inflationary effect of the increase in the money stock. The labor supply schedule and as a consequence the aggregate supply schedule will shift to the left to the positions given by $N^s(M_1^e, g_0^e, t_0^e, \bar{\imath}_0^e, \ldots)$ and $y^s(M_1^e, g_0^e, t_0^e, \bar{\imath}_0^e, \ldots)$, as shown in Figure 11.2. As the decline in aggregate supply puts further upward pressure on the price level, the labor demand schedule shifts out to $N^d(P_1)$. The new equilibrium is where output and employment have returned to their initial levels, y_0, N_0, while the price level and the money wage are permanently higher at W_1, P_1, respectively. Notice that the return to the initial levels of output and employment takes place in the short run when expectations are rational.

The new classical analysis differs from the Keynesian or mone-

---

[4]Expected changes in oil prices or other supply-side factors, for example, would also affect the expected price level.

Figure 11.2 Effects of an Increase in the Money Stock: The New Classical View

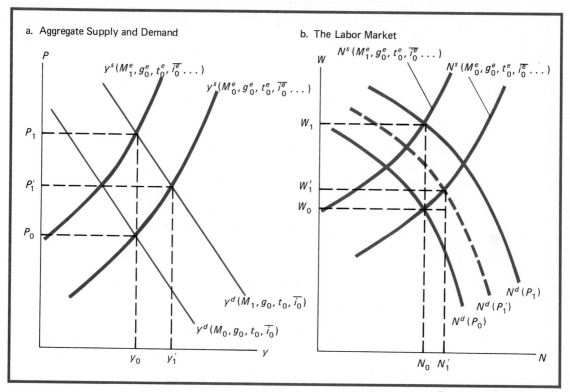

a. Aggregate Supply and Demand

b. The Labor Market

The increase in the money stock shifts the aggregate demand curve from $y^d(M_0, g_0, t_0, \bar{\imath}_0)$ to $y^d(M_1, g_0, t_0, \bar{\imath}_0)$. By itself, this change would increase output to y_1' and the price level to P_1'. The increase in the price level would shift the labor demand schedule from $N^d(P_0)$ to $N^d(P_1')$ and employment would rise to N_1'. However, since the increase in the money stock was fully anticipated, there is also an increase in the *expected* money stock. This increase in the expected money stock will shift the aggregate supply schedule to the left from $y^s(M_0^e, g_0^e, t_0^e, \bar{\imath}_0^e)$ to $y^s(M_1^e, g_0^e, t_0^e, \bar{\imath}_0^e)$ and also shift the labor supply schedule to the left from $N^s(M_0^e, g_0^e, t_0^e, \bar{\imath}_0^e)$ to $N^s(M_1^e, g_0^e, t_0^e, \bar{\imath}_0^e)$. These shifts cause employment and output to fall back to their initial levels (y_0 and N_0).

tarist analysis in that with the new classical assumption of rational expectations, labor suppliers are assumed to perceive correctly the increase in price which will be a consequence of the increase in the money stock. They demand proportionately higher money wages. The labor market will return to equilibrium only after the money wage and price level have increased in the same proportion, the real wage is unchanged, and consequently employment and output are back at their initial levels. Put differently, in

THE NEW CLASSICAL ECONOMICS

the Keynesian or monetarist analysis the increase in the money stock leads to an increase in employment and output in the short run, that is, until labor suppliers correctly perceive the increase in the price level that comes as a result of the expansionary monetary policy action. In the Keynesian or monetarist view, since expectations about prices depend on the past behavior of prices, adjusting only slowly to current conditions, this short-run period where the increase in the money stock affects output and employment can be of considerable length. If expectations are rational, however, labor suppliers cannot be systematically "fooled" by anticipated changes in aggregate demand policy. Such policy actions will not affect output and employment, even in the short run.

Thus the new classical assumption of rational expectations has very dramatic implications for macroeconomic policy. If expectations are formed rationally, then anticipated aggregate demand policy actions will not affect real output or employment, even in the short run. Notice that since the public will learn any systematic "rules" of policy action, such as the hypothetical response of the money stock to employment mentioned above, any such set of systematic policy actions will come to be anticipated and will not affect the behavior of output or employment over time.[5] This is the new classical policy conclusion which was stated at the beginning of the chapter. The values of real variables such as output and employment will be insensitive to systematic changes in aggregate demand management policies. This conclusion is of extreme importance because if it is accepted, there is clearly no useful role for aggregate demand policies aimed at stabilizing output and employment.

So far we have been assuming that the increase in the money stock was anticipated either because it was announced or because it was a systematic policy response that could be predicted. Now consider the effects of an *unanticipated* increase in aggregate demand. To be specific we again consider the effects of an increase in the money stock from M_0 to M_1, but the analysis would be similar for an unanticipated increase in aggregate demand from another source. The short-run effects of this unanticipated increase in the money stock—what can be termed a *monetary surprise*—can also be explained with reference to Figure 11.2. As before, the increase in the money stock will shift the aggregate demand schedule from $y^d(M_0, g_0, t_0, \bar{\imath}_0)$ to $y^d(M_1, g_0, t_0, \bar{\imath}_0)$. As the price level rises to P'_1, the labor demand schedule will also shift out to the right, to

---

[5]That the public would learn systematic policy "rules" follows from the assumption of rational expectations. Estimates of such rules could be made on the basis of past policy behavior. Since such estimates would be helpful in predicting policy actions and consequently in predicting the behavior of prices and other variables, the rational economic agent would be assumed to use the information.

$N^d(P_1')$. If the increase in the money stock is unanticipated, these are the only curves that will shift in the short run. The additional shift to the left in the labor supply curve and consequently the shift to the left in the aggregate supply curve shown in Figure 11.2, where the increase in the money stock was anticipated, will *not* occur for an unanticipated increase in the money stock. When the increase in the money stock is not anticipated, it does not affect the labor suppliers' expectation of the value the aggregate price level will take on over the current period. This is why the labor supply curve does not shift.

When the increase in the money stock is unanticipated, the new classical model would indicate that output and employment will be affected. In Figure 11.2, output will rise from y_0 to y_1' and employment will increase from N_0 to N_1', results identical to those of the Keynesian or monetarist analysis of such an increase in aggregate demand. Since the increase in the money stock is unanticipated, it cannot affect even the rational expectation of the price level. For the short run, even assuming rational expectations, labor suppliers will not perceive the inflationary effect of the increase in aggregate demand. This was the assumption in the Keynesian or monetarist view *for any change in aggregate demand*. The new classical economists deny that anticipated changes in aggregate demand can affect output and employment, but their view of the effects of unanticipated changes in aggregate demand does not differ from that of the Keynesians or monetarists.

Note, however, that the results here are those for the short run. Even though the policy change was unanticipated, in future periods economic agents would find out that policy had in fact changed. In particular, labor suppliers would observe that the money stock had increased and would revise upward their price forecasts. In the long run the labor supply schedule, and consequently the output supply function, would shift left as shown in Figure 11.2. Output and employment would return to their initial levels. Again here there is no fundamental difference between the Keynesian (or monetarist) and new classical analyses of the effects of an *unanticipated* change in aggregate demand.

This analysis of the effects of an unanticipated monetary policy action illustrates an important difference between the new classical theory and the original classical theory explained in Chapters 3 and 4. In the new classical model economic agents are assumed to be rational but they do not have perfect information; they make mistakes in predicting the price level, and such mistakes cause short-run deviations of output and employment from their natural (full-information) rates. In the classical model economic agents were assumed to have perfect information. Labor suppliers knew the real wage. In effect, in the classical system there were no monetary (or other) surprises. There were no deviations from the supply-determined natural rates of output and employment.

The New Classical Policy Conclusions

We can now restate the new classical policy conclusion in a clearer manner. The new classical economists believe that real output and employment will be unaffected by systematic, and therefore predictable, changes in aggregate demand policy. In both the Keynesian and monetarist models, changes in aggregate demand policies affect output and employment because labor suppliers fail to perceive correctly the effects on the price level of such policy changes. The new classical economists assume that expectations are rational and consequently that labor suppliers will not make such systematic mistakes in their price forecasts. If the policy action is anticipated, so too will be the price effects of that policy. Although the new classical economists assume that expectations are rational, they do not assume that economic agents have perfect information. Unanticipated changes in aggregate demand, whether policy induced or from other sources, will affect real output and employment. Labor suppliers will not be able to perceive the effects on the price level as a result of such unanticipated changes in aggregate demand.

The new classical view that unanticipated aggregate demand changes will affect output and employment still does not provide any meaningful role for macroeconomic stabilization policy. To see this, consider the new classical economists' view of the proper policy response to a decline in private sector demand, for example, an autonomous decline in investment demand. We have already analyzed the Keynesian view of the proper policy response to such a shock (Section 10.2). The Keynesians would argue that a decline in private sector demand should be offset by an expansionary monetary or fiscal policy action to stabilize aggregate demand, output, and employment.

The effects of the decline in investment demand are depicted in Figure 11.3. The decline in investment demand shifts the aggregate demand schedule from $y^d(\bar{\imath}_0)$ to $y^d(\bar{\imath}_1)$ in Figure 11.3a.[6] This will cause output to decline from y_0 to y_1'. The price level will fall from P_0 to P_1' and as a result the labor demand curve in Figure 11.3b will shift downward from $N^d(P_0)$ to $N^d(P_1')$. Whether there are additional effects from the decline in investment demand will depend in the new classical view on whether the decline was or was not anticipated. To begin, we assume that it was anticipated.

***

[6]The positions for the aggregate demand schedule and other schedules continue to depend on all the variables discussed above, including policy variables, but for notational simplicity the labels on the schedules in the graph contain only the variables that are assumed to change.

MACROECONOMIC MODELS

Figure 11.3 Effects of an Autonomous Decline in Investment Demand: A New Classical View

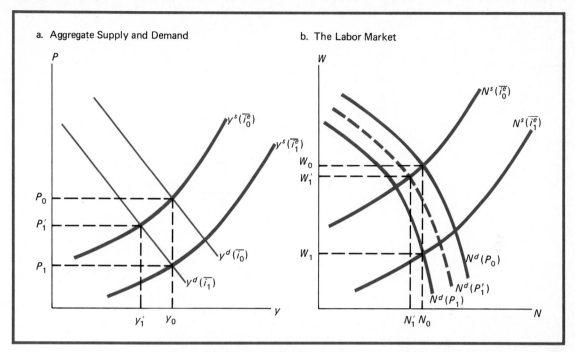

a. Aggregate Supply and Demand

b. The Labor Market

An autonomous decline in investment demand shifts the aggregate demand schedule from $y^d(\bar{I}_0)$ to $y^d(\bar{I}_1)$. This shift would reduce output from y_0 to y'_1 and lower the price level from P_0 to P'_1. The fall in the price level shifts the labor demand schedule from $N^d(P_0)$ to $N^d(P'_1)$ which causes employment to fall from N_0 to N'_1. These are the only effects if the decline in investment demand was not anticipated. If the decline in investment demand was anticipated, the expected level of autonomous investment $(\bar{I}^e)$ will also fall (from $\bar{I}^e_0$ to $\bar{I}^e_1$). The aggregate supply schedule will shift from $y^s_0(\bar{I}^e_0)$ to $y^s(\bar{I}^e_1)$ and the labor supply schedule will shift from $N^s(\bar{I}^e_0)$ to $N^s(\bar{I}^e_1)$. Those shifts cause output and employment to return to their initial levels.

In that case, labor suppliers will anticipate the decline in the price level that will come as a result of the decline in aggregate demand. Labor suppliers, now expecting the price level to be lower, will supply more labor at a given money wage, since with the lower expected price level, a given money wage corresponds to a higher expected real wage. This fall in the expected price level shifts the labor supply curve to the right in Figure 11.3b [from $N^s(\bar{I}^e_0)$ to $N^s(\bar{I}^e_1)$]. As a consequence, the aggregate supply schedule shifts to the right in Figure 11.3a [from $y^s(\bar{I}^e_0)$ to $y^s(\bar{I}^e_1)$]. There is a further decline in the price level to P_1, and therefore a further downward shift in the labor demand schedule to $N^d(P_1)$. At the new *short-run* equilibrium, the money wage and price level have fallen sufficiently to restore employment and output to their initial levels, N_0 to y_0.

This analysis is just the reversal of our previous analysis of an anticipated increase in aggregate demand coming as a result of an increase in the money stock. In the new classical system, output and employment are not affected by anticipated changes in aggregate demand, even in the short run. Consequently, there is no need for a stabilization policy response to an anticipated demand change such as a decline in investment demand. In the new classical view the economy is self-stabilizing with respect to such shocks.

But what if the decline in investment demand had not been anticipated? In that case the labor suppliers would not have foreseen the price decline that resulted from the decline in aggregate demand. The labor supply curve (Figure 11.3b) and the aggregate supply curve (Figure 11.3a) would have remained at $N^s(\bar{\iota}_0^e)$ and $y^s(\bar{\iota}_0^e)$, respectively. The decline in investment demand would have caused output and employment to decline to the levels given by y_1' and N_1'. Would not an offsetting policy action to raise aggregate demand back to its initial level be called for in this case?

The answer is that such a policy response would be desirable but not feasible. The decline in investment demand was by definition unanticipated. With the assumption of rational expectations this means that the decline could not have been predicted by economic agents on the basis of *any* available information. The policymaker, like any other economic agent, would have been unable to foresee the investment decline in advance. He could not have acted to raise aggregate demand to offset the decline. Once the investment decline has occurred and has had its effect on output, the policymaker could act to raise aggregate demand if the low investment level was expected to be repeated in future periods. If low investment was *expected* to continue in future periods, however, there would be no need for a policy response since private agents would also hold this expectation. At this point the shift in the labor supply and aggregate supply schedules would take place. In other words, as long as the shock is unanticipated, the policymaker lacks the knowledge needed to act to offset the shock. Once the shock is anticipated by the policymaker, it is anticipated by other economic agents, including labor suppliers, and there is no need to offset the shock.

The foregoing analysis indicates that in the new classical view there is no useful role for aggregate demand policies aimed at stabilizing output and employment. The new classical economists policy conclusions are strongly noninterventionist, just as were those of the classical economists. In this respect the new classical

MACROECONOMIC MODELS

economists agree with the monetarists, although, as a comparison of this chapter with the preceding two will show, the new classical economists reach their noninterventionist policy conclusions for somewhat different reasons. Concerning monetary policy, the new classical economists arrive at the same position as the monetarists, generally favoring a constant growth rate in the money stock as the optimal policy. Such a policy rule would do away with unanticipated changes in the money stock, which can have little stabilization value and are likely to move the economy away from the natural rate of output and employment by causing economic agents to make price forecast errors. In addition, a constant rate of growth in the money stock would contribute to stability in the inflation rate, and if the constant money growth rate was low, to a low inflation rate as well.

In the case of fiscal policy, as long as we are concerned with effects on aggregate demand, again the new classical view favors stability and avoidance of excessive and inflationary stimulus.[7] Excessive and erratic government deficit spending should be avoided. There is much in the new classical economics that is favorable to a policy of balancing the budget at a desirable level of spending and taxation—the desirable level being chosen on grounds such as optimum division of GNP between private and public expenditures. The choice would not be made on stabilization grounds since the level of real GNP would be independent of such a systematic policy choice.

11.2 A BROADER VIEW OF THE NEW CLASSICAL POSITION

So far we have concentrated on the rather striking policy conclusion reached by the new classical economists and on the central role of the rational expectations hypothesis in producing this conclusion. It is because of this striking policy conclusion—the independence of real variables from systematic aggregate demand policy actions—that so much attention has been focused on the new classical economics. Several Keynesian economists have in fact argued that the rational expectations assumption and the policy conclusion following from it are really all that is new about the new classical economics. This is not the position of the new classical economists themselves. They view their attack on Keynesian economics as much more far reaching than simply a proposal for

[7]Fiscal policy will also have certain supply-side effects, which are considered below. Consideration of such effects will only reinforce the policy conclusion stated in the text.

an alternative treatment of expectations formation. In this section we examine some of these broader aspects of the new classical position. In doing so, we will also bring out the classical roots of the new classical theory.

The new classical economists are highly critical of Keynesian economics as a whole. In one summary of their position, new classical economists Robert Lucas and Thomas Sargent use terms such as "fundamentally flawed," "wreckage," "failure on a grand scale," and "of no value" to describe major aspects of the neo-Keynesian theoretical and policy analysis.[8] The very title of their paper, "After Keynesian Macroeconomics," suggests their view that a total restructuring of macroeconomics is required. The basis for such a restructuring they believe can be found in the classical economics.

Lucas, Sargent, and other new classical economists are critical of the theoretical foundations of the Keynesian system. They argue that Keynes's model was one where "rules of thumb" such as the consumption function and Keynesian money demand function replaced sounder classical functions based on individual optimizing behavior. Generally, they believe that the classical system was more carefully constructed from a theory of rational choices by individual households and businesses. The Keynesian model is made up of more ad hoc elements, which were failed attempts at explaining the observed behavior of the economy in the aggregate. A good example of this failing of the Keynesian system is in the handling of expectations. The Keynesian system uses a rule of thumb whereby the expected current price is expressed as a function of the past behavior of prices. Such an assumption is not derived on the basis of individuals making optimal use of information and implies, in general, that economic agents choose to ignore useful information in making their price forecasts. The new classical economists make the alternative assumption that expectations are rational, which they argue to be consistent with optimal use of information by the economic agents in the model.

The new classical economists are also critical of Keynes's assumption that wages are "sticky," meaning, as they interpret this assumption, that wages "are set at a level or by a process that could be taken as uninfluenced by the macroeconomic forces he proposed to analyze." We have already considered the arguments that the Keynesians advance in support of the assumption of wage rigidity. The new classical economists do not find these arguments convincing. They favor the classical view that markets, including

---

[8]Robert Lucas and Thomas Sargent, "After Keynesian Macroeconomics," in *After the Phillips Curve: Persistence of High Inflation and High Unemployment* (Boston: Federal Reserve Bank of Boston, 1978).

the labor market, "clear"; prices, including the wage rate, which is the price of labor, move to equate supply and demand.

The new classical economists argue that fruitful macroeconomic models should rectify the failures of Keynesian economics by consistently adhering to the assumptions that:

1. Agents act in a optimal fashion; that is, they act in their own self-interest.
2. Markets clear.

They believe that the classical model adhered to these assumptions and is a basis for future work in macroeconomics.

Why, then, did Keynes dispense with these assumptions? In the new classical view, Keynesian economics was a response to the supposed failure of classical economics to explain the problem of unemployment and the realtionship between unemployment and aggregate demand. Recall that the classical aggregate supply schedule was vertical. With such a vertical supply schedule, aggregate output was totally dependent on supply factors. The equilibrium classical model was abandoned by Keynes because it did not explain the prolonged deviations of output and employment from full-employment levels. The classical model also failed to explain why these deviations from full employment were related to movements in the price level. Specifically, high levels of employment and output were associated with rising price levels, whereas low levels of employment and output were associated with declining price levels. Such behavior is explainable in the Keynesian system, where increases in aggregate demand increase the price level as well as the levels of output and employment. The empirical evidence seems to support the notion of an upward-sloping, not a vertical, aggregate supply curve.

The new classical economists argue that the classical model can explain both the deviations of employment from full-employment levels and the positive relation between output and price changes if one incorporates the assumption of rational expectations into the classical system. Recall that the classical theory of the labor market, which was the basis for the classical vertical aggregate supply function, assumed that labor suppliers knew the real wage, implying that labor suppliers had *perfect information* about the value the aggregate price level would take on over the short run. The new classical economists would substitute the assumption that labor suppliers make a rational forecast of the aggregate price level. In this case, as we saw above, systematic, and hence anticipated, changes in aggregate demand will not affect output and employment, but unanticipated changes in aggregate demand will. Such unanticipated changes in aggregate demand can provide an explanation for deviations of employment from the full-employment level. Notice also that unanticipated increases in aggregate demand will increase price as well as output and employment, with the reverse effect for unanticipated decreases in demand. Thus, with the rational expectations assumption, the classical system can explain the positive relationship between output changes and price changes.

This substitution of the assumption of rational expectations for the classical assumption of perfect information does not require substantive changes in the noninterventionist classical policy conclusions, for as we saw earlier in this chapter meaningful aggregate demand management policies involve *systematic* variations in aggregate demand, and these have no effect on output and employment in the new classical view. The new classical economists believe that the updated classical model with the rational expectations assumption substituted for the perfect information assumption provides a starting point for the construction of useful macroeconomic models.

11.3 THE KEYNESIAN RESPONSE

The theme which runs through the Keynesian response to the new classical criticisms is that although there is much that is valid in the points they raise, especially concerning the weakness of the Keynesian treatment of expectations formation, it is still, as the neo-Keynesian Robert Solow, puts it "much too early to tear up the IS–LM chapters in the textbooks of your possibly misspent youth."[9] The neo-Keynesians continue to believe that Keynes provided the basis for a useful framework in which to analyze the determinants of output and employment. They continue to believe in the usefulness of activist policies to stabilize output and employment.

In this section we analyze the countercritique of the new classical economics provided by the neo-Keynesians. On each of the points raised in this countercritique, the new classical rejoinder is presented. The major areas in which the neo-Keynesians have raised objections to the new classical view are as follows.

The Question of Persistence

In the preceding section we saw that the new classical model, with the concept of rational expectations, could provide an explanation of deviations of employment from the full-employment level. Unanticipated declines in aggregate demand would move output and

---

[9]Robert Solow, "Alternative Approaches to Macroeconomic Theory: A Partial View," *The Canadian Journal of Economics*, August, 1979. Another useful paper in this area by Solow is "On Theories of Unemployment," *American Economic Review*, March 1980, pp. 1–11.

employment below the full-employment levels. The Keynesians argue that whereas such an explanation might be plausible for temporary departures from full employment, it is not adequate to explain the persistent and substantial deviations from full employment that we have actually experienced. An unanticipated decline in investment demand, such as we considered above (Figure 11.3), might well cause output and employment to decline over a short period, let us say one year. By the next year, however, this decline in aggregate demand would be seen to have taken place; it would no longer be unanticipated. Labor suppliers would recognize that the aggregate price level had declined. Consequently, the shifts to the right in the labor supply curve and the aggregate supply curve discussed above (see Figure 11.3) would restore employment and output to their initial levels.

This being the case, how can the new classical model explain unemployment rates of 10 percent or more in Great Britain for the entire period 1923–39 or during the Great Depression of the 1930s in the United States, where the unemployment rate exceeded 14 percent for 10 consecutive years? In the more recent past, how can such a theory explain the movement of the unemployment rate from 4.8 percent in the fourth quarter of 1973 all the way to a peak of 8.8 percent in the second quarter of 1975, with a decline to below 7 percent only in the third quarter of 1977? The Keynesians argue that such persistently high unemployment does not fit the new classical explanation. To explain such experiences, one must accept the Keynesian view that the money wage is sticky downward for the reasons offered in Chapter 8. The labor market does not clear and involuntary unemployment results.

The response of the new classical economists to this criticism is that while the source of the unemployment, the unanticipated change in aggregate demand, will be of short duration as the Keynesians point out, there is no reason why the effects of such a shock will not persist. Consider, for example, the response to an unanticipated decline in aggregate demand. Assume that after one year or so everyone recognizes that demand has fallen, so that the change is no longer unanticipated. Declines in output and employment will have occurred. The new classical economists argue that it will take time before such declines are reversed. Firms that have already cut output levels will not find it optimal to immediately restore production to the levels before the shock because of the costs of adjustment of output levels. Workers who have become unemployed will not find it optimal to take the first job offer that comes along but will engage in a search for the best job opportunity. As a consequence of such adjustment lags, the new classical economists argue that quite lengthy deviations from full employment such as the United States experienced during the mid-1970s can be explained even though the shocks that cause such deviations are short-lived.

What about the depressions in Great Britain and the United States in the 1930s? One proponent of the new classical position, Robert Barro, has tentatively explained the severity of at least the U.S. experience by the extent of the largely unanticipated monetary collapse during the early years of the Depression, when the money stock fell by one-third. The slow recovery is viewed as a result of the massive government intervention during the New Deal period, intervention that subverted the normal adjustment mechanisms of the private sector.[10]

The Keynesians remain unconvinced that adjustment lags provide a sufficient explanation of persistent and severe unemployment. They believe that if one accepts the classical or new classical frameworks, one can only explain episodes such as the Great Depression as a result of factors on the supply side which in their view are the only factors in the classical or new classical model that could cause prolonged unemployment. If markets clear and there is no involuntary unemployment, then as Modigliani puts it, to the classical or new classical economists "what happened to the United States in the 1930s was a severe attack of contagious laziness."[11]

The Extreme Informational Assumptions of Rational Expectations

The Keynesians accept the new classical economists's criticism of price expectations formulations, which assume that economic agents use only information about past prices in making price forecasts. Such rules are naive because they assume that economic agents neglect other available and potentially useful information in making their forecasts. Such naive assumptions about expectations came into use in the 1950s and early 1960s when the inflation rate was both low and stable. In these circumstances such naive price forecasting rules might have been reasonable approximations of the way people made forecasts, since good forecasts could in fact have been made on the basis of the past behavior of prices. With the high and volatile inflation of the 1970s, it is harder to believe that economic agents did not find it worthwhile to make more sophisticated forecasts.

Still, many of the Keynesians argue that the rational expectations assumption errs in the direction of assuming that economic

---

[10]See Robert Barro, "Second Thoughts on Keynesian Economics," *American Economic Review*, 69 (May 1979), p. 57. Examples of such New Deal interventions could be NRA codes to fix prices and wages, agricultural policies to restrict output and raise prices, and increased regulation of the banking and securities industry which might have hindered the raising of funds for investment.

[11]Franco Modigiani, "The Monetarist Controversy, or Should We Forsake Stabilization Policies?" *American Economic Review*, 67 (March 1977), p. 6.

agents are unrealistically sophisticated forecasters, especially when rational expectations are assumed for the individual suppliers of labor. Keynesians criticize the assumption that individuals use *all* available relevant information in making their forecasts. Such an assumption ignores the costs of gathering information.

The rational expectations theory also presumes that individuals use available information intelligently. They know the relationships that link observed variables with the variables they are trying to predict. They are also able to estimate the systematic response pattern of policymakers. For example, if the monetary policymaker typically responds to rising unemployment by increasing the money stock, the public will come to anticipate such policy actions. They will also be able to predict the price effects of such anticipated monetary policy actions. Many Keynesians deny that individual labor suppliers possess such knowledge of both the working of the economy and the behavioral patterns of policymakers.

If the economy, including the behavior of policymakers, had been stable and subject to little change for a long period of time, it is perhaps not unreasonable to believe that economic agents would come to know more about the nature of the underlying relationships that govern policy variables and economic aggregates. The rational expectations assumption might then be realistic in a long-run equilibrium model, but the Keynesians argue that it is not realistic in the short run. In the short run the cost of gathering and processing information may be high enough so that labor suppliers making forecasts of the aggregate price level or inflation rate do not find it worthwhile to use much information over and above the past behavior of prices. The Keynesians would not make an unqualified defense of such naive rules and would agree that more research is needed on expectations formation. Many Keynesians would, however, given the current state of knowledge, regard such naive rules as better approximations than the rational expectations hypothesis.

If expectations are not rational, there is a role for aggregate demand management policy aimed at stabilizing output and employment. Even systematic changes in aggregate demand will affect output and employment in this case since they will not be predicted by economic agents. If private-sector aggregate demand is unstable, as the Keynesians believe it is, there is a need for stabilization policy. Further, the monetary and fiscal policymaking authorities can be assumed to be able to forecast systematic changes in private sector aggregate demand. These policymaking authorities *do* gather what they consider to be all the available and important information on variables they wish to forecast and control. They also invest considerable resources in trying to estimate the relationships that characterize the economy. The Keynesians would regard the rational expectations assumption as reasonably correct when applied to the policymakers. The policymakers can design policy changes to offset what are to the public unanticipated changes in private-sector aggregate demand. Notice that these stabilization policies, *even though they are systematic,* do affect output and employment. Since the expectations of private-sector economic agents are not rational, the actions of the policymakers will not be anticipated. In essence this role for stabilization policy stems from an information advantage on the part of the policymaker.

The Keynesians conclude that

> macroeconomic models based on the assumptions of the rational expectations hypothesis do not demonstrate the short-run ineffectiveness of policy, therefore, because they are not really short-run models. The information availability assumption of the rational expectations hypothesis implicitly places such models in a long-run equilibrium context in which their classical properties . . . are not surprising.[12]

In rebuttal, the new classical economists have defended the rational expectations assumption. They would admit that the rational expectations hypothesis is "unrealistic," but as Bennett McCallum argues: "All theories or models are 'unrealistic' in the sense of being extremely simplified descriptions of reality. . . . So the true issue is: of all the simple expectational assumptions conceivable, which one should be embodied in a macroeconomic model to be used for stabilization analysis."[13] The new classical economists favor the rational expectations assumption over formulations which assume that individuals form price expectations on the basis of the past history of prices because the rational expectations hypothesis is consistent with individual optimizing behavior—a property they feel all relationships in economic models should have.

The Auction Market Characterization of the Labor Market

In the new classical view, as in the original classical theory, the money wage is assumed to adjust to clear the labor market—to equate labor supply and demand. In contrast, the Keynesian assumption is that the money wage is sticky downward. Most of the response to a decline in aggregate demand, and consequently the

[12]Benjamin Friedman, "Optimal Expectations and the Extreme Informational Assumptions of 'Rational Expectations' Macromodels," *Journal of Monetary Economics,* January 1979, pp. 39–40.

[13]This quotation is from McCallum's useful nontechnical exposition, "The Significance of Rational Expectations Theory," *Challenge Magazine* January–February 1980, p. 39.

demand for labor, will come in the form of a reduction in employment rather than a drop in the money wage. The reasons advanced by the Keynesians to explain the downward rigidity of the money-wage were discussed in Chapter 8. These include laborers' reluctance to accept money wage cuts which will be viewed by each group of workers as declines in their wages relative to other groups of workers. Also important are explicit and implicit contracts in the labor market which fix, or at least limit the flexibility of, the money wage over considerable periods of time.

The most fundamental objection the Keynesians have to the new classical economics is over this question of the flexibility of the money wage—and more broadly over the new classical characterization of the labor market as an auction market. In the auction market characterization of the labor market, with many buyers and sellers, labor is bought and sold with continuous market clearing. The Keynesian view of the labor market is one where more long-term arrangements are made between buyers and sellers and where long-term relationships develop between particular buyers and sellers. Generally, the form of such relationships has been to fix the money wage paid to labor while leaving the employer free to adjust hours worked over the course of the explicit or implicit contract. Layoffs or hours reduction are considered an "acceptable" response on the part of the employer to a fall in demand. Pressure for wage cuts or replacing current workers with unemployed workers who will work for lower wages is not. This contractual Keynesian view of the labor market then explains wage stickiness on the basis of the institutional mechanisms that characterize the labor market.[14] Much work is currently under way, investigating the theoretical reasons labor market institutions such as these have developed. Even without such theoretical foundations, the Keynesian argue that such institutional mechanisms *do exist,* and they criticize the new classical economists for ignoring these elements of reality, which their model cannot explain.

The new classical economists agree that the labor market is at least in part characterized by long-term contracts. They deny,

[14]For an excellent discussion of this contractual view of the labor market, see Arthur Okun, *Prices and Quantities* (Washington, D.C.: Brookings Institution, 1981). As Okun summarized this view:

It is the central theme of this analysis that most prices and wages are not set to clear markets in the short run, but rather are strongly conditioned by longer-term considerations involving customer-supplier and employer-worker relations. These factors insulate wages and prices to a significant degree from the impact of shifts in demand so that the adjustment must be made in employment and output (p. 233).

As can be seen from this statement, Okun would extend this (implicit) contractual view to product markets as well as labor markets to explain why prices as well as wages are sticky, and why some product markets, as well as labor markets, fail to clear in modern economies.

however, that the existence of such contracts has, of itself, any implication for whether the labor market will clear—that is, for whether or not there will be involuntary unemployment. They deny that the terms of labor contracts are so rigid that employers and employees cannot affect changes desirable to both parties. For example, if the money wage specified is too high to maintain the market clearing level of employment, workers could give up other provisions in the contract, increase the work done per hour, or in extreme cases allow revision of the wage in some fashion.

The new classical economists also criticize the Keynesians for simply taking the contracting process as given. Perhaps there have been long-term fixed-money-wage contracts in past periods when price changes were slow and predictable. The new classical economists argue that with current higher and more variable inflation rates, labor market institutions, including the form of labor contracts, will adapt. One might expect labor contracts to become shorter in duration and to have the money wage more closely indexed to the price level. Thus, even if long-term contracts were a significant source of wage stickiness in the past, they may not be in the future. Overall, while the new classical economists would probably not deny that fixed-money-wage labor contracts cause some deviation of employment from the market clearing levels, they do not believe that this deviation is significant.

11.4 THE CURRENT STATE OF THE DEBATE

The new classical economics presents a challenge to the neo-Keynesian orthodoxy of a very fundamental nature. On the theoretical level the new classical economists question the soundness of the Keynesian model, arguing that many of its relationships are not firmly based on individual optimizing behavior. As an example, the new classical economists point to the naive treatment of price expectations in the Keynesian model. Further they criticize what they consider arbitrary assumptions of the Keynesians concerning wage stickiness and consequent involuntary unemployment.

The new classical economists believe that useful macroeconomic models can be constructed by modifying the classical model, which they believe was based on individual optimizing behavior, to incorporate the rational expectations concept in place of the classical assumption of perfect information. With this change, they believe that the classical model is capable of explaining fluctuations in output and employment while retaining the assumption that markets clear.

On policy questions, the new classical economists maintain that output and employment are independent of systematic and, therefore, anticipated changes in aggregate demand. Since meaningful aggregate demand management policies to stabilize output and employment consist of such systematic changes in aggregate demand, the new classical economists see no role for such policies. They arrive at noninterventionist policy conclusions similar to those of the original classical economists.

The Keynesians criticize the new classical theory on several grounds. They argue that the new classical model cannot explain the prolonged and severe unemployment experienced by the United States and other industrialized countries. They claim that the rational expectations assumption ascribes an extreme and unrealistic availability of information to market participants. Finally, and most important, they criticize the auction market characterization of the labor market in the new classical model. The Keynesians believe the labor market is much more a contractual market and that the nature of these contractual arrangements leads to wage rigidities and consequent involuntary unemployment.

In support of their position, the new classical economists cite the failure of Keynesian economics to explain the simultaneously high unemployment and inflation of the 1970s. Table 11.1 shows unemployment and inflation rates for the United States for the years 1973–80, together with figures for the rate of growth in the money stock and the government deficit. According to the new classical economists, if the Keynesian theory were correct, the large government deficits and the high rates of growth in the money stock in this period should have produced low unemploy-

Table 11.1 Unemployment, Inflation, Money Growth, and Government Deficits, 1973–1980

Year	Unemployment Rate[a]	Inflation Rate[b]	Money Growth Rate[c]	Government Deficit[d]
1973	4.9	6.2	7.3	5.6
1974	5.6	11.0	4.9	11.5
1975	8.5	9.1	4.6	69.3
1976	7.7	5.8	5.5	53.1
1977	7.0	6.5	7.5	46.4
1978	6.0	7.7	8.2	29.2
1979	5.8	11.3	7.8	14.8
1980	7.1	13.5	6.4	61.2

[a]Civilian unemployment rate (percent).
[b]Annual percentage rate of change in the consumer price index.
[c]Annual percentage rate of growth in M1-B (currency plus deposit balances on which checks can be written).
[d]Federal government budget *deficit* (spending minus tax revenues, billions of current dollars).

ment. The high rates of unemployment are, in their view, clear evidence against the Keynesian interpretation.

The Keynesians own explanation of the high unemployment and inflation in the 1970s, as we have seen (Chapter 8), ascribes a key role to supply disturbances, primarily to the large increases in the world price of oil and other basic commodities. Such supply shocks can be expected to increase prices while reducing output and employment. Other things being unchanged, high rates of growth in the money stock and large government deficits *would*, the Keynesians believe, have resulted in high rates of growth in output and employment, but during the 1970s other things, namely supply conditions, were not unchanged.

At present the empirical evidence does not clearly favor one side or the other in this debate between the new classical and Keynesian economists. Much current empirical and theoretical research in macroeconomics is aimed at resolving the important issues in this controversy.

Review Questions

1 Explain the concept of *rational expectations*. How does this view of how expectations are formed differ from the assumption made in previous chapters that workers formed expectations of current and future price levels on the basis of past information about prices?

2 Explain the implications of the rational expectations assumption for the effectiveness of economic stabilization policy.

3 Contrast the new classical and neo-Keynesian views of the way in which labor markets function.

4 Within the new classical framework, how could you explain a sustained departure from high-employment output such as that experienced by the United States in the mid-1970s?

5 Compare the new classical and monetarist positions concerning the usefulness and effectiveness of aggregate demand management policies to stabilize output.

6 Even within the new classical model, anticipated policy actions such as an increase in the money stock will affect *nominal* income. Explain why the adjustment of economic agent's expectations which offsets the real effects of such a policy change does not offset the nominal effects as well.

7 Why attach the adjective "new" to "classical" in describing the model in this chapter? How does this analysis differ from the classical model of Chapters 3 and 4?

8 Comment on the following statement. Do you agree or disagree with the view expressed concerning the effectiveness of systematic or anticipated fiscal policy actions within a new classical economic framework? Explain.

> The new classical economics or rational expectations theory provides a convincing explanation of the inability of systematic monetary policy to affect real income or employment. The situation is quite different, however, with fiscal policy actions such as increases in government spending, which will affect real output and employment whether they are anticipated or not—the difference between monetary and fiscal policy being that monetary policy affects aggregate demand and, hence, output by *inducing* private economic agents to change their demands for output. With rational expectations this effect will be offset. An increase in government spending affects aggregate demand directly and there is no way for the private sector to offset its effects on income and employment.

9 How would a supply shock such as the exogenous increase in the price of oil that was analyzed in Section 8.5 affect the aggregate price level and the level of real output in the new classical model?

Selected Readings

BARRO, ROBERT, "Unanticipated Money Growth and Unemployment in the United States," *American Economic Review*, 67 (March 1977), pp. 101–15.

LUCAS, ROBERT, "Understanding Business Cycles," in Karl Brunner and Alan Meltzer, eds., *Stabilization of the Domestic and International Economy*. Amsterdam: North-Holland, 1977.

LUCAS, ROBERT, and SARGENT, THOMAS, "After Keynesian Macroconomics," in *After the Phillips Curve: Persistence of High Inflation and High Unemployment*. Boston: Federal Reserve Bank of Boston, 1978. See also the "Comment on Lucas-Sargent" by Benjamin Friedman and the "Summary and Evaluations" by Robert Solow and William Poole in this volume.

McCALLUM, BENNETT, "The Significance of Rational Expectations Theory," *Challenge Magazine*, January–February 1980, pp. 37–43.

MILLER, PRESTON; NELSON, CLARENCE; and SUPEL, THOMAS, "The Rational Expectations Challenge to Policy Activism," in *A Prescription for Monetary Policy*. Minneapolis: Federal Reserve Bank of Minneapolis, 1976.

OKUN, ARTHUR, "Inflation: Its Mechanics and Welfare Costs," *Brookings Papers on Economic Activity*, No. 2, 1975, pp. 351–90.

Poole, William, "Rational Expectations in the Macro Model," *Brookings Papers on Economic Activity*, No. 2, 1976, pp. 463–514.

Sargent, Thomas, "Rational Expectations, the Real Rate of Interest, and the Natural Rate of Unemployment," *Brookings Papers on Economic Activity*, No. 2, 1973, pp. 429–72.

Sargent, Thomas, and Wallace, Neil, "Rational Expectations and the Theory of Economic Policy," *Journal of Monetary Economics*, 2 (April 1976), pp. 169–83.

Solow, Robert, "On Theories of Unemployment," *American Economic Review*, 70 (March 1980), pp. 1–11.

Solow, Robert, "Alternative Approaches to Macroeconomic Theory," *Canadian Journal of Economics*, 12 (August 1979), pp. 339–54.

12

We have now completed our analysis of the major schools of macroeconomic theory. The original classical macroeconomic model was presented. Then the Keynesian attack on the classical economics was discussed. The Keynesian macroeconomic model, which dominated macroeconomic analysis from the early post–World War II era until the late 1960s, was considered in detail. Finally, we analyzed the challenges to this Keynesian orthodoxy, the models of the monetarists, and the new classical economists.

In this chapter we give an overview of the theories considered in earlier chapters, attempting to clarify the areas of agreement and disagreement among these various schools of macroeconomic theory.

12.1 THEORETICAL ISSUES

It is again convenient to center our discussion on the aggregate supply–aggregate demand framework we have used to characterize the various economic models. The first of the models we considered, the classical model, viewed output as completely determined by supply factors. This view is embodied in the vertical aggregate supply schedule shown in Figure 12.1a.

Central to the classical theory of output and employment were what we termed the classical labor market assumptions. Both labor supply and demand depend only on the real wage, which

classical →

322

MACROECONOMIC MODELS: A SUMMARY

was known to all market participants. The money wage was perfectly flexible and moved to equate demand and supply in the labor market. Increases in aggregate demand would cause prices to rise which, other things being equal, would be a spur to production. To clear the labor market, however, the money wage would have to rise proportionately with the price level. The real wage would then be unchanged and consequently the levels of employment and output would be unchanged in the new equilibrium.

In the classical system, then, the role of aggregate demand was to determine the price level. The classical theory of aggregate demand was an implicit theory based on the quantity theory of money. The quantity theory provided a proportional relationship between the exogenous quantity of money and the level of nominal income. In the Cambridge form this relationship was

$$M = kPy \qquad (12.1)$$

With k treated as a constant, changes in the quantity of money resulted in proportional changes in nominal income (Py). With real income (y) fixed, the full adjustment came in the level of prices.

This relationship provided the classical aggregate demand schedule drawn in Figure 12.1*a*. The economic process behind this theory of aggregate demand was that if, for example, there was an excess supply of money ($M > kPy$), there would be a corresponding excess demand for commodities driving up the aggregate price level. Equilibrium between money demand and supply would imply that there was no spillover to the commodity market caus-

Figure 12.1 Theories of Aggregate Demand and Supply

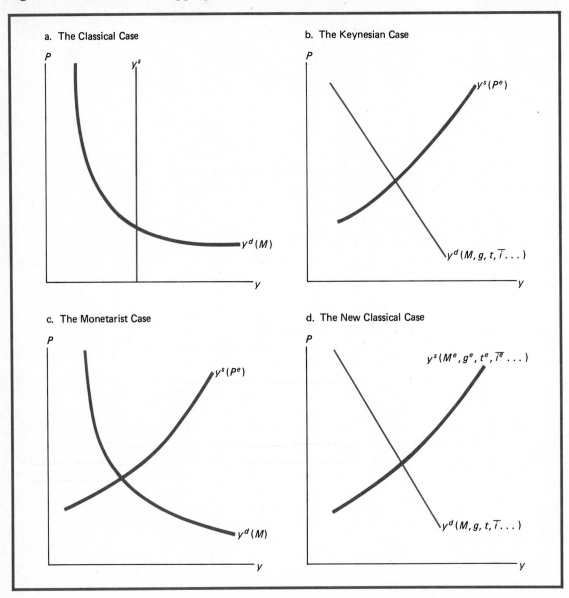

a. The Classical Case

b. The Keynesian Case

c. The Monetarist Case

d. The New Classical Case

ing a change in the price level. The classical economists had a monetary theory of aggregate demand.

In its simplest and most extreme form, the Keynesian model is the antithesis of the classical theory. In a simple Keynesian model, such as that discussed in Chapter 5, supply plays no role in output determination. The aggregate supply curve implied by such sim-

324

ple Keynesian models would be horizontal, indicating that supply is no constraint on the level of production, an assumption appropriate, if ever, only to situations where production is well below capacity levels. On the demand side, the simple Keynesian model (again see Chapter 5) concentrated on the determinants of autonomous expenditures: government spending, taxes, and autonomous investment demand. Monetary factors were neglected. This simple model highlights a central notion in Keynesian economics, the importance of aggregate demand in the determination of output and employment.

But this simple Keynesian model was an incomplete representation of Keynes's work. Additionally, the Keynesian theory has been modified and refined over the period since Keynes wrote. The modern neo-Keynesian model allows for both the influence of supply factors on output and the influence of monetary factors on aggregate demand. Still the neo-Keynesian model remains "Keynesian" in that aggregate demand is important in determining the level of output.

On the supply side the neo-Keynesian view is illustrated by the aggregate supply schedule shown in Figure 12.1*b*. In contrast to the vertical classical supply curve, the Keynesian aggregate supply function slopes upward to the right. Increases in aggregate demand that shift the aggregate demand schedule out to the right will increase both price and output. In the short run, an increase in the price level will cause firms to supply a higher level of output because the money wage will not rise proportionately with price.

The money wage is assumed to adjust only incompletely due to institutional features of the labor market as well as labor suppliers' imperfect information about the aggregate price level and, hence, about the level of real wage. In the long run, labor suppliers will come to perceive the price effects of changes in aggregate demand and wages will rise proportionately with prices. Institutional factors such as explicit and implicit labor market contracts which impart stickiness to the money wage will impede but not prevent this eventual adjustment in the level of the money wage. In the long run, the Keynesian aggregate supply schedule will converge to the vertical classical supply function. The Keynesian focus is, however, on the short run.

On the demand side (the y^d schedule in Figure 12.1*b*) the neo-Keynesian model provides a role for monetary factors (M) as well as fiscal policy variables (g and t) and other autonomous elements of aggregate demand (e.g., autonomous investment, $\bar{\imath}$). The Keynesian theory of aggregate demand is an *explicit* theory, in contrast to the *implicit* theory of the classical economists, in that the level of aggregate demand is found by first determining the level of the components of aggregate demand, consumption, investment, and government spending. Then we sum these to find aggregate demand. Money affects aggregate demand, primarily the investment component of aggregate demand, by influencing the level of the interest rate. There is no reason to believe that such monetary effects on aggregate demand are small. Neither is there reason to believe that monetary influences are dominant. Money is one of several important influences on aggregate demand in the Keynesian system.

There are, then, two important differences between the Keynesian and classical frameworks.

1. In the classical model output and employment are completely supply determined, whereas in the Keynesian theory in the short run, output and employment are determined jointly by aggregate supply and demand. In the Keynesian system, aggregate demand is an important determinant of output and employment.
2. Aggregate demand in the classical model is determined solely by the quantity of money. In the Keynesian system, money is one of a number of factors that determine aggregate demand.

These two issues, the role of aggregate demand in determining output and employment and the relative importance of monetary and other factors as determinants of aggregate demand, are also the ones that divide the Keynesians and the later schools of macroeconomic theory we have considered.

The major controversy between the monetarists, whose view of aggregate supply and demand is represented in Figure 12.1c, and the Keynesians has centered on point 2, the degree to which monetary forces dominate the determination of aggregate demand. The monetarists have taken the Cambridge version of the quantity equation [equation (12.1)] as the basis for their own strong quantity theory view that money is the dominant influence on aggregate demand and, therefore, nominal income.

On the supply side there is no fundamental difference between the monetarist and the Keynesian theories, although it has taken some time for this fact to be recognized. In both the monetarist and Keynesian models, the aggregate supply schedule slopes upward to the right in the short run and approaches the vertical classical formulation only in the long run. In both models changes in aggregate demand will affect output in the short run. But agreement on this issue has not kept the monetarists and Keynesians from reaching substantially different conclusions about the usefulness of aggregate demand management policies to stabilize output and employment in the short run—as will be discussed below.

The new classical view of the determination of aggregate supply and demand is illustrated in Figure 12.1d. The issue dividing the

MACROECONOMIC MODELS

new classical economists and the Keynesians concerns point 1 above, the degree to which aggregate demand plays a role in determining the level of real output. The new classical economists believe that systematic and, therefore, predictable changes in aggregate demand will not affect the level of real output. Such changes will be anticipated by rational economic agents. The aggregate demand curve and the aggregate supply schedule will shift upward, symmetrically raising the price level but leaving real output unchanged. To reflect this dependence of the aggregate supply schedule on expected changes in the determinants of aggregate demand and consequently the rational expectation of the price level, the aggregate supply schedule in Figure 12.1d is shown as depending on the expected level of the money stock (M^e) as well as expected values of fiscal policy variables and other possible determinants of demand (g^e, t^e, $\bar{\imath}^e$, . . .).

Unanticipated changes in aggregate demand, for example an increase in the money stock (M) which could not have been predicted (M^e is unchanged), will shift the aggregate demand curve without shifting the aggregate supply schedule. Such unanticipated changes in aggregate demand will cause labor suppliers to make price forecast errors and will therefore affect output and employment. In this respect the new classical model is a modification of the original classical model, where there was *no* role for aggregate demand in determining output and employment. The modification is the substitution of the rational expectations assumption in the new classical analysis for the classical assumption of perfect information. In the classical analysis there were no price forecast errors on the part of labor suppliers. Labor suppliers and demanders both had perfect information about the price level. In effect, there were assumed to be no unanticipated shifts in aggregate demand.

On the demand side there is no clear difference between the new classical and Keynesian positions (compare the y^d schedules in Figures 12.1b and d). Differences may emerge as more work is done to develop a complete new classical model, since as we have seen the new classical economists do not believe that the Keynesian theory of aggregate demand is based on a sound-choice theoretic basis. Note also that there is no reason why a new classical economist might not take a monetarist position on the determinants of aggregate demand.

From the above it should be clear that the monetarist–Keynesian dispute and the Keynesian–new classical dispute revolve around the same issues that separated the Keynesians from the classical economists. The Keynesian revolution was an attack on the classical supply-determined, full-employment theory of output and employment, as well as an attack on the quantity theory of money. The new classical economists and the monetarists have modified these two aspects of classical economics and have used these modified versions of the classical model to attack the Keynesian system. The two issues listed as points 1 and 2 above, which in terms of Figure 12.1 concern the slope of the short-run aggregate supply function and the determinants of the position of the aggregate demand function, have been the central issues in the macroeconomic controversies of the past 50 years.

12.2 POLICY ISSUES

Given the classical roots of the monetarist and new classical theories, it should not be surprising that these modern theories share the noninterventionist policy conclusions of the original classical theory. In contrast, the Keynesians are policy interventionists favoring activist aggregate demand management to stabilize output and employment.

In the classical system, output and employment are self-adjusting to the *supply*-determined full-employment levels. There was clearly no role for interventionist aggregate demand stabilization policies. In the new classical model, unanticipated shifts in aggregate demand do affect output and employment. Sensible stabilization policies, however, would have to consist of systematic reaction patterns to the state of the economy. Such systematic shifts in aggregate demand would be anticipated by the public and, therefore, would not affect output or employment. Consequently, the new classical economists also view aggregate demand stabilization policies as ineffective.

The monetarists believe that *monetary* policy actions, whether anticipated or not, will affect output and employment in the short run. Still, they arrive at the same noninterventionist policy conclusions as the classical and new classical economists. Like the classical economists, the monetarists believe that the private sector is stable if left free from destabilizing government policy actions. Further, since in the monetarist view aggregate demand is determined predominantly by the money stock, the best way to stabilize aggregate demand is to provide stable growth in the money stock. Rather than interventionist stabilization policies, the monetarists favor a constant growth rate policy for the money stock.

Ranged against this noninterventionist view is the Keynesian position that a private enterprise monetary economy is unstable in the absence of government policies to regulate aggregate demand. The Keynesians favor activist monetary and fiscal policies to offset shocks to private aggregate demand. In recent years, when there have been substantial supply shocks to the economy, the Keynesians have favored the use of aggregate demand policies to try to offset the output and employment effects of these shocks as well.

Thus, although we have considered four different schools of macroeconomic theory, on the major policy issue the controversy is between two positions, the noninterventionist position, with roots in the original classical system, and the Keynesian interventionist position. On this policy issue, as with the theoretical issues discussed above, the controversy is a long-standing one. In modern form it extends back over the 50 years since the Keynesian attack on the classical orthodoxy. But there were heretics before Keynes and the origins of the policy and theoretical controversies discussed here date back to the early 1800s.

How can such controversies proceed for so long without resolution? In economics we have no opportunity for controlled laboratory experiments aimed at settling such controversies. We cannot, for example, construct an economy, let the money stock grow for 10 years at a constant rate, and then see if the monetarist predictions are verified. To test theories we must examine events in the real world, where many factors vary at the same time. The resulting data are open to different interpretations. In the high inflation and unemployment of the 1970s, the new classical economists find evidence of the massive failure of Keynesian economics. The monetarists see the delayed results of past monetary excess. The Keynesian see mainly the unavoidable effects of a series of severe supply shocks.

Failure to resolve the continuing controversies in macroeconomics is unsettling even if it is not surprising. This failure contributes to the popular (mis?) conception of macroeconomists as a quarrelsome group, who must not know all that much if they can agree on so little. The present chapter and the preceding ones in Part II present areas of agreement as well as controversy. An attempt has been made to show that the controversies center on well-defined issues that have their basis in theoretical differences in the underlying models. Still, the student of macroeconomics is left with the choice of which view of the macroeconomy he or she finds to be the most plausible.

Review Questions

1   Suppose that investment demand in a given economy is predicted to be weak next year, let us say 10 percent below this year's level due to an exogenous shock. All other components of aggregate demand are predicted to be at levels comparable to this year's. These levels were consistent with high employ-

ment and relatively stable prices. For each of the macroeconomic systems listed below, explain the effects of this exogenous fall in aggregate demand and explain the proper policy response implied by the model; that is, what action should the policymaker take?

a. The classical model.
b. The neo-Keynesian model.
c. The monetarist model.
d. The new classical model.

2   The question of what information market participants possess at any point in time and how quickly they learn—what can be termed the information structure of the model—is a distinguishing feature of the different macroeconomic systems we dealt with. With reference to the major frameworks covered in this Part (classical, Keynesian, monetarist, new classical), explain the differing assumptions about the information market participants possess and the degree to which these differing assumptions account for the different policy conclusions one derives from these models.

3   Which of the frameworks that we have considered do you view as the most useful in explaining the behavior of the economy and providing proper prescriptions? Defend your choice.

extensions of the models

chapter 13

The chapters in Part III consider refinements and extensions of the models in Part II. We begin in this chapter with a further examination of the determinants of the private sector's demand for output: consumption spending and investment spending. In Chapters 14 and 15 we take a more detailed look at money demand and money supply. Chapter 16 extends our previous models to analyze a longer-run horizon. Chapter 17 extends the models by considering an open economy, one that trades with other nations.

13.1 CONSUMPTION

Early Empirical Evidence on the Keynesian Consumption Function

Household consumption expenditures account for approximately two-thirds of gross national product. In Part II we saw that the consumption to income relationship—the consumption function—was a key element in the Keynesian theory of income determination. The starting point for Keynes's theory of consumer behavior was the following concept:

> The fundamental psychological law, upon which we are entitled to depend with great confidence both *a priori* from our knowledge of human nature and from the detailed facts of experience, is that men are disposed, as a rule and on the average, to increase their consumption as their income increases, but not by as much as the increase in their income.[1]

[1] John M. Keynes, *The General Theory of Employment, Interest and Money* (New York: Harcourt, Brace and Company, Inc., 1936), p. 96.

CONSUMPTION AND INVESTMENT SPENDING

This psychological law translates into the Keynesian consumption function:

$$C = a + bY_D \qquad a > 0, \quad 0 < b < 1 \qquad \textbf{(13.1)}$$

where C is real consumption and Y_D is real disposable income, which equals real GNP minus taxes. The parameter b is the marginal propensity to consume (MPC), which measures the increase in consumption per unit increase in disposable income ($\Delta C/\Delta Y_D$). The *intercept*, a, measures consumption at a zero level of disposable income. The consumption function (13.1) is shown graphically in Figure 13.1.

Because of the intercept, the Keynesian consumption function is not a proportional relationship between consumption and income, that is, consumption is not a constant fraction of disposable income. The ratio of consumption to income is termed the *average propensity to consume*, APC, which from (13.1) can be seen to be given by

$$\text{APC} = \frac{C}{Y_D} = \frac{a}{Y_D} + b \qquad \textbf{(13.2)}$$

The APC is greater than the MPC, by the amount a/Y_D. It also follows from (13.2) that the APC declines as the level of income increases. This implies that as income rises, households consume a smaller fraction of income, which is to say that they save a larger fraction of income. The ratio of saving to income is termed the

Figure 13.1
Simple Keynesian
Consumption Function

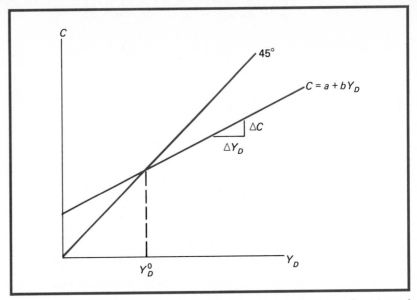

The Keynesian consumption function shows consumption as a function of disposable income. The intercept (*a*) gives the level of consumption corresponding to a zero level of disposable income. The slope of the consumption function (*b*) is the marginal propensity to consume ($\Delta C / \Delta Y_D$).

average propensity to save (APS) and is equal to $(1 - \text{APC})$, or

$$\text{APS} = 1 - \frac{a}{Y_D} - b = \frac{-a}{Y_D} + (1 - b) \qquad (13.3)$$

which can be seen to increase as disposable income rises. In Figure 13.1, below the income level Y_D^0, consumption exceeds disposable income. In this range the APC is greater than 1 and the APS is negative. Above income level Y_D^0, the APC is less than 1 and the APS is positive. Total consumption increases less than proportionately with Y, so the APC declines and the APS rises as we move to higher-income levels in the graph.

The version of the consumption function described above has been called the *absolute income hypothesis;* consumption is assumed to react rather mechanically to actual current levels of income. Keynes advanced this hypothesis about consumption, as we have seen, on the basis of "knowledge of human nature" and "detailed facts of experience." Early followers of Keynes attempted to provide a stronger empirical basis for this form of the consumption function—with mixed results.

Using statistical techniques and annual data for a short period,

1929–41, Keynesian economists obtained the following type of estimate for the consumption function:[2]

$$C = 26.5 + 0.75Y_D \qquad (13.4)$$

In (13.4) the estimate of the MPC (b) is 0.75 and estimate of the intercept (a) is $26.5 billion. The positive value of the intercept (a) confirmed the Keynesian view that the average propensity to consume ($a/Y_D + b$) exceeded the marginal propensity to consume (b). Equation (13.4) implies that the APC declines as income rises. At a level of disposable income equal to $100 billion, the APC estimated from (13.4) would be 1.015 (26.5/100 + 0.75), implying that the APS is negative (−0.015), but at an income level of 200, the APC would be 0.883 (26.5/200 + 0.75). An estimated consumption function such as (13.4) seemed to predict annual levels of consumer expenditures during this period (1929–41) reasonably well.

Further support for the Keynesian form of the consumption function came from comparative studies of family budgets. As one looked at budgets for families at progressively higher income levels, the absolute amount of consumption increased ($b > 0$) but by less than the increase in income ($b < 1$). Also, families at higher income levels consumed a smaller proportion of income, indicating that the APC declined as income rose.

The fact that the proportion of income that is saved apparently increased as income rose led some early Keynesians to worry about secular stagnation in the economy. As the ratio of saving to income increased, these economists worried that aggregate demand would fall short of output. Recall that saving is a *leakage* from the circular flow of income and expenditure. Aggregate demand would be inadequate unless the fall in the C/Y_D ratio (rise in the S/Y_D ratio) were balanced by growth in the other components of aggregate demand: government spending and investment. In the absence of such growth these economists feared that aggregate demand would fall short of full-employment output and stagnation would result.[3] Whether such a secular decline in the ratio of consumption to income would have led to chronically deficient levels of aggregate demand is a matter of conjecture. The fact has turned out to be that although there has been continued growth in real GNP in the United States and other industrialized countries, there has been no tendency for the APC to decline and the APS to rise. The shares of consumption and saving in income have been

[2]This estimate is taken from Gardner Ackley, *Macroeconomic Theory* (New York: Macmillan, 1961), p. 226. Data for the equation are in 1954 constant dollars.

[3]For an example of this stagnationist thesis, see Alvin Hansen, "Economic Progress and Declining Population Growth," *American Economic Review*, 29 (March 1939).

relatively constant for over a century, as became apparent when estimates of GNP and output shares extending back into the nineteenth century became available in the early post–World War II period.

Data from an early study by Simon Kuznets for real national income (Y), real consumption (C), and the ratio of the two (C/Y) are given in Table 13.1. The data are overlapping decade averages of annual figures. As can be seen from the table, there was no downward trend in the ratio of consumption to income even though national income grew from an average of $9.3 billion in the 1869–78 decade to $72.0 billion in the 1929–38 decade. Nor is there evidence of a downward trend in the average propensity to consume in more recent years. The APC (C/Y_D) was 0.93 in 1950, 0.92 in 1960, 0.89 in 1970, and 0.92 in 1980. The Kuznets data, as well as later estimates, strongly suggested that the secular or long-run relationship between consumption and income was a proportional one, as illustrated in Figure 13.2.

Additionally, data from the early post–World War II period showed that quarter-to-quarter changes in consumption were not well explained by quarter-to-quarter movements in income. Gardner Ackley, for example, examined 22 quarter-to-quarter changes in consumption and income. He found that in five quarters the changes in consumption and income were in opposite directions. In 10 of the cases where consumption and income did change in the same direction, the change in consumption *exceeded* the change in income. In only 7 of the 22 quarters were the movements in consumption and income consistent with a short-run marginal

Table 13.1 **Consumption and National Income, 1869–1938**[a]	Years	Y	C	C/Y
	1869–78	9.3	8.1	0.87
	1874–83	13.6	11.6	0.85
	1879–88	17.9	15.3	0.85
	1884–93	21.0	17.7	0.84
	1889–98	24.2	20.2	0.83
	1894–1903	29.8	25.4	0.85
	1899–1908	37.3	32.3	0.87
	1904–13	45.0	39.1	0.87
	1909–18	50.6	44.0	0.87
	1914–23	57.3	50.7	0.88
	1919–28	69.0	62.0	0.90
	1924–33	73.3	68.9	0.94
	1929–38	72.0	71.0	0.99

[a]Y, national income, billions of dollars; C, consumption expenditure, billions of dollars.
Source: Simon Kuznets, *National Product Since 1869* (New York: National Bureau of Economic Research, 1946), p. 119.

EXTENSIONS OF THE MODELS

Figure 13.2
Long-Run
Consumption Function

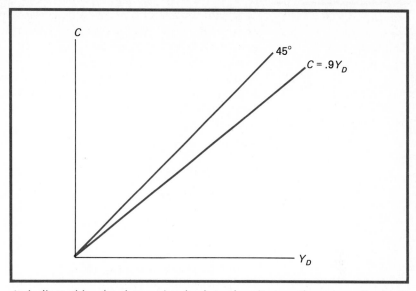

As indicated by the data going back to the nineteenth century, the long-run consumption function is shown as a proportional relationship with an $MPC = APC$, both approximately 0.9.

propensity to consume $(\Delta C/\Delta Y_D)$ which is positive and less than 1.[4] This erratic short-run behavior of consumption indicated that either the relationship of consumption to current income in the short run was not as mechanical as predicted by the absolute income hypothesis, or that other variables were influencing consumption behavior.

We can then summarize the early evidence about the consumption function as follows. Evidence from short-run annual time series data (e.g., 1929–41) and family budget studies seemed to support the Keynesian hypothesis about consumption—the absolute income hypothesis—as represented by (13.1). Time series data for a longer time period (e.g., 1869–1938) suggest that the consumption income relationship is a proportional one rather than the nonproportional relationship given by (13.1). There is therefore a need to reconcile long-run evidence on the consumption function with the short-run time series evidence and cross-sectional evidence from family budget studies. Finally, the erratic quarter-to-quarter movements of consumption relative to income which were noted above cast doubt on the closeness of the consumption–income relationship in the short run. Resolving these puzzles posed by the early empirical evidence on consumer behavior has been the task of the modern theory of the consumption function.

[4]See Ackley, *Macroeconomic Theory*, pp. 253–54.

The Life Cycle Theory of Consumption

To see how post-Keynesian consumption theories have tried to reconcile the somewhat disparate implications from different data sources, we will consider one of these theories, the *life cycle theory* of consumption, in some detail. We then compare the conclusions of this theory with another explanation of the same phenomena, Milton Friedman's *permanent income hypothesis.*[5]

The life cycle hypothesis about consumption was developed by Franco Modigliani, Albert Ando, and Richard Brumberg.[6] As stated by Modigliani:

> The point of departure of the life cycle model is the hypothesis that consumption and saving decisions of households at each point of time reflect a more or less conscious attempt at achieving the preferred distribution of consumption over the life cycle, subject to the constraint imposed by the resources accruing to the household over its lifetime.[7]

An individual's or household's level of consumption will depend not just on his current income but also, and more important, on his long-term expected earnings. Individuals are assumed to plan a lifetime pattern of consumer expenditure based on expected earnings over their lifetime.

To see the implications of this theory for the form of the consumption function, we first look at a simplified example. Consider an individual of a given age who is in the labor force, has a life expectancy of T years, and who plans to remain in the labor force for N years. Our representative consumer might, for example, be 30 with a life expectancy of 50 (additional) years, plans to retire after 40 years, and, therefore with expected years in retirement equal to $(T - N)$, or 10. We will make the following assumptions about the individual's plans. The individual will be assumed to desire a constant consumption flow over his lifetime. Further, we will assume that he intends to consume the total amount of his lifetime earnings plus current assets; he plans no bequests. Finally, we will assume that the interest paid on his assets is zero; current saving results in dollar-for-dollar future consumption.

---

[5]For another reconciliation of the long-run and short-run evidence on the consumption function, see James Duesenberry, *Income, Saving, and the Theory of Consumer Behavior* (Cambridge, Mass.: Harvard University Press, 1949).

[6]Two early papers on the life cycle hypothesis are: Franco Modigliani and Richard Brumberg, "Utility Analysis and the Consumption Function: An Interpretation of Cross Section Data," in K. Kurihara, ed., *Post-Keynesian Economics*, (N.J.: Rutgers University Press, 1954), pp. 388–436; and Albert Ando and Franco Modigliani, "The Life Cycle Hypothesis of Saving: Aggregate Implications and Tests," *American Economic Review*, 53 (March 1963), pp. 55–84.

[7]Franco Modigliani, "The Life Cycle Hypothesis of Saving, the Demand for Wealth and the Supply of Capital," *Social Research*, 33 (June 1966), pp. 160–217, p. 162.

These assumptions are purely to keep the example simple and are relaxed below.

These assumptions imply that consumption in a given period will be a constant proportion, $1/T$, of expected *lifetime* resources. The individual plans to consume his lifetime earnings in T equal installments. The consumption function implied by this simple version of the life cycle hypothesis is

$$C_t = \frac{1}{T}[Y_t^1 + (N-1)\bar{Y}^{le} + A_t] \tag{13.5}$$

C_t is consumption in time period t. The term in brackets is expected lifetime resources, which consist of

$Y_t^1 =$ the individual's labor income in the current time period (t)
$\bar{Y}^{le} =$ the average labor income expected over the future $N - 1$ years during which the individual plans to work
$A_t =$ the value of presently held assets

It can be seen from (13.5) that according to the life cycle hypothesis, consumption will depend not only on current income but also on expected future income, and current asset holdings (i.e., current wealth). In fact, the life cycle hypothesis suggests that consumption would be quite unresponsive to changes in current income (Y_t^1) which did not also change average expected future income. From (13.5), for example, we can compute

$$\frac{\Delta C_t}{\Delta Y_t^1} = \frac{1}{T} = \frac{1}{50} = 0.02$$

An increase in income that was expected to persist through the work years would mean that $\bar{Y}^{le}$ also rose and the effect on consumption would be much greater:

$$\frac{\Delta C_t}{\Delta Y_t^1} + \frac{\Delta C_t}{\Delta \bar{Y}^{le}} = \frac{1}{T} + \frac{N-1}{T} = \frac{N}{T} = \frac{40}{50} = 0.8$$

A one-time or transient change in income of, say, $100 will have the same effect as a change in wealth (note that $\Delta C_t/\Delta Y_t^1 = \Delta C_t/\Delta A_t = 1/T$) of the same amount. Lifetime resources will go up by $100 and this will be spread out in a planned consumption flow of $100/T = 100/50 = 2$ per period in our example, where the individual expects to live for 50 additional years. A permanent increase in income of $100 will lead to an increase of consumption of $80 in each of the remaining periods, including the 10 planned periods of retirement. The increase of $80 in each of these 10 retirement years, a total of $800, is financed by a saving of $20 $(100 - 80)$ in each of the 40 remaining working years.

Generally, the life cycle hypothesis attempts to account for the observed dependence of consumption and saving behavior on the individual's position in the life cycle. Young workers entering the labor force have relatively low incomes and low (possibly negative) saving rates. As income rises in middle age years, so does the saving rate. Retirement brings a fall in income and begins a period of *dissaving* (negative saving rates). This time profile of consumption and saving is depicted in Figure 13.3. Here the desired pattern of consumption is taken to rise mildly with time instead of the constant desired consumption pattern assumed in our individual example. The pattern of income rises more sharply, though, and the typical individual smoothes out his consumption flow by a short period of early dissaving, a period of positive saving, then a somewhat longer period of dissaving in retirement.

The general form of the aggregate consumption function implied by the life cycle hypothesis is

$$C_t = b_1 Y_t^1 + b_2 \overline{Y}^{le} + b_3 A_t \tag{13.6}$$

where the variables C_t, Y_t^1, $\overline{Y}^{le}$, and A_t are as defined for (13.5) but should now be interpreted as economy-wide averages. If the simplifying assumptions made above of no bequests, zero interest on saving, and a uniform consumption pattern over time are relaxed, the parameters b_1, b_2, and b_3 will no longer be simply functions of N and T as were the coefficients in (13.5). Still, in the aggregate

Figure 13.3
Income and Consumption Over the Life Cycle

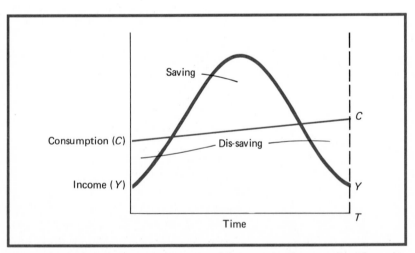

The level of consumption is shown as rising gradually over the life cycle. Income rises sharply over the early working years, peaks and then declines, especially with retirement. This pattern of consumption and income results in periods of disaving in the early working years and late stage of the life cycle, with positive saving over the high-income middle period of the life cycle.

consumption function (13.6), as in the case of (13.5), consumption depends not just on current labor income (Y^1_t), but also on future expected labor income ($\bar{Y}^{le}$) and wealth (A_t). It will also be true in the aggregate, as in the simplified individual example, that the response to a *transient* or one-time increase in labor income (an increase in Y^1_t) will be quite small, much less than the response to a permanent income change (an increase in Y^1_t *and* $\bar{Y}^{le}$).

To use (13.6) to study actual aggregate consumer behavior, some assumption must be made about the way in which individuals form expectations concerning lifetime labor income. In a study for the United States, Ando and Modigliani make the simple assumption that expected average future labor income is just a multiple of current labor income:

$$\bar{Y}^{le} = \beta Y^1_t \qquad \beta > 0 \tag{13.7}$$

According to this specification, individuals revise their expectation of future expected labor income $\bar{Y}^{le}$ by some proportion β of a change in current labor income. Substitution of (13.7) for $\bar{Y}^{le}$ in the aggregate consumption function (13.6) yields

$$C_t = (b_1 + b_2\,\beta)Y^1_t + b_3 A_t \tag{13.8}$$

A representative statistical estimate of the equation based on the work of Ando and Modigliani is the following:

$$C_t = 0.72Y^1_t + 0.06A_t \tag{13.9}$$

An increase in current labor income of $100 *with the assumed effect on future labor income* will increase consumption by $72. An increase in wealth of $100 will increase consumption by $6. As noted above, an increase in income which was shown to be temporary and therefore which would *not* affect future expected labor income would have the same effect as an increase in wealth. Thus according to this estimate, the marginal propensity to consume out of such a transient income flow is on the order of 0.06, the marginal propensity to consume out of wealth.

The life cycle hypothesis can explain some of the puzzles that emerged from the early empirical work on consumption functions. According to the life cycle hypothesis, the relationship between consumption and current income would be nonproportional, as seemed to be the case in *short-run* time series estimates [see (13.4)]. The intercept of the function would measure the effect of wealth [$0.06A_t$ in (13.9)]. But the intercept would not be constant over time, such short-run consumption functions would be shifting upward over time as wealth grew. Such upward shifts in the short-run consumption function (SCF) are illustrated in Figure 13.4. The shifting short-run consumption functions trace out a long-run consumption function (LCF).

Figure 13.4
Short-Run and Long-
Run Consumption
Functions

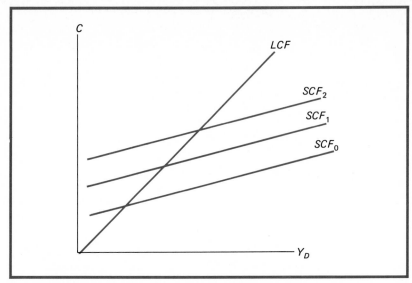

As wealth increases over time, the non-proportional short-run consumption function shifts upward (from SCF_0 to SCF_1 then to SCF_2) to trace out
the long-run proportional consumption income relationship (LCF).

To the degree that the ratios of wealth and labor income to disposable personal income are relatively constant over time, the life
cycle consumption function [equation (13.9)] is also consistent
with the evidence from long-run time series data that the long-run
consumption–income relationship (LCF in Figure 13.4) is proportional, with the APC(C/Y_D) relatively stable in the neighborhood of
0.9. To see this, first note that the ratio of labor income to disposable personal income has been approximately 0.88, that is, $Y_t^1 =
0.88Y_D$. The ratio of wealth to disposable income is approximately
4.75; $A_t = 4.75Y_D$. Substitution of these expressions for A_t and Y_t^1 in
the estimated aggregate consumption function (13.9) yields

$$C_t = 0.72(0.88Y_D) + 0.06(4.75Y_D)$$
$$= 0.63Y_D + 0.29Y_D$$
$$= 0.92Y_D$$

or

$$\frac{C_t}{Y_D} = 0.92$$

which is approximately the average value of the APC over the
post–World War II period.

The life cycle hypothesis also provides an explanation of the
evidence from cross-sectional family budget studies showing that

higher-income families consume a smaller proportion of income (have a lower APC) than do lower-income families. A larger proportion of high-income families might be expected to be those who are in their peak earning years, that is, in the "humped" portion of Figure 13.3. It is in this range that according to the life cycle hypothesis income should exceed consumption by the greatest amount and the APC should therefore be lowest. Conversely, a sample of low-income families would have a high proportion of new entrants to the labor market and retirees, groups that tend to dis-save. These groups with high APCs would push up the APC for the sample of low-income families.

Finally, the life cycle hypothesis provides an explanation of why quarter-to-quarter movements in consumption do not closely mirror quarter-to-quarter movements in income, the other anomalous finding of early research on the consumption function. The change in income from any given quarter to the next will surely be the result in large part of one-time factors that will not affect individuals' perceptions of lifetime average income. We have seen that such transient income changes have little impact on consumer behavior according to the life cycle hypothesis. It is not surprising, therefore, that quarter-to-quarter changes in consumption and income are not closely related.

While the life cycle hypothesis provides an explanation of several puzzling features of the consumption–income relationship, the approach is not without its critics. Gardner Ackley, for example, points out that the life cycle theory assumes that each household in making consumption decisions has at all times "a definite, conscious vision"

> of the family's future size and composition, including the life expectancy of each member;
> of the entire lifetime profile of the income from work of each member—after the then applicable taxes;
> of the present and future extent and terms of any credit available to it;
> of the future emergencies, opportunities, and social pressures which will impinge upon its consumption spending.[8]

Further, each household must hold such a vision with enough certainty that it would be worthwhile to use this vision as a basis for rational planning of consumption decisions. Ackley finds these assumptions to be unrealistic. In essence, Ackley will not accept the point of departure for the life cycle hypothesis, Modigliani's statement which was quoted above, that consumption and saving

[8]Gardner Ackley, "Discussion" of a paper by James Tobin and Walter Dolde, in *Consumer Spending and Monetary Policy: The Linkages* (Boston: Federal Reserve Bank of Boston, 1971).

decisions of households "reflect a more or less conscious attempt at achieving the preferred distribution of consumption over the life cycle."

Another criticism of the life cycle approach is that it fails to recognize the presence of *liquidity constraints*. Even if a household or individual possessed a concrete vision of future income, there is very little opportunity in real-world capital markets for borrowing for any long period on the basis of this future income. As a result, consumption may be much more responsive to changes in current income, whether temporary or not, than would be predicted on the basis of the life cycle hypothesis. The response of consumption to current income, however, may not be the simple mechanical one predicted by the "absolute income" hypothesis. The consumption pattern of younger households whose consumption is limited by such liquidity constraints may be very responsive to changes in current income. The consumption of older households with more accumulated wealth may not be responsive to temporary variations in current income. Small temporary changes in income may be financed out of a buffer of liquid assets, but larger changes may cause liquidity constraints to become binding and begin to affect consumption behavior. Consideration of liquidity constraints on households therefore leads one to believe that current income may be a more important influence on consumption than would be predicted on the basis of the life cycle hypothesis, but the consumption-to-current income relationship may be more complex than predicted by Keynes's absolute income hypothesis.[9]

Policy Implications of the Life Cycle Hypothesis

As mentioned at the beginning of this section, the consumption function is an important element in Keynesian macroeconomic theory. Fluctuations in the unstable investment component of private aggregate demand are assumed to be amplified and transmitted throughout the economy by the induced consumption response to the initial income change; this is the multiplier process. A change in government spending would have multiplier effects, again with induced effects on consumption. A change in taxes in the Keynesian system would affect disposable income and therefore consumption, but this effect was also predicated on the absolute income hypothesis about consumer expenditures. In this subsection we examine the changes required in the Keynesian analysis of the multiplier process and the effects of fiscal policy

[9]Ackley's view that households do not have sufficient knowledge on which to base lifetime consumption plans also could imply a greater role for current income as a determinant of consumption. In the absence of worthwhile forecasts of future resources and needs, consumption may respond somewhat automatically to available income, with saving determined by rules of thumb to protect against a "rainy day."

when consumption is assumed to be determined according to the life cycle hypothesis instead of the absolute income hypothesis. We also consider the implications of the life cycle hypothesis for the effectiveness of monetary policy.

Fiscal Policy and the Multiplier Process

The key element in the Keynesian analysis of the multiplier effects of changes in investment or fiscal policy variables is the response of consumption to current income. According to the life cycle hypothesis, consumption is determined primarily by expected lifetime income and wealth. A change in current income will of itself have little influence on consumer behavior. In the empirical work of Ando and Modigliani discussed above, it was assumed that expected future income is proportional to current income. If this assumption is correct, we would expect a strong response of consumption to current income, since changes in current income cause proportional changes in expected lifetime income as well. Ando and Modigliani's estimate of the consumption function [equation (13.9)] implies that the marginal propensity to consume out of current labor income is 0.72. This value is high enough to be consistent with the earlier Keynesian multiplier analysis and to imply strong effects for changes in taxes and government spending. In other empirical work by Modigliani, expected lifetime income is assumed instead to depend on a weighted average of the past 12 quarters' income levels.[10] With this assumption as well, the response of consumption to income was strong enough to produce results consistent with earlier Keynesian analysis. For example, there were strong effects for tax and government spending changes within a year. The life cycle hypothesis does not therefore seem to imply an essential modification of the general Keynesian multiplier or fiscal policy analysis.

There is one modification required in the Keynesian view of fiscal policy effects if the life cycle hypothesis is adopted in place of the absolute income version of the consumption function. According to the life cycle hypothesis, current income has a strong effect on consumption only because of the assumption that changes in current income affect expected average lifetime income. This will clearly not be the case where the change in current income is known to be transient, as would be the case with a change in tax rates or government transfer payments which is explicitly temporary. In the second quarter of 1975, for example, $8 billion was paid out to taxpayers as a one-time rebate in order to

---

[10]See Franco Modigliani, "Monetary Policy and Consumption," in *Consumer Spending and Monetary Policy: The Linkages* (Boston: Federal Reserve Bank of Boston, 1971).

stimulate aggregate demand. According to the life cycle theory, such a one-time payment would *not* affect expected future income and would therefore have very little effect on consumption. Keynesian advocates of the life cycle hypothesis favor permanent, not temporary, changes in tax policy as measures to manage aggregate demand.

Even temporary tax changes may have strong effects, however, if liquidity constraints are important in determining consumption as discussed above. If a household would choose a higher level of consumption if it were not constrained in the amount that can be borrowed, then a $200 rebate such as was received in 1975 would increase consumption by up to $200. The rebate would reduce the liquidity constraint. On the question of the efficacy of temporary tax changes as a stabilization tool, therefore, it appears that the crucial issue is the importance of liquidity constraints as a determinant of aggregate consumption. We will return to this question when fiscal policy instruments are considered in more detail in Chapter 18.

Monetary Policy and Consumption

In our analysis of monetary policy effects, the main focus of the discussion was on investment. The life cycle hypothesis implies that monetary policy may have important direct effects on consumption as well. According to the life cycle hypothesis, household wealth is one of the main determinants of consumption. Monetary policy affects household wealth and therefore consumption. Monetary policy actions affect wealth both directly by changing the quantity of money that is a component of household net wealth and by affecting interest rates and consequently the market value of other assets, such as government and private bonds and corporate equities (stocks). In Chapter 6 we analyzed the relationship between the interest rate and the market value of bonds. An increase in the interest rate resulting from a tight money policy will cause bond prices to fall and, hence, cause households to suffer capital losses on bonds. A decline in interest rates due to an expansionary monetary policy will cause bond prices to rise, with resulting capital gains on bonds. Equity prices would also be expected to move inversely with interest rates. Equities pay streams of dividends, and with higher market interest rates, the price investors will be willing to pay for a equity with a given dividend flow will fall.

Tight money policies will therefore reduce wealth and consumption, whereas expansionary policies will have the opposite effects. Empirical work by Modigliani, mentioned above, indicates that monetary policy effects on consumption are a large component of the overall effects of monetary policy. In the Federal

Reserve–Massachusetts Institute of Technology statistical model developed by Modigliani (and many others), this wealth effect on consumption accounts for 34 percent of the effects of a monetary policy action in the first year after the policy shift and 45 percent of the effect after four years.

The hypothesis that liquidity constraints are important in the determination of consumption provides an additional channel by which monetary policy might affect consumption. Tight money policies will result in larger down-payment requirements and stricter credit standards for consumer credit and increase the severity of the liquidity constraint facing many households. Expansionary monetary policies will make credit more available and reduce liquidity constraints. A graphic illustration of how consumption may be affected by liquidity constraints, whether real or only perceived, came in the spring of 1980. The Federal Reserve, in an effort to reduce the growth of consumer credit, instituted a number of credit controls. There are indications that the public overreacted and feared that credit would simply become unavailable. Owing in part to this expected liquidity constraint, real consumer expenditure fell by 10.5 percent at an annual rate in the second quarter of 1980!

The Permanent Income Hypothesis

An alternative explanation of consumer behavior is the permanent income hypothesis suggested by Milton Friedman.[11] The permanent income hypothesis has in common with the life cycle hypothesis the property that long-term income is assumed to be the primary determinant of consumption. Friedman postulates that consumption is proportional to permanent income:

$$C = kY^p \qquad (13.10)$$

where Y^p is permanent income and k is the factor of proportionality ($k > 0$). Permanent income is expected average long-term income from both "human and nonhuman wealth," that is, both expected labor income (the return to human wealth or human capital) and expected earnings from asset holdings (nonhuman wealth).

Friedman would not expect this consumption equation to predict consumption perfectly because, in addition to the part of consumption determined on the basis of permanent income, there will be in any period a random element to consumption which Friedman termed "transitory" consumption. Similarly, there will, in any period, be a transitory component of income; measured income will not in general equal permanent income for the individ-

---

[11]Milton Friedman, *A Theory of the Consumption Function* (Princeton, N.J.: Princeton University Press, 1957).

ual or in the aggregate. We can then write measured income (Y) as

$$Y = Y^p + Y^t$$

where Y^t is transitory income, which may be either positive or negative, causing measured income to exceed or fall short of permanent income. According to the permanent income hypothesis, it is only the permanent component of income that influences consumption. Consumption, even the transitory component of consumption referred to above, is independent of transitory income. As with the life cycle theory, in order to implement the permanent income hypothesis, some assumption must be made about how individuals form long-term expectations about income. In applications of the permanent income hypothesis, Friedman and other researchers have assumed that permanent income is a weighted moving average of actual past incomes. It has not been generally assumed that permanent income is proportional to current income, the assumption made by Ando and Modigliani for the case of expected lifetime labor income in work on the life cycle hypothesis.

The permanent income hypothesis can also be used to explain the puzzles about the consumption–income relationship which were discussed earlier. The permanent income hypothesis is consistent with the proportional long-run consumption function (APC constant) and the nonproportional short-run consumption function (APC declines as Y increases) found in the time-series data. In the long run, income growth is dominated by changes in permanent income, with positive and negative transitory changes in income canceling out. The long-run consumption–income relationship will therefore be approximately the proportional relationship given by (13.10) with constant APC equal to k. In the short run, years of high income will in general be years when the transitory component of income is positive. Since consumption rises only with increases in permanent income, in these high-income years the ratio of consumption to measured income [APC $= C/Y = C/(Y^p + Y^t)$] will be low. In low-income years when, in general, transitory income is negative, permanent income will be above measured income and the ratio of consumption, which depends on permanent income, to measured income will be high (the APC will be high).

The evidence from the cross-sectional budget studies that high-income families have a lower APC than low-income families is also consistent with the permanent income hypothesis. A sample of high-income families at a given time is likely to contain more than a proportionate number of families experiencing positive transitory income flows ($Y^t > 0$). Since the consumption levels of these families depend only on their permanent incomes, the measured

EXTENSIONS OF THE MODELS

APCs for these families will be low, bringing down the average APC for the high-income group. On the other hand, a group of families with a low income at a given point in time will contain a disproportionate share of families with a negative transitory income component and, hence, a high measured APC. This will push up the average APC for the low-income group.

Finally, the permanent income hypothesis is consistent with the failure of quarter-to-quarter movements of consumption to follow closely such short-run movements in income. Quarter-to-quarter income changes will contain many transitory income changes to which consumption does not respond.

The policy implications that follow from the permanent income hypothesis are similar to those that follow from the life cycle hypothesis in many respects. Generally, however, advocates of the permanent income hypothesis have been more pessimistic about the efficacy of fiscal policy, especially tax policy, as an instrument for control of aggregate demand.[12] It is easy to understand the source for this pessimism in the case of explicitly temporary tax cuts or tax increases. Such policy shifts will cause changes only in the transitory component of income and therefore will be ineffective in controlling consumption and aggregate demand.[13] Pessimism about the effectiveness of permanent changes in tax policy appears to stem not from any implications of the permanent income hypothesis itself but from the assumption made about how individuals estimate permanent income. If, as often assumed, permanent income is estimated as a weighted average of past incomes *and responds only slowly* to changes in current income (resulting from tax changes or any other source), consumption will not respond quickly to even a permanent change in tax policy. If the estimate of permanent income is responsive to a change in current income, or if a change in tax rates, perceived as permanent, independently causes such an estimate to be revised, there is no reason why tax policy should not be effective, even accepting the permanent income hypothesis.

13.2 INVESTMENT SPENDING

The second category of private demand for output we consider is investment demand. Investment in the national income accounts includes business fixed investment (purchases of durable equip-

---

[12]See, for example, Robert Eisner, "What Went Wrong," *Journal of Political Economy*, 70 (May–June 1971), pp. 629–41.

[13]This disregards the possible effect of liquidity constraints that was discussed above.

ment and structures), residential construction investment, and changes in business inventories. Additionally, our discussion of consumption in Section 13.1 is most appropriately applied to household expenditures on nondurable consumer goods, services, and the *service flow* from consumer durable goods. These categories measure the flow of goods used up by the household sector in a given period and it is this quantity that the theories discussed in Section 13.1 are intended to explain. Consumer *expenditures* as measured in the national income accounts, however, include purchases of consumer durable goods (automobiles, refrigerators, televisions, etc.), not the service flow from these goods. Therefore, we will also deal briefly in this chapter with the factors that determine the timing of such consumer durable goods purchases, which are best considered a form of household investment.

We deal first with business fixed investment, the largest component of investment. The other components of investment are discussed below.

Business Fixed Investment

Business fixed investment is important in two respects. First, investment spending is a significant component of total aggregate demand ($327 billion in 1981, 11.2 percent of GNP). The importance of investment to cyclical movements in income is even more than in proportion to its size as a share in GNP because it is one of the more volatile components of GNP. This fact was recognized by Keynes, among others, and variations in fixed business investment are an important element in many theories of the cyclical behavior of output.

Figures for (gross) business fixed investment both in absolute terms and as a share of GNP are given in Table 13.2. The variability of business fixed investment as a share of GNP is evident from the table, although in the post–World War II period this variability is considerably less than prior to the war. Over this postwar period business fixed investment has ranged between 9 and 12 percent of GNP.

The second important macroeconomic role for business fixed investment follows from the fact that net fixed business investment measures the amount by which the stock of capital increases in each period; that is,

$$K_t - K_{t-1} = I_{n,t} \tag{13.11}$$

where K is the capital stock and $I_{n,t}$ is net fixed investment. Business fixed investment is therefore important in the process of longer-run economic growth. In this chapter we focus primarily on the role of investment as a component of aggregate demand, although the growth role of investment cannot be ignored completely. In Chapter 16 the role of investment in the growth proc-

Table 13.2
Business Fixed Investment, 1929–1981, Selected Years[a]

Year	Business Fixed Investment	Business Fixed Investment as share of GNP
1929	10.6	0.103
1933	2.4	0.043
1939	5.9	0.065
1940	7.5	0.075
1943	5.0	0.026
1945	10.1	0.048
1950	27.3	0.095
1955	38.5	0.096
1960	48.5	0.096
1965	72.7	0.105
1970	103.9	0.105
1971	107.9	0.100
1972	121.0	0.102
1973	143.3	0.108
1974	156.6	0.109
1975	157.7	0.101
1976	174.1	0.101
1977	205.5	0.107
1978	242.0	0.112
1979	279.7	0.116
1980	296.0	0.113
1981	327.1	0.112

[a]Figures are for gross business fixed investment.
Source: *Economic Report of the President,* 1982.

ess—the role of investment in changing aggregate supply over time—is examined.

In previous chapters, investment was assumed to depend negatively on the interest rate,

$$I = I(r) \qquad \text{(13.12)}$$

Investment was also assumed to depend positively on the expected future profitability of investment projects. In the discussion here we explain the effect on investment of changes in the level of output. The role of the interest rate, as well as other factors that influence the cost of capital to the firm, will also be discussed in more detail.

Investment and Output: The Accelerator Relationship

As noted above, net investment measures the change in the capital stock. (In the remainder of this section the term "investment" will be used to mean business fixed investment.) Most investment theories therefore first explain the desired stock of capital. Investment is then explained as a response to deviations of the actual capital stock from the desired level. It is not hard to see that the desired capital stock would depend on the level of output. Higher levels of output would lead firms to demand a larger stock of capital, one of the factors used to produce output. The *accelerator model* is a simple representation of this relationship.

The accelerator model specifies the desired capital stock as a multiple of the level of output:

$$K_t^d = \alpha Y_t \qquad \alpha > 0 \qquad (13.13)$$

In the simplest form of the accelerator model, net investment is assumed to be set equal to the difference between the desired capital stock and the stock of capital inherited from the preceding period. If we ignore depreciation of the existing capital stock for the moment, we would then have

$$I_{n,t} = K_t^d - K_{t-1} \qquad (13.14)$$

The stock of capital inherited from the last period will be the desired capital stock based on income in the last period:

$$K_{t-1} = K_{t-1}^d = \alpha Y_{t-1} \qquad (13.15)$$

Therefore, we can rewrite (13.14) as

$$I_{n,t} = K_t^d - K_{t-1} = \alpha Y_t - \alpha Y_{t-1} = \alpha(Y_t - Y_{t-1})$$

$$I_{n,t} = \alpha \Delta Y_t \qquad (13.16)$$

The level of investment spending will depend on the rate of change in output.

This simple version suggests a crucial feature of the accelerator model. From (13.13), α can be seen to be the desired capital/output ratio:

$$\alpha = \frac{K_t^d}{Y_t} \qquad (13.17)$$

Assume, for example, that this ratio is 2. In this case every one-dollar change in the rate of growth in output (ΔY_t) will cause a two-dollar change in investment. Investment would then be expected to exhibit considerable instability over the business cycle. Further, recall from our discussion of the Keynesian model in Chapter 5 that changes in investment (in this case due to changes in ΔY) will have multiplier effects on income. Thus the simple accelerator theory, together with the multiplier process, can explain cyclical fluctuations output.[14] A shock to output growth would

[14]An early model of the interaction of the accelerator and the Keynesian multiplier was constructed by Paul Samuelson, "Interactions Between the Multiplier Analysis and the Principle of Acceleration," *Review of Economics and Statistics*, 21 (May 1939), pp. 75–78, reprinted in M. G. Mueller, ed., *Readings in Macroeconomics* (New York: Holt, Rinehart and Winston, 1966).

EXTENSIONS OF THE MODELS

cause investment to change, with resulting multiplier effects on the level of equilibrium output and therefore further effects on investment via the accelerator. As with the simple theory of the Keynesian multiplier in Chapter 5, however, considerable modification of the accelerator theory of investment is required before we can use the theory to explain the investment process in the real economy.

A first modification that would make the simple accelerator model more realistic would be to allow for lags in the adjustment of the actual capital stock to the level of the desired capital stock. Suppose that the period to which we apply the model is a calendar year. Also assume that due to an increase in output there is an increase in the desired capital stock. Investment projects will be planned to eliminate this discrepancy between the actual and desired capital stock. In addition to what we may call the direct cost of the investment projects, there will be *adjustment costs* which it is reasonable to assume will rise quickly as the rate of investment is increased. Examples of such costs of adjustment include plant shutdowns or hiring of overtime labor to install equipment, extra cost of speeding plant construction (overtime, etc.), and disruption of production if management concentrates solely on expediting investment projects. If such costs of adjustment do rise rapidly as the pace of investment is quickened, it will be optimal for firms to adjust the actual capital stock to the desired capital stock slowly over time, closing only a portion of the gap between the two within one period.

To reflect this adjustment lag, we modify (13.14) as follows:

$$I_{n,t} = \lambda(K_t^{\mathrm{d}} - K_{t-1}) \qquad 0 < \lambda < 1 \tag{13.18}$$

Using (13.13), we have

$$I_{n,t} = \lambda(\alpha Y_t - K_{t-1}) \tag{13.19}$$

where since the actual capital stock is not equated to the desired capital stock in each period, K_{t-1} will *not* in general equal K_{t-1}^{d}. Equation (13.19) specifies a *partial adjustment* mechanism where a fraction (λ) of the gap between the desired and actual capital stock is filled each period by investment. Since only a portion of the desired change in the capital stock is accomplished within one period, in a given period investment will be responding to changes in income during a number of previous periods. Equation (13.19) implies a slower response of investment to changes in current income and hence implies that investment will be less volatile in the short run than would be the case with the simple accelerator relationship [equation (13.16)]. Equation (13.19), which is termed the *flexible accelerator* model of investment, appears more consistent with the observed behavior of investment. Although investment is a volatile component of GNP (see Table 13.2), it is not as volatile as the simple accelerator model would predict.

The flexible accelerator model can also be modified to allow for variations in the speed with which investment is undertaken to fill the gap between the desired and actual capital stock (the λ parameter). This is obviously a choice variable to the firm and may be influenced by credit conditions, including the level of the interest rate, tax considerations, and other variables. One would expect, for example, that other things being equal, less investment would be undertaken to eliminate discrepancies between the actual and desired capital stock when the interest rate (cost of borrowing) was high than when the interest rate was low. Thus the flexible accelerator model is not inconsistent with the assumption made in Part II that investment was negatively related to the interest rate. In the following subsection we will see an additional role for the interest rate, and other factors influencing the cost of capital to the firm, in determining investment.

Investment and the Cost of Capital

Even the flexible version of the accelerator theory of investment assumes that the desired capital stock is a fixed multiple of output ($K^d = \alpha Y$). This specification ignores the fact that different levels of output can be produced with the same level of capital by varying the labor input, that is, by varying the capital/labor ratio (K/N) and therefore the desired capital output ratio (α). The optimal choice of a capital–labor mix to produce a given output will depend on the ratio of the two factor costs, the ratio of the cost of capital to the real wage. We would expect the amount of capital used to produce a given output to be positively related to the real wage and negatively related to the cost of capital. The relevant real wage for the investment decision is not the current real wage but the average real wage expected over the lifetime of the capital goods being purchased. If it is assumed that this variable does not change significantly in the short run, then the only modification we need to make to the flexible accelerator model is to take account of the relationship between the cost of capital and the desired capital stock.

In our discussion of the flexible accelerator model, it was pointed out that the timing of investment would be expected to depend on credit conditions, including the level of the interest rate. The argument above indicates that it is the overall level of investment, not just the timing of investment, which would be expected to depend on the interest rate and more broadly on all factors that affect the cost of capital. This follows since the desired capital/labor and therefore capital output ratio (α) will depend on the cost of capital. We would therefore expect an investment function of the general form

$$I_{n,t} = I(Y_t, CC_t, K_{t-1}) \tag{13.20}$$

where CC is a measure of the cost of capital, which we now consider in more detail.

In deciding on its desired capital stock, the firm is comparing the marginal productivity of additional units of captial with what may be termed the *user cost of capital,* the cost to the firm of employing an additional unit of capital for one period.[15] What elements comprise this user cost of capital? If the firm must borrow to finance the purchase of capital goods, the interest rate is the cost of borrowing. If the capital goods are purchased with previously earned profits that have not been distributed to stockholders (retained earnings), the interest rate represents the opportunity cost of the investment project, since alternatively the firm could have invested its funds externally and earned that interest rate. In either case the interest rate is an element of the user cost of capital.

So far in our discussion we have assumed that investment depends on the nominal rate of interest (an exception is the discussion of Irving Fisher's model in the Appendix to Chapter 4). If inflation is expected, however, we need to distinguish between the *nominal* interest rate (r) and the real interest rate, where the *real* interest rate (ϕ) is defined as the nominal rate minus the expected inflation rate ($\dot{p}^e$), that is,

$$\phi = r - \dot{p}^e \tag{13.21}$$

It is the real rate of interest on which the level of investment will depend. If, for example, the firm borrows at a nominal rate of 10 percent, then at the end of one year it will have to repay 110 dollars for each 100 dollars borrowed. If over the year the firm expects the average price level to rise by 10 percent, then the expected real value of the sum to be repaid, its expected value in terms of goods and services at the end of the year, will be just equal to the value of the $100 the firm borrowed. The real interest rate will be zero ($r - \dot{p}^e = 10$ percent $- 10$ percent $= 0$). Looked at slightly differently, the expected amount of output the firm would

---

[15]The firm's choice of the optimal capital stock is made in a manner analogous to the firm's choice of the level of labor input in the short run. For the case of the labor input, the firm employs labor to the point where the marginal product of labor is equated with the real wage—the user cost of labor. For the case of capital, the desired capital stock is the level that equates the marginal product of capital with the user cost of capital. In the case of capital, though, we assume that due to costs of adjustment, the actual capital stock adjusts to the desired capital stock with a lag.

have to sell to repay $110 at the end of one year is just equal to the amount that would generate $100 at the beginning of the year if prices (including the firm's product price) are expected to rise 10 percent during the year. Therefore, real borrowing costs would be zero if the nominal rate were 10 percent.

If inflation rates are low and steady, as they were in the United States from 1953 to 1966, the nominal rate will not be seriously misleading as a measure of the cost of capital. It is when inflation rates are high and variable and when people come to anticipate inflation, as was certainly the case in the later U.S. experience, that it becomes important to distinguish between the nominal and real interest rate and to remember that the latter is the relevant borrowing cost for the investment decision.

An additional element of the user cost of capital is the depreciation rate. A certain proportion (δ) of the capital stock is used up (worn out) in the production process during each period, and this depreciation rate is a cost to the firm of using capital goods.

To this point, then, we can express the user cost of the capital as

$$CC = \phi + \delta = r - \dot{p}^e + \delta \qquad (13.22)$$

Equation (13.22) requires one further modification, due to the effects of tax programs on the cost of capital. There are a number of government tax programs which offset a portion of the user cost of capital. We will summarize the effects of these programs by assuming that the government subsidizes investment purchases of capital goods at the rate τ, where τ is a positive proportion of the cost of the investment good ($0 < \tau < 1$). The effective cost of capital to the firm is then

$$CC = (1 - \tau)(r - \dot{p}^e + \delta) \qquad (13.23)$$

Perhaps the most obvious form of such a subsidy is an *investment tax credit*. The Kennedy administration, for example, instituted an investment tax credit in 1962 whereby a corporation's tax liability to the federal government was reduced by 7 percent of the amount of its fixed investment expenditure.[16] The government was, in effect, paying a 7 percent subsidy for investment purchases ($\tau = 0.07$). The effective user cost of capital to the firm is 93 percent of the cost without the tax credit ($1 - \tau = 0.93$).

Tax programs other than investment tax credits can also affect the user cost of capital. The corporate income tax reduces the after-tax profits generated by an investment project. If each of the items that comprise the cost of capital (interest costs and depreciation) is fully tax deductible, then the after-tax cost of capital is

[16]The tax credit was only 3 percent for utilities, and the full 7 percent was only for equipment with a life of eight years. The details of the program are not crucial to the discussion.

also reduced proportionately. For example, with a 48 percent corporate tax rate each dollar in pretax profits will bring only 52 cents in after-tax profits; each dollar of interest expense or depreciation will reduce tax liabilities by 48 cents and, effectively, cost the firm 52 cents. Thus if all elements of the cost of capital are fully deductible, as a first approximation we would expect the effect of the corporate income tax on investment to be neutral.[17] An additional way of reducing the effective user cost of capital to the firm is to make a part of the cost of capital *more* than 100 percent deductible in the early years after the investment is undertaken. This is the idea behind accelerated depreciation allowances. For example, in the United Kingdom 100 percent of the cost of an investment project can be deducted from a corporation's tax liability as depreciation in the year the investment is made. Actual depreciation will, of course, occur only over the course of many years. By giving firms such early tax savings governments reduce the effective user cost of capital and hope to encourage investment.

To summarize our discussion of fixed investment to this point, we have developed an investment function of the following general form:

$$I_{n,t} = I(Y_t, r_t, \dot{p}_t^e, \tau_t, K_{t-1}) \qquad \textbf{(13.24)}$$

Net investment (I_n) depends on income and the variables r, $\dot{p}^e$, and τ, which represent elements of the user cost of capital, where we have omitted the depreciation rate δ, which we assume to be constant over time. Given the level of the lagged capital stock an increase in income (Y), the expected rate of inflation ($\dot{p}^e$), or the tax subsidy to investment (τ), will all increase net investment. Increases in the nominal interest rate will cause investment expenditures do decline.

Monetary and Fiscal Policy and Investment

In Part II we analyzed the effects of monetary and fiscal policies on the level of investment. Here we consider some modifications and extensions of that analysis suggested by the investment theory in the previous subsections. First we reexamine fiscal policy effects.

Fiscal policy effects on investment were indirect and perverse in our analysis in Part II. For example, we found that an increase in government spending in order to increase aggregate demand would raise the interest rate and "crowd out" private investment

---

[17]We say "as a first approximation" since there are some additional interrelationships between corporate taxes and the level of the firm's profits, which we consider in Chapter 16. There we examine the arguments of a number of economists to the effect that the interaction of the corporate income tax and inflationary monetary and fiscal policies has significantly lowered after-tax corporate profitability and discouraged investment.

expenditures. Tax cuts would do the same. This crowding out was an offset to the intended effects of the policy. The analysis in this chapter suggests that by combining an expansionary fiscal policy, for example a cut in the personal income tax, with a tax policy such as an investment tax credit to stimulate investment, these unfavorable effects of fiscal policy on investment can be prevented. The personal income tax cut stimulates aggregate demand, pushing up both income and the nominal interest rate. The rise in the nominal interest rate increases the user cost of capital. The role of the investment tax credit is to offset this rise in the user cost of capital. Additionally, the analysis above suggests that tax policy toward investment (setting τ) provides an alternative tool to monetary policy as a means of stabilizing investment demand. Both types of policy work by changing the effective cost of capital to the firm.

A final implication for fiscal policy of our analysis in this chapter is that expansionary fiscal policy actions may on net stimulate rather than crowd out private investment expenditures, even ignoring changes in the tax treatment of investment. This is because expansionary fiscal policies will increase Y and therefore stimulate investment via the accelerator mechanism. This effect may be quantitatively more important than any negative effect via a fiscal policy–induced increase in interest rates. Which effect dominates clearly depends on the importance of output growth versus the cost of capital as determinants of investment. Those economists who conclude that output growth is the primary variable explaining investment argue that the best way to stimulate investment is to keep the economy operating at a high rate.[18] Where investment performance has been poor, as it was in the United States during much of the 1970s, economists holding this view attribute low investment to the economy's being below full capacity. Other economists stress the importance of the cost of capital and see low investment as due to unfavorable effects of government policies. We will return to this question when the relationships among capital formation, inflation, and tax policies are discussed in Chapter 16.

As regards monetary policy, the only modification of our previous analysis results from the distinction that we previously ignored between the nominal and the real rates of interest. Since it is the latter rate that is relevant for the investment decision, monetary policy must affect the real rate of interest in order to affect the level of investment. In the Keynesian or monetarist system, where the expected inflation rate depends primarily on the past history of inflation and, further, is assumed to change only slowly over

[18]See, for example, Peter K. Clark, "Investment in the 1970's: Theory, Performance and Prediction," *Brookings Papers on Economic Activity*, No. 1, 1979.

time, changes in the nominal rate will mean changes in the real rate in the short run. The expected inflation rate, which is the difference between the two interest rate concepts, will be relatively constant in the short run. Thus our previous analysis is substantively unchanged. Within the new classical view, anticipated monetary policy actions will quickly affect price expectations and will not affect the real rate of interest, even in the short run. This is one further aspect of the new classical view that anticipated monetary policy actions do not affect real variables, and is consistent with our earlier analysis.

Other Components of Investment

We turn now to the other components of investment in the national income accounts: residential construction investment and inventory investment. As noted at the beginning of this section, we will also discuss the determinants of consumer durable goods expenditures. Residential construction investment and inventory investment, although they are relatively small as components of GNP, are important in explaining the cyclical variation of income. The determinants of residential construction investment and inventory investment are somewhat different from those of fixed business investment and therefore we discuss these categories of investment separately. Consumer durable goods expenditures, especially new-automobile purchases, are also important to the explanation of the cyclical behavior of income, as will be explained below.

Residential Construction Investment

Residential construction investment is expenditure for the construction of new housing units. In recent years residential construction investment has varied between 3.6 and 5.4 percent of GNP (see Table 13.3). Houses have a life of 40 to 50 years. As a consequence, the stock of housing units is very large relative to the flow supply of new housing units. Also, there is a well-developed resale market for housing units. These two properties of the housing market have important implications for determinants of residential construction investment.

Figure 13.5 illustrates the determination of the price of houses and the quantity of new housing units supplied. In Figure 13.5a the *stock* supply of houses (H_s^s), which includes *all* existing houses, is plotted as a vertical schedule against the price of houses (P^H).[19] The schedule is vertical because the stock of existing houses at any point in time is given. The demand for houses is plotted as a downward-sloping function of the price of houses. The price of houses is

---

[19]We are here ignoring differences in the prices of new and existing houses as well as among different types of houses.

Figure 13.5 Determination of the Price of Houses and the Level of Residential Construction

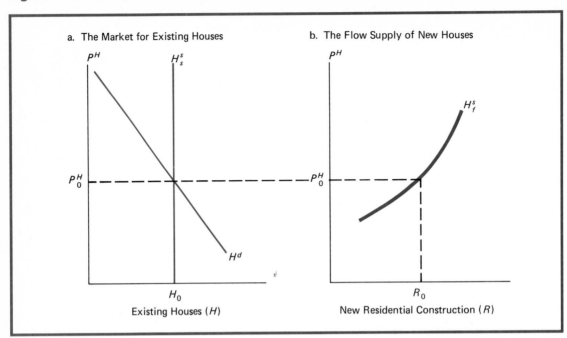

a. The Market for Existing Houses

b. The Flow Supply of New Houses

The equilibrium price of houses, P_0^H, is determined in Part *a* at the point where the demand for houses is equal to the fixed supply of existing houses. At price P_0^H, the flow supply of houses, which is residential construction investment, is shown in Part *b* to equal R_0.

determined at the intersection of the supply and demand curves, P_0^H in the graph. In Figure 13.5*b* the supply of *newly constructed* houses, the *flow* supply of houses, is shown to depend positively on the price of houses. It is this flow supply of new houses that is counted as residential construction investment (R) in the national income accounts. At a price level of P_0^H, the level of residential construction investment would be R_0, as shown in Figure 13.5*b*.

For a given stock of existing houses, the price of houses and quantity of new houses produced will depend on the state of housing demand, the H^d schedule in Figure 13.5*a*, as well as on factors that affect the position of the flow supply schedule for houses (H_f^s) in Figure 13.5*b*.

In the long run the demand for houses depends largely on demographic factors such as the rate of growth in the population and the rate of formation of new households. The coming to adulthood of the post–World War II baby-boom generation and tendency toward one-member households in the 1970s, for example, were strong stimuli to housing demand. Housing demand also depends

EXTENSIONS OF THE MODELS

on income, where, as in our discussion of consumption, the appropriate income variable is a smoothed measure of expected lifetime average income or permanent income. Whereas demographic factors and income are the major long-term determinants of housing demand, the primary variables causing recent short-run swings in housing demand and consequently in residential construction investment have been credit market conditions.

Most housing purchases are financed by long-term (20- to 30-year) mortgage borrowing. Thus the mortgage rate of interest has an important effect on the effective cost of the house as measured by the monthly mortgage payment the homeowner will have to make. Here again, though, it needs to be recognized that the appropriate interest measure is a real interest rate, the nominal rate minus the expected inflation rate. In this case the relevant expected inflation rate is the expected increase in the price of houses. If, for example, the mortgage rate is 12 percent and the expected rate of price increase for houses is 10 percent, the real borrowing cost would be 2 percent.[20] Increases in mortgage interest rates for given rates of expected appreciation in housing prices would be expected to decrease housing demand and therefore the price of houses. Consequently, the level of residential construction investment (new housing construction) would decline.

During recent "tight money" periods, in addition to high interest rates, a scarcity of mortgage funds, and consequently *credit rationing* in the mortgage market, has also lowered housing demand. As explained in Section 6.1, the largest proportion of mortgage lending is done by savings and loan associations and mutual savings banks. These financial intermediaries raise their funds primarily from depositors. The interest rates they pay to their depositors are constrained by federally imposed rate ceilings, called rate Q ceilings after the regulation imposing them. Rate Q ceilings have been liberalized substantially in recent years and are currently being phased out. To the present, however, the existence of these rate ceilings has meant that during periods of high *market* rates the interest rates paid by savings and loans and mutual savings banks have not been competitive, and investors have withdrawn funds and put them directly into money market instruments such as short-term government bonds. As a result, the savings and loans and mutual savings banks have had to curtail mortgage lending. They have done this in part through credit rationing by means of setting high down-payment ratios, refusing loans to only marginally qualified buyers, refusing to lend for con-

---

[20]The mortgage will be for a long term. The expected rate of appreciation in housing prices, which is subtracted from the mortgage rate, must be for the time horizon over which the borrower expected to hold the mortgage, which may of course not be for the full term.

struction of non-owner-occupied housing, and at times simply staying out of the market completely. As a result, in times of high market interest rates, mortgage money is not only expensive but to many it becomes unavailable.[21]

The effects on the housing market of a period of "tight" money, meaning high interest rates and reduced availability of mortgage funds, are illustrated in Figure 13.6. The tight money conditions

[21]There is an additional factor which makes it hard for many individuals to obtain mortgage loans when nominal interest rates are high. It was argued above that it is the real rate, equal in this case to the mortgage rate minus the expected rate of increase in housing prices, that is relevant for housing demand. If the nominal rate is high, however, even if due to inflation the real rate is not high, individuals will find that they want to borrow, but since the high nominal rate means a high monthly mortgage payment, they cannot obtain a loan unless they have a high income. This follows because many financial institutions will not make loans where the monthly payment exceeds a specified proportion of the borrower's disposable income.

Figure 13.6 Effects of Tight Money Conditions on the Housing Market

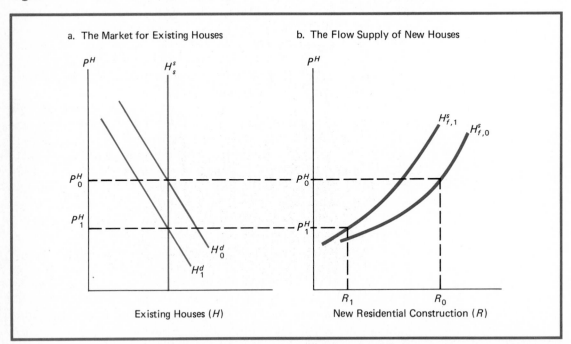

High interest rates and reduced availability of mortgage funds shift the demand schedule for the existing stock of houses down from H_0^d to H_1^d (Part a). The price of existing houses declines from P_0^H to P_1^H. The tight money conditions also shift the supply schedule for new houses to the left from $H_{f,0}^s$ to $H_{f,1}^s$ (Part b). Due to this shift in the flow supply schedule for new houses and the movement down the supply schedule due to the price fall, residential construction declines from R_0 to R_1.

EXTENSIONS OF THE MODELS

reduce the overall demand for houses, as illustrated by the shift of the demand schedule from H_0^d to H_1^d in Figure 13.6a. As a consequence, the price of houses falls from P_0^H to P_1^H. Additionally, as shown in Figure 13.6b, the high interest rates cause a shift to the left in the flow supply schedule, from $H_{f,0}^s$ to $H_{f,1}^s$. This shift reflects the fact that builders must borrow funds to finance the building of houses. High interest rates on these construction loans add to the cost of building houses. This is a shift to the left in the flow supply function. Because of the effect on both overall housing demand and the flow supply of new houses, residential construction investment declines from R_0 to R_1 in Figure 13.6b.

Credit conditions have always been of vital importance to the housing market in the short run. Until the late 1960s, this appeared to lead to a *countercyclical* pattern of residential construction. As the economy went into a recession, the demand for credit to finance other types of expenditures, such as business fixed investment and consumer durable purchases, eased, more funds flowed into the mortgage market, and interest rates fell. Residential construction investment increased. Correspondingly, tight money conditions in the later stages of boom periods discouraged residential construction investment. This pattern of residential construction investment had an overall stabilizing effect on the economy. In recent years, however, residential construction activity has had a strongly *procyclical* pattern, as can be seen from Table 13.3, which shows residential construction investment *as a*

Table 13.3 Residential Construction, Housing Starts, and the Level of Economic Activity	Year	Residential Construction as a Percentage of GNP	Housing Starts (millions)	Unemployment Rate (%)
	1965	4.47	1.51	4.5
	1966	3.77	1.20	3.8
	1967	3.58	1.32	3.8
	1968	3.99	1.55	3.6
	1969	4.05	1.50	3.5
	1970	3.74	1.47	4.9
	1971	4.72	2.08	5.9
	1972	5.38	2.38	5.6
	1973	5.13	2.06	4.9
	1974	4.03	1.35	5.6
	1975	3.57	1.17	8.5
	1976	4.19	1.55	7.7
	1977	4.99	1.99	7.0
	1978	5.16	2.02	6.0
	1979	4.91	1.75	5.8
	1980	4.01	1.29	7.1
	1981	3.60	1.08	7.6

Source: *Economic Report of the President,* 1982.

percentage of GNP, housing starts, and the unemployment rate, annually for the 1965–81 period. Residential construction declined as a percent of GNP during the tight money period following what has been called the "credit crunch" of 1966, which occurred while the economy was at a high employment level. Following that, each subsequent significant decline in residential construction coincided with a recession period, a slight decline in the mild recession of 1970 and sharper declines in the 1974–75 and 1980 recessions. The declines in housing *starts* during the two most recent recessions have been even more dramatic.

What has caused this switch from a countercyclical to a procyclical pattern of activity in the housing sector? The key factor appears to be that the recessions of the 1970–80 decade were inflationary recessions, whether due to the impact of supply shocks, as the Keynesians would argue, or due to the lagged effect of previous overexpansion of demand, as the monetarists and new classical economists claim. In response to the inflation, monetary policy, at least as measured by nominal interest rates and credit availability in the mortgage market, was extremely restrictive during these recessions. The response of the housing market to such tight money conditions has been much as depicted in Figure 13.6. This contraction in residential construction activity has been an important element in explaining output declines in these two recent U.S. recessions.

Before ending our discussion of residential construction investment, one implication of our analysis for monetary policy should be noted. The sensitivity of the housing market to credit conditions increases the effectiveness of monetary policy as measured by the size and speed of its impact on aggregate demand. But the large impact on the housing industry is an illustration of the differential effects of monetary policy; the housing sector is hit much harder than other sectors are by tight money policies. This creates a equity problem in the use of monetary policy, in that it is scarcely fair to create a depression in the housing market, with bankruptcies for construction firms and high unemployment among construction workers, just to engineer a modest cut in aggregate demand. We will return to this problem when we look at monetary policy more carefully in Chapter 19.

Inventory Investment

Firms hold inventories both of goods that will be used in the production process and of finished goods awaiting sale. Changes in the stock of such business inventories comprises inventory investment, a small but cyclically volatile component of GNP. A firm's demand for both inventories of materials used in production and inventories of final goods will depend on the level of the firm's sales. In the aggregate, desired inventories (IN^d) are generally assumed to be proportional to expected sales (S^e), that is,

$$IN_t^d = \gamma S_t^e \qquad \gamma > 0 \qquad (13.25)$$

If we assume that actual inventories are adjusted to the desired level with a lag, due to costs of adjustment, we can specify inventory investment (ΔIN) as

$$\Delta IN_t = IN_t - IN_{t-1} = \lambda_1(IN_t^d - IN_{t-1}) \qquad 0 < \lambda_1 < 1 \quad (13.26)$$

We can rewrite (13.26) as

$$\Delta IN_t = \lambda_1(\gamma S_t^e - IN_{t-1}) \qquad (13.27)$$

From (13.27) we expect a *positive* relationship between inventories and expected sales or the general level of economic activity. There is, however, another aspect to the inventory–sales relationship.

In our earlier discussion of the Keynesian model, we made a distinction between intended and unintended inventory investment or accumulation. As discussed there, when aggregate demand falls short of output, the difference shows up as an unintended accumulation of business inventories which is counted in the national income accounts as inventory investment. This suggests a *negative* relationship between sales and inventory investment to the degee that sales differed from the expected level of sales, the sales level on which the firms' production decisions were based. Taking account of this additional relationship results in the following specification for inventory investment

$$\Delta IN_t = \lambda_1(\gamma S_t^e - IN_{t-1}) + \lambda_2(S_t^e - S_t) \qquad (13.28)$$
$$0 < \lambda_1 < 1 \qquad 0 < \lambda_2 < 1$$

The first term is as in the preceding equation. The second term specifies that at least a portion of the amount by which sales (S) fall short of (or exceed) expected sales (S^e) shows up as an unintended increase (decrease) in business inventories.

From (13.28) we would expect that as sales vary over the business cycle, the following pattern of inventory investment would emerge. As sales start to fall off in a downturn, to the degree that the change was unanticipated, business inventory investment would increase. This would be an unintended inventory accumulation [the second term in (13.28)]. In the later stages of the downturn, as the drop in sales becomes anticipated (S^e falls), we would expect to observe a rather sharp drop in inventory investment or even to see inventory disinvestment as firms try to cut inventories. A reverse pattern will be evidenced following an upturn. Thus inventory investment would move in a procyclical way but lagging the cycle somewhat. Often, in fact, such inventory fluctuations comprise a large portion of the variation in GNP over the cycle.

Table 13.4 Inventory Investment During Two Recent Recessions and Recoveries (billions of dollars at an annual rate)

Inventory Investment and the Change in Real GNP (1974:I–1976:II)

Year:Quarter	1974:I	1974:II	1974:III	1974:IV	1975:I	1975:II	1975:III	1975:IV	1976:I	1976:II
Change in real GNP	−12.4	−5.7	−7.6	−17.2	−29.9	18.4	32.5	9.1	26.2	15.5
Inventory investment	13.7	12.9	2.3	6.8	−22.0	−25.1	4.9	−3.6	14.5	18.3

Inventory Investment and the Change in Real GNP (1979:I–1980:IV)

Year:Quarter	1979:I	1979:II	1979:III	1979:IV	1980:I	1980:II	1980:III	1980:IV
Change in real GNP	14.1	−6.5	14.8	2.4	11.3	−38.6	8.6	13.7
Inventory investment	24.3	33.1	13.3	−0.8	2.5	7.4	−16.0	−17.4

Source: *Economic Report of the President*, 1982.

This cyclical pattern of inventory investment is illustrated in Table 13.4, which shows the behavior of real income and inventory investment during the two most recent periods of recession and recovery. As can be seen from the table, inventory investment remained positive (the level of inventories continued to increase) while real GNP declined throughout 1974. Inventory investment then turned sharply negative in 1975 as firms tried to restore desired inventory sales ratios. Inventory investment turned strongly positive again only after the recovery was well under way in 1976. Again in the 1979–80 period, there were signs of unintended inventory accumulation when GNP declined in the second quarter of 1979 and again, though to a lesser extent, in the second quarter of 1980. There was a sharp run-off of inventories just as GNP growth resumed in the third quarter of 1980. Table 13.4 also illustrates the sharp swings that occur in inventory investment, for example a net change of $28.8 billion at an annual rate from the fourth quarter of 1974 and the first quarter of 1975.

Finally on the subject of inventories, something should be said about the role of the interest rate in determining the level of inventory investment. In the older literature on the business cycle, one strand of thought, due primarily to the British economist R. G. Hawtrey, stressed the dependence of inventory investment on the interest rate. Higher interest rates would increase the carrying cost of inventories and therefore reduce inventory investment. Monetary policy, by changing the interest rate, could then potentially eliminate the cyclical volatility of inventory investment and thereby lessen the overall cyclical variation in GNP. Post-Keynesian empirical studies of inventory investment had until recently found no role for interest rates in inventory investment functions. Some recent studies that employ data from the 1970s, when there was a great deal of variability in interest rates, have found significant negative interest rate effects on the level of inventory investment.[22] This recent work suggests that interest rate effects on investment may provide an additional channel whereby monetary policy affects aggregate demand.

Consumer Durable Goods Expenditures

Consumer durable goods include items such as automobiles and household appliances. Consumer durable good expenditures have averaged approximately 9 percent of GNP in recent years. The proper durable goods variable for the consumption theories con-

[22]See, for example, F. Owen Irvine, "Retail Inventory Investment and the Cost of Capital," *American Economic Review*, 71 (September 1981), pp. 633–48; and Dan Bechter and Stephen Pollock, "Are Inventories Sensitive to Interest Rates?" Federal Reserve Bank of Kansas City *Economic Review*, April 1980, pp. 18–27.

sidered in Section 13.1 is the service flow from durable goods, sometimes measured as depreciation of the stock of consumer durables. Because of the difficulty of accurate measurement of depreciation of consumer durables, the national income accounts include all expenditures on durables under consumption. Still, from a theoretical standpoint, expenditure on consumer durables net of depreciation of the stock of durables should be viewed as a form of investment by households.

One reason it is important to distinguish consumer durable expenditures from the service flow from durables is that whereas the service flow, as part of consumption, will depend on expected lifetime or permanent income, the timing of expenditures on durables will be much more responsive to current income. Fluctuations in consumer expenditures on durable goods, especially automobiles, have been a prime factor in recent recessions in the United States. In the 1980 recession, for example, consumer expenditures on durable goods fell by 11 percent between the first and second quarters. This drop in consumer expenditures of $24.5 billion at an annual rate comprised approximately 70 percent of the total drop in GNP.

Both the 1974–75 and 1980 recessions followed large increases in energy prices, including the price of gasoline. In early 1974 and in the spring and summer of 1979, there were also shortages of gasoline. The high price of gasoline and supply disruption led to a fall in consumer demand for new domestically produced automobiles as consumers cut overall automobile purchases and also switched to more-fuel-efficient imports. *Real* (1972 dollars) expenditures on new domestic automobiles in 1974–75 averaged only 79 percent of the 1973 level. During the second quarter of 1980, real expenditures on automobiles were running at 66 percent of the level of 1978, although in this latter period tight credit conditions were probably more important in explaining the drop than conditions in the energy market. Declines in the demand for domestically produced automobiles have contributed substantially to the past two recessions. Unemployment in the automobile industry and the industries that are suppliers of the automobile industry have risen much more than in proportion to the national average in both recessions.

If consumer durable goods expenditures are responsive to changes in current income, changes in tax rates could be used to regulate aggregate demand even if consumption (purchases of consumer nondurables, services, and the service flow from consumer durables) did not respond strongly to tax-induced changes in disposable income. Consumption might not respond if the tax change were temporary and consumption depended on expected lifetime or permanent income, but there could be a strong effect on the timing of consumer durable expenditures from even a temporary tax change. Recent one-time rebate schemes have been aimed at affecting "big ticket" consumer durable expenditures on appliances and automobiles. Additionally, monetary policy might be used to affect the level of consumer durable expenditures. As was the case with inventory investment, empirical research in the United States for the 1950s and 1960s did not reveal much evidence of a systematic negative relationship between interest rates and the level of consumer durable expenditure. More recent work, however, does suggest that monetary policy affects consumer durable goods expenditure both via interest rates and more broadly by affecting the overall liquidity position of households.[23] Tight money policies, for example, will, as we have seen previously, lower the values of long-term bonds and corporate equities, causing a decline in household wealth and therefore a decline in the willingness to borrow to finance purchases of durables. This recent research indicates that effects on consumer durable expenditures are an additional way in which monetary policy affects aggregate demand.

13.3 CONCLUSION

It would be satisfying to close this discussion of aggregate demand by drawing some definite conclusions as to whether private-sector demand is unstable, as the Keynesians believe, or whether, as the monetarists believe, the private sector is "shock absorbing." Clearly, several components of aggregate demand—business fixed investment, residential construction investment, inventory investment, and consumer durable goods expenditures—exhibit considerable variability over the cycle. But is the source of this variability inherent within these expenditure functions, or are these categories of expenditure simply responding for the most part to policy-induced shocks? The data themselves reveal little about the relative quantitative importance of policy-induced shocks versus shocks originating with private-sector demand itself. Monetarists and Keynesians have quite different interpretations of the cyclical instability of aggregate demand described in this chapter.

[23]See, for example, two papers by Frederick S. Mishkin, "Illiquidity, Consumer Durable Expenditure, and Monetary Policy," *American Economic Review*, 66 (September 1976), pp. 642–53, and "What Depressed the Consumer? The Household Balance Sheet and the 1973–75 Recession," *Brookings Papers on Economic Activity*, No. 1, 1977, pp. 123–64.

Review Questions

1   Explain the essential elements of the life cycle theory of consumer behavior.

2   Explain why the existence of "liquidity constraints" facing certain households would have an important implication for the life cycle theory of consumption.

3   What are the implications of the life cycle theory of consumer behavior for the effectiveness of fiscal policy actions?

4   Explain the permanent income theory of consumer behavior. Compare the permanent income hypothesis with the life cycle theory of consumption.

5   How do the life cycle hypothesis and the permanent income hypothesis resolve the apparent contradiction between the short-run data, which suggest a nonproportional relationship between consumption and income, and the long-run data, which suggest a proportional relationship?

6   Do the more detailed specifications of consumption in this chapter lead you to believe that monetary policy would be more or less effective than was suggested by our previous analysis? Do they indicate that fiscal policy is likely to be more or less effective, again relative to our previous analysis?

7   Explain the relationship between output and investment that is implied by the *accelerator* theory. How do costs of adjustment affect the model?

8   What elements comprise the cost of capital relevant to the firm's investment decision? Explain the way in which this cost of capital can be influenced by monetary and fiscal policy actions.

9   As regulation Q ceilings on the rates that savings and loan associations pay depositors are phased out, we might expect to see the housing sector be somewhat less drastically affected by periods of "tight" money. Comment.

10 Distinguish between consumption of durables and consumer purchases of durable goods. Why might it be important to make this distinction?

11 Explain the way in which you would expect inventory investment to respond to an increase in sales during a period when GNP rises rapidly.

12 Do the more detailed specifications of fixed business investment and the other components of investment lead you to believe that monetary policy will be more or less effective than was suggested by our previous analysis? Do they indicate that fiscal policy is likely to be more or less effective, again relative to our previous analysis?

Selected Readings

CONSUMPTION

ACKLEY, GARDNER, *Macroeconomic Theory and Policy*. New York: Macmillan, 1978, Chaps. 16 and 17.

ANDO, ALBERT, and MODIGLIANI, FRANCO, "The Life Cycle Hypothesis of Saving: Aggregate Implications and Tests," *American Economic Review*, 53 (March 1963), pp. 55–84.

DUESENBERRY, JAMES, *Income, Saving and the Theory of Consumer Behavior*. Cambridge, Mass.: Harvard University Press, 1949.

EVANS, MICHAEL, *Macroeconomic Activity*. New York: Harper & Row, 1969, Chaps. 2–3.

FRIEDMAN, MILTON, *A Theory of the Consumption Function*. Princeton, N.J.: Princeton University Press, 1957.

KEYNES, JOHN M., *The General Theory of Employment, Interest and Money*. New York: Harcourt, Brace and Company, Inc., 1936, Chaps. 8–10.

MAYER, THOMAS, "The Propensity to Consume Permanent Income," *American Economic Review*, 56 (December 1966), 1158–77.

MISHKIN, FREDERICK, S., "What Depressed the Consumer? The Household Balance Sheet and the 1973–75 Recession," *Brookings Papers on Economic Activity*, No. 1, 1977, pp. 123–64.

MODIGLIANI, FRANCO, "The Life Cycle Hypothesis of Saving, the Demand for Wealth and the Supply of Capital," *Social Research*, 33 (June 1966), pp. 160–217.

MODIGLIANI, FRANCO, "Monetary Policy and Consumption," in *Consumer Spending and Monetary Policy: The Linkages*. Boston: Federal Reserve Bank of Boston, 1971.

MODIGLIANI, FRANCO and STEINDEL, CHARLES, "Is a Tax Rebate an Effective Tool for Stabilization Policy?" *Brookings Papers on Economic Activity*, No. 1, 1977, pp. 175–209.

TOBIN, JAMES, and DOLDE, WALTER, "Wealth Liquidity and Consumption," in *Consumer Spending and Monetary Policy: The Linkages*. Boston: Federal Reserve Bank of Boston, 1971.

FIXED BUSINESS INVESTMENT

ACKLEY, GARDNER, *Macroeconomic Theory and Policy*. New York: Macmillan, 1978, Chaps. 18 and 19.

BISCHOFF, CHARLES, "Business Investment in the 1970's: A Comparison of the Models," *Brookings Papers on Economic Activity*, No. 1, 1971, pp. 13–63.

CLARK, PETER K., "Investment in the 1970's: Theory, Performance and

Prediction," *Brookings Papers on Economic Activity*, No. 1, 1979, pp. 73–113.

EVANS, MICHAEL, *Macroeconomic Activity*. New York: Harper & Row, 1969, Chaps. 4 and 5.

EISNER, ROBERT, and STROTZ, R. H., "Determinants of Business Inventory," in Commission on Money and Credit, *Impacts of Monetary Policy*. Englewood Cliffs, N.J.: Prentice-Hall, 1964. Reprinted (in part) in N. F. Keiser, ed., *Readings in Macroeconomics*. Englewood Cliffs, N.J.: Prentice-Hall, 1970, pp. 133–40; and in Arnold Zellner, ed., *Readings in Economic Statistics and Econometrics*. Boston: Little Brown, 1968, pp. 463–516.

KNOX, A. D., "The Acceleration Principle and the Theory of Investment: A Survey," *Economica*, 19 (August 1952), pp. 269–97. Reprinted in M. G. Mueller, ed., *Readings in Macroeconomics*. New York: Holt, Rinehart and Winston, 1967, pp. 114–33.

SAMUELSON, PAUL, "Interactions Between the Multiplier Analysis and the Principle of Acceleration," *Review of Economics and Statistics*, 21 (May 1939), pp. 75–78. Reprinted in M. G. Mueller, ed., *Readings in Macroeconomics*. New York: Holt, Rinehart and Winston, 1966.

OTHER COMPONENTS OF INVESTMENT

BLINDER, ALAN S., "Inventories and the Structure of Macroeconomic Models," *American Economic Review*, 71 (May 1981), pp. 11–16.

EVANS, MICHAEL, *Macroeconomic Activity*. New York: Harper & Row, 1969, Chaps. 6–8.

FELDSTEIN, MARTIN, and AUERBACH, ALAN, "Inventory Behavior in Durable-Goods Manufacturing: The Target Adjustment Model," *Brookings Papers on Economic Activity*, No. 2, 1976, pp. 351–96.

HYMANS, SAUL H., "Consumer Durable Spending: Explanation and Prediction," *Brookings Papers on Economic Activity*, No. 2, 1970, pp. 173–99.

JAFFEE, DWIGHT M., and ROSEN, KENNETH T., "Mortgage Credit Availability and Residential Construction," *Brookings Papers on Economic Activity*, No. 2, 1979, pp. 336–76.

JUSTER, THOMAS F., and WACHTEL, PAUL, "Inflation and the Consumer," *Brookings Papers on Economic Activity*, No. 1, 1972, pp. 71–114.

chapter 14

We have already considered the demand for money in our discussion of the classical, Keynesian, and monetarist theories. The treatment of money demand in those chapters, however, was limited to the simplest money demand specifications. The discussion of these specifications was confined to issues of general importance for the overall model. In this chapter we take a more detailed look at the demand for money.

As a starting point, let us review our previous analysis of money demand. The classical economists concentrated on the role of money as a medium of exchange (i.e., a generally accepted means of payment). In doing so they confined their attention to what Keynes termed the "transactions" demand for money. With uncertain as well as planned transactions taken into account, this medium of exchange function of money can also incorporate what Keynes called the "precautionary" demand for money.

In the form developed by the Cambridge economists (Section 4.1), the classical money demand function can be expressed as

$$M^d = kPy \tag{14.1}$$

Money demand (M^d) was proportional to nominal income (the price level P times real income y). The proportion of income held in the form of money (k) was considered to be relatively stable as long as we were considering equilibrium positions. In the alternative Fisherian version of the classical theory,

$$MV = Py \tag{14.2}$$

MONEY DEMAND: THEORY AND EVIDENCE

the velocity of money, equal to $1/k$, was assumed to be stable, again when equilibrium positions of the economy were considered.[1] An important feature of this classical analysis was that the interest rate was not considered to be an important determinant of money demand.

Keynes's theory of money demand considered the role of money as a "store of value" in addition to its role as a medium of exchange. The store of value function of money means simply that money is one possible asset in which one can hold wealth. In analyzing this store of value function of money, Keynes was led to view money as one asset in an individual's portfolio and to consider the manner in which an individual divides his wealth between money and alternative assets. Keynes lumped all these assets that were alternatives to holding money into one category, which he termed "bonds." The important variable that Keynes believed would determine the split of an individual's portfolio between money as bonds was the interest rate, the return on bonds. At a high rate of interest the forgone interest payments that would result from holding money instead of bonds would be high. Further, in Keynes's view, when the interest rate was high relative to some reasonably fixed view of the normal level of the interest rate, the public would expect a future decline in the interest rate. Such

---

[1] In "transition periods" when the economy was out of equilibrium, the velocity of money, and hence k, was assumed to fluctuate, depending on the anticipated inflation rate (see the appendix to Chapter 4).

a decline in the rate of interest would mean a capital gain on bonds.[2] Both because of the high forgone interest payments and the fact that at a high interest rate a future capital gain on bonds was likely, Keynes believed that a high interest rate would result in a low demand for money as a store of value. As the interest rate declined, the demand for money as an asset would increase. Thus, according to Keynes's theory, the demand for money would be expected to vary inversely with the rate of interest. This is Keynes's theory of the speculative demand for money.

Keynes also considered the transaction demand for money and the precautionary demand for money. Both of these demands grew out of the means of payment function of money, as noted above. Keynes viewed income as the primary variable determining the amount of money held due to both the transactions and precautionary motives, higher values of income increasing the amount of money held for each purpose.

The Keynesian money demand function can be expressed as

$$M^d = L(y, r) \tag{14.3}$$

Money demand depends on both the level of income *and the interest rate*. The fact that in the Keynesian view money demand was a function of the interest rate as well as the level of income was of considerable importance in explaining the differences in policy conclusions between the classical and Keynesian models. If the demand for money is simply proportional to income as in (14.1) and (14.2), then nominal income is completely determined by the supply of money. With k fixed in (14.1), for example, an increase in the money stock (M) must in equilibrium result in a proportional increase in nominal income, as can be seen by writing the equilibrium condition

$$M = M^d = kPy \tag{14.4}$$

from which it follows that

$$\Delta M = k\Delta Py$$

$$\frac{1}{k} \Delta M = \Delta Py \tag{14.5}$$

Note that with k fixed, nominal income can change *only* when the quantity of money changes, as can be seen from (14.5). Factors such as fiscal policy actions or autonomous changes in investment demand have no role in income determination. In terms of the IS–LM analysis of Chapters 6 and 7, this is the classical case of the vertical LM, where fixing the supply of money fixes the level of

---

[2]The relationship between bond prices and interest rate changes is discussed in Section 6.1.

income, with shifts in the IS schedule affecting only the level of the interest rate.

With the Keynesian form of the money demand function, income is no longer proportional to the quantity of money. Factors other than changes in the quantity of money, including fiscal policy changes and autonomous shifts in investment demand, can cause changes in income. Again in terms of the IS–LM analysis, the LM curve is upward sloping, not vertical. Shifts in the IS curve will change the level of income. The relative importance of monetary factors and the other determinants of income (factors that shift the IS curve) will depend on the slopes of the IS and LM schedules, as discussed above (see Table 7.2).

In the monetarist view, the interest rate theoretically belongs in the money demand function. Empirically, the monetarists do not believe that the interest elasticity of money demand is high. They believe that the LM schedule, although not vertical, is quite steep. For this reason, among others, they believe that money is the dominant influence on nominal income.

The role of the interest rate in determining money demand is then a question with important policy implications. Keynes's followers have not been satisfied with Keynes's own theory of the relationship between the interest rate and money demand—his theory of the speculative demand for money. They have advanced additional reasons for the dependence of money demand on interest rates. This neo-Keynesian theory of money demand also extends Keynes's analysis of the transactions demand for money. These extensions of the Keynesian theory are discussed in Sections 14.2 and 14.3. Beginning in the mid-1970s, money demand functions constructed on the basis of this neo-Keynesian theory began to "misbehave." The actual behavior of money demand began to diverge seriously from the predictions of the theory. Specifically, the uncooperative public insisted on holding much less money than the theory predicted they would, a puzzle for macroeconomists which has been termed "The Case of the Missing Money." The possible reasons for this puzzling recent behavior of money demand are discussed in Section 14.4. Section 14.5 briefly summarizes the current state of the theory of money demand. Prior to presenting theories of money demand it is useful to discuss the question of the definition of "money."

14.1 THE DEFINITION OF MONEY

The Functional Definition of Money

We have already mentioned the two primary functions of money, those of a medium of exchange and a store of value. Additional functions that money traditionally performs in an economy are those of a unit of account and a standard of deferred payment. The unit of account function means that prices are generally quoted in terms of the monetary unit (e.g., in the United States, prices are in dollars and cents). Similarly, the standard of deferred payment function refers to the fact that debts are denominated in terms of the monetary unit.

Money can be defined for a given economy as the financial asset or assets that perform the functions noted above. For the United States this procedure does not, however, lead to a generally agreed upon definition of money. Further, a series of recent innovations in the financial sector have greatly complicated the question of which assets should be defined as money. We will see that the question of difficulties in defining money is linked to the puzzle of "missing money" referred to above, so it is worthwhile to discuss these difficulties in some detail.

To start with, consider the definition of money for the U.S. economy given the financial system that existed in the 1960s. The main disagreement at that time was in how strictly actually to require an asset to be used in exchange in order to be classified as money. The "strict constructionists" would classify as money only those assets directly used in exchange transactions. In our economy this would have meant currency held by the public and demand deposits. Currency consists of the notes and coins held by the public. Demand deposits are commercial bank deposits against which one can write a check. This narrow definition of money was termed M1 in the official monetary statistics.

What might be termed the "loose constructionist" position would broaden the definition of money to include other bank deposits which, although they cannot be directly used in transactions, can be easily converted to currency or demand deposits. To give one example, savings deposits at commercial banks are available on demand, but checks cannot be written on them.[3] A trip to the bank or for some accounts a telephone call is all that is required to convert the savings deposits to demand deposits or currency. Such deposits are then highly *liquid*, where the term "liquid" means that the asset can be quickly converted to the medium

---

[3]Technically, banks can impose a waiting period for withdrawal from savings accounts, but this is not done in practice. There is a distinction between *savings deposits* and *time deposits*. Time deposits are certificates of deposit which generally pay a higher rate of interest than savings deposits but carry fixed maturity dates ranging from 30 days to several years. Since the government mandates penalties for early withdrawal from such accounts, time deposits are substantially less *liquid*, in the sense explained in the remainder of this paragraph, than are savings deposits.

of exchange without loss of value.[4] The loose constructionists would include in the definition of money highly liquid deposits at commercial banks and other depository institutions (e.g., savings and loan associations, mutual savings banks, credit unions). Among those preferring a broader definition of money there was still a question of where to draw the line in deciding which highly liquid assets to include in the definition of money. Some economists favored broadening the definition of money to include savings deposits and small time deposits at commercial banks, but no additional assets. This procedure results in the definition of money which in the old official statistics was designated M2. Still broader measures were constructed adding savings and small time deposits at the other depository institutions and adding large time certificates of deposits (CDs).[5] These successively broader measures were designated with higher M numbers (M3, M4, M5) in the old official definitions. The successively broader monetary aggregates generally added less liquid assets.

Innovations in the Deposit Market

Recent innovations in the financial sector have blurred the distinctions between different types of deposits at commercial banks and between deposits at commercial banks and other financial institutions, distinctions that were the basis for the old definition of the monetary aggregates. These changes necessitated a redefinition of the *monetary aggregates.*

The most important innovations that have taken place in the deposit market involve the evolution of new substitutes for commercial bank demand deposits as a medium of exchange. Savings and loan associations and mutual savings banks, as well as commercial banks, presently offer interest-paying NOW (negotiated order of withdrawal) accounts, which allow the depositor to write a checklike draft on his deposits.[6] Credit union share drafts are similar checkable deposits at institutions other than commercial banks. With the old definition of the monetary aggregates, these checkable deposits at credit unions, savings and loan associations, tions, and mutual savings banks would not have been included in M1, the narrow definition of the money stock, which included only checkable deposits at commercial banks.

[4]An example of a relatively nonliquid asset would be an automobile, which could be sold within a short period (one day, for example) only with a probable sacrifice in the sale price, if one could find a buyer at all. The automobile cannot be quickly converted to the medium of exchange without loss of value.
[5]Large CDs are those issued in denominations of $100,000 or more.
[6]Banking regulations were modified to permit the offering of NOW accounts nationwide beginning in January 1981. Previously, such accounts could be offered only in New York and New England.

Other innovations have clouded the distinction between deposit types at the same institution. Commercial banks, for example, now offer ATS (automatic transfer from saving) accounts, where funds are automatically transferred from a designated savings account to cover a check written on a demand deposit account. The savings deposits in such accounts therefore become balances available for use in transactions. Telephone transfer accounts, which allow money to be moved in response to a telephone request between savings accounts and checkable accounts at commercial banks or other depository institutions, also make savings and checking account balances less distinguishable. NOW accounts and credit union share draft accounts also have properties of both checking accounts and saving accounts (since they are interest bearing, at times at the same rate as passbook accounts on which checks may not be written). Clearly, many balances in some so-called savings accounts are then as liquid as checking account balances, but under the old definition such balances would not be included in M1.

Further complicating the definition of money has been the development of two close substitutes for demand deposits, neither of which is a bank deposit. The first of these asset types are the money market mutual funds. These funds sell shares to the public, invest in short-term liquid assets, and then let shareholders withdraw money (redeem their shares) by writing checks drawn on a designated bank. The individual's investment in the fund is equivalent to a checkable deposit, although typically with a fairly high minimum for each check ($250 to $500).

Money market funds provide a substitute for checking or savings accounts for individuals. Another newly developed substitute for demand deposits, repurchase agreements (RPs), are important as a substitute for business demand deposit holdings.[7] A typical type of RP transaction is a loan, usually an overnight loan or other short-term loan, from a corporation (or other nonbank institution) to a commercial bank; the loan is secured by government securities owned by the bank. When the loan is repaid, the ownership of the security reverts back to the bank; the security is repurchased. Corporate customers of a commercial bank can transfer funds from their demand deposit account to their RP account with little cost. In effect, they reclassify their deposit at the bank as a short-term loan to the bank. Prior to spending these funds, they must be transferred back to the demand deposit account, but RPs are certainly a close substitute for the demand deposits since such a transfer can be rearranged quickly and at low cost.

[7]Such RP transactions are not entirely new, but only in recent years has the volume of such transactions been high enough to be of importance for the question of the proper definition of money.

One might wonder why such a range of transaction balance accounts have developed. The answer is that since 1933 the payment of interest on demand deposits at commercial banks has been prohibited by law. This prohibition does not apply to the newly developed substitutes for demand deposits. NOW accounts, for example, pay interest, although at rates that are subject to government set ceilings. There are no restriction on the interest rate that money market mutual funds may pay. Interest rates on RP transactions are also unrestricted.[8]

The Redefined Monetary Aggregates

The growth of all these new substitutes for demand deposits created a need for revision of the definitions of the monetary aggregates. The revised official definitions of monetary aggregates for the U.S. monetary statistics are given in Table 14.1. The rationale for the new definitions, as with the old ones, is to have a series of money measures ranging from a very narrow or "strict constructionist" definition to much broader measures.

As with the old definitions, the M1 aggregate is aimed at measuring the "strict constructionist" concept of money—financial instruments actually used in transactions. The new M1 consists of currency plus demand deposits at commercial banks—the old

[8]The timing of these innovations in the deposit market has not been accidental. The high nominal interest rates in the 1970s greatly increased the opportunity cost of holding money in non-interest-bearing checking accounts and created increased pressure on both financial institutions and the government agencies that regulate these institutions to provide interest-bearing transactions accounts.

Table 14.1 Revised Monetary Aggregates[a] (billions of dollars, October 1981)

M1	432.9
M2	1789.3
M3	2151.0

[a]Composition of the Money Stock Measures is as follows:
M1: Averages of daily figures for (1) currency outside the Treasury, Federal Reserve Banks, and the vaults of commercial banks; (2) traveler's checks of non-bank issuers; (3) demand deposits at all commercial banks other than those due to domestic banks, the U.S. government, and foreign banks and official institutions less cash items in the process of collection and Federal Reserve float; and (4) negotiable order of withdrawal (NOW) and automatic transfer service (ATS) accounts at banks and thrift institutions, credit union share draft accounts (CUSD), and demand deposits at mutual savings banks.
M2: M1 plus savings and small-denomination time deposits at all depository institutions, overnight repurchase agreements at commercial banks, overnight Eurodollars held by U.S. residents other than banks at Caribbean branches of member banks, and money market mutual fund shares.
M3: M2 plus large-denomination time deposits at all depository institutions and term RPs at commercial banks and savings and loan associations.

M1—plus other checkable deposits, such as NOW accounts, ATS accounts, and credit union share drafts.[9]

The new M2 definition includes all the assets in M1 plus overnight RPs, money market mutual fund shares, savings deposits at all depository institutions, and small time deposits (denomination of less than $100,000) at all depository institutions. The M2 measure includes in the definition of money other highly liquid assets which, although generally not directly used in transactions, can easily be converted to demand deposits or currency. Money market mutual funds do not quite fit into this category since checks can be written on such accounts. Studies have shown, however, that the turnover rates on such accounts are quite low, and thus they are not in fact being extensively used for transactions purposes. Consequently, the monetary authority treats them like savings accounts.

The broadest of the money aggregates M3 is equal to M2 plus large-denomination time deposits and RPs that have some term to maturity. These additional assets on average are less liquid than those included in the narrower money stock measures.

The discussion above should make it clear that there is no unique definition of money for the U.S. economy, a fact that has important implications for the proper conduct of monetary policy, which is discussed in Chapter 19. Also, we will need to be careful to specify which assets we are considering as money in our analysis below of the various theories of money demand.

14.2 THE THEORY OF THE TRANSACTIONS DEMAND FOR MONEY

An important motive for holding money in both the classical and Keynesian theories of money demand was the transactions motive. Money is a medium of exchange and individuals hold money for use in transactions. The fact that money is not only *used* in transactions but that positive sums of money are being held at any point in time for transaction purposes is due to the imperfect synchronization of income receipts and expenditures. Money is held to bridge the gap between receipts and expenditures. Theories of the

---

[9]Here and below we omit discussion of some of the minor items included in the definitions given in the table. For a detailed discussion of the new definitions of the monetary aggregates, see "The Redefined Monetary Aggregates," *Federal Reserve Bulletin*, February 1980. For an intermediate period the Federal Reserve tabulated two M1 measures. The first, which was referred to as M1-A, was essentially the old M1 measure (currency plus demand deposits at commercial banks); the second, M1-B, included other checkable deposits (NOW accounts, ATS accounts, and credit union share drafts).

transaction demand for money have generally assumed that income is a good measure of the volume of transactions and, as a consequence, that the transaction demand for money varies positively with income. In the classical theory income was the only systematic determinant of the transactions demand for money. Since the transactions motive, stemming from the role of money as a medium of exchange, was the major role of money considered in the classical theory, the classical money demand function ($M^d = kPy$) expressed money simply as a function of income.

We saw above that the Keynesian money demand function [$M^d = L(y, r)$] expressed money demand as a function of both income and the interest rate, an increase in the interest rate being expected to reduce the level of money demand for a given income level. Keynes's own theory of the relationship of money demand and the interest rate was the theory of the *speculative demand for money* and concerned money's role as a store of value. It was noted above that the transactions demand might also be expected to be negatively related to the level of the interest rate. Individuals would economize on their holdings of transactions balances at higher interest rates. Extensions of Keynes's theory of the demand for money developing this relationship between the transactions demand for money and the interest rate are the subject of this section. In the next section we discuss extensions of Keynes's theory of the demand for money as a store of wealth.

Before beginning our discussion of these theories of the demand for money, two points are worth noting. First, as just explained, there is no unique definition of money. For the purposes of the transactions demand for money, the relevant concept of money is the narrow definition confined to those assets actually used in transactions—the M1 definition of money. When we turn to consideration of money as a store of wealth, a broader definition of money such as M2 or M3 will be relevant. Second, many of the theories of money demand are often stated in terms of the behavior of households. But money is also held by firms and by the government sector. As of 1977, for example, the government and business sectors accounted for approximately 40 percent of money holdings (old M1 definition). This fact has implications for the theories we discuss.

The Inventory-Theoretic Approach to Money Demand

The extensions of Keynes's theory of the transactions demand have followed an *inventory-theoretic approach*. The transactions demand for money has been regarded as the inventory of the medium of exchange (money) that will be held by the individual or firm. The theory of the optimal level of this inventory has been developed by

William Baumol and James Tobin along the lines of the theory of the inventory holdings of goods by a firm.[10]

To explain the inventory-theoretic approach, we consider first the example of an individual who receives an income payment of Y dollars *in cash* at the beginning of the period ($t = 0$). To be concrete, suppose that the individual has a monthly income payment of $1200. We further assume that the individual spends this income at a uniform and perfectly predictable rate throughout the period. By the end of the monthly period ($t = 1$), cash holdings have fallen to zero. This time profile of money holdings is depicted in Figure 14.1. The average inventory of money held during the period will equal $Y/2$, in this case $600 ($1200/2), which is also the amount that will be held at the midpoint of the period ($t = \frac{1}{2}$). This follows from the assumption that expenditures take place at a uniform rate over the period.

[10]William Baumol's article "The Transactions Demand for Cash: An Inventory-Theoretic Approach" appeared in the *Quarterly Journal of Economics* 66 (November 1952), pp. 545–56. James Tobin's article "The Interest-Elasticity of the Transactions Demand for Cash" appeared in the *Review of Economics and Statistics*, 38 (August 1956), pp. 241–47.

Figure 14.1
Individual Money Holdings (No Bond Market Transactions)

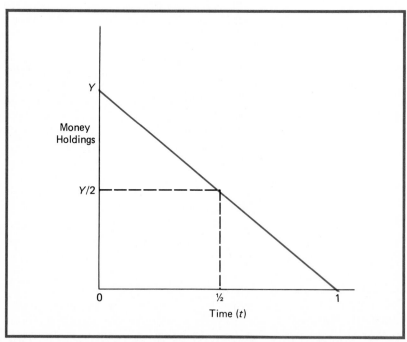

The individual receives income in cash of Y dollars at the beginning of the period. The income payment is spent at an even rate over the period. Average holdings of cash equal the holdings at the midpoint of the period $Y/2$.

EXTENSIONS OF THE MODELS

From Figure 14.1 the relationship between the level of income and the average level of money holdings can be seen. The higher the initial income payment, the higher the average level or inventory of money holdings. The inventory-theoretic approach also suggests that the level of the inventory holding of money will depend on the carrying cost of the inventory. In the case of money, the relevant carrying cost is the interest forgone by holding money and not bonds, net of the cost to the individual of making a transfer between money and bonds, which we will call the *brokerage fee*.[11] The time profile of money holdings shown in Figure 14.1 assumes that throughout the month the individual holds all of the unspent income payment received at the beginning of the month in the form of money. Alternatively, he could invest a proportion of the initial income payment in bonds and then sell the bonds when additional money was needed for transactions.[12]

If the individual invested half of the income payment in bonds at the beginning of the month and then sold the bonds when his cash holdings were exhausted at midmonth, the time profile of his money holdings would be as depicted in Figure 14.2. At the beginning of the month money holdings are $Y/2$ (Y minus bond purchase of $Y/2$). Money holdings are then run down to zero by the midpoint of the period at uniform rate. Average money holdings for the first half of the period are therefore $Y/4$. At the midpoint of the period, the bonds are sold. Money holdings return to $Y/2$ and are then spent at a uniform rate over the last half of the period. The average money holding for the second half of the period is again $Y/4$. Thus the average money holding for the period as a whole is $Y/4$, which is lower than $Y/2$ for the case where no bonds are held. The average bond holding for the period is $Y/4$ (the average of $Y/2$ for the first half of the period and zero for the second). If the monthly interest rate on bonds is r percent and there is a fixed brokerage fee for each transaction in the bond market of b dollars, then the net profit (Pr)

[11]Some components of the money stock (M1) do pay interest, NOW accounts and credit union share drafts for example, but the interest rates on such accounts are fixed by government regulation at levels well below the market interest rate. The interest forgone by holding these deposits instead of bonds is then the differential between the market interest rate and such deposit rates. It will simplify our analysis, without changing our conclusions, to neglect such interest payments on deposits.

[12]Notice that since money here is defined to be actual transactions balances (M1), such assets as savings deposits, money market mutual funds, or RPs are *not* considered as money. These assets are then included in "bonds," so the choice the individual faces can be thought of as one between holding transactions balances or, for example, holding savings deposits, which pay interest but require periodic trips to the bank to convert the savings deposits to transactions balances. The "brokerage" cost in this case is a time cost. For the wealthy individual or business firm, the interest-earning asset which is the alternative to holding money might be an actual short-term bond such as a marketable government security, and the brokerage cost is an actual broker's fee for buying or selling the bonds.

Figure 14.2
Individual's Money
Holdings (Two Bond
Market Transactions)

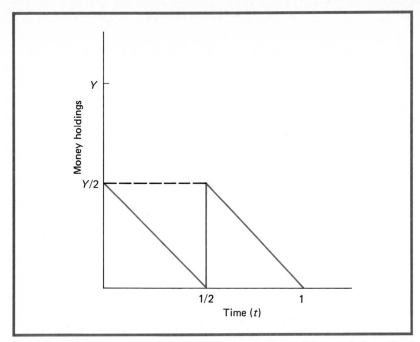

The individual receives Y dollars at the beginning of the period, half of which ($Y/2$) is used to purchase bonds. The other half is spent at an even rate over the first half of the period. The bonds are sold at $t = 1/2$ and the cash received ($Y/2$) is spent at an even rate during the second half of the period. Average cash holdings are $Y/4$ ($Y/2 \div 2$) in each half of the period and, therefore, for the period as a whole.

from the one bond purchase and one sale (number of transactions, n, equal 2) is

$$\Pr(n = 2) = r\frac{Y}{4} - 2b \qquad (14.6)$$

The first term is the interest earning on the average bond holding. The second term is the transactions cost, which equals the broker-age fee times the number of bond market transactions.

If, instead, the individual chose to engage in three transactions ($n = 3$) in the bond market, the optimal strategy would be to buy an amount of bonds equal to $\frac{2}{3}Y$ at the start of the period, sell bonds equal to $\frac{1}{3}Y$ when initial money holdings of $\frac{1}{3}Y$ are exhausted at $t = \frac{1}{3}$, and then sell the remaining amount of bonds, $\frac{1}{3}Y$, when money holdings are again exhausted at $t = \frac{2}{3}$.[13] The time profile of

[13]Notice that a specific strategy of purchases and sales is being considered here, namely a strategy where, after the initial bond purchase, sales are evenly spaced across the time period. Such a strategy can be shown to be the optimal one in the sense that it enables the individual to maximize his average holdings of bonds and,

EXTENSIONS OF THE MODELS

money holdings over the period would in this case be as shown in Figure 14.3. From the preceding example and the figure, it can be seen that for this case average money holdings are equal to $Y/6$ ($Y/3 \div 2$ for each third of the time period). Average bond holdings equal $Y/3$ ($\frac{2}{3}Y$ for the first third of the period, $\frac{1}{3}Y$ over the second third, zero for the last third) and net profit from the bond transactions equals

$$\Pr(n = 3) = r\frac{Y}{3} - 3b \tag{14.7}$$

Average money holdings, average bond holdings, and net profit can be expressed in terms of the number of bond market transactions (n).

In the general case, average money holdings (M) will be

$$M = \frac{1}{2n}Y \tag{14.8}$$

In the examples above, for $n = 2$, money holdings were $Y/4$ ($= \frac{1}{2(2)}Y$) and for n equal 3 money holdings were $Y/6$ ($= \frac{1}{2(3)}Y$). Average bond holdings (B) can be expressed as

$$B = \frac{n-1}{2n}Y \tag{14.9}$$

For the cases considered above, average bond holdings were $Y/4$ ($= \frac{2-1}{2(2)}Y$) for $n = 2$ and $Y/3$ ($= \frac{3-1}{2(3)}Y$) for $n = 3$.

The general expression for net profits is

$$\Pr = r\frac{n-1}{2n}Y - nb \tag{14.10}$$

The first term in this expression is the interest earnings on bonds equal to the interest rate (r) times average bond holdings $\left(\frac{n-1}{2n}\right)Y$, which is given by (14.9). The second term is again transaction costs, the brokerage fee (b) times the number of transactions (n). By substituting $n = 2$ and $n = 3$ into (14.10), we can get (14.6) and (14.7) for our previous examples.

From these results it can be seen that for a given income payment the choice of how much money (or how many bonds) to hold is determined by the choice of n. Determining the optimum n will

---

hence, interest earnings for a given number of transactions. For a proof of this, see Tobin, "Interest-Elasticity," or Thomas Dernburg and Judith D. Dernburg, *Macroeconomic Analysis* (Reading, Mass.: Addison-Wesley, 1969), pp. 31–32. The Dernburg and Dernburg book contains a good mathematical exposition of the inventory-theoretic approach to the transactions demand for money.

Figure 14.3

Individual's Money
Holdings (Three Bond
Market Transactions)

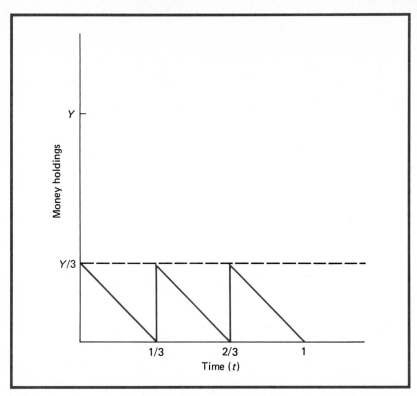

In this case ($n = 3$) two-thirds of the income payment is invested in bonds at the beginning of the period. The remaining one-third Y ($Y/3$) is spent at an even rate over the first third of the period. Bond sales of $Y/3$ are made at $t = 1/3$ and $t = 2/3$ with cash receipts again spent at even rates. Average money holdings are $Y/6$ ($Y/3 \div 2$) for each third of the period and, therefore, for the period as a whole.

determine the optimal money and bond holdings for the individual. Economic theory tells us that the individual will choose n such that net profits from bond sales (Pr) are maximized. He will increase the number of transactions in the bond market until the point is reached where the marginal interest earnings from one additional transaction are just equated with the constant marginal cost, which will be equal to the brokerage fee.

The determination of the optimal number of bond transactions for an individual to undertake is depicted graphically in Figure 14.4. The marginal cost (MC) of an additional transaction, which is the brokerage fee (b), is by assumption constant, hence the horizontal marginal cost schedule in Figure 14.4.

What about the marginal revenue schedule? When we considered going from zero bond market transactions to one purchase

Figure 14.4

Determination of the Optimum Number of Bond Market Transactions

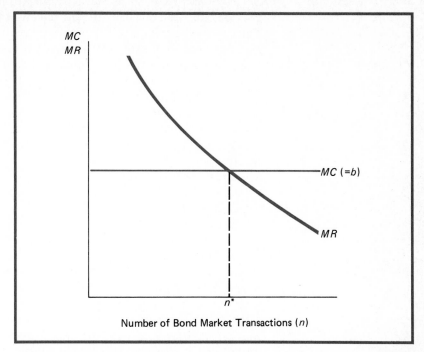

The optimum number of bond transactions (*n**) is chosen to equate the declining marginal revenue of additional bond market transactions *(MR)* with their constant marginal cost *(MC)*.

and sale above, we found that interest earnings increased from zero to $r(Y/4)$. A further increase to three bond market transactions increased average bond holdings from $Y/4$ to $Y/3$ and therefore interest earnings rose from $r(Y/4)$ to $r(Y/3)$, a further, though smaller increase in interest earnings of $r(Y/12)$ [note that $r(Y/12) = r(Y/3) - r(Y/4)$]; the marginal revenue of the third transaction is then $r(Y/12)$. Now consider the marginal revenue from a fourth bond market transaction. Using the formula given above [equation (14.9)] for average bond holdings, we can compute bond holdings which result from four bond market transactions,

$$B = \frac{n-1}{2n}Y = \frac{4-1}{2(4)}Y = \frac{3}{8}Y$$

Therefore, interest earnings will be $r\frac{3}{8}Y$ for four bond market transactions. The marginal revenue of the fourth transaction will be $r\frac{Y}{24}$ [note that $r(Y/24) = r(3/8)Y - r(Y/3)$]. The marginal revenue from the fourth bond market transaction is positive but is less than

MONEY DEMAND   **389**

the marginal revenue from the third transaction $[r(Y/24) < r(Y/12)]$. This is the general case. The increment to interest earnings from an additional bond market transaction declines as the number of bond market transactions increases. The marginal revenue schedule is downward sloping, as shown in Figure 14.4.

The optimal number of bond market transactions is determined at the point where the marginal revenue schedule intersects the horizontal marginal cost schedule, at n^* in Figure 14.4. Beyond this point the marginal gain in interest earned from increasing the number of bond market transactions is not sufficient to cover the brokerage cost of the transaction.

The choice of n determines the split of money and bond holdings *for a given income payment*. We can see how various factors affect the demand for money and bonds by seeing how they affect n. Factors that increase (decrease) n will, for a given income, increase (decrease) average bond holdings and decrease (increase) average money holdings. Figure 14.5a shows the effect on n of an increase in the interest rate from r_0 to r_1. This increase in the interest rate shifts the marginal revenue schedule upward from $MR(r_0)$ to $MR(r_1)$ in Figure 14.5a. At a higher interest rate an additional bond market transaction will increase bond holdings by the same amount as before but will increase interest earnings on the bond holding by a greater amount. The individual responds by engaging in more bond market transactions; the optimum number of bond market transactions rises from n_0^* to n_1^*. The average bond holding over the period increases. The average money holding over the period declines. This is the effect referred to in previous chapters as economizing on transactions balances at higher interest rates. The inventory-theoretic approach to the transactions demand for money provides a theoretical basis for this negative relationship between money demand and the interest rate.

The inventory-theoretic approach to the transactions demand for money also suggests that the demand for money and bonds will depend on the cost of making a transfer between money and bonds, what we have termed the brokerage fee (b). Figure 14.5b illustrates the effect on the optimum number of bond transactions (n) as a result of an increase in the brokerage fee from b_0 to b_1. The increase in the brokerage fee increases the marginal cost of bond market transaction and consequently lowers the number of such transactions, from n_0^* to n_1^* in Figure 14.5b. The increase in the brokerage fee increases the transactions demand for money and lowers the average bond holding over the period. This follows since an increase in the brokerage fee makes it more costly to switch funds temporarily into bond holdings.

Changes in the interest rate or brokerage fee affect the split of a given income payment between money and holdings. What is the

Figure 14.5

Factors Determining
the Optimum Number
of Bond Market
Transactions (*n**)

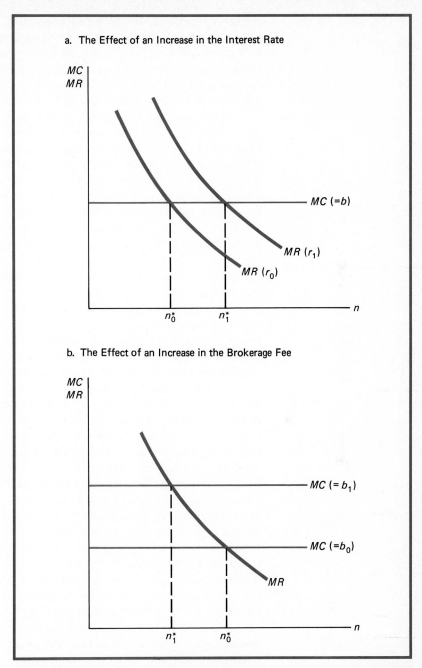

a. The Effect of an Increase in the Interest Rate

b. The Effect of an Increase in the Brokerage Fee

Part *a:* an increase in the interest rate from r_0 to r_1 shifts the marginal revenue curve to the right from $MR(r_0)$ to $MR(r_1)$. The optimal number of bond market transactions increases from n_0^* to n_1^*. Part *b:* an increase in the brokerage fee from b_0 to b_1 shifts the marginal cost schedule up from $MC(=b_0)$ to $MC(=b_1)$. The optimal number of bond market transactions falls from n_0^* to n_1^*.

effect of changing the level of income (Y)? We have already mentioned one effect. For a given n which determines the split between money and bonds, an increase in Y increases both the demand for money and bonds. For the cases considered above, for example with n equal 2, the average money and bond holdings are both $Y/4$ and clearly depend positively on Y. However, an increase in Y will *not* leave n unchanged. As Y rises, the marginal revenue from each additional bond transaction will increase, since each bond transaction will be for a greater amount and will therefore result in a greater increase in interest earnings. With the assumption of a fixed brokerage fee, the marginal cost of a transfer will be constant. The increase in income will then increase n. Graphically, this effect is the same as for the increase in the interest rate in Figure 14.5a; the MR schedule shifts to the right along a fixed MC schedule. Given the assumptions made here, it can be shown that the increase in n will not be so great as to cause money holdings to decline on net as income rises. *An increase in income will increase the holdings of both bonds and money.* It will be true that with the increase in n, the split between the two assets will move toward a higher proportion of bonds and lower proportion of money. As a consequence, an increase in income will cause the transactions demand for money to rise less than proportionately with income.

There is one qualification to the foregoing analysis. We have so far not constrained n to be an integer, but clearly it must be. You cannot engage in 6.89 bond market transactions and, more important, you cannot engage in 0.14 transaction or any number less than 2. If a comparison of marginal cost and marginal revenue indicates that the optimal level of transactions is less than 2, no transactions will be undertaken. For individuals with relatively modest incomes this situation seems quite likely. The brokerage cost will be high enough (even if it is just a time cost of switching between savings deposits and transactions deposits) that the individual will simply hold the money he needs for transactions throughout the whole period. In our example above, where the pay period is 1 month and monthly income was $1200, if the *monthly* interest rate is $\frac{1}{2}$ of 1 percent (0.005 as a decimal), then for $n = 2$, average bond holdings would be $300 ($Y/4$) and interest earnings would be $1.50 ($300 $\times$ 0.005). It is easy to see that the brokerage cost may exceed this amount and cause the individual to forgo any bond market transactions. For one group in the economy, those with relatively low incomes, the transactions demand for money may, therefore, simply be proportional to income and independent of the interest rate and brokerage fee. For wealthier individuals and especially for firms, however, brokerage costs will not prohibit bond market transactions such as those discussed above.

To summarize, in the aggregate the transactions demand for money can be written as follows:

$$M^d = L(y, r, b) \tag{14.11}$$

where an increase in aggregate income (y) or the brokerage fee (b) will increase money demand for transactions purposes and an increase in the interest rate will lower money demand for transactions purposes. The last two arguments ($r, b,$) are likely to be relevant only to firms and relatively high income individuals, but since these groups hold a substantial proportion of the money stock, these variables may be of considerable importance.

The Inventory-Theoretic Approach to Money Demand Continued: The Case of Uncertainty

In the preceding subsection we derived an expression for the transactions demand for money under the assumption that the stream of transactions the individual will undertake can be perfectly predicted at the beginning of the period. Here we relax that assumption and recognize that there is an element of uncertainty concerning the expenditures which will have to be undertaken over a given period. By doing so we can provide a rationale for Keynes's precautionary demand for money. In addition, we will see what effect changes in the degree of uncertainty about necessary future expenditures would have on the demand for money.

The standard type of example used to explain the precautionary motive for holding money is that of a man starting on a business trip. He would have a certain amount of money with him for planned transactions but would also carry some additional money in case there were unexpected expenditures, car repairs for example. If he did not do so, he might incur some cost, such as a missed business appointment, while he tried to arrange to obtain money to pay for car repairs or other unexpected expenditures. The modern business manager probably carries so many credit cards that the story has become unrealistic, but the point it makes is relevant. We hold money over and above that required for planned expenditures due to uncertainty about the volume of expenditures that will prove necessary. We do so because there is a cost to being without the money needed to finance unforeseen expenditures—what can be termed the cost of being *illiquid*. The higher our money holdings, the less likely it is that we will incur such a cost.

The level of uncertainty about the future stream of expenditures will therefore be one factor determining the level of money demand. For one class of money holders, business corporations, uncertainty concerning both receipts and expenditures provides the primary motive for holding money. Rather than receiving an income payment on the first of a given month and making payments over the month, a typical corporation is continually receiving income and making expenditures. If there is a significant non-synchronization of receipts and expenditures, for a reasonably large corporation the gain in holding bonds instead of keeping idle money balances is likely to be large, even net of brokerage fees. The major factor causing corporations to hold transactions balances in the form of money is uncertainty about the pattern of receipts and expenditures. It is to guard against the costs of illiquidity due to unexpected excess of expenditures over receipts that corporations have a large transactions demand for money. An implication of this that will be of importance below is that any changes which enable the corporation to reduce the uncertainty about future receipts and expenditures will reduce the corporate transactions demand for money.

The role of uncertainty in determining the transactions demand for money can be illustrated by modifying the graphical analysis in Figure 14.4. With uncertainty about the level of expenditures over the course of the period, putting more funds into bonds and less into money will increase the probability of becoming illiquid and incurring some cost. We can model this as an additional marginal cost to increasing the number of bond market transactions (n) and therefore lowering money holdings.

Specifically, let the probability of illiquidity (i.e., the probability that the individual or firm will not have sufficient money to finance a necessary expenditure) be given by $p(M, \mu)$. M is the amount of money held, which will negatively affect the probability that an individual will become illiquid. The term μ is a measure of the uncertain variability of expenditure. The higher the value of μ, the more likely that expenditures deviate greatly from the predicted pattern, and for a given holding of money, the more likely it is that an individual becomes illiquid. The last element to be specified is the cost of becoming illiquid. For simplicity let us assume this cost is equal to b, the brokerage cost. If the firm or individual becomes illiquid, he has to make an unplanned sale of bonds to raise money to finance an expenditure and incurs an extra brokerage cost.

With these modifications the marginal cost of engaging in an additional bond market transaction (increasing n) can be expressed as

$$\text{MC} = b + \Delta p(M, \mu)b \qquad (14.12)$$

The marginal cost includes the fixed brokerage fee (b), as before. Additionally, an increase in the number of bond market transactions will in the presence of uncertainty decrease the holdings of money and thus increase the probability of illiquidity [$\Delta p(M, \mu)$ will be positive]. This increase in the probability of becoming

EXTENSIONS OF THE MODELS

illiquid times the cost of becoming illiquid (b) is an additional marginal cost of a bond market transaction.

The determination of the optimal number of bond market transactions in the presence of uncertainty is depicted graphically in Figure 14.6. The marginal cost curve is higher than the corresponding schedule for the case of no uncertainty, where marginal cost is simply the brokerage fee b. The marginal cost schedule is upward sloping since we assume that the *increase* in the probability of illiquidity that comes from each additional bond transaction will become greater the higher the value of n, and hence the further money holdings have been drawn down.

The optimum number of bond market transactions is now given by n^{**}, where the new MC schedule intersects the MR schedule. Compared with the case where there is no uncertainty about the pattern of expenditures (MC = b), the number of bond market transactions is reduced, which means that average bond holdings are lower and average money holdings are higher. This increase in money holdings due to the decline in the number of bond market

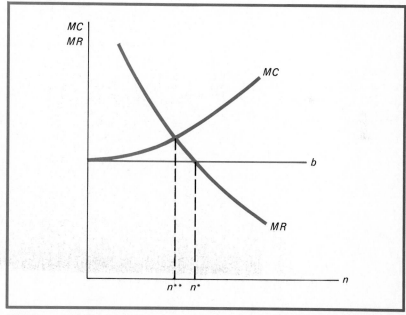

Figure 14.6
Determination of the Optimum Number of Bond Market Transactions in the Presence of Uncertainty About Expenditures

With uncertainty about the stream of transactions and the resulting chance of becoming illiquid, the marginal cost of each transaction exceeds the brokerage fee. Due to the higher marginal cost of an additional bond market transaction, the optimal number of bond market transactions in the presence of uncertainty (n^{**}) will be lower than in the case of no uncertainty (n^*).

transactions from n^* to n^{**} is the *precautionary* demand for money.

Finally, consider the effects of a change in μ, the degree of uncertainty about the stream of expenditures that will have to be undertaken. It seems reasonable to assume that an increase in μ will shift the MC schedule upward, as shown in Figure 14.7. With more uncertainty about the pattern of expenditures (a higher value of μ), any increase in n can be expected to cause a greater increase in the probability of illiquidity. If this is the case, then an increase in μ (from μ_0 to μ_1) will lower n^{**} (from n_0^{**} to n_1^{**} in Figure 14.7) and increase the demand for money. Correspondingly, any reduction in the uncertainty of the pattern of expenditures for an individual or firm will enable the individual or firm to increase its holdings of bonds and reduce their demand for money.

Summary

Our analysis to this point results in a demand for money function subsuming Keynes's transaction and precautionary demand for money, which is of the following form:

$$M^d = L(y, r, b, \mu) \qquad (14.13)$$

Figure 14.7

Effect of an Increase in the Uncertainty About the Pattern of Expenditures (μ)

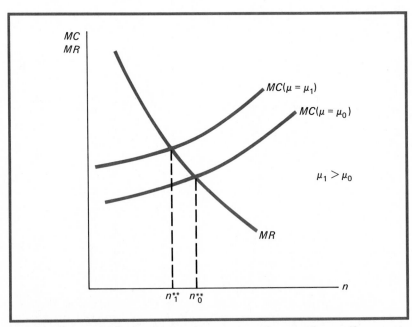

An increase in uncertainty about the pattern of expenditures (from μ_0 to μ_1) shifts the marginal cost schedule upward [from $MC(\mu = \mu_0)$ to $MC(\mu = \mu_1)$]. The optimal number of bond market transactions falls (from n_0^{**} to n_1^{**}).

The demand for money depends positively on the level of income (y), the level of the brokerage fee (b), and on the uncertainty about the pattern of expenditures (μ). Money demand depends negatively on the rate of interest. The money demand functions used in previous chapters omitted the last two arguments in (14.13). Implicitly, these were assumed to be constant in the short run and thus not to affect the analysis. This has also been the usual assumption in empirical work on money demand. But in recent years there have been systematic changes in both μ and b, and such changes are a major element in the puzzle of missing money we will consider in Section 14.4. Prior to that we consider some modifications that have been made in Keynes's theory of the demand for money as a store of wealth.

14.3 EXTENSIONS OF KEYNES'S THEORY OF THE DEMAND FOR MONEY AS A STORE OF WEALTH

Keynesian economists working in the 1950s followed Keynes's approach to the theory of the demand for money in that they considered the function of money as a store of value or wealth in addition to the means of payment function. They modified and extended Keynes's analysis, however, to remedy what they saw as weaknesses in his theory of the speculative motive for money demand.

Keynes's original theory of the speculative demand for money had been criticized on two grounds. First, recall that Keynes's theory implies that the individual investor would hold *all* of his wealth in bonds (other than the amount of money held as transaction balances) as long as the interest rate is above the "critical rate," a rate below which the expected capital loss on bonds outweighed the interest earnings on bonds. If the interest rate fell below this critical rate, the investor would transfer all his wealth to money.[14] Keynes's theory cannot therefore explain why an individual investor holds both money balances *and* bonds as stores of wealth, but such *portfolio diversification* does occur.

Second, according to Keynes's theory, investors hold money as an asset when the interest rate is low because they expect the interest rate to rise—returning to a *normal* level. A crucial element of Keynes's theory was the existence of a fixed or at least only slowly changing *normal* level for the interest rate, around which the ac-

[14]See the analysis of the speculative demand for money in Section 6.1, especially in Figure 6.3.

tual interest rate fluctuated. Figure 14.8 shows the behavior of the long- and short-term interest rates for the United States for the period 1920–78. The assumption of a normal level of interest rates around which the actual rates fluctuate is more consistent with interest-rate behavior for the period before Keynes wrote *The General Theory* in 1936 than afterward. In the period since 1950, there has been a pronounced upward trend in interest rates. In such a circumstance, Keynes's particular assumption that investors always expect a return of interest rates to some normal level would require modification. At a minimum the normal level would itself have to be assumed to be changing over time. Neo-Keynesian economists have modified Keynes's original theory in a way that explains why portfolio diversification takes place which does not depend on Keynes particular assumption about investor expectations of a return of the interest rate to a "normal" level. The start-

Figure 14.8 Long- and Short-Term Interest Rates

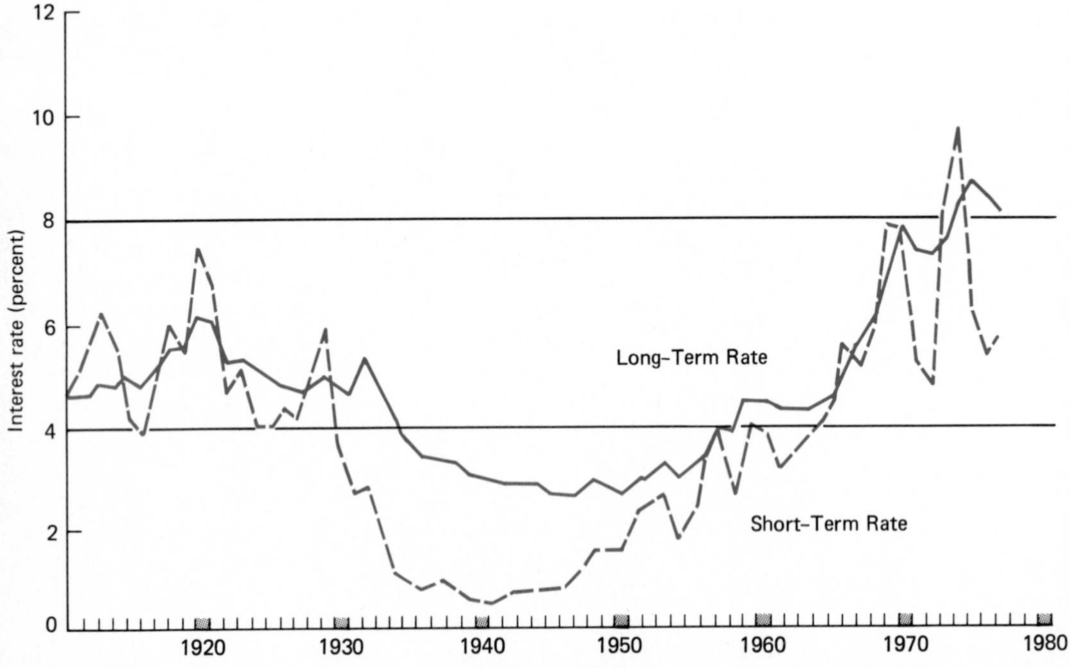

The long-term rate is Standard and Poor's AAA Corporate Bond Rate. The short-term rate is for prime commercial paper (4 to 6 months).

ing point of this portfolio theory of money demand is the work of James Tobin.[15]

The Demand for Money as Behavior Toward Risk

Tobin analyzes the individual's allocation of his portfolio between money holdings and bond holdings. The transaction demand for money is assumed to be determined separately along the lines of the analysis of the preceding section, and the demand for money considered here is solely the demand for money as a store of wealth.

In Tobin's theory the individual investor has no fixed normal level to which he always expects interest rates to return. We can assume that he believes capital gains or losses to be equally likely; that is, the *expected* capital gain is zero. The best expectation of the return on bonds is simply the interest rate (r). But note that this interest rate is only the expected return on bonds. The actual return will in general include some capital gain or loss, since the interest rate will generally not remain fixed. Thus bonds pay an expected return of r, but they are a risky asset—their actual return is uncertain.

Money, in contrast, is a safe asset. Money's nominal return of zero is lower than the expected return on bonds, but there are no capital gains or losses when money is held. Tobin argues that an individual will hold some proportion of his wealth in money because by doing so he lowers the overall riskiness of his portfolio below what it would be if he held all bonds. The overall expected return on the portfolio would clearly be higher if the portfolio were all bonds, but if the investor is *risk averse*, he will be willing to sacrifice higher return, to some degree, for a reduction in risk. The demand for money as an asset is explained as aversion to risk.

Tobin's theory can be explained more precisely with reference to Figure 14.9. In the upper quadrant on the vertical axis we measure the expected return to the portfolio; on the horizontal axis the riskiness of the portfolio is measured. The expected return on the portfolio is the total interest earning on bonds which depends on the interest rate and the proportion of his portfolio that the individual places in bonds. The total risk the individual takes depends on the uncertainty concerning bond prices—the uncertainty concerning future interest rate movements—as well as on the proportion of his portfolio placed in bonds, the risky asset. We denote the expected total return R and the total risk of the portfolio σ_T. If the individual holds all his wealth (Wh) in money and none in bonds,

---

[15]Tobin's original article on this subject, "Liquidity Preference as Behavior Towards Risk," appeared in the *Review of Economic Studies*, 25 February 1958, pp. 65–86.

Figure 14.9 Determination of the Optimum Portfolio

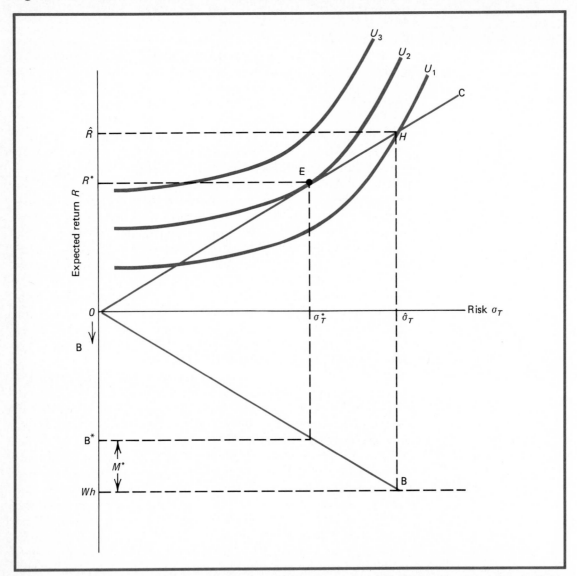

The upper quadrant of the figure shows the determination of the individual's optimum portfolio allocation. At point E the risk-expected return trade-off the individual faces in the market, reflected in the slope of the line C, is just equal to the terms on which he is willing to accept increased risk in return for an increase in expected return, given by the slope of his indifference curve (U_2). The lower quadrant shows the bond and money holdings (B^*, M^*) which correspond to this choice of risk and expected return.

the portfolio will have zero expected return and have zero risk. This portfolio allocation is shown at the origin (point O) in Figure 14.9. As the proportion of bonds in the portfolio increases, portfolio return and risk both rise. The terms on which the individual investor can increase the expected return on the portfolio (R) at the cost of increasing risk (σ_T) are represented by the line C.[16] As the investor moves along C, more bonds and less money are being held.

The lower quadrant of Figure 14.9 shows the allocation of the portfolio between bonds and money which results in each risk–return combination. Bond holdings (B) are measured on the vertical axis. The amount of bonds held in the portfolio increases as we go *down* the vertical axis to a maximum of Wh, the total amount of wealth. The difference between bond holdings and total wealth is the demand for money as an asset (M). The schedule B in the lower portion of the graph shows the relationship between total risk of the portfolio (σ_T) and the proportion of the portfolio held in bonds, with higher levels of risk associated with higher proportions of bonds in the portfolio.

To find the optimum portfolio allocation, we need to consider the preferences of the investor. We assume that the investor is risk averse; that is, whereas he wishes to receive a higher return on the portfolio, he also wants to avoid risk. He will accept a higher level of risk only if compensated by an increase in expected return. Formally, we assume that the investor's utility function is

$$U = U(R, \sigma_T) \tag{14.14}$$

where an increase in expected return (R) increases utility and an increase in risk (σ_T) decreases utility. On the basis of this utility function we can draw indifference curves for the investor, U_1, U_2, U_3 in Figure 14.9, showing the terms on which he is willing to accept more risk if compensated by receiving a higher expected return. Each point along one of these curves represents a given level of utility. As we move from U_1 to U_2 to U_3, we are moving to higher levels of utility—higher levels of R and lower levels of σ_T. The curves are drawn sloping upward to represent a risk-averse investor who will take on more risk only if compensated by a higher return. Further, the curves become steeper as we move to the right, reflecting the assumption of *increasing risk aversion*, by which is meant that the more risk the individual has already taken on, the greater the increase in expected return he will require before being willing to accept an additional increase in risk.

---

[16] Let σ be a measure of the uncertainty about the price of a given bond, the total risk on the portfolio can be measured by $\sigma_T = \sigma B$. Total return is $R = rB$ so the slope of the C line is $\Delta R / \Delta \sigma_T = r / \sigma$. Note that the C schedule here bears no relationship to the consumption function in previous chapters, which was also denoted by the letter C.

We now have all the elements needed to determine the optimal portfolio allocation between money and bonds. The individual investor will move to the point along the C schedule where that schedule is just tangent to one of his indifference curves. At this point the terms on which he is *able* to increase expected return on the portfolio by accepting more risk, given by the slope of the C schedule, will be equated to the terms on which he is *willing* to make this trade-off, given by the slope of his indifference curve. This is the point of utility maximization. In Figure 14.9 this tangency occurs at point E, with expected return R^* and total risk on the portfolio of σ_T^*. From the lower quadrant it can be seen that this risk–return combination is achieved by holding an amount of bonds equal to B^* and by holding the remainder of wealth M^* in the form of money.

The demand for money is then what Tobin terms "behavior towards risk"—the result of attempting to reduce risk below what it would be if all wealth were held in bonds. In Figure 14.9 such an all-bonds portfolio would incur risk of $\hat{\sigma}_T$ and earn expected return of $\hat{R}$, point H in the graph. This portfolio yields a lower level of utility than that represented by bond holdings of B^* and money holdings of M^*. The reason for this can be seen from the graph. As we move farther along the C schedule past point E, the incremental expected return on the portfolio from holding additional bonds is insufficient to compensate the investor for the additional risk he incurs (the slope of the C schedule is lower than that of the U_2 schedule). Movement to point H takes him to a lower indifference curve, U_1 in Figure 14.9.

Money Demand and the Rate of Interest

Tobin's theory has the implication that the amount of money held as an asset will depend on the level of the interest rate. This relationship between the interest and asset demand for money is depicted in Figure 14.10. The effect of an increase in the interest rate will be to improve the terms on which the expected return on the portfolio can be increased by accepting greater risk. At a higher interest rate a given increase in risk, which corresponds to a given increase in the amount of bonds in the portfolio, will result in a greater increase in expected return on the portfolio. In Figure 14.10, increases in the interest rate from r_0 to r_1, then to r_2, will rotate the C schedule in a counterclockwise direction from $C(r_0)$ to $C(r_1)$, then to $C(r_2)$.[17] The point of portfolio optimization shifts from point E to point F and then to point G in the graph. In response to the increase in the interest rate, the individual will increase the proportion of his wealth held in the interest-bearing

[17]As explained in footnote 16, the slope of the C schedule is r/σ; thus an increase in r will increase the slope of the C schedule.

Figure 14.10 Asset Demand for Money and the Rate of Interest

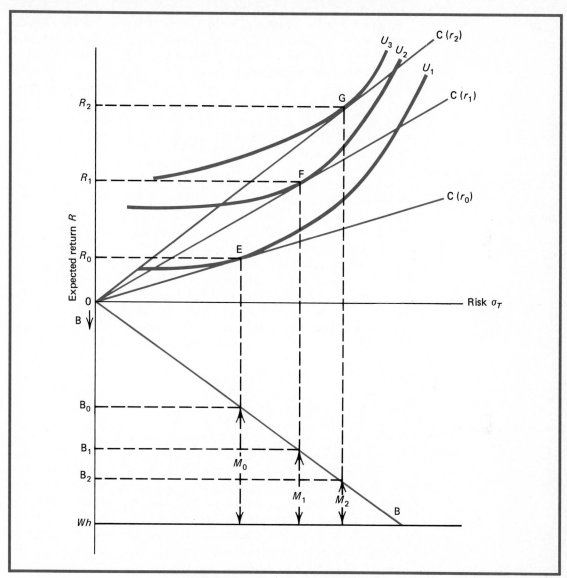

Increases in the interest rate (from r_0 to r_1 and then r_2) make the C schedule steeper by increasing the expected return which can be gained by undertaking increased risk. The individual responds by undertaking more risk and earning higher expected return (the equilibrium point moves from point E to F then to G). Holdings of the risky asset, bonds, increase (from B_0 to B_1 then to B_2); money holdings decline (from M_0 to M_1 then to M_2).

asset, bonds (from B_0 to B_1 to B_2), and will decrease his holding of money (from M_0 to M_1 to M_2).

Tobin's theory implies, as did Keynes's original theory of the speculative demand for money, that the demand for money as a store of wealth will depend negatively on the interest rate.[18] Within Tobin's framework an increase in the rate of interest can be considered an increase in the payment received for undertaking risk. It is therefore not surprising that when this payment is increased, the individual investor is willing to undertake more risk by putting a greater proportion of his portfolio into the risky asset, bonds, and thus a smaller proportion into the safe asset, money.

Is Tobin's Theory a Theory of Money Demand?

Tobin's theory of portfolio behavior apparently shows why there is a demand for money as a store of wealth and also explains the phenomenon of portfolio diversification, which Keynes's theory of the speculative demand for money did not explain. Tobin's theory, as did Keynes's, implies that the demand for money as an asset will depend negatively on the level of the rate of interest.

Recently, however, questions have been raised about the relevance of Tobin's portfolio theory to the question of the demand for *money*. Tobin's theory explains why individuals hold safe assets even when their return is lower than the risky alternative assets, but there are safe assets other than money. Does Tobin's theory explain why there is an asset demand for money? If we restrict ourselves to a narrow definition of money such as currency plus commercial bank demand deposits (the old M1), the answer is no. The investor seeking a safe asset for portfolio diversification would not choose these zero return assets, since there are other safe assets—commercial bank time deposits for example—which pay interest and, hence, are superior. Therefore, Tobin's theory does not explain the interest elasticity of such a narrowly defined money demand. Belief that the demand for currency or demand deposits depends on the interest rate must rest on the analysis of the preceding section, which showed that the transactions demand for money depends on the interest rate. If we broaden the definition of money to include assets such as NOW accounts, savings deposits,

---

[18]The conclusion that an increase in the interest rate will result in a decline in money demand does require one additional assumption. As explained in the text, a rise in the interest rate on bonds improves the terms of the trade-off between risk and return, making bonds more desirable. This corresponds to the usual *substitution* effect in consumer demand theory. There is also an *income* effect, however, which may work in the opposite direction. With a higher interest rate a given return can now be achieved with a lower proportion of bonds in the portfolio. This income effect may lead the investor to lower the demand for bonds and increase the security gained from holding money. In the terms of consumer demand theory, risk may be an inferior good. In the text we make the typical assumption that the substitution effect dominates any possible negative income effect.

time deposits, and money market fund shares, Tobin's theory does become relevant. These are interest-bearing safe assets and may be used in diversified portfolios. Thus Tobin's theory does provide a motive for the demand for money and an explanation of the interest elasticity of broader money aggregates.

14.4 THE CASE OF MISSING MONEY

Our analysis of the transactions and precautionary demands for money (Section 14.2) left us with the following specification for money demand:

$$M^d = L(y, r, b, \mu) \qquad (14.15)$$

where y is the level of income, r the interest rate, b the brokerage cost, and μ is a measure of the uncertainty concerning transactions that will have to be undertaken in the current period. Our consideration of the role of money as a store of wealth—Tobin's portfolio theory (Section 14.3)—would not suggest any modification of this money demand function as long as a narrow definition of money demand was adopted, since as just explained, Tobin's theory becomes relevant only when the broader definitions of money are considered. If a broader definition of money is adopted, Tobin's analysis suggests an additional reason for expecting the demand for money to depend on the interest rate, since his analysis implies that the demand for money as a store of wealth will decline with an increase in the interest rate. Tobin's analysis also indicates that uncertainty about bond prices, and hence the risk involved in buying bonds, may be an additional determinant of money demand (again only for the broader money aggregates).

In practice, a simplification of (14.15) has become the conventional specification of the money demand function. This simple form is that used in the earlier Keynesian theoretical models in Part II:

$$M^d = L(y, r) \qquad (14.16)$$

Money demand has been taken to depend on income and on an interest rate, usually a short-term interest rate. Although the preference for this specification has never been unanimous, this type of money demand function performed well in predicting actual money holdings up until 1973 and it was widely used for empirical work and in policy formation.

But beginning in 1974, equations such as (14.16) began to "misbehave." Such equations, when estimated by statistical procedures and used to predict the public's holding of money, began to seriously overpredict the amount of money the public was holding.[19] Given the level of income and the interest rate, the public was holding less money than these equations predicted it should. The question of why this was happening has been called the "case of missing money."

The failure of the conventional money demand function indicates a possible instability in money demand, and such instability would have important theoretical and policy implications. Clearly, an unstable money demand function would be a matter of importance to the monetarists. A central proposition of monetarism is that there is a stable relationship between money demand and income (among other variables), assuring that changes in the *supply* of money will have predictable effects on nominal income. But it is not only to the monetarists that unstable money demand would be important. In the Keynesian view as well, monetary factors—factors determining the position of the LM schedule—are an important determinant of income. If the demand for money is unstable, there are unpredictable shifts in the LM schedule which need to be offset by monetary or other policy actions.[20] Finally, we will see in a later chapter that instability in money demand has important implications for the proper conduct of monetary policy by the central bank.

Table 14.2 shows the amount by which one version of the conventional money demand function overpredicted money demand for each quarter from the beginning of 1975 through the first quarter of 1979, as well as the size of the error as a percent of the total money stock. The figures in the table are for the old M1 definition of money, and in fact, the major source of the overprediction of money demand seems to have come from the demand deposit component of M1. It can be seen that the conventional money demand function goes badly off track in the 1975–76 period, with the percentage overprediction in money demand reaching 10.5 percent by the end of the fourth quarter of 1976. The prediction error remains at about this level until there is another spurt late in 1978, with the prediction error reaching 15.5 percent in the first quarter of 1979. These prediction errors are both large and systematic. It is also useful to note that tests of separate money demand functions for

[19]For a detailed description of empirical work on the demand for money, see David Laidler, *The Demand for Money*, 2nd ed. (New York: Dun-Donnelley, 1979); and John Boorman, "The Evidence on the Demand for Money: Theoretical Formulations and Empirical Results," in Boorman and Thomas Havrilesky, *Current Issues in Monetary Theory and Policy*, 2nd ed. (Arlington Heights, Ill.: AHM Publishing Corp., 1980). Empirical evidence on the recent problems in predicting money demand is contained in Stephen Goldfeld's article "The Case of Missing Money," *Brookings Papers on Economic Activity*, No. 3, 1976; and in Richard Porter, Thomas Simpson, and Eileen Mauskopf, "Financial Innovations and the Monetary Aggregates," *Brookings Papers on Economic Activity*, No. 1, 1979, pp. 213–29.
[20]The effect on the LM schedule of a shift in money demand is explained in Section 6.2.

Table 14.2
Overprediction of Money Demand from a Conventional Money Demand Function[a]

Year: Quarter	Overprediction of Money Demand (billions of dollars)	Prediction Error as a Percent of Total
1975:1	12.6	4.5
1975:2	15.2	5.3
1975:3	16.9	5.8
1975:4	21.9	7.4
1976:1	26.1	8.8
1976:2	28.3	9.3
1976:3	31.6	10.3
1976:4	32.7	10.5
1977:1	34.3	10.8
1977:2	36.3	11.2
1977:3	36.7	11.1
1977:4	37.4	11.1
1978:1	38.3	11.2
1978:2	39.4	11.2
1978:3	40.5	11.3
1978:4	45.1	12.5
1979:1	55.7	15.5

[a]The definition of money here is the old M1 definition (currency plus demand deposits).

Source: Richard Porter, Thomas Simpson, and Eileen Mauskopf, "Financial Innovations and the Monetary Aggregates," *Brookings Papers on Economic Activity*, No. 1, 1979, Table 1, p. 214.

businesses and households (not reported in the table) indicated that the overprediction of money demand was most serious for the case of businesses.

Although the case of missing money has not been solved completely, we do have some indications about the causes of the puzzling behavior of money demand in recent years. Two factors which may have caused money demand to fall short of predicted levels are (1) declines in the brokerage fee for moving from demand deposits to other interest-bearing assets (b) and (2) improvements in cash management practices on the part of firms, which lower the uncertainty about expenditures that will have to be made (μ). Notice that these two variables, the brokerage fee and a measure of the uncertainty of transactions, are not included in the conventional money demand function [equation (14.16)], even though the theory of the transactions demand for money implies that they will have a role in money demand. If brokerage costs have been declining and firms have reduced the uncertainty about their transactions through better cash management practices—both changes that would reduce money demand—it would not be surprising that the conventional money demand function, which does not take account of these changes, would overpredict money demand.

There is evidence that brokerage fees have been declining in recent years. This has come in part due to the development of the new substitutes for demand deposits discussed in Section 14.1; especially important in this respect has been the growth of the RP market. Transactions costs of going from demand deposits to RPs are low and until recently RPs were not included in the definition of money. They are still not included in M1. The increased substitution of RPs for demand deposits would lower the demand for money below the predictions of the conventional money demand function. RPs are held overwhelmingly by businesses and the growth of the RP market may help to explain the especially large overprediction of the business sector's demand for money. The growth of money market funds played a similar role in causing a decline in individual holdings of demand deposits over the 1975–80 period. The brokerage cost of buying a government bond might make it unprofitable for an individual to economize on demand deposits by temporarily transferring funds into such a bond. There is no explicit "brokerage" fee to shifting funds in and out of a money market fund, however, and the time cost of such transactions is low. Again, until recently such money market funds were not included in the money aggregates and they still are not in M1.

There is also evidence that cash management practices on the part of both large and small businesses improved over the mid- and late 1970s. This development was in response to the record high levels of short-term interest rates during this period (see Figure 14.8). These high interest rates increased the incentives for cash managers to economize as much as possible on the holding of non-interest-bearing demand deposits. To do this they have made investments in cash management techniques which enable them to forecast their short-term cash flows (receipts and expenditures) more accurately, to process receipts as quickly as possible, and in some cases to delay disbursements as long as possible.[21] With these reductions in the uncertainty about their cash flow (μ), firms were able to reduce their transactions demand for money—holding instead short-term bonds, RPs, and other interest-bearing assets. Once the initial investment had been made to institute such cash management procedures, they continued to be used even when short-term interest rates declined.

This combination of lower brokerage fees and improved cash management techniques on the part of firms can explain the bulk of the overprediction of money demand by conventional money demand functions, which neglected both phenomena.

Given that past sources of unpredictability in money demand

---

[21]Examples of such cash management procedures are given in Porter, Simpson, and Mauskopf, "Financial Innovations."

EXTENSIONS OF THE MODELS

can be reasonably well explained, is there reason to believe that we will be able to do better in predicting the future course of money demand? Part of the past problem seems to have been one of properly defining money rather than an instability of money demand. The revised definitions of the monetary aggregates have at least partially solved that problem. Further innovations in the financial sector may, however, create needs for further revisions, and while such financial innovations are under way, it is difficult to gauge their impact and know how to adjust the monetary aggregates.[22] It seems unlikely that difficulties in measuring the proper concept of money are at an end. It is equally unlikely that future changes in cash management practices will be highly predictable; hence future difficulty in measuring business demand for money seems likely. Overall, the likely prospect appears that money demand will continue to be difficult to predict for at least the near-term future. The consequences of this for the proper conduct of monetary policy are discussed below.

14.5 THE CURRENT STATE OF THE THEORY OF MONEY DEMAND

A summary of the state of the theory of money demand several years ago would have approached the subject as one where a reasonable consensus had been reached. Money demand had been shown theoretically and empirically to depend on income and the interest rate. The conventional form of the money demand function discussed in the preceding section performed well. The recent failure of this conventional money demand function has led to renewed interest in the money demand function.

On some issues there still is a consensus. There is agreement that income is an important determinant of money demand. The interest elasticity of money demand is also well established as both a theoretical and an empirical matter. Keynes correctly criticized the classical economists for failing to consider the interest rate as a determinant of money demand. Empirical estimates of the value of the interest elasticity of money demand are not, however, sufficiently precise to settle convincingly the dispute between the Keynesians and monetarists about the slope of the LM schedule (see Section 9.2), the monetarists generally believing the (abso-

---

[22]As was noted above, many of the financial innovations of the 1970s were responses to the prohibition of interest payment on demand deposits as well as other legal ceilings on rates that can be paid on savings and time deposits. The Monetary Control Act of 1980 begins a process of phasing out such ceilings, a process that may begin a new round of innovations in the deposit market.

lute) value of the interest elasticity to be low (steep LM schedule), the Keynesians believing the interest elasticity of money demand to be relatively high (LM schedule relatively flat).

The recent problems in predicting money demand have not led economists to view the existing theory of money demand as fundamentally flawed. As the discussion above should illustrate, the source of these recent difficulties can be found in the effects of innovations in the financial sector—the growth of new substitutes for demand deposits and the development of new cash management techniques by businesses. These changes have required a redefinition of the money aggregates and are leading economists to renewed interest in the question of what should be considered to be "money." In terms of the theory of money demand, more attention needs to be focused on the previously neglected determinants of money holdings: brokerage fees and the uncertainty of transactions flows. More attention also needs to be focused specifically on the demand for money by businesses, and this will require a more disaggregated analysis of money demand.

Review Questions

1   Explain why recent innovations in the financial sector have necessitated changes in the definition of money aggregates (the old M1, M2, M3, etc.). Without going into all the details of the definitions of the new aggregates, explain how the proposed new aggregates are aimed at taking account of these changes.

2   What is the most important difference between the classical and Keynesian theories of money demand?

3   According to the inventory-theoretic approach to the transactions demand for money, how would you expect the amount of money an individual demanded for transactions purposes to be affected by:
    a. An increase in the interest rate paid in bonds.
    b. An increase in the brokerage fee for bond market transactions.
    c. An increase in income.
    d. An increase in the length of the payment period, for example from a week to a month.

4   Explain the modifications of the inventory-theoretic approach to the transactions demand for money which are required when we assume that the stream of transactions faced by the individual is uncertain.

5 Show how James Tobin's theory explains the demand for money as an asset as "behavior towards risk." How does Tobin's theory differ from Keynes's formulation of the asset demand for money; Keynes's theory of the speculative demand for money? In what respects are Tobin's and Keynes's theories similar?

6 Within Tobin's theory of the demand for money, explain how the optimal portfolio (the choice of money and bond demand) would be affected by an increase in uncertainty about the price of bonds.

7 Explain the nature of the recent difficulties in predicting money demand. How would you explain the source of these difficulties?

Selected Readings

BAUMOL, WILLIAM, "The Transaction Demand for Cash: An Inventory-Theoretic Approach," *Quarterly Journal of Economics*, 66 (November 1952), pp. 545–56.

BERKMAN, NEIL, "The New Monetary Aggregates: A Critical Appraisal," *Journal of Money, Credit and Banking*, 12 (May 1980), pp. 134–54.

GOLDFELD, STEPHEN, "The Case of Missing Money," *Brookings Papers on Economic Activity*, No. 3, 1976, pp. 683–730.

LAIDLER, DAVID, *The Demand for Money*, 2nd ed. New York: Dun-Donnelley, 1977, Chaps. 2–5.

PORTER, RICHARD; SIMPSON, THOMAS; and MAUSKOPF, EILEEN, "Financial Innovations and the Monetary Aggregates," *Brookings Papers on Economic Activity*, No. 1, 1979, pp. 213–29.

SIMPSON, THOMAS, "The Redefined Monetary Aggregates," *Federal Reserve Bulletin*, 66 (February 1980), pp. 97–114.

SURREY, M. V. C., *Macroeconomic Themes*. London: Oxford University Press, 1976, Chap. 4.

TOBIN, JAMES, "The Interest-Elasticity of Transactions Demand for Cash," *Review of Economics and Statistics*, 38 (August 1956), pp. 241–47.

chapter 15

So far we have been assuming that the supply of money is exogenously determined by the central bank. In this chapter we consider the money supply process in more detail. The structure of the central bank in the United States, the *Federal Reserve System*, is discussed and the Federal Reserve will be shown to have a pivotal role in determining the supply of money. The banking system and the nonbank public will, however, also be seen to play a part in determining the money stock. The realism of our previous assumption that the money stock was exogenous will be seen to depend on the behavior of the Federal Reserve. Since it is in the power of the Federal Reserve to offset in large part the actions of the other participants in the money supply process (the banking system and the nonbank public), the money stock is potentially an exogenous policy variable. For reasons explained below, the Federal Reserve has not always chosen to offset such private-sector actions, and the actual determination of the money stock has resulted from both private-sector and Federal Reserve actions. In this chapter we restrict ourselves to a consideration of the way the money supply is determined under different assumptions about the way in which the Federal Reserve behaves. In a later chapter we consider the question of how the Federal Reserve *should* behave—the question of *optimal* monetary policy.

We begin in Section 15.1 with a discussion of the structure of the Federal Reserve system and the tools that the Federal Reserve uses for monetary control. In Section 15.2 we consider the relationship between bank reserves and deposits, a vital linkage in the process

THE MONEY SUPPLY PROCESS

of Federal Reserve control over the money stock. In Section 15.3 we return to the question raised above concerning the relative roles of the nonbank public, the banking system, and the Federal Reserve in determining the money stock. Section 15.4 summarizes our analysis of the money supply process.

15.1 THE FEDERAL RESERVE SYSTEM

The Structure of the Central Bank

The U.S. system of central banking was established by the Federal Reserve Act of 1913.[1] Unlike the European countries, which have a single central bank, the United States has a system of Federal Reserve banks, one for each of 12 Federal Reserve districts. Each Federal Reserve Bank is named for the city in which it is located: The Federal Reserve Bank of New York, The Federal Reserve Bank of Chicago, The Federal Reserve Bank of San Francisco, and so forth. For some of the functions of central banking this regional character of our system is of importance, but the making of macroeconomic policy has become centralized in Washington in two policy-making groups.

The first of these groups is the Board of Governors of the Federal

[1]For a more detailed discussion of the structure of the Federal Reserve System and the evolution of central banking in the United States, see Lester Chandler and Stephen Goldfeld, *The Economics of Money and Banking* (New York: Harper & Row, 1977), Chaps. 8 and 9.

Reserve. The Board is composed of seven members (governors) appointed by the President of the United States with the advice and consent of the Senate for a term of 14 years. One member of the board is appointed by the President as Chairman of the Board. When this post has been held by forceful individuals, the chairman has been the dominant figure in monetary policy formation.

The second central monetary policymaking group is the Federal Open Market Committee. The most important method by which the Federal Reserve controls the money stock is the purchase and sale of government securities in the "open market," the open market being the market of dealers in government securities located in New York City. We will see below how the Federal Reserve uses open market purchases or sales of securities to increase or decrease the *legal reserves* of the banking system. Since banks are required to hold fixed proportions of their deposits in the form of legal reserves, such *open market operations* can be used to control the deposit component of the money stock. The Open Market Committee controls open market operations. The Open Market Committee is composed of 12 voting members: the seven members of the Board of Governors and five of the presidents of the regional Federal Reserve Banks. The presidents of the regional banks serve on a rotating basis, with the exception that the president of the New York Bank, the bank charged with actually carrying out open market operations, is always a voting member of the Open Market Committee.

Federal Reserve Control of the Money Stock

Recall that the monetary aggregates discussed in Chapter 14 consisted of currency held by the public plus various classes of bank deposits. To simplify our discussion, let us assume to begin with that there is only one deposit type—a commercial bank demand deposit. Currency in the United States consists primarily of Federal Reserve notes—paper money issued by the Federal Reserve System.[2]

To control the demand deposit component of the money stock, the Federal Reserve sets legal reserve requirements on demand deposits. Federal Reserve legal reserve requirements specify that banks must hold a certain percentage of their demand deposit liabilities either in the form of vault cash (currency) or as deposits at regional Federal Reserve Banks. Given the existence of legal reserve requirements, the Federal Reserve can control the money stock by regulating the supply of legal reserves. Technically setting reserve requirements and fixing the level of reserves only sets a ceiling on the level of deposits. If, for example, the required re-

---

[2]A small and diminishing fraction of currency is composed of U.S. Treasury Notes. It will do no harm in our discussion to neglect this item.

serve ratio is 20 percent and reserves are set at $60 billion, then the maximum amount of demand deposits would be $300 billion. In fact, since legal reserves (currency or deposits at regional Federal Reserve Banks) do not pay interest, banks will hold few reserves beyond those required by Federal Reserve regulations. Thus the actual level of deposits will be close to the maximum value supportable by a given reserve level.

A convenient starting point for an analysis of Federal Reserve control of bank deposits via control of legal reserves is the balance sheet summarizing the assets and liabilities of the Federal Reserve System. A simplified version of this balance sheet is shown in Table 15.1. The primary assets held by the Federal Reserve are U.S. government securities. A much smaller item on the asset side of the balance sheet, but one that we return to later in the discussion, is the amount of loans to commercial banks; these are the *borrowed reserves* of the banking system. On the liability side the two major items are Federal Reserve notes outstanding, which make up the bulk of U.S. paper currency, and bank reserve deposits. This latter item consists of the deposits held at the Federal Reserve Banks by the banking system to satisfy legal reserve requirements.

These two items on the liability side of the Federal Reserve balance sheet (currency plus bank reserve deposits) form what is termed the *monetary base*, since together they provide the foundation for the money stock.[3] Currency is directly included in the money stock if held by the (nonbank) public. The portion of currency held as bank reserves plus bank reserve deposits provide the reserves supporting the deposit component of the money stock. The Federal Reserve controls the quantity of its liabilities, which means that it can control the monetary base and therefore control bank reserves and the money stock.

[3]The monetary base is often referred to as the stock of *high-powered money,* since a given base supports a much larger money stock.

Table 15.1 Balance Sheet of Federal Reserve Banks, May 1980 (billions of dollars)	Assets		Liabilities	
	U.S. government securities	129.7	Federal Reserve notes	111.5
	Loans to commercial banks	1.0	Bank reserve deposits	32.7
	Other assets	23.0	Other liabilities and capital	9.5
	Total assets	153.7	Total liabilities and capital	153.7

Source: *Federal Reserve Bulletin,* June 1980.

MONEY SUPPLY PROCESS

The Tools of Federal Reserve Control of Bank Reserves

In this section we discuss the major tools the Federal Reserve uses to control bank reserves.[4] In the Section 15.2 the process by which changes in bank reserves affect the level of bank deposits is explained. One point should be noted before proceeding. When the Federal Reserve takes some action changing the monetary base, an action increasing the base for example, the net effect of this action on bank reserves depends on how much of the increase in the base goes into increased currency holding by the (nonbank) public. The behavior of the public's currency holdings then influences the ultimate effect of Federal Reserve actions on the level of bank reserves and, hence, deposits. This influence is explained in the next section, but for now we will assume that the public's holding of currency is fixed. With this assumption changes in the monetary base produce dollar-for-dollar changes in the quantity of bank reserves.

There are three major tools that the Federal Reserve uses to control the reserve position of banks.

Open Market Operations

The first of these, open market operations, was referred to above. To see how an open market action by the Federal Reserve affects bank reserves, consider the example of an open market purchase of a government security worth $1000.

Government securities comprise the major part of Federal Reserve assets, as can be seen from Table 15.1. The purchase of the additional security will increase the government security item on the asset side of the Federal Reserve's balance sheet by $1000. To pay for this security the Federal Reserve writes a check on itself, drawn on the New York Federal Reserve Bank. A key point to note here is that the Federal Reserve, by writing this check, does not reduce the balance in *any* account. The Federal Reserve simply creates a new liability against itself. What happens to the check? Let us suppose that some individual investor sold the security to the Federal Reserve. He will take the check he receives and deposit it in his account at a commercial bank, Chase Manhattan Bank in New York for example.

Chase Manhattan will then present the check to the New York Federal Reserve Bank for payment. The Federal Reserve will credit the Chase Manhattan account balance at the New York Federal Reserve Bank by $1000. The open market purchase results in an increase of an equal amount in bank reserve deposits with the Federal Reserve. The effects of the open market purchase on the balance sheet of the Federal Reserve are summarized in Table 15.2.

---

[4]Hereafter we drop the adjective "legal" when referring to bank reserve assets that satisfy reserve requirements.

EXTENSIONS OF THE MODELS

Table 15.2	Assets	Liabilities
Effect on the Federal Reserve's Balance Sheet of a $1000 Open Market Purchase	Government securities +1000	Bank reserve deposits +1000

In a similar manner, a sale of government securities in the open market will reduce bank reserve deposits by an equal amount. In this case the Federal Reserve receives a check drawn on a commercial bank by the individual who purchased the security. The Federal Reserve lowers that bank's deposit balance at a regional Federal Reserve Bank by the amount of the check. Such open market purchases and sales of securities provide a flexible means of controlling bank reserves, and open market operations are, as noted above, the most important of the Federal Reserve's tools of monetary control.

The Discount Rate

The Federal Reserve Open Market Committee oversees open market operations. The remaining tools of monetary control are administered by the Board of Governors of the Federal Reserve System. The first of these is the Federal Reserve *discount rate*, the interest rate charged by the Federal Reserve on its loans to banks. The Federal Reserve raises or lowers this rate to regulate the volume of such loans to banks. To see the effect on bank reserve deposits of changes in the volume of loans from the Federal Reserve, consider the effect of a loan of $1000 from the Federal Reserve to a bank. The effects on the Federal Reserve's balance sheet are shown in Table 15.3.

The asset item "loans to banks" increases by $1000. The proceeds from the loan are credited to the account of the borrowing bank at the Federal Reserve. At this point bank reserve deposits increase by $1000. By lowering the discount rate, the Federal Reserve can encourage banks to borrow and increase the borrowed

Table 15.3	Assets	Liabilities
Effect on the Federal Reserve's Balance Sheet of a $1000 Loan to a Bank	Loans to banks +1000	Bank reserve deposits +1000

component of bank reserve deposits. Raising the discount rate has the reverse effect.

The Required Reserve Ratio

The third tool that the Federal Reserve uses to control the bank's reserve position is the level of the required reserve ratio—the percentage of deposits banks must hold as reserves. Changes in this policy instrument do not change the level of total bank reserves, but by changing the required reserve ratio on deposits, the Federal Reserve changes the quantity of deposits that can be supported by a given level of reserves. Increases in the required reserve ratio reduce the quantity of deposits that can be supported by a given amount of reserves. Consider our previous example, where reserves were set at $60 billion, so that with a 20 percent reserve requirement the maximum level for demand deposits was $300 billion. If the required reserve ratio were increased to 25 percent, the maximum level of deposits, with reserves unchanged at $60 billion, would be $240 billion. The increase in the required reserve ratio from 20 percent to 25 percent would have the same effect as a reduction in reserves (e.g., via an open market sale of securities) from $60 billion to $48 billion (48 = 0.20 × 240).

15.2   BANK RESERVES AND BANK DEPOSITS

So far we have seen how the Federal Reserve can use open market operations, changes in discount rate, and changes in the required reserve ratio on deposits to affect the reserve position of banks. In this section we examine the process whereby changes in reserves affect the level of deposits in the banking system. Again a convenient starting point is with a balance sheet, in this case one for the commercial banking system.

A simplified form of the consolidated balance sheet for all commercial banks is shown in Table 15.4. On the asset side, the first item is cash assets of commercial banks. Reserves (vault cash plus deposits at the Federal Reserve) come under this category, but other items are included as well (e.g., bank deposits at other banks). Reserves as of the time period for which the table was compiled (May 1980) totaled $43.9 billion, of which all but $135 million were required reserves. As explained above, banks hold very few excess reserves since reserve assets do not pay interest. The other major items on the asset side of the ledger are loans by the commercial banks, which include loans to consumers and businesses and the banks' holdings of both government and private securities. The major liabilities of the commercial banks are deposits, both demand and savings plus time deposits.

Table 15.4	Assets		Liabilities	
Consolidated Balance Sheet for the Commercial Banking System, May 1980 (billions of dollars)	Cash assets, including reserves	103.6	Demand deposits	370.1
	Loans	856.8	Time and savings deposits	686.8
	U.S. Treasury securities	93.9	Other liabilities and capital	338.4
	Other securities	199.3		
	Other assets, including cash assets in process of collection	141.7		
	Total assets	1395.3	Total liabilities and capital	1395.3

Source: *Federal Reserve Bulletin,* June 1980.

A Simple Model of Deposit Creation

Now consider the effects on the bank of an increase in reserves. Let us return to our example of the Chase Manhattan Bank. Recall our assumption that the Federal Reserve had purchased a $1000 security from an individual, making payment with a check drawn on the New York Federal Reserve Bank. The individual had deposited the check in his account at the Chase Manhattan Bank. When the check is presented for payment at the New York Federal Reserve Bank, Chase Manhattan's reserve deposits at the New York Federal Reserve increase by $1000. To this point the effects on Chase Manhattan's balance sheet as a result of this open market purchase by the Federal Reserve are as shown in Table 15.5. Demand deposits and reserves have both increased by $1000. For simplicity we will continue to assume that there is a uniform reserve requirement of 20 percent. In that case, the increase in reserves will consist of an increase of $200 in required reserves (0.20 × 1000) and an increase of $800 in excess reserves, as shown in Table 15.5.

Table 15.5, however, gives only the initial effects of the open market purchase on Chase's balance sheet. The position described in Table 15.5 will not be an equilibrium for Chase because the bank will not, in general, wish to increase *excess* reserves. Since reserves

Table 15.5	Assets		Liabilities	
Initial Effect on Chase Manhattan Bank's Balance Sheet from a $1000 Open Market Purchase	Reserves	+ 1000	Demand deposits	+ 1000
	Required reserves + 200			
	Excess reserves + 800			
	Total assets	+ 1000	Total liabilities	+ 1000

do not pay interest, the bank will convert the excess reserves, which are in the form of deposits at the New York Federal Reserve, into interest-earning assets. In doing so, a process of deposit creation whereby the initial increase in reserves of $1000 causes deposits to increase by a multiple of that initial increase will be set in motion.

In describing this process it will be convenient to begin by making some simplifying assumptions. First, we will continue to assume that the public's holdings of currency remain unchanged. None of the initial increase in the monetary base, which was in the form of bank reserves, is siphoned off into increased currency holdings by the public. Second, we assume that the quantities of time and savings deposits are fixed. There are legal reserve requirements on time and savings deposits as well as on demand deposits, and if the quantities of such deposits change, some of the newly created bank reserves would be channeled into reserves to back these new deposits. We ignore this complication for now. Finally, we assume that the banking system's *desired* level of excess reserves is constant. The effect of altering this assumption is also examined below.

Having made these assumptions, we are ready to describe the process of deposit creation. The Chase Manhattan Bank in our example has $800 in excess reserves which it wants to convert into earnings assets. The bank can do this by either increasing loans or purchasing additional securities. Neither of these actions will produce any lasting effect on the liability side of the ledger; there is no effect on the *equilibrium* level of Chase Manhattan's demand deposits. If the bank buys a new security, this clearly does not change deposits. If the bank makes a loan, temporarily it may credit the amount of the loan to the checking account of the customer, and this would increase deposits. But the customer would not borrow just to increase his checking account balance. Suppose that the loan was to a consumer who used the proceeds to buy a new boat. The consumer pays for the boat with a check drawn on Chase Manhattan, and when this transaction is completed, deposits at Chase will have returned to their initial level (before the loan).

The consumer's check will be deposited in the account of the firm that sold him the boat. This firm's checking account balance, let us suppose at the Bank of New York, increases by $800. The Bank of New York presents the check to Chase for payment—the check clears through the Federal Reserve System—which results in a transfer of funds from Chase's account at the New York Federal Reserve Bank to the account of the Bank of New York at that Federal Reserve Bank. At this point the $800 in excess reserves is eliminated from the Chase Manhattan Bank's balance sheet—the banks reserve deposits have declined by $800. The Chase Manhat-

Table 15.6
Final Effects on Chase Manhattan Bank's Balance Sheet from a $1000 Open Market Purchase

Assets			Liabilities	
Reserves		+200	Demand deposits	+1000
Required reserves	+200			
Loans		+800		
Total assets		+1000	Total liabilities	+1000

tan Bank's balance sheet is now at its final position, where the effects of the open market operation are as shown in Table 15.6. On the liability side, demand deposits are higher by the $1000 deposit of the original individual who sold a government security to the Federal Reserve. Required reserves are higher by $200 (= 0.20 × 1000). Earning assets of the bank, loans in our example, have risen by $800.

While we are now finished with Chase Manhattan's balance sheet, the process of deposit creation is not complete. Table 15.7 shows the effects on the Bank of New York's balance sheet to this point. Because of the deposit by the boat manufacturer, demand deposits are up by $800. After the check has cleared through the Federal Reserve System, $800 has been transferred to the Bank of New York's reserve account. Thus reserves are increased by $800, of which only $160 (0.20 × 800) is required to back the increase in deposits. The Bank of New York, finding itself with $640 of excess reserves, will attempt to convert them into interest earnings asset by proceeding in the same manner as did Chase Manhattan. The bank will increase its volume of loans or buy additional securities.

Suppose in this case that the bank uses the $640 of excess reserves to purchase a security, a corporate bond, for example. The final position of the Bank of New York will be as shown in Table 15.8. Deposits remain up by $800, increasing required reserves by $160. As soon as the Bank of New York pays for the security with a check drawn upon itself and that check clears the Federal Reserve System, the bank's excess reserves will be zero. Earning assets will be increased by $640 and the bank will be in equilibrium.

Table 15.7
Initial Effects on the Bank of New York's Balance Sheet

Assets			Liabilities	
Reserves		+800	Demand deposits	+800
Required reserves	+160			
Excess reserves	+640			
Total assets		+800	Total liabilities	+800

Table 15.8	Assets			Liabilities	
Final Effects on the Bank of New York's Balance Sheet	Reserves		+160	Demand deposits	+800
	Required reserves	+160			
	Securities		+640		
	Total assets		+800	Total liabilities	+800

The process of deposit creation continues beyond this point, however, because the individual who sold the corporate bond to the Bank of New York has deposited the proceeds of the check he received for $640 in his demand deposit account at some other commercial bank. That bank now has excess reserves of $512, the $640 minus the $128 of reserves required to back the deposit. Another round of deposit creation will ensue.

The initial increase of $1000 in reserves began a process of deposit creation whereby deposits of $1000, then $800, then $640, then $512 resulted from the banking system's attempts to convert what were initially excess reserves into earning assets. The individual bank's attempt to rid itself of excess reserves, under the assumptions made to this point, simply transfers the reserves to another bank, together with creating a deposit at that bank. The newly created deposits increase required reserves by 20 percent of the increase in deposits; thus at each round in the process the newly created deposit is 20 percent smaller than for the previous round. The process will stop when all the new reserves have been absorbed in required reserves. With a $1000 increase in reserves and a required reserve ratio of 20 percent, the new equilibrium will be reached when the quantity of demand deposits has increased by $5000 ($1000 = 0.20 × $5000). At this point required reserves will have increased by $1000. There will no longer be any excess reserves in the system. The expansion of bank credit and resulting creation of new bank deposits will come to an end.

More generally, an increase in reserves (R) of ΔR will cause deposits to increase until required reserves have increased by an equal amount. The increase in required reserves is equal to the increase demand in deposits times the required reserve ratio on demand deposits; that is,

$$\text{increase in required reserves} = \text{rr}_d \Delta D \qquad (15.1)$$

where rr_d is the required reserve ratio and ΔD is the increase in demand deposits. For equilibrium, then,

$$\text{increase in reserves} = \text{increase in required reserves} \qquad (15.2)$$

$$\Delta R = \text{rr}_d \Delta D \qquad (15.3)$$

EXTENSIONS OF THE MODELS

Therefore,

$$\Delta D = \frac{1}{rr_d} \Delta R \qquad (15.4)$$

The increase in deposits will be a multiple ($1/rr_d$) of the increase in reserves. In our previous example with ΔR equal to 1000 and rr_d equal to 0.2 (a 20 percent reserve requirement), we have, from equation (15.4),

$$\Delta D = \frac{1}{0.2}(1000) = 5000 \qquad (15.5)$$

the result reached above.

From (15.4) we can also define a *deposit multiplier*, giving the increase in deposits per unit increase in bank reserves:

$$\frac{\Delta D}{\Delta R} = \frac{1}{rr_d} \qquad (15.6)$$

The deposit multiplier for the simple case considered so far is equal to the reciprocal of the required reserve ratio on demand deposits. For rr_d equal to 0.2 in our example, the deposit multiplier would be 5. Demand deposits increase by 5 dollars for each one-dollar increase in reserves.

This simple form of the deposit multiplier results from the simplifying assumptions made above and will have to be modified when we relax those assumptions. What follows generally is that given the system of fractional legal reserve requirements, an increase in reserves will cause deposits to increase by a multiple of the reserve increase. All of our analysis can of course be reversed to consider the effects of an open market sale of securities which will lower bank reserves and begin a process of deposit contraction. Also note that a similar process of deposit creation would result from a reduction in the Federal Reserve discount rate, which would increase borrowed reserves, or from a lowering of reserve requirements, which although it would not change total reserves would create excess reserves in the banking system at the initial level of deposits. The balance sheet changes for such policy actions would be somewhat different than those shown in Tables 15.5 to 15.8, but the general effect would be the same. Both of these additional expansionary policies would cause both bank credit and bank deposits to increase.

The relationship just derived between reserves and deposits can be restated as a relationship between the monetary base (MB) and the money supply (M^s). The monetary base is equal to currency held by the public plus bank reserves. Thus far we are assuming that currency holdings of the public are constant, so that the change in the monetary base equals the change in reserves ($\Delta \text{MB} = \Delta R$). The change in the *money supply* will in this case be just equal to the change in bank deposits, again since currency held by the public is held constant ($\Delta D = \Delta M^s$). As a consequence we can write a *money multiplier* giving the increase in the money supply per unit increase in the monetary base:

$$\frac{\Delta M^s}{\Delta \text{MB}} = \frac{\Delta D}{\Delta R} = \frac{1}{\text{rr}_d} \tag{15.7}$$

which in this simple case is just equal to the deposit multiplier. This expression will also require modification when we relax some of our simplifying assumptions, and generally the money multiplier will not be equal in value to the deposit multiplier. It will generally be the case that a given increase in the monetary base will cause the money stock to rise by a multiple of the increase in the base.

As described so far, the process of deposit or money creation must seem somewhat mechanical. New doses of reserves are converted via simple multipliers into new deposits and the money supply increases. Simple models such as that developed in this section are helpful in explaining the close relationship between bank deposits and bank reserves but tell us little about the economic processes behind the process of deposit and money creation. Before going on to more complex models of deposit creation, it is worthwhile to stop and consider the nature of these processes.

When banks find themselves with excess reserves following a Federal Reserve open market purchase of securities, they attempt to convert those excess reserves into interest-earning assets. They attempt to expand bank credit by making more loans and purchasing securities. To increase the volume of its lending, a bank offers lower interest rates on loans and perhaps adopts lower standards of credit worthiness. In buying securities, banks bid up the prices of such securities; they bid down the interest rate on securities. Among the earning assets banks buy are mortgages; thus in times of credit expansion, mortgage interest rates will also fall. Federal Reserve open market purchases, as well as other expansionary policy actions that increase bank reserves, will therefore lead to credit expansion and a general decline in interest rates. This is the other side of the process of deposit and money creation.

Deposit Creation: More General Cases

In addition to possibly obscuring the economic process involved, simple models such as that in the preceding section overstate the degree of precision in the relationship between Federal Reserve policy actions and resulting changes in the stock of deposits or money. In this section we take note of some of the complexities involved in this relationship.

First consider the effect of modifying our assumption that the public's currency holdings are constant throughout the process of deposit creation. Instead, assume, as seems likely to be the case, that as the quantity of demand deposits grows, the public also chooses to hold an increased amount of currency. In this case some of the increase that occurs in the monetary base due to an open market purchase will end up not as increased bank reserves, but as an increase in the public's holding of currency.

Suppose for simplicity that the public holds a fixed ratio of currency to demand deposits, for example one dollar in currency per four dollars in demand deposits ($CU/D = 0.25$, where CU denotes currency). Now, the individual who in our example sold the $1000 bond to the Federal Reserve will not deposit the full $1000 in his checking account. He will deposit only $800, keeping the remaining $200 as currency ($200/800 = 0.25 = CU/D$). Bank reserves will increase by only $800 as a result of the $1000 open market operation. Further, at each stage in the deposit creation, as demand deposits rise the public's demand for currency will increase in order to maintain a constant currency/demand deposit ratio. There will at each stage be a further leakage from bank reserves into currency.

As a consequence of the fact that reserves will increase by less, the increase in deposits for a given increase in the monetary base will be lower when the public's holding of currency rises than for the case where it is fixed. The increase in the money stock will also be lower. This follows because each dollar of the base that is part of bank reserves backs a multiple number of dollars in deposits— five in our example of a 20 percent reserve requirement—while each dollar of the monetary base that ends up as currency held by the public is simply *one* dollar of the money stock. The more of the increase in the base that goes into bank reserves, the higher will be the money multiplier.

Relaxing our assumption that banks do not change their desired holdings of excess reserves provides an additional reason to expect that the expression derived in the preceding subsection $(1/rr_d)$ is an overstatement of the true money multiplier. It appears likely that as deposits rise, banks will increase their excess reserves. Excess reserves are held as a buffer against unexpected deposit flows, and as deposits increase, so does the potential volume of such deposit flows. Additionally, as we have discussed, the process of deposit expansion leads to a drop in the level of interest rates. The cost of holding excess reserves is the interest forgone by not using these funds to purchase interest-bearing assets. As the interest rate falls, this cost becomes lower. Banks are likely to respond by holding more excess reserves.

If some of the increase in bank reserves ends up as new excess reserves, the quantity of deposits created by a given increase in reserves will be smaller than for the case where excess reserves are constant. Generally, the higher the bank's desired excess reserve/demand deposit ratio (ER/D), the lower will be the money multiplier.

Next consider the effect of modifying the assumption that the public's holdings of time and savings deposits are fixed. Again, the more realistic assumption would be that the public increases its time and savings deposits together with its holdings of demand deposits. Since there are legal reserve requirements on time and savings deposits, if the public increases its holdings of such deposits, some of the increase in the monetary base will go to reserves to back up these deposits and less will be available to support an increase in demand deposits. The effect of this on the money multiplier depends on how money is defined.

If the money stock is narrowly defined to include only currency plus demand deposits (M1), then the money multiplier will be smaller for the case where time deposits and savings deposits increase than for the case where they are fixed. This follows since with some reserves now going to satisfy reserve requirements on new time and savings deposits, fewer are available to support an increase in demand deposits. As a consequence, the increase in demand deposits and in the narrowly defined money stock per unit increase in the base is reduced.[5] If, however, we define money more broadly to include time and savings accounts (M2, for example), then the larger the proportion of the increase in deposits going into time and savings deposits, the *larger* will be the value of the money multiplier (defined as $\Delta M2/\Delta MB$). The reason for this is that the required reserve ratios for time and savings deposits are lower than for demand deposits. The larger the proportion of the increase in deposits that occurs in the deposits with the lowest required reserve ratio, the greater is the increase in deposits that can be supported by a given increase in the monetary base.

The discussion in this subsection leads to the conclusion that the expression for the money multiplier will be much more complex than the one derived in the preceding subsection. We would instead expect that the money multiplier (*m*) *for the narrowly defined money stock (M1)* would be a function of the following form:

$$m = \frac{\Delta M^s}{\Delta MB} = m(\mathrm{rr}_d, \mathrm{CU}/D, \mathrm{ER}/D, \frac{\mathrm{SD} + \mathrm{TD}}{D}, \mathrm{rr}_{sd}, \mathrm{rr}_{td}) \quad (15.8)$$

[5]Once the changes in reserve requirements specified by the Monetary Control Act of 1980 are fully phased in, only nonpersonal time deposits (e.g. deposits held by corporations or state and local governments) will be subject to legal reserve requirements. Consequently, increases in only such nonpersonal time deposits will necessarily siphon off reserves that might otherwise support checkable deposits that are included in M1.

EXTENSIONS OF THE MODELS

The money multiplier (m) would depend negatively on the required reserve ratio on demand deposits (rr_d) as before, but on the following additional factors as well:

1. The public's desired currency/demand deposit ratio (CU/D); as explained above, the higher the currency/demand deposit ratio, the lower the money multiplier.
2. The excess reserve/demand deposit ratio (ER/D); as also explained above, the higher the bank's desired excess reserve/demand deposit ratio, the lower the money multiplier.
3. The public's desired ratio of savings plus time deposits to demand deposits [(SD + TD)/D]; the higher the public's desired ratio of savings plus time deposits to demand deposits, the greater the proportion of the increase in the monetary base that will become required reserves for time and savings deposits and, hence, not be available to support an increase in demand deposits. Since we are defining the money multiplier for the narrowly defined money stock, any increase in this variable lowers the money multiplier.
4. The required reserve ratios for savings and time deposits (rr_{sd}, rr_{td}); the higher the required reserve ratios on savings and time deposits, the more reserves will be needed to support any increase in savings or time deposits and, hence, not be available to back an increase in demand deposits. Thus an increase in either rr_{sd} or rr_{td} will lower the money multiplier.

If the value of the money multiplier (m) in (15.8) were known, the Federal Reserve could then predict the change in the money stock that would result from a given change in the monetary base:

$$\Delta M^s = m \, \Delta \text{MB} \qquad (15.9)$$

The same information can be expressed slightly differently by defining a *money supply function* giving the supply of money corresponding to a given level of the monetary base:

$$M^s = m \cdot \text{MB} \qquad (15.10)$$

Equation (15.10) would replace our previous assumption that the money stock was given exogenously. Prior to introducing the complications discussed in this subsection, a money supply function in the form of (15.10) would still imply that the money stock was exogenously set by the Federal Reserve as long as the monetary base was controlled by the Federal Reserve. This is true because prior to our discussion in this section, the money multiplier (m) depended only on the required reserve ratio on demand deposits, which was set exogenously by the Federal Reserve. With both the monetary base and the money multiplier set by the Federal Reserve, there would be no role for the public or the banking system in determining the money supply. The more complicated expression for the money multiplier given by (15.8) contains variables determined by the (nonbank) public [CU/D and (SD + TD)/D] and by the banking system (ER/D), implying that even if the Federal Reserve set the monetary base exogenously, the level of the money supply will not be exogenous; it will depend to a degree on the behavior of the public and banking system.

15.3 WHO CONTROLS THE MONEY STOCK?

What, then, can be said about the relative importance of the Federal Reserve, the banking system, and the nonbank public in determining the money stock? To begin with, let us continue to assume that the monetary base is set exogenously by the Federal Reserve. In that case, the reason that the Federal Reserve would not have perfect control over the money stock would be because, as just explained, the value of the money multiplier depends to some extent on the behavior of the banking system and the public. How great is the loss of control due to these sources?

If we are considering a short period of time, one to two months for example, it would appear that uncertainty about the money multiplier results in a serious loss of money stock control for the Federal Reserve. The variables that affect the money stock and are outside the direct control of the Federal Reserve—the currency/deposit ratio, the excess reserve/deposit ratio, and the saving plus time deposit/demand deposit ratio—cannot be predicted with great precision in the short run. Notice that although in our discussion we made simplifying assumptions such as a fixed currency/deposit ratio, in fact the currency, excess reserve, and savings plus time deposit/demand deposits ratios are *variables* that depend on the decisions of the banking system and public. These decisions depend in turn on the behavior of other economic variables in the system. To give some examples, the excess reserve/deposit ratio will depend on the cost of holding such reserves—the interest rate that could be earned on loans and securities. The savings plus time deposit/demand deposit ratio will depend on the interest rates paid on savings and time deposits relative to other market rates, as well as on various factors affecting the growth of NOW accounts, ATS accounts, and so on. Precise control of the money stock in the very short run would require highly accurate predictions of these variables, among others. Although no one would deny that movements in the monetary base are an important determinant of money growth from month to month, uncertainty concerning

EXTENSIONS OF THE MODELS

short-run variations in the money multiplier makes precise monetary control quite difficult over such a time horizon.[6]

When considering a longer period, six months to one year for example, difficulties in monetary control due to uncertainty about the money multiplier are less serious. Although the Federal Reserve may not be able to predict in a given month the response of the money stock to a given change in the monetary base, the policymakers can monitor the month-to-month behavior of the money stock and make the adjustments in the monetary base required to achieve the desired average rate of growth in the money stock over a period of several months. To see how this might be done, consider the following example.

Suppose that the Federal Reserve wished to achieve a growth rate for the money stock (M1) of 5 percent for a given calendar year. If no change in the money multiplier was expected, the Federal Reserve could attempt to achieve this target by increasing the monetary base at an annual rate of 5 percent. Assume that in February of the year in question, the data received show that for January, with a 5 percent growth (all growth rates expressed at annual rates) in the monetary base, the money stock grew by only 1 percent. There had been a fall in the money multiplier. The Federal Reserve could then in February and the following months cause the monetary base to grow by more than 5 percent to offset this fall in the money multiplier. If the action taken in one month was insufficient to get the money stock back on the 5 percent growth path, a further adjustment to the growth rate in the monetary base could be made. Arthur Okun has quoted P. T. Barnum as saying that the trick to keeping a lamb in a cage with a lion is to have a large reserve supply of lambs. The Federal Reserve's control over the money stock rests on a similar supply of actions that can be taken to offset any undesired movements stemming from other sources. Even over periods as long as six months or one year, such control is not perfect. If the Federal Reserve set a target growth rate for the money stock of 5 percent and concentrated all its policy actions on achieving that target, we might end up with growth

---

[6]There is one additional difficulty in short-run control of the money stock which should be mentioned. Even if the Federal Reserve is trying to control the monetary base—the assumption we are making here—it will not be possible to do so with absolute precision on a month-to-month basis. One reason for this is that the monetary base includes borrowed reserves. Although the Federal Reserve can influence bank borrowing via changes in the discount rate and can offset any undesired changes in borrowed reserves through open market operations, there will be some time lags before such adjustments are made. As a consequence, month-to-month movements in the monetary base will to some extent depend on the borrowing behavior of commercial banks as well as on the policy actions of the Federal Reserve.

of 4.8 percent or 5.2 percent. We would not, however, end up with 3 percent or 7 percent.

In actual historical experience the Federal Reserve has announced growth-rate targets for six to twelve month periods and has ended up wide of the mark. If, as is argued above, the Federal Reserve *can* control the money stock with a reasonable degree of precision, what explains the failure of the Federal Reserve to hit its own pre-announced money growth targets? Why in practice has the Federal Reserve not closely controlled the money stock over much of the recent past?

Above we assumed that the Federal Reserve controlled the monetary base and *concentrated its policy actions* on achieving a money stock target. The reason monetary growth targets are not achieved in practice is quite simply that the Federal Reserve is unwilling to concentrate all its efforts on this one policy goal. The Federal Reserve has also been interested in the behavior of other financial market variables, the most important being interest rates. Conflicts arise between hitting target levels of money stock growth and achieving desirable behavior of these other variables. When such conflicts arise, the Federal Reserve has often chosen to miss the money growth target rather than accept what is viewed as the cost of hitting such targets, the resulting undesirable behavior of interest rates. We consider this choice between money stock targets and interest rate targets at greater length in Chapter 19, but the essence of the conflict between achieving target levels of the money stock and desirable behavior of the interest rate can be explained at this point.

Figure 15.1*a* reproduces an earlier graph showing the demand and supply schedules (M^s and M^d) for money intersecting to determine the equilibrium interest rate r^*. We assume as we did earlier that the money supply is exogenous. In terms of the analysis of this chapter, we assume that the Federal Reserve uses control of the monetary base to achieve its money stock target (M^*). Also suppose that the equilibrium interest rate r^* shown in Figure 15.1*a* is regarded by the Federal Reserve as the desired level of the interest rate.

Now consider the effects of shifts in the money demand schedule, as shown in Figure 15.1*b*. Such shifts could result from changes in income, which change money demand for a given interest rate. Alternatively, such shifts could represent the effects of actual shifts in the money demand *function*—changes in the amount of money demanded at given levels of both income and the interest rate—due, for example, to the development of the new money substitutes discussed in Chapter 14. Such changes in the demand for money might shift the money demand schedule to positions such as M_1^d (an increase in money demand) or M_2^d (a decline

Figure 15.1

Interest Rate Versus
Money Stock Control

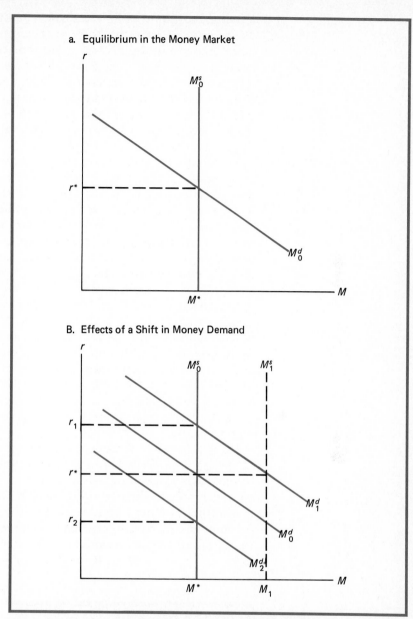

a. Equilibrium in the Money Market

B. Effects of a Shift in Money Demand

Part *a* shows money market equilibrium with interest rate r^* and level of the money stock M^*. If, however, as shown in Part *b* the money demand function shifts from M_0^d to either M_1^d or M_2^d, then if the Federal Reserve keeps the money stock at M_0^s the interest rate must diverge from the target level r^*. Alternatively, the Federal Reserve could accommodate the shift in money demand, to M_1^d, for example, by causing the money stock to move to M_1^s. In this case the money stock target, M^*, will not be achieved.

in money demand) in Figure 15.1b. What will the Federal Reserve do in response to such shifts? If they stick to their money stock target and maintain the money stock at M^*, the interest rate will move away from r^*, the Federal Reserve's desired level for the interest rate. A decline in money demand (a shift in the money demand schedule from M_0^d to M_2^d) would cause the interest rate to fall to r_2; an increase in money demand (a shift in the money demand schedule from M_0^d to M_1^d) would cause an undesirable rise in the interest rate to r_1.

The Federal Reserve can prevent or mitigate these undesirable movements in the interest rate only by changing the monetary base, and, hence, the money supply. In the case of an increase in money demand, the Federal Reserve could, by increasing the monetary base, move the money supply to the level given by the M_1^s schedule in Figure 15.1b. This increase in the money stock would produce equilibrium in the money market at the desired interest rate r^*. The Federal Reserve would, however, miss the money stock target; the money stock would be M_1, which is above M^*. This is a case where the Federal Reserve is *accommodating* the public's increased demand for money. The Federal Reserve supplies new money balances in order to keep the increased demand for money from pushing up the interest rate. Notice that with such accommodation, neither the money supply nor the monetary base are any longer being set exogenously. They are responding to the behavior of the public.

To the degree that the Federal Reserve engages in such accommodation, the public will have a large role in determining the value of the money stock even over periods of six months to a year. In the extreme case where the Federal Reserve "pegs" the interest rate at a fixed level for a long period of time, as was done in the United States in the early post–World War II period,[7] the monetary authority plays a completely passive role in the money supply process, having to supply whatever amount of money is required to maintain the desired level of the interest rate.

15.4 SUMMARY

Prior to this chapter we made the assumption that the money supply was set exogenously by the monetary authority. In the first sections of this chapter we considered the way in which the U.S. monetary authority, the Federal Reserve, controls the monetary

[7]See the discussion in Section 9.2.

EXTENSIONS OF THE MODELS

base (currency plus bank reserve deposits) and the linkages between control of the monetary base and control of the money stock. What we have seen is that due to uncertainty about the value of the money multiplier, precise Federal Reserve control of the money stock in the very short run (one or two months) is quite difficult. The behavior of the public and the banking system will have a substantial influence on such short-term variations in the money stock. Over longer periods (six months to a year, for example), the Federal Reserve can control the money stock with reasonable precision by altering the monetary base to offset any undesirable changes in the money stock due to the behavior of the banking system or (nonbank) public. When the Federal Reserve does not control the money stock over such longer periods, the failure to do so is one of will rather than ability.

The reason why the Federal Reserve does not always concentrate solely on controlling the money stock is that to do so would result in what the Federal Reserve regards as undesirable fluctuations in the interest rate. To prevent such undesirable interest rate movements, the Federal Reserve at times accommodates changes in the public's demand for money with the effect that the monetary base and the money stock are no longer exogenous. The reasons for the Federal Reserve's concern over fluctuations in interest rates and the relative desirability of controlling interest rates or the money stock are topics we return to in Chapter 19 when we analyze the Federal Reserve's operating procedures in more detail.

Review Questions

1   What are the major policymaking bodies within the Federal Reserve System? Explain their composition and functions.

2   Suppose that the Federal Reserve wants to increase bank reserves. Explain the various measures which could be taken to achieve that end. In each case illustrate the linkage between the Federal Reserve's policy action and the level of bank reserves.

3   What is the maximum amount of the increase in demand deposits that can result from a $1000 increase in legal reserves if the required reserve ratio for demand deposits is 25 percent? Explain exactly how this increase comes about in a commercial banking system. Give several reasons why the actual increase may fall short of the theoretical maximum.

4   Suppose that the level of the required reserve ratio on demand deposits were 0.10. Also assume that the public's hold-

ings of currency and savings plus time deposits are constant, as are bank's desired excess reserves. Analyze the effects on the money stock of a $1000 open market sale of securities by the Federal Reserve. In your answer, explain the role of the commercial banking system in the adjustment to this monetary policy action.

5 Explain the concept of the money multiplier. What factors determine the size of the money multiplier?

6 Within the IS–LM curve model used in Chapters 6 and 7, show how income and the interest rate will be affected by each of the following changes.
   a. An increase in the required reserve ratio for demand deposits.
   b. An open market sale of securities by the Federal Reserve.
   c. A decrease in the Federal Reserve discount rate.

7 In the text it was argued that the Federal Reserve would find it very difficult to exert close control of the rate of growth in the money stock over very short periods but would be able to achieve much greater control over somewhat longer periods. What are the nature of the difficulties in short-run monetary control, for example on a month-to-month basis? Why are these difficulties less serious over longer periods?

8 Within the IS–LM curve model, illustrate the nature of the conflict the Federal Reserve faces between trying to control the money stock and trying to achieve "desirable" levels of the interest rate.

Selected Readings

BALBACH, ANATOL, and BURGER, ALBERT, "Derivation of the Monetary Base," Federal Reserve Bank of St. Louis Review, 58 (November 1976), pp. 2–8. Reprinted in Thomas Havrilesky and John Boorman, Current Issues in Monetary Theory and Policy, 2nd ed. Arlington Heights, Ill.: AHM Publishing Corp., 1980.

CACY, J. A., "The Choice of a Monetary Policy Instrument," Federal Reserve Bank of Kansas City Economic Review, May 1978, pp. 17–35.

HAVRILESKY, THOMAS, and BOORMAN, JOHN, Monetary Macroeconomics. Arlington Heights, Ill.: AHM Publishing Corp., 1978, Chaps. 1–3.

JORDAN, JERRY, "Elements of Money Stock Determination," Federal Reserve Bank of St. Louis Review, 51 (October 1969), pp. 10–19. Reprinted in Thomas Havrilesky and John Boorman, Current Issues in Monetary

Theory and Policy, 2nd ed. Arlington Heights, Ill.: AHM Publishing Corp., 1980.

chapter 16

The changes in output discussed in previous chapters were short-run changes in actual output for a given level of potential or capacity output. In this chapter we consider the determinants of output movements over longer periods of time. First, we examine the determinants of the long-run equilibrium rate of growth in output. Next, we look at factors that determine the time path of output in what can be called the intermediate run, a period too long to be accurately represented by the short-run models of Part II, but not necessarily a period characterized by the assumptions we will make concerning long-run equilibrium growth. This intermediate period analysis might, for example, ask which factors will be important in determining the growth rate for the United States over the decade of the 1980s.

When dealing with the short run, we have seen in previous chapters that there is much controversy over the relative importance to be attached to aggregate supply and demand as determinants of output. In the case of long-run equilibrium economic growth, it is clear that supply factors—factors determining the growth of potential income—are of predominant importance. Substantial income growth over long periods has been due to growth of factor supplies (the labor force and capital stock) and to changes in technology which increase output per unit of factors employed. When we consider periods of intermediate length we will see that there are again differences of opinion between those who believe that demand factors still play a role and those who emphasize the importance of the supply side.

436

THE SUPPLY SIDE: INTERMEDIATE- AND LONG-TERM ECONOMIC GROWTH

We begin with an analysis of long-run equilibrium growth, what is called "steady-state growth" (Section 16.1), and then consider output determination over intermediate-run periods (Section 16.2). This chapter concludes with an analysis of the Reagan administration's supply-side policies to influence economic growth over such intermediate-run periods—policies that have been termed "Reaganomics" (Section 16.3).

16.1 LONG-RUN STEADY-STATE GROWTH

Growth and the Aggregate Production Function

Over the period 1870–1969, national income in the United States increased at an annual rate of 3.7 percent. Per capita output increased at an annual rate of 1.9 percent. What factors account for such sustained growth? One way to approach this question employs the notion of the aggregate production function seen in previous chapters. The aggregate production function relates the level of output to the level of factor inputs.

For the purposes of this chapter, the aggregate production function can be written as

$$Y = A(t)F(K, N) \tag{16.1}$$

Equation (16.1) differs from our previous expressions for the aggregate production function in two respects. First, there is the additional term $A(t)$. This term represents technological change, which is taken to simply depend on time; that is, as time passes, the $A(t)$ term will increase, meaning that more output is produced for a given amount of factor inputs. In (16.1) the $A(t)$ term enters multiplicatively. With this specification, technological change is assumed not to affect the relative marginal productivities of the two factors, as determined by the $F(K, N)$ part of the production function. In other words, technological change results in equal increases in the productiveness of both factors. Such technological change is termed *neutral* (favoring neither capital or labor) technological change. Robert Solow, in a study of shifts in the aggregate production function over time, found evidence that for the U.S. technological change had in fact been neutral. We will restrict our analysis to this case.[1]

A second difference between (16.1) and previous specifications of the production function in Part II is the absence of the bar over the K variable in (16.1), indicating that here we are not assuming that the capital stock is constant. This reflects the fact that we are now dealing with the long run.

On the basis of (16.1) we can follow Solow's method in the above-mentioned study and write the following specification for the growth in output over time:

$$\frac{\dot{Y}}{Y} = \frac{\dot{A}}{A} + w_k\frac{\dot{K}}{K} + w_n\frac{\dot{N}}{N} \qquad (16.2)$$

where the dot over a variable indicates the time rate of change in that variable (e.g., $\dot{N}$ is the rate at which the labor force is increasing). Equation (16.2) specifies the proportional rate of increase in output ($\dot{Y}/Y$) as depending on the proportional rates of technological change ($\dot{A}/A$) and the proportional rates of change in the capital stock and number of workers employed ($\dot{K}/K$ and $\dot{N}/N$). The weights (w_k, w_n) attached to these latter two variables are their shares in national output, reflecting their importance in the production process. From (16.2), the growth in output can be seen to depend [as should also be apparent from (16.1)] on the rate at which technological progress occurs over time and the rate at which factor supplies are growing over time.

If the production function given by (16.1) exhibits what are termed *constant returns to scale*, it can be written in an alternative form that will provide some insights into the way in which each of the factors mentioned above enters into the growth process. Constant returns to scale mean that if all inputs rise in some propor-

[1]See Robert Solow, "Technical Change and the Aggregate Production Function," *Review of Economics and Statistics*, 39 (August 1957), pp. 312–20. We make further reference to Solow's findings below. Also relevant to the discussion here are Chaps. 1 and 2 of Solow's book, *Growth Theory* (London: Oxford University Press, 1970).

tion, output will increase in the same proportion. A doubling of the amount of both capital and labor used in production would, for example, just double the amount of output produced. In essence, we assume that the productivity of the inputs is not affected by scale. With constant returns to scale it will follow that for a given technology, fixing $A(t)$, output per worker (Y/N) will depend only on the amount of capital employed per worker, the capital/labor ratio. Letting q equal output per worker (Y/N) and k equal capital per worker (K/N), we can rewrite (16.1) as

$$\frac{Y}{N} = A(t)f\left(\frac{K}{N}\right)$$

or

$$q = A(t)f(k) \qquad (16.3)$$

where $f(k)$ is the function relating output per worker to the capital/labor ratio, for a given technology—what is often called the *intensive* form of the aggregate production function.

The relationship given by (16.3) is shown graphically in Figure 16.1. The state of technology is assumed to be given by $A(t_0)$, which fixes the position of the production function relating output per worker to capital per worker. As we move out to the right along the production function, output per worker increases with the increase in capital per worker (k). The shape of the production function in Figure 16.1 reflects the assumption that there are diminishing returns to increases in capital per worker. The increment to output per worker declines with successive increases in capital per worker.[2] At an assumed initial capital/labor ratio of k_0, output per worker would be q_0 in the figure.

Figure 16.2 illustrates the process of growth in output per worker between two points of time, t_0 and t_1. Technological change causes the production function to shift upward from $A(t_0)f(k)$ to $A(t_1)f(k)$. By itself, this technological change would increase output per worker, at the initial capital labor ratio k_0, from q_0 to q'_1 in Figure 16.2. Additionally, however, we assume that the capital/labor ratio increases over time, a process called *capital deepening*. This is illustrated in the graph by a movement to a capital/labor ratio of k_1. As a result, output per worker increases further, to q_1.

The framework illustrated in Figure 16.2 [the graph of (16.3)] suggests that the growth of output per worker is the result of two factors:

[2]Notice this assumption of diminishing returns to increases in capital intensity is not at odds with our assumption that the production process exhibits constant returns to scale. The latter assumption refers to the effect of proportional increases in *all* factors of production. Diminishing returns to increases in capital intensity refer to the effects of increases in the amount of one factor (capital) per unit of the other factor (labor).

Figure 16.1

Aggregate Production Function: Equation (16.3)

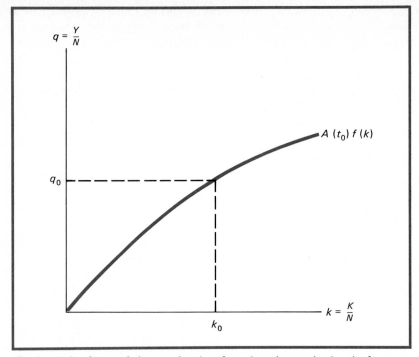

The *intensive* form of the production function shows the level of output per worker ($q = Y/N$) corresponding to each capital/labor ratio ($k = K/N$) for a given technology ($A(t_0)$). As the capital/labor ratio rises, output per worker increases but at a declining rate, reflecting diminishing returns to increases in capital per worker.

1. Technological change which increases output per worker for a given capital/labor ratio.
2. Capital deepening as the capital/labor ratio increases.

If we are considering the growth rate in total output, as opposed to output per worker, growth in the labor force is an additional source of growth.

Sources of Economic Growth

The analysis in the preceding subsection indicates that the economic factors that determine a country's long-run equilibrium growth rate will be those that affect the rate of technological change, labor force growth, and rate of capital formation. Influences on these magnitudes are the ultimate sources of economic growth. Here we will examine some estimates compiled by Edward Denison on the importance of the different sources of growth in the United States. First, however, a rather paradoxical result will be explained. This result is that the *long-run equilibrium* growth rate will *not* depend on a nation's saving rate ($s = S/Y$).

Figure 16.2
Growth in Output per
Worker

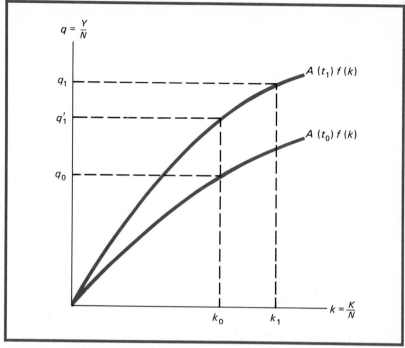

$q = \dfrac{Y}{N}$

q_1

q'_1

q_0

$A(t_1)\,f(k)$

$A(t_0)\,f(k)$

k_0 k_1

$k = \dfrac{K}{N}$

Output per worker increases from q_0 to q'_1 as the result of technological progress as the production function shifts upward from $A(t_0)\,f(k)$ to $A(t_1)\,f(k)$. There is a further increase in output per worker from q'_1 to q_1 as a result of an increase in the capital/labor ratio from k_0 to k_1.

The Equilibrium Growth Rate and the Saving Rate

The independence of a nation's growth rate from the saving rate is at first surprising, since one would expect the saving rate to affect the rate of capital formation and therefore the equilibrium growth rate. To see why the equilibrium growth rate does not depend on the saving rate, let us analyze the effect of an increase in the saving rate within the production function framework of the preceding section.

In Figure 16.3, assume that initially the saving rate is s_0, and that the economy is in equilibrium with the capital/labor ratio k_0 and output per worker equal to q_0. Consider the ray marked $1/\alpha_0$ coming from the origin and intersecting the production function at a level of output per worker equal to q_0. Each point along the line corresponds to a constant ratio of the variable on the vertical axis Y/N to the variable on the horizontal axis K/N, that is, a constant output/capital ratio, since

Figure 16.3
Effects of an Increase
in the Saving Rate

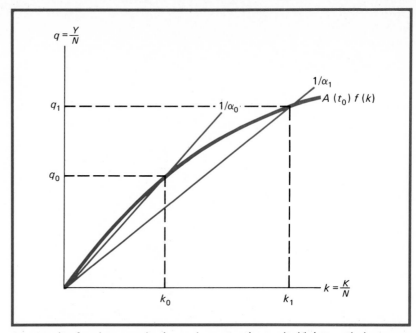

As a result of an increase in the saving rate, the capital/labor ratio increases
from k_0 to k_1. Output per worker increases from q_0 to q_1. The capital/
output ratio rises from α_0 to α_1. Once q_1 is reached there is no further
increase in output per worker. The initial equilibrium growth rate in output is restored.

$$\frac{Y}{N} \div \frac{K}{N} = \frac{Y}{K} = \frac{1}{\alpha}$$

where α is the capital/output ratio (K/Y). Initially, then, the
capital/output ratio is α_0 in Figure 16.3.

Now consider the effect of an increase in the saving rate to some
higher value s_1 (say 15 percent of income as opposed to 10 percent
of income). Initially, the economy was assumed to be in equilibrium at the capital/labor ratio k_0, which means that capital and
labor were growing at the same rate. With the increase in the saving rate, the rate of capital formation will initially increase. To see
this clearly we need to specify the relationship between capital
formation and the saving rate. The rate of capital formation can be
written as

$$\frac{\dot{K}}{K} = \frac{I}{K} - \frac{D}{K} \qquad (16.4)$$

where I is gross investment and D is depreciation. Since in long-
run equilibrium, output will grow as supply grows, we ignore the

problem of inadequate demand. We will assume that all saving (S) will be channeled into investment ($I = S$). Also assume that depreciation is a constant fraction (δ) of the capital stock. Using these facts, we can rewrite (16.4) as

$$\frac{\dot{K}}{K} = \frac{S}{K} - \frac{\delta K}{K} = \frac{sY}{K} - \frac{\delta K}{K} \tag{16.5}$$

where the second equality follows from the fact that saving is equal to the saving rate times the level of income. From (16.5) it follows that an increase in the saving rate (s) will initially increase the rate of capital formation.

Since the rate of capital formation has increased with no change in the rate of growth in the labor force, the capital/labor ratio will rise. A new equilibrium will be reached, as shown in Figure 16.3, at capital/labor ratio k_1 and with higher output per worker q_1. Once this adjustment is made, however, there will be no further increase in output per worker and since labor force growth is unchanged, the equilibrium growth rate will have returned to its initial level.

To see why this has happened, look at the ray labeled $1/\alpha_1$ originating at the origin and crossing the production function at the new level of output per worker q_1 in Figure 16.3. As explained above, each point along such a ray corresponds to a fixed capital/output ratio. The $1/\alpha_1$ ray is flatter than the initial $1/\alpha_0$ ray, indicating that the ratio of Y/N to K/N, the output/capital ratio is lower after the increase in the saving rate. The capital/output ratio (K/Y) is therefore *higher*. At a higher capital/output ratio, a larger saving rate ($s = S/Y$) is required just to maintain a constant growth rate in the capital stock. Once the capital/output ratio reaches α_1, capital formation will have returned to the initial equilibrium rate equal to the growth rate in the labor force. There will be no further increases in either output per worker or the capital/labor ratio.

The effect on the rate of economic growth will be as shown in Figure 16.4. Assume that the equilibrium growth rate for income is g. If the rise in the saving rate occurs at time t_0, the growth rate ($\dot{Y}/Y$) will rise temporarily as the economy moves from the initial level of output per worker q_0 to the higher level of output per worker q_1. As this new higher level of output per worker is reached, the growth rate will return to g, as shown at time t_1 in Figure 16.4. The increase in the saving rate causes a temporary period of faster growth but does not affect the equilibrium growth rate.

None of the above implies that the saving rate is unimportant in the growth process. The temporary period during which a change in the saving rate does affect the growth rate (from t_0 to t_1 in Figure 16.4) may be a substantial period in calendar time. In Section 16.2, when we discuss growth over intermediate-run time periods, we

Figure 16.4
Effect on the Growth
Rate from an Increase
in the Saving Rate

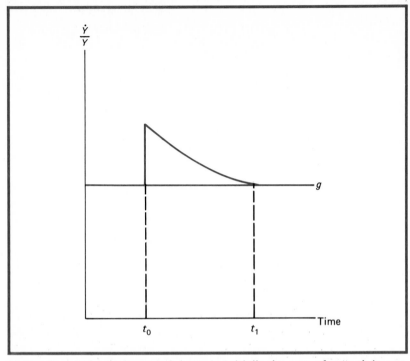

At the time t_0 the saving rate increases. Initially the rate of growth in output rises. This is the period where output per worker is increasing from q_0 to q_1 as shown in Figure 16.3. At time t_1, when output per worker has reached q_1 in Figure 16.3, the initial equilibrium growth rate g has been restored.

return to the discussion of the saving rate. Also, notice that even after the full adjustment to a change in the saving rate (after we reach t_1 in Figure 16.4 and k_1 and q_1 in Figure 16.3), the higher saving rate has resulted in a *permanent* increase in capital per worker and output per worker. An economy with a higher saving rate will therefore have a higher standard of living due to a more capital-intensive production process. The analysis above suggests only that when looking at the determinants of the long-run equilibrium rate of growth, the key factors will be the growth rate of the labor force and the rate of technological change.

Sources of Growth in the United States

Table 16.1 summarizes Edward Denison's findings concerning the sources of economic growth in the United States for the 1929–69

EXTENSIONS OF THE MODELS

Table 16.1

Denison's Estimates of the Sources of U.S. Economic Growth, 1929–1969: Contribution to Annual Growth Rate (Percentage Points)

Total factor input		1.40
Labor	1.05	
Capital	0.35	
Output per unit of input		1.82
Growth in national income		3.22

Source: Edward, Denison, *Accounting for United States Economic Growth: 1929–69* (Washington, D.C.: Brookings Institution, 1974), Table 8.2, p. 111.

period.[3] As the table indicates, national income grew at an *annual* percentage growth rate of 3.22 percent over the period. Of that growth, Denison attributes 1.40 percentage points to the growth of total factor inputs (capital and labor) and 1.82 percentage points to the growth of output per unit of factor input. Of the growth due to increases in the quantity of factor inputs, Denison attributes 1.05 percentage points of growth to growth in the labor input and 0.35 percentage point to growth in capital.

In Denison's measures, growth in the labor input is not just growth in the number of hours of labor input; it also includes growth due to an increase in the quality of the labor input. In fact, Denison attributes nearly half of the growth in national income due to growth in the labor input (0.49 of the 1.05 percentage points) to the higher educational achievements of the labor force. Capital's contribution to growth is rather small. In part, this is because not all increases in the quality of the capital input are considered growth due to capital formation, but rather some are counted as growth due to technological change. Only to the degree that quality increases result in a higher price for the capital good do they show up in Denison's measures of growth due to capital.

Growth in output per unit of factor input accounts for 1.82 percentage points of national income growth, or 57 percent of total growth according to Denison's estimates. Much of this, 1.11 percentage points, Denison attributes to advances in knowledge (other than those that show up in the measured capital and labor inputs), what we have been calling technological change. Denison attributes 0.43 percentage point of annual economic growth to "economies of scale," increases in factor output per unit of input due to increases in the scale of the production process. Denison finds then that rather than the *constant returns to scale* we as-

[3]The estimates in the table are Denison's estimates of the sources of growth in nonresidential business output, which does not encompass all of national income. These measures are presented instead of those for all of national income because the conceptual measures of input and output are best for this sector.

sumed in the preceding section, the U.S. economy has had *increasing returns to scale;* even given the state of technology, an increase in the quantity of inputs has produced more than a proportional increase in output.[4]

In analyzing the relative importance of different factors contributing to U.S. economic growth, we should not let the individual trees hide the forest, the forest in this case being the magnitude of the overall growth that has taken place. As Denison states:

> In 1929 production of goods and services in the United States exceeded that in any country during any previous year of world history, yet it was only one-fourth as large as U.S. production today [1974]. Thus three quarters of the entire increase in the annual output in this land area since its first habitation has been achieved in the brief period since 1929.

Unfortunately, in the course of our discussion of the growth process in intermediate-run periods, we will have to examine why U.S. economic growth has slowed dramatically since the close of the period covered by Denison's study.

16.2 DETERMINANTS OF OUTPUT GROWTH IN INTERMEDIATE-RUN PERIODS

In this section the factors that determine the growth of output over periods longer than the short-run periods analyzed in Part II, but not necessarily periods where the economy is in long-run equilibrium, are examined. The short-run period in our earlier analysis was characterized by the assumptions of a constant capital stock, a fixed labor force, and an unchanged technology. Output changes came as the level of employment varied. When considering changes in output in the intermediate run, perhaps over 10 to 15 years rather than over a cycle of perhaps 2 to 4 years, we are not entitled to these assumptions. Variations in the rates of capital formation, growth in the labor force due to growth in the working age population as well as changes in labor force participation rates, and variations in the rate of technological change will be factors determining growth rates of output in the intermediate run. What about the importance of demand? Economists who accept the classical or new classical view see little direct role for ag-

---

[4]The portion of annual growth in output per unit of factor input not explained by technological change or economies of scale is attributed by Denison to improved resource allocation and a number of additional minor influences, such as weather (in farming) and labor disputes.

gregate demand as a significant factor in determining the growth path of output over periods of intermediate length. In the original classical theory, aggregate demand did not even play a role in determining output in the short run. In the new classical model, only unanticipated demand changes affect output. Therefore, only deviations of demand growth from the average rather than the average rate of growth in demand over a period of 10 to 15 years itself would affect output.

The situation is somewhat different with respect to the monetarist and neo-Keynesian views. As we have explained, the long-run equilibrium growth rate is supply determined, but both the monetarists and neo-Keynesians believe that changes in demand may affect output over periods of several years. If we look at any 10- to 15-year period, the average rate of growth may be affected by demand induced recessions or expansions within that period. Demand factors might be used to explain why the growth rate of GNP was approximately zero for the 1929–39 decade of the Great Depression. Unstable growth in aggregate demand might also be used by a monetarist or neo-Keynesian to explain why growth in real GNP averaged 3.1 percent in the decade from 1969 to 1979, a period during which there were two recessions, compared with an annual growth of 4.3 percent in the 1960s, where there was a sustained expansion from February of 1961 to December of 1969.

It is the case, then, that, as with analysis of the short run, there is considerable disagreement over the relative importance of supply and demand in explaining the determination of output over intermediate-run periods. One position, which we will call the "supply-side" view, ascribes predominance to supply-side factors as determinants of the behavior of output. The other position, which can be termed the neo-Keynesian position, maintains, as James Tobin has said, that God gave us two eyes so that we could watch both supply and demand. Prior to examining both these views of output growth in the intermediate run, it will be useful to look back over the growth performance of the U.S. economy in recent years to see what phenomena both the supply-siders and neo-Keynesians are attempting to explain.

Recent U.S. Economic Growth

The growth experience of the United States in recent years is summarized in Table 16.2, which is drawn from a study by J. R. Norsworthy, M. J. Harper, and K. Kuntze. Our primary interest will be with growth in the period since 1965. Figures from 1948–65 are shown for purposes of comparison. The table shows that a slowdown in the growth rate in output occurred in the 1973–78 period. Real output rose at an annual rate of only 2.62 percent compared to average rates between 3.71 and 3.77 in the two previ-

**Table 16.2
Recent U.S. Growth
Experience**

Item	Annual Average Percentage Growth Rate		
	1948–65	1965–73	1973–78
1. Gross domestic output	3.71	3.77	2.62
2. Labor productivity	3.32	2.32	1.20
3. Total hours of labor input	0.38	1.44	1.42
4. Net capital stock	2.62	3.67	2.05

Source: J. R. Norsworthy, M. J. Harper, and K. Kuntze, "The Slowdown of Productivity Growth: Analysis of Some Contributing Factors," *Brookings Papers on Economic Activity*, No. 2, 1979, p. 390.

ous subperiods shown in the table. Looking at the second line of the table, it can be seen that the rate of growth in labor productivity (output per manhour in the private business sector) began to decline in the second subperiod in the table, 1965–73, and then declined further in the 1973–78 period. In the final years of the 1970s (figures not in the table) there was an absolute reduction in the *level* of labor productivity, a decline at an annual rate of 0.6 percent during the 1978–80 period.

Two factors appear to have delayed the decline in the growth rate in output until 1973. The first was the increase in the rate of growth of the labor input in the 1965–73 period, as shown in line 3 of the table. The second was the increase in the rate of capital formation during that period, which can be seen from line 4 in the table, showing the growth rate in the net capital stock. After 1973 the rate of capital formation declined and the growth rate in the labor input stabilized. The decline in productivity growth intensified and as a result the growth rate in output declined.

The facts that both supply-side economists and neo-Keynesians must try to explain are, therefore:

1. The U.S. growth rate has slowed in recent years (since 1973).
2. The decline has been accompanied by a fall in labor productivity which began as long ago as the mid-1960s.
3. Since 1973 there has also been a decline in the rate of capital formation.

Their differing explanations of these events reflect the different theories advanced by the supply-side economists and neo-Keynesians concerning the determinants of output growth in the intermediate run. These differing views of the factors determining growth lead to somewhat different policy conclusions although we will also find areas of agreement.

The Supply-Side Position

The theoretical origins of supply-side economics lie in the classical theories examined in Chapters 3 and 4. In particular, for the intermediate run, economists favorable to the supply-side position accept the classical view that output is determined by real variables on the supply side of the economy—growth of factor supplies and changes in technology. They also adhere to a classical view of the savings–investment process, where the interest rate is a crucial variable. Most fundamentally, the supply-side economists share the classical economists faith in the free enterprise capitalist system and dislike of government intervention in the economy. To analyze these ideas in more depth, we begin by stating some propositions of the supply-side economics. We then explain each proposition in terms of its classical roots and show how each applies to current U.S. economic problems and policies. In the next subsection we examine the neo-Keynesian critique of supply-side economics.

The following four propositions are important elements of supply-side economics.[5]

1. Output growth in the intermediate run is predominantly supply determined by rates of growth in factor supplies and the rate of technological change.
2. The rate of growth of the capital input is determined primarily by the incentives for saving and investment, the incentives being the *after-tax* returns to saving and investment.
3. The rate of growth in the labor input, while in the long run determined by demographic factors, can also be affected significantly by incentives, in this case by changes in the after-tax real wage.
4. Excessive government regulation of business has discouraged capital formation, contributed to the slowdown in the growth of labor productivity, and reduced the U.S. growth rate.

Let us examine each proposition in turn.

[5]Elements of the supply-side position may be found in: George Gilder, *Wealth and Poverty* (New York: Basic Books, 1981), especially Chaps. 4, 15–16; Paul Craig Roberts, "The Breakdown of the Keynesian Model," *The Public Interest*, 52 (Summer 1978), pp. 20–33; Arthur B. Laffer and Jan P. Seymour, eds., *The Economics of the Tax Revolt: A Reader* (New York: Harcourt Brace Jovanovich, 1979); and Laurence Meyer, ed., *The Supply-Side Effects of Economic Policy* (St. Louis: Center for the Study of American Business, 1981). The last two sources also contain critiques of the supply-side positions. Two useful analyses of supply-side economics are James Barth, "The Reagan Program for Economic Recovery: Economic Rationale (A Primer on Supply-Side Economics)," *Federal Reserve Bank of Atlanta Review*, September 1981, pp. 4–14; and John Tatom, "We Are All Supply-Siders Now!" *Federal Reserve Bank of St. Louis Review*, 63 (May 1981), pp. 18–30.

Intermediate-Run Output Growth Is Supply Determined

It was pointed out in Section 16.1 that in the long run, economic growth depends on supply factors. The supply-side economists believe that this is also true of growth in the intermediate run. Clearly, this would follow in the original classical model, where even in the short run output is supply determined. Intermediate-run growth in the classical model is illustrated in Figure 16.5. Output increases from y_0 to y_1 to y_2 as the supply curve shifts to the right, reflecting growth in factor supplies and changes in technology. If the aggregate demand schedule remains at y_0^d in Figure 16.5, prices will fall successively to P_1 and then P_2. If instead, demand is increased via growth in the money stock proportional to the growth in output, the price level can be maintained at P_0. Whichever is the case, the growth in output is determined solely by the size of the shift in the supply curve.

Figure 16.5
Intermediate-Run
Growth in the
Classical System

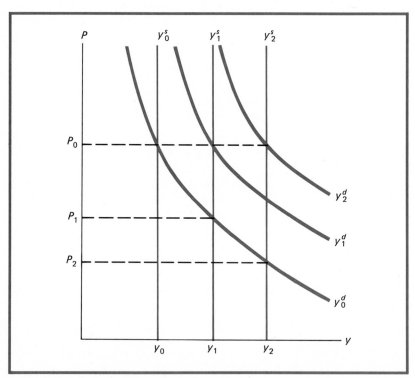

Growth in factor supplies shifts the supply curve to the right (from y_0^s to y_1^s then y_2^s). If demand is unchanged, the price level falls (from P_0 to P_1 then to P_2). Appropriate increases in the quantity of money would increase demand sufficiently (from y_0^d to y_1^d then to y_2^d) to maintain the initial equilibrium price level (P_0). In any case the growth of output is supply determined.

It would be overly restrictive to say that Figure 16.5 necessarily represents the supply-side view of intermediate-run growth. Some, perhaps most, supply-side economists would accept that demand plays a role in the *short-run* determination of income; the very short-run aggregate supply curve is upward sloping to the right rather than vertical as the classical economists would have drawn it. Consequently, to avoid short-run disruptions many supply-side economists would favor a policy strategy where demand was raised sufficiently to avoid the need for deflation (the fall in prices from P_0 to P_2 in Figure 16.5). Still, a central element in the supply-side position is that for *intermediate-run* periods, growth in output is supply and not demand determined.

A final element of the supply-side economists' view of the role of aggregate demand in the intermediate-run growth process is their belief that overexpansion of aggregate demand *retards* growth. They believe that the inflation caused by excessive aggregate demand growth inhibits investment and saving and weakens the work incentives to labor suppliers. As we will see below, in the supply-side economists' view, these negative growth effects of inflation are due to the fact that the tax system is not set up to adjust adequately for inflation.

The Levels of Saving and Investment Depend on After-Tax Rates of Return to These Activities

The supply-side economics stresses the importance of the after-tax rate of return to investment as a primary determinant of investment and therefore of the rate of capital formation. The after-tax rate of return is the pretax profit rate multiplied by 1 minus the rate at which profits are taxed. Similarly, the after-tax return for saving is believed by supply-side economists to be an important influence on the saving rate. Here the relevant rate of return is the after-tax *real* rate of interest, which equals the after-tax nominal interest rate (the nominal rate multiplied by 1 minus the rate at which interest payments are taxed) minus the expected inflation rate.

This view of saving and investment is again a very classical notion. Recall our discussion of the theory of interest in the classical model, as illustrated in Figure 16.6. The equilibrium (real) interest rate is shown to be determined by the intersection of the savings and investment schedules. This reflects the assumption we make for the moment that the government deficit $(g - t)$ is zero. Otherwise, government deficit bond financing would be an additional demand for loanable funds. The position of the investment schedule is shown to depend on cp, the pretax corporate profit rate, and

Figure 16.6

Classical Theory of Interest

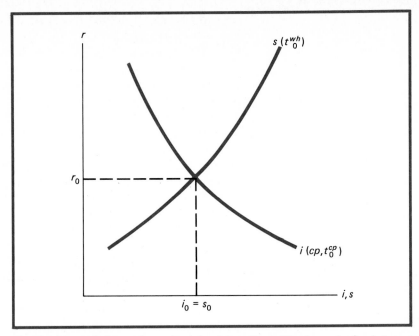

The position of the saving schedule depends on the tax rate for interest and dividend income (t_0^{wh}). The position of the investment schedule depends on the effective tax rate on corporate profits (t_0^{cp}) as well as on the pre-tax corporate profit rate (cp). These tax rates, t_0^{wh} and t_0^{cp}, will, therefore, affect the value of the equilibrium real interest rate (r).

t^{cp}, the effective tax rate on corporate profits, to be explained below. The position of the saving schedule depends on t^{wh}, the rate of taxation of individual income earned on accumulated savings (wealth). In the simple classical model, income earned from accumulated savings would simply be interest income on bonds. In the real economy, t^{wh} would also represent tax rates on dividend income and tax rates on capital gains due to changes in asset prices. In our earlier analysis we were interested in establishing that the interest rate (r) was determined by what the classical economists called the forces of productivity and thrift, productivity being reflected in the profit rate and therefore the position of the investment schedule, thrift reflected in the position of the saving schedule (both for a given structure of taxes). Here the important point is that productivity and thrift, *as well as the structure of taxes*, are in the classical view the determinants of saving, investment, and consequently the determinants of the rate of capital formation.

Supply-side economists need not accept the particular specification of the saving and investment functions in our simple version of the classical system. In actually trying to predict the level of investment spending for the United States in a particular year in the 1980s, for example, a supply-side economist would use a much more complex investment function than that plotted in Figure 16.6. He would, for example, take account of factors such as lags and costs of adjustment discussed in our more detailed analysis of investment theory (Section 13.2). The essentially classical feature in the supply-side economists' view of the savings–investment process is their stress on the importance of rates of return as influences on the rates of saving, investment, and thus capital formation. Where else might one put the emphasis? The answer is on income and, hence, on aggregate demand; we will see that the neo-Keynesians believe that the level of income is the most important determinant of investment. Investment can best be kept high according to this neo-Keynesian view by keeping the economy at a high rate of capacity utilization. The neo-Keynesians do not ignore rates of return, nor do the supply-side economists ignore income as a determinant of saving or investment. It is a matter of emphasis, and the supply-side economists clearly place the emphasis on rates of return as incentives to saving and investment.

If one stresses the importance of incentives for saving and investment, one is led to seek the source of the decline in the rate of U.S. capital formation in the post-1973 period in factors which weakened these incentives. One is led to seek the solution to slow capital formation in increased incentives for savers and investors. Martin Feldstein and a number of other economists claim that the interaction of inflation and the current U.S. tax system have weakened these incentives in recent years. Feldstein and Lawrence Summers have argued that increases in the inflation rate raise the effective tax rate on corporate income and, therefore, lower the after-tax rate of return on investment in two important ways.[6]

The first of these effects that inflation has on the effective tax rate on corporate income is due to the standard inventory procedure followed by most firms, the so-called first in–first out system (FIFO). Under FIFO, as items are used up from an inventory of raw materials, or finished goods are sold from inventory, it is assumed that goods are being used or sold in the order in which they were purchased or produced; first in are first out. The true costs to the firm of using up materials or selling finished goods is the *replace-*

[6]See Martin Feldstein and Lawrence Summers, "Inflation and the Taxation of Capital Income in the Corporate Sector," *National Tax Journal*, 32 (December 1979), pp. 445–70.

ment cost, not the cost when they were originally acquired. When inflation is taking place, FIFO *understates* true costs of production, overstates profits, and hence results in an increase in the firm's corporate tax liability.

The second reason why inflation raises the effective tax rate on corporate income is due to depreciation laws. Firms can deduct depreciation of capital investments only at *original* costs. In inflationary periods, as with inventories, the true cost of depreciating capital is the replacement cost. This cost is understated by depreciation at original or "historic" cost, so profits are overstated and, through this channel too, the *effective* corporate tax liability is increased. Feldstein and Summers estimate that the effect of these two factors is huge. They estimate that due to the FIFO inventory accounting system and historic cost depreciation, inflation increased the corporate tax liability in 1977 by $32 billion dollars, 50 percent of total corporate income taxes.

Feldstein and Summers also argue that the combination of inflation and the U.S. tax system reduce the incentives to save. The income tax that an individual pays is based on the *nominal* interest, dividends, or capital gains that he earns on his invested savings. Two examples will illustrate how increased inflation and taxation of nominal interest payments or capital gains lower the real return on saving. Suppose that initially the nominal interest rate is 6 percent and the rate of inflation is 2 percent (a pretax real rate of 4 percent). At a 50 percent marginal tax rate, an individual investor would have an after-tax *nominal* return of 3 percent [6 percent $\times (1 - t^{wh}) = 6$ percent $\times (1 - 0.5)$] and an after-tax real return of 1 percent (3 percent $-$ 2 percent). Now suppose that the nominal interest rate were 16 percent with an inflation rate of 12 percent (again a pretax real rate of 4 percent). The after-tax nominal return will be 8 percent [16 percent $\times (1 - 0.5)$], which means that the after-tax real return is now -4 percent.

Or consider the case of taxation of nominal capital gains, on corporate equities for example. Suppose that an individual purchased a share of stock at a price of $100 in 1967 and sold it in 1980 for $200. Since the price level rose by over 150 percent in this period while the price of the stock doubled, or rose 100 percent, the individual's real return is negative even before taxes. Still, he must pay a capital gains tax on the nominal capital gain (of $100), increasing the size of his real loss. Feldstein and Summers, among others, argue that taxing of nominal capital gains and interest earnings during inflationary periods results in an increased effective tax rate on real returns and will retard saving.

The effects of overtaxing both corporate profits and the return to saving during inflationary time periods are illustrated in Figure 16.7. Suppose that we move from a period of relatively low inflation rates such as the 1950s and 1960s to a period of higher inflation rates such as the 1970s. Because of use of the FIFO inventory accounting system and historic cost depreciation, this results in an increase in the effective tax rate on corporate profits from t_0^{cp} to t_1^{cp} in Figure 16.7. For a given before-tax profit rate cp, this increase in the effective tax rate will shift the investment schedule to the left as shown in the graph. Further, owing to the taxing of nominal interest payments and capital gains, the effective tax on the return to saving is increased from t_0^{wh} to t_1^{wh}, which shifts the saving schedule to the left in Figure 16.7. After the adjustment to a new equilibrium, saving and investment are reduced from the levels i_0 and s_0 to the levels shown as s_1 and i_1 in Figure 16.7. The rate of capital formation is thus reduced by the interaction of inflation and the current U.S. tax system.

It was noted above that the supply-side economists believe that excessive (inflationary) growth in aggregate demand might actually retard growth in output. The interaction of inflation, the tax

Figure 16.7

Inflation, the Tax System, and the Saving–Investment Process

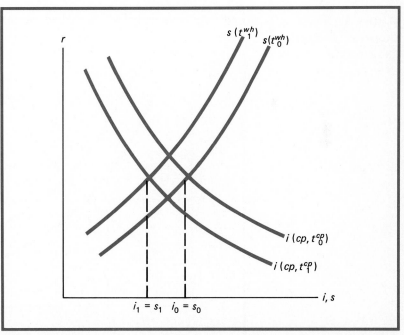

An increase in the effective corporate tax rate due to increased inflation causes the investment schedule to shift leftward from $i(cp, t_0^{cp})$ to $i(cp, t_1^{cp})$. An inflation-induced increase in the effective tax rate on interest income and capital gains shifts the saving schedule leftward from $s(t_0^{wh})$ to $s(t_1^{wh})$. The equilibrium levels of saving and investment fall from $i_0 = s_0$ to $i_1 = s_1$.

system, and the level of capital formation is one reason for this supply-side view of the negative growth effect of inflationary rates of increase in aggregate demand. According to supply-side economists, overly expansionary *fiscal* policies have discouraged capital formation in an additional way. What the supply-side economists would regard as excessive growth in government spending has resulted in perennial federal government budget deficits with an effect in the capital market as illustrated in Figure 16.8. Government borrowing to finance a deficit $(g - t)$ increases the demand for loanable funds, now given by the $i(cp, t_1^{cp}) + (g - t)$ schedule in Figure 16.8. As the government competes with private borrowers, the interest rate is driven up from r_1 to r_2 and investment declines from i_1 to i_2. This is the "crowding out" process described in previous chapters. Of course, the government need not borrow from the public to finance a deficit; the alternative would be to finance the deficit via new money creation. But in the supply-side view this would lead to increased inflation, which also would discourage investment and saving, for reasons just discussed.

Figure 16.8
Government Budget Deficits and the Level of Investment

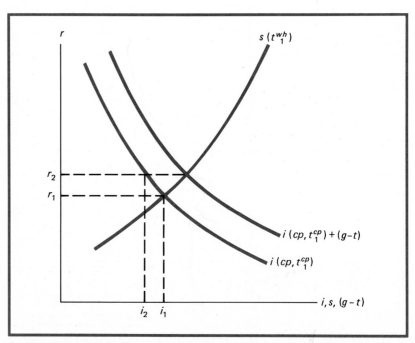

A bond-financed government deficit $(g - t)$ is a demand for loanable funds in addition to the private demand. This additional demand for loanable funds pushes the interest rate up from r_1 to r_2. Consequently, investment declines from i_1 to i_2.

Labor Supply Is Responsive to Changes in the After-Tax Real Wage

Supply-side economists argue that labor supply is responsive to changes in *after-tax* real wages. Here again the supply-side view is rooted in the classical economics. Figure 16.9 illustrates the determination of equilibrium employment in the classical system and the effect of a change in the after-tax real wage as a result of a change in the income tax rate t^y. Initially assume that the income tax rate is set at t_0^y. The labor supply curve is given by $N^s(t_0^y)$ and intersects the labor demand curve at N_0, the equilibrium level of employment.

Now assume that the income tax rate is raised to the higher level, t_1^y. According to the supply-side view, labor supply depends on the after-tax real wage, which will equal $(1 - t^y)W/P$. For example, with a marginal tax rate of 0.20, the after-tax real wage will be 0.80 times the pretax real wage. The marginal income tax rate thus forms a "wedge" between the wage paid by the employer W/P and the wage received by the worker $(1 - t^y)W/P$. An increase in the tax rate from t_0^y to a higher level t_1^y would cause the labor

Figure 16.9

Taxes and Labor Supply in the Classical System

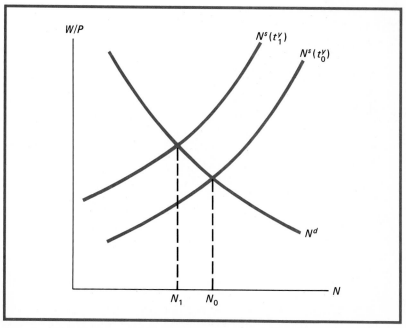

An increase in the income tax rate from t_0^y to t_1^y reduces the after-tax real wage and causes the labor supply schedule to shift to the left. The level of employment declines from N_0 to N_1.

supply schedule to shift to the left from $N^s(t_0^y)$ to $N^s(t_1^y)$. Less labor would be supplied at each level of the pretax real wage because with a higher tax rate a given pretax real wage represents a *lower* after-tax real wage. Employment declines from N_0 to N_1.

The supply-side economists believe that rising marginal tax rates in the United States have increased the size of this "wedge" which the income tax creates between the real wage paid by the employer and the (after-tax) wage received by the employee. They claim that work incentives have been reduced, with negative effects on employment and output. Here again inflationary aggregate demand policies and a tax system not well designed to cope with the effects of inflation deserve much of the blame. The income tax system is progressive, so as *nominal* incomes go up due to inflation, individuals move into higher marginal tax brackets. According to the supply-side view, inflation-induced increases in tax rates have been an important cause of labor supply shifts such as that depicted in Figure 16.9.

Government Regulation Has Contributed to the Slowdown in the U.S. Growth Rate

The supply-side economists argue that the proliferation of government regulation of business has contributed significantly to the slowdown in U.S. growth. There is no doubt that there was a new wave of government regulatory activity which began in the late 1960s. New agencies were set up and laws passed for such purposes as pollution control, protection of worker safety, consumer product safety, and pension reform. Supply-side economists argue that this increase in government regulatory activity has slowed economic growth in two ways.

First, complying with such regulations increases the cost of producing a given output. Increases in government regulation will therefore have the same effects as the supply shocks considered in Chapter 8. The aggregate supply curve will shift to the left, reducing output. Note that some of the increase in cost will come from having to employ workers not directly for production of output, steel for example, but having them clean smokestacks to comply with pollution controls, eliminate on-the-job safety hazards, or otherwise comply with regulations. Thus the increase in government regulation is a possible factor explaining the decline in the growth of labor productivity.

Second, supply-side economists argue that government regulatory activity has retarded capital formation, at least capital formation that contributes to increased productivity in terms of measured output. Lawrence Summers estimates that expenditures on pollution control absorbed approximately 20 percent of net investment in 1979.[7] More generally, supply-side economists argue that the proliferation of regulations has discouraged investment by increasing the uncertainty about the future profitability of investment projects. Will a plant be built and then have some costly emission control system imposed on it as clear air standards are changed? Will future price controls in the energy area lower profits of producing energy products or disrupt supplies of energy inputs? Such questions arise due to possibilities of regulatory changes and may cause investment projects to be postponed.

Supply-Side Policy Recommendations

The supply-side economists want to reduce the role of government in the economy and "let the market work." The market, they believe, will work in the sense that incentives will be provided that will foster noninflationary economic growth. Other supply-side economists' policy recommendations are aimed at mitigating the unfavorable effects that inflation has had on saving and capital formation. The latter policy recommendations are really short-run measures, for the supply-side economists believe that the basic remedy to this problem lies in ending the government policies that cause inflation. Among specific policy proposals consistent with supply-side economics are the following:

1. Substantial reductions in the personal income tax are proposed as a means of increasing labor supply. (In terms of Figure 16.9, the aim is to shift the labor supply curve to the right by reducing the marginal income tax rate, t^y.) For example, the tax bill originally sponsored by Representative Jack Kemp and Senator William Roth, and incorporated as a plank in President Reagan's campaign platform in 1980, called for 10 percent reductions in personal income tax rates in each of three successive years. These cuts would be aimed at reducing the size of the "wedge," discussed above, that the income tax creates between the real wage payment by the employer and the after-tax real wage received by the worker.

2. Corporate income tax laws should be changed to eliminate the increase in the effective tax rate on corporate income which is created by inflation. This could be done by changing depreciation rules to allow calculation of depreciation at replacement rather than historic cost and by elimination of taxes on nominal inventory profits due to inflation. Alternatively, accelerated depreciation allowances and overall reductions in the corporate income tax could be enacted to offset the inflation-caused increase in the effective tax rate on corporate income. These proposals are aimed

[7]See Lawrence Summers, "Tax Policy and Corporate Investment," in Meyer, *Supply-Side Effects.*

at increasing the after-tax return to investment and therefore stimulating capital formation. (In terms of Figure 16.7, the aim of the policy is to shift the investment schedule to the right by reducing the effective corporate tax rate, t^{cp}.)

3. In a similar vein, the supply-side economists suggest that the tax laws should be changed to encourage saving. Taxing real not nominal capital gains, interest payments, and dividend income would eliminate the increase in the effective tax rate on the return to saving that results from inflation. A more drastic proposal would be to eliminate taxes on such forms of income—the argument for this being that saving takes place out of income, which is taxed as it is earned. To tax the returns which an individual then earns on that saving is "double taxation."

As evidence that reductions in a combination of personal and business taxes will stimulate economic growth without inflation, the supply-side economists point to the U.S. experience following the Kennedy–Johnson 1964 tax cut. Supply-side economist Paul Craig Roberts argues that the tax cut, which amounted to a reduction of almost 20 percent in individual tax liabilities and almost 10 percent in corporate tax liabilities, stimulated saving and investment and increased the incentives for labor supply. The result, Roberts concludes, was a supply-led expansion of output and employment with little increase in the inflation rate.[8]

4. The supply-side economists want to halt the growth in government regulation, which they believe to be increasing costs, and consequently prices, as well as discouraging capital formation. Proposals in this area are for a one-year moratorium on all new regulations and various modifications of existing regulations with an eye to increasing cost effectiveness.

5. Finally, since they believe that inflation has perverse effects on capital formation, the supply-side economists argue for noninflationary aggregate demand management. They favor policies aimed at balancing the federal budget and stabilizing money growth rates. There is a potential conflict between balancing the budget and the large income tax cuts proposed by the supply-side economists and there is a difference of opinion among the supply-side economists as to which goal should receive precedence. Some argue that the tax cuts should come only if matched by spending cuts, in which case the tax cuts will not affect the budget deficit; the goal of budget balance and tax cuts are not in conflict. Others may be regarded as more optimistic. They believe that the output gains as a result of cuts in tax *rates* will be so large that *revenues*

---

[8]See Paul Craig Roberts, "Reagan's Tax-Cut Program: The Evidence," *Wall Street Journal*, May 21, 1981, and "The Economic Case for Kemp-Roth," in Laffer and Seymour *Economics of the Tax Revolt*.

will not fall. Therefore, reductions in the income tax rate will not produce deficits even if there are no spending cuts. This issue of whether spending cuts should be regarded as a necessary precondition for tax cuts was a key one in the debate over the Reagan Administration's fiscal policy program in 1981.

The Neo-Keynesian Critique of Supply-Side Economics

We have stressed the classical roots of the supply-side economics. In fact, the supply-side economics can be regarded as the intermediate-run counterpart to the monetarist and new classical attacks on the neo-Keynesian orthodoxy which had become dominant by the mid-1960s, those attacks also being based on classical notions. In this section we analyze the neo-Keynesian critique of the supply-side position. We examine the neo-Keynesian view of each of the supply-side propositions discussed in the preceding section, considering the associated supply-side policy propositions as we go along.

The Supply-Determined Nature of Intermediate-Run Growth

As noted above, the neo-Keynesian position is that for periods of a decade or so, both supply and demand factors are important in determining output growth. In explaining the lower growth in the United States in the 1970s, for example, James Tobin sees as the primary causes, supply shocks, the most important from the energy sector, and monetary policy "overkill," the latter term meaning overly restrictive monetary policy actions that were imposed to slow the economy when a slowdown was already under way. Such mistimed monetary actions are blamed in part by Tobin for the severity of the recessions of the 1970s, which resulted in the lower growth rate for the decade.[9] The neo-Keynesians do not agree with the supply-side idea that inflationary growth in aggregate demand was important in reducing the growth rate in real output.

Saving and Investment and After-tax Rates of Return

On the question of whether depressed rates of return have lowered saving, investment, and capital formation, there are areas of agreement and disagreement between the supply-side economists and the neo-Keynesians.

Neo-Keynesian economists do not deny that capital formation is important to growth or that the slowdown in net capital formation has been one cause of the growth slowdown of the 1970s, al-

---

[9]See James Tobin, "Stabilization Policy Ten Years After," *Brookings Papers on Economic Activity*, No. 1, 1980, pp. 19–71.

though some would argue that slower capital formation can explain relatively little of the slowdown in output growth. Nor do the neo-Keynesians oppose tax policies to stimulate investment. Tobin points out, for example, that it was during the Kennedy Administration, a highpoint of Keynesian influence, that the first investment tax credit was passed.

Still, in the neo-Keynesian view, the primary explanation for the slowdown in net capital formation in the 1970s lies in the low levels of output growth during that period, which caused investment demand to lag. In the neo-Keynesian view, then, *for the most part* causation runs from low output to low investment rather than in the reverse direction. The low output levels are ascribed, as explained above, to supply shocks and, at times, overly restrictive monetary policies.

What about the role of incentives for saving and investment? Although not ignoring the effects of changes in after-tax returns on investment demand, many neo-Keynesians seem to accept the evidence from studies such as Peter Clark's, which was cited in Chapter 13, that output is the key variable determining investment.[10] The best way to encourage investment, then, is to keep the economy near the full-capacity level of output. In the case of saving, the neo-Keynesians would not deny that the rate of return (after taxes) is a determinant of saving. Nor would most neo-Keynesians deny that a decline in this rate of return may have caused the decline in the saving rate which did occur in the late 1970s. They believe, however, as Tobin states, that "an explanation of the slowdown in business capital formation in the 1970's may be sought in investment demand rather than saving supply" and as explained above, it is income as a determinant of investment that is the key to capital formation.

The Effect of Income Tax Cuts on Labor Supply

Most neo-Keynesian economists do not believe that "vast increases" in labor supply will result from lowering marginal income tax rates. They do not believe that current income tax rates are a serious impediment to labor supply. As evidence that they are not, neo-Keynesian economists cite the high labor-force-participation ratios in Western European countries (West Germany, for example), where marginal tax rates are substantially higher than in the United States. Further, they point out that although with a progressive income tax, inflation will push individuals into higher tax brackets, actual tax rates paid will increase only if the tax schedule is unchanged. If, instead, Congress periodically low-

---

[10]Peter Clark, "Investment in the 1970's: Theory, Performance and Prediction," *Brookings Papers on Economic Activity*, No. 1, 1979, pp. 73–113.

ers tax rates to offset the effects of inflation (or for some other reason), actual marginal tax rates may not rise. According to estimates cited by James Tobin, the federal marginal rate of personal income tax averaged over all brackets was actually lower in 1975 than in 1960—18.0 percent compared with 18.8 percent. In the 1975–80 period there does appear to have been some "bracket creep" due to inflation, with the average marginal tax rate increasing to 21.6 percent. But Tobin finds no evidence of a weakened "propensity to supply labor in recent experience."[11] In fact, he suggests that it is strange to be worrying over the problem of disincentives to work when labor force participation ratios have *risen* to record levels in the late 1970s. For example, the aggregate labor force participation ratio was 59.6 percent in 1957, 60.1 percent in 1969, and 63.7 percent in 1979.[12]

In rebuttal, the supply-side economists could point to the large increase in payroll taxes over recent years. Payroll (social security) taxes are an additional element in the "wedge" between the wage paid by the employer and that received by the worker. Such taxes have risen dramatically from a combined tax rate (on the employer and employee) of 6.0 percent on the first $4800 of wage income in 1960 to 13.30 percent on the first $29,500 of wage income in 1981. Additionally, the supply-side economists point to recent empirical studies which indicate that, given secular trends that have increased labor force participation rates, there are negative effects of income and payroll tax rates on labor supply.[13]

The issues, then, would appear to be the empirical ones of whether recent increases in marginal tax rates have been of a magnitude sufficient to have created an important work disincentive and, further, whether reductions in marginal tax rates on the order of the Kemp–Roth proposal would affect labor supply strongly enough to increase employment and output substantially.

The neo-Keynesian analysis of the effects of a proposal such as

[11]See James Tobin, "The Reagan Economic Plan—Supply-Side, Budget and Inflation," in *The Reagan Economic Plan* (San Francisco: Federal Reserve Bank of San Francisco, 1981).

[12]See Daniel Hamermesh, "Transfers, Taxes, and the NAIRU," in Meyer, *Supply-Side Effects*. It should be noted, however, that the rise in the aggregate labor force participation rate is due to a remarkably large increase in the labor force participation rate for adult women, which rose from 36.5 percent in 1957 to 50.6 percent in 1979. The labor force participation rate for males aged 25 to 54 declined from 97.2 percent in 1957 to 94.4 percent in 1979. For males 55 and over, the labor force participation rate declined from 63.4 percent in 1957 to 46.7 percent in 1979. Tax effects may have been a factor in these declines in male labor force participation. Even so, the neo-Keynesians might argue that it is growth in the aggregate labor input which is relevant as a determinant of output growth.

[13]See, for example, Jerry Hausman, "Income and Payroll Tax Policy and Labor Supply," in Meyer, *Supply-Side Effects;* or Jerry Hausman, "Labor Supply," in Henry Aaron and Joseph Pechman, eds., *How Taxes Affect Economic Behavior* (Washington, D.C.: Brookings Institution, 1981).

the Kemp–Roth tax cut is illustrated in Figure 16.10. Recall from our analysis in Chapters 5 to 8 that in the neo-Keynesian view, an income tax cut would increase consumer disposable income and consumption demand. The aggregate demand curve would shift out to the right from a position such as $y^d(t_0^y)$ to $y^d(t_1^y)$ in Figure 16.10, where t_0^y is the tax rate prior to the tax cut and t_1^y is the tax rate after Kemp–Roth. This *demand-side* effect of the tax cut would cause output to increase from y_0 to y_1 and cause the price level to rise from P_0 to P_1. The neo-Keynesians would agree that there would be some stimulus to labor supply due to the initial increase in the after-tax real wage following the tax cut. The labor supply curve, and hence the aggregate supply curve, would shift to the right as a result of the tax cut. In the neo-Keynesian view, however, this effect would be minor; the responsiveness of labor supply to changes in income tax rates is believed by them to be small. The supply curve would shift from $y^s(t_0^y)$ to a position such as $y^s(t_1^y)$ in Figure 16.10. This shift would further increase income

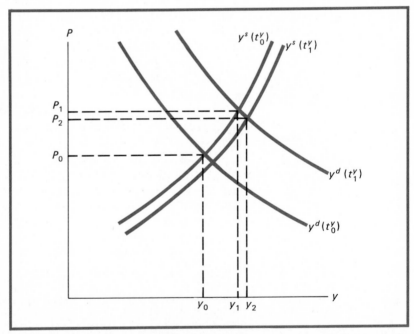

Figure 16.10

Kemp–Roth Tax Cut Proposal: A Neo-Keynesian View

The tax cut shifts the aggregate demand schedule from $y^d(t_0^y)$ to $y^d(t_1^y)$. This *demand effect* causes the price level to increase to P_1 and the level of real output to rise to y_1. The tax cut also causes the supply schedule to shift to the right, from $y^s(t_0^y)$ to $y^s(t_1^y)$, but in the neo-Keynesian view this supply effect is small. Output rises to the slightly higher level y_2; the supply effect causes the price level to fall to P_2, a level below P_1 but above the pre-tax cut level P_0.

EXTENSIONS OF THE MODELS

to y_2 and slightly moderate the upward movement in the equilibrium price level, which would now be P_2 instead of P_1. But this *supply-side effect* is secondary; the demand-side effect dominates.

Kemp–Roth in the neo-Keynesian view is no "free lunch." Income tax cuts can increase income substantially by stimulating aggregate demand; this is standard doctrine. But since in the neo-Keynesian view the demand-side effect is dominant, the tax cut will, unless there is considerable slack in the economy, put upward pressure on prices as well.

What about evidence from the period following the 1964 tax cut which the supply-side economists cite in support of a Kemp–Roth type of tax proposal? The neo-Keynesians agree that the tax cut "delivered a powerful stimulus to economic expansion" but believe that "the record is crystal clear that it was its stimulus to demand, the multiplied impact of its release of over $10 billion of consumer purchasing power and $2 billion of corporate funds," which provided the stimulus.[14] Their analysis of the effects of the 1964 tax cut is as depicted in Figure 16.10. Supply factors are viewed as a clearly secondary factor in the expansionary effects of the tax cut. In the neo-Keynesian view the success of the 1964 tax cut in producing a relatively noninflationary expansion stemmed from the fact that there was considerable slack in the economy at the time of the tax cut. In terms of Figure 16.10, it was the fact that we were on a relatively flat portion of the aggregate supply schedule, rather than any significant shift to the right in the aggregate supply schedule, which was responsible for the tax cut's relatively small effect on the price level.

None of the above implies that the neo-Keynesians oppose the use of tax policy to affect supply. In considering tax policies to influence aggregate supply, however, neo-Keynesian economists have been most favorable to cuts in excise taxes or employer's contributions to payroll taxes. Reductions in these taxes will cause business costs to decline. The neo-Keynesians believe that this is more likely to have a favorable effect on the aggregate supply curve than income tax cuts, which rely on a response in labor supply.

Regulation as a Source of Inflation and Slow Growth

With regard to the effects of government regulation on inflation and growth, the issues are broad ones and it would be incorrect to argue that there is *a* neo-Keynesian position which contrasts with

[14]On the neo-Keynesian interpretation of the 1964 tax cut, see Walter W. Heller, "The Kemp–Roth–Laffer Free Lunch," *Wall Street Journal*, July 12, 1978, reprinted in Laffer and Seymour, *Economics of the Tax Revolt*; and Arthur M. Okun, "Measuring the Impact of the 1964 Tax Cut," in Walter W. Heller, ed., *Perspectives on Economic Growth* (New York: Random House, 1968).

the supply-side position. As stated above, there is no doubt that there has been a tremendous growth in government regulation in the period since the late 1960s. There is also no doubt that complying with many of these regulations is quite costly to firms and that much of the cost is passed on to consumers. Robert Crandall estimates the cost of pollution controls mandated by EPA (Environmental Protection Agency) regulations at $25.3 billion in 1977 and likely to rise to $44.7 billion (in 1977 dollars) by 1983. He estimates the cost of complying with major OSHA (Occupational Safety and Health Administration) regulations at $4.2 billion for 1977.[15] Nor is it doubtful that many of the regulations are cost ineffective in that more efficient ways exist for achieving the same benefits.

Both supply-side economists and neo-Keynesians favor some restructuring of regulations to make them more cost effective. Robert Crandall in the study cited above, for example, argues that reliance on engineering controls rather than work practices or personal protective equipment makes compliance with OSHA regulations overly costly. In the area of environmental regulation most economists believe that using taxes or subsidies rather than standards to achieve given goals will allow market incentives to work so that pollution is reduced with a minimum loss in efficiency.[16]

Economists who would go less far than the supply-siders in massive dismantling of the regulatory structure that arose since the 1960s either believe the benefits are greater than the supply-side economists believe or that the costs, in terms of lost growth, are lower. Additionally, they may be more optimistic about the possibility for improvement in regulatory effectiveness. The prospective benefits from these new regulations include cleaner air, cleaner water, safer workplaces, and safer consumer products. These are, of course, desirable to all, but there are differences of opinion as to the degree to which government intervention in the economy is needed to achieve them.

As for the cost of regulation in terms of intermediate-run growth, there is also room for a divergence of opinion. The study by Norsworthy, Harper, and Kuntze, cited above, estimated that 0.03 percentage point of the 1.0 percentage point decline in the growth rate of labor productivity between the 1948–65 and 1965–73 periods, and another 0.09 percentage point of the further 1.12 percentage point decline between 1973 and 1978 were due directly to required pollution abatement investment. Edward Denison estimates that mandated expenditures for pollution abatement low-

[15]Robert Crandall, "Federal Government Initiatives to Reduce the Price Level," *Brookings Papers on Economic Activity*, No. 2, 1978, pp. 401–40.
[16]See, for example, the discussion in Lester Thurow, *The Zero Sum Society* (New York: Basic Books, 1980), Chapters 5 and 6.

ered the annual percentage growth rate in national income by 0.18 percentage point, while worker safety and health regulation cut an additional 0.09 percentage point from the growth rate.[17] These are modest, although not insignificant amounts. But Denison also finds that much of the slowdown in growth cannot be explained by *any* of the factors he considers. He finds a large unexplained "residual" drop in the growth rate due to factors not measured explicitly. One cannot rule out overregulation by government in many areas in addition to pollution control and worker safety (the areas measured by Denison) as factors responsible for the otherwise unexplainable portion of the decline in the growth rate.

The Proper Conduct of Aggregate Demand Management Policy

We have seen that the supply-side economists stress the negative effects of inflation on growth and favor stable low money growth rates and a balanced federal budget. No group of economists are for inflationary policies per se, but some neo-Keynesians argue that at times in the 1970s, monetary policy was overly restrictive in an attempt to combat the inflationary effects of supply shocks. In general, the neo-Keynesians still favor activist policies to restrict the economy when demand is excessive *and* to stimulate the economy when aggregate demand is weak. Supply shocks, such as those in the energy sector in 1974–75 and again in 1979–80, as we have seen (Section 8.6), create a dilemma for the policymaker confronted by both inflation and unemployment. The neo-Keynesians would argue that the policymaker must still make the choice of the degree to "accommodate" the supply shock by raising aggregate demand, therefore keeping employment relatively high but worsening the inflation situation, or following restrictive policies that minimize inflation but increase the rise in unemployment. In such times variability in aggregate demand policy, as measured by budget deficits or money growth rates, is not necessarily bad. To the degree that the supply-side economists' proposals for aggregate demand mean rules for money growth and budget balance, these proposals are antithetical to the neo-Keynesian position.

16.3 REAGANOMICS: AN APPLICATION OF SUPPLY-SIDE THEORY

To the degree that the election outcome was determined by economic factors, voters in the United States in 1980 appeared ready

[17]See Edward Denison, *Accounting for Slower Economic Growth* (Washington, D.C.: Brookings Institution, 1979).

for an experiment with supply-side economics. The economic platform on which Ronald Reagan ran included several of the key supply-side policy prescriptions.[18] In this section we will consider the Reagan economic program—often referred to as Reaganomics. We will also look at the criticisms of the Reagan program, as voiced by a number of neo-Keynesian economists. The behavior of the economy over the first eighteen months following the initial implementation of the Reagan program will be examined.

Elements of President Reagan's Economic Recovery Plan

Each of the major facets the Economic Recovery Plan advanced by the Reagan Administration was based on the supply-side propositions discussed above. These major elements of the Reagan program were:

Personal Income Tax Reductions

The Reagan Administration adopted a revised version of the Kemp-Roth bill. As enacted by Congress the Reagan tax cut bill reduces marginal income tax rates, in three stages, by a total of 23 percent. The bill also lowers the top rate on income earned from capital from 70 to 50 percent. Beginning in 1985 the tax bill indexes tax brackets to inflation to prevent "bracket creep." As discussed in Section 16.2, in the view of supply-side economists such income tax cuts should increase labor supply and therefore output (supply-side proposition 3).

Personal income tax cuts should also increase personal saving. The reduction in the maximum tax bracket from 70 to 50 percent was especially aimed at increasing saving. Additionally, to encourage saving the tax act extended the opportunity to use IRA accounts to all households. IRA accounts allow for deposit of $2000 ($4000 for a two-worker couple) to a retirement account. Contributions to these accounts are deductible from taxable income, with taxes paid as withdrawals are made after retirement. Accumulated interest on IRA accounts is also tax-free until withdrawal.

Reductions in Business Taxes

The Reagan Administration's tax act had several features aimed at encouraging business investment by increasing the after-tax return to investment. The most important of these was the *accelerated cost recovery system* (ACRS) which was a set of accelerated depreciation allowances for business plants and equipment. To

---

[18]While the rationale for the central elements of the Reagan economic program is supplied by the supply-side theory, questions have been raised about whether the program, as implemented, is actually an application of supply-side economics. We return to this question below.

give an example, a piece of industrial equipment which could have been depreciated over an 8.6 year period before the tax act could be depreciated over a 5 year period under the act's provisions.

Accompanying these accelerated depreciation allowances was a leasing system whereby firms without taxable income (e.g. firms with losses not profits) could through leasing arrangements, in return for compensation, transfer their tax deductions under the new tax act to profitable firms. Finally, with regard to business taxation, the investment tax credit for certain types of equipment was increased.

These business tax cuts were aimed at offsetting the inflation-induced increase in the effective tax rate on business profits which was discussed in Section 16.2. Such tax cuts are consistent with the supply-side view (proposition 2) that the way to encourage capital formation is by increasing the after-tax return to investment.

Reductions in Nondefense Government Spending

According to the supply-side view, the personal and business tax cuts should increase aggregate supply and, therefore, produce non-inflationary real output growth. Also, it was hoped that such growth would increase the tax base and therefore increase tax revenues to offset, in large part (or completely), the loss in revenue due to the lower tax rates. However, to assure that demand was not overly stimulated, and to keep the budget deficit as small as possible, the Reagan program proposed cuts in nondefense government spending. Cuts were proposed in areas such as housing, education, and income maintenance programs. Such cuts in nondefense spending were also needed, in part, to finance a proposed increase in defense spending. Finally, the cuts in nondefense spending were in line with the view expressed by one supporter of the Reagan program that

> There are a great many federal spending programs, transfer programs, and regulations which the people don't want, which have an unfavorable effect on the public's spendable real incomes. We should make a list of all the rat holes that the government is pouring money into today, and we should eliminate them.[19]

In addition to the tax cuts, therefore, the Economic Recovery Act of 1981, cut *projected* 1982 nondefense spending by an amount on the order of $30–40 billion, with further cuts proposed for future years.

[19]Robert Hall, "The Reagan Economic Plan: Discussion," in *The Reagan Economic Plan* (San Francisco: Federal Reserve Bank of San Francisco, 1981), p. 16.

Reductions in Governmental Regulation

Again consistent with the supply-side view that government regulation of the economy in areas such as air quality, worker safety, and consumer product safety has been overly costly and has retarded growth (proposition 4), the Reagan administration began a regulatory review. The aim was to eliminate "wasteful or outdated regulation and to make necessary regulation more efficient and more flexible." Some specific regulatory initiatives early in the Reagan Administration were a shift in some responsibilities for air pollution control to the states, decontrol of petroleum markets, a proposal to abolish the Department of Energy, and an Executive Order calling for a cost–benefit analysis before issuing any new federal regulation.

Viewing the Reagan program near the end of the first year of the Administration, Paul Craig Roberts, supply-side economist and the Assistant Secretary of the Treasury, concluded that

> Much has been accomplished in a short period of time. Federal spending is coming under control and incentives to work, and save and invest are being restored. Inflation is falling, the dollar has been riding high in the foreign exchange markets, and the price of gold is down from panic levels. . . I am confident that the Administration will see its program succeed.[20]

Neo-Keynesian critics of the supply-side position were, as might be expected, less sanguine about the prospects for the Reagan economic recovery plan.

Neo-Keynesian Doubts about Reaganomics

Many criticisms of the Reagan economic program concern *micro-economic* questions. These include questions about the effects of tax and spending cuts on income distribution, as well as questions about the proper allocation of resources between the public and private sector, and within the public sector between defense and nondefense spending. While important, these questions fall, for the most part, outside the subject matter of macroeconomics. The analysis here is confined to questions raised by a number of neo-Keynesian economists about whether the Reagan program can achieve its announced goal of a high level of noninflationary economic growth. These neo-Keynesian economists believe that the Reagan program will not achieve this goal in large part because the monetary-fiscal policy mix within the Reagan program is faulty.

---

[20]Paul Craig Roberts, "Will Reaganomics Unravel," in Thomas J. Hailstones, ed., *Viewpoints on Supply-Side Economics* (Richmond, Virginia: Robert F. Dame, 1982), p. 238.

Focusing only on the fiscal policy part of the Reagan program, James Tobin terms it "neutral" in effect. Tobin views the proposed tax and spending changes from the standpoint of their effects on aggregate demand and sees the spending cuts, in large part, as cancelling out the expansionary effects of the tax cuts. If the latter rounds of spending cuts are not made and the tax cut package remains unchanged, then the effect on demand would become more expansionary. Tobin is implicitly denying that the incentive effects of the tax cut (on saving and labor supply) will have important independent expansionary effects on output.

But in Tobin's view, even with an expansionary fiscal policy, rapid output growth could not be achieved given the Reagan Administration's monetary policy projections. The Reagan Administration's program called for a reduction in the rate of growth in the money supply to approximately one-half of the 1980 rate of 6.3 percent by 1986. This was the anti-inflationary part of the economic recovery plan. While the supply-side tax cuts were to stimulate output, a reduction in money growth would lower the inflation rate.

Tobin among others has questioned whether such slow money growth could accommodate rapid growth in output. For example, the Administration projected (in March of 1981) that in 1982 real output would grow by 4.2 percent, the inflation rate would be 8.3 percent, and therefore nominal GNP would rise by approximately 12.5 percent. For 1983 and 1984 the projected growth rates in nominal income were 12.4 and 10.8 percent, respectively. Tobin doubts that such nominal income growth can be achieved when, according to projections for monetary policy, money growth will be in the range of 2.0–to 5.5 percent over that period. Given the equation of exchange, $MV \equiv Py$, such rapid growth in nominal income (Py) with such slow growth in money (M) would require an increase in velocity (V) on the order of 8 percent per year, a level "beyond historical experience."

The neo-Keynesians do not believe that velocity is constant in the short-run. As we have seen (Section 9.2), in the Keynesian theory a rise in the rate of interest would cause less money to be demanded for a given income level; therefore a given money stock could support a higher nominal income level. In the Keynesian theory, velocity (Py/M) is *positively* related to the level of the interest rate. In the Reagan projections, however, interest rates were supposed to drop sharply over the 1980–85 period, from 11.5 percent in 1980, for the short-term interest rate, to 6.0 percent in 1985. Of itself, this would cause velocity to *fall*, not rise. Tobin concludes that monetary and fiscal policy are pulling in opposite directions in the Reagan economic program and that, consequently

The outlook, I am afraid, is for continued stagflation, with disappointing results on all fronts—inflation, unemployment, real output, interest rates, and capital formation. We will unwind the Great Society, redistribute income regressively, withdraw the Federal commitment to the environment, and we will have little or no macro-economic progress to show. The Program will not fulfill the promises that have led the country to support it. I wish I knew what will happen when the Administration, Congress, and public confront this reality.[21]

Reaganomics: Some Early Evidence

Table 16.3 shows the level of a number of major macroeconomic variables for the first six quarters of the Reagan Administration. The general characterization of the course of the economy over this period is as follows.

Inflation: The rate of inflation slowed, as shown by the figures in the table for the GNP deflator ($\dot{P}$). The same slowdown was evident in data for the consumer price index which rose 12.4 percent in 1980, 8.9 percent in 1981, and 5.1 percent (at an annual rate) over the first six months of 1982.

Output and Employment: As can be seen from the data for real GNP ($\dot{Y}$), after rapid growth in the first quarter, the economy moved into a recession in mid-1981. The unemployment rate rose to a post World War II high of 9.5 percent by May of 1982. The investment column reveals that, despite tax incentives, investment fell sharply during the recession.

The Budget Deficit and Interest Rates: Due to the tax cut and

[21]Tobin, "The Reagan Economic Plan," p. 13.

Table 16.3 Recent U.S. Economic Performance: Selected Quarterly Data	Year: Quarter	$\dot{P}$	U	$\dot{Y}$	I	T-G	r^s
	1981: 1	10.9	7.4	7.9	221.6	−46.6	14.4
	1981: 2	6.8	7.4	−1.5	229.5	−47.2	14.8
	1981: 3	9.0	7.4	2.2	233.4	−55.7	15.1
	1981: 4	8.8	8.4	−5.3	218.9	−100.0	12.0
	1982: 1	4.3	8.8	−5.1	195.4	−126.4	12.8
	1982: 2	5.3	9.5	1.3	200.5	−108.9	12.4

$\dot{P}$ = percentage change in the GNP deflator
U = civilian unemployment rate (percent)
$\dot{Y}$ = percentage change in real GNP
I = real investment (billions of 1972 dollars)
T-G = federal government budget surplus (+) or deficit (−)
r^s = interest rate on 3-month treasury bills

Sources: *Federal Reserve Bulletin*, Federal Reserve Bank of St. Louis, *National Economic Trends*

more important the fall in tax revenues as a result of the recession, the federal budget deficit (T-G column) rose rapidly in the first half of 1982. In the budget agreed upon for fiscal 1982 (September 1982–September 1983) the projected budget deficit was $103.7 billion. The large budget deficit has been blamed, especially by monetarist economists who believe that bond-financed budget deficits directly push up interest rates (Section 9.3), for the failure of interest rates to fall significantly. As can be seen from Table 16.3, the interest rate (r^s) had fallen only to 12.4 percent by the spring of 1982 despite the recession (which lowered income growth and therefore growth in money demand) and the drop in the inflation rate.

With the exception of the inflation rate, the Reagan economic program did not achieve the optimistic projections for 1981–82 made in the early months of the administration. Unemployment has gone higher than projected and output growth is below the projected level. Interest rates have not fallen as quickly as projected and the budget deficit has risen far above the targeted level.

Still, it is too early to assess the longer-effects of the Reagan economic program. At the end of the period covered by the data in Table 16.3, the second of the three phases of the personal income tax cut was just going into effect. The business tax cuts had been in place less than one year. Regulatory reform was mostly in the review stage. A more complete assessment of Reaganomics must await data from several more years.

Even when enough time has elapsed to permit a more thorough assessment of the Reagan economic program, this policy experiment will not lead to a conclusive verdict on the validity of the supply-side theories. Already in the first year after the program had gone into effect, questions were being raised about whether, as implemented by Congress, the program was actually supply-side economics in practice. Due to delays in enacting the personal income tax cuts and the effects of "bracket creep," for example, Paul Craig Roberts, who by the summer of 1982 had left the administration, argued that there had really been little effective tax relief. He concluded that, "The administration has badly mismanaged the tax-cut issue."[22] By the summer of 1982 Congress was considering various tax increases due to concerns about the rising federal deficit. Such tax increases were strongly opposed by the supply-side economists. As was noted in Chapter 12, the historical record provides few clearcut tests of economic theories.

[22]Paul Craig Roberts, "How to Break the Stalemate over the Budget," *Wall Street Journal*, May 3, 1982.

Review Questions

1 Explain why it is that the long-run equilibrium rate of growth in output is independent of the saving rate (*S/Y*). Would you expect that the rate of growth in output over intermediate-run periods would also be independent of the saving rate?

2 According to Denison's estimates, which factors were the most important in accounting for the growth in real output over the 1929–69 period?

3 Explain the relationships between the supply-side economists' theoretical propositions and the classical macroeconomic theory.

4 Outline the main features of a supply-sider's prescription for policies to foster noninflationary economic growth over the decade of the 1980s. How do these policy prescriptions differ from those of the neo-Keynesians?

5 Compare the neo-Keynesian and supply-siders' positions on the effects of a Kemp–Roth type tax cut.

6 Compare the neo-Keynesian and supply-siders' positions on the determinants of saving, investment, and capital formation.

7 Within the supply-side theory, what is the proper role for aggregate demand management policies?

8 Compare the neo-Keynesian and supply-side economists' interpretations of the effects of the 1964 tax cut.

9 Supply-side factors are important to *both* a neo-Keynesian and a supply-sider's explanations of the behavior of price and output during the decade of the 1970s, although in quite different ways. Comment.

Selected Readings

Long-Run Growth

DENISON, EDWARD, *Accounting for United States Economic Growth: 1929–69.* Washington, D.C.: Brookings Institution, 1974.

DIXIT, A. K., *The Theory of Equilibrium Growth.* London: Oxford University Press, 1976.

SOLOW, ROBERT, "Technical Change and the Production Function," *Review of Economics and Statistics*, 39 (August 1967), pp. 312–20. Reprinted in

M. G. Mueller, ed., *Readings in Macroeconomics.* New York: Holt, Rinehart and Winston, 1967.

SOLOW, ROBERT, *Growth Theory.* London: Oxford University Press, 1970.

STIGLITZ, JOSEPH E., and UZAWA, HIROFUME, eds., *Readings in the Modern Theory of Economic Growth.* Cambridge, Mass.: MIT Press, 1969.

Intermediate-Run Growth and Supply-Side Economics

BARTH, JAMES, "The Reagan Program for Economic Recovery: Economic Rationale," Federal Reserve Bank of Atlanta *Economic Review,* September 1981, pp. 4–14.

DENISON, EDWARD, *Accounting for Slower Economic Growth.* Washington, D.C.: Brookings Institution, 1979.

FELDSTEIN, MARTIN, "Does the United States Save Too Little?" *American Economic Review,* 67 (February 1977), pp. 116–21.

FELDSTEIN, MARTIN, and SUMMERS, LAWRENCE, "Inflation and the Taxation of Capital Income in the Corporate Sector," *National Tax Journal,* 32 (December 1979), pp. 445–70.

LAFFER, ARTHUR B., and SEYMOUR, JAN P., eds., *The Economics of the Tax Revolt: A Reader.* New York: Harcourt Brace Jovanovich, 1979.

MEYER, LAURENCE H., ed., *The Supply-Side Effects of Economic Policy.* St. Louis: Center for the Study of American Business, 1981.

NORSWORTHY, J. R.; HARPER, M. J.; and KUNTZE, K., "The Slowdown of Productivity Growth: Analysis of Some Contributing Factors," *Brookings Papers on Economic Activity,* No. 2, 1979, pp. 387–421.

ROBERTS, PAUL CRAIG, "The Breakdown of the Keynesian Model," *The Public Interest,* 52 (Summer 1978), pp. 20–23.

TATOM, JOHN, "We Are All Supply-Siders Now!" Federal Reserve Bank of St. Louis *Review,* 63 (May 1981), pp. 18–30.

TOBIN, JAMES, "Stabilization Policy Ten Years After," *Brookings Papers on Economic Activity,* No. 1, 1980, pp. 19–71.

chapter 17

In previous chapters international economic transactions were ignored. We have, in effect, assumed that the economy we were analyzing was a *closed* economy having no dealings with the rest of the world. In this chapter we extend our analysis to *open* economies which trade with other nations. We will consider some new questions, such as the factors that determine a country's levels of imports and exports, capital flows,[1] and exchange rate. We will also examine the necessary modifications of our previous analysis when our focus is extended to open and, hence, interdependent economies.

Proceeding this far without considering the foreign sector of the economy was justified only by the fact that for the United States the foreign sector is relatively small. For example, in 1979 the volume of imports equaled approximately 9 percent of GNP.[2] But the foreign sector has grown rapidly in recent years. The volume of imports equaled only 3 percent of GNP in 1961. The growing U.S. dependence on foreign oil is one striking manifestation of the increasing interdependence of the United States and other economies.

---

[1]In previous chapters the term "investment" has been used exclusively to refer to purchases of physical capital goods. The term "capital" referred to those physical goods themselves. In the discussion of international economic relations, the term "capital flows" refers to exchanges of financial assets involving individuals in different countries, as well as direct investment such as the purchase of a plant in another country.

[2]For a more open economy such as Belgium or the Netherlands, the volume of imports exceeds 50 percent of GNP.

MACROECONOMICS OF OPEN ECONOMIES

We will begin, as we did with closed-economy macroeconomics, with the question of measurement.

17.1 THE U.S. BALANCE OF PAYMENTS ACCOUNTS

Economic relations between the United States and other nations are summarized in the U.S. balance of payments accounts. On one side of the accounts all earnings from the foreign activities of U.S. citizens and the U.S. government are recorded as credits, while on the other side of the ledger expenditures abroad are recorded as debits. By the usual principles of double-entry bookkeeping, each credit must be matched by an equal debit, and vice versa. For example, each expenditure abroad, each debit, is financed in some fashion; the source of financing is recorded as a credit. A first conclusion, then, is that the balance of payments always balances.

We will, however, want to look at several concepts of deficits or surpluses in the balance of payments. Since in the total the balance of payments is always balanced, these imbalances must be the result of excluding some items from the calculation. The reason why it is of interest to look at such subtotals in the balance of payments accounts will become clear as we go along.

Table 17.1 gives a summary of the U.S. balance of payments accounts for 1978. Let us start at the top, and then as we proceed

Table 17.1   U.S. Balance of Payments, 1978 (billions of dollars)

	Credit (+)	Debit (−)	Balance (−) deficit (+) surplus
Current account			
Exports (+) and imports (−)	218.024	−228.909	
Net transfers		−5.076	
Current account balance			−15.961
Capital account			
Capital inflows (+)	32.103	−59.620	
and outflows (−)			
Capital account subbalance			−27.517
Statistical discrepancy			+11.446
Official reserve transactions balance			−32.032
Financing of official reserve transaction balance			
Reduction in U.S. official reserve assets			0.872
Increase in foreign official assets in U.S.			31.160
Total official reserve transactions			+32.032

down the list of items we will stop at various points and see whether the subgroup of transactions *above the line,* or to that point, is in balance; that is, are credits and debits equal for that subgroup of transactions?

The first group of items in the table comprise what are called *current account* transactions. The first items here are exports and imports of goods and services. The goods category includes such transactions as sales of U.S. machinery to Japan (an export) or the purchase of a Japanese car by a U.S. citizen (an import). Examples in the services category would be banking services or other professional services provided by the U.S. to foreign citizens (a credit), services provided to U.S. firms by foreign shippers (a debit), or interest and dividend earnings by U.S. citizens on foreign stocks and bonds (a payment for capital services and a credit in our balance of payments). The other transactions in the current account are net transfers. Recorded here are private and government transfer payments made between the United States and other countries. Such payments include U.S. foreign aid payments (a debit) and private or government pension payments to persons living abroad (a debit). Any such transfer to a U.S. citizen from abroad would be a credit on this line.

If we stop, or draw the line, at this point we can compute the *current account balance.* In the table it can be seen that in 1978 the current account was in deficit by $15.961 billion. Imports ex-

EXTENSIONS OF THE MODELS

ceeded exports by $10.885 billion and the net debit for transfers was an additional $5.076 billion. On current account U.S. citizens spent approximately $16 billion more than was earned in international transactions.

The next entries in the table record *capital account* transactions. Capital inflows (credits) are purchases of U.S. assets by foreign citizens. Such capital inflows include purchases by foreigners of U.S. private or government bonds, stocks, and bank deposits. Additionally, foreign direct investments in the United States, such as Volkswagon's building of a plant in Pennsylvania, are capital inflows in the balance of payments. Purchases by U.S. citizens of financial assets or direct investments in foreign countries are capital outflows (debits) in the balance of payments. In 1978 there was a net capital outflow or capital account deficit of $27.517 billion.

The last item prior to considering the method by which the net current and capital account deficit is financed is the statistical discrepancy. All international transactions are not properly recorded and the statistical discrepancy or error and omissions term is the amount that must be added to reconcile the recorded deficit and the entry we discuss next, the financing of the net current plus capital account deficit. In effect, the statistical discrepancy is the term added to make the total balance of payments balance.

If we stop and draw the line after the errors and omissions term, we can compute the *official reserve transactions* balance. All the items above the line represent international economic transactions undertaken by private U.S. citizens or the U.S. government for some motive independent of the effect of the transaction on the balance of payments. A U.S. citizen buys a Japanese car or a share of stock in a German company because he prefers them to their domestic counterparts. The U.S. government may give foreign aid to another government to stabilize the political situation in that country. All the items above the line where we stopped and computed the official reserve transactions balance are what, from the point of view of the balance of payments accounts, can be termed *autonomous* or independently motivated transactions. But what happens if when we add up all such autonomous transactions there is a deficit or surplus? How is a deficit financed? What becomes of the proceeds from a surplus?

In answering these questions it is best to begin by recognizing that all expenditures by U.S. citizens on foreign goods, services, or assets and all foreign transfers payments—all debits in the balance of payments accounts—also represent demands for foreign currencies. This demand for foreign currencies in the aggregate is termed the demand for *foreign exchange*. The U.S. citizen buying a Japanese car pays for it in dollars, but the Japanese exporter will expect to be paid in yen. So dollars must be exchanged for yen in

the *foreign exchange market,* the market in which national currencies are traded one for another. To take another example, if a U.S.
citizen buys a share of stock on the German stock exchange, a
broker must convert the buyer's dollars into marks before actually
making the purchase. Thus the total expenditure of U.S. citizens
abroad represents a demand for foreign exchange. Looked at from
the point of view of the dollar, we can also state that the total
foreign expenditure of U.S. citizens represents an equal supply of
dollars in the foreign exchange market.

Similarly, all foreign earnings of U.S. citizens reflect equal
earnings of foreign exchange. American exporters, for example,
will expect to be paid in dollars, and to buy our goods foreigners
must sell their currency and buy dollars. Total credits in the balance of payments accounts are then equal to the supply of foreign
exchange or, what is the same thing, the demand for dollars.

What does it mean when, as in Table 17.1, we find that having
summed up all the *autonomous* transactions, we have a deficit? In
1978, for example, the debits exceeded the credits by approximately $32 billion. This means that considering only autonomous
transactions the demand for foreign exchange in that year exceeded the supply by $32.032 billion. Equivalently, the supply of
dollars exceeded the demand by this amount.

The question above of how a deficit is financed is then the question of how the $32.032 billion in foreign exchange was made
available to enable U.S. citizens to make payments in excess of
their earnings abroad. Or again put in terms of the dollar, who
absorbed the $32.032 billion excess supply? The answer is that
central banks performed these actions by their official reserve
transactions, as shown in the last two lines of Table 17.1.

The first of these items is a reduction in U.S. official reserve
assets. Official U.S. reserve assets are composed of gold, holdings
of foreign currencies, and SDRs (special drawing rights), which
are a reserve asset created by the International Monetary Fund.[3]
Part of the deficit (excess demand for foreign exchange) was financed by sale of these reserve assets. The U.S. central bank by
this sale was providing foreign exchange and was buying up a part
of the $32 billion excess supply of dollars. The rest (and in 1978 the
bulk) of the deficit was financed by foreign central bank increases
in their holdings of dollars. This is the last item in the table, "Increases in foreign official assets in U.S." Foreign central banks
provided $31.160 billion worth of foreign exchange. They bought

[3]The International Monetary Fund (IMF) is an agency that was set up near the
end of World War II to administer the international monetary agreements signed at
that time. These agreements, the Bretton Woods agreements, are discussed in Section 17.2.

up dollars, which they then held in bank deposits or U.S. securities. These holdings are part of their reserves.

We will analyze why central banks *intervene* in the foreign exchange markets in the next section. For now let us summarize what we have found out about balance of payments deficits.

1. If all items are included (and accurately measured), there will be no deficit or surplus in the balance of payments accounts. Since each expenditure (debit) is by definition matched by some credit (source of financing), the accounts balance by definition.

2. If we draw the line at some point before all items are taken into account, we can calculate the amount by which, for items above the line, there is an excess of debits over credits (a deficit) or alternatively an excess of credits over debits (a surplus).

3. The most important concept of a deficit is where we draw the line after all "autonomous" transactions. The deficit or surplus computed at this point is called the *official reserve transaction balance* and shows the amount of *accommodating* central bank transactions which were required to finance a deficit or absorb a surplus in the U.S. payments balance.[4]

17.2 EXCHANGE RATES AND THE MARKET FOR FOREIGN EXCHANGE

The Foreign Exchange Market

We return now to the question of how and why central banks intervene in foreign exchange markets to finance balance of payment imbalances. For simplicity we will assume that there are only two countries, the United States, whose domestic currency is the dollar, and Germany, with the mark as the domestic currency unit. The *exchange rate* in this simple situation is the relative price of the two currencies, which we will express as *the price of the mark in terms of dollars.* If, for example, the price of the mark is 0.25 dollar, then 4 marks trade for 1 dollar; at 0.40 dollar the exchange rate (price of the mark) is higher and 2.5 marks equal 1 dollar. It will be important to remember that with the exchange rate expressed in this manner, a higher exchange rate means that the price of foreign currency (or foreign exchange) has risen. When the exchange

---

[4]The example considered above was the financing of a deficit in the U.S. balance of payments. If there had been a surplus, the two items below the line (the last two items in Table 17.1) would have shown a net increase in U.S. official reserve assets and a decline in foreign official reserve assets in the United States just equal to the amount of the surplus.

rate rises, we say that the foreign currency has *appreciated* or the dollar has *depreciated*. Alternatively, a fall in the exchange rate means that the price of foreign exchange (price of the marks) has declined. The mark has *depreciated* while the dollar has *appreciated*.

The exchange rate will be determined in the market for foreign exchange where the currencies are traded. In Figure 17.1 we represent graphically the supply and demand curves for foreign exchange plotted against the exchange rate (π). As was explained above, all foreign expenditures by U.S. citizens (imports, purchases of foreign assets, and foreign transfers) are demands for foreign exchange. How will this demand for foreign exchange vary with the price of foreign exchange? As drawn in Figure 17.1, the demand curve (D_{fe}) is downward sloping, indicating that as the price of foreign exchange (price of marks) rises, the demand for foreign exchange falls. This is because a rise in the price of foreign

Figure 17.1
Foreign Exchange
Market

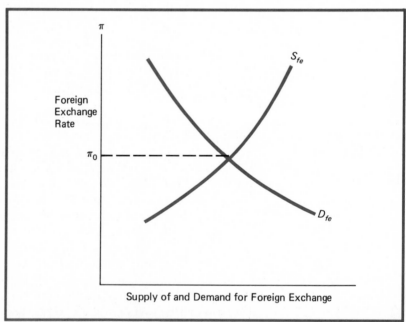

The demand schedule for foreign exchange is downward sloping plotted against the exchange rate (π) since the demand for foreign exchange to finance imports will fall as the exchange rate rises, making foreign goods more expensive. The supply schedule for foreign exchange is upward sloping reflecting the assumption that the foreign exchange proceeds from export sales rise as the exchange rate rises, making domestic goods less expensive to foreign buyers. The equilibrium value of the exchange rate is π_0, the rate which will equate demand and supply.

EXTENSIONS OF THE MODELS

exchange will increase the cost in terms of dollars of purchasing foreign goods. Imports will therefore decline and less foreign exchange will be demanded. Note that here we are holding all prices other than the exchange rate constant. Suppose that you are considering the purchase of a German camera that costs 200 marks. If the exchange rate, the price of the mark in terms of dollars, is 0.25, the camera will cost $50 (200 marks = $50 at 4 marks to the dollar). If the exchange rate rises to 0.5, the camera will cost $100 (200 marks = $100 at 2 marks to the dollar). The higher the exchange rate, the higher the dollar cost of imported goods and the lower the demand for foreign exchange.

What about the demand for foreign exchange for the purchase of foreign assets and for foreign transfers? With respect to the latter, there seems no reason for a definite relationship between the amount of foreign transfers and the exchange rate. It is not clear what effect the change in the exchange rate would have on foreign aid programs, pension payments to persons living abroad, or gifts to foreign nationals. In the case of purchases of foreign assets, an increase in the exchange rate will, as in the case of imported goods, push up the price in dollars of the foreign stocks or bonds. The rise in the exchange rate will also result in a proportional increase in the interest or dividend payment on the foreign bond or stock, again as measured in dollars. For example, a German bond costing 1000 marks and paying interest of 100 marks per year will cost $250 and pay interest of $25 per year at an exchange rate of 0.25 (4 marks = 1 dollar). At an exchange rate of 0.5 (2 marks = 1 dollar), the bond will cost $500 and pay interest of $50 per year. In either case the bond represents an asset that pays a return of 10 percent per year. Consequently, we would not necessarily expect any effect on the demand for foreign assets as a result of a change in the exchange rate.[5] The downward slope of the demand for foreign exchange schedule therefore results only from the fact that imports decline as the exchange rate rises.

The supply schedule for foreign exchange is drawn with a positive slope in Figure 17.1, which reflects the assumption that the supply of foreign exchange increases as the exchange rate rises. As the exchange rate (price of marks) rises, U.S. export goods become less expensive to Germans in terms of marks. Again here we are holding all other prices, including the dollar price of U.S. exports, fixed. Thus U.S. wheat, for example, which sells for $4 a bushel

---

[5]It would be the expectation of a change in the exchange rate that would trigger changes in the demands for foreign versus domestic assets. If, for example, you expected the price of the mark to rise from 0.25 dollar today to 0.50 dollar next week, you would buy the German bond discussed in the text now for $250 and could sell it next week for $500. For now, however, we are not allowing for expected changes in the foreign exchange rate.

would cost a German 16 marks per bushel at an exchange rate of 0.25 (4 marks = 1 dollar) but only 8 marks at an exchange rate of 0.5 (2 marks = 1 dollar).

The demand for our exports should therefore increase as the exchange rate rises. Notice, however, that a given *dollar* volume of exports earns less foreign exchange (fewer marks) at the higher exchange rate. If, for example, the exchange rate rose by 10 percent and as a result the *dollar* volume of exports rose 10 percent, earnings of foreign exchange would be unchanged. The United States would be selling 10 percent more but earning 10 percent fewer marks on each sale.

For the supply of foreign exchange to increase as the exchange rate rises, the foreign demand for our exports must be more than *unit elastic*, meaning simply that a 1 percent increase in the exchange rate (which results in a 1 percent decline in the price of the export good to Germans) must result in an increase in demand of more than 1 percent. If this condition is met, the dollar volume of our exports will rise more than in proportion to the rise in the exchange rate and earnings of marks (the supply of foreign exchange) will increase as the exchange rate rises. This is the assumption we make in Figure 17.1.[6]

Exchange Rate Determination: Flexible Exchange Rates

So far we have said nothing about intervention by central banks in this market for foreign exchange. Let us assume for the moment that there is none and see how the exchange rate is determined in the absence of such intervention. In this case we would expect the exchange rate to move to clear the market, to equate the demand for and supply of foreign exchange. In Figure 17.1, this equilibrium exchange rate is π_0. It is important to note that since the exchange rate moves to equate supply and demand in the foreign exchange market, there is no balance of payments deficit in the official reserve transactions sense. The autonomous elements in the balance of payments account, those above the line where the official reserve transactions balance is computed, are equated by the adjustment of the exchange rate. Such a system of exchange rate determination where there is no central bank intervention is a *flexible exchange rate system* or, as it is sometimes called, a *floating rate* system. An exchange rate system or regime is a set of international rules governing the setting of exchange rates. A completely flexible or floating rate system is a particularly simple set of rules for the central banks of different countries to follow; they do nothing to affect directly the level of their exchange rate. The exchange rate is market determined.

[6]Empirical support for this assumption is provided by Hendrik Houthakker and Stephen Magee, "Income and Price Elasticities in World Trade," *Review of Economics and Statistics*, 5 (May 1969), pp. 111–25.

EXTENSIONS OF THE MODELS

To better understand the workings of a flexible exchange rate system and why the official reserve transactions balance will be zero with such a system, we examine the effect of a shock that increases the demand for foreign exchange. Suppose that there is an increase in the U.S. demand for imported goods. For example, assume that an increase in energy prices causes an increased demand for fuel-efficient foreign cars. The effect of this increase in import demand would show up in the foreign exchange market as a shift to the right in the demand schedule for foreign exchange, for example, from D_{fe}^0 to D_{fe}^1 as illustrated in Figure 17.2. At a given exchange rate, there is a greater demand for imports in the United States and correspondingly a greater demand for foreign exchange to finance the increase in imports. At the initial equilibrium exchange rate π_0, there is now an excess demand for foreign exchange (shown as XD_{fe} in Figure 17.2). To clear the market, the exchange rate must rise to the new equilibrium value π_1.

The rise in the exchange rate will cause the quantity of imports demanded to decline since the dollar price of imported goods will rise with the exchange rate. Also, the quantity of exports de-

Figure 17.2
Effect in the Foreign Exchange Market of an Increase in the Demand for Imports

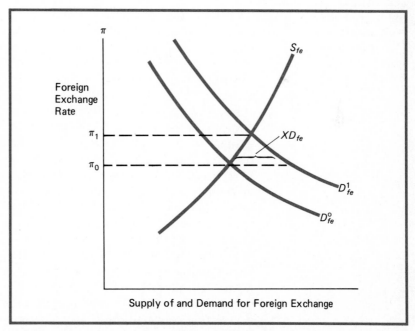

An autonomous increase in import demand shifts the demand schedule for foreign exchange from D_{fe}^0 to D_{fe}^1. At the initial equilibrium exchange rate there is now an excess demand for foreign exchange (XD_{fe}). The exchange rate rises to π_1 to requilibrate supply and demand in the foreign exchange market.

manded will increase since the rise in the exchange rate will make U.S. exports less expensive to foreigners. This adjustment in the exchange rate eliminates an incipient balance of payments deficit due to the excess of desired U.S. expenditures abroad (the demand for foreign exchange) over earnings abroad (the supply of foreign exchange) which existed at π_0. At the new equilibrium with the higher exchange rate (π_1), the supply and demand for foreign exchange are again equal. The increase in import demand has led not to a balance of payments deficit but to a depreciation of the dollar.

The official reserve transaction balance for the United States has not been zero in recent years. As Table 17.1 indicates, the United States had a $32 billion official reserve transaction balance deficit in 1978. We have not then had a *completely* flexible exchange rate system. The current international monetary system is discussed below. Prior to that it is useful to discuss the working of the foreign exchange market under the polar opposite of a completely flexible rate system, a system of *fixed* or *pegged* exchange rates. The current system will be seen to be a mixture of the two extremes.

Exchange Rate Determination: Fixed Exchange Rates

An international monetary system is a set of rules organizing exchange rate determination and agreeing on which assets will be official reserve assets. An example of a fixed exchange rate system was the post–World War II Bretton Woods system. The international monetary agreements that comprise this system were negotiated near the end of the war (at Bretton Woods, New Hampshire). The International Monetary Fund (IMF) was set up to administer the Bretton Woods system. According to IMF rules, the United States was to set a parity or par value for its currency in terms of gold. Other nations would set parities for their currencies in terms of dollars, which with the dollar tied to gold also fixed the gold value of these other currencies. The United States agreed to maintain convertibility between the dollar and gold at the fixed price (originally $35 per ounce). Other countries agreed to maintain convertibility (after a period of postwar adjustment) with the dollar and other currencies but not with gold. The other countries agreed to maintain their exchange rates vis-à-vis the dollar within a 1 percent range on either side of the parity level. The differential responsibility of the United States as against other IMF members concerning convertibility into gold seemed sensible in that at the time the United States had approximately two-thirds of the official world gold reserves.

To see how a system of fixed exchange rates functions, we will examine the way in which a country can "peg" or fix the level of its exchange rate. To do so we return to our two-country example and assume that the United States wants to fix its exchange rate against the mark, which we are using to represent the currencies of the rest of the world. We will ignore the 1 percent margin just mentioned and assume that the U.S. central bank wishes to fix an exact par value for the dollar; let us say that an exchange rate of 1 mark equals 0.4 dollar (2.5 marks = 1 dollar). The working of the foreign exchange market with this fixed exchange rate system is illustrated in Figure 17.3.

We will assume that this official fixed exchange rate 0.4 (1 mark = 0.4 dollar) is below the equilibrium exchange rate in a flexible rate system, the equilibrium rate in Figure 17.3 being 0.5 (2 marks = 1 dollar). At the fixed exchange rate in such a situation the dollar would be said to be *overvalued* and the mark would be said to be *undervalued*. What is meant by this is that if the exchange rate were market determined, the price of the mark relative to the dollar (the exchange rate) would have to rise to clear the market. What prevents this from happening?

Recall that the demand and supply schedules that we constructed for the foreign exchange market measure only *autono-*

Figure 17.3
Foreign Exchange
Market with Fixed
Exchange Rate

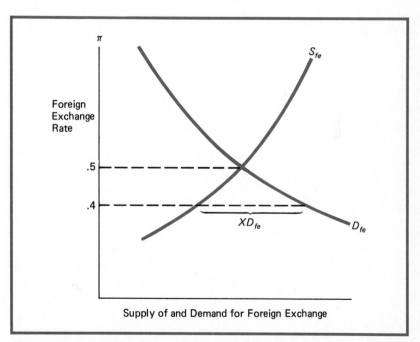

If, in a fixed exchange rate system, the official exchange rate ($\pi = .4$) is below the market equilibrium rate ($\pi = .5$), there will be an excess demand for foreign exchange, XD_{fe}. To keep the exchange rate from rising, domestic or foreign central banks must supply an amount of foreign exchange equal to XD_{fe}.

mous transactions; they do not take account of accommodating transactions undertaken by central banks to finance payments imbalances. It is precisely such intervention by central banks that is required to peg the exchange rate at a nonequilibrium value such as 0.4 dollar in Figure 17.3. To keep the rate at 0.4, the United States must stand ready to buy and sell dollars at that exchange rate. That this will fix the exchange rate (price of the mark) at that level should be clear. If the U.S. central bank will buy marks for 0.4 dollar the exchange rate cannot fall below that point since no one would sell elsewhere for less. Similarly, the exchange rate cannot rise above 0.4 since the central bank will be willing to sell marks at that price.

In the situation depicted in Figure 17.3, with the exchange rate below the equilibrium rate, there is an excess demand for foreign exchange (shown of XD_{fe}). To keep the exchange rate from rising, the central bank must supply foreign exchange (i.e., buy dollars in exchange for marks).

In the balance of payments accounts such intervention will appear as a deficit in the official reserve transactions balance. The deficit is financed by a decline in U.S. official reserve assets as the central bank's holding of foreign currencies, in our example marks, declines, or as the central bank uses another reserve asset, such as gold, to buy marks which are then sold for dollars in the foreign exchange market. (This is the first of the two items below the line in Table 17.1.)

Alternatively, the German central bank may be the one to intervene to keep the exchange rate between the dollar and the mark fixed. The German central bank would supply the necessary marks (buy up the necessary amount of dollars) to keep the price of the mark from rising above 0.4 dollar. The German central bank would then find itself with an increased holding of dollars. Under the Bretton Woods system, the German central bank could then demand that the United States exchange these dollars for gold or SDRs, in which case this intervention in the foreign exchange market would also show up in our balance of payments as a decline in official U.S. reserve assets. The German central bank might instead simply keep the dollars, for example as bank deposits in the United States. In this case the results of the German central bank's intervention in the foreign exchange market would appear in our balance of payments account as an increase in foreign official reserve assets in the United States (the last item in Table 17.1).

There is an important point to note here. It would be sensible for the German central bank to increase its holdings of dollars rather than demand payment in gold or SDRs because the dollar itself is used by other countries as a reserve asset. Assume instead that the country with a fixed exchange rate was Mexico, with pesos as their currency. Then, if the German central bank intervened and purchased pesos to stabilize the exchange rate with Mexico, it is less likely that the German central bank would want to hold the pesos as a reserve asset. It is more likely that they would ask the Mexican central bank to exchange the pesos for gold or SDRs. Thus, for most countries balance of payments deficits will result in declines in their official reserve assets. Consequently, they have a limited ability to sustain such deficits without running out of reserves. When deficits arise, such countries must adopt some policy to keep the deficit from persisting.

Exchange Rate Determination: A Managed Float

The current international monetary system, to the extent that one can call the current arrangement a system at all, is a system of neither completely fixed or completely flexible exchange rates. As an IMF official described the situation at one point:

> We have 10 countries floating with different degrees of intervention; we have 8 countries floating as a bloc, maintaining a very close relationship among themselves, but with no obligation whatsoever to defend a rate with respect to the dollar; and we have 24 countries that have pegged their currencies with respect to the dollar; 14 with respect to the French franc; and 11 with respect to the pound; and we have 53 countries that have either declared central rates or par value which they defend by intervening in any of the 3 above-mentioned currencies.[7]

This statement indicates that the current situation is a cross between a fixed and a flexible exchange rate system, what has come to be called a *managed* or *dirty float*.

In the case of the dollar this means that the U.S. central bank allows the price of the dollar to float in response to market forces, as in the flexible rate case. At times, however, the central bank intervenes to prevent what it views as disruptive movements in the exchange rate. The interpretation of "disruptive" has varied somewhat over time. In the 1974–80 period there were frequent interventions in the foreign exchange market by the U.S. central bank. For example, in November of 1978 there was a massive support program for the price of the dollar coordinated by the U.S. government. In 1981 the Reagan administration announced that there would be central bank intervention only when necessary to prevent disorder in the foreign exchange market initiated by crisis situations following events such as the shooting of President Reagan, the assassination of Egypt's President Sadat, or the declaration of martial law in Poland. Following the adoption of this strict

---

[7]Statement by Richard H. Arrazu, Alternate Executive Director, IMF, quoted in Marina v. N. Whitman, "The Current and Future Role of the Dollar: How Much Symmetry?" *Brookings Papers on Economic Activity*, No. 3, 1974, p. 577.

interpretation of what constituted a "disruptive" movement in the exchange rate, there were several quarters in which no U.S. central bank intervention in the foreign exchange market took place.

Even in the absence of U.S. central bank intervention, the price of the dollar does not float freely with the current exchange rate system. This is true because foreign central banks buy or sell dollars to influence the price of their currencies relative to the dollar. For example, in 1981 European central banks sold dollars from their reserve holdings to slow the rise in the price of the dollar which would have meant a fall in the price of their currencies. The current system remains a *managed* or *dirty float*.

How did the international monetary system become so disorganized, and should this lack of organization be a cause of concern? The second of these questions is best left for Section 17.4, where the relative merits of different exchange rate systems will be considered. The question of how the current international monetary system or lack of a system emerged is the question of why the Bretton Woods system disintegrated.

Central to the Bretton Woods system was the set of fixed exchange rates and the key currency role of the dollar. Par values set for currencies were not assumed to be fixed for all time; the Bretton Woods system was to be one of adjustable pegs. A country was to be able to change its exchange rate if it found that there was a "fundamental disequilibrium" in its balance of payments. Such changes were to be made in consultation with the IMF. Countries with chronic deficits would be expected to *devalue* their currencies, which means to lower the par value of the currency in terms of the dollar, and since the dollar's value in terms of gold was fixed to also lower the currency's value in terms of gold. Countries with persistent surpluses would *revalue* their currencies at higher par values in terms of the dollar and gold.

In fact, adjustments in exchange rates proved extremely difficult. Countries with persistent surpluses were under no pressure to revalue their currencies. Governments of countries with persistent deficits found it politically difficult to devalue, since a decline in the value of the currency was taken as a sign of the failure of a government's economic policy. Also, rumors that a currency was to be devalued led to waves of speculation against the currency, as speculators sold the currency with an eye to buying it back after it had been devalued. Because of these difficulties in making adjustments in the par values of currencies, over the Bretton Woods period some countries (e.g., Great Britain) developed chronic balance of payments deficits and others (e.g., Germany), chronic surpluses.

Most damaging to the system, the United States developed into a chronic deficit country, an indication that the dollar was over-

EXTENSIONS OF THE MODELS

valued. To devalue the dollar, which since the dollar was convertible into gold at the fixed par value meant a rise in the price of gold, presented special difficulties because of the key currency role played by the dollar within the Bretton Woods system. But the growing deficits in the U.S. balance of payments were creating a glut of dollars on the market. The problem became acute in the late 1960s and especially in 1971. Throughout the 1960s the United States had had deficits on the official reserve transactions balance. As long as such deficits were not too large, foreign central banks were willing to hold the dollars created by these deficits since the dollar served as a reserve currency. In this process, as described in Section 17.2, foreign central banks intervened in the foreign exchange market. They sold their currency, obtained dollars, and held them as an official reserve asset. Such dollar reserves, which constituted claims on the United States, rose from $21.0 billion in 1960 to $38.5 billion in 1968. To some extent the deficits of the 1960s were also financed by a decline in U.S. official reserve assets. The U.S. official gold stock fell from $17.8 billion in 1960 to $10.9 billion in 1968.

In the late 1960s, the U.S. balance of payments position worsened. Severe inflationary pressure developed in the United States due to government spending on the Vietnam war, which was not adequately financed by increased taxes. This increased inflation worsened the U.S. balance of payments in the following way. Prices in the United States rose faster than prices in other industrial countries. With the exchange rate fixed, this meant that our export goods became more expensive to foreigners while the price of foreign imports fell relative to domestic goods prices in the United States. As a consequence, the demand for our exports fell and our demand for imports rose; our balance of payments deficit increased. In 1971 the deficit on the official reserve transaction balance was $29.8 billion!

Foreign central banks could not continue to absorb so many dollar reserves. Nor could they demand payment from the United States in gold since the U.S. gold stock had fallen to $10.9 billion by 1968. The glut of dollars and the presumption that eventually the dollar would have to be devalued led to a lack of confidence in the dollar as an asset.

In 1972 the dollar was devalued, with the price of gold increased to $38. A new set of par values for other IMF member currencies was established. Attempts to defend the new set of par values had collapsed, however, by 1973. Again an upward surge of inflation in the United States and loss of confidence in the dollar were proximate causes of the problems in maintaining a set of fixed currency values. Also, beginning in 1973–74, huge increases in oil prices led to large balance of payments deficits for the industrialized oil-consuming nations and surpluses for the oil-producing countries. Exchange rate adjustments were required to restore equilibrium. The system of a managed float that emerged in the 1970s has been the mechanism by which exchange rate adjustments necessitated by the declining strength of the dollar and rising oil prices have been achieved.

17.3 THE BALANCE OF PAYMENTS AND THE LEVEL OF ECONOMIC ACTIVITY

In this section we analyze the relationships between items in the balance of payments—imports, exports, and capital flows—and the level of economic activity. For the present our attention will be confined to the fixed exchange rate case.[8] We will see the potential conflicts that can arise for a country between pursuing domestic goals and maintaining balance of payment equilibrium, conflicts between *internal equilibrium* and *external equilibrium*. This discussion will be useful for our evaluation in the next section of the relative merits of different exchange rate systems.

The Effects of Imports and Exports on Equilibrium Income

To start, consider the role of imports and exports within the simplest of the Keynesian models of Part II, the model in Chapter 5. This simple Keynesian model neglected both the money market and the effects of changes in wages and prices. Equilibrium output was determined completely by aggregate demand. The condition for equilibrium in the model specified that output must equal aggregate demand,

$$Y = C + I + G \tag{17.1}$$

where as before Y is output, C is consumption, I is desired investment, and G is government spending.

To extend this condition to an open economy, we must add to aggregate demand exports (X), which are foreign demands for domestic output. Also, since imports (Z) are included in $C, I,$ and G but are *not* demands for domestic goods, we must subtract out imports. The resulting condition for equilibrium output in an open economy is

$$Y = C + I + G + X - Z \tag{17.2}$$

As in Chapter 5, we will take investment and government spend-

---

[8]The flexible exchange rate case is discussed in the appendix to this chapter, which also contains a more detailed analysis of the fixed rate case. The adjustment of the exchange rate to external shocks in the flexible rate case is discussed in Section 17.4.

ing as exogenous—as autonomous expenditure components. Consumption will again be given by the consumption function

$$C = a + bY \qquad (17.3)$$

where, since they play no essential role in our discussion, we have left out taxes and therefore do not need to distinguish between GNP and disposable income ($Y_D = Y - T$). To compute equilibrium output for the open economy case, we need to specify the determinants of imports and exports.

To simplify our analysis we will assume that imports consist solely of consumption goods. The demand for imports will be assumed to depend on income and to have an autonomous component

$$Z = u + vY \qquad u > 0, \quad 0 < v < 1 \qquad (17.4)$$

The parameter u represents the autonomous component of imports. The parameter v is the marginal propensity to import, the increase in import demand per unit increase in GNP, a concept analogous to the marginal propensity to consume (b) in (17.3).

The demand for our exports will be a part of the foreign demand for imports. The foreign demand for imports will depend on the level of *foreign* income, being determined by an import demand function analogous to (17.4). From the point of view of this country, foreign income and, hence, the demand for our exports will be considered exogenous.

Additional variables that one would surely expect to influence both our demand for imports and foreign demand of our exports are the relative price levels in the two countries and the level of the exchange rate. These variables will determine the relative costs of the two countries' products to citizens of either country. Note that for now we are assuming that price levels and the exchange rate are fixed. Below, the effects on imports and exports of changes in the domestic price level or exchange rate will need to be examined.

With imports given by (17.4) and exports assumed to be exogenous, we can compute equilibrium income from (17.2), as follows:

$$Y = C + I + G + X - Z \qquad (17.2)$$

$$Y = \overbrace{a + bY}^{C} + I + G + X \overbrace{-u - vY}^{-Z}$$

$$Y - bY + vY = a + I + G + X - u$$

$$(1 - b + v)Y = a + I + G + X - u$$

$$\bar{Y} = \frac{1}{1 - b + v}(a + I + G + X - u) \qquad (17.5)$$

One way to examine the effects of allowing for foreign trade in the model is to compare (17.5) with the equivalent expression for equilibrium income from the closed economy model in Chapter 5. This expression, omitting the tax variable (T), can be written as

$$\bar{Y} = \frac{1}{1-b}(a + I + G) \tag{17.6}$$

[see equation (5.15)]. In both (17.5) and (17.6) equilibrium income is expressed as the product of two terms (as explained in Chapter 5), the autonomous expenditure multiplier and the level of autonomous expenditures. Consider how each of these is changed by adding imports and exports to the model.

Take first the autonomous expenditure multiplier $\left(\dfrac{1}{1-b+v}\right)$ in (17.5) as opposed to $\left(\dfrac{1}{1-b}\right)$ in (17.6) for the closed economy model. Since v, the marginal propensity to import, is greater than zero, the multiplier in (17.5), $\left(\dfrac{1}{1-b+v}\right)$ will be *smaller* than the multiplier in (17.6), $\left(\dfrac{1}{1-b}\right)$. To give an example, if $b = 0.8$ and $v = 0.3$, we would then have

$$\frac{1}{1-b} = \frac{1}{1-0.8} = \frac{1}{0.2} = 5$$

and

$$\frac{1}{1-b+v} = \frac{1}{1-0.8+0.3} = \frac{1}{0.5} = 2$$

From these expressions it can be seen that the more open an economy is to foreign trade (the higher is v), the lower will be the autonomous expenditure multiplier.

As discussed in Chapter 5, the autonomous expenditure multiplier gives the change in equilibrium income per unit change in autonomous expenditures. It follows, therefore, that the more open an economy is (the higher v), the smaller will be the response of income to aggregate demand shocks such as changes in government spending or autonomous changes in investment demand. The reason for the decline in the value of the autonomous expenditure multiplier with a rise in v can be explained with reference to our discussion of the multiplier process in Chapter 5. A change in autonomous expenditures, a change in government spending for example, will have a direct effect on income and have an induced effect on consumption with a further effect on income. The higher the value of v, the larger the proportion of this induced effect on consumption that will be a change in demand for *foreign*, not domestic, consumer goods. The smaller will be the induced effect on demand for domestic goods and, hence, on domestic income. The increase in imports per unit of income constitutes an additional *leakage* from the circular flow of (domestic) income at each round of the multiplier process and reduces the value of the autonomous expenditure multiplier.

Now consider the second term in the expression for equilibrium income in the open economy case [equation (17.5)], the level of autonomous expenditures. In addition to the elements for a closed economy $(a + I + G)$, autonomous expenditures for the open economy include the level of exports and the autonomous component of imports. Recall that autonomous components of aggregate demand are those that are not directly determined by income. Rather, shifts in the components of autonomous expenditures affect the level of aggregate demand *for a given level of income* and result in changes in equilibrium income. Thus changes in the level of exports and autonomous changes in import demand are additional shocks that will change equilibrium income.

From (17.5) we can compute the multiplier effects of changes in X and u.

$$\frac{\Delta \bar{Y}}{\Delta X} = \frac{1}{1 - b + v} \qquad (17.7)$$

$$\frac{\Delta \bar{Y}}{\Delta u} = \frac{-1}{1 - b + v} \qquad (17.8)$$

An increase in the demand for our exports is an increase in aggregate demand for domestically produced output and will increase equilibrium income just as would an increase in government spending or an autonomous increase in investment.[9]

In contrast, an autonomous increase in import demand, an increase in u, is seen to cause a decline in equilibrium income. An autonomous increase in import demand represents a shift from demand for domestic goods to demand for foreign goods. For example, because of the large rise in gasoline prices, U.S. consumers shifted demand from domestic to foreign automobiles. As such, the autonomous increase in import demand is a *decline* in demand for domestic output and causes equilibrium income to decline.

To summarize, an increase in the demand for our exports will have an expansionary effect on equilibrium income, whereas an autonomous increase in imports will have a contractionary effect on equilibrium income. Clearly, this should not be interpreted to

[9]Note that from (17.5) we can compute

$$\frac{\Delta \bar{Y}}{\Delta G} = \frac{\Delta \bar{Y}}{\Delta I} = \frac{1}{1 - b + v}$$

mean exports are good and imports harmful in their economic effects. Countries import goods that can be more efficiently produced abroad, and trade increases the overall efficiency of the worldwide allocation of resources. The expansionary effect of increases in exports and contractionary effect of increases in imports do, however, explain why at times nations have tried to stimulate the domestic economy by subsidizing exports and restricting the flow of imports.

The Level of Economic Activity and the Trade Balance

The specifications of imports and exports in the preceding subsection have implications for the relationship between the trade balance [exports (X) − imports (Z)] and the level of economic activity. This relationship is illustrated in Figure 17.4. The export demand schedule is horizontal when plotted against the level of income, reflecting the fact that export demand is exogenous. The import demand schedule is upward sloping since the demand for imports depends positively on income. The slope of the import demand schedule is the marginal propensity to import (v).

As shown in Figure 17.4, exports and imports will be equal if income is at the level $Y_{TB=0}$ (the trade balance will be zero). This level of income generates import demand just equal to the exoge-

Figure 17.4

Trade Balance and the Level of Economic Activity

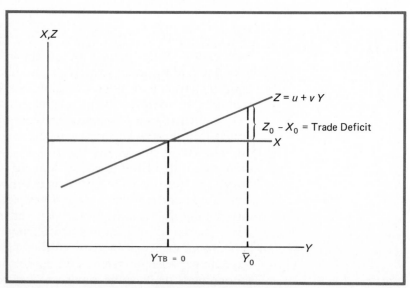

The level of income which equates imports (Z) with the exogenous level of exports (X) is $Y_{TB=0}$. There is no reason to believe that the equilibrium level of income is equal to $Y_{TB=0}$. For example, if $\bar{Y}_0$ is the equilibrium level of income, imports will exceed exports and there will be a deficit in the trade balance $(Z_0 − X_0)$.

EXTENSIONS OF THE MODELS

nous level of exports. But, notice that there is no reason to expect that $Y_{TB=0}$ will be an equilibrium level of income. The equilibrium level of income will be determined by (17.5) and may be either above or below the level that equates imports and exports. For example, in Figure 17.4 assume that the equilibrium level of income is at $\bar{Y}_0$, above $Y_{TB=0}$. At income level $\bar{Y}_0$, imports exceed exports and there is a trade deficit.

We have seen in earlier chapters how aggregate demand management policies can, at least in the Keynesian view, be used to affect equilibrium income. Such policies could then in principle be used to move equilibrium income to the level $Y_{TB=0}$, where exports equal imports. If the other current account items and the capital account were in balance, this would be a position of what we will call *external balance* for the economy, which in a fixed exchange rate system means balance of payments equilibrium (official reserve transactions deficit equals zero). In terms of Figure 17.4, the policymaker could, for example, use a restrictive fiscal policy such as a tax increase to reduce income from $\bar{Y}_0$ to $Y_{TB=0}$.

But policymakers also have domestic goals. Within the Keynesian framework, aggregate demand management policies are to be used to pursue unemployment and inflation goals—to achieve *internal balance*. The problem, and the important point to note here, is that there is no reason to believe that the level of income which produces external balance is the level that is optimal with regard to domestic goals. Suppose, for example, that in Figure 17.4, the optimal level from the point of view of domestic goals is $\bar{Y}_0$. If a restrictive fiscal policy were used to lower income to $Y_{TB=0}$, a undesirably high unemployment rate would result and internal balance would be disturbed. But if income is maintained at $\bar{Y}_0$, there will be a trade deficit; the economy will not have external balance.

We see then that *under a fixed exchange rate system, potential conflicts arise between the goals of internal balance and external balance.* In particular, countries may find that expansionary policies, which might be desirable from the point of view of reducing the unemployment rate, lead to income levels too high to balance the trade account and may therefore lead to balance of payments problems.

Capital Flows and the Level of Economic Activity

The primary determinants of the level of capital flows between nations are expected rates of return on assets in each of the countries. With a fixed exchange rate system the effects of expected exchange rate movements on asset returns can be ignored (except at times when there is speculation that the official exchange rate is to change). Interest rates in the various countries will be measures of relative rates of return. If we take the rate of return in other countries as given, the level of the capital flow into a particular country will depend positively on the level of its interest rate (r); that is,

$$F = F(r) \qquad\qquad (17.9)$$

where F is the net capital inflow (a negative value of F represents a net outflow or deficit on capital account).[10] The way in which the changes in the level of economic activity will affect the balance on the capital account will therefore depend on how the interest rate varies with the change in economic activity.

Consider first increases in economic activity caused by expansionary monetary policies. As was explained in Chapter 7, an expansionary monetary policy will stimulate aggregate demand and, hence, income by *lowering* the rate of interest. The effect of the lower rate of interest will be unfavorable to the balance on capital account. The amount of investment in the United States by foreigners will decline and U.S. investment abroad will increase as foreign assets become relatively more attractive. (Remember here that the foreign interest rate is assumed to be unchanged.) In the preceding section we saw that increases in income for any reason increased imports while leaving exports unchanged and therefore worsened the trade balance. If the increase in income is the result of an expansionary monetary policy, it follows that both the trade balance and the capital account will deteriorate.

Now suppose alternatively that the increase in economic activity was the result of an expansionary fiscal policy or another nonmonetary shock to aggregate demand such as an autonomous increase in (domestic physical) investment. As income rises there is a consequent increase in the demand for money, and with a fixed money stock the interest rate will rise (see Section 7.1). In this case the increase in income is accompanied by an increase in the interest rate. Consequently, while the balance of trade worsens, the rise in the interest rate will stimulate a capital inflow. Whether the overall effect on the balance of payments is favorable or unfavorable will depend on the relative strength of these two effects of the fiscal policy–induced expansion: the favorable effect on the capital account or the unfavorable effect on the trade balance.

We find therefore that in a fixed exchange rate system, conflicts may arise between domestic goals such as low unemployment and the goal of external balance as measured by balance of payments equilibrium. The conflict is especially severe with respect to monetary policy, where expansionary policy actions have unfavorable

---

[10]Capital flows include purchases of shares of stock in other countries and direct investments as well as purchases of bonds, the asset that earns the interest rate (r). Thus other variables that influence the expected returns on stocks and direct investments might be included in a more complex specification of the capital flow function. For simplicity, we restrict our attention here to the simple function (17.9).

EXTENSIONS OF THE MODELS

effects on both the trade balance and the capital account. Expansionary fiscal policies may also lead to balance of payments problems if their unfavorable effect on the trade balance outweighs their favorable effect on the capital account. Although there is no overwhelming empirical evidence on the question, U.S. policymakers appear to believe that expansionary fiscal policies have unfavorable balance of payments effects. Excessive government budget deficits were, for example, often cited as a cause of U.S. balance of payment difficulties during the pre-1973 period of fixed exchange rates.

The reason for this presumption that any expansionary policy is likely to lead to a deterioration in the balance of payments may be due to a final relationship between the balance of payments and the level of economic activity which needs to be taken into account. Unless the economy is far from full employment, expansionary aggregate demand policies, whether monetary or fiscal in nature, will cause the price level to rise. With a fixed exchange rate, an increase in the domestic price level will, for a constant foreign price level, increase imports and cause exports to decline. Foreign goods will be relatively cheaper to U.S. citizens and our exports will be more expensive to foreign buyers. This *price effect* on the balance of trade reinforces the directly unfavorable effect that an economic expansion has on the trade balance.[11]

17.4 THE RELATIVE MERITS OF FIXED VERSUS FLEXIBLE EXCHANGE RATES

In Section 17.2 we left unanswered the question of whether the collapse of the Bretton Woods fixed exchange rate system and the ensuing greater, but by no means total, flexibility of exchange rates should be a cause of concern. The answer to this question depends, at least in part, on the relative merits of fixed versus flexible exchange rates, a question that has long been debated by economists and central bankers. To provide a context in which to discuss this question, it was first necessary to explain the interrelationships between the balance of payments and the level of economic activity as well as the potential conflicts between the goals of internal and external balance which can arise in a fixed exchange rate system. A major advantage cited by advocates of a flexible exchange rate system is that with flexible exchange rates there can be no conflict between balance of payments equilibrium

[11]Macroeconomic policy in an open economy and the interrelationships among balance of payments adjustment, the interest rate, and the level of economic activity are discussed further in·the appendix to this chapter.

and domestic policy goals. With flexible exchange rates, the exchange rate will adjust automatically to equate the supply and demand for foreign exchange. A flexible rate system therefore removes the balance of payments constraint on domestic policy instruments, leaving these instruments to be used in pursuit of domestic goals.

To see this, consider the case of a country that begins in a situation of balance of payments equilibrium but with an unacceptably high unemployment rate. Suppose that the situation in the foreign exchange market is as shown in Figure 17.5. In the initial situation the supply and demand curves for foreign exchange are assumed to be S_{fe}^0 and D_{fc}^0. respectively. The foreign exchange market is in equilibrium at the exchange rate π_0, which will be assumed to be the par value for the country's currency within a fixed exchange rate system.

Suppose now that in order to alleviate the high unemployment (from which we have supposed the country to be suffering) the policymakers embark on an expansionary monetary policy. The

Figure 17.5
Effect of an
Expansionary
Monetary Policy in the
Foreign Exchange
Market: Fixed and
Flexible Exchange
Rates

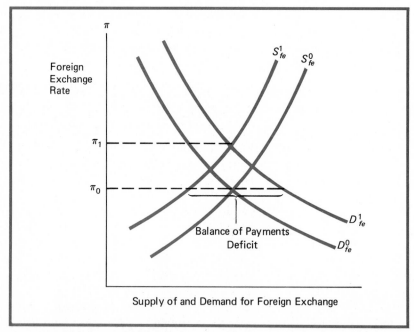

An expansionary monetary policy shifts the demand curve for foreign exchange to the right from D_{fe}^0 to D_{fe}^1 and shifts the supply curve for foreign exchange to the left from S_{fe}^0 to S_{fe}^1. With a fixed exchange rate system, there will be a balance of payments deficit as indicated in the figure. With a flexible exchange rate, the exchange rate rises to π_1 to clear the foreign exchange market and therefore eliminate the balance of payments deficit.

EXTENSIONS OF THE MODELS

expansionary monetary policy will reduce the domestic interest rate and increase domestic income and the price level. As discussed above, the demand for imports will rise due to both the increase in income and the increase in the domestic price level. Further, the decline in the domestic interest rate will make domestic assets less attractive and domestic investors will shift to foreign assets. The increase in both the demand for imported goods and foreign assets represents increased demands for foreign exchange. In terms of Figure 17.5, the demand schedule for foreign exchange will shift from D_{fe}^0 to D_{fe}^1 as a result of the expansionary monetary policy.

The expansionary monetary policy will also affect the supply of foreign exchange. The monetary policy–induced decline in the interest rate will cause foreign investors to buy fewer of the country's assets, and the rise in the domestic price level will reduce export demand. The supply of foreign exchange schedule in Figure 17.5 will shift from S_{fe}^0 to S_{fe}^1. With the exchange rate fixed at the par value π_0, the increase in demand and the reduction of supply in the market for foreign exchange will result in a balance of payments deficit (excess of demand for foreign exchange over the supply of foreign exchange), as shown in Figure 17.5. The country's foreign exchange reserves will dwindle and the expansionary policy may have to be abandoned.

In contrast, with a flexible exchange rate system, the increase in demand and decline in supply in the foreign exchange market as a result of the expansionary monetary policy will cause the exchange rate to rise. As the exchange rate rises, the quantity of foreign exchange demanded will fall and the quantity of foreign exchange supplied will increase. A new equilibrium will be reached at exchange rate π_1, where the balance of payments deficit will have been eliminated (the demand and supply for foreign exchange rate are again equal). With a flexible exchange rate system there will be no need to abandon the anti-unemployment expansionary monetary policy. It is in this sense that *a flexible exchange rate system frees domestic policy from a balance of payments constraint.* The exchange rate moves to maintain balance of payments equilibrium, and domestic monetary and fiscal policies can be used to pursue domestic goals.

A further and a related advantage of a flexible exchange rate system is that it will insulate an economy from certain shocks. To see this, consider the example of a country that is inititally in a state of macroeconomic bliss, with an optimal level of unemployment, an optimum price level, and equilibrium in the balance of payments. Now suppose that there is a recession abroad and foreign income declines. Since import demand by foreigners, which is the demand for this country's exports, depends on foreign income, it will fall with the foreign recession. In the foreign exchange market this decline in export demand will show up as a shift to the left in the supply of foreign exchange schedule. As shown in Figure 17.6, the supply curve shifts from S_{fe}^0 to S_{fe}^1 as a result of the foreign recession.

In a fixed exchange rate system, the country would find itself with a balance of payments deficit equal to distance $A - B$ in Figure 17.6. Also, since changes in exports have multiplier effects on the level of income, as seen in Section 17.3, the decline in exports would lead to a fall in domestic income. The foreign recession would spread at home.

In a system of flexible exchange rates the excess demand for foreign exchange (equal to the balance of payments deficit $A - B$) which resulted from the foreign recession would cause the exchange rate to rise. The new equilibrium would be at point C with the higher exchange rate π_1. The increase in the exchange rate eliminates the balance of payment deficit. Notice another aspect

Figure 17.6
Insulation of the Domestic Economy in a Flexible Exchange Rate System

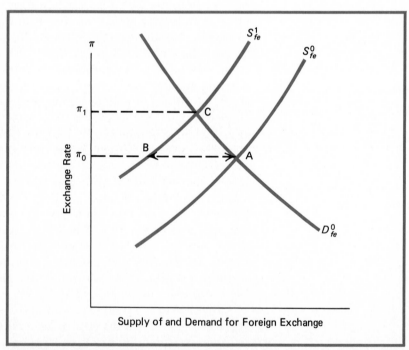

Supply of and Demand for Foreign Exchange

A foreign recession results in a fall in exports and a shift to the left in the supply of foreign exchange schedule from S_{fe}^0 to S_{fe}^1. With a fixed exchange rate system there will be a balance of payments deficit $(A - B)$. In a flexible exchange rate system, the exchange rate will rise to π_1 to clear the foreign exchange market.

of the adjustment to a new equilibrium. As we go to point C, the increase in the exchange rate stimulates export demand and lowers import demand. These changes have expansionary effects which work in opposition to the contractionary effect on domestic income from the recession-induced fall in export demand.[12] *The exchange rate adjustment thus works to offset the contractionary effect on the domestic economy which comes as the result of a foreign recession.* It is in this sense that a system of flexible exchange rates works to insulate an economy from certain external shocks.[13]

Given the advantages of a flexible exchange rate system in freeing domestic policy instruments from a balance of payments constraint and insulating an economy from certain foreign shocks, what case can be made for the alternative of a fixed rate system? Advocates of fixed exchange rates argue that such a system will provide a more stable environment for the growth of world trade and international investment. This is claimed to be so since in a fixed rate system business managers can more easily gauge what their returns will be in terms of their own currency. They need not worry about exchange rate fluctuations during the interim period between the time when goods are sold or foreign assets purchased and when a return is realized. Proponents of fixed exchange rates also worry about the effects that speculators may have in a system of floating rates. Will not the effect of speculation be wild gyrations in currency values—"excessive turbulence in exchange markets"? Moreover, rather than viewing the balance of payments constraint that a fixed rate system imposes on domestic policy instruments as a liability, some proponents of fixed exchange rates regard this as an asset of the system. They believe that the *discipline* which the balance of payments places on policymakers acts as an effective counterweight to the otherwise overly inflationary tendencies of modern democratic governments.[14]

As for the insulation of the economy from foreign shocks that is provided by a flexible exchange rate, proponents of a fixed exchange rate point out that this insulation is incomplete. Whereas a flexible exchange rate will insulate the domestic economy from foreign shocks that affect demand, such as the foreign recession discussed above, it will not insulate the economy from the effects of supply shocks. This was demonstrated by the inflationary reces-

---

[12]That the fall in import demand will be expansionary can be seen from the multiplier expression given in (17.8). Note that the fall in imports here is equivalent to a decline in u in (17.4), a fall in the demand for imports for a given level of income, in this case caused by a rise in the exchange rate.

[13]For further discussion on this point, see Section A.4 of the appendix to this chapter.

[14]The supply-side economists, whose position on domestic issues was examined in Chapter 16, propose a return to the nineteenth-century fixed exchange rate system, the gold standard, for just this reason. See the appendix to Chapter 19.

sion throughout the industrialized nations which followed the oil price shock of 1974.

Proponents of flexible exchange rates counter the argument that uncertainty due to possible exchange rate fluctuations will impede international trade and investment by pointing out that traders and investors can *hedge* by making transactions in the *forward* market. For example, a U.S. merchant who will receive payment for his goods in German marks in one month can contract in the forward market to exchange the marks for dollars then, at the one-month-forward rate set today, thereby eliminating exchange rate risk. As for the adverse effects of speculation in a flexible rate system, proponents argue that speculators must ultimately lose money and go out of business if their actions are destabilizing. To make profits speculators must buy currencies when they are low in price and will subsequently rise and correspondingly sell when they are high and set to fall. In doing so, speculators should smooth, not exacerbate, fluctuations in currency values.

What evidence has been provided by our experience with greater flexibility in exchange rates in the post-1973 period? One problem has been large fluctuations in currency values. For example, the change in the price of the dollar relative to major foreign currencies such as the French franc and the German mark has exceeded 2 percent per month in the post-1973 period. Still, world trade and investment have continued to grow rapidly over the period, indicating that economic agents have found ways, including hedging in forward markets, to operate in this uncertain environment. Further, the current system (or nonsystem) has successfully rechanneled the high current account surpluses of the oil-exporting nations, which amounted to almost one-fourth of a *trillion* dollars in the 1975–79 period.

Should world economic conditions in the 1980s prove to be substantially more tranquil than in the 1970s, attempts may be made to return to a system of pegged exchange rates, although undoubtedly one with greater flexibility of rates than existed in the Bretton Woods system. Central bankers seem always to have been attracted by the at least superficial certitude and stability of fixed exchange rates. For the present, however, the different degrees of dependence on foreign oil among industrialized countries and the variability in the degree to which different countries have tried to use accommodative aggregate demand policies to offset the employment effects of energy-related supply shocks (see Section 8.6), virtually demand that nations accept flexibility in the relative prices of their currencies.[15]

[15]For discussions of the issues in the fixed versus flexible exchange rate debate in light of our experience with greater exchange rate flexibility, see Jacques R. Artus and John H. Young, "Fixed Versus Flexible Exchange Rates: A Renewal of the

Review Questions

1   Why do the balance of payments accounts always balance?

2   Explain the way in which the official reserve transactions balance is computed. How would a deficit in the official reserve transactions balance be financed?

3   Explain how the exchange rate for a country is determined under:
a. A fixed exchange rate system.
b. A flexible exchange rate.
c. A managed or dirty float.

4   Analyze the effects of an autonomous fall in the demand for a country's exports under fixed and flexible exchange rate systems. In each case indicate the effects on the country's balance of payments and on the exchange rate.

5   If central banks never intervened in foreign exchange markets, could there be deficits or surpluses in a country's balance of payments?

6   Describe the Bretton Woods system of exchange rate determination which was set up at the end of World War II and lasted until 1973.

7   Why is the multiplier from the simple Keynesian model smaller for the case of an open economy than for a closed economy? How is the value of the multiplier related to the marginal propensity to import [v in equation (17.4)]?

8   Explain the relationship between the trade balance and the level of economic activity in a fixed exchange rate system. Why does this relationship create a potential conflict between the goals of internal and external balance?

9   Taking account of both the effect on the trade balance and the capital account, explain the relationships between balance of payments equilibrium and both expansionary monetary and fiscal policies within a fixed exchange rate system.

10   "Adoption of a system of flexible exchange rates would free monetary and fiscal policy for use in attaining domestic goals

---

Debate," *IMF Staff Papers*, 26 (December 1979), pp. 654–98; and Rudiger Dornbush, "Exchange Rate Economics: Where Do We Stand?" *Brookings Papers on Economic Activity*, No. 1, 1980, pp. 143–85, with accompanying discussion by William H. Branson and Marina v. N. Whitman.

of full employment and price stability." Do you agree or disagree with this statement? Explain.

11 What are some of the relative advantages or disadvantages of fixed versus flexible exchange rates?

12 Illustrate graphically the effects in the foreign exchange market of an expansionary monetary policy carried out by the *foreign* country in our two-country framework. Consider both the cases of a fixed and a flexible exchange rate.

Selected Readings

ARTUS, JACQUES R., and YOUNG, JOHN H., "Fixed Versus Flexible Exchange Rates: A Renewal of the Debate," *IMF Staff Papers*, 26 (December 1979), pp. 654–98.

BRYANT, RALPH C., *Money and Monetary Policy in Interdependent Nations*. Washington, D.C.: Brookings Institution, 1980.

DORNBUSH, RUDIGER, "Exchange Rate Economics: Where Do We Stand?" *Brookings Papers on Economic Activity*, No. 1, 1980, pp. 143–85.

DORNBUSH, RUDIGER, *Open Economy Macroeconomics*. New York: Basic Books, 1980.

DORNBUSH, RUDIGER, and KRUGMAN, PAUL, "Flexible Exchange Rates in the Short-Run," *Brookings Papers on Economic Activity*, No. 3, 1976, pp. 537–75.

FRIEDMAN, MILTON, "The Case for Flexible Exchange Rates," in Milton Friedman, *Essays in Positive Economics*. Chicago: University of Chicago Press, 1953.

JOHNSON, HARRY G., "The Case for Flexible Exchange Rates, 1969," Federal Reserve Bank of St. Louis *Review*, 51 (June 1969), pp. 12–24.

KINDLEBERGER, CHARLES P., "The Case for Fixed Exchange Rates, 1969," in *The International Adjustment Mechanism*. Boston: Federal Reserve Bank of Boston, 1969.

McKINNON, RONALD I., *Money in International Exchange: The Convertible Currency System*. New York: Oxford University Press, 1979.

MEADE, JAMES E., *The Balance of Payments*. Vol. 1: *The Theory of Economic Policy*. London: Oxford University Press, 1951.

STERN, ROBERT M., *The Balance of Payments: Theory and Economic Policy*. Chicago: Aldine, 1973.

WHITMAN, MARINA V. N., "The Current and Future Role of the Dollar: How Much Symmetry?" *Brookings Papers on Economic Activity*, No. 3, 1974, pp. 539–83.

WHITMAN, MARINA V. N., "Global Monetarism and the Monetary Approach to the Balance of Payments," *Brookings Papers on Economic Activity*, No. 3, 1975, pp. 491–536.

An Open Economy Macroeconomic Model

ere we will consider monetary and fiscal policy in open econo-mies in more detail. We will see further examples of the con-flicts that can arise for policymakers between considerations of internal and external balance in a system of fixed exchange rates. We will illustrate why those conflicts do not arise in a flexible exchange rate system. The way in which a flexible rate system provides a degree of insulation from foreign shocks will also be clarified. In order to carry on this analysis, we begin by modifying the IS–LM curve model used in Chapters 6 and 7 to take account of the foreign sector.

A.1 AN OPEN ECONOMY IS–LM MODEL

The closed economy IS–LM model consisted of the following two equations:

$$M = L(Y, r) \qquad (A.1)$$

$$S(Y) + T = I(r) + G \qquad (A.2)$$

Equation (A.1) is the money market equilibrium or LM schedule and (A.2) is the goods market equilibrium or IS schedule. The model simultaneously determines the nominal interest rate (r) and the level of *real* income (Y), with the aggregate price level held constant. What changes will be required in order to analyze an open economy?

When we consider an open economy, the LM schedule will not need to be changed. Equation (A.1) states that the *real* money stock, which we will assume to be controlled by the domestic policymaker, must in equilibrium equal the real demand for money. It is, of course, the nominal stock of money that the policymaker controls, but with the assumption of a fixed price level, changes in the nominal money stock are changes in the real money stock as well.

The equation for the IS schedule (A.2) is derived from the goods market equilibrium condition for a closed economy:

$$C + S + T \equiv Y = C + I + G \qquad \text{(A.3)}$$

which when C is subtracted from both sides reduces to

$$S + T = I + G \qquad \text{(A.4)}$$

If we add imports (Z) and exports (X) to the model, (A.3) is replaced by[1]

$$C + S + T \equiv Y = C + I + G + X - Z \qquad \text{(A.5)}$$

and the IS equation becomes

$$S + T = I + G + X - Z \qquad \text{(A.6)}$$

If we bring imports over to the left-hand side and indicate the dependence of variables on income and the interest rate, the IS equation for an open economy can be written as

$$S(Y) + T + Z(Y) = I(r) + G + X \qquad \text{(A.7)}$$

By a derivation analogous to that in Chapter 6, the open economy IS schedule can be shown to be downward sloping, as drawn in Figure A.1. High values of the interest rate will result in low levels of investment. To satisfy (A.7), at such high levels of the interest rate, income must be low so that the levels of imports and saving will be low. Alternatively, at low levels of the interest rate, which result in high levels of investment demand, for goods market equilibrium saving and imports must be high; therefore, Y must be high.

Notice that the levels of taxes, government spending, and exports are taken as given; these are the factors that shift the IS schedule. Expansionary shocks such as an increase in government spending, a cut in taxes, or an increase in export demand will shift the IS schedule to the right. An autonomous increase in investment [a shift in the $I(r)$ function] also would shift the IS schedule to the right, as would an autonomous *decline* in import demand.

---

[1]Private transfer payments to foreigners should also appear on the left-hand side of (A.5), but we will ignore this relatively minor item in our model.

Figure A.1
Open Economy IS–LM
Model

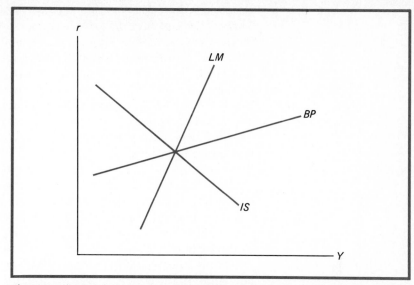

The *LM* schedule shows the combinations of *r* and *Y* which are points of equilibrium for the money market and the *IS* schedule shows combinations of *r* and *Y* that clear the goods market. The *BP* schedule shows the combinations of *r* and *Y* that will equate supply and demand in the foreign exchange market at a given exchange rate.

An autonomous decline in import demand [a fall in u in equation (17.4)] is expansionary because it is a shift in demand away from foreign goods to domestically produced output.

In addition to the IS and LM schedules, our open economy model will contain a balance of payments equilibrium schedule, the BP schedule in Figure A.1. This schedule plots all the interest rate–income combinations that result in balance of payments equilibrium at a given exchange rate. By balance of payments equilibrium is meant that the official reserve transaction balance is zero. The equation for the BP schedule can be written as

$$X(\pi) - Z(Y, \pi) + F(r) = 0 \qquad \text{(A.8)}$$

where here we have made explicit the dependence on the exchange rate (π) of both imports and exports.[2] Equation (A.8) states that the sum of the trade balance $(X - Z)$ plus the capital inflow (F), which depends positively on the interest rate, must be zero for balance of payments equilibrium.

The BP schedule will be positively sloped as shown in Figure A.1. As the level of income rises, import demand increases whereas

[2]Recall that π is the price of foreign currency measured in dollars. A rise in π will make imports more expensive and cause import demand to decline. A rise in π will make our exports less expensive to foreign buyers and export demand will rise.

export demand does not. To maintain balance of payments equilibrium the capital inflow must increase, which will happen if the interest rate is higher. Now consider factors that will shift the BP schedule. An increase in π will shift the schedule horizontally to the right. For a given level of the interest rate, which fixes the capital flow, at a higher exchange rate a higher level of income will be required for balance of payments equilibrium. This is because the higher exchange rate encourages exports and discourages imports; thus a higher level of income which will stimulate import demand is needed for balance of payments equilibrium. Similarly, an exogenous rise in export demand or fall in import demand will shift the BP schedule to the right. If exports rise, for example, at a given interest rate which again fixes the capital flow, a higher level of income and therefore of imports is required to restore balance of payments equilibrium. The BP schedule shifts to the right.

Having constructed the open economy IS–LM model, we can now analyze the effects of various policy actions. To begin with, we will assume that the exchange rate is fixed.

A.2   MONETARY AND FISCAL POLICY IN AN OPEN ECONOMY: FIXED EXCHANGE RATES

Monetary Policy: Fixed Exchange Rates

Consider the effects of an expansionary monetary policy action, an increase in the money stock from M_0 to M_1, as illustrated in Figure A.2. The increase in the money stock shifts the LM schedule to the right, from $LM(M_0)$ to $LM(M_1)$. The equilibrium point shifts from E_0 to E_1 with a fall in the interest rate from r_0 to r_1 and an increase in income from Y_0 to Y_1. What has happened to the balance of payments? First, note that all points below the BP schedule are points of balance of payments deficit, while all points above the schedule are points of surplus. As we move from an equilibrium point on the BP schedule to points below the schedule, for example, we are increasing income and/or reducing the interest rate and therefore causing a deficit in the balance of payments. Consequently, as we move from point E_0 to point E_1 following the increase in the money stock, the balance of payments moves into deficit. As discussed in Section 17.3, the expansionary monetary policy increases income, which stimulates imports and lowers the interest rate, which causes a capital outflow (F declines).

It is the fact that beginning from a point of equilibrium, an expansionary monetary leads to a balance of payments deficit that raises potential conflicts between domestic policy goals and external balance. If at point E_0 in Figure A.2 the level of income, Y_0, is

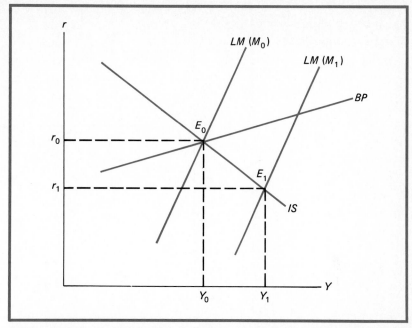

An increase in the quantity of money will shift the *LM* schedule from
$LM(M_0)$ to $LM(M_1)$. The equilibrium point shifts from E_0 to E_1. The rate of
interest falls and the level of income rises. The new equilibrium point is
below the *BP* schedule, indicating that the expansionary monetary policy
has caused a deficit in the balance of payments.

low relative to full employment, then the move to point E_1 and
income level Y_1 may well be preferable on domestic grounds. But
at point E_1 there will be a deficit in the balance of payments, and
with limited exchange reserves, such a situation cannot be indefi-
nitely maintained.

**Fiscal Policy: Fixed
Exchange Rates**

The effects of an increase in government spending from G_0 to G_1
for the fixed exchange rate case are illustrated in Figure A.3. The
increase in government spending shifts the IS schedule to the right
from $IS(G_0)$ to $IS(G_1)$, moving the equilibrium point from E_0 to E_1
in the graph. Income rises from Y_0 to Y_1 and the interest rate rises
from r_0 to r_1. As shown in Figure A.3, at the new equilibrium point
we are above the BP schedule; there is a balance of payments surplus. We get this result because in Figure A.3 the BP schedule is
flatter than the LM schedule. If, alternatively, the BP schedule
were steeper than the LM schedule, as drawn in Figure A.4, it can
be seen that an expansionary fiscal policy action would lead to a
balance of payments deficit.

The BP schedule will be steeper the less responsive capital flows

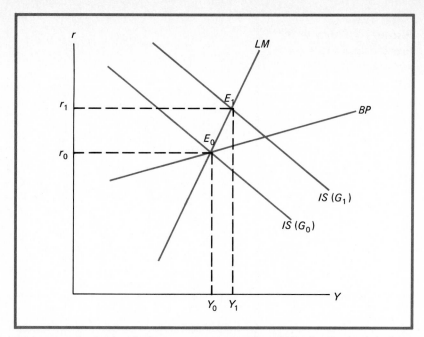

An increase in the level of government spending shifts the IS schedule from
$IS(G_0)$ to $IS(G_1)$. The equilibrium points shifts from E_0 to E_1. The level of
income and the interest rate rise. The new equilibrium point is above the
BP schedule which indicates that with a fixed exchange rate *for the case
where the BP schedule is flatter than the LM schedule* the expansionary
fiscal policy results in a surplus in the balance of payments.

are to the rate of interest. The smaller the increase in the capital
inflow for a given increase in the interest rate, the larger will be
the rise in the interest rate required to maintain balance of payments equilibrium as we go to a higher income (and hence import)
level; that is, the steeper will be the BP schedule. The BP schedule
will also be steeper the larger the marginal propensity to import [v
in equation (17.4)]. With a higher marginal propensity to import, a
given increase in income will produce a larger increase in imports.
For equilibrium in the balance of payments, a larger compensa-
tory increase in the capital inflow and consequently a larger rise in
the interest rate will be required.

The expansionary fiscal policy action depicted in Figures A.3
and A.4 causes income to increase, which leads to a deterioration
in the trade balance and causes the interest rate to rise, which
results in an improvement in the capital account. The foregoing
discussion indicates that the steeper the BP schedule, the larger
the unfavorable effect (the effect on imports and the trade balance)

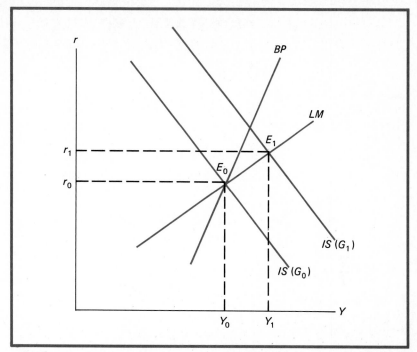

As in Figure A.3, an increase in the level of government spending shifts the *IS* schedule to the right, increasing both income and the rate of interest. In this case where the *BP* schedule is steeper than the *LM* schedule, the new equilibrium point (E_1) is below the *BP* schedule. The expansionary fiscal policy results in a balance of payments deficit.

and the smaller the favorable effect (on capital flows). Therefore, the steeper the BP schedule, the more likely it becomes that an expansionary fiscal policy action will lead to a balance of payments deficit.

Finally, notice that it is the slope of the BP schedule relative to the slope of the LM schedule that determines whether an expansionary fiscal policy action will result in a balance of payments surplus or deficit. Given the slope of the BP schedule, the steeper the LM schedule, clearly the more likely it is that the LM schedule will be steeper than the BP schedule—the condition for a surplus to result from an expansionary fiscal policy action. This follows since *ceteris paribus* the steeper the LM schedule, the larger the increase in the interest rate (which produces the favorable capital inflow) and the smaller the increase in income (which produces the unfavorable effect on the trade balance) as a result of the expansionary fiscal policy action.

A.3 MONETARY AND FISCAL POLICY IN AN OPEN ECONOMY: FLEXIBLE EXCHANGE RATES

Monetary Policy: Flexible Exchange Rates

We turn now to the case where the exchange rate is completely flexible; there is no central bank intervention. The exchange rate adjusts to equate supply and demand in the foreign exchange market. Consider first the same monetary policy action analyzed above, an increase in the quantity of money from M_0 to M_1. The effects of this expansionary monetary policy action in the flexible exchange rate case are as illustrated in Figure A.5.

The initial effect of the increase in the money stock—the effect prior to an adjustment in the exchange rate—is to move the economy from point E_0 to point E_1. The interest rate falls from r_0 to r_1.

Figure A.5
Monetary Policy with a Flexible Exchange Rate

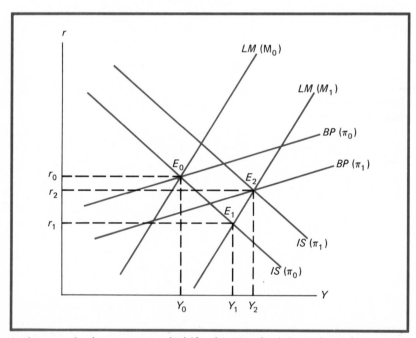

An increase in the money stock shifts the *LM* schedule to the right, moving the equilibrium point from E_0 to E_1. The point E_1 is below the *BP* schedule where there is an incipient balance of payments deficit. In the flexible exchange rate case, the exchange rate will rise, causing the *BP* schedule to shift to the right from $BP(\pi_0)$ to $BP(\pi_1)$ and the *IS* curve to shift right from $IS(\pi_0)$ to $IS(\pi_1)$. The final equilibrium point will be at E_2 with an income level Y_2, above Y_1 the new equilibrium for a fixed exchange rate.

Income rises from Y_0 to Y_1 and we move to a point below the BP schedule where there is an *incipient* balance of payments deficit. In a flexible exchange rate system, the exchange rate will rise (from π_0 to π_1) to clear the foreign exchange market. (This is the adjustment shown earlier in Figure 17.5.) The rise in the exchange rate will, as explained above, shift the BP schedule to the right; in Figure A.5 the schedule shifts from $BP(\pi_0)$ to $BP(\pi_1)$. The rise in the exchange rate also causes the IS schedule to shift to the right, from $IS(\pi_0)$ to $IS(\pi_1)$ in Figure A.5 because exports rise and imports fall with an increase in the exchange rate. The new equilibrium is shown at point E_2, with the interest rate r_2 and income at Y_2. The exchange rate adjustment reequilibrates the balance of payments following the expansionary monetary policy and eliminates the potential conflict between internal and external balance.

Notice also that the rise in income as a result of the expansionary monetary policy action is greater in the flexible rate case than in the fixed rate case. In the fixed exchange rate case income would rise only to Y_1 in Figure A.5 or Figure A.2. With a flexible exchange rate, the rise in the exchange rate will further stimulate income by increasing exports and reducing import demand (for a given income level). Monetary policy is therefore a more potent stabilization tool in a flexible exchange rate regime.

<table>
<tr><td>

Fiscal Policy: Flexible Exchange Rates

</td><td>

Figure A.6 illustrates the effects of an increase in government spending from G_0 to G_1 for the flexible exchange rate case. The initial effect—meaning again the effect prior to the adjustment in the exchange rate—is to shift the IS schedule from $IS(G_0, \pi_0)$ to $IS(G_1, \pi_0)$ and move the economy from E_0 to E_1. The interest rate rises (from r_0 to r_1) and income increases (from Y_0 to Y_1). With the slopes of the BP and LM schedules as drawn in Figure A.6 (with the BP schedule flatter than the LM schedule), an incipient balance of surplus results from this expansionary policy action. If this is the case, the exchange rate must *fall* (from π_0 to π_1) to clear the foreign exchange market. A fall in the exchange rate will shift the BP schedule to the left in Figure A.6, from $BP(\pi_0)$ to $BP(\pi_1)$. The IS schedule will also shift left, from $IS(G_1, \pi_0)$ to $IS(G_1, \pi_1)$ since the fall in the exchange rate will lower the level of exports and stimulate import demand. The exchange rate adjustment will *in this case* work as a partial offset to the expansionary effect of the fiscal policy action. The new equilibrium point will be at Y_2, which is above Y_0 but below Y_1, the level that would have resulted in the fixed exchange rate case.

There is not, however, a general relationship between the potency of fiscal policy and the type of exchange rate regime as there was with monetary policy. If the BP schedule is steeper than the

</td></tr>
</table>

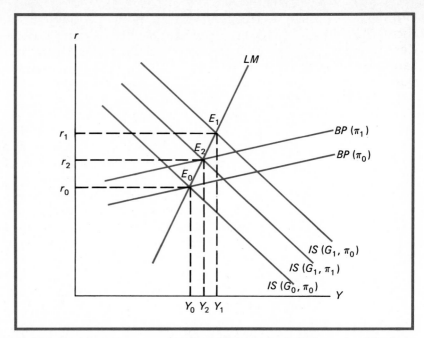

An increase in government spending shifts the *IS* schedule to the right from $IS(G_0, \pi_0)$ to $IS(G_1, \pi_0)$ moving the equilibrium point from E_0 to E_1. With the *BP* schedule flatter than the *LM* schedule, E_1 is above the initial *BP* schedule, $BP(\pi_0)$. There is an incipient balance of payments surplus and the exchange rate will fall, shifting the BP schedule to the left to $BP(\pi_1)$ and shifting the *IS* schedule to the left from $IS(G_1, \pi_0)$ to $IS(G_1, \pi_1)$. The final equilibrium will be at E_2 with income level Y_2, below Y_1 the new equilibrium for a fixed exchange rate.

LM schedule, as we saw in Figure A.4, an expansionary fiscal policy will, for a given exchange rate, cause a balance of payments deficit. With an incipient balance of payments deficit in the flexible exchange rate regime, the exchange rate must rise to restore equilibrium in the foreign exchange market. The BP schedule and the IS schedule will shift to the right and reinforce the initial expansionary effect of the increase in government spending. In this case, as illustrated in Figure A.7, the expansionary fiscal policy action has a *larger* effect on income than it would have in the fixed exchange rate case (income rises to $Y_2 > Y_1$). Therefore, although we can say unambiguously that the potency of monetary policy increases as we go from fixed to flexible exchange rates, no definite statement can be made about the relative effectiveness of fiscal policy in the two exchange rate regimes.

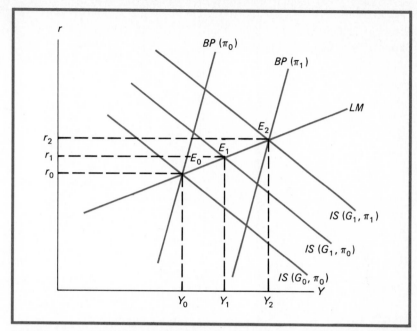

As in Figure A.6 the increase in government spending shifts the *IS* schedule to the right, moving the equilibrium point from E_0 to E_1. With the *BP* schedule steeper than the *LM* schedule there is an incipient balance of payments deficit at E_1 and the exchange rate rises. The *IS* and *BP* schedules shift to the right to the new equilibrium point E_2 where the level of income Y_2 is above Y_1, the new equilibrium for a fixed exchange rate.

A.4 INSULATION OF THE ECONOMY FROM FOREIGN SHOCKS UNDER FLEXIBLE EXCHANGE RATES

As a last application of our open economy IS–LM model, we examine how a flexible exchange rate system can insulate the domestic economy from certain foreign shocks. We will consider the same shock discussed in Section 17.4, a fall in export demand due to a recession abroad. The effects on the domestic economy from such a shock are illustrated in Figure A.8.

The initial effect of the fall in export demand from X_0 to X_1 will be to shift the IS schedule to the left, from $IS(X_0, \pi_0)$ to $IS(X_1, \pi_0)$. The BP schedule will shift upward to the left since with a lower exogenous export demand a higher interest rate (with a higher capital inflow) and/or a lower level of income (with a lower level of

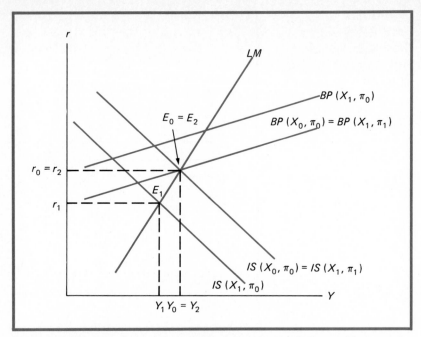

A fall in exports shifts the IS schedule to the left which would move the equilibrium point from E_0 to E_1. At E_1 there is an incipient balance of payments deficit so the exchange rate rises. The IS and BP schedules shift to the right and the final point of equilibrium is at E_2 which coincides with the initial equilibrium point E_0.

imports) will be required for balance of payments equilibrium *at the initial exchange rate*. The economy moves from point E_0 to point E_1. The level of income initially falls to Y_1. Also, since E_1 is below the new BP schedule, the economy is at a point where there is an incipient balance of payments deficit. This would be the final result if the exchange rate were fixed. The foreign recession would depress income at home and create a balance of payments deficit.

With a flexible exchange rate, the incipient balance of payments deficit will cause a rise in the exchange rate. A rise in the exchange rate (from π_0 to π_1) will, as we have seen in earlier examples, cause the IS and BP schedules to shift to the right. In this simple IS–LM model, the rise in the exchange rate will cause these schedules to shift all the way back to their initial levels [i.e., $IS(X_1, \pi_1) = IS(X_0, \pi_0)$ and $BP(X_1, \pi_1) = BP(X_0, \pi_0)$]. The domestic economy will be completely insulated from foreign shocks to export demand. In more complicated models this complete insulation may not occur.[3] As a general point, however, it does hold that exchange

[3]The intuition behind the complete insulation result here is as follows. The rise

518   EXTENSIONS OF THE MODELS

rate adjustments that occur in a flexible exchange rate system provide a degree of insulation to the economy against certain foreign shocks: shocks that affect aggregate demand.

Review Questions

1 Explain why the BP schedule in Figure A.1 is upward sloping. What factors will cause a shift in the BP schedule? Explain.

2 Within the open economy IS–LM model, analyze the effects of the following policy actions for both the fixed and flexible exchange rate cases.
a. A decline in the money stock from M_0 to M_1.
b. A decrease in government spending from G_0 to G_1.
Include in your answer the effects of the policy action on both income and the interest rate, as well as the effects on the balance of payments and exchange rate.

3 Suppose that, rather than a foreign recession, the external shock to hit the economy was an expansionary boom abroad. Explain the effects that this shock would have on the domestic economy in both a fixed and, alternatively, a flexible exchange rate regime.

---

in the exchange rate, which is just sufficient to shift the BP schedule back to the initial position $BP(\pi_0, Y_0)$, will just restore the trade balance to its initial level for each point along the BP schedule. This means that this rise in the exchange rate has caused a rise in exports and a fall in imports, which just counterbalances the initial drop in exports. From this it follows that the rise in the exchange rate is just sufficient to return the IS schedule to its initial level—the rise in exports and fall in imports due to the rise in the exchange rate just counterbalances the effect *on aggregate demand* from the initial drop in exports. The new equilibrium is the same as the initial equilibrium, with both the capital flow and the trade balance back at their initial levels.

economic policy

chapter 18

The two chapters in Part IV extend our discussion of macroeconomic stabilization policy. The macroeconomic effects of monetary and fiscal policies were analyzed in the previous chapters on macroeconomic models, but in those chapters the policy actions we considered were simple and in some cases unrealistic policy shifts, a "lump-sum" change in the level of tax collections, for example. In the next two chapters we take a more detailed look at the policymaking process. We examine the goals of macroeconomic policy and the optimum ways in which the policy process should be designed to achieve these goals—questions of optimal economic policy. In dealing with these questions we return to the issue of whether policy should be conducted by rules (e.g., the constant money growth rule of the monetarists) or by discretion (e.g., the activist policy prescription of the neo-Keynesians). Arguments concerning the role of political goals, as opposed to desirable social goals, as the determining factors in the behavior of macroeconomic policymakers are also discussed. Such political influences on the macroeconomic policy process, particularly on fiscal policy, are advanced as arguments in favor of policy by rules, not by discretion. Additionally, another class of stabilization policies, "incomes policies," will be examined. Incomes policies are attempts by the government to achieve desirable behavior of prices and money wages by direct intervention in the price- and wage-setting process. They have been applied as an alternative or a supplement to monetary and fiscal policies which influence prices and wages indirectly by affecting aggregate demand and/or sup-

FISCAL AND INCOMES POLICIES

ply. We begin in this chapter with an examination of fiscal and incomes policies.

Chapter 19 will examine monetary policy. An appendix to this Part provides a listing, along with a brief description, of major macroeconomic policy actions for the period since the Great Depression of the 1930s.

18.1 THE GOALS OF MACROECONOMIC POLICY

What are the goals of macroeconomic policy? Low unemployment and price stability seem to be agreed upon as policy goals, although as we saw in Part II, there is considerable disagreement concerning the ability of policymakers to achieve these goals via aggregate demand management. There are also differences of opinion about the relative weights that should be assigned to each of these goals. Economic growth as a policy goal is perhaps more controversial. Fostering rapid growth is still an announced goal of U.S. macroeconomic policy, but there are those who point to the costs of growth and see merits in slow or even zero economic growth. Measures of external balance—deficits or surpluses in the foreign balance of payments and movements in the exchange rate—are also considerations in macroeconomic policymaking, but these are more constraints on policy actions than goals in themselves. A potential balance of payments deficit, for example, could be, as we saw in Chapter 17, a factor inhibiting expansionary policy actions to decrease unemployment in a fixed exchange rate system.

Suppose that we were to agree that the goals of macroeconomic policy should be to achieve target levels of inflation, unemployment, and economic growth. The question of optimal conduct of macroeconomic policy would then be one of how to set the policy *instruments,* variables such as the levels of government spending and various tax rates in the case of fiscal policy, in order to come as close as possible to achieving the target levels for these goal variables. One way of formulating this problem in theory is to assume that the policymaker minimizes a social loss function of the following form:

$$L = a_1(U - U^*)^2 + a_2(\dot{P} - \dot{P}^*)^2 + a_3(\dot{y} - \dot{y}^*)^2 \qquad \textbf{(18.1)}$$
$$a_1, a_2, a_3, > 0$$

In this equation L is the social welfare loss which comes as a result of deviations of the macroeconomic goal variables from the target levels, the costs of excessively high unemployment for example. The goal variables themselves are the level of unemployment (U), the inflation rate $(\dot{P})$, and the rate of growth in real income $(\dot{y})$. The target levels for these variables are $U^*, \dot{P}^*$, and $\dot{y}^*$, respectively. In the particular form given by (18.1) the loss in social welfare depends on the squared deviations of the goal variables from the target levels. This implies that the welfare loss from a given increase in the deviation of a goal variable from the target level increases as we get further from the target level; large deviations from desired levels receive especially heavy weights. The coefficients $(a_1, a_2,$ and $a_3)$ in (18.1) represent the relative weights attached to the different targets.

Equation (18.1) is only one possible representation of the social loss function relevant to macroeconomic policies. The key assumption for this type of formulation of the optimal policy problem is simply that the policymaker minimizes some social welfare loss function. The problem is then to find the setting of the instruments that results in the minimum loss. One can further investigate whether there are various rules, such as the constant money growth rule, which outperform more activist policy prescriptions.

18.2 THE GOALS OF MACROECONOMIC POLICYMAKERS

There is a growing literature questioning the realism of the preceding formulation of the optimum policy question. One criticism of this formulation is that it is too mechanistic to describe policy formation in practice. In the case of fiscal policy, few of the participants in policy decisions could specify the precise loss function they are trying to minimize. Few could, for example, quantify the relative weights they put on the different goal variables [a_1, a_2, a_3 in equation (18.1)]. This criticism is not a particularly telling one. The same criticism could, for example, be levied against the microeconomic theory of consumer choice. Few consumers can write out their utility function. Still the theory based on the assumption that consumers maximize utility may provide a decent explanation of their behavior.

Recent critics of the view of the macroeconomic policymakers as acting to minimize some form of a social welfare function have a more fundamental objection than just the overly mechanical nature of this view. These critics who espouse what is called the *public choice* view of policymaker behavior argue that policymakers act to maximize their own welfare or utility rather than acting for the social good.[1] As Gordon Tullock, a proponent of the *public choice* view, puts it: "Bureaucrats are like other men. . . . If bureaucrats are ordinary men, they will make most (not all) their decisions in terms of what benefits them, not society as a whole."[2] Rather than a social loss function such as that given by (18.1), the relevant loss function is one that measures variables of direct importance to policymakers. In the case of elected officials making fiscal policy decisions, this alternative approach to the policymaking problem emphasizes votes as the central goal variable motivating policymakers.

Within this public choice framework, one representation of the appropriate loss function that the policymaker seeks to minimize would be

$$L = b_1 \text{VL} \qquad b_1 > 0 \tag{18.2}$$

where VL is vote loss and b_1 is the weight given to votes lost. Equivalently, the policymaker could be assumed to maximize votes gained. Macroeconomic goal variables enter the picture because the behavior of the economy affects votes.

For example, vote loss might be represented as

$$\text{VL} = c_0 + c_1(U - U^*)^2 + c_2(\dot{P} - \dot{P}^*)^2 + c_3(\dot{y} - \dot{y}^*)^2 \tag{18.3}$$

The macroeconomic goal variables and their target levels are the same as in (18.1). The parameters c_1, c_2, and c_3 represent the loss of votes resulting from deviations of the macroeconomic goal varia-

---

[1]More generally, the term *public choice* can be defined as the application of choice theoretic economic theory to political decision making. See, for example, Dennis Mueller, "Public Choice: A Survey," *Journal of Economic Literature*, 14 (June 1976), pp. 395–433.

[2]Gordon Tullock, *The Vote Motive* (London: Institute of Economic Affairs, 1976).

bles from target levels. This particular representation assumes that vote loss depends on the squared deviation from the target level, assuming as above that an especially heavy weight is given to large deviations from desired target levels. The c_0 parameter represents all other influences on voter behavior (e.g., foreign policy questions, other domestic issues).

Let us suppose that vote loss is given by (18.3) and the policymaker acts to minimize vote loss; the relevant loss function is (18.2). Will policy actions differ from those that would result from the policymaker acting more altruistically and minimizing the social loss function given by (18.1)? Advocates of the public choice view of policymaker behavior argue that they would. To see why, we first examine the condition necessary for behavior in the two cases to be the same and then explain why the advocates of the public choice view do not believe that this condition will be met in practice.

First assume that voter behavior is governed by what we may call *collective rationality*, by which is meant that vote loss *due to macroeconomic concerns* is proportional to social welfare loss. This means simply that where macroeconomic variables affect voting behavior, voters reward or punish incumbent politicians depending on their performance in minimizing social welfare loss. In this case the optimal strategy to minimize vote loss [equation (18.2)] is to minimize social welfare loss [equation (18.1)].[3] As has been recognized in the public choice literature, it is when this type of collective rationality does not exist that the behavior of the vote-maximizing policymaker will deviate from social welfare–maximizing behavior.

The following hypotheses about voter behavior have been advanced in the public choice literature.[4]

1. *Voters are myopic.* Advocates of the public choice view argue that voting behavior will be heavily influenced by the state of the economy over the few quarters before the election and that the level of economic activity, not the inflation rate, will be the variable whose recent performance determines votes. "Incumbent politicians desire re-election and they believe that a booming pre-election economy will help to achieve it."[5] As a consequence, we have a "political business cycle," where aggregate demand is overly stimulative in the preelection period, with inflation following after the election.

---

[3]Mathematically, in this case c_1, c_2, and c_3 in (18.3) are proportional to a_1, a_2, and a_3 in (18.1). Therefore, the same setting of the policy instruments that minimizes (18.1) will minimize (18.3).

[4]See, for example, James M. Buchanan and Richard E. Wagner, *Democracy in Deficit* (New York: Academic Press, 1977); and Edward R. Tufte, *Political Control of the Economy* (Princeton, N.J.: Princeton University Press, 1978).

[5]Tufte, ibid, p. 5.

ECONOMIC POLICY

2. *Unemployment is more likely to result in vote loss than is inflation.* The inflation process is presumed to be sufficiently complex and ill understood that politicians can avoid blame for inflation more easily than they can in the case of unemployment: "At any moment of time the inflation is blamed on events which are not under the control of the political party in power, but ideally on the political party previously in power."[6] As a consequence, advocates of the public choice view argue that elected officials will rarely respond to inflation with restrictive policies but will respond to unemployment with expansionary policies. The fiscal policy process will have an inflationary bias.[7]

3. *Deficit bias of the budget process.* This inflationary bias is reinforced by the inherent bias toward budget deficits that public choice writers believe to be characteristic of democratic government fiscal policies. For example, as James Buchanan and Richard Wagner argue:

> Elected politicians enjoy spending public monies on projects that yield some demonstrable benefits to their constituents. They do not enjoy imposing taxes on these same constituents. The pre-Keynesian norm of budget balance served to constrain spending proclivities so as to keep governmental outlays roughly within the revenue limits generated by taxes. The Keynesian destruction of this norm, without an adequate replacement, effectively removed the constraint. Predictably politicians responded by increasing spending more than tax revenues, by creating budget deficits as a normal course of events.[8]

Various groups of voters, in Buchanan and Wagner's view, perceive the direct benefits to them from the spending programs, but put little weight on the indirect costs that come through the inflationary effects of government deficit spending.

Because of this combination of vote-maximizing policymakers and the features of voter behavior described above, the budget process generates overly inflationary budget deficits. According to this public choice view, the resulting consequences, in addition to the high inflation, are high interest rates, low rates of capital formation and economic growth, and undesirable enlargement of the government sector.

If we accept the public choice characterization of the fiscal policy process, how can this inflationary bias in the process be corrected? Buchanan and Wagner, from whose book we quoted above,

---

[6]Morris Perlman, "Party Politics and Bureaucracy in Economic Policy," in Tullock, *Vote Motive*, p. 69.

[7]In terms of (18.1), and (18.3), these public choice writers argue that although inflation does cause significant social welfare loss [a_2 in (18.1) may be large], inflation does not result in much of a vote loss [c_2 is small in (18.3)]. Therefore, the vote-maximizing policymaker does not respond.

[8]Buchanan and Wagner, *Democracy in Deficit*, pp. 93–94.

believe that we must restore the "pre-Keynesian norm of budget balance"; we must avoid *all* deficit spending. They favor an amendment to the U.S. Constitution that would require the Congress and President to balance the budget. A balanced budget amendment would, they believe, eliminate the inflationary effects of federal deficit spending. Also, since new or expanded government spending programs would have to be financed by new taxes in a balanced budget system, the growth of the government sector would be curtailed by such an amendment. In the public choice view, optimal fiscal policy is not a question of designing policies to stabilize the macroeconomy. It is rather imposing rules on the policymakers that eliminate the destabilizing effects of deficit spending. As might be expected, neo-Keynesian economists do not agree with this policy prescription. Their criticisms of such a budget balancing amendment will be considered below. Prior to that, however, several issues pertaining to fiscal policy are discussed.

18.3 THE FEDERAL BUDGET

Two fiscal policy variables, the levels of government spending and tax collections, were included in the theoretical models considered in Part II. The government spending variable there (G) was the government spending component in national income, which includes both federal and state and local government spending on *currently produced goods and services*. The tax variable (T) included both federal and state and local tax collections. Fiscal stabilization policy is conducted primarily by the federal government. States and localities have limited abilities to run budget deficits. The levels for both their expenditures and revenues are determined by local needs and the state of the economy rather than being set to influence macroeconomic goals. Therefore, our discussion here focuses on federal budget policy.

Table 18.1 gives total receipts and expenditures by the federal government in selected years. The figures show that, at least when measured in current dollars, there has been a rapid growth in both tax receipts and expenditures in recent years. The figures also show that the budget has been continually in deficit for over a decade.

Table 18.2 explores the growth in the expenditure side of the federal budget in further detail. Column 1 gives total government expenditures divided by GNP. It can be seen that government spending as a proportion of GNP increased from 0.195 or just less than 20 percent in 1962 to 0.229 or just less than 23 percent in 1980. This figure must, however, be interpreted with care. Total federal government expenditures include transfer payments,

	Year	Receipts	Expenditures	Surplus or Deficit (−)
Table 18.1 **Receipts and Expenditures of the Federal Government[a] (billions of dollars at an annual rate)**	1954	63.7	69.8	−6.0
	1956	78.0	71.9	6.1
	1958	78.7	88.9	−10.3
	1960	96.1	93.1	3.0
	1962	106.2	110.4	−4.2
	1964	114.9	118.2	−3.3
	1966	141.8	143.6	−1.8
	1968	174.4	180.5	−6.0
	1970	191.9	204.3	−12.4
	1971	198.6	220.6	−22.0
	1972	227.5	244.3	−16.8
	1973	258.6	264.2	−5.6
	1974	287.8	299.3	−11.5
	1975	287.3	356.6	−69.3
	1976	331.8	384.8	−53.1
	1977	375.1	421.5	−46.4
	1978	431.5	460.7	−29.2
	1979	494.4	509.2	−14.8
	1980	540.8	602.0	−61.2

[a]Figures may not sum to total due to rounding.
Sources: *Economic Report of the President, 1981;* Federal Reserve Bank of St. Louis, *Monetary Trends*

Table 18.2   Selected Components of Government Expenditures, Various Years

	(1)	(2) Federal Government Purchases of Goods and Services	(3) Transfer Payments to Persons (billions	(4) Transfer Payments to Persons	(5) Grants to State and Local Governments (billions	(6) Grants to State and Local Government
Year	Government Expenditures ÷ GNP	÷ GNP	of dollars)	÷ GNP	of dollars)	÷ GNP
1962	0.195	0.113	25.6	0.045	8.0	0.014
1964	0.185	0.102	27.9	0.044	10.4	0.016
1966	0.190	0.104	33.5	0.044	14.4	0.019
1968	0.207	0.112	46.0	0.053	18.6	0.021
1970	0.206	0.096	61.3	0.062	24.4	0.025
1971	0.205	0.089	72.7	0.067	29.0	0.027
1972	0.205	0.086	80.5	0.068	37.5	0.032
1973	0.199	0.077	93.3	0.070	40.6	0.031
1974	0.209	0.077	114.5	0.080	43.9	0.031
1975	0.230	0.079	146.3	0.094	54.6	0.035
1976	0.224	0.075	158.4	0.092	61.1	0.036
1977	0.220	0.075	169.6	0.088	67.5	0.035
1978	0.214	0.071	181.8	0.084	77.3	0.036
1979	0.211	0.070	204.9	0.085	80.4	0.033
1980	0.229	0.076	245.2	0.093	87.3	0.033

Source: *Economic Report of the President, 1981.*

grants in aid to state and local governments, interest payments on the national debt, and subsidy payments to business, in addition to purchases of goods and services. Only the last of these is an element of GNP.

If we want to see the fraction of current output that is purchased by the federal government, the relevant measure is federal government purchases of currently produced goods and services divided by gross national product. This statistic is given in column 2 of Table 18.2. Measured in this way the share of the federal government sector in GNP has not grown but has instead declined from 0.113 or 11.3 percent in 1962 to 0.076 or 7.6 percent in 1980.[9]

Columns 3 to 6 of the table show the components of *total* government expenditures which account for the growth in the ratio of government expenditures to GNP: transfer payments to persons and grants in aid (transfers) to state and local governments, expressed both in dollar amounts (billions) and as proportions of GNP. Together these items were just less than 6 percent expressed as a proportion of GNP in 1962. By 1980 this figure had risen to over 12 percent. While the federal government has not been purchasing a higher percentage of gross national product, it has greatly increased transfer payments and grants (transfers) to state and local governments, and therefore influenced the way in which income, and hence output, is distributed. The increase in transfer payments represents the growth in such programs as social security, including Medicare; welfare and other income security programs; federal aid to education; and revenue-sharing programs with states and localities.[10]

Viewed from the standpoint of stabilization policy, the federal budget can be seen to contain three types of items that can be varied to affect macroeconomic goal variables: government purchases of goods and services, government transfer payments (including grants to state and local governments), and government tax receipts. In Part II we analyzed the effects of changes in government spending, which in those models was spending on goods and services only, and changes in tax receipts. In the models in Part II, tax receipts were net of transfers (taxes minus transfer payments); therefore, an increase in transfer payments would have just the opposite effects in those models as a reduction in taxes. In the next section we will reverse the question and instead of asking how changes in taxes or government expenditures affect

[9]State and local government purchases of goods and services have increased as a proportion of GNP in recent years. If one takes the proportion of GNP purchased by all levels of government (federal, state, and local) as a measure of resources absorbed by the public sector, this proportion has declined ony slightly, from 0.209 in 1962 to 0.204 in 1980.

[10]The Reagan administration's attempt to slow the growth in such transfer payments in the post–1980 period is discussed in Section 16.3.

income, we will examine how the level of income affects items in the federal budget. In doing so, we will see the way in which changes in the government budget work as an *automatic stabilizer* for the level of economic activity. In the following section, we consider the question of the measurement and optimal design of *discretionary* or activist fiscal policies.

18.4 THE ECONOMY AND THE FEDERAL BUDGET: THE CONCEPT OF AUTOMATIC FISCAL STABILIZERS

In order to consider the way in which the level of economic activity affects the government budget, we need to modify our assumption that the level of net tax receipts (gross tax receipts minus government transfer payments) is exogenous. An assumption more in line with reality is that the schedule of tax *rates* is exogenously set, but the level of net tax collections depends on the level of income.[11] With this assumption, we can specify *net* tax collections (T) as determined by the following *net tax function*

$$T = t_0 + t_1 Y \qquad t_0 < 0, \quad t_1 > 0 \tag{18.4}$$

where t_0 and t_1 are parameters that represent the tax structure. The parameter t_1 is the marginal net income tax rate, giving the increase in taxes (net of transfers) per unit increase in income ($t_1 = \Delta T / \Delta Y$). If the tax system were proportional, the other parameter in the tax function t_0 would be zero; tax collections would simply be equal to $t_1 Y$. Notice that in this case the marginal tax rate $\Delta T / \Delta Y$ would be equal to the average tax rate T/Y, both being given by t_1. The negative term t_0 allows the average tax rate, which from (18.4) would be $\left(\dfrac{t_0}{Y} + t_1 \right)$, to be less than the marginal rate (t_1). The negative term t_0 also allows for transfers, negative net taxes, which are independent of income.

From the net tax function given by (18.4) it clearly follows that as income rises, net tax collection increases and the government budget surplus increases (or the deficit declines). This follows since at higher levels of economic activity, more tax revenue will be collected at any given set of tax rates. The positive relationship between *net* tax revenues and the level of economic activity also

---

[11]Even this assumption will be only an approximation. The level of tax collections will also depend on the composition of income, since different components of income (profits and wages, for example) are taxed at different rates. Additionally, current marginal income tax rates are progressive (i.e., they rise with income); therefore, even tax rates are not truly exogenous.

results from the fact that transfer payments, especially payments for unemployment compensation, decline as the level of economic activity rises. On the expenditures side of the budget, in the absence of discretionary policy shifts there is no reason to expect government spending (G) to respond to changes in the level of economic activity.[12] Our previous assumption that government spending was exogenous can be maintained.

Consequently, the net effect of a rise in the level of income will be to increase the federal budget surplus or to decrease the size of an existing deficit. An expansion in the level of economic activity therefore causes fiscal policy, as measured by the budget surplus, to become more restrictive. This works to dampen the expansion. Similarly, a shock that causes the level of economic activity to fall will automatically result in a decline in the federal budget surplus or a rise in the deficit, which will cushion the fall in income. This is the essence of the concept of *automatic fiscal stabilizers*.

To examine the functioning of automatic fiscal stabilizers in more detail, we return to the multiplier analysis of the Keynesian model in Chapter 5. In that chapter we considered the way in which aggregate demand responded to exogenous shocks such as changes in autonomous investment demand or government spending. In effect, automatic fiscal stabilizers work by reducing the response of aggregate demand, and hence income, to such exogenous shocks. To show this, we analyze the effects on the multiplier expressions, the expressions giving the aggregate demand response to these shocks, which come as a result of allowing for endogenous changes in net tax revenues.

The equilibrium condition for income from Chapter 5 is

$$Y = C + I + G \qquad (18.5)$$

Consumption (C) was assumed to be given by

$$C = a + bY_D \qquad (18.6)$$

where Y_D is disposable income, defined as national income minus net tax collections $(Y - T)$. Investment, government spending, and the level of tax collections were all taken to be exogenous in that simple version of the Keynesian system. Similar to the procedure followed in Chapter 5, we can substitute (18.6) into the equilibrium condition for income given by (18.5), and using the definition of Y_D, we can compute an expression for equilibrium income $(\bar{Y})$:

$$\bar{Y} = \frac{1}{1 - b}(a - bT + I + G) \qquad (18.7)$$

---

[12]Here and below, the term "government spending" refers to federal government purchases of goods and services only, with transfer payments included in the net tax variable.

From (18.7) we can compute the effects on equilibrium income of exogenous changes in investment (I), government spending (G), and *exogenous* tax collections (T) as follows:

$$\frac{\Delta \bar{Y}}{\Delta I} = \frac{1}{1-b}$$

$$\frac{\Delta \bar{Y}}{\Delta G} = \frac{1}{1-b} \tag{18.8}$$

$$\frac{\Delta \bar{Y}}{\Delta T} = \frac{-b}{1-b}$$

The task here will be to see how these expressions are modified when the net tax function given by (18.4) is substituted for the assumption that tax collections are exogenous.

To begin, consider the form of the consumption function given by (18.6) with our new assumption about taxes. Using the definition of disposable income ($Y_D = Y - T$) and with T defined by (18.4), we can write the consumption function as

$$C = a + b(Y - T)$$

$$= a + bY - bt_0 - bt_1 Y$$

$$= a - bt_0 + (b - bt_1)Y$$

$$= a - bt_0 + b(1 - t_1)Y \tag{18.9}$$

Substituting (18.9) into the equilibrium condition for equilibrium income given in (18.5), we can derive the revised expression for the equilibrium level of income as follows

$$\bar{Y} = \overbrace{a - bt_0 + b(1 - t_1)Y}^{C} + I + G$$

$$\bar{Y}[1 - b(1 - t_1)] = a - bt_0 + I + G$$

$$\bar{Y} = \frac{1}{1 - b(1 - t_1)}(a - bt_0 + I + G) \tag{18.10}$$

As was the case with the previous expression (18.7), equation (18.10) specifies equilibrium income as determined by an autonomous expenditure multiplier, in this case $\frac{1}{1 - b(1 - t_1)}$, and the autonomous influences on income given by $a - bt_0 + I + G$. As above, we can compute the effects on equilibrium income of a change in investment or in the level of government spending.

$$\frac{\Delta \bar{Y}}{\Delta I} = \frac{\Delta \bar{Y}}{\Delta G} = \frac{1}{1 - b(1 - t_1)} \tag{18.11}$$

Note that the autonomous expenditure multiplier and hence the effect on income from a change in autonomous expenditures (changes in I or G, for example) is *smaller* for the case where tax collections depend on income than for the case where the level of tax collections is exogenous; that is,

$$\frac{1}{1 - b(1 - t_1)} < \frac{1}{1 - b}$$

To give an example, if b, the marginal propensity to consume, were equal to 0.8 and t_1, the marginal tax rate, were 0.25, we would have

$$\frac{1}{1 - b} = \frac{1}{1 - 0.8} = 5$$

$$\frac{1}{1 - b(1 - t_1)} = \frac{1}{1 - 0.8(1 - 0.25)} = \frac{1}{1 - 0.6} = 2.5$$

In this example the marginal tax rate of 0.25 cuts the value of the multiplier in half.

The presence of a marginal net income tax rate lowers the effect on equilibrium income of shocks to autonomous expenditure, such as an autonomous change in investment demand. It is in this sense that the income tax functions as an automatic stabilizer. The reason for this stabilizing effect of an income tax can be explained with reference to our earlier discussion of the multiplier process (Section 5.5). An initial shock to investment demand, for example, will change income and have an induced effect on consumption spending. It is this induced effect on consumption demand that causes equilibrium income to change by a multiple of the original change in investment demand. With a marginal income tax rate of t_1, each one-dollar reduction in GNP will reduce an individual's disposable income, the determinant of consumption, by only $(1 - t_1)$ dollars, since the individual's tax liability will fall by t_1 dollars. Since disposable income will be affected less per unit change in GNP, the induced effects on consumer demand will be smaller at each round of the multiplier process. The total effect on income of a change in autonomous investment, which consists of the original shock to investment plus the induced effects on consumption, will therefore be smaller where there is a marginal income tax rate relative to the case where tax collections were assumed to be exogenous.[13]

---

[13]Suppose, for example, that the fall in autonomous investment is 100 units. With tax collections exogenous, this initial drop in GNP would reduce disposable income by 100 units. In our example above, with the MPC(b) equal to 0.8, the first round–induced decline in consumption would be 80 units. With a marginal tax rate of 0.25, the decline of 100 units in GNP would reduce disposable income by

The automatic response of taxes and transfers to the level of economic activity has been a substantial stabilizing force in the U.S. economy over the post–World War II period, generally moving the budget sharply into deficit during recessions, with falling deficits or at times (in the 1950s) surpluses during expansionary periods. The increased size of the federal budget in the postwar period relative to the prewar period has increased the effectiveness of automatic fiscal stabilizers; in terms of our tax function, the marginal net tax rate is higher now than it was in a period such as the 1920s, and thus the multiplier is lower. Empirical estimates indicate that automatic fiscal stabilizers have offset from one-fourth to over one-half of the cyclical fluctuations in income during the postwar period.[14]

Substituting the net tax function given by (18.4) for the assumption that the level of tax collections is exogenous also requires a modification of the analysis of the effects of discretionary tax changes in the model. Since such discretionary fiscal policy actions are considered in the next section, it is worthwhile here to consider the nature of this modification. In the revised expression for equilibrium income given by (18.10), tax policy is represented by two variables: t_0, the intercept of the tax function, and t_1, the marginal income tax rate.

The closest analogue to a lump-sum change in tax collections in the revised income equation is a change in t_0. Such a change could represent a lump-sum tax rebate to each taxpayer, for example, or a lump-sum change in transfer payments. From (18.10) the effects of a change in t_0 can be computed as

$$\frac{\Delta \bar{Y}}{\Delta t_0} = \frac{1}{1 - b(1 - t_1)}(-b) = \frac{-b}{1 - b(1 - t_1)} \qquad (18.12)$$

Taking account of the change in the autonomous expenditure multiplier, this expression is the same as the tax multiplier where tax collections were exogenous [see equations (18.8)]. Again, the effect of a tax change, here a change in the intercept of the tax function, will be opposite in sign from the effect of a change in government spending or autonomous investment given by (18.11). An increase in t_0, for example, will cause equilibrium income to fall. Also, the effect of a one-dollar change in t_0 is smaller in absolute value than the effect of a one-dollar change in I or G. This is due, as in the

---

only 75 units; the first round decline in consumption would be only 60 units (0.75 × 0.8).

[14]Empirical studies of the effectiveness of automatic fiscal stabilizers are: Wilfred Lewis, Jr., *Federal Fiscal Policy in Postwar Recessions* (Washington, D.C.: Brookings Institution, 1962); and Peter Eilbott, "The Effectiveness of Automatic Stabilizers," *American Economic Review*, 61 (June 1966), pp. 450–65.

earlier case, to the fact that at a given level of GNP (Y), a one-dollar change in taxes will change autonomous expenditures [the term in parentheses in (18.10)] by only b (<1) dollars, with the remaining ($1 - b$) dollars absorbed by a change in saving. A one-dollar change in government spending or autonomous investment will change autonomous expenditures by one full dollar.

By inspection of (18.10), equilibrium income can also be seen to depend on the marginal tax rate t_1. An increase in t_1 will lower the autonomous expenditure multiplier, and therefore lower equilibrium income, given the values of the autonomous expenditure components. The way in which equilibrium income is affected by a change in the marginal income tax rate can perhaps best be seen graphically. Figure 18.1 illustrates the effects of an increase in the marginal tax rate from t_1 to t_1'. Figure 18.1a shows the effect of the increase in the tax rate on the consumption function.

With an income tax, consumption is given by (18.9). Before the increase in the marginal tax rate, the consumption line is $C = (a - bt_0) + b(1 - t_1)Y$ in the graph. The increase in the income tax rate rotates the function downward to the schedule $C = (a - bt_0) + b(1 - t_1')Y$. The new consumption line is flatter, indicating that a given increase in Y will cause consumption to rise by less with the higher tax rate. This follows since with a higher tax rate a given increase in Y, national income, will cause a smaller increase in disposable income and hence in consumption. Figure 18.1b shows the effect on equilibrium income from the rise in the tax rate. Since the consumption function rotates downward as in Figure 18.1a, the $C + I + G$ line also rotates downward, from ($C + I + G$) to ($C + I + G$)'. The effect of this is to cause equilibrium income to fall from Y to Y' in the figure. The higher tax rate lowers aggregate demand (at any positive level of income) and causes equilibrium income to fall.

18.5 DISCRETIONARY FISCAL POLICY AND THE CHOICE OF A FISCAL INSTRUMENT

In addition to functioning as an automatic stabilizer, federal budget items are one set of policy instruments that can be used for activist or discretionary management of aggregate demand. In this section we discuss two issues concerning such discretionary fiscal policy. The first is the measurement of discretionary fiscal policy actions. The second is the choice of a particular fiscal policy instrument (i.e., the relative merits of using government purchases, transfer payments, or tax rates) to affect aggregate demand. From the discussion in Part II it should be clear that these

Figure 18.1
Effect of an Increase
in the Marginal
Income Tax Rate (t_1)

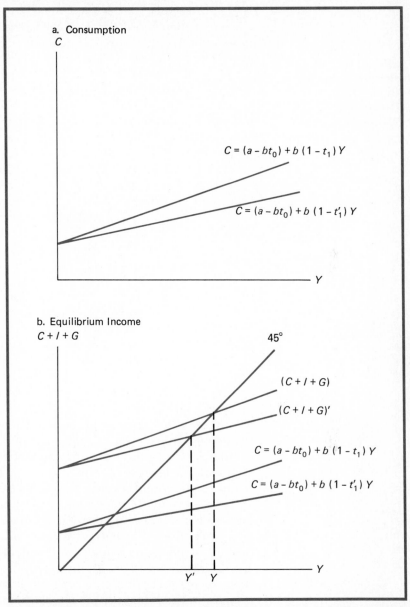

a. Consumption

$C = (a - bt_0) + b(1 - t_1)Y$

$C = (a - bt_0) + b(1 - t_1')Y$

b. Equilibrium Income

45°

$(C + I + G)$

$(C + I + G)'$

$C = (a - bt_0) + b(1 - t_1)Y$

$C = (a - bt_0) + b(1 - t_1')Y$

An increase in the income tax rate from t_1 to t_1' rotates the consumption function downward in Part *a*. Consequently, the $C + I + G$ schedule in Part *b* also rotates downward from $(C + I + G)$ to $(C + I + G)'$. Equilibrium output declines from Y to Y'.

issues, especially that of the choice of a fiscal instrument, are of interest primarily to the neo-Keynesians, since neither the monetarists nor the new classical economists favor the use of activist aggregate demand management policies.

Measuring Discretionary Fiscal Policy Actions

Policymakers designing fiscal policies as well as individuals in and out of government trying to evaluate fiscal policy require measures of the degree to which discretionary fiscal policy is expansionary or restrictive. One candidate as a measure of discretionary fiscal policy would be the actual government budget deficit, the amount by which tax collections fall short of total government expenditures (inclusive of transfers). Expansionary fiscal policies such as tax cuts or increases in government spending would increase the budget deficit, whereas restrictive policy actions such as spending cuts or tax increases would reduce the size of the deficit. In much public discussion the budget deficit is, in fact, used as a summary measure of the stance of fiscal policy.

The discussion of the preceding section indicates, however, that the federal budget deficit depends in part on the level of economic activity. Thus changes in the budget deficit reflect not only discretionary fiscal policy actions but also endogenous movements due to changes in the level of economic activity. A summary measure of discretionary policy alone must remove the endogenous influences on the government budget deficit. Measures of the *high-employment* government budget deficit have been constructed for this purpose. Figures for the high-employment government budget deficit are based on measures of spending and net taxes at *potential* or *high-employment* income. The effect of this is to provide a standardized measure of the budget deficit which will not depend on the actual level of economic activity. Endogenous movements in tax revenues and transfer payments which result from the fact that the economy is not at the level of potential income will, by their construction, not affect the high-employment deficit measures—measures that correct for such movements. In principle, then, movements in the high-employment government budget deficit will result only from discretionary fiscal policy actions such as changes in government purchases of goods and services and changes in the schedules for tax rates and transfer payments.

Since, as was noted in the preceding section, the automatic adjustments in the government budget in response to changes in the level of economic activity are substantial in magnitude, high-employment budget measures that correct for such movements often differ significantly from actual budget measures. An examination of the behavior of the actual deficit and the high-employment deficit during the latter part of the Eisenhower administration in the 1950s will provide one example of the different conclusions about fiscal policy that would be reached depending on which budget measure one considered.

Quarterly figures for both the actual and high-employment budget deficits and for the unemployment rate are given in Table 18.3. The recession that began late in 1957 moved the actual budget substantially into deficit; this was the automatic stabilizing effect of a reduction in tax revenues and higher unemployment compensation payments. The high-employment budget was in surplus throughout the recession, although the decline in the size of the surplus in 1958 reflects some small expansionary, discretionary fiscal policy actions. As measured by the high-employment budget surplus, discretionary fiscal policy became more restrictive in 1959 and into 1960. This restrictive discretionary fiscal policy was one factor cited as a cause of the abortive recovery of

Table 18.3 Budget Deficits and Unemployment Rates, 1957–1961 (billions of dollars at annual rates)

Year Quarter	Actual Budget Surplus (+) or Deficit (−)	High-Employment Budget Surplus (+) Deficit (−)	Unemployment Rate (%)
1957 I	4.3	5.7	3.9
II	2.5	5.8	4.1
III	2.6	7.2	4.2
IV	−1.5	7.0	4.9
1958 I	−8.1	6.7	6.3
II	−12.4	5.1	7.4
III	−10.8	4.3	7.3
IV	−9.8	2.4	6.4
1959 I	−4.2	6.0	5.8
II	0.8	8.1	5.1
III	−1.0	8.7	5.3
IV	−0.6	10.5	5.6
1960 I	7.1	14.6	5.1
II	5.6	15.0	5.2
III	1.5	14.2	5.5
IV	−0.6	15.1	6.3
1961 I	−4.9	13.1	6.8
II	−4.5	13.3	7.0
III	−3.8	11.9	6.8
IV	−1.9	12.1	6.2

Sources: Actual and high-employment budget measures are taken from Keith Carlson, "Estimates of the High Employment Budget: 1947–67," Federal Reserve Bank of St. Louis *Review,* 49 (June 1967) pp. 6–14. The unemployment figures are from the Commerce Department's publication *Business Statistics,* 1973.

the economy in 1959–60 and new recession that began in mid-1960.[15] As a result of this new recession, the automatic stabilizing effect on the budget produced actual budget deficits beginning with the fourth quarter of 1960. But as can be seen from the high-employment budget column, discretionary fiscal policy was restrictive throughout the 1960–61 period.

Overall during this period (1957–61) an observer looking at the actual budget deficit would conclude that fiscal policy worked in a countercyclical fashion, moving substantially into deficit during recessionary periods. An observer looking at the high-employment budget would conclude that *discretionary* fiscal policy actions were only timidly countercyclical in the 1958 recession and were restrictive in 1959–60. Movements in the actual budget deficit during this period reflected both the effects of automatic fiscal stabilizers and the effects of sometimes perverse discretionary policy actions.

Table 18.4 shows the annual actual and high-employment budget deficits for the 1973–81 period, again accompanied by figures for the unemployment rate. Although both measures of the budget were in deficit throughout the period, a comparison of the two budget measures indicates that the exceptionally high deficits of 1975–77 were to a substantial degree the result of the low level of economic activity. The same was true in 1980 and 1981. The high-employment budget indicates that discretionary fiscal policy became more expansionary as unemployment rose both in 1975

[15]Fiscal policy actions during this period are described in Lewis, *Federal Fiscal Policy*, Chaps. 6 and 7.

Table 18.4 Annual Budget Deficits and Unemployment Rates, 1973–1981

Year	Actual Budget Surplus (+) or Deficit (−) (billions of dollars)	High-Employment Budget Surplus (+) or Deficit (−) (billions of dollars)	Unemployment Rate (%)
1973	−5.6	−11.3	4.9
1974	−11.5	−0.8	5.6
1975	−69.3	−29.1	8.5
1976	−53.1	−20.1	7.7
1977	−46.4	−23.1	7.0
1978	−29.2	−15.7	6.0
1979	−14.8	−2.2	5.8
1980	−61.2	−18.3	7.1
1981	−62.4	−2.7	7.6

Sources: Federal Reserve Bank of St. Louis, *Monetary Trends; Federal Reserve Bulletin.*

ECONOMIC POLICY

and 1980, but not in 1981 when the spending cuts of the Reagan economic program came into effect more quickly than the tax cut part of the program (see Section 16.3).

The usefulness of the high-employment budget concept is that it provides an indication of the degree to which movements in the federal budget are due to discretionary actions, as opposed to being the result of changes in the level of economic activity. There are, however, a number of deficiencies in such high-employment budget measures. As potential income grows over time, tax revenues, even at the potential or high-employment income level, will grow endogenously. The high-employment budget deficit will decline unless there are offsetting discretionary changes in spending. Moreover, inflation will also affect tax revenues and therefore the budget deficit even standardized at the potential output level. Consequently, even the high-employment budget deficit is subject to endogenous influences; it will not in practice measure only discretionary fiscal actions.

Additionally, one would ideally want a measure of the thrust of fiscal policy to measure the *effect* of fiscal policy. Such a measure of fiscal impact must take account of the differing multipliers attached to different budget items. The income tax multiplier would, for example, based on our analysis above, be expected to be smaller than the government expenditures multiplier. If we use the high-employment budget deficit, we are implicitly assuming that all budget items receive the same weight in measuring the impact of fiscal policy. It is only the size of the deficit that matters, not the policy mix that produces a given deficit. Economists concerned about this defect of even high-employment budget measures have proposed alternative *weighted high-employment* deficit concepts. In such weighted budget deficit measures, components are weighted by their income multipliers prior to calculating the deficits. The difficulty arises, however, that there will be different measures of the weighted high-employment deficit depending on the models used to derive the multipliers used as weights.[16]

The difficulties discussed above indicate that even the high-employment deficit is a highly imperfect measure of discretionary fiscal policy actions. Nevertheless, high-employment budget figures are useful in forming a rough breakdown of the budget into movements that reflect discretionary policy actions and those that result from automatic responses of taxes and transfers to the level of economic activity.

[16]See Alan Blinder and Robert Solow, "Analytical Foundations of Fiscal Policy," in Alan Blinder *et al., The Economics of Public Finance.* (Washington, D.C.: Brookings Institution, 1974) for a useful discussion of weighted high-employment deficit measures as well as other difficulties with high-employment budget measures.

The Choice of a Fiscal Instrument

The next question we consider concerning discretionary fiscal policy is the choice of a fiscal policy instrument. Given that the decision has been made to change aggregate demand via a fiscal policy action, which possible fiscal policy instrument should be used to effect the change: government purchases of goods and services, transfer payments to persons, grants to state and local governments, or income or other tax rates.[17] To date, there has been a preference on the part of policymakers and a number of economists for income tax rate changes as the major instrument for fiscal policy actions.[18] The reasons for this preference are discussed next and some dissenting views are noted.

The choice of income tax rates as a fiscal instrument is in large part a choice by default. The other budget items are believed to be constrained by the need to meet other goals of budget policy to an extent which greatly limits their potential as instruments for stabilization policy. The level of government purchases of goods and services is determined mostly on the basis of a decision about the desired allocation of output between the public and private sectors rather than on grounds of the appropriate degree of fiscal stimulus. Substantially increasing defense spending or doubling the number of postal employees simply to stimulate demand would result in a suboptimal allocation of resources. Government transfer payments are constrained by distributional goals. Substantial cuts in social security pension payments during inflationary periods and then raises in them during recessions would, for example, be rejected on grounds of equity, whatever the merit of such a policy on stabilization grounds.

There is some latitude for varying levels of both government purchases and transfers for stabilization purposes. The timing of public works projects can be geared to the cyclical behavior of the economy. Similarly, planned modifications of schedules of transfer payments can be initiated at times when they will have appropriate aggregate demand effects. Still, both government purchases and transfers have been regarded as insufficiently flexible to perform as the major instruments of fiscal stabilization policy.

Personal income tax rates can be varied without such unfavorable effects on resource allocation and income distribution. Changes in income tax rates affect aggregate demand by changing household disposable income and consumption. Income tax changes should therefore affect demand for a wide range of prod-

---

[17]The prior choice of whether a desired change in aggregate demand should be accomplished by fiscal policy or monetary policy is discussed in Section 19.4.

[18]See, for example, the discussion in Arthur M. Okun, "Rules and Roles for Fiscal and Monetary Policy," in James Diamond, ed., *Issues in Fiscal and Monetary Policy* (Chicago: DePaul University Press, 1971).

ucts, with small effects on the allocation of resources among product groups. The changes in the structure of tax rates can also be designed to leave the distribution of income relatively unchanged. There is, in principle then, no reason why frequent changes in income tax rates should not be used to regulate the level of aggregate demand. Changes in income tax rates do require legislative approval, which can be a time-consuming process, but legislative approval is also required for changes in the levels of government purchases or transfer payments. This significant lag in the implementation of any fiscal policy action helps explain why monetary rather than fiscal policy has often been used to control aggregate demand, as explained in Chapter 19.

In recent years doubts have been voiced about the effectiveness of changes in income tax rates, even when they can be made in a timely manner. Briefly, the argument has been made that if there were frequent changes in income tax rates, such changes would be regarded as temporary and would not have much effect on "permanent" or "life cycle" income as discussed in Chapter 13. Such changes in tax rates would therefore have little effect on consumption. It does appear that if tax rates were varied frequently, consumers would come to see such changes as movements around a "permanent" level of tax rates. Thus, whether frequent changes in tax rates would be effective would depend on the response of consumption expenditures to *transient* income. In Chapter 13 it was pointed out that consumption expenditures will respond to even temporary changes in income if consumers are "liquidity constrained" due to their low ability to borrow against future earnings. Also, as discussed in Chapter 13, consumption expenditures include purchases of consumer durable goods, and even the permanent income or life cycle hypotheses about consumption do not deny that the timing of such purchases may depend on current income whether transient or permanent.

There have been a number of empirical studies of the effectiveness of temporary tax rate changes. In a recent paper summarizing the results of those studies, Walter Dolde concluded that "most of the evidence points to a relative effectiveness on consumer expenditures of 50 to 90 percent of permanent tax changes."[19] It should also be noted that fiscal policy may have been sufficiently

---

[19]See Walter Dolde, "Temporary Taxes as Macro-economic Stabilizers," *American Economic Review*, 69 (May 1979), pp. 81–85. In another recent study Alan Blinder estimated the effects of temporary tax changes as near the lower end of Dolde's range (50 to 90 percent of the effect of an equivalent permanent change) in the first year after the policy change but near the upper end of that range during the second year after the policy shift, indicating that temporary tax policy changes work with a longer lag than do permanent changes. See Alan Blinder, "Temporary Income Taxes and Consumer Spending," *Journal of Political Economy*, 89 (February 1981), pp. 26–53.

unsystematic in the past as to make it difficult for consumers to distinguish permanent from temporary tax changes, as long as the latter are not specifically announced as temporary. A given tax rate change for stabilization purposes may therefore have the effects of a permanent tax rate change even though it will be reversed at a later (but unspecified) date.

One final objection to the use of income tax rates as an instrument of aggregate demand management policy should be considered. One who accepts the Kemp–Roth or supply-side view of the effects of tax rates (see Section 16.2) would not favor increases in income tax rates as an anti-inflation measure. Such an increase in the income tax rate would cause aggregate supply to decline as workers cut labor supply at a given money wage rate. Upward pressures on money wages, and eventually on prices, would result. Adherents of the supply-side view believe that these unfavorable effects outweigh the effect of the income tax–induced decline in aggregate demand. They favor a system of permanently low income tax rates to foster employment and economic growth. Neo-Keynesian economists who advocate the use of income tax rates as a countercyclical device assume, as we have seen, that these supply-side effects are of secondary importance—that the demand effect is dominant.

In the preceding section we concluded that automatic fiscal stabilizers eliminated a substantial portion of the cyclical fluctuation in income during the post–World War II period. What can be said about the record for discretionary fiscal policy during the postwar period? The record appears to be a mixed one, with cases of successful policy action and other cases where discretionary fiscal actions were procyclical (i.e., were a factor increasing the magnitude of the cyclical fluctuation in income). During two of the postwar recessions (1953–54, 1960–61), for example, discretionary fiscal policy actions were clearly contractionary and contributed to the magnitude of the recession. An overly expansionary fiscal policy in the 1967–68 period when the economy was already at a high level of economic activity was a factor contributing to the acceleration in inflation that occurred during that period. Examples of successful stabilization policies often cited by advocates of activist fiscal policy are the income tax cut of 1964, which gave strength to the sluggish recovery from the 1960–61 recession, and the tax cut of 1975, which came just at the low point of the 1974–75 recession and aided the subsequent recovery.

18.6 THE NEO-KEYNESIAN OBJECTION TO CONSTITUTIONAL BUDGET BALANCE AMENDMENTS

In Section 18.2 we explained the case made by economists who accept the *public choice* view of the budget process in favor of constitutional amendments to require a balanced federal budget. Also noted there was the fact that neo-Keynesian economists are critical of such amendments. The material covered in the preceding two sections (18.4 and 18.5) provides the basis for an explanation of the neo-Keynesian criticisms.

The role of the tax-transfer system as an automatic fiscal stabilizer, which was explained in Section 18.4, requires that the budget be allowed to go into deficit (or surplus) at appropriate points in the business cycle. During a recession, as the level of economic activity falls, the budget *should* go into deficit. To raise tax rates or cut expenditures at such a time would only exacerbate the recession. The neo-Keynesians cite the 1932 tax increase as an example of the misguided fiscal policies that result from pursuing the goal of a balanced budget. The Hoover administration raised tax *rates* substantially in 1932 to try to balance the budget at a time when tax *revenues* were falling due to the depression. The tax rate increase came at a time when the unemployment rate was 24 percent! The policy did not succeed in balancing the actual budget because of the sharp decline in income, due in part to the tax increase.

Besides impeding the working of automatic fiscal stabilizers, an amendment requiring federal budget balance would limit the ability of policymakers to take discretionary countercyclical fiscal actions. As just explained, the record of success with such discretionary fiscal policy measures is a mixed one. No doubt the neo-Keynesians would agree that some of the failures of discretionary fiscal policy stem from the types of interactions between the political process and macroeconomic policymaking stressed in the public choice analysis of the budget process. Neo-Keynesians opposed to constitutional budget balance amendments argue, however, that the record for discretionary policy is not uniformly bad and that the cost of interfering with the functioning of automatic fiscal stabilizers through such amendments is great.[20]

[20]See, for example, James Tobin, "Comment from an Academic Scribbler," *Journal of Monetary Economics,* 4 (August 1978). The historical record is, of course, subject to varying interpretations. Economists favorable to the public choice view and, consequently, to a balanced budget rule, view the record of discretionary fiscal policy in a much less favorable light and see automatic fiscal stabilizers as less crucial. See, for example, Buchanan and Wagner, *Democracy in Deficit.*

18.7 INCOMES POLICIES

Fiscal policy or monetary policy can be used to control aggregate demand and thus, at least in the neo-Keynesian view, to affect the rates of unemployment and inflation. *Incomes policies* are policies that intervene more directly in the wage–price setting process, with an aim to restraining inflation. Examples of such incomes policies include voluntary wage and price guidelines, mandatory wage and price controls, and tax-based incomes policies (TIP), which use the tax system to penalize (or reward) business and labor for inflation increasing (or restraining) behavior.

The current argument in favor of an incomes policy appears to be as follows. We begin with a situation where both the inflation rate and level of unemployment are undesirably high. The cost of reducing inflation via a restrictive aggregate demand policy is viewed as large measured in terms of forgone output and higher unemployment. An incomes policy, it is asserted, can be used in concert with restrictive aggregate demand policy to reduce inflation with a smaller cost in terms of unemployment than if the restrictive aggregate demand policy alone were employed.

We will analyze this argument somewhat further below. The case against incomes policies will then be considered. Finally, some evidence from the U.S. experience with incomes policies in the early 1970s will be examined. First, however, it is useful to describe in more detail the types of incomes policies that have been enacted or advocated in recent years.

Voluntary wage and price guidelines were employed by the Kennedy and Johnson administrations in the 1962–66 period and more recently by the Carter administration. With this type of incomes policy the government sets standards or guideposts for acceptable levels of wage and price increases. There is no explicit enforcement procedure. Informally, pressures of various sorts are put on business and labor to adhere to the guidelines. Such pressures include publishing names of violators, threats to use antitrust policies, government contract cutoffs or other measures to punish firms whose price increases exceed the guideline, as well as suggestions that mandatory controls will replace voluntary ones if guidelines are not followed.

Mandatory wage–price controls were applied during both World War II and the Korean War. Peacetime wage–price controls were instituted by President Nixon in August 1971 and were in effect to some extent until April 1974. This most recent program began with a three-month freeze on all prices (other than those of certain raw materials) and wages from August to November of 1971 (termed Phase I). This was followed by a period (Phase II) of enforced standards for price increases (2.5 percent) and wage increases (5.5 percent) administered by Price and Pay Boards, which could make merited exceptions. This period of enforced standards lasted from the end of the freeze in November 1971 to the end of 1972. It was followed by less stringent sets of regulations beginning in 1973 (Phase III and Phase IV), a temporary freeze in the summer of 1973, and the eventual dismantling of controls in 1974.

The idea of a tax-based incomes policy (TIP) was proposed by economists Henry Wallich and Sidney Weintraub.[21] There are a number of variants of TIP, but they take the same general approach: the use of the tax system to penalize firms or workers for inflationary behavior (the stick approach) or to reward them for noninflationary behavior (the carrot appraoch). In one of the "stick" versions of TIP, for example, the corporate income tax rate paid by a firm would be increased by a specified amount for each 1 percent that the wage increase granted by the firm exceeded an established guideline rate, the obvious goal being to stiffen the resistance of firms to worker demands for inflationary wage increases. An example of the carrot approach is the *wage insurance* plan proposed by the Carter administration in 1978. According to this plan, workers who settled for wage increases at or below the wage guideline would receive a certain percentage income tax rebate proportional to the amount by which the inflation rate exceeded the price guideline. This plan was aimed at reducing the hesitancy of one group of workers to adhere to a wage guideline because they feared that other workers would not do the same and hence the guideline policy would not reduce inflation. One advantage claimed for TIP relative to mandatory wage–price control programs is greater flexibility. A firm in a growth industry, for example, which needs to increase wages rapidly to expand its labor force can do so under TIP, although with a "stick" version of TIP only with some additional cost, whereas with a strict mandatory ceiling on wage increases it could not.

The Case for Incomes Policies

The case for incomes policies rests on certain assumptions about the nature of the inflationary process, the most basic of these assumptions being that there is a high degree of inertia in the wage- and price-setting mechanism. A wage–price inflation gathers momentum and then is to a degree self sustaining. A key element in explaining this inertia is the psychology of inflationary expectations. Proponents of incomes policies argue that inflationary expectations are in large part "backward looking," depending on

[21]See Henry Wallich and Sidney Weintraub, "A Tax-Based Incomes Policy," *Journal of Economic Issues*, 5 (June 1971), pp. 1–19. See also the papers in "Innovative Policies to Slow Inflation," *Brookings Papers on Economic Activity*, No. 2, 1978.

past inflation. Therefore, after a period of significant inflation, whether resulting from too rapid demand growth or in recent years from energy-related shocks to aggregate supply, expectations of future inflation become entrenched. The expectation of high inflation leads to high money wage demands, high wage settlements, and further inflation—a wage–price spiral.

To see how advocates of incomes policies believe that such policies work to restrain inflation, consider the effect of temporary, mandatory wage and price controls on an economy suffering from the type of wage–price spiral just described. Specifically, we assume that wage and price controls are imposed in a situation where past inflation rates had been high—due to supply shocks or past (not current) high rates of growth in demand—but where the cause of current inflation was primarily high inflationary expectations and, hence, strong upward pressure on money wages.

In Figure 18.2, the Phillips curve apparatus from Chapter 10 is used to depict the situation in the absence of wage–price controls and the effects of controls. Recall from the discussion in Chapter 10 that the position of the short-run Phillips curve depends on the level of the expected inflation rate. An increase in the expected inflation rate will shift the short-run Phillips curve upward to the right; a decline in expected inflation will shift the curve downward. Let us suppose that without the freeze the expected inflation rate would be $\dot{P}_0^e$, with the short-run Phillips curve given by the $PC(\dot{P}_0^e)$ schedule in Figure 18.2. Assume that the economy is initially at point A, with the unemployment and inflation rates at U_0 and $\dot{P}_0$, respectively. In the short run a reduction in the inflation rate could be accomplished by lowering aggregate demand and moving the economy to a point such as B, with an inflation rate of $\dot{P}_1$ and unemployment rate U_1. The goal of wage and price controls accompanying the restrictive aggregate demand policy would be to lower the expected inflation rate, to $\dot{P}_1^e$, for example, shifting the Phillips curve to a position such as $PC(\dot{P}_1^e)$, and therefore allowing the same reduction of the inflation rate at a smaller cost in increased unemployment. With the short-run Phillips curve at $PC(\dot{P}_1^e)$, the inflation target $\dot{P}_1$ can be reached at point C, with an unemployment rate of $\bar{U}_1$, below U_1.

As our analysis in Chapter 10 indicated, with a lower actual inflation rate, inflationary expectations would eventually decline, even in the absence of wage and price controls. The role of temporary wage and price controls is to speed up the decline in what are assumed to be "backward-looking" inflationary expectations by providing a period of relative price stability and signaling the private sector that an anti-inflationary program is in effect. The role for TIP would be to encourage compliance with voluntary guide-

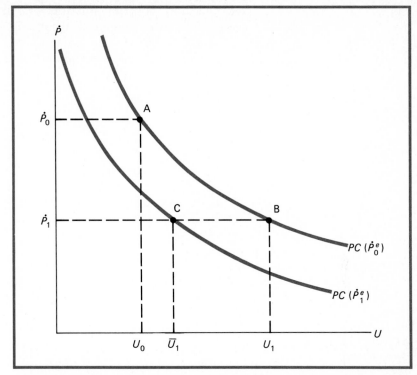

With the short-run Phillips curve given by $PC(\dot{P}_0^e)$, to reduce inflation from $\dot{P}_0$ to $\dot{P}_1$ requires an increase in unemployment from U_0 to U_1. An incomes policy is aimed at lowering the expected inflation rate to shift the short-run Phillips curve downward to $PC(\dot{P}_1^e)$ and allow inflation to be reduced to $\dot{P}_1$ with unemployment rising only to $\bar{U}_1$.

lines and therefore accomplish this same result without mandatory controls.

The Case Against Incomes Policies

Critics of incomes policies argue that there are important harmful side effects from such policies and deny that incomes policies will achieve their intended goal of reducing inflation while minimizing the associated unemployment costs.

Consider the side effects first. Critics of incomes policies point out that the price system plays an important role in allocating resources. Attempts to interfere with free market price setting will distort relative prices and therefore the allocation of resources. To accomplish an efficient allocation of resources, relative prices of some goods should rise over time and others should fall. To freeze all prices at some specified level, for example, clearly inhibits the process. A mechanism can of course be made to provide "merited" exceptions from controls, but this substitutes a bureaucracy for the marketplace in making decisions that affect resource allocation. Incomes policies are also criticized as an infringement on economic freedom, limiting the ability of individuals to bargain for the price their product or labor services will bring in the market. Some critics see a progressive process whereby controls lead to inefficiency, which leads to demands for additional controls, with a progressive loss of economic and eventually personal freedoms as the state comes to dominate the economy.[22]

Moreover, critics maintain that incomes policies simply do not work. Price and wage controls will be evaded by firms and workers. Product quality can be lowered as a substitute (e.g., larger holes in the doughnut) for price increases. Difficult to measure fringe benefits can be granted in place of wage increases (e.g., more coffee breaks). The administrative cost of a comprehensive enforcement procedure is argued to be prohibitively high.

Even if incomes policies could temporarily hold down prices and wages, critics argue that prices will simply rise faster in the post-controls period to catch up for time lost during controls. We examine some evidence below on whether this was the case for the United States during the period after wage–price controls were weakened in 1973. The argument that there will be a "price bubble" in a post-controls period implicitly attacks the view of inflationary expectations as backward looking, the view on which the case for an incomes policy is based. If inflationary expectations are instead forward looking, as for example they are with the rational expectations assumption discussed in Chapter 11, then at the end of a control period, if controls have been keeping price below the equilibrium level, firms and workers will expect renewed inflation. Wage demands and consequently price inflation will ensue.

Finally, note that if expectations are rational, the whole short-run Phillips curve analysis on which the case for incomes policies is based requires serious modification. There is no need for an incomes policy to aid in the transition to a noninflationary regime. The policy conclusion that followed from the rational expectations assumption, together with the other aspects of the new classical economics, was that real variables such as unemployment and real output are independent of the systematic component of aggregate demand management policies. A disinflation policy that is pre-announced and followed should *not*, in the rational expectations view, increase unemployment. The only effect of such a policy should be on the price level and other nominal variables. One

---

[22]See, for example, the discussion in Milton Friedman, *Free to Choose* (New York: Harcourt Brace Jovanovich, 1979), Chap. 2.

will not find any new classical economist who is sympathetic to the use of incomes policies.

The 1971–1974 Price Stabilization Program

The U.S. experiment with mandatory price and wage controls during the early 1970s, which was described at the beginning of this section, provides evidence on the effectiveness of incomes policies. This experiment with a incomes policy had a somewhat different rationale than that described above, where an incomes policy is one element in a disinflation program. When Phase I of the Nixon administration controls policy took effect, the inflation rate was 5 percent, a rate considered high at the time. After controls went into effect, however, both monetary and fiscal policy became *more* expansionary rather than more restrictive. The logic behind this incomes policy seemed to have been to use controls as an anti-inflationary device so that aggregate demand policy could be used to lower the unemployment rate, which was 6 percent in the quarter during which controls began. There is little evidence that the program succeeded.

Reasonable estimates of the effects of the mandatory phases of the wage and price control program in 1971–72 show that the annual inflation rate was reduced by approximately two percentage points by the controls program.[23] The same estimates indicate, however, that there was a post-control "bubble" in the inflation rate which erased this gain, so that by mid-1975 the price level was about where it would have been with no controls. In terms of having a lasting effect on the inflation rate, the wage–price stabilization program failed.

To some, the experience of 1971–74 is taken as evidence that incomes policies will not work. A more narrow interpretation of the evidence from that period is that incomes policies cannot be used to control inflation while expansionary aggregate demand policies are used to stimulate employment. Incomes policies are not a substitute for restrictive aggregate demand policies as a cure for inflation. Those proposing incomes policies today suggest the use of such programs, in concert with restrictive aggregate demand policies in a disinflation program.[24] The role of income policies, as discussed above, is to minimize the unemployment cost of such a disinflationary process by helping to reduce inflationary

---

[23]See, for example, Robert Gordon, "The Impact of Aggregate Demand on Prices," *Brookings Papers on Economic Activity*, No. 3, 1975, pp. 613–662. See also Lawrence Davidson, "Large Changes: Pitfalls in Econometric Practice," *Journal of Economic Issues*, 15 (June 1979), pp. 329–45. Davidson estimates that controls had a somewhat smaller impact, especially in 1972.

[24]See James Tobin, "Are New Classical Models Plausible Enough to Guide Policy?" *Journal of Money, Credit and Banking*, 12 (November 1980, Part 2), especially pp. 792–95.

expectations. Critics of incomes policies would expect such policies to prove as unsuccessful in this role as they have (in the view of the critics) in past applications.

Review Questions

1 Some economists who accept the public choice view of the fiscal policymaking process have concluded that a constitutional amendment to mandate a balanced federal budget would be desirable. Summarize their arguments in favor of such an amendment. Explain the neo-Keynesian objections to such an amendment.

2 Summarize the trends in the level and composition of federal government expenditures during the period 1962–80.

3 Explain the concept of an automatic fiscal stabilizer. Give examples.

4 Explain the concept of the high-employment budget surplus or deficit. Discuss the usefulness and the limitations of the concept.

5 Why do many economists favor changes in tax rates over changes in government spending on goods and services or transfer payments as an instrument of fiscal policy? What difficulties are there in using changes in tax rates as a policy instrument?

6 Suppose that within the simple Keynesian model used in Section 18.4, the level of government spending (G) was 100, the level of investment (I) was 75 and consumption (C) was given by

$$C = 25 + 0.8\,Y_D.$$

Net taxes (T) are given by the tax function

$$T = 50 + 0.25Y$$

Calculate equilibrium income ($\bar{Y}$). Now suppose that the intercept of the net tax function (t_0) decreases from 50 to 40. Find the new level of equilibrium income.

7 Give some examples of incomes policies.

8 Explain the current rationale for an incomes policy as part of a disinflation program.

9 Summarize the arguments against the use of incomes policies.

Selected Readings

FISCAL POLICY

Bach, George L., *Making Monetary and Fiscal Policy*. Washington, D.C.: Brookings Institution, 1971.

Blinder, Alan, and Solow, Robert, "Analytical Foundations of Fiscal Policy," in Alan Blinder et al., *The Economics of Public Finance* (Washington, D.C.: Brookings Institution 1974).

Buchanan, James M., and Wagner, Richard E., *Democracy in Deficit*. New York: Academic Press, 1977.

Dolde, Walter, "Temporary Taxes as Macro-economic Stabilizers," *American Economic Review*, 69 (May 1979), pp. 81–85.

Heller, Walter W., *New Dimensions of Political Economy*. New York: Norton, 1967.

Lewis, Wilfred, *Federal Fiscal Policy in Postwar Recessions*. Washington, D.C.: Brookings Institution, 1962.

Musgrave, Richard, *The Theory of Public Finance*, New York: McGraw-Hill, 1959, Chaps. 1–4, and 17–22.

Okun, Arthur M., "Rules and Roles for Fiscal and Monetary Policy," in James Diamond, ed., *Issues in Fiscal and Monetary Policy*. Chicago: DePaul University Press, 1971.

Okun, Arthur M., "Monetary–Fiscal Activism: Some Analytical Issues," *Brookings Papers on Economic Activity*, No. 1, 1972, pp. 123–163.

Ott, David V., and Ott, Attiat, F., *Federal Budget Policy*. Washington, D.C.: Brookings Institution, 1969.

Stein, Herbert, *The Fiscal Revolution*. Chicago: University of Chicago Press, 1969.

Stein, Herbert, "Balancing the Budget," in William Fellner, ed., *Contemporary Economic Problems*, 1979. Washington, D.C.: American Enterprise Institute, 1979.

INCOMES POLICIES

Goodwin, Crawfurd, ed., *Exhortation and Controls*. Washington, D.C.: Brookings Institution, 1975.

Okun, Arthur M., "Efficient Disinflationary Policies," *American Economic Review*, 68 (May 1978), pp. 348–52.

Okun, Arthur M., and Perry, George L., ed., "Innovative Policies to Slow Inflation," special issue, *Brookings Papers on Economic Activity*, No. 2, 1978. Also in book form as *Curing Chronic Inflation*. Washington, D.C.: Brookings Institution, 1978.

Shultz, George, and Aliber, Robert, eds., *Guidelines, Informal Controls, and the Market Place*. Chicago: University of Chicago Press, 1966.

Wallich, Henry, and Weintraub, Sidney, "A Tax-Based Incomes Policy," *Journal of Economic Issues*, 5 (June 1971), pp. 1–19.

Weber, Arnold, *In Pursuit of Price Stability: The Wage–Price Freeze of 1971*. Washington, D.C.: *Brookings Institution*, 1973.

19

In this chapter we focus on the conduct of monetary policy. We will be especially concerned with the question of the optimal way in which monetary policy should be carried out—an issue over which there has been considerable controversy in recent years. Two aspects of this question will be considered. The first is that of the optimal *strategy* for monetary policy—the plan that links the policy instruments controlled by the Federal Reserve to the ultimate policy goals. The second aspect of the optimal monetary policy question is the choice of a policy instrument or operating target in the short run—the optimal *tactics* or operating procedure for monetary policy. Additionally, in this chapter the relative merits of monetary and fiscal policy as stabilization tools are considered. Finally, we return to the issue of rules versus discretion in policymaking as it pertains to monetary policy. Prior to considering these topics, it will be useful to expand on our earlier description of the monetary policymaking process.

19.1 THE MONETARY POLICYMAKING PROCESS

The structure of the Federal Reserve System was discussed in Chapter 15. For purposes of macroeconomic policy it was explained that the policymaking bodies within the Federal Reserve system were the Board of Governors of the Federal Reserve and the Open Market Committee. The Board of Governors is composed

MONETARY POLICY

of seven governors appointed by the President of the United States with Senate confirmation to terms of 14 years, with one of the governors designated by the President as Chairman for a four-year term. The Open Market Committee has 12 voting members, the seven governors and five of the presidents of the 12 regional Federal Reserve Banks. The presidents of the regional Federal Reserve Banks serve on a rotating basis with the exception that the president of the New York Federal Reserve Bank is a permanent voting member.

As discussed in Chapter 15, open market operations are the major tool used by the Federal Reserve in conducting monetary policy, and our discussion in this chapter focuses on the behavior of the Open Market Committee. Adjustments in the Federal Reserve discount rate and the levels of reserve requirements are made by the Board of Governors to supplement, or at times substitute for, open market operations.

In light of our discussion in Chapter 18 concerning the interaction of macroeconomic policymaking and democratic politics, it is worthwhile to consider the relationship of the Federal Reserve and other government policymaking bodies. The striking feature of the Federal Reserve's situation is the considerable degree of independence given to the monetary policymaking authority. The 14-year terms for which the governors are appointed and the fact that they cannot be reappointed provide insulation from the political process. The Chairman of the Board of Governors is appointed for a four-year term but this term is not concurrent with that of the President of the United States. Therefore, an incoming President does not immediately get to appoint his choice of Chairman. The other members of the Open Market Committee, the regional bank presidents, are appointed by the directors of the regional banks with the approval of the Board of Governors.

In recent years Congress has passed legislation requiring periodic reports from the Federal Reserve on the conduct of policy, but monetary policy decisions such as the target growth rate in the money stock or target level for the short-term interest rate are not subjects on which Congress legislates. These decisions are made by the Open Market Committee. Further, the Federal Reserve is independent of the budget appropriations process, since its expenses are paid by its interest earnings on holdings of government securities.

All this is not to say that the Federal Reserve is completely autonomous or that monetary policy is conducted in a completely nonpolitical setting. The Chairman of the Board of Governors comes up for reappointment (as chairman) during the course of a President's term. Also, since relatively few members of the Board of Governors serve out their full terms, most recent Presidents have had the opportunity to make several appointments to the board and, therefore, to influence the conduct of monetary policy. Furthermore, the Federal Reserve's independence is itself the result of congressional legislation and the Federal Reserve has recognized that new legislation could weaken this independence. In fact, at times when there is a severe conflict between the Federal Reserve and the administration or Congress over the proper course of monetary policy, bills to limit Federal Reserve independence are often proposed in Congress. The Federal Reserve recognizes this threat and the fact that there are limits to how far it can go in pursuing goals that deviate from those of Congress and the President. Even taking account of these constraints, however, the degree of independence of the Federal Reserve is sufficient that in our discussion below we consider how the monetary policy authority itself makes policy decisions and determines optimal policy.

The Open Market Committee meets on a monthly basis. At these meetings they review the current domestic and international economic situation. They also consider forecasts of the Federal Reserve staff concerning future economic events. On the basis of this information they formulate a "directive" to the *Open Market Desk* at the New York Federal Reserve Bank, explaining how open market operations should be conducted over the next month. The questions of an optimal monetary policy strategy and tactics can then be viewed as the choice of a directive by the Open Market

Committee. In the next two sections (19.2 and 19.3) we deal with two important issues concerning the optimal choice of an Open Market Committee directive.

19.2 THE STRATEGY OF MONETARY POLICY: INTERMEDIATE TARGETING ON THE MONETARY AGGREGATES

The Concept of Intermediate Targeting

The ultimate "target" variables that the monetary authority attempts to control are macroeconomic goal variables such as the unemployment rate, inflation rate, level of real GNP, foreign exchange rate, and the foreign balance of payments. Rather than simply adjusting monetary policy instruments on the basis of past observations on these variables and forecasts of their future behavior, in the short run the Federal Reserve has adopted a strategy of trying to influence these ultimate targets by hitting target rates of growth in monetary aggregates (M1, M2, M3). Monetary aggregates have assumed the role of *intermediate targets* in this Federal Reserve strategy.

An intermediate target is a variable that the Federal Reserve controls not because the variable is necessarily important in its own right, but because by controlling the variable the policymakers believe they are influencing the ultimate policy targets in a predictable way. In the case of domestic targets, with a monetary aggregate as an intermediate target, the implicit assumption in Federal Reserve's strategy is that higher rates of growth in the money stock will, other things being equal, increase inflation while lowering unemployment (raising the level of economic activity) in the short run. Slower monetary growth rates will, again *ceteris paribus,* be associated with lower inflation rates and higher short-run rates of unemployment.

What is the rationale for such intermediate targeting? Even if there is a predictable relationship between money growth rates and ultimate economic targets that the Federal Reserve wants to control, why use an intermediate target rather than controlling the ultimate targets directly? To understand the possible usefulness of the intermediate targeting approach, we must recognize the fact that monetary policy must be made under conditions of imperfect information and, therefore, uncertainty about the behavior of the economy. If the ultimate targets of policy can be observed at less frequent intervals than financial market variables such as interest rates, bank reserves, and monetary aggregates, then as information about such financial market variables becomes available, it can be used to adjust the previous policy setting. The intermediate targeting approach is one way of employing such financial market information.

As currently implemented by the Federal Reserve, intermediate targeting proceeds as follows. At the beginning of each calendar quarter, the Open Market Committee chooses the money growth rate target that it views as consistent with its ultimate policy goals for the next year. The committee makes this choice on the basis of past data and staff forecasts of the behavior of the economy for given money growth rates. After this choice is made, monetary policy during the quarter proceeds *as if the chosen money growth target is the ultimate target of monetary policy*. Policy actions within the quarter are aimed at hitting this money target. At the beginning of the next quarter the money target is reviewed and adjusted on the basis of new forecasts and the experience within the quarter.

To see how this process works, recall from Chapter 15 that the money stock (M1 definition) can be expressed as the monetary base (MB) times the money multiplier (m):

$$M^s = m \cdot \text{MB} \tag{19.1}$$

where

$$m = m(\text{rr}_d, \frac{\text{CU}}{D}, \frac{\text{ER}}{D}, \frac{\text{SD} + \text{TD}}{D}, \text{rr}_{\text{sd}}, \text{rr}_{\text{td}}) \tag{19.2}$$

The money multiplier depends on a number of variables, such as the required reserve ratios on demand deposits (rr_d) and the currency/deposit ratio (CU/D) (see Section 15.1). The variables that determine the money multiplier are themselves functions of other economic variables, such as interest rates and the level of income. If the Federal Reserve is using a monetary aggregate such as M1 as an intermediate target, then within the quarter, open market operations will be aimed at providing sufficient growth in the monetary base to achieve the target growth rate in the money stock. The Federal Reserve will monitor weekly money stock figures and offset the effects on the money stock of unpredicted changes in the money multiplier or in the monetary base (via changes on bank borrowing of reserves, for example). The financial market information they react to is then the weekly money stock figures and they use this information in a particular way—to adjust open market operations in order to hit the money stock target.

The Inefficiency of Intermediate Targeting

The question arises as to whether such intermediate targeting on a monetary aggregate is the optimal way to adjust the policy setting as current-quarter financial market information becomes available. The answer is that viewed from a theoretical standpoint, in general it is not. Using a monetary aggregate as an intermediate target is in general an inefficient monetary policy strategy.[1] To see why, we will first consider a case where such intermediate targeting *is* optimal. This case is depicted within the IS–LM framework in Figure 19.1. For simplicity, suppose that the Federal Reserve has only one ultimate target, the level of real income (y), the desired level of which is (y^*). Also assume that in a given quarter, based on its forecasts, the monetary policy authority concludes that the target level of income will be achieved if the money stock is set at M^*.

The LM schedule in Figure 19.1 is vertical, reflecting an assumption that the demand for money is totally interest inelastic. Money demand depends only on income. Further, we assume that the demand for money function is perfectly stable. There are no shifts in the function—no changes in the amount of money demanded for a given income level. On the supply side, the Federal

[1]For a good analysis of the issues discussed in this subsection, see Benjamin Friedman, "The Inefficiency of Short-Run Monetary Targets for Monetary Policy," *Brookings Papers on Economic Activity*, No. 2, 1977, pp. 293–318.

Figure 19.1
Optimal Case for Intermediate Targeting on a Monetary Aggregate

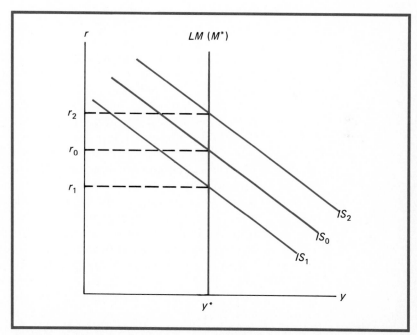

If the demand for money function is totally interest inelastic and perfectly stable, then by hitting the money stock target M^* the Federal Reserve will fix the vertical *LM* schedule at *LM*(M^*). Income will be at the target level y^* regardless of the position of the *IS* schedule.

Reserve is assumed to offset changes in the money supply that come as a result of the behavior of the banking system. Thus, if the Federal Reserve achieves its target level of the money stock (M^*), the LM schedule will be perfectly stable at LM (M^*) in Figure 19.1. This means that successfully hitting the intermediate target for the money stock will in fact mean successfully hitting the ultimate income target (y^*).

To see this, consider the situation depicted in the figure. We assume that the Federal Reserve cannot predict with certainty the position of the IS schedule. Assume that the predicted position for the curve is IS_0. Real sector demand factors such as exports, autonomous investment, and government spending may turn out to be weaker than predicted, causing the IS schedule to be to the left of IS_0, at IS_1. Alternatively, such real sector demand factors may be stronger than predicted, causing the IS schedule to be at a position such as IS_2, to the right of IS_0. By targeting on the money stock, the Federal Reserve assures that the vertical LM schedule will be fixed at $LM(M^*)$ and consequently income will be at y^*, regardless of the position of the IS schedule. We said above that when the Federal Reserve uses a money aggregate as an intermediate target then within the quarter, policy proceeds as if the chosen money stock target *was* the ultimate target of monetary policy. In the case depicted in Figure 19.1, hitting the money stock target guarantees hitting the income target. The implicit assumption behind intermediate targeting on the money stock is indeed valid. This is the optimal case for such intermediate targeting.

Notice that while hitting the money stock target guarantees that we will hit the income target, unpredicted shocks that shift the IS schedule will cause volatility in the interest rate. If the actual position of the IS schedule is IS_1 or IS_2 instead of the Federal Reserve's predicted position IS_0, the interest rate will be r_1 or r_2 instead of the predicted level r_0. If the Federal Reserve also has an interest rate target—if, for example, r_0 is in some sense the "desirable" level of the interest rate—the Federal Reserve will have to miss the interest rate target to hit the money stock target. Generally, interest rate volatility will be one cost of adhering to money stock targets. We return to this issue below.

Figure 19.2 illustrates cases where achieving the money stock target will not in general mean that the income target will be achieved. In Figure 19.2a we still assume that if the Federal Reserve hits its money stock target, it will fix the position of the LM curve. For this to be the case we must still assume that the money demand function is perfectly stable. There are no unpredictable shifts in money demand that will shift the LM schedule for a given value of the money stock. In Figure 19.2a we do not assume that

Figure 19.2

Cases Where
Intermediate
Targeting on the
Money Stock Is
Suboptimal

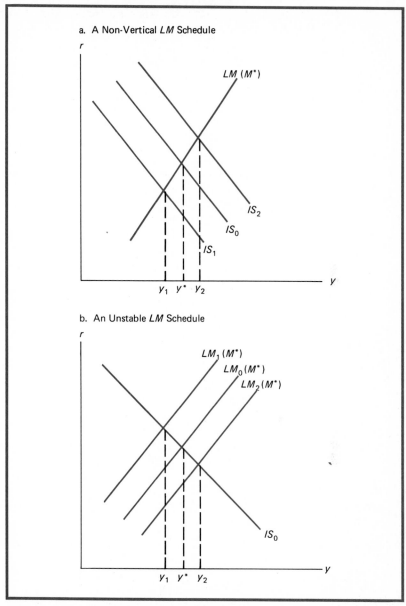

a. A Non-Vertical *LM* Schedule

r

LM (*M**)

*IS*₂

*IS*₀

*IS*₁

*y*₁ *y** *y*₂

y

b. An Unstable *LM* Schedule

r

*LM*₁ (*M**)

*LM*₀ (*M**)

*LM*₂ (*M**)

*IS*₀

*y*₁ *y** *y*₂

y

Part *a*. A non-Vertical *LM* Schedule. If money demand is not totally interest inelastic and the *LM* schedule is upward sloping to the right, then hitting the money stock target will cause income to be at the target level *y** only if the *IS* schedule is at the predicted position *IS*₀. If, due to unpredicted shocks, the *IS* schedule is instead at *IS*₁ or *IS*₂, income will be away from *y** at *y*₁ or *y*₂ even though *M* is at *M**. Part *b*. An Unstable *LM* Schedule. We assume that the Federal Reserve hits the money stock target *M** which, based on its forecast of money demand, should set the *LM* schedule at *LM*₀(*M**) and hit the income target *y**. If, due to an unpredicted shock to the money demand function, the *LM* curve shifts either to *LM*₁(*M**) or *LM*₂(*M**), income will be at *y*₁ or *y*₂ and the income target will be missed even if the money stock is at the target level *M**.

money demand is totally interest inelastic; the LM schedule is therefore not vertical.

In this case notice that even though the Federal Reserve achieves its target level of the money stock, it will hit the ultimate income target only if the IS curve is at the predicted position IS_0—only if the Federal Reserve's real sector forecast, on which the choice of the money stock target was predicated, was correct. If real sector demand was weaker than predicted and the IS schedule was at IS_1 in Figure 19.2a instead of IS_0, income would be at y_1, below y^*. If real sector demand was stronger than predicted and the IS schedule was at IS_2, income would exceed the target level. In both cases the income target is missed even though the Federal Reserve hits the money stock target M^*. With a nonvertical LM schedule fixing, the money stock does not fix the level of income.

In Figure 19.2b we consider a case where the money demand function is not perfectly stable. There are unpredicted shifts in money demand for given levels of income and the interest rate. Such shocks to money demand shift the LM schedule. In this case even if the Federal Reserve hits its money stock target, the LM schedule will not be fixed. In Figure 19.2b assume that based on a forecast of money demand, the Federal Reserve predicts that the LM schedule will be at $LM_0(M^*)$. To isolate the effects of uncertainty about money demand more clearly, let us assume that the Federal Reserve's forecast about the real sector is correct: the predicted and actual position of the IS curve is IS_0.

If the Federal Reserve is using the money stock as an intermediate target and hits the money stock target (M^*), it will be the case that it will hit the income target (y^*) only if the prediction of money demand is correct—only if the LM schedule is at $LM_0(M^*)$ as predicted. This can be seen in Figure 19.2b. If there is an unpredicted shock that increases the demand for money above the predicted level and the LM schedule is at $LM_1(M^*)$ instead of $LM_0(M^*)$, the level of income (y_1) will fall short of the target level.[2] In the reverse case, where an unpredicted shock reduced money demand below the predicted level and the LM curve was at a position such as $LM_2(M^*)$, the level of income would be y_2 above the target level. Again here, hitting the money stock target does not guarantee that the income target will be hit.

There is another important reason why achieving a money stock target may not in practice result in achieving a real income target. The IS–LM curve model depicts the equilibrium *real* income and the interest rate, but so far we have not mentioned the behavior of

---

[2]By a shock that reduces (or increases) money demand is meant a shift in the money demand function which reduces (or increases) the quantity of money demanded for a given level of income and the rate of interest. The way in which shifts in the money demand function shift the LM schedule is explained in Section 6.2.

the price level. As we saw in Chapter 8, changes in the price level will shift the LM schedule. Increases in the price level will reduce the *real* value of the money stock (M/P) for a given nominal money stock, shifting the LM schedule to the left. Reductions in the price level increase the real value of the money stock, shifting the LM schedule to the right. As a consequence, with a variable price level *any* unforeseen shock that affects aggregate demand or aggregate supply and hence the price level will shift the position of the LM schedule for a given *nominal* money stock. Hitting a particular *nominal* money stock target will not be sufficient to pin down the position of the LM schedule, even if there are no unpredictable shocks to money demand. Consequently, hitting such a money stock target will certainly not guarantee hitting a real income target. To see this we examine the effects of an unexpected shock to aggregate supply such as that caused by an autonomous increase in the world price of oil, which we analyzed in Section 8.5.

The effects of such an unanticipated oil price increase are illustrated in Figure 19.3. Here we will assume that the Federal Reserve maintains the money stock at the target level M^* which in the absence of unanticipated shocks is consistent with the target income level y^*. The rise in the price of oil will, as we have seen, shift the aggregate supply schedule to the left from a position such as y_0^s in Figure 19.3a to the position y_1^s. Output declines to y_1 and the price level rises to P_1. In Figure 19.3b it can be seen that this increase in the price of oil will shift the LM schedule from $\text{LM}_0(M^*)$ to $\text{LM}_1(M^*)$. This shift in the LM schedule occurs even though the Federal Reserve hits the money stock target M^*. Hitting the money stock target does not result in achieving the target level of income (y^*).

The examples provided so far show only that intermediate targeting is an *imperfect* procedure in that it will not generally be the case that successfully maintaining the money stock at the target level will assure hitting the income target. This is not sufficient to show that such intermediate targeting is *inefficient* or suboptimal in the sense that it produces a less desirable result than some alternative strategy.

To see that in the general case intermediate targeting on a monetary aggregate is not only imperfect but inefficient, recall the two basic elements in the procedure. First, with a monetary aggregate as an intermediate target, the *only* current-quarter information to which monetary policy responds are the observations on the money stock. Second, with such a strategy the Federal Reserve responds to the observations on the money stock in a particular manner. They conduct open market operations with the goal of hitting the quarterly money stock target, *acting as if the money stock target is the ultimate target of monetary policy.*

Figure 19.3
Effects of an
Aggregate Supply
Shock with a
Monetary Aggregate
as an Intermediate
Target

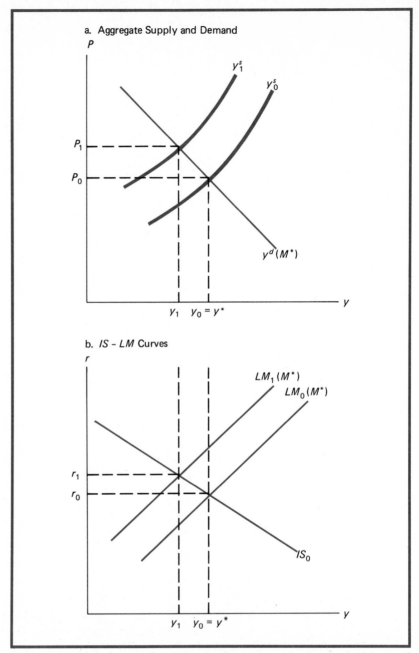

a. Aggregate Supply and Demand

An unfavorable supply shock shifts the aggregate supply schedule from y_0^s
to y_1^s in Part a. If the money stock is held at the target level, the aggregate
demand schedule does not shift; income falls below the target level to y_1
and the price level rises to P_1. The LM schedule in Part b shifts left from
$LM_0(M^*)$ to $LM_1(M^*)$ due to the price increase. The income target is missed
even though the money stock target is hit.

ECONOMIC POLICY

These two features of the process are responsible for its inefficiency. An optimal procedure would take account of *all* relevant available current-quarter information. On the basis of this complete information set, a forecast would be made of the effects of current-quarter shocks on the level of income. Open market operations would then be conducted to offset these predicted disturbances. Such a process can be termed *direct targeting* on the ultimate policy target or targets, in this case income. In such a process current quarter observations on monetary aggregates and other financial market variables play the role of *information variables*, variables used in forecasting current period shocks to the system. Such a direct targeting approach will not in general involve setting and hitting specific money stock targets. Reference to one of the examples above may clarify how the objectives of hitting a money stock target and following a direct targeting approach will at times call for different strategies of open market operations.

Consider the case of the unanticipated supply shock depicted in Figure 19.3. If open market operations are carried out with the goal of achieving the money stock target (M^*), the rise in prices that occurs as a result of the supply shock will cause the LM schedule to shift from $LM_0(M^*)$ to $LM_1(M^*)$. If, instead, the direct targeting procedure is followed, the Federal Reserve will recognize from current information that there is upward pressure on interest rates and on the money stock as the rising price level decreases the available *real* money stock.[3] Since we assume that the Federal Reserve cannot forecast the supply shock, the policymakers would not be able to pinpoint the exact source of this tightness in financial markets. Without being more specific about the exact information available to the policymaker and without developing the theory of the optimal use of information somewhat further than will be done here, it is not possible to determine the exact policy response. What can be said, however, is that with direct targeting the optimal policy will be to "lean against the wind" to some degree and respond to such tightness in financial markets by allowing the *nominal* money stock to rise above the target level M^*.

The effect of this policy strategy is illustrated in Figure 19.4. As in Figure 19.3, the unanticipated supply shock will shift the aggregate supply schedule from y_0^s to y_1^s in Figure 19.4a. For a given

[3]Other signs indicating that a shock had occurred which was lowering the level of economic activity would come from monthly observations on variables such as unemployment, industrial production, and capacity utilization rates. But note that some current-quarter data would be open to conflicting interpretation. Monthly observations of the price level, for example, would show a price increase, but this could indicate either a supply shock or a shock to aggregate demand. The supply shock would tend to cause income to fall below the target level. If the price rise were from shock that strengthened aggregate demand, the tendency in the absence of a policy response would be to overshoot the target level.

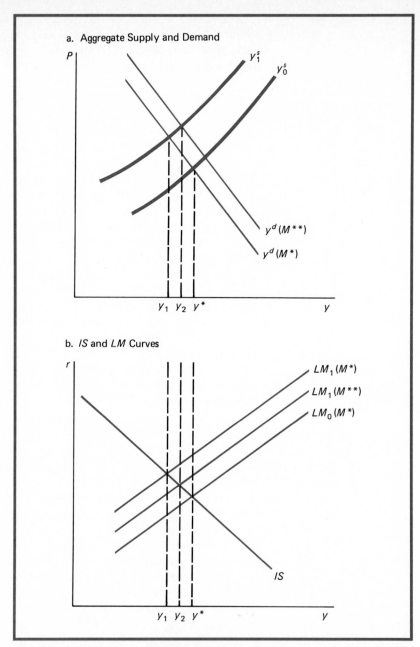

Figure 19.4
Alternative Monetary Policy Responses to an Unanticipated Supply Shock

a. Aggregate Supply and Demand

b. *IS* and *LM* Curves

As in Figure 19.3, the supply shock shifts the aggregate supply curve from y_0^s to y_1^s; income falls to y_1 and the price level rises to P_1. The increase in the price level shifts the *LM* schedule leftward from $LM_0(M^*)$ to $LM_1(M^*)$ if the money stock is maintained at the target level (M^*). If, in response to evidence of tightness in the money market, the Federal Reserve allows the money stock to rise (to M^{**}) above the target level, the *LM* schedule will shift from $LM_1(M^*)$ to $LM_1(M^{**})$. The aggregate demand schedule will therefore shift to the right from $y^d(M^*)$ to $y^d(M^{**})$ and income will rise (to y_2) back toward the target level (y^*).

nominal money stock, the target level M^*, the price increase shifts the LM schedule from $LM_0(M^*)$ to $LM_1(M^*)$. Income declines from y^* to y_1. If the Federal Reserve is taking account of all available current information, it will respond to the tightness in the money market (rising interest rate, excess demand for money, etc.) by allowing the nominal money stock to rise above M^* to a level we denote M^{**}. This increase in the nominal money stock will shift the LM schedule to a position such as $LM_1(M^{**})$ in Figure 19.4b and thus shift the aggregate demand schedule to a position such as $y^d(M^{**})$ in Figure 19.4a. Real income will decline only to the level y_2, which is closer to the target level of income y^*.

The example in Figure 19.4 is only an illustration, but it is true in general that intermediate targeting on a monetary aggregate is an inefficient strategy. This inefficiency results partly from the fact that the intermediate targeting approach fails to utilize *all* the relevant current period information. Second, the data that are used, observations on the monetary aggregate, are used inefficiently since the intermediate targeting approach is based on the generally incorrect assumption that hitting the money stock target is equivalent to hitting the ultimate monetary policy targets.

The Case for Intermediate Targeting on a Monetary Aggregate

If in theory intermediate targeting on a monetary aggregate is an inefficient strategy, why in practice is such a procedure employed? In recent years the Federal Reserve has, in fact, placed increased emphasis on control of such intermediate targets. In 1980, when because of uncertainty about the effects of financial innovations on the growth rates of various monetary aggregates, the Federal Reserve chose temporarily not to announce money growth targets for the coming year, there was widespread objection in Congress. In response the Federal Reserve assured Congress that it was still committed to the intermediate targeting process and announced a new set of money growth targets. Why is there this commitment to a seemingly inefficient strategy?

One group strongly supporting the strategy of intermediate targeting on monetary aggregates are the monetarists. The monetarists, as we have seen, go further and advocate setting a *constant* money growth rate target. Recall from the preceding subsection that the ideal case for the intermediate targeting approach was where the LM schedule was vertical and the money demand function was perfectly stable. The monetarists believe that the LM schedule is quite steep and that money demand is quite stable; therefore, it is natural for them to favor the intermediate targeting approach.

The monetarists must recognize that supply shocks such as that analyzed in Figure 19.3 will cause the intermediate targeting approach to fail to perform ideally. They also recognize that even if a stable money demand function exists, recent innovations in financial markets cause problems in defining and measuring money demand. Any measured concept of money demand will display some instability as institutional changes take place. Consequently, even many monetarists would agree that as a theoretical matter intermediate targeting on a monetary aggregate is not optimal. To Milton Friedman and other monetarists these problems are "second-order" effects and, as Friedman has said: "We must not in this area as in others let the best be the enemy of the good." In fact, the monetarist criticism of the Federal Reserve is that it has not placed sufficient emphasis on hitting money growth targets.

Nonmonetarists who do not believe that the LM schedule is steep and, given the recent innovations in financial market, believe that *measured* money demand is subject to significant instability have less reason to favor intermediate targeting on a monetary aggregate. The neo-Keynesian economists, who believe that supply shocks have had an important effect on aggregate economic activity, would see an additional source of inefficiency in this intermediate targeting approach, as discussed above.

Still there is considerable support among nonmonetarists for the intermediate targeting approach. The reason is not that these economists reject the view that such intermediate targeting is inefficient, but they believe that it is less inefficient than other *feasible* strategies. Implicitly, such economists accept that the optimum or "first best" strategy of processing all important current information and "direct targeting" on the ultimate target variables is too complex a process for policymakers. Intermediate targeting on a monetary aggregate will at least prevent large destabilizing swings in money growth. Consequently, many nonmonetarist economists view such intermediate targeting as the best *feasible* strategy—as a "second best" alternative.

Other nonmonetarists do not favor the intermediate targeting approach. In addition to the theoretical argument that such intermediate targeting is suboptimal, they raise the pragmatic objection that there are a number of money aggregates and it is not at all clear which should be used as an intermediate target. In practice, the Federal Reserve sets target ranges for several monetary aggregates (M1, M2, M3), and at times the targets are conflicting. For example, in mid-1981, M1 growth was below the lower end of its target range whereas M2 growth exceeded the upper bounds of its range. Does such a situation call for an easing or tightening of open market operations? Critics of intermediate targeting on monetary aggregates doubt that in this era of financial innovation any one aggregate provides a reliable measure of "money" and, hence, should be given primacy in formulating policy. They believe that more emphasis should be put on interest rates and overall measures of credit rather than monetary aggregates. They favor the *direct targeting* approach while acknowledging that there are difficulties in its implementation.

What about the policymakers themselves; why has the Federal Reserve adopted the intermediate targeting approach? In part the Federal Reserve has acted in response to pressure from the monetarists. In part the policymakers have been responding to criticism from Congress and elsewhere as a result of the past instability in money growth. But an additional factor has been the desire within the Federal Reserve for more quantifiable short-run guidelines for policy. The monetary aggregates serve this function and are believed by many to be good measures of the thrust of monetary policy. Especially important here is the Federal Reserve's presumption that there is a close link between money growth and inflation, a view that over intermediate-run periods the inflation rate will be no higher than is accommodated by the money growth rate. This belief, together with concern over the secular rise in the inflation rate (see Table 1.3), has led the Federal Reserve to place increased emphasis on monetary aggregates as intermediate targets.

In closing this discussion, however, we should note that there is some controversy over how strong a commitment the Federal Reserve really has to hitting money stock targets. We mentioned above that the monetarists are critical of the Federal Reserve for failing to hit announced money stock targets. We will see in the next section that in 1979 the Federal Reserve modified its procedures for hitting such targets, but in practice monetary policy is not as mechanical as the description of the intermediate targeting approach above might imply. For better or worse, monetary policy is still guided by human beings rather than by rules.

19.3 THE TACTICS OF MONETARY POLICY: INTEREST RATE VERSUS RESERVE CONTROL

As mentioned above, the Federal Reserve has been criticized for failing to hit pre-announced money growth targets. In order to gain firmer control over the monetary aggregates, the Federal Reserve changed its operating procedure on October 6, 1979. The *strategy* of intermediate targeting remained unchanged but the *tactics* by which this strategy was to be accomplished were changed. Prior to October 1979, the Federal Reserve pursued its money stock targets using interest rates as an *instrument*. After October 1979, the Federal Reserve switched to a procedure of controlling the money stock through control of bank reserves. In the next two subsections, monetary control under the two procedures is described. We then evaluate the relative merits of the two approaches.

Monetary Control with an Interest Rate Instrument

The procedure followed during most of the 1970s was to control the money stock by closely controlling the level of one short-term interest rate. The rate of interest the Federal Reserve controlled was the federal funds rate, which is the interest rate that banks charge each other for overnight loans of reserves. Since short-term rates move together, by controlling this rate the Federal Reserve was effectively controlling the general level of short-term interest rates. The way in which the Federal Reserve pursued money stock targets via interest rate control is illustrated in Figure 19.5.

Consider the Federal Reserve's directive to the Open Market Desk for a given month. Based on forecasts of the level of economic activity (both real income and price changes) as well as any special factors, the Federal Reserve would have a prediction of the position of the money demand schedule drawn as a function of the interest rate. In Figure 19.5, assume that the predicted position of the schedule is M_0^d. If the money stock target is M^* in the graph, the interest rate consistent with hitting the money target is r^*. If the Federal Reserve is using the interest rate as an instrument to control the money stock, the Open Market Committee would instruct the Open Market Desk to keep the federal funds rate within a narrow band centered on r^*.

How would the Open Market Desk keep the federal funds rate close to r^* given that this is a rate determined by banks' borrowing and lending of excess reserves? Federal Reserve control over the federal funds rate is exerted by increasing and decreasing the supply of reserves. Suppose, for example, that at a federal funds rate of r^*, there is an excess demand for federal funds, by which we mean that the volume of reserves banks want to borrow exceeds the volume other banks desire to lend. This would place upward pressure on the federal funds rate and in the absence of Federal Reserve action, the funds rate would rise until demand (desired borrowing) equaled supply (desired lending).

If the Federal Reserve were maintaining the Federal funds rate at r^*, they would intervene and increase the supply of reserves by an amount sufficient to equilibrate the federal funds market at r^*. The typical way of increasing reserves would be through open market purchases of government securities. Similarly, if there was an excess supply in the federal funds market (desired lending of reserves exceeded desired borrowing), the Federal Reserve would reduce the volume of reserves in the system to keep the federal funds rate from falling below the target level r^*. In this fashion the

570

Figure 19.5
Monetary Control
with an Interest Rate
Instrument

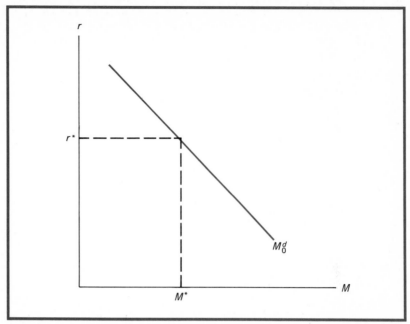

Based on the predicted position of the money demand schedule M_0^d, the Federal Reserve would choose the interest rate level r^* as consistent with achieving the money stock target M^*.

Federal Reserve would keep the federal funds rate very close to r^*, which if their money demand prediction is correct is the rate consistent with hitting the money stock target M^*.

Two points need to be noted concerning this procedure of using an interest rate instrument for money stock control. First, it should be recognized that if the Federal Reserve's prediction of the position of the money demand schedule is in error, the money stock target will be missed. The Federal Reserve's money demand forecast may be in error because the forecast of the level of economic activity, an important determinant of the level of money demand, is wrong or because there is some unpredicted shock which shifts the money demand *function*. Figure 19.6 illustrates one such case. Assume again that the Federal Reserve's forecast for the position of the money demand schedule is at M_0^d and the money stock target is M^*. The level of the federal funds rate consistent with this money stock target *and this forecast of the position of the money demand schedule* is r^*. Suppose, however, that the level of economic activity and therefore the demand for money exceeds the Federal Reserve's prediction; the *actual* position of the money demand schedule is at M_1^d in Figure 19.6. If the Federal Reserve maintains the federal funds rate at r^*, the money stock

Figure 19.6
Interest Rate
Instrument with Errors
in Prediction of
Money Demand

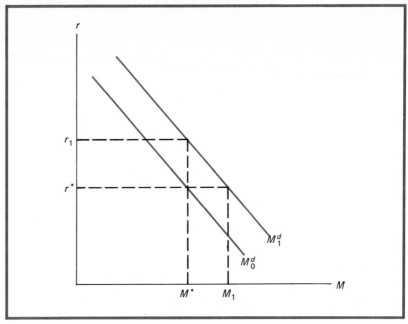

As in Figure 19.5, the Federal Reserve's prediction of the position of the money demand schedule is M_0^d and the interest rate target is therefore r^* to achieve the money stock target M^*. If the actual position of the money demand function is M_1^d, then with the interest rate held at r^* the money stock will rise above the target level to M_1. A higher interest rate of r_1 would be required to achieve the money stock target M^*.

will be at M_1 above the target level. A higher interest rate target of r_1 would have been required to hit the money stock target M^*.

The second point to note about the use of an interest rate instrument for monetary control is that when such a procedure is followed, the Federal Reserve loses control over the quantity of bank reserves. In order to keep the federal funds rate at the target level, the Federal Reserve must stand ready to increase reserves whenever there are market pressures pushing the funds rate above the target rate and to decrease reserves whenever market pressure would push the funds rate below the target level. The quantity of reserves is *demand determined*, depending on the banking system's reserve demand as expressed in the federal funds market.

Monetary Control with a Reserve Instrument

An alternative means of controlling the money stock is to control the supply of reserves directly. To do this the Federal Reserve would first calculate the quantity of reserves consistent with desired growth in the monetary aggregates. The Federal Reserve would also need to take account of the public's demand for currency. Then open market operations would be conducted to provide growth in the monetary base just sufficient to supply bank reserves and currency consistent with hitting the target growth rates in the money aggregates. This reserve supply approach to monetary control is essentially the process described in Chapter 15, where we assumed that the Federal Reserve controlled the monetary base.

When control of bank reserves is the procedure for monetary control, Federal Reserve errors in predicting the strength of money demand, whether due to prediction errors about the level of economic activity or unpredicted shocks to the money demand function, will be a less serious problem than when an interest rate instrument is employed. To see why, consider the example in Figure 19.6. The Federal Reserve was assumed to have underpredicted the level of economic activity and therefore the level of money demand. If an interest rate is being used as an instrument to control the money supply, then to maintain the target level for the federal funds rate, the Federal Reserve must expand the supply of reserves, allowing the money stock to increase to M_1, above the target level M^*. If the supply of reserves is the instrument, the level of reserves will not be increased in this situation. If the Federal Reserve also controls the supply of currency, the monetary base will be unaffected by the Federal Reserve's prediction error. The money stock target may still be missed since the *money multiplier*, which relates the level of the monetary base to the money stock, may be affected by the level of economic activity and other factors, but by holding the level of reserves and the monetary base constant the Federal Reserve restricts the possible variation in the money stock.

Although control of the supply of reserves will limit the response of the money stock to unpredicted shocks to the money demand function or unpredicted changes in the level of economic activity, such reserve control will magnify the interest rate response to such shocks. Again consider the unpredicted increase in the demand for money that we have been discussing. The increase in money demand will cause banks to need more required reserves. With the federal funds rate as the policy instrument, the Federal Reserve supplies the additional reserves to keep the federal funds rate from rising above the target level. It is this increase in the supply of reserves that allows the money stock to rise above its target level, but this procedure does keep the interest rate stable. If the supply of reserves is the instrument, then as the unpredicted increase in money demand increases the banks' demand for required reserves, there will be an excess demand for federal funds and the federal funds rate will rise. Thus whereas the use of the supply of reserves as a policy instrument will limit the response of the money stock to unpredicted shocks to the money demand function or level of economic activity, it will increase the volatility of the federal funds rate and consequently of other short-term interest rates as well.

A Comparison of the Two Operating Procedures

As mentioned above, the Federal Reserve shifted from using an interest rate to using a reserve instrument for control of the money stock in October 1979. Looking at the reasons for this shift is a useful way of explaining the relative merits of these two operating procedures.

The proximate cause for the shift to a reserve instrument was the Federal Reserve's failure to hit its money growth rate targets over much of 1979 using the federal funds rate as an instrument. Table 19.1 shows the target and actual growth rates for the money stock (old M1 definition) for various two-month intervals between December 1978 and September 1979. As can be seen from the table, at the beginning of this period M1 growth was well below the target level. The Federal Reserve was not particularly concerned about these "misses." At the time and later, the slow money growth during this period was attributed to a downward shift in the demand for money for a given level of economic activity—what we have termed an unpredicted shock to the money demand function.[4] As we saw in Section 19.2 (see Figure 19.2*b* and

[4]The apparent cause of the downward shift in money demand at this time was the shift into interest-paying substitutes for demand deposits such as money market funds and RPs in response to rising interest rates. Since these substitutes were not included in the definition of monetary aggregates, at the time their growth appeared as a decline in money demand.

Table 19.1
Target and Actual Money Growth Rates (M1)[a]

Time Period[b]	Target Range	Actual Rate
December 1978/January 1979	2–6	−0.8
February/March 1979	3–7	0.4
March/April 1979	4–8	10.1
April/May 1979	4–8	9.5
May/June 1979	0–5	7.9
July/August 1979	$2\frac{1}{2}$–$6\frac{1}{2}$	8.6
August/September 1979	4–8	9.1

[a]Growth rates are percentages at *annual* rates.
[b]Target ranges at a given meeting are set for a two-month period, but if a meeting occurs after one month, the target is often changed. Thus some of the two-month intervals above are overlapping.
Source: Figures are taken from Richard Lang, "The FOMC in 1979: Introducing Reserve Targeting," Federal Reserve Bank of St. Louis *Review* 62 (March 1980), pp. 2–25, Table 1.

ECONOMIC POLICY

the accompanying discussion), when there are such unpredicted shocks to the money demand function, hitting the money stock target does not guarantee hitting the ultimate target. In fact, in the face of such instability in money demand, use of an interest rate instrument (the federal funds rate) is desirable. As a member of the Board of Governors, Henry Wallich explained this incident,

> In case of an instability of the demand for money, a funds-rate strategy is preferable. It automatically offsets variations in the demand for money and prevents any inappropriate changes in interest rates that would otherwise result. This was the case, for instance, last fall and winter. There occurred a downward shift in the demand for money relative to GNP. By staying with a funds rate strategy, the Federal Reserve prevented this decline in the demand for money from lowering interest rates at an inappropriate time and so exacerbating the inflation.[5]

If the Federal Reserve is using a federal funds rate instrument, then when there is instability in money demand, the money stock target will be missed, but by maintaining the target level of the interest rate the Federal Reserve cushions the rest of the economy from the effects of the shock.

The situation was quite different beginning in the spring of 1979. Beginning in the March/April period, actual money growth exceeded the Federal Reserve's target range. Rather than reflecting instability in the money demand function, this rapid money growth seemed to be due to a rate of increase in the level of economic activity above the rate predicted by the Federal Reserve. As in the example considered in the preceding subsection (see Figure 19.6 and the accompanying discussion), the level of money demand exceeded the Federal Reserve's forecast because of the underprediction of the level of economic activity, and in order to hold the federal funds rate at the target level, the Federal Reserve had to increase the quantity of bank reserves. This enabled the money stock to increase at rates above the target range. In this case, rather than insulating the rest of the economy from the effects of a shock in financial markets, to keep the interest rate fixed at the target level, the Federal Reserve increased reserves, allowing the money stock to increase and thereby fueling inflation.

Use of a reserve instrument in this case would have been preferable, since with a fixed supply of reserves we have seen an unforeseen increase in the level of economic activity would push up the federal funds rate, thereby working to slow economic activity and inflation. When the Federal Reserve concluded in the fall of 1979

[5]Henry Wallich, "A New Strategy for the Federal Reserve," *Challenge Magazine*, January–February 1980, pp. 49–51.

that excessive growth in economic activity was responsible for the excessive money growth, a switch was made from using the federal funds rate instrument to the procedure of reserve control.

The Federal Reserve has recognized that this new procedure will make the federal funds rate, and hence other interest rates, more volatile than they have been in the past when the federal funds rate was the instrument. To the degree that one believes that interest rate instability has undesirable effects, this must be counted as a disadvantage of the reserve control procedure. The Federal Reserve view has been that there are undesirable effects from interest rate instability. Sharp fluctuations in interest rates are believed to lead to disorderly financial markets. Dealers who must temporarily assume ownership of securities that will then be placed in the market play an important role in organizing security markets. Frequent sharp fluctuations in interest rates and therefore in the price of bonds will greatly increase the risk accompanying such dealer activity and will in the Federal Reserve's view disrupt the efficient functioning of security markets. Weighed against this cost is the fact that, as we have already seen, the reserve control procedure will in many cases eliminate short-run instability in the money growth rate that would result if an interest rate were the instrument.

To summarize, the use of the federal funds rate as an instrument of money stock control has the advantage that it will increase the stability of interest rates, which will, at least in the view of the Federal Reserve, facilitate the efficient functioning of financial markets. Use of the federal funds rate instrument will also insulate the real sector of the economy from the effects of unpredictable shifts in the money demand function—changes in the quantity of money demanded at a given level of income and the interest rate. Given the difficulty in forecasting the pace of innovation in the financial sector, and therefore the growth in money substitutes, this last advantage of an interest rate instrument is of considerable importance.

The use of a reserve control procedure has the advantage that it should result in more stability in money stock growth. This advantage is particularly important when owing to unpredicted shifts in the level of economic activity, use of an interest instrument would result in procyclical behavior of the money stock. With an interest rate instrument the Federal Reserve was led to allow over-expansionary increases in the money stock when economic activity was unexpectedly strong in 1979, contributing to the high rate of inflation during that period. Similarly, if economic activity was unexpectedly weak, with an interest rate instrument money stock growth would decline undesirably. Use of a reserve instrument would lessen such procyclical swings in money growth rates.

576

As our discussion should make clear, which of the two operating procedures one favors depends in large part on the economic situation one believes to be confronting the policymakers. Given its view of the economic situation in late 1979 and 1980, the Federal Reserve concluded that the paramount danger was in allowing a procyclical and inflationary growth in the money stock. The monetary policymakers therefore chose to switch to a reserve control procedure. As circumstances change, this decision may be reversed. Although the strategy of intermediate targeting on a monetary aggregate seems entrenched with considerable support from Congress, the choice of the tactics of monetary policy would appear more dependent on the course of economic events.[6]

19.4 MONETARY VERSUS FISCAL POLICY AS STABILIZATION TOOLS

This section deals with the relative merits of monetary versus fiscal policy as stabilization tools. Since we are considering the choice of policy tools, we are implicitly dealing with discretionary or activist policies. Thus the issue considered here is one of interest primarily to the neo-Keynesians. Monetarist and new classical economists do not favor the use of either type of discretionary policy to stabilize output and employment.

Within the neo-Keynesian framework (see Chapters 7 and 8), both monetary and fiscal policy actions affect output, employment, and the price level. Both types of policy tools are effective in this sense. The choice between them must be made on grounds other than the ability of the policy action to affect the policy goal variables. The argument has been made by some neo-Keynesian economists that generally, and especially where restrictive policies are required, fiscal policy action should be favored over monetary policy action. Monetary policy should be kept near the "middle of the road." Those espousing this view point to various undesirable "side effects" of monetary policy actions, which we discuss below.[7] This view has considerable support among economists, yet in practice monetary policy has not been kept to the middle of the road. In fact, in the case of restrictive policy actions, monetary policy has been relied on to a greater extent than fiscal

---

[6]For a lively exchange of views on the new money stock control procedures see "Money, Credit and Banking Debate: Is the Federal Reserve's Monetary Control Policy Misdirected?" *Journal of Money, Credit and Banking*, 14 (February 1982), pp. 119–147.

[7]For a good explanation of this view, see Arthur M. Okun, "Rules and Roles for Fiscal and Monetary Policy," in James Diamond, ed., *Issues in Fiscal and Monetary Policy* (Chicago: DePaul University Press, 1971).

policy. We return to this disparity between the theory and the practice of stabilization policy after discussing the side effects of monetary policy actions.

The Side Effects of Monetary Policy

In previous chapters we have discussed the process whereby restrictive monetary policies will raise interest rates and discourage business investment spending and residential construction investment. Periods of tight money and rapidly rising interest rates are, as we have seen (Section 13.2), especially disruptive in the housing market because of deposit rate ceilings and consequent credit rationing.[8] Of course, as the investment component of aggregate demand declines, income will fall, with a resulting decline in consumer expenditures. Still, the effects of restrictive monetary policies will fall heavily on investment spending, with a resulting harmful effect on the rate of capital formation and longer-run economic growth.

Expansionary monetary policies obviously do not have these negative effects on capital formation and disruptive effects on housing due to credit unavailability. Such stimulative policies can, however, be argued to encourage excessive activities in these sectors. In general, it seems reasonable to believe that socially optimal rates of business investment and housing construction are most likely to be achieved if wide swings in monetary policy are avoided.

Sharp movements in interest rates which accompany major shifts in monetary policy also have significant effects on prices of financial assets. Periods of tight money, for example, result in increases in interest rates and hence declines in capital values of bonds and corporate equities (see Section 6.1). The random distribution effects caused by such capital losses or, in the case of expansionary monetary policy, capital gains, are another undesirable side effect of monetary policy.

A final important side effect for monetary policy actions is the effect on the balance of payments. Restrictive monetary policies will produce rising interest rates and as a consequence stimulate capital inflows. Capital inflows will improve the balance of payments in a fixed exchange rate system and lead to an increase in the price of the dollar (fall in the exchange rate) in a flexible rate system. Alternatively, expansionary monetary policies lower interest rates, leading to capital outflows with the reverse effects. Notice that here the side effect likely to be regarded as unfortunate by the policymaker comes from an expansionary monetary policy. The negative effect of the capital outflow on the balance of pay-

[8]Tight money during the 1978–80 period caused a decline in housing starts from a level of over 2 million in 1978 to an annual rate of approximately 900,000 by May 1980.

ments in a fixed exchange rate system is in particular likely to limit severely the potential for expansionary monetary policies in countries experiencing balance of payments difficulties (see Section 17.3).

Having catalogued the side effects of monetary policies, we should note that fiscal policies are not without side effects of their own. In the discussion in Chapter 18 of the choice among fiscal policy instruments, it was argued that on grounds of flexibility and lack of allocative side effects, changes in tax rates and to a lesser extent transfer rates would in general circumstances be preferred to changes in government purchases as a macroeconomic stabilization tool. We can therefore restrict our discussion here to the side effects of such changes in tax and transfer rates.

Tax rate or transfer rate changes affect aggregate demand by changing disposable income and consequently consumer spending on a broad array of products. Therefore, such fiscal policy actions would not be expected to fall disproportionately on any one sector in the way that tight money policy affects business investment and housing. We have seen, though, that expansionary fiscal policies increase interest rates and crowd out private expenditures. Thus such policies also have adverse effects on capital formation and growth. However, if such expansionary fiscal policies are used at appropriate times (i.e., when the economy would otherwise be well below full capacity), such crowding out might be expected to be minor. Also, at such times an accommodating monetary policy can be used to nullify this unfavorable side effect. Recall that the interest rate increase that comes with an expansionary fiscal policy results from an increase in the demand for money as income increases (see Section 7.1). The Federal Reserve can expand the money stock sufficiently to provide the required increase in transaction balances to keep the interest rate, and therefore investment, unaffected by fiscal policy actions.

The crowding-out effect of expansionary fiscal policies does suggest that the worst possible combination of policies from the point of view of capital formation and growth would be an overly expansionary fiscal policy which forced monetary policy to be restrictive in order to restrain inflation. Of interest for our discussion of the policy mix in practice is the fact that this mix of expansionary fiscal policies, with the burden of inflation fighting placed on monetary policy, seems to have been characteristic of recent U.S. experience.

Fiscal policy actions will also have effects on our external balance. Expansionary fiscal policy actions, if accompanied by higher interest rates (no accommodating monetary policy), will stimulate capital inflows. Alternatively, restrictive policy actions will produce capital outflows if interest rates fall and may thus cause declines in the price of the dollar or balance of payments deficits, depending on the exchange rate regime. These side effects are less serious than in the case of monetary policy, since accommodating monetary policies can again offset the interest rate effects of fiscal policy actions.

Even in the absence of such accommodation, the fiscal actions themselves produce effects on the *trade balance* that will work to offset the effects on capital flows. A restrictive fiscal policy action, a tax increase for example, would with a fixed exchange rate cause a decline in interest rates and a capital outflow. Such a policy action would also cause income to fall, reducing the demand for imports and improving the trade balance. To the degree that the inflation rate was lowered by the restrictive policy action, our export performance should also improve, further offsetting the negative effect of this fiscal policy action on the balance of payments.[9]

On net, many neo-Keynesian economists have concluded that the undesirable side effects of sharp swings in monetary policy, especially the disruptive effects in the housing market, on balance sheets, and on capital formation, outweigh undesirable side effects from fiscal policy actions. They have therefore favored an activist fiscal policy that would allow monetary policy to stay on a middle-of-the-road course. This desire for stability in monetary policy is one factor explaining the support among some neo-Keynesian economists for setting intermediate money growth targets. These economists do not favor the constant money growth rule of the monetarists, but they do want to avoid sharp swings in monetary policy.

The Policy Mix in Practice

Despite the recognition that there are significant adverse side effects to deviations of monetary policy from a middle-of-the-road stance, especially sharp deviations toward restrictive monetary policies, recent U.S. experience has been characterized by several instances of sharp swings to monetary tightness. Such restrictive shifts in monetary policy occurred in 1966, 1969, 1974, and again in 1979–80. In each case the Federal Reserve felt that inflation was such a serious problem that a highly restrictive policy was required. In the 1966 episode, the source of the inflationary pressure was an overly stimulative fiscal policy, specifically the Vietnam war spending imposed on an economy already at or near full employment. In the later episodes fiscal policy either remained expansionary or was in the Federal Reserve's view insufficiently re-

[9]Notice that in the case of monetary policy, the effects on the trade balance will reinforce rather than offset the effect on capital movements. An expansionary monetary policy, for example, will with a fixed exchange rate lower the interest rate, causing a capital outflow *and* increase income, with a resulting increase in imports and deterioration of the trade balance.

strictive to allow monetary policy to remain in the middle of the road. There is ample evidence from each of these episodes of the undesirable side effects of monetary policy, particularly of the disruption of the housing industry and financial markets, with effects on capital formation.

Why does the policy mix in practice differ from the desirable mix in theory? There are at least two reasons for this disparity. The first is the necessary lag in implementing fiscal policy actions. Any substantial change in fiscal policy requires legislative action. Passing such legislation is an inherently time-consuming process, with hearings and voting by both houses of Congress. More seriously, legislation requires that agreement be reached both in Congress and between Congress and the administration on the need for action, the appropriate degree of stimulus or restraint, the choice of a fiscal instrument, and the details of the program. In practice, such agreement is at times difficult to achieve, and inaction results.

To give one example, as spending on the Vietnam war increased in 1966–67, the Johnson administration sought a tax increase. With the economy already at virtually full employment, there was a need for such a restrictive action to keep aggregate demand from rising excessively and creating inflationary pressures. But Wilbur Mills, then chairman of the House Ways and Means Committee, favored a cut in nondefense spending to finance the increased war spending. As a consequence, restrictive fiscal policy action was delayed until the spring of 1968, when a tax increase was finally approved.

Also making the implementation of restrictive fiscal policies difficult in recent years is the fact that the problem of inflation has been encountered during periods of high unemployment. One need not completely accept the public choice view of policymaker behavior to believe that popularly elected officials will find it difficult to agree on restrictive policies in the presence of high rates of unemployment. In the past two periods of increasing inflation, fiscal policymakers began to implement restrictive budgetary measures, but as unemployment figures rose these measures were abandoned. Monetary policy, which can be implemented quickly and which is somewhat more insulated from the political process, has in recent years been left to take responsibility for combatting inflation, regardless of the unfavorable side effects that result.[10]

[10]As noted at the beginning of this section, the question of the relative merits of monetary and fiscal policy as discretionary stabilization tools is one of interest primarily to the neo-Keynesians—the only group we have considered that favors the use of such discretionary policies. The discussion of this section has, therefore, been from a neo-Keynesian viewpoint. It is worth noting that the supply-side economists, whose position we describe in Chapter 16, would disagree with this analy-

19.5 RULES VERSUS DISCRETION IN MONETARY POLICY

One way to avoid sharp swings in monetary policy would be to adopt a constant money growth rate rule. The monetarists and others proposing such a constant money growth rule thus see their case bolstered by the adverse side effects of sharp swings in monetary policy and the Federal Reserve's tendency to engineer such rapid shifts in response to inflation. They argue that in the past, rather than consistently maintaining a low rate of growth in the money stock, the Federal Reserve has allowed inflationary money growth for long periods; then when the inflation problem gets out of hand we have "brief bouts of monetary stringency." One reason the monetarists believe the Federal Reserve often tolerates inflationary money growth concerns the relationship between government deficit spending and monetary policy. In the absence of accommodating Federal Reserve actions, government deficit spending will put upward pressure on interest rates as the level of economic activity is expanded and as the government sells bonds to finance the deficit. The Federal Reserve, because of its concern about the disruptive effects that interest rate instability will have on financial markets, responds by increasing the money stock.[11]

If the fiscal policy actions are overly expansionary to begin with, resulting from the attempt of elected officials to gain votes by sponsoring various spending programs, as alleged in the public choice view, the Federal Reserve is exacerbating an already overly inflationary process. This inflationary effect of federal government deficit spending on money growth can be prevented if the Federal Reserve is committed to a constant money growth policy. This is another reason why Milton Friedman and other monetarists favor a constitutional amendment forcing the Federal Reserve to follow a constant money growth rule.[12] Buchanan and Wagner, whose

---

sis. In the supply-side view, increases in tax rates should be avoided since they have unfavorable effects on aggregate supply. Therefore, a mix of an expansionary fiscal policy (if it is due to low tax rates, not excessive government spending) to stimulate aggregate supply and a restrictive monetary policy to restrain demand *would* be desirable. On this question, see Martin Feldstein, "Tax Rules and the Mismanagement of Monetary Policy," *American Economic Review*, 70 (May 1980), pp. 182–86; see also the accompanying comment by Alan Blinder, pp. 189–90.

[11]In terms of our IS–LM curve model, an increase in the federal budget deficit, whether created by increasing government spending or lowering taxes, would shift the IS schedule to the right, increasing income and pushing up the interest rate. To keep the interest rate from rising, the Federal Reserve would shift the LM schedule to the right, *accommodating* the expansionary fiscal policy shift.

[12]Friedman's proposed amendment would not quite force the Federal Reserve to maintain a *constant* money growth rate, which would in practice be impossible, but it does limit growth in the monetary base to the narrow range of between 3 and 5 percent.

public choice view of the federal budget process was examined in Chapter 18, favor an amendment restricting Federal Reserve action which is quite similar in spirit to Friedman's.

We have seen above that the neo-Keynesian economists are aware of the harmful side effects of sharp swings in monetary policy. They are also aware of the political pressures on the budget process and, less directly, on the Federal Reserve itself. Even taking account of these factors, most neo-Keynesian economists still oppose monetary policy by rules and favor discretionary policy. The reasons for their opposition to such money growth rules, whether constitutionally mandated or not, are much the same as their objections to constitutional amendments to balance the federal budget, as discussed in Chapter 18.

The neo-Keynesians believe that the private capitalist economy is unstable in the absence of government regulation of aggregate demand. They do not believe that aggregate demand is wholly or even predominantly determined by monetary factors. Thus constant money growth will not stabilize aggregate demand. Given the need they see for activist stabilization policies, they view the cost of adopting constitutionally mandated rules for monetary or fiscal policy as unacceptably high.[13] Instead, they favor living with the policy mistakes, politically motivated or not, which are inevitable in a regime of discretionary monetary and fiscal policy. The issue of rules versus discretion in monetary or fiscal policy is then closely entwined with the conflict between the activist and noninterventionist policy positions which has been central to most of our policy analysis.

The view of many neo-Keynesians that monetary policy should not diverge sharply from the middle of the road is not inconsistent with their opposition to constant money growth rules. In the first place the neo-Keynesians would not measure stability in monetary policy simply in terms of money growth rates. They believe that interest rates and overall credit measures also need to be taken into account. Second, the neo-Keynesian prescription for monetary policy would avoid sharp swings in policy but not rule out all discretionary monetary policy actions. On the contrary, neo-Keynesian economists such as Arthur Okun have suggested that monetary policymakers "make small and prompt adjust-

[13]Neo-Keynesian economists and others have also questioned the effectiveness of constitutional amendments or laws that restrict macroeconomic policymakers. If, for example, there is a law or constitutional amendment restricting the growth of the monetary base or a specific monetary aggregate, it is argued that the Federal Reserve would simply expand or contract credit when it felt such action was required, using means that did not affect that aggregate. To quote Arthur Okun: "The proposal to control political officials with a non-discretionary rule reminds me of the suggestion to catch birds by pouring salt on their tails. Neither the political officials nor the birds will cooperate."

ments in the light of the best current evidence and analysis." Monetary policy should "lean against the wind" while, hopefully, appropriate fiscal policy actions ensure that the wind does not become a gale.

Review Questions

1 What is the Open Market Committee? What role does this committee play in formulating monetary policy?

2 Evaluate the arguments for and against the strategy of intermediate targeting on a monetary aggregate.

3 Why is it natural for a monetarist economist to favor the policy strategy of intermediate targeting on a monetary aggregate?

4 In October 1979 the Federal Reserve shifted from using the federal funds rate to the use of total bank reserves as an instrument to control the money stock. Explain the reasons for this choice.

5 Explain the relative advantages and disadvantages of the federal funds rate and the level of bank reserves as instruments to use for money stock control.

6 Would an increase in the instability of money demand favor the use of the federal funds rate or level of reserves as an instrument of money stock control?

7 In the text, unfavorable side effects were cited as reasons for avoiding sharp swings in monetary policy. What are these side effects of monetary policy actions? Are there similar side effects for fiscal policy actions?

8 Here and in earlier chapters the question of rules versus discretion in policymaking has been central to our policy analysis. Pertaining to monetary policy, outline the monetarist position in favor of rules. Then outline the neo-Keynesian arguments in favor of discretion. Evaluate the two positions.

Selected Readings

AXILROD, STEPHEN H., "New Monetary Control Procedure: Findings and Evaluation from a Federal Reserve Study," *Federal Reserve Bulletin,* April 1981, pp. 277–90.

AXILROD, STEPHEN H., and LINDSAY, DAVID E., "Federal Reserve System

Implementation of Monetary Policy: Analytical Foundations of the New Approach," *American Economic Review*, 71 (May 1981), pp. 246–52.

BACH, G. L., *Making Monetary and Fiscal Policy*. Washington, D.C.: Brookings Institution, 1971.

BRUNNER, KARL, "The Control of Monetary Aggregates," in *Controlling Monetary Aggregates III*. Boston: Federal Reserve Bank of Boston, 1981.

CAGAN, PHILLIP, "The New Monetary Policy," in William Fellner, ed., *Contemporary Economic Problems*, 1980. Washington, D.C.: American Enterprise Institute, 1980.

Davis, Richard G., "Implementing Open Market Policy with Monetary Aggregate Objectives," in *Monetary Aggregates and Monetary Policy*. New York: Federal Reserve Bank of New York, 1974.

FRIEDMAN, BENJAMIN, "The Inefficiency of Short-Run Monetary Targets for Monetary Policy," *Brookings Papers on Economic Activity*, No. 2, 1977, pp. 293–318.

FRIEDMAN, MILTON, "Monetary Policy: Theory and Practice," *Journal of Money, Credit and Banking*, 14 (February 1982), pp. 98–118.

LOMBRA, RAYMOND E., "Monetary Control: Consensus or Confusion," *Controlling Monetary Aggregates*. Boston: Federal Reserve Bank of Boston, 1981.

LOMBRA, RAYMOND E., and TORTO, RAYMOND G., "The Strategy of Monetary Policy," Federal Reserve Bank of Richmond, *Economic Review*, 61 (September–October 1975), pp. 3–14.

MODIGLIANI, FRANCO, "The Monetarist Controversy, or Should We Forsake Stabilization Policies?" *American Economic Review*, 67 (March 1977), pp. 1–19.

OKUN, ARTHUR, "Rules and Roles for Fiscal and Monetary Policy," in James Diamond, ed., *Issues in Fiscal and Monetary Policy*. Chicago: DePaul University Press, 1971.

PIERCE, JAMES L., and THOMSON, THOMAS, "Some Issues in Controlling the Stock of Money," in *Controlling Monetary Aggregates II: The Implementation*. Boston: Federal Reserve Bank of Boston, 1972.

POOLE, WILLIAM, "The Making of Monetary Policy: Description and Analysis," *Economic Inquiry*, 13 (September 1975), pp. 253–65.

Appendix

A Return to the Gold Standard: The Supply-Sider's Prescription for Monetary Policy

In this chapter we have been concerned primarily with the monetarist and neo-Keynesian views on optimal monetary policy. Here we examine the prescription of the supply-side economists for the proper conduct of monetary policy.

As we saw when we examined the position of the supply-siders in Chapter 16, they believe that inflationary aggregate demand management policies, including monetary policies, have had a detrimental effect on economic growth. To remedy this situation, the supply-siders propose a return to the *gold standard*. The gold standard is a system in which the value of a country's currency is fixed in terms of gold and in which that currency is convertible into gold. If a number of countries all fix their currency values in terms of gold, which in turn fixes the relative values of those country's currencies, the gold standard becomes an international monetary system of fixed exchange rates. The primary benefit of the gold standard is that of price stability over the long run, which explains its attractiveness to the supply-side economists. For various reasons, which we will analyze below, most neo-Keynesians and monetarists do not find a return to gold so attractive.

A return to the gold standard has been given recent consideration. Bills to establish various types of gold standard have been introduced in Congress and a recent law was passed creating a *Gold Commission* to make recommendations concerning the proper role of gold in the domestic and international monetary systems. Here we examine the functioning of a gold standard and then consider the arguments for and against a return to gold.

A.1 THE WORKINGS OF A GOLD STANDARD

A Pure Gold Coin Standard

There are a number of versions of the gold standard. The strictest would be a pure gold coin standard where gold is, in fact, the only domestic or international currency. This would be an example of a pure *commodity money standard* in which the quantity of money and the price of other goods in terms of the commodity money (in terms of gold in this case) are determined solely by the supply and demand for the commodity.[1] The resource costs of such a commodity money standard are high since substantial resources must be used for production of the commodity money; in a pure gold coin standard these costs would be the resources tied up in gold discovery and mining. Consequently, such pure commodity money standards have been rare in practice. Still, it is worthwhile to illustrate the way in which such a system assures long-run price stability and limits government's ability to pursue inflationary monetary and fiscal policies. These are the features proponents of less rigid versions of the gold standard hope to preserve.

To see how the gold standard leads to long-run price stability, consider the effects of an increase in the supply of gold, due for example to new gold discoveries. The increase in the money stock would in the short run drive up the cost of goods and services, including the price of labor services. The rise in these prices would be an increase in the cost of gold production, which would cause the quantity of new gold produced to decline. Further, with the fall in the price of gold relative to other commodities, more gold would go into nonmonetary uses (jewelry, dentistry, industrial uses). Together, the decline in production and increase in consumption would cause the supply of gold money to decline and the initial rise in the price level would be reversed. It is important to note that the adjustments in gold production and consumption described above may take a long time. The gold standard will produce long-run but not short-run price stability.

The gold standard, especially an international gold standard, does, however, substantially limit the ability of the government to follow inflationary monetary and fiscal policies, even in the short run. Under a pure gold coin standard, there would be no need for a central bank since the only money would be the commodity money—the gold coins. The government could be taken out of money creation process. Also, the government clearly could not

[1]Useful discussions of the workings of a pure commodity standard are: Milton Friedman, "Commodity Reserve Currency," in *Essays in Positive Economics* (Chicago: University of Chicago Press, 1953), pp. 204–50; and Michael David Bordo, "The Classical Gold Standard: Some Lessons for Today," Federal Reserve Bank of St. Louis *Review*, 63 (May 1981), pp. 2–17.

finance expenditures in excess of taxation by printing money. Such deficit spending could proceed only if the government spent previously accumulated gold coins or sold bonds to the public. In either case, if such deficit spending proved inflationary, under a gold coin standard two countervailing processes would be set in motion.

The first of these is similar to the adjustment just considered for the case of the gold discovery. The rise in the price level and therefore fall in the relative price of gold would lead to a decrease in gold production and rise in gold consumption; the supply of gold coins would decline, reversing the increase in the price level. But as noted above, this adjustment might be quite slow. Under an international gold standard, however, there is an adjustment that would occur more quickly. As the price level in the United States, for example, rose, the value of gold in terms of commodities in the United States would fall, but gold value in terms of goods abroad would not. Gold will therefore flow out of the United States as U.S. citizens import more and foreigners buy fewer of our goods. As gold flows out of the United States, our price level will fall back to its initial level. The nineteenth-century economists referred to this latter adjustment as the *price-specie-flow* mechanism.

A Managed Gold Standard

As noted above, because of high resource costs, pure gold coin or other commodity standards are rarely seen in practice. The classical gold standard that existed in the United States, Great Britain, and in many continental European countries during much of the nineteenth and the early part of the twentieth centuries was, instead, a *managed gold standard*. It is to such a managed gold standard that proponents of gold argue that we should return. The essential features of such a system are as follows.

The nineteenth-century gold standard was an international system, and each country that adhered to the gold standard fixed the price of its currency in terms of gold, thereby fixing exchange rates between national currencies. But domestically, each country had separate noncommodity monies, paper currencies, and bank deposits, the use of which reduced the resource costs of a pure gold coin standard. To maintain the "discipline" of the gold standard, countries would maintain fixed ratios of gold to domestic money. Further, the central bank maintained convertibility of gold and other components of the money stock, which means that paper currency would be redeemed on demand with gold by the central bank. Therefore, although gold was not the only money, the growth in the gold stock limited the growth in the money stock. In theory at least, the managed gold standard could be as effective as the pure gold coin standard in maintaining long-run price stability.

To see how such a managed gold standard might also preserve the limitations that the pure gold coin standard placed on a government's ability to follow inflationary aggregate demand policies, consider the effects in such a system of the same inflationary government fiscal policy action analyzed above. Suppose that, either financed by bond sales or expenditure of previously hoarded gold or currency, the government begins to spend more and prices begin to rise. As in the case of the pure commodity standard, the price rise would make gold worth less domestically, while it maintained its previous value in terms of goods abroad. Since all domestic money was convertible into gold, individuals would obtain gold and purchases of imported goods would rise while exports would fall; the domestic gold supply would decline. If the total domestic money stock was fixed in proportion to the stock of gold, the money stock would then fall until the original price level was restored and, consequently, the gold outflow ceased.

Thus if central banks adjusted the money stock in response to gold inflows and outflows, the managed gold standard could function much as the pure gold coin standard. The price-specie-flow mechanism referred to above would still be operative.

In practice, central banks did not always adhere to the "rules of the game" and adjust the domestic money stock in response to gold inflows or outflows. Instead, at times, they *sterilized* such gold flows. A gold inflow was, for example, simply added to gold reserves in excess of reserves needed to back the domestic money stock—what was termed the *gold cover*. In the case of a gold outflow, previously held excess gold reserves would be used to maintain the gold cover. Central banks would not in effect accept the "discipline of the gold standard." In such situations a managed gold standard becomes undistinguishable from the monetary system we have had since the demise of the classical gold standard, which is a managed *fiduciary money system*. This is a system whereby the central bank maintains control of the money stock, which consists of paper currency and bank deposits—the liabilities of the central bank and commercial banking system. Such a managed fiduciary system of domestic money stock control was the assumption underlying all the monetary policy analysis in the text.

A.2 SHOULD WE RETURN TO THE GOLD STANDARD

The supply-side economists's case for a return to the gold standard can be simply stated. The supply-side economists believe that a return to the gold standard would produce the long-run price stability which they regard as essential to the success of their policies to stimulate aggregate supply. The return to gold would, they think, put an end to inflationary government aggregate demand management policies.

The critics of a return to the gold standard, a group that includes most monetarist and neo-Keynesian economists, believe that considerable short-run instability of both price and output would result from a return to gold. The record of the nineteenth-century gold standard era does in fact reveal considerable short-run instability. Figure A.1 shows the behavior of the wholesale price index for the United States over the period 1800–1979. Ignoring the Civil War period and its aftermath (1861–78), during which the gold standard was suspended, and also ignoring the decade of the 1930s, during which the gold standard disintegrated, the short-run behavior of the price level certainly seems no more stable during the gold standard period than afterward. The striking difference is in the trend in the price level, which was mildly downward in the gold standard period but more sharply upward in post-gold standard period.

The gold standard era was also marked by numerous monetary crises and recurrent recessions. Over the 1815–1914 period there were 14 financial crises in the United States or Great Britain, five of which spread to both countries. In addition, there were 14 recessions in the United States and nine in Great Britain which did not involve financial panics or crises.[2]

Opponents of a return to gold believe that there would be even more short-run instability with a gold standard under current conditions. Monetarists worry especially that a return to a gold standard would lead to instability in money stock growth. Under a gold standard, the money stock must be adjusted proportionately with changes in the domestic gold supply. Monetarists and other critics of gold argue that the supply as well as the price of gold are highly unstable and to tie the money stock to gold would be destabilizing.

There are several reasons for believing that the supply of gold would prove to be unstable under a gold standard. The principal gold-exporting nations are South Africa and the USSR. Soviet gold exports are highly variable, depending on their import needs. Critics of gold also worry that political factors might affect the behavior of either of these gold exporters. Other than new gold production, which in recent years has fallen short of the nonmonetary use of gold, changes in official gold reserves under a gold standard would depend on the demand for gold for hoarding and

[2]See Edward M. Bernstein, "Back to the Gold Standard?" *The Brookings Bulletin*, 17 (Fall 1980), pp. 8–12.

Figure A.1 Wholesale Price Index for the United States, 1800–1979

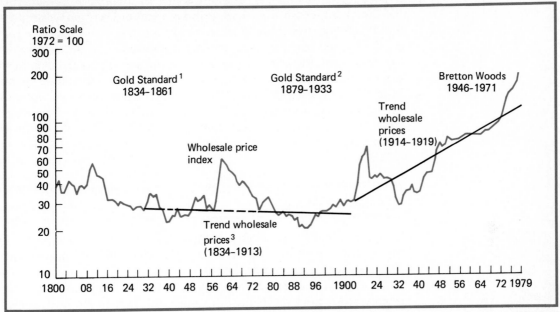

From Michael David Bordo, "The Classical Gold Standard: Some Lessons for Today," Federal Reserve Bank of St. Louis *Review,* 63 (May 1981), p. 9.

investing. If there were sharp shifts in this demand, as there have been in recent years, gold reserves and consequently the domestic money supplies in countries that adhered to the gold standard would also have to fluctuate sharply. Instability in the money stock would result in instability in prices and output.

Opponents of a return to gold also point to the difficulty of effecting a return to a gold standard. One particular problem is the question of the proper price for gold. Too high a price will mean that a country will be flooded with gold, with a resulting inflationary rise in the money stock. Too low a price and there will be a deflationary gold outflow. The United Kingdom returned to the gold standard at too low a price for gold (too high an exchange rate for the pound) in 1925 and as a result suffered what has been called "a lost decade" for the British economy, with deflation and high unemployment. Various methods have been suggested for choosing the proper price, but critics of the return to gold are not convinced of their merits.

To summarize, then, the supply-side economists favor a return to the gold standard because it will foster long-run stability of the price level and impose anti-inflationary discipline on monetary and fiscal policy. Most monetarist and neo-Keynesian economists oppose a return to gold, believing that there would be considerable short-run instability of price and output under a gold standard and believing that there are serious difficulties in successfully resuming a gold standard. For the neo-Keynesians, the opposition to a return to gold is in line with their opposition to fixed policy rules. The gold standard is viewed by them as a particularly "barbaric" rule. The monetarists favor a rule for the conduct of monetary policy, but in their view the gold standard imposes the wrong rule. They favor a *managed fiduciary standard*, where the central bank attempts to achieve a constant rate of growth in the money stock.

A.3 CONCLUSION

In its final report to Congress in April 1982, the Gold Commission referred to at the beginning of this appendix recommended against a return to a gold standard. More in line with the monetarist position, the Commission suggested further study of a rule for money stock growth. The Gold Commission did recommend the minting of a U.S. gold coin, but the coin would not have a fixed dollar value and would not be legal tender. This latter recommendation drew criticism from opponents of a return to a gold standard who felt that the minting of a gold coin would be perceived as a first step to establishing a formal link between the dollar and gold. The discussion of a return to the gold standard is likely to continue in future years with interest in the question waxing and waning in direct proportion to the degree of instability or stability provided by our present monetary standard.

Historical Appendix
Selected Major
Macroeconomic Policy Actions,
1929–81

Throughout the book we have discussed actual macroeconomic policy actions in the context of the theories we were considering. Here, as background for that discussion, a number of important macroeconomic policy actions taken by the U.S. government during the period since the Great Depression are listed and briefly described. References are given to the sections of the text where these policy episodes are discussed further. At the end of the appendix is a list of books dealing with economic policy in the United States over the period.

1929–1933

Monetary Collapse during the Depression: Over the period 1929–1933, the Federal Reserve allowed the money stock (M1) to decline by 30 percent. This monetary collapse is viewed by the monetarists as *the* cause of the Depression. Neo-Keynesians certainly regard it as an important contributing factor to the sharp decline in economic activity during this period.

1932

The Hoover Tax Increase: In 1932, with the unemployment rate at 24 percent, President Hoover initiated large increases in both excise and income taxes. Taxes were increased in order to balance the Federal budget in the wake of falling tax revenues due to the Depression (Sections 5.1, 18.6).

1933

Launching the New Deal: Upon taking office the Roosevelt administration enacted a broad program to combat the Depression. Included in the early stages of the program were efforts to raise prices, or at least to stem the decline in prices, such as the Agricultural Adjustment Act (AAA) and National Recovery Act (NRA). Public works programs, such as the Tennessee Valley Authority (TVA) and Works Progress Administration (WPA), were a second part of the program. A third part of the program was financial sector reform including initiating a system of deposit insurance and regulation of security markets.

1933

The United States Leaves the Gold Standard: As part of his plan to raise the U.S. domestic price level, Roosevelt took the U.S. off the gold standard, breaking the link of the dollar price to gold. The move prompted one of his economic advisors to assert, "this is the end of Western civilization." Great Britain had left the gold standard in 1931. Several continental European countries, led by France, remained on the gold standard for a few more years, but the classical gold standard was to collapse completely during the 1930s. (On the workings of the classical gold standard and current proposals for a return to a gold standard, see the appendix to Chapter 19). Western civilization apparently survived the demise of the gold standard, but international economic relations were badly disorganized in the 1930s.

1937–1938

Restrictive Monetary and Fiscal Policies: The economic recovery in the U.S. had been proceeding from 1933 to 1937, with the unemployment rate dropping from 25.2 percent in 1933 to 14.3 percent in 1937. In 1937–38, however, both monetary and fiscal policies became highly restrictive. There followed a sharp decline in economic activity, with the unemployment rate rising to 19.1 percent in 1938. Fiscal policy became restrictive with tax increases and spending reductions aimed at balancing the federal budget. Roosevelt had never been comfortable with the notion of deficit spending and thought that by 1937 the recovery had proceeded far enough to allow a more *conventional* balanced budget policy to be followed. The Federal Reserve tightened monetary policy by doubling the required reserve ratios on deposits. The reason for the Federal Reserve's action was that the level of excess reserves in the system had gotten quite high, and the policymakers feared that their ability to control the money stock through control of bank reserves (Sections 15.2 and 15.3) had been weakened.

1940–1942

World War II Defense Build-Up: Federal government purchases of goods and services for national defense increased from $1.2 billion in 1939 to $49.4 billion in 1942. This massive defense build-up finally ended the Great Depression. The unemployment rate fell to 4.7 percent in 1942, then 1.9 percent in 1943.

1942	**Wartime Wage and Price Controls:** Following a sharp rise in both wholesale and retail prices in 1940–42, general wage and price controls were instituted in 1942. The controls remained in effect until the second half of 1946.
1945	**The Bretton Woods Agreements:** The international monetary agreements signed at Bretton Woods, New Hampshire near the end of World War II set up a fixed exchange rate system where the dollar's value was fixed in terms of gold and convertible into gold. Other currencies had par values in terms of the dollar and were convertible into dollars. This international monetary system was to last until 1973 (Section 17.2).
1946	**The Employment Act:** Congress explicitly took responsibility for maintaining high levels of employment and production while also maintaining the purchasing power of the dollar (limiting inflation) by passage of the Employment Act.
1951	**Korean War Price and Wage Controls:** The beginning of the Korean War, in 1950, triggered a wave of panic buying by consumers and firms recalling the shortages of World War II. Prices rose quickly and price and wage controls, along with restrictive fiscal policy actions, were put into effect in 1951.
1951	**Federal Reserve–Treasury Accord:** Beginning in 1942 the Federal Reserve had been pegging the level of interest rates on government securities in order to help the Treasury market debt. In March of 1951, the Treasury and Federal Reserve reached an Accord whereby the Federal Reserve would no longer agree to peg interest rates, though it would still cooperate in marketing federal government debt (Section 9.2). The Accord allowed the Federal Reserve to pursue an independent monetary stabilization policy.
1953–1960	**Fiscal Policy in the 1950s:** The record of fiscal policy in the 1950s illustrated the importance of *automatic fiscal stabilizers* (Section 18.4) as the budget went into deficit during recessions and surplus with peaks in economic activity. Such fiscal stabilizers had become more important because of the larger size of the federal government budget in this period relative to the pre-World War II period. Discretionary fiscal policy actions were used during this period to a lesser extent than in later years.
1961–1964	**The New Economics of the Kennedy–Johnson Period:** The Kennedy Administration came into office with a program to speed recovery from the recession which had begun in 1960. Included in

the program were an investment tax credit (Section 13.2), an increase in government spending, and tax cuts for persons and businesses (Section 16.2). The anti-inflationary part of the program was a set of voluntary wage and price guidelines. By the first half of 1965 the unemployment rate had declined to 4.8 percent (from 6.9 percent for the first half of 1961).

1965–1967

Inflationary Vietnam War Spending: With the beginning of the Vietnam War, government spending on national defense rose from $49.4 billion in 1965 to $71.5 billion in 1967. Since this increase was not adequately financed by higher tax revenues, the federal deficit rose by approximately $14 billion over this period. With the economy already at a high-employment level, the rate of inflation increased.

1966

A Credit Crunch: The expansionary fiscal policy and higher inflation rate in 1965–66 put increased pressure on the Federal Reserve. The resulting tightening of monetary policy led to a "credit crunch." Credit demand exceeded supply and interest rates rose sharply. With ceilings on deposit rates paid by financial intermediaries, deposits declined, with resulting credit rationing in the housing market (Sections 6.1, 13.2, and 19.4).

1968

The Income Tax Surcharge: Finally, in the spring of 1968, a 10 percent income tax surcharge was legislated to aid in financing the Vietnam War. Passage of the surcharge had been held up due to disagreement between President Johnson, who favored the surcharge, and some Congressional leaders, who favored cuts in nondefense spending to fund the war (Section 19.4).

1971

President Nixon's "New Economic Policy": The Nixon Administration came into office pledged to reduce the inflation rate. Restrictive monetary and fiscal policies in 1969–70 led to increased unemployment but did little to slow inflation. In August of 1971 President Nixon announced several policy actions. First was a system of wage and price controls, beginning with a 3-month freeze on prices and wages (Section 18.7). Second was a series of moderately expansionary fiscal policy shifts. Finally, convertibility between the dollar and gold was suspended and a 10 percent surtax on imports imposed to deal with a growing international balance of payments deficit (Section 17.2).

1973

The Move to Floating Exchange Rates: After an attempt to establish a viable new set of fixed exchange rates in 1972 (The Smithsonian Agreements), the dollar was allowed to *float* in 1973. The

Bretton Woods system of fixed exchange rates had been replaced by a managed floating of major world currencies (Section 17.2).

1975

The Anti-Recession Tax Cut: A large tax cut, consisting of a one-time rebate and a reduction in personal income tax rates, was passed at just the low-point of the severe 1974–75 recession. Both the rebate portion of the 1975 tax cut and the temporary income tax surcharge in 1968 gave rise to a controversy over the effectiveness of temporary changes in tax policy (Sections 13.2 and 18.5).

1979

Shift in the Federal Reserve's Operating Procedure: On October 6, 1979 the Federal Reserve announced a shift in the tactics of monetary policy. Previously the Federal Reserve had attempted to control the money stock via control of the federal funds rate. As of 1979, the Federal Reserve shifted to total reserves as an instrument through which it would seek to control the money stock (Section 19.4).

1981

The Reagan Economic Recovery Program: The Reagan Administration's program consisted of a set of business and personal tax cuts, cuts in nondefense spending, increases in defense spending, and regulatory reform (Section 16.3) aimed at fostering noninflationary economic growth. The rationale for much of the program came from the theories of the supply-side economists (Section 16.2), but questions have been raised about whether as implemented the program was in fact supply-side economics in practice.

Selected Readings

BACH, GEORGE L., *Making Monetary and Fiscal Policy.* Washington: The Brookings Institution, 1971.

BLINDER, ALAN S., *Economic Policy and the Great Stagflation.* New York: Academic Press, 1981.

FRIEDMAN, MILTON and SCHWARTZ, ANNA, *A Monetary History of the United States, 1867–1960.* Princeton, New Jersey: Princeton University Press, 1963.

GORDON, ROBERT A., *Economic Instability and Growth: The American Record.* New York: Harper and Row, 1974.

KINDLEBERGER, CHARLES P., *The World in Depression, 1929–39.* Berkeley, California: University of California Press, 1973.

STEIN, HERBERT, *The Fiscal Revolution in America.* Chicago: University of Chicago Press, 1969.

TEW, BRIAN, *The Evolution of the International Monetary System, 1945–77.* London: Hutchison and Company, 1977.

TRIFFIN, ROBERT, *Our International Monetary System: Yesterday, Today, and Tomorrow.* New York: Random House 1968.

index

C

Cambridge approach to quantity theory, 59–61, 87, 231, 248, 323, 326, 374
Capital account of balance of payments
definition of, 479
in 1978, 478
Capital flows
determinants of, 497–499
in international economic relations, 476n
Capital goods in GNP, 14
Capital stock
growth of, 438, 441–444, 445
in production function, 39
Carlson, Keith, 539n
Carter administration, incomes policies during, 546, 547
Cash balances approach to quantity theory, *see* Cambridge approach
Certificates of deposit (CDs), 379
Chandler, Lester, 413n
Churchill, Winston, 95
Clark, Peter K. 358n, 462
Collective rationality in voter behavior, 526
Conservative Party (British), 95
Constant growth rate rule, 262–266
Constant returns to scale, 438–439
versus increasing returns to scale, 445–446
Consumer demand, theory of, 46
analogy to labor supply, 211n
analogy to money demand theory, 404n
Consumer durable goods
expenditure, 366–369
as investment component of aggregate demand, 124
in national income accounts, 350
see also Consumption
Consumer price index (CPI)
compared to PPI and GNP deflator, 26–27
description of, 26
as measure of inflation, 7–8
Consumption
component of GNP, 15–16, 102
fiscal policy and, 344–346
-income relationship, 332–349
absolute income hypothesis, 334–337

Keynesian consumption function, 102–104, 332–337
life cycle theory, 338–347, 543
permanent income hypothesis, 347–349, 543
monetary policy and, 346–347
see also Consumer durable goods expenditure
Corporate income tax
effective tax and inflation, 451–456
investment and, 356–357
Cost reducing tax policies, 230
Council of Economic Advisors, 27–28
Crandall, Robert, 466
Credit controls of 1980, 347
Credit crunch of 1966, 364, 580, 596
Credit rationing, 361
"Crowding out," 70, 181–182, 184, 187, 258–261, 357–358, 456, 579
Currency/Deposit ratio, 425, 428
Current account of balance of payments, 478

D

Davidson, Lawrence, 551n
Denison, Edward, 440, 444–446, 466–467
Deposit multiplier, 423
Deposits
as components of monetary aggregates, 381–382
innovations in, 379–382
relationship to bank reserves, 418–428
reserve requirements, 414–415
see also specific types of deposits
Depreciation
accelerated allowances for, 357, 468–469
as charge against GNP, 14, 18
in 1933, 16n
Devaluation, 490–491
Discount rate, 417–418
Disequilibrium analysis
classical, 36
Fisher's model, 79–90
Disposable personal income
consumption and, Keynesian view, 102–104
definition of, 19
national income and, 20

OSHA (Occupation Safety and
Health Administration), 466
Output
cyclical fluctuations in, 233, 350,
352–353, 365–366, 535, 544
growth of
1870–1969, 437
1953–1981, 4–5
potential real
compared to actual GNP, 1956–
1980, 29–31
definition of, 27
estimation of, 27–28
see also Gross National Product;
National Income

P

Pegging of interest rates, 244–247,
251, 432
Perlman, Morris, 527n
Perpetuities, 64, 126, 130, 245
Personal income
definition of, 19
national income and, 19–20
in 1980, 20–21
Phelps, Edmund, 270n
Phillips, A. W. H., 274n
Phillips curve
Keynesian view, 281–286
monetarist view, 274–279
role of temporary wage price
controls and, 548–549
Pigou, A. C., 36, 59–60
Pollock, Stephen, 366n
Pollution control, cost of, 458–459,
466
Porter, Richard, 406n, 408n
Portfolio diversification, 397
Portfolio effect, 259
Price expectations
as cost push factor, 224–227
Keynesian view, 213–215, 297
monetarist view, relationship to
Phillips curve, 274–278
rational expectations concept, 297,
312–14, 327
Price indices, *see* Consumer price
index; GNP deflator; Product
price index
Price level
and the quantity of money,
classical view, 56–61

Price and Pay Boards, 547
Price-specie-flow mechanism, 588
Private sector
classical view of inherent stability,
76
Keynesian view of instability, 287,
290–291, 328, 369
monetarist view of stability, 240,
291, 328, 369
Producer price index (PPI)
description of, 26
compared to CPI and GNP
deflator, 26–27
Product market equilibrium
schedule, *see* IS curve
Production function
in classical theory, 39–41, 47–48,
200
long run growth and, 437–444
Public choice view of policymaker
behavior, 525–528
Public works projects
Keynesian-classical debate on, 233
for stabilization purposes, 542

Q

Quantity theory of money, 56–63;
see also Money

R

Rational expectations, 297, 312–314,
327
Reagan administration, 530n
campaign platform, Kemp-Roth
proposal in, 459
economic recovery plan of, 468–
469, 541, 597
early effects of, 472–473
neo-Keynesian critique, 470–472
policy on central bank
intervention in foreign market,
489
Reaganomics, 437; *see also* Reagan
administration, economy
recovery plan of
Real wage
equilibrium, 47
expected, 214
labor supply and, 46, 211

Tobin, James, 4, 343n, 384, 399, 447, 461, 462, 463, 551n, 577n
  on balanced budget amendment, 545
  on Reaganomics, 471–472
  on theory of money demand, 399–405
Transaction balance accounts
  Automatic Transfer from Savings (ATS), 380
  credit union share draft accounts, 380
  money market mutual funds, 380
  NOW accounts, 126n, 379–381
  Repurchase Agreements, (RPs), 380–381
Transfer payments
  increase in, 529–530
  for stabilization purposes, 542
Treasury
  pegging of interest rates, 244
Tufte, Edward R., 526n
Tullock, Gordon, 525

U

Unemployment
  data, 6, 7, 9, 92, 280, 317, 539, 540
  effects on voter behavior, public choice view, 527
  frictional (seasonal), 28
  genesis of as economic policy question, 92–97
  incomes policies effects on, 546–551
  inflation and, 8–10
    trade-off between, see Phillips curve
  money wage and, 71–76, 204–211, 214
  natural rate theory of, 270–291
  persistence of, Keynesian-new classical debate, 311–312, 317–318
  potential output estimates and, 28
Unintended inventory accumulation, 101, 365
U.S. Department of Commerce, 15n, 20

User cost of capital, 355–357
USSR, as principal gold exporter, 590
Utilization rates
  and estimates of potential output, 28

V

Velocity of money, 57–58
  implications for Reagan administration program, 471
  Keynesian view, 242–243
  monetarist view, 252–253
Vietnam war, as source of inflationary pressure, 29, 491, 580–581, 596
Voter behavior hypotheses, 526–527

W

Wage bargain, 211
Wage Insurance Plan of 1978, 547
Wage and price controls, 546–552, 595
Wage and price guidelines, 546
Wages, see Money wage; Real wage
Wagner Richard E., 526–528, 545n, 582–583
Wallace, Neil, 295
Wallich, Henry, 547, 575
Weintraub, Sidney, 547
Wholesale Price Index, 590–591
Works Progress Administration (WPA), 594
World War II
  defense build-up during, 594
  GNP during, 17, 238
  monetary policy during, 244
  wage and price controls during, 546, 595

Y

Young, John H., 504n